KAY FRANCIS

I Can't Wait To Be Forgotten

Her Life On Film & Stage

By Scott O'Brien

Foreword by Robert Osborne

KAY FRANCIS

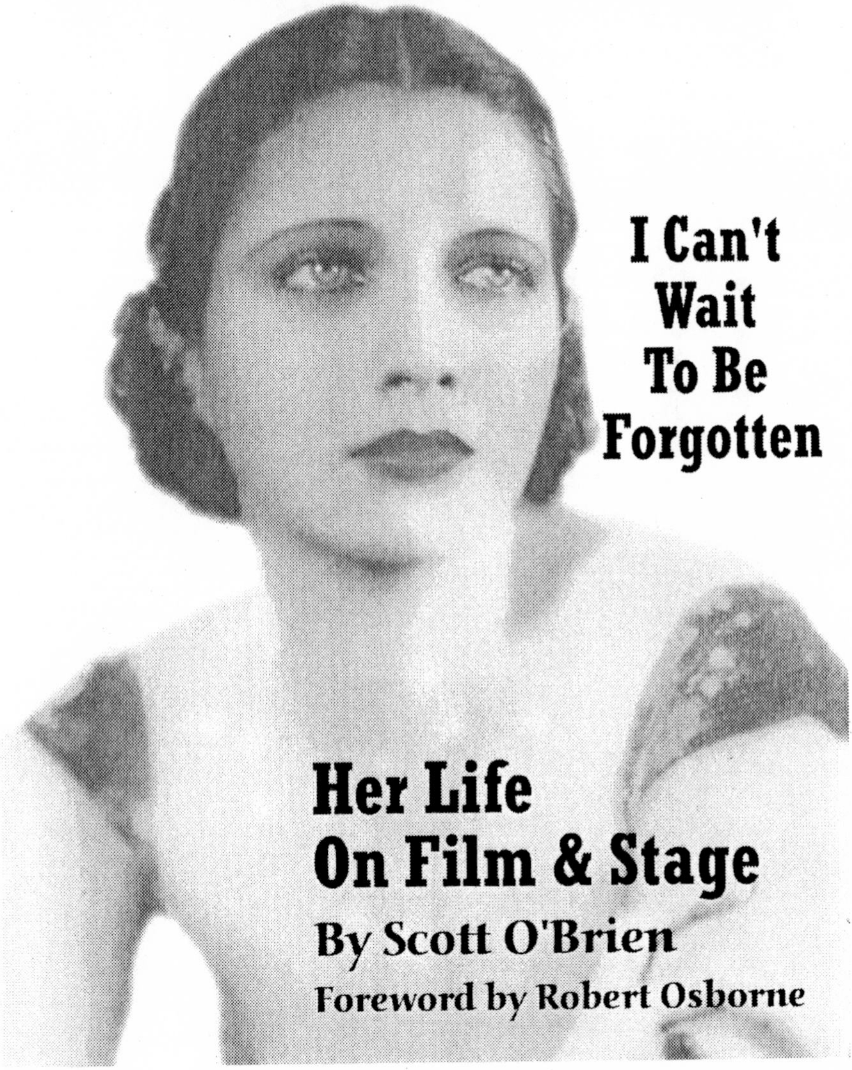

I Can't
Wait
To Be
Forgotten

Her Life
On Film & Stage

By Scott O'Brien

Foreword by Robert Osborne

BearManor Media
2006

Kay Francis: I Can't Wait To Be Forgotten;
Her Life on Film and Stage
© 2006 Scott O'Brien
Foreword © 2006 by Robert Osbourne

For information, address:

BearManor Media
P. O. Box 750
Boalsburg, PA 16827

bearmanormedia.com

Cover design by John Teehan

Typesetting and layout by John Teehan

Published in the USA by BearManor Media

ISBN—1-59393-036-4

Table of Contents

To Jetti and Lou Ames
with love and gratitude

Kay Francis was a box-office bonanza for Warner Brothers. "Kay Francis is my favorite actress," declared columnist Walter Winchell. "She has intellect and charm." Both qualities are captured here by the camera of Elmer Fryer (1932). (Warners)

Foreword
by Robert Osborne

Of all the grand dames, glamour queens, divine divas and fascinating females who dominated the golden age of cinema, Kay Francis was one of the most striking, most popular and most fun to have around. Yet for too many unfathomable reasons, today she's one of the most forgotten and underrated of all those ladies. A wide patch of the population still knows Crawford, Davis, Stanwyck, Dietrich and others who reigned mightily in films of the 1930s but few are familiar with the elegant, dark-haired lady who once outdrew them all at the box-office.

Before Bette Davis began her reign as "the fourth Warner Brother" in 1938 with *Jezebel*, Kay Francis was the most important female star at that studio. A few other contenders came and went (Ruth Chatterton, Ruby Keeler and Dolores Del Rio among them) but Kay—after a healthy run at Paramount in 19 films, including *The Cocoanuts* with the Marx Brothers, and Lubitsch's *Trouble in Paradise*—had moved to the Burbank lot, helping the Warner boys to pay the mortgage for several years.

At Warners, there was a Kay Francis "formula" as much as there was a "Joan Crawford" formula at MGM and then, later, another when Crawford herself moved over to the Warner lot. With Kay, the fans were never satisfied unless she (a) wore stunning gowns, (b) suffered in love, (c) remained gallant and true, (d) did the right thing at the fade-out, even if it meant giving up the great love of her life, be it a husband, a swain or a child. The public ate it up—time and time again.

And it was her popularity with the public that ultimately seemed to doom her. As her hold on film fans grew stronger, so did her salary and she was soon making far more money per week than any of her bosses. Rare is the businessman who enjoys having an employee getting so rich on his dime (or, in this case, the studio's thousand-dollar bills). Because of that high fee she commanded week in and week out, the Warners ultimately decided to ditch her and promote someone whose salary was considerably smaller, one of them was that unusual, feisty girl who recently signed with the studio named Davis.

But Kay didn't ditch easily, and that eventually hurt her career severely. Warners hesitated to fire Kay—if they did they'd have to pay her off, at an astoundingly high fee. So they tried to get her to quit. After promising to cast her in an important script, *Tovarich*, they gave that to freelancer Claudette Colbert instead and started casting Kay in inferior, second-rate projects, assuming she'd refuse to do them and bolt—at which

i

point no payoff would be required. To their dismay, she did all the B and C status films without a squawk. Then the studio began squashing her billing, putting her name in small print below the titles and in far less prominent size type than her co-stars. Still, she stayed and worked. She was determined to collect that high-level salary she'd been promised until her contract was finished. That made her bosses even more furious. "I wanted the money," she told Bette Davis many years later, in explaining why she'd let Warner Bros. humiliate her during her final years there. "I never cared about the money," retorted Davis. "I wanted the career." (Nearly 20 years later, Jack L. Warner was still smarting about having lost the money battle with Kay. In the 1950s, there was talk about casting her in an important role in a Warner film, a part which would have been ideal for her, but J.L.W. wouldn't even consider hiring her for it.)

But there's no question that the substandard quality of many of those scripts is one reason her work isn't as widely known today as that of her peers. It's also why her fame has been allowed, unfortunately, to fade from view. As wonderfully entertaining as many of her movies remain (notably *One Way Passage, Jewel Robbery, Confession* and *It's a Date*) and how expert she is in them, the fact is she never had a *Mildred Pierce* to her credit as Crawford did, no *Double Indemnity* like Stanwyck, no *Dark Victory* like Davis. Nor did Kay Francis ever make a film in Technicolor, which for years was a requirement in order for a movie to get wide exposure on television.

Hopefully, this new book on Kay Francis will stimulate more curiosity about her and pique people's interest in seeing her films. We love her at Turner Classic Movies, and show many Kay Francis films each year. One of our missions has always been to make it possible for people to get to know the work and personas of those wonderfully charismatic and talented stars from the past who tend to be overlooked these days—like Kay Francis. With her, once seen, it's easy to understand what all the shouting was about.

When she was delivering the goods as only she could—usually draped in some outlandish outfit designed by Orry-Kelly which no sane person would ever wear in real life, in any era, except maybe to a Halloween party—she was a marvel to behold, a symbol of glamour, style and femininity which, of course, is what moviegoers of her era wanted to see. Today's moviegoers revere realism in their films. In Kay's day, it was a time when most moviegoers were more akin to Tennessee Williams' Blanche Dubois when in *A Streetcar Named Desire* she says, "I don't want realism...I want *magic*."

Magic is what Kay Francis gave us.

She stands high among the great stars of her time and I'm delighted this new book has been written to help give her the kind of full-scale attention she deserves.

At long last Kay.

— *Robert Osborne*
Host of the Turner Classic Movies
television network

Prologue

In the early 1970s, after seeing a San Francisco revival of the1937 film *Confession* starring Kay Francis, I was smitten with her. Why on earth hadn't I ever heard of her? I found the natural understatement of her acting and the charisma of her unique personality, captivating. I began the venture of tracking down her films, and gathering anything written about her, reviews, articles, plus any anecdotes worth saving. After I wrote a career article on Kay for a 1996 issue of *Films of the Golden Age*, San Francisco writer Mick LaSalle (author of *Complicated Women*, a tribute to pre-Code Hollywood) encouraged me to do a Kay Francis biography. In January 2003, I finally took the plunge. The project truly came together upon contacting one of Kay's closest friends, Jetti Preminger Ames, who had worked with Kay on stage in 1945's *Windy Hill*. Jetti provided an insightful look into Kay's retirement years. I also received some very touching responses from the young people Kay had contact with during her studio years: Billy Mauch, Jimmy Lydon, Gloria Jean, and Sybil Jason, who had played Kay's daughter in two films. These child actors, now in their 70s and 80s, respected and adored Kay. It's no wonder. She loved children.

Things got even more interesting after I contacted two of the offspring of Kay's first husband, Dwight Francis. Lesley Francis (granddaughter of poet Robert Frost), rendered a fascinating portrait of her father, whom she never saw until she was in her teens. Henry "Thins" Francis, a product of Dwight's third marriage, provided two wonderful photos of Kay from 1921-22—the earliest I had ever seen. I also contacted the son of Kay's last fiancé, Erik Barnekow. He offered an affecting, yet tragic account of his father's strange disappearance out of Kay's life in 1939.

The book's title? "I Can't Wait to be Forgotten" is taken from an interview Kay gave to Dick Mook in the fall of 1938. It was her last interview on a Warner Brothers set. Mook listened as she held back the tears and let go of her ties with the studio that had made her a star. Little did she realize that her dreams for a life with Erik Barnekow would also evaporate into thin air. It would be under the storm clouds of World War II that Kay would again "find herself."

1

The journey of writing Kay's biography was full of the unexpected. Out of the thin air, just when I had begun to do research on Kay's portrayal of Florence Nightingale in *The White Angel*, I was contacted by Paula Ferguson (professor, RN and PhD. in the nursing field). She was a Nightingale expert! Ms. Ferguson was extremely generous with her knowledge. In September 2003, I found myself flying to Daytona Beach to introduce the 1936 film at the Florida Nurses Foundation's annual fund-raiser. As the audience watched Kay on screen, they could see that even with a hampered script and censors breathing down her neck, she managed an eloquent, focused performance. The big screen magnified her naturalness as an actress. That night she got a standing ovation. Afterwards, I was surrounded with queries about Kay Francis.

In June 2004, I spent an evening on Nantucket Island with Jetti Preminger Ames and her husband Lou -- I found myself face-to-face with two people who really loved and cared about Kay. They both reflected the very qualities that initially drew them to her—humor, intelligence and generosity of spirit. And this was *before* happy hour. They were eager to share their stories about Kay Francis, the godmother of their two sons.

Soon after visiting Jetti and Lou, I spent several days at the Wesleyan University Cinema Archives in Middletown, Connecticut. With the excellent assistance of archivist Joan Miller, I had access to the calendar-diaries that Kay had kept from 1922-1953. I read fragments, bits and pieces, of Kay's emotional jottings. They were filled with the "stuff" of her life. The pages not only listed her social engagements, but were her personal venue for letting off emotional steam. The diary was her personal process for, hopefully, letting go and moving on to enjoy what she called the "little moments" that meant so much to her.

The remarkable aspect of Kay's diaries was her frank remarks about her love life. These were usually written in shorthand. Wesleyan University hired a translator, who managed to decipher, not all, but a good deal of these entries. These translations provided a glimpse of a young woman who helped define what made the Jazz Age generation so unique. No shrinking violet, Kay pursued romantic love, as well as sexual relationships, with gusto and no apologies. After bobbing her hair in 1924, she joined thousands of others of her generation into a brave new territory. She took up smoking and drinking in public—courageous acts for a young woman in the 1920s. She turned heads, mostly of the attractive male variety. From 1925-1930, it was a marathon of love for Kay, but that was certainly not her focus. She had a vision for a career on stage. She never claimed to be stage-struck, but simply stated that stage was her business. When her "business" was transferred to Hollywood and the world of filmmaking, Kay took her liberated lifestyle along with her. What Kay valued, many would find scandalous. It's what made her unique. It's what made her human. And, as a result of her intelligent mind and perceptiveness, there was always more laughter than tears. Perhaps that's just why she saved her diaries—to have them on hand for a rainy day and a good laugh, or cry, about all her escapades.

"Whenever I think of Kay," wrote her friend and reporter Dick Mook, "the first thing I think of is her laugh...It is a deep guffaw that seems to come right from the pit of her stomach. You can hear it all over the set or all over any room she happens to be in."[1] "The thing I envy most about Kay Francis is not her appearance, her ability, nor her position," said Kay's co-star, Patricia Ellis. "It is her laugh. I've never heard anyone laugh so whole-heartedly or who seemed to enjoy laughing as much as she."[2] Some things for Kay were no laughing matter. Kay expected nothing of people except fair play. "When she doesn't get it," noted reporter Frances Kellum, "the rankle goes deep."[3] The rankle from her court battle with Warner Brothers in 1937 became embedded in her as a permanent fixture. Author James Robert Parish would later comment on Kay's battle with the studio, saying, "In the entire history of American films it was one of the meanest put-downs ever carried out against a luminary."[4] I was hoping to get some insight from her diary as to what exactly happened—but I was met with a series of blank diary pages during the trial. She was so stunned; she couldn't even bring herself to write about it. After her conflict with Warner Brothers, Kay put her career on the "back burner" and allowed herself to consider whatever opportunities came her way. The whole episode acted as a catalyst that allowed her the capacity and compassion for helping others during a war-torn world.

I relied a great deal on the initial research done by George Eells in his 1976 work *Ginger, Loretta and Irene Who?* Eells had interviewed many individuals from Kay's early days in New York, a few co-stars, her last romantic partner Dennis Allen, and Kay's lawyer Arnold L. Weissberger. Eells' work was a cornerstone which enabled me to venture for more information. As with most biographers, Eells had a hypothesis about Kay, which he aimed to prove, calling her a "Sellout." He also pictured her as a bitter, alcoholic recluse after 1952. "Just how true was this?"—I had to ask myself. I discovered a completely different Kay Francis in retirement.

I decided early on to allow the voice of Kay Francis to tell her story as much as possible. Her interviews and diaries were consistently revealing. Kay's friends, co-workers and contemporaries, in their own words, provided vivid and authentic impressions of Kay Francis the person and Kay Francis the actress. I am indebted to the assistance from both my friends, Martha Hunt and Carole Davis. These women spent hours proofreading the manuscript and helped to bring it into what Carole called a "reader friendly" experience. Also, very helpful in the research process were: G.D. Hamann, for his assistance with Los Angeles press reports on Kay; my sister, Amy O'Brien Shepherd did the preparation for the acquisition of FBI files that concerned Kay; Nona Davis, at FBI headquarters in D.C.; fashion consultant Mary Oliver, with her descriptions and detail about Kay's wardrobe; multilingual interpreter Dan Fowler, who helped with information on Raquel Meller; Mike Rinella whose extensive research on Kay's stage work was shared most willingly; and, the Sonoma County Library in acquiring news and reviews on microfilm from the east coast. Thanks also to: Andrew Potter, of the Royal Academy Library in London, for access to a copy of the 1925 portrait of Kay by Sir George Kelly; Katherine Le Blanc of the Skowhegan Free Public Library for publicity from Kay's 1952 *Theatre* tour; Budget Films of Los Angeles for providing rare outtakes from Kay's Warner films; my good friend Tim Buell for his book loans; John Drennon for his generous supply of Kay clippings, photos and pressbooks; Jim King, who created a fantastic Kay Francis Website that provided much advanced publicity for the book; ditto, to Paul Meienberg and San Francisco's "Thursday Night Film Noir," for inviting me as special guest to introduce Kay's Monogram *noir* films; and to my partner, Joel Bellagio for being a good soundboard and tolerating my Kay-mania.

Kay's story truly couldn't have been as complete or as honest without the help of Jetti Preminger Ames and her husband Lou. They are an amazingly warm and generous couple who shared a treasured simpatico with Kay during her final years. My publisher, Ben Ohmart, must be congratulated on his impressive effort to keep the stories from Hollywood's past alive and *in print*. BearManor Media has a unique library that reflects Ben's genuine affection for the Golden Age of film, radio and television.

The strangest and most surprising coincidence while writing Kay's biography, came to the fore while I was doing her genealogy. I was aware that on my great-grandmother O'Brien's side there was a Benjamin Gibbs—what I didn't know is that his grandfather was Kay's great-great-great-great grandfather! Kay is now "Cousin Kay," albeit a very distant cousin. Close friends, for some reason, weren't surprised when I told them the news.

What impressed me the most about Kay as an individual was her ability to be herself at a time when men and women were confined to very strict moral and social restrictions. After her exposure and participation in the unapologetic, liberated lifestyle of "Jazz Age New York," Kay was puzzled by what she found in Hollywood. All the fuss and interest in her private life amazed her. She stuck to her guns and lived her life as she saw fit. It took courage and self-assurance. Kay had enough savvy to realize that being honest about her affairs would have had the ladies of Middle America swallowing their teacups—especially, after the clampdown by the Catholic Legion of Decency and the Production Code Administration in the early 1930s. As a sexually liberated, and in her case, fertile woman, without the benefits of birth-control, Kay endured multiple abortions. Kay, who loved children, had the integrity *not* to bring a child into a lifestyle that was not conducive to the benefits of hearth and home. For decades fan-magazines fictionalized the "love-lives" and "perfect marriages" of film stars. This was disorienting for the American public. Readers and filmgoers paid the price for trying to mirror something that didn't exist. Kay looked in the mirror and refused to create lies for public consumption.

Elizabeth Wilson, for a 1937 issue of *Silver Screen,* commented on Kay's vitality, her interest in people and her willingness to embrace change and adventure. Wilson then zeroed in on Kay's dilemma with interviewers:

> There are two things which magazine and newspaper writers always want to interview Kay Francis about—her love life and clothes—and those happen to be the two subjects on which she is just about as communicative as a clam…She has the most terrific private life complex I have ever seen in any actress…it really is a shame that she is so fussy about her private life…[5]

Well, it isn't a shame any longer. At last, we are able to discover the public *and* private Kay Francis. She was a woman who followed her own instincts—and allowed herself to be entirely of this world with all the attendant urges and frailties. In the process she discovered her own humanity.

Chapter 1
Katharine Edwina Gibbs

> I was born in Oklahoma City by mistake. My dad and mother had
> gone out there on probably the most unusual of business deals. Dad, always
> the master of the magnificent gesture, had heard that he could buy up the
> Sioux Indian ponies, thousands of 'em for polo! He had planned to a nicety
> just how many ponies he'd keep for his own string, and how many he'd sell
> and how much money he'd make. He got out there, on his last dollar, and
> learned that the government controlled the whole shebang. So, while he
> and Mother were wondering what to do in Oklahoma City, when you're
> broke, I was born. And, in the meantime, he became the manager of a local
> hotel, so that solved the immediate problems of food and board. Nothing
> fazed Mother, the darling.[1]

Kay's explanation of how she came to be born in Oklahoma City and under what
circumstances was, for her, a most revealing bit of information. She rarely mentioned her
father, or talked about her humble beginnings. Columnist and future TV giant Ed Sullivan
cornered Kay in the fall of 1937, as she curled up on a couch in the library of her friend,
the prolific screenwriter, Donald Ogden Stewart, and got surprisingly candid responses.
Kay was still recovering from a court battle with Warner Brothers. They were intentionally
blackballing her into finishing out her contract in run-of-the-mill B programmers. The
whole episode shocked the Hollywood community. Kay was "Queen of the Lot"—the
only female on Warners' roster of stars who was listed among the major box-office attractions. Kay was angered, hurt, and she was struggling with the humiliation. Donald Ogden
Stewart (who would later have his own struggle being blacklisted during Hollywood's
Communist witch hunt), understandably offered Kay refuge. Just before Kay's ruckus
with the studio she had engaged the hospital room next Stewart's after he had suffered a
serious skull fracture. She spent the early morning hours consulting with physicians for
several days as he hovered between life and death.[2] Stewart considered Kay's gesture a
token of true friendship and it fully illustrates Kay's giving nature.

When Sullivan asked her if she had any regrets, Kay let off some steam. "Yes," she
said, firing away. "I'm sorry that I haven't the amazing nerve I had when I was about
nineteen years old…Ed, if I had that much gall now…I'd just sweep through this town

and people would be so overpowered by my sheer assurance that they'd bow and salaam to me in the streets." Kay's ability to regain some of that self-assurance would continue to elude her for a few more years. After what she had been through, to deny her humble beginnings seemed inconsequential. Fortunately, the many tidbits she offered Sullivan that day allowed me to tap into a plethora of information.

Kay Francis' early years have been shrouded in mystery and fabrication. Kay was protective and resourceful when talking about her childhood. Hints of exclusivity, private schools and privileges attempted to veil the reality of a single mother's determined struggle to do her best for an attractive, talented young daughter. Perhaps it was this "cover" that encouraged such far-fetched rumors that Kay's mother, actress Katharine Clinton, had come from Trinidad and was the daughter of a black mother and a white father.[3] Curiously enough, Maya Angelou, in her autobiographical *I Know Why the Caged Bird Sings*, tells of her own fantasy and that of her brother's, that Kay Francis was the mother they were intermittently separated from. Growing up as black children in a rural Arkansas community, they found solace and comfort from Kay Francis' image flickering on the big screen of movie palaces—and eagerly awaited each attraction that starred their "Mother Dear," Kay Francis.[4]

In truth, Kay's heritage isn't exotic. Her mother, Katharine Clinton Franks, born on May 17, 1874, was a product of her father's second marriage. Kay's Grandfather Franks had wandered the wild west and made his living scouting out the boomtowns of the frontier.[5] At some point Mr. Franks ventured East again, as Kay told Ed Sullivan that her mother came from Chicago. While residing in the town of Galena, Illinois, the youthful Franks was bequeathed a 17th-century portrait of actress Nell Gwynne that had been stolen from the Royal Bedchamber of Windsor Castle. The painting of Gwynne, who was the mistress of Charles II, had been a royal commission painted by Sir Peter Lely. Over the years the painting of Nell managed to survive a strange history of fires and the jealousy of Franks family wives. In the1920s, when *Nell* fell into Kay's safekeeping, she acknowledged an affinity for the actress-courtesan, and commented, "I find Nell, with her strange smile and her look of knowing so much more than she would ever tell, a fascinating person. But I shan't be afraid of her or jealous...And if she brings excitement in her wake, as she has done before...well, I don't mind excitement! I rather like it."[6] Coincidentally, Nell brought Kay good luck. In 1925, Kay herself posed for the Principal Painter for the British Monarchy, Sir Gerald Kelly, one of England's most admired artists of the 20th Century.

As for the Clinton side of Kay's family, her mother confirmed that Lawrence Clinton arrived at Ipswich, Bay of Cod, Massachusetts in 1665, making Kay a ninth-generation American.[7] Once ashore, Lawrence married a woman fourteen years his senior who paid to release him as an indentured servant. His libido dissolved that unhappy union when he was convicted of ravishing another woman. He then sired a son, Jacob, from yet *another* affair, for which he was ordered to pay 20 pence of corn for child support. Not long after Jacob was born, Lawrence was found guilty of "fornicating" with a woman named Mary Wooden. He married Mary, who died after bearing him two more children. Lawrence married a third time, to a widow named Margaret Painter

Morris. They had six children. Around 1707, the fertile Lawrence *finally* put his plow to rest. He died near Newport, Rhode Island.[8] From which of Lawrence Clinton's sons Kay is a descendant is unknown.

Kay also told Ed Sullivan that her father, Joseph Sprague Gibbs, came from a little town outside of Detroit. Records verify that he was born in 1862 in Homer, Michigan, 90 miles west of Detroit. In the 1880 census 18-year-old Joseph was living at home with his parents, Volney and Helen Wooley Gibbs.[9] Kay's father was named after his grandfather, Joseph Gibbs, and his grandmother, Polly Sprague Gibbs, who was born in Connecticut. Joseph and Polly and their eight children had relocated to Michigan in 1848. Joseph, a Freemason, was influential in organizing one of the state's oldest Masonic Lodges (a secret fraternal order that emphasizes the practice of charity). The Gibbs line establishes Kay as a ninth-generation American on both sides of her family.[10] The Sprague line reinforces the 9th-generation lineage with the arrival of Francis Sprague in Plymouth, Massachusetts, on the ship *Anne*, in 1623. Sprague was known among the Puritans as one of the "Strangers" (Puritans referred to themselves as the "Saints"). Had she known, Kay would have prided herself that Sprague acquired one of the first liquor licenses in the area and opened one of New England's first inn-taverns. Despite the fact that Puritan officials monitored the intake of liquor for each patron and that Francis Sprague lost his license at least twice for "drinking overmuch and tolerating too much jollity," he died one of the ten wealthiest men in New England.[11] Sprague's son, Joseph, carried on the family tradition and was found guilty of drinking, gambling and "uncivil reveling." He spent many hours in the punishment stalls known as stocks. In addition, "to the dishonor of God and the offense of the government," Joseph brought his mare into the parlor of a friend's house, presumably to celebrate the birth of one of his seven children.[12] Two hundred years later, his descendant, Kay's father, pulled the same "offense" in the hotel where she was newly born. A slightly tipsy Joseph Sprague Gibbs galloped his mare up the staircase and into the room where mother and baby Kay lay resting.[13]

With such an ancestry, it is fitting that Kay kept her liquor cabinet well-stocked, was an ace poker player, and enthusiastically claimed her share of husbands and lovers. She inherited her grandfather Frank's love of travel, and, although she died a wealthy woman, one *cannot* overlook Kay's charitable nature that seems to echo down from her great-grandfather Joseph Gibbs' association with the Freemasons.

Kay's theatrical heritage may have paled next to the Barrymores', but her mother's acting career was strongly influenced by some of the finest talent in the American Theatre. Katharine Clinton Franks attended Kemper Hall, a preparatory and collegiate school for young ladies on the shores of Lake Michigan, in Kenosha, Wisconsin. Katharine graduated in the class of 1894 under the tutelage of the Sisters of St. Mary. Kemper Hall's *Alumnae Messenger* for April 1945, noted, "Kay Francis comes rightly by her histrionic talent, for we read in old Kodaks of her mother's ability in dramatics." Katharine then ventured to study elocution at the Chicago Conservatory. The *Alumnae Messenger* for May 1898, made note that Katharine, "gave a very successful reading at Elgin, Illinois, on April 10, 1898." Her expertise with speaking, vocabulary, and succinct communication was a powerful influence on Kay, who always expressed herself intelligently.

Soon after her Chicago studies, Katharine met the giant among theatrical producers, Augustine Daly. She dropped her surname, becoming Katharine Clinton, and made her stage debut in a musical comedy he produced. She also appeared in Daly's melodrama, *The Great Ruby*. Daly, who died the following year, in 1899, had become the most respected playwright, producer and director of his era, in spite of his tendency to tamper with the text of established classics. Although Daly's influence on Katharine's career was short-lived, his protégée, Ada Rehan, noted Katharine's talents and used her in productions after Daly's death. From Limerick, Ireland, Rehan, under Daly's coaching, was recognized as one of America's greatest actresses.

So it was that Katharine Clinton, with her soft shining black hair, large lustrous brown eyes, and eager ambitions, came under Rehan's influence. By October 1900, Katharine was cast in a play by Eugene W. Presbrey, titled *Marcelle*, an epoch presentation set in the court of Louis XV and the new frontier in Quebec. Blanche Walsh starred. Presbrey was better known for his adaptation of the 1903 hit *Raffles* (which Kay filmed in 1930). When *Marcelle* opened in New York, *The New York Times* remarked, "The last act is full of action, and in it Miss Walsh rose to real emotional heights and scored a great personal success...Katharine Clinton, as Mira, has a few bits that were well done, but none of the other women had even a chance to shine."[14] During the 1903-04 season at New York's Lyric Theatre, Katharine was encouraged to play in such successes as Shakespeare's *Merchant of Venice* (as Jessica, daughter of Shylock). Rehan produced *Merchant* in association with theatrical legend Otis Skinner. (Twenty-one years later, Kay Francis would make her own Broadway debut in Shakespeare's *Hamlet*.)

Katharine Clinton's career flourished, as did her romance with a businessman-hotel manager, Joseph Sprague Gibbs. The two were married, December 7, 1903.[15] Kay revealed to Ed Sullivan that her parents married at "The Little Church Around the Corner."[16] This Episcopal Church in New York got its name from a curious incident in 1870. When actor George Holland passed away, his fellow thespian Joseph Jefferson was rebuffed when arranging for a funeral. He was told there was a little church around the corner where "they do that sort of thing." "God Bless 'The Little Church Around the Corner!'" Jefferson exclaimed. His benediction fostered the church's close-knit relationship with people of the theatre. With Katharine's established theatrical career, the Episcopal Church "around the corner" was a logical choice for the couple's ceremony.

Based on the census information from Michigan, Joseph would have been forty-one at this time, and his marriage to Katharine (age 29) would have been his third. Gibbs was on the move frequently. Thirteen months after their marriage, the couple was residing in Oklahoma City when Kay was born. Katharine Edwina Gibbs entered the world stage at one o'clock in the morning on Friday the 13th of January 1905.[17] Kay's middle name is for her Uncle Edwin (her mother's half-brother). As with many actresses of Kay's era, there has always been confusion about her actual birth date. Kay clarified the year in a 1939 interview with her longtime intimate, interviewer Dick Mook:

> When I first came out here [Hollywood] I was under contract to Paramount. I have never been sensitive about my age and was perfectly willing to have it published. But, Paramount said, "No!" They merely publicized the fact I was born on Friday, the 13th of January. Reporters consulted

almanacs and found the 13th of January fell on Friday in the years 1899 and 1911. One made me younger and the other older. They arbitrarily selected 1899 as the year of my birth. Actually, it was 1905 and I am 34.[18]

Kay's close friend for the last 20 years of her life, Jetti Ames, substantiated this claim, saying, "It's 1905. There's no reason Kay would lie to me."[19] Many reference books still use the 1899 date. Photos from the collection of Henry Francis, Kay's first husband's son, verify the 1905 date. A photo from 1921 shows a smiling 16-year-old Katharine Gibbs (date and age noted on the back) enjoying the beach on a summer break. Upon viewing the 1910 census for New Jersey, all doubts about 1905 being the date can be put to rest. The census shows Katharine E. Gibbs, age five, born in Oklahoma, attending the Institute of Holy Angels in Fort Lee.[20]

Kay's mother, Katharine Clinton Franks (1874—1957), in a 1902 stage production.

Joseph and Katharine Gibbs soon relocated to Denver where infant Kay made her stage debut in the reputable Denver theatre group run by Margaret Fealy. Kay's mother reported:

> Kay first appeared on the stage in Denver. Margaret Fealy had a dramatic school in that city and needed a baby for the farce comedy, *Jane*, which she was about to produce. We lived near Mrs. Fealy, so she suggested that I allow Kay to appear in the performance. Kay's father and I stood in the wings as Kay was about to be carried on the stage. Suddenly it occurred to him that she might cry at the wrong moment, so he poked a pacifier into her mouth. Would she deign to use it? No, she calmly discarded it and endured the rest of the show tolerantly. With such a start I haven't been at all surprised to view Kay's success in pictures.[21]

As part of Kay's theatrical résumé, Margaret Fealy was the founder of Denver's Tabor Grand School of Acting. The *Denver Times* reported that prominent national stars and managers attended many of the school's performances, "all of whom lavish in their praise of...the excellent system used by Mrs. Fealy."[22] Kay's nonchalant baby debut in *Jane* was at either Denver's Elitch's Gardens, or the Tabor Grand Opera House. One of the most famous names to hail from Fealy's instruction was Douglas Fairbanks, Sr.

On the move again, Kay and her family relocated to Santa Barbara and then on to Los Angeles. Joseph Gibbs was connected with hotels in Los Angeles, Santa Barbara and Yosemite. Kay's mother later reminisced, saying, "We had a horse and buggy in Los Angeles, and as soon as Kay was old enough to see and enjoy things out of doors, she used to beg for afternoon rides. It was so beautiful here then. There were so many more orange groves and gardens before the city grew large. I don't believe, even though a baby, Kay will ever forget a rough and muddy journey in our first auto over the then terrible roads to San Francisco."[23]

When Kay was four, the Gibbs family returned to New York, where Katharine resumed her stage work. Some sources claim that Joseph and Katharine split up around this time (1909), but Katharine told of a performance where Gibbs was present. "One evening my husband bought two box seats and brought Kay to a Boston theater where I was playing. Before the drop of the third curtain, I died a dramatic death. Just when we had brought the audience to a pitch of intense sobbing, Kay rose in the box and in a shrill baby voice called, 'Don't be frightened! Mother's only acting.' The hysteria of the audience turned into loud laughter and we had to ring down the curtain."[24]

Kay reiterated the story, stating that she was *not* with her father, but with a family friend:

> Mother had to be shot just before the third act curtain and when the big scene came, the audience was properly keyed up for it. The shot was fired. Mother cried out tragically. She staggered and fell while the slayer watched horrified at this deed, and the audience gripped its chair-arms. The atmosphere was stifling with silence and tenseness. Then I turned to the friend who was 'minding' me, and piped up, 'don't be frightened—mother's not really dead—she's only acting!' My childish voice carried everywhere in the theatre. The audience became hysterical with laughter…The part I remember best is the spanking I received in the dressing-room. After that episode I saw mother's portrayals from the wings—not from out front.[25]

Kay contended that as a small child she was "excitable, spoiled, and had a terrible temper." Through her mother's discipline, Kay (gratefully) achieved balance. Kay spent many months on tour with her mother. Katharine performed with Boston's Castle Square Stock Company (where Alfred Lunt got his start), while Kay got a rather intermittent and disjointed education in convent schools.[26] Touring would fill the final years of Kay's *own* theatrical career, but with much greater success. Unfortunately, Katharine Clinton's struggle as a single mother (Joseph Gibbs' whereabouts were unknown once Kay started school), restrained her ambitions for a stage career. It wasn't until 1921 that she returned to Broadway, playing Mme. Lebas, in Denys Amiel and Andre Obey's *The Wife With the Smile*. (In 1928, Katharine's final stage appearance was at Broadway's Klaw Theatre in Clifford Pember and Ralph Cullinan's *Caravan*.)[27]

Kay's friend, Jetti Ames, recalled Kay saying her father "was a big mistake for her mother and deserted them."[28] In her mid-forties Kay told friends that she didn't know where her father was and didn't care. Kay never had a good word for him. Joseph Sprague Gibbs was indeed a tall order. At 6' 4", he gave Kay distinction as the tallest leading lady (5' 7") in Hollywood during the 1930s. He also gave her a half-sister that she probably never knew existed. It is unknown what happened to his first wife, Hattie Adeline Darrow, whom he married in 1884. His second marriage, to Mary Connelly in 1894, produced a daughter, Helen, who was born in 1897. Records from Calhoun County show that Mary Connelly Gibbs died in 1907. It is unknown what happened to Kay's half-sister, Helen.[29] Obviously, Joseph left behind his little family in Michigan before Mary died, and started a second family with third wife Katharine Clinton Franks. After he left Kay and her mother, census records from 1910 show that Joseph had relocated to Moravia, California where he was the landlord of a hotel.[30] The only reminder he left behind for Kay was reflected in the mirror. She was always tall for her age and stood out from her peers. Kay saw this as an asset, saying, "Even as a girl I was tall, but my mother instilled the sensible attitude. Rather than making me self-conscious, she kept reminding me that my father had been six feet four, that height was admirable. She held the motto: 'Whatever You Are, Be.' And I have patterned my philosophy on it."[31]

Kay actually saw herself as a blend of both her parents. "I was called Katharine for my mother," Kay said, "and I look a good deal like her, but I got my height from my father." With her father out of the picture, Kay looked for male mentors elsewhere, and later commented, "To a great extent I think it's the men she comes in contact with who shape a woman's outlook and even her personality. There was Peter, for instance."[32] Kay met Peter, a neighbor, when she was twelve (1917). Kay was fascinated by Peter's travels and absorbed his "straight-from-the-shoulder" philosophy. Their frequent conversations, or "hedge talks" as they called them, took place near a row of boxberry between their houses. "Play square, Kay. Always," he told her, "then you'll have no regrets. You know how glad you were that you told the grocer about those two extra apples he put in the bag accidentally—because then he gave you three for being honest. Life's pretty much like that. In the end it gives you something extra for playing the game fairly…" Kay's co-stars during the 1930s, William Powell and George Brent, admired and acknowledged the fact that Kay had what was then considered to be a "man's point of view." Kay claimed it was from Peter that she learned how to speak a man's language, be direct, and cut through all the annoying feminine tricks and foibles. She avoided tears to gain a point and refused to lead a man on merely for a whim. Throughout her life, Kay followed the "code of ethics" that Peter so willingly helped formulate. *Playing the game fairly…*[33] became something essential to Kay as an adult. In 2004, Kay's friend and confident, Jetti Ames, concurred. "Kay was so warm and genuine…but, don't ever lie to her! That's one thing she would not tolerate. She expected honesty from those close to her."[34]

At fourteen, Kay continued her education at Miss Fuller's School for Young Ladies in Ossining, New York. The school had been attended by many famous women including author Faith Baldwin.[35] Kay's lack of conventional education, however, proved her undoing at Miss Fuller's. A few years later, in a rare interview, Kay's mother was defensive about Kay's mediocre success at the school.

> She failed in geometry and I was pleased over that…And I've always thought it ridiculous for an attractive glamorous woman to study Latin and Greek. I wanted her to do well in piano. But what possible use would geometry be? She was like her father. He was a clear thinker and possessed excellent judgment. Kay has that too. Every daughter is one half her father by inheritance…I attribute the fact that her career has been one of the steadiest and most evenly regulated rises in filmdom to the calm, wise brain she inherited from her father. Kay's father had a great personality. And you must remember, Kay has the greatest gift in the world for an actor—personality. That's a star's most valuable asset.[36]

Kay herself once said that at Miss Fuller's it was "Katie-did" when she was good and "Katie-didn't" when she performed poorly. "Mostly it was Katie-didn't," she acknowledged.[37] As the school's resident tomboy, Kay's claim to fame at Miss Fuller's was for the art of climbing. The whole school witnessed this talent at an ungodly hour one morning. "She climbed from her window to the roof of the dormitory on a dare. She just managed to get a grip on the rain gutter when her feet swung clear of the window ledge. She clung as long as she could and then started to fall. A protruding nail caught her bloomers and there she hung—suspended in midair. She was just out of reach of rescuing hands…So she hung while the Ossining Fire Department was hastily summoned. They had the only ladder in town long enough to reach her."[38]

The gallantry of firemen rescuing the fair Katie Gibbs appealed to Kay. Her lifelong fascination with chivalry was again spurred on the afternoon of September 18, 1919. World War I had just ended less than a year earlier. New York City was waiting for the return of General Pershing. Kay liked telling the story:

> It was at the time General Pershing came back from France. Remember the excitement? The big parade in New York? I started following it at eleven in the morning and I was still following it at three that afternoon! My family had lost me entirely and they were frantic, but I was having a marvelous time—marching right behind the band! I dote on bands…swinging along to that band of General Pershing's was one of the greatest thrills I've ever had—until a horse stepped on my foot! Somebody caught hold of me…Somebody about ten feet tall. He hoisted me to his shoulder for the rest of the parade, then took me home in a taxi after we'd had some ice cream. Who was he? A hard-bitten, old army sergeant to the rest of the world—but a white-plumed prince to me![39]

Although Kay's shenanigans did not warrant a visit to Ossining's Sing Sing prison, her mother soon sought a different sort of confinement for Kay. The hoydenish antics were considerably cooled down when Kay entered the cloistered environment of the Cathedral School of St. Mary in Garden City, Long Island. She was enrolled there from September 1920, until May 1921. She earned a 77 in conduct and 80s in all her other courses. She excelled with a 98 in spelling and failed again in geometry. She also managed to find affinity with more ladylike pursuits. Jetti Ames recalled that Kay "always stressed that her ability to sew and do needlework so well was due to her early years with the nuns. The nuns encouraged her with these skills. Kay did a lot of work with her hands. She did beautiful needlepoint. Although her mother moved frequently, because she couldn't pay the rent, she sought a Catholic school because she felt Kay would get a better education there."[40] Mrs. Gibbs' positive experience at Kemper Hall influenced this decision. She also hoped a better environment might make up for the times when the going got rough for her and Kay.

During her mother's touring years on the road, Kay's education included the harsher realities outside the atmosphere of nuns and a Catholic education. George Eells noted:

> Kay spent much of her childhood touring with her mother, moving from one broken-down rooming house to another. She never forgot those barn-

storming years when they were so desperately poor that they frequently filled up on salty popcorn and drank water to save the cost of dinner...As an adult, Kay would sometimes speak of those early experiences to close friends..."That was a pretty dreadful time of life for Kay," Mrs. Dwight Wiman said. "I know her mother had an awful lot of odd jobs. Some of the things Kay told me I wouldn't repeat. They were horrible. It was all very third-rate."[41]

Any offense that Kay's society friends felt about her upbringing, or lack of it, was possibly the bias of a sheltered elite. Eells description and Wiman's impression of Kay's early years overlook the fact that theatre trouping in the early 1900s was typically a rugged experience for *anyone* who braved the territory. The important thing is that from 1910 on, Kay's mother made sure Kay was off the road and in school when it was affordable. Kay's early experience with the uncertainties accompanying poverty, would later influence many of her career decisions. She made no bones about it. She took her work seriously, but her main focus as a star was the financial reward. Whether Kay felt any ambivalence toward her mother from these childhood experiences is unlikely. Once Kay's own career took off, she certainly took excellent care of her mother financially, although she did not encourage her to visit the movie sets or mix with her friends. Years later, Kay's friend Beatrice Stewart impulsively stopped at Kay's house and was greeted at the door by a "perfectly beautiful little woman—snow-white hair, charming—[Stewart] said, 'Oh, I'm sorry. I'm Beatrice Stewart. I wonder if I could see Miss Francis.' And she said, 'Of course, I'm Kay's mother.'"[42] Stewart gave Kay a dressing down afterwards and wondered why Kay wouldn't let friends meet her perfectly charming mother.

The curious thing about Kay's early years was the absence of any family support. Where was Uncle Edwin? What about Katharine Franks' parents? Surely, if they could afford private schooling for her, they must have been well off. Perhaps her decision to go on stage caused a rift in the family? After all, becoming an actress at that time was not considered *de rigueur*. Whatever the story, no family members were around at all by the time Kay was a star. Her mother wrote in 1936, "Kay and I are the last two living relatives in our entire family. Not only is this a tie of sympathy, but we have a deep respect and regard for each other. Kay and I are everything to each other."[43]

While at Cathedral School, Kay helped present a three-act play with another student, Katherine "Katty" Stewart. Kay had a trouser-role as the male lead. The script, titled *You Never Can Tell*, had Katty as "the female lead, because she was the author," Kay explained years later. "And, I played the leading male role, because I was the tallest girl in the class."[44] At the time (1921), 16-year-old Kay wasn't contemplating a stage career, but instead fancied herself becoming a trapeze artist. Kay's mother fancied her daughter becoming something else entirely, recalling, "I wanted Kay to be a pianist. We began her musical education when she was very young and found her to be a natural musician...few of her fans know how very accomplished she is in this other sphere. Kay became very proficient in memorizing and made an unusually fine pianist...in her teens she played quite exquisitely. I wanted her to study the pipe organ, for picture houses were just installing organs and I felt this would open a new career for musicians."[45]

Instead of returning for her senior year at Cathedral in the fall of 1921, or playing the pipe organ for the flickers, Kay took a six-month course at a business college coinci-

Katie Gibbs 1921 (age 16). On summer break from Cathedral School (where she ran the 100-yard dash in 12 seconds flat). (Courtesy of Henry Francis)

dentally called the Katherine Gibbs Secretarial School. Kay enrolled at her mother's request that she prepare to earn a living. (The school, founded in 1911, is still reputable, and as of 2005 has campuses in several states.) Kay excelled in stenography and typing. Upon graduation she had a brief assignment, at thirty dollars a week, for businessmen Charles McAlpine Pyle and Emerson MacMillan.[46] She later maintained that she was a "most excellent secretary" and "well worth every penny of the salary" paid to her![47]

Kay then landed the posh position as companion-secretary to Juliana Cutting, a prominent arranger for social and debutant events among blue-bloods. Kay made many useful social connections from her association with Cutting. Elsa Maxwell mentioned Cutting in an article about Kay, saying Cutting was, "that very industrious lady who discovered that while marriages might be made in heaven, coming-out parties succeed— or flop—on earth. That one of those eligible young men would prefer Juliana's beautiful secretary to her homely clients was likewise foreordained."[48] (Maxwell was referring to Allan Ryan, who would actually enter Kay's life a few years later.)

1921-22 turned into a whirlwind year for Kay, with many transitions. Her first big romance was the "real thing." She noted in her combination diary-engagement calendar for January 4, 1922: "Met Dwight Francis through Lyn. Tea date expected?"[49] Dwight showed up two days later and invited her to a dance. Her engagement calendar was filled with tea dates, walks and dinners with Dwight. On April 22 Dwight told Kay that he loved her. After his confession, Kay noted: "Off for my fifth weekend with Dwight and I love him—I think."[50] Kay told reporter Dick Mook that she had first noticed Dwight during the pre-nuptial festivities of her "cousin" Bea Lockwood. Bea's husband had been living with Dwight, most likely in New York where Kay's life was centered.[51] George Eells gave some background on Kay's new beau:

James Dwight Francis, whose surname Kay always retained, was the handsome, wellborn son of a Pittsfield, Massachusetts family. He attended Phillips-Exeter Academy and in 1915 entered Harvard, but his interest was not so much in educating himself as living it up, and he left in 1919 without a degree. By the time he came into Kay's life he was drinking well beyond his financial means, but his background and charm blinded her to the dangerous implications of his frequently lurching gait.[52]

Kay's diaries confirm her innocence and are imbued with the glow of sentiment. An old photograph from May 30, 1922 shows the romantic duo "sneaking a weekend in Atlantic City, N.J." (inscription on back). Kay is seated, while Dwight stands at her side. At seventeen she has a finish and elegance about her. Sporting a scarf-trimmed, upturned brim hat, ankle-length wool skirt and coat-length jacket, young Kay looked very much a lady. She had a "way with clothes" even at this tender age. At twenty-five, Dwight looked quite dashing. His charm, good looks and social position had literally swept Kay off her feet into a romantic euphoria. After spending six weekends together, Kay noted in her diary, "I think I am a mother."[53] Two weeks later she entered: "My baby died or rather our baby."[54] By the end of the summer Kay had met Dwight's parents in Pittsfield, where she was also introduced to his aunts and uncles. On October 27, she recorded their engagement and in November she noted, "GOT MY RING!"[55] The couple was married on Wednesday, December 4, 1922, at St. Thomas Church, 5th Avenue, New York. Kay and Dwight walked down the aisle past the High Gothic-styled stonework of columns and arches. With such a solid foundation and storybook setting for a ceremony, hopes for the newlyweds looked promising. They also shared the same birthday, January 13. Pittsfield's *Berkshire Eagle* reported on December 5, 1922:

> The marriage of Miss Katharine Gibbs, daughter of Mrs. Katharine Clinton Gibbs and the late Joseph Sprague Gibbs of Los Angeles and J. Dwight Francis of Pittsfield and New York, son of Mr. and Mrs. Henry A. Francis of this city was solemnized yesterday in New York City at St. Thomas's church at 12:30 o'clock by Dr. Stires.
>
> The bride was given away by Dr. Stuart Hart…the bride wore a gown of grey crepe-de-chine, a black picture hat and carried a shower bouquet of pink roses and lilies of the valley. Miss Mary Strong of Ossining, N.Y., was maid of honor…the best man was Fred G. Crane, Jr., of Dalton.
>
> Following the ceremony, Mr. Francis' uncle gave a wedding breakfast at the Metropolitan club for the bridal party and a few relatives. Mr. and Mrs. Francis left for a trip to the Scacquit club on Cape Cod and will be at home after January, at 21 West 49th Street, New York City.

The *Berkshire Eagle* failed to mention that Kay was an hour late for her own wedding. She stopped on her way to St. Thomas to listen to a marching band! "I couldn't resist," Kay later explained. Her fixation on band music would follow her to Hollywood where she enthusiastically declared, "Every morning I play band music on the gramophone while I'm making up to set me right for the day!"[56]

The day after the wedding, Kay and Dwight motored in the New England countryside, had lunch at Saybrook, and spent the night at the Biltmore in Providence, Rhode Island. The next few days were spent relaxing, playing bridge, golfing and going to the opera. They spent their first night in their own home in New York on December 17. For her final entry in 1922 Kay wrote, "My most wonderful year—1922!"[57]

Thanks to Dwight's parents, he and Kay were able to enjoy the opera season: *Tristan and Isolde* (always Kay's personal favorite), *Aida, Lucia di Lammermoor, Romeo and Juliet,* and *Boris Godunov* with the famous Russian bass Chaliapin. Then there was a recital with the famous dance interpreter Ruth St. Denis. As far as the movies were concerned, Kay made a point of seeing her idol Pola Negri vamping outrageously in 1923's *Bella Donna.* During the summer of 1923, Kay and Dwight took time out for tennis, polo, the beach and swimming. Kay noted that she weighed in at 116 pounds in her bathing suit. In the first few months of her marriage, it would appear that Kay had visits to her home from *both* her parents and mentions both "Mother" and "Dad" coming by on separate occasions. The Dad she referred to in her diaries was Dwight's father. She was fond of Dwight's parents and called them "Mom" and "Dad." Mr. Francis was a frequent visitor to Kay and Dwight's apartment during their marriage. Kay's mother told an interviewer in the 1930s that Kay's father had died in 1918.[58] Kay's wedding announcement listed her father as "the late Joseph Sprague Gibbs." However, the uncertainty surrounding the exact date of Gibbs' demise remained clouded when he was listed as a possible survivor in Kay's will, dated 1967.[59] Perhaps the mystery of Joseph's death is resolved by a source that lists his death in St. Louis, Missouri (January 1919). This account makes sense, as it mentions he left behind a wife (#4) *and* two more half-sisters for Kay: Virginia, age four, and Helen, age three.[60]

Dwight Francis and Katharine Gibbs, May 30, 1922. "Sneaking a weekend in Atlantic City." At seventeen Kay displayed a distinctive grace and elegance. (Courtesy of Henry Francis)

While Dwight worked in the family's New York office (woolen business) at $180 a month, Kay avoided boredom and housework by finding herself a job. She worked half a day and her salary was $15 a week, which is exactly what she paid her maid Maud. Kay later mused to reporter Dick Mook,

Good old Maud…She did everything—cleaned the apartment, cooked, laundered. Why, she used to do the washing in our bath-tub! We had two rooms, a kitchenette and bath, and paid $75 a month for it out of Dwight's $180. Maud used to take a basket and go over on Ninth Avenue to market because we couldn't afford to buy in the markets on Sixth! But we went to the opera. Oh, yes! That was part of the family tradition. Dwight's family had money, plenty of it, but *we* didn't. They would pay for a membership to the opera club for him but not for a maid.[61]

After several months, Kay and Dwight relocated to the family home in Pittsfield where they occupied a six-room house. Kay felt as if she had been imprisoned after living amid all the excitement and distractions of the big city. When she was able to escape to New York, she was jubilant. Kay also elaborated to Mook on her domestic situation. She laughed,

> We had two cars alright. The family gave them to us. Family front had to be kept up. But I did all my own housework. I hated every dust rag I owned and took a very hearty and very personal dislike to every egg I fried and every potato I boiled. I am still the world's worst cook. But we belonged to the country club and all that sort of thing. New England families are conservative and we were no different from all other 'young marrieds'...but the fact that misery had company didn't help me any. It just wasn't the sort of life I had planned for myself and I simply couldn't adapt myself to it.[62]

Kay later mentioned that Dwight was almost as much a romantic as she was and that he had innate charm, an innate feeling for things. Instead of buying her the usual kind of engagement ring, he gave her a ring that had been in his family for generations -- an exquisitely cut diamond flanked by two sapphires, in an old-gold setting. Each month, on the date of their wedding anniversary, Dwight would send Kay a carefully selected white gardenia. Also, on a positive note, Kay felt the marriage transformed her from a long-legged gawky girl to a poised young woman. However, once relocated in Pittsfield, the young couple fought as much as they loved. She was *anything* but content. Kay later confessed they weren't good companions. They could find no common tastes. She loved the theatre and he couldn't stand it. She was quoted later as saying, "There can be a great romantic love between two people, but it cannot last unless there are other bases of enjoyment. There *must* be companionship. I learned that the first time I married."[63] Kay reported that she walked out after one of their quarrels and never went back. Dwight taught Kay the danger of placing her own happiness in someone else's hands. She looked to Dwight for happiness and stability—something he could not provide. Ultimately, she discovered happiness was found in herself. In 1934, Kay wrote an article titled, "My Design for Happiness," in which she sagely advised:

> I'll begin with happiness and what *I* mean by the word. People mean so many different things. I believe that happiness lies within yourself and cannot be altered, increased or abated, really by an external influence or by any person. I may get excitement, pleasure and many other emotions from outside stimuli and persons, but happiness in its essence is within myself.[64]

On a trip to New York in May 1924, Kay helped celebrate her mother's birthday and a few days later made a significant change in her appearance. She bobbed her hair. It was a stunning look for Kay. In July, she started smoking. Both of these actions were considered symbols of liberation for women of Kay's generation. Her steps into this new "self-awareness" were at the very moment the 1920s started to roar. Any excitement she felt about these changes was tentative. Kay was encouraged to have an abortion by Dwight, who she found out was a hopeless philanderer. Wagging tongues in the small town of Pittsfield goaded her into an unforgiving attitude regarding Dwight's escapades. Had she simply been blinded by his good looks and charm? The couple was always short on funds. Dwight refused to give up the Squadron A or any of his other clubs. Kay contributed what she could to their household expenses. Coupled with Dwight's manhandling and wandering eye, Kay regretfully decided to divorce him. After their divorce, James Dwight Francis' matrimonial path had similar results for his future wives. His persona was best described to me in April 2003, by his daughter, Lesley Lee Francis. Lesley Lee is the granddaughter of poet Robert Frost. Her mother, Lesley Frost, married James Dwight Francis in 1928, three years after he divorced Kay. Their marriage lasted about as long as Dwight's union with Kay, although it did produce two daughters. Lesley Lee saw little of her father and had this to say,

> I really didn't know my father. I never had any dealings with Kay. My father was gone before I was born. My mother got total custody. He did not even have visitation rights. And what she gave up for that was no alimony and no child support, which made her life very difficult. My mother wouldn't have anything to do with Dwight. He liked women, and I think that's basically what broke up all the marriages. My mother didn't put up with it very long. Nothing she ever said to me suggested that he was abusive, or that he was an alcoholic. He did go into a terrible depression over the loss of all the money that was given to him by his father and his uncle. It was supposed to set him up in business, but he lost everything. It was the *women* that were the problem. He thought that every one of them was the "big love of his life." These weren't one night stands. These were always big things. Women found him very attractive. By the time I met him (late 1940s)...he looked terrific. He was married to Henrietta [third wife], but he was having an affair with another woman who was at the table with us! He would invite "the mistress" to dine with them at the Hotel Pierre! He was pretty open about these things. I think at that point Henrietta had had enough. I don't like womanizers. The *ego* of this man. He sets up this dinner with these two daughters of his, he had not seen since they were born...a big fancy dinner and he invites his wife, three sons, two daughters and his *mistress*! *Excuse me*! I have no regard for the man at all. What I do think is that he was a womanizer and furthermore he wasn't a very serious provider.[65]

Kay's friend Beatrice Ames Stewart recalled years later, "I'd been aware of Katie Gibbs before her marriage but actually met her in Paris...Katie was getting a divorce but at the family's request kept their name. They loved her so and realized how much in love she was with that poor, dreary, sodden offspring of theirs. She felt badly about leaving him, but she couldn't stand the beatings. So his aunt (Kay later referred to her as Gertrude Tobin) took her to Paris, and the family paid for the divorce. He was her real love. Oh, I could tell you about Katie, but I wouldn't. She wouldn't like it. I will say I don't think she ever stopped loving him."[66]

Kay expressed her own private reactions to Dwight in emotionally charged diary entries from October 1924—"Dwight is *such* a cad!!"—"This marriage is over I'm afraid!!"[67] It wasn't long before nineteen-year-old Kay found herself looking for love on the rebound. She had met a man named Paul, thought he was "charming," and by December they were having long discussions. "Wonderful conversation with Paul," she wrote. "We talked and will be talking again. We want to sleep together. Thank you dear God!"[68] Not surprisingly, Kay's feelings for Paul waned by the time she sailed on the Atlantic Transport liner *Minnetonka* for Cherbourg on February 28, 1925.[69] In Europe, she found new distractions as she hobnobbed amongst the elite (Dwight's aunt had social connections). Kay's final divorce decree was granted in Paris on April 23, 1925.[70] She was kept busy with many male admirers in Europe, but something about her feelings for Dwight had staying power. David Lewis, the lover and partner of James Whale (director of 1931's *Frankenstein*), was associate producer for Kay's 1938 feature *Secrets of an Actress*. He was quoted as saying, "[Kay] married several times and had many lovers but she never really recovered from that first marriage. The affection was still there."[71]

The affection was still there. Indeed, Kay's emotional ties with the Francis family remained kindled for years afterwards. In 1932, she told an interviewer, "I adored [Dwight's] family. One of my most treasured friends of today is his mother."[72] In 1934, Dwight's mother was outraged and came to Kay's defense when the town mayor of Pittsfield banned Kay's film *Dr. Monica*. In 2003, Dwight's son Henry (from his third marriage) said, "My mother, Henrietta, told me that Kay adored my grandfather and namesake, Henry A. Francis, and that Kay kept the Francis name solely because of her fondness for Henry."[73] During the peak of her Hollywood career, Kay wistfully recalled her marriage to Dwight, saying, "It's a rather wonderful thing to be married very young and know that ecstatic happiness that belongs to the 'teen's. I suppose I'd do it all over again."[74] Whether or not Kay had fully recovered from the emotional strain of divorce, upon her return to New York she discovered, once again, what she thought was true love. But Kay kept this next whirlwind romance and marriage a secret for years to come.

❋ JAMES DWIGHT FRANCIS ❋
Born: January 13, 1897, Pittsfield, Mass.
Died: January 25, 1988, Edgartown, Mass.
Married to Kay Francis: December 13, 1922—April 23, 1925
    James Dwight Francis was the only child of Henry A. and Agnes Bartlett Francis. Henry and his two brothers had a very successful textile business. According to Dwight's daughter, Lesley Francis, "They made a lot of money. One of the brothers was a designer. A big chunk of their fortune was lost in the Depression, the crash."

Dwight grew up in Pittsfield and attended Harvard for two years, Class of 1919. Daughter Lesley clarified this event saying, "Now there's some question about *how* he graduated. He left Harvard before he graduated and joined the Lafayette Escadrille, 41st Pursuit Squadron. A lot of young men coming back from the war were given honorary degrees." (Note: this famous WWI squadron was formed in 1916 by two Harvard graduates. The pilots were based in France (1916-1918) and fought against the Jagdstaffeln of Germany *prior* to the United States entry into WWI.) Son Henry Francis confirmed that his father Dwight received a "war diploma."

After his divorce from Kay in 1925, Dwight walked into a Pittsfield bookstore and met Lesley Frost, daughter of the poet Robert Frost. Lesley was managing the bookstore The Open Book. They were married on September 3, 1928, and had two daughters, Elinor (1929) and Lesley (1931). The couple separated before Lesley was born and divorced in 1932. Daughter Lesley noted it was Dwight's philandering that broke up the marriage. On the plus side, Lesley noted, "Dwight loved to go off to Europe, be in the Alps. He was a real athlete, a good skier." After his divorce from Lesley Frost, Dwight lived in Europe for four years. In 1936 he married Mrs. Henrietta Rossiter Van Deventer, which also ended in divorce. Lesley gave some details on this marriage. "His third wife was very, very rich. They had three wonderful sons. Henrietta wanted us [Lesley and Elinor] to keep in touch with them. They are remarkable. Henry 'Thins' Francis is a classical jazz pianist. Robert is a full professor at University of Washington. I think Dwight stayed around pretty much during the time the boys were growing up."

Dwight's obituary in the *New York Times,* January 26, 1988, read:

J. Dwight Francis died January 25, 1988. Age 91, in Edgartown, MA. He grew up in Pittsfield, MA. and graduated from Harvard in 1919. His principal business activity was as an investment counselor. For much of his life he explored the world with a spirit of adventure, absorbing and enjoying most of the intellectual and artistic disciplines. He is survived by his five children.

Chapter 2

On Broadway – "Lying a Lot, To the Right People"

The *S. S. Lapland*. Built in Belfast, Ireland, for Red Star, the *Lapland* was the largest ship for the line when it was launched in 1908. The *Lapland* made headlines in April 1912, when she rescued 167 crew members who survived the Titanic's sinking. In June 1917, she was requisitioned as a troop ship and fitted to accommodate 3,000 soldiers. The handsome two-funneled, four-mast vessel had carried honeymooners Mary Pickford and Douglas Fairbanks across the Atlantic for their 1920 honeymoon. In 1925, the *Lapland* carried the hopes and dreams of a 20-year-old divorcee, Katharine Gibbs Francis. She had dined and danced with the Prince of Wales.[1] She supped with Queen Wilhelmina at the Royal Palace at The Hague.[2] She went to the *Folies Bergere* and she had seen Chevalier perform at the Palace Theatre. Turning heads wherever she went, her dance card was always full. With the *Lapland*'s history and her minor triumphs in Europe Kay was triggered to make a momentous decision before she completed her voyage. She had a premonition that would launch a whole new career. Kay recalled,

> It was an awfully rough crossing…and the closer we got to the Statue of Liberty, the more certain I became that I needed a job. The third day out I was the only woman on deck. Sitting in the rain and wind on the top deck, I had a sudden feeling of tremendous self-confidence. I felt very *indomitable*. All I could think of to decide about was a career. So, I determined to make good. And at nothing so simple as stenography. Mother had impressed me with the difficulties and travail of the theater. That would be the *real* triumph, I thought. It was the stage or nothing, from then on.[3]

Kay had not left her role as stenographer behind without some distinction. After she walked out on Dwight, she found herself mixing among the elite as secretary for the financial secretaries of the wives of W. K. Vanderbilt (railroad magnate, yachtsman and holder of the America's Cup) and Dwight Morrow (famous lawyer, banker and Ambassador to Mexico under Coolidge). Kay more aptly described her Vanderbilt-Morrow connection, saying, "I was the secretary to the two elderly ladies who handled income tax for Mrs. Morrow, Mrs. Vanderbilt and Mrs. Pratt and a lot of other wealthy women."[4] Nonetheless, Kay never underestimated the time she spent employed as secretary. She later wrote about it in her perceptive and eloquent style:

The more I think of it, the more I am convinced that being a secretary had much to do with my subsequent career. The habit of self-discipline I gained in the business world has been of the utmost use in my acting career. Women have as a habit and a heritage the idea that their chief aim is to attract, and to arouse emotional response. In the business world, this expression of personality must be controlled. A good feminine office worker realizes that the airing of her personal grievances, jealousies, fits of melancholy or even of exuberance must be brought under control. *At that very moment* she is learning to become *an actress*. She conquers something which is inherent and traditional in her sex; by assuming an attitude of cheerful reserve, of impersonal, good-humored composure. She is enacting a part on life's stage."[5]

During her divorce proceedings in Europe, Kay's connections with bluebloods placed her in company with what author F. Scott Fitzgerald called the "lost generation"—well-to-do, aimless American youngsters who were living the high life on their parents' bank accounts. From reading her diaries, the young, impressionable Kay seemed a little lost herself and overwhelmed by the partying, drinking, and sexual recklessness. Men were drawn to her like a magnet, using flattery, calling her "perfect" and "noble," only to take advantage of her inexperience. Her lack of expertise as a playgirl finally caught up with her. She even shocked *herself*. July 8—"My seventh man—God I hate myself!" July 16—"Another operation! My God who is the father!"[6] As sobering as the ordeal was, her quest to fill the empty space in her heart that Dwight had left followed her wherever she went. In Paris it was Alec, Dave, and Charlie. The alcohol flowed freely. Kay would frequently find herself sick from drinking and her wealthy, arrogant, selfish boyfriends lost in a stupor or passed out in their apartments. Kay never stopped to think about what she was doing, because her behavior was reflected in the lives of the youthful faces that surrounded her. On her return home aboard the *S. S. Lapland* Kay was forced to take time out. The era's quintessential flapper, F. Scott Fitzgerald's wife Zelda, thought unconventional women to be happier if they avoided a career of hard work. However, Kay's recent European whirlwind acted as a catalyst for her to *do something*. She was motivated to escape the aimless lives of the acquaintances that had surrounded her in Europe and opted for *both* the career and the unconventional lifestyle. Kay refused financial support from Dwight and had to deal with basic realities. She would later proclaim, "I don't believe a woman who can support herself should take alimony."[7]

As mistress of her own fate, Kay wasted no time. She debarked in New York on the 26th of September and spent the following day visiting her mother and artist-friend Charlie Baskerville. On September 29, with her courage up, Kay had the pluck to start at the top of her new profession. Obviously, Kay's stage resume was sorely lacking. However, she figured she could at least *play* the part of an experienced actress. "I had...smart clothes," she reminisced later. "I bought them at the places in Paris that copied the famous *modistes*. I figured out that the only place to use clothes and the ability to wear them was the theater."[8] The indomitable feeling she experienced on the *S. S. Lapland*, reemerged to carry her right into the office of theatrical legend and producer Al H. Woods. Before she knew it, Kay was staring Woods in the face. She searched her memory for names of theaters her mother had played in and gave Woods a long story, impressive enough to make him reach for a script. Woods said, "Sweetheart, you're just the type for Poppy in

'Shanghai Gesture.'"⁹ Could Kay fill the shoes of Poppy—the spoiled, young woman "out for excitement" in Shanghai? Kay later confessed she was,

> Lying furiously...that I had played stock at Kansas City and in amateur Shakespearean companies. He asked me to read the part and I was...*very* bad. 'Sweetheart,' he said, 'You go home and get the wavers out of your voice.' The next day I knew the jig was up and demanded that he get Mrs. Leslie Carter, poor dear, to read her part with me. 'I'll call your bluff,' he said, amused at my nerve, and at 3 o'clock that afternoon I was in her apartment. 'You're too tall! Three inches too tall!,' she told me. 'In the last act when I kill you, it would look ridiculous for little me even to attempt it—sort of a canary chasing the cat idea.' I was *so happy* that I didn't have to read the part to him and John Colton, that I was delighted at the bad news."¹⁰

Shanghai Gesture, lurid exotic fare, would premier on Broadway in February 1926, without Kay and without the indomitable Mrs. Leslie Carter. "The Poor Dear," as Kay referred to Mrs. Carter, had been called the "American Sarah Bernhardt" at the turn of the century—riveting audiences in what one critic termed "a wholly absorbing exhibition of hysterical acting." At the Newark tryout of *Shanghai Gesture*, Carter's faltering memory betrayed her consistently, and, at the end of the performance, Woods sent actor Lowell Sherman backstage to notify the actress that she was too old for the part. She heard the cruel emissary without saying a word. She walked to her dressing room mirror and gazed searchingly at her reflection. "Too...old," she murmured.¹¹ Ironically, before Kay had left Warner Brothers in 1939, the studio had purchased a story for her based on the memoirs of Mrs. Leslie Carter. Kay's rift with the studio put the role in the hands of her friend Miriam Hopkins. The film was released as *The Lady with Red Hair* in 1940.

As "delighted" as Kay was at not getting the part in *Shanghai Gesture*, she grabbed the chance to understudy one of Broadway's great actresses, Katharine Cornell, in a sentimental play of love, sacrifice (and syphilis!) titled *The Green Hat*. Artist Charles Baskerville had introduced Kay to Edgar Selwyn, who made the arrangements. "Luckily she never went on," Baskerville commented. "She couldn't act for sour apples, but she was physically a similar type to Cornell."¹² *The Green Hat* opened in September of 1925, just before Kay's return from Europe. Cornell's co-star, Leslie Howard, would later team successfully with Kay on film and radio in Hollywood.

Kay's premonitions about a Broadway debut materialized on November 9, 1925. "It didn't last long," she commented later.¹³ Still, it was the beginning of a résumé. James Light staged the modern-dress version of Shakespeare's *Hamlet*, a controversial production, which played at the Booth Theatre. Kay wrote, "It struck me that the whole *idea* of the play implied taking a chance. Perhaps the manager might be willing to take a chance on a newcomer as well? Fortified by this theory, I went to see him, persuaded him to let me read some lines in a tryout against several other aspirants—and came off with a part."¹⁴ Kay admitted lying to actor-producer Basil Sydney when he asked if she had even read *Hamlet*. "*Know it!*" she repeated incredulously. "Why Mr. Sydney, I *played* the part as a child!" Sydney signed her. Soon after rehearsals started, he stopped speaking to her. He finally thawed after Kay, through her connections with publisher Conde Nast, got Sydney's photo prominently displayed in *Vanity Fair*. *Hamlet* was declared almost unanimously one of the most successful theatrical experiments up to that time. Basil Sydney was cast a Hamlet and Helen Chandler, who would become best remembered as the starry-eyed victim of Bela Lugosi in *Dracula*, played Ophelia. No one took note of Kay in the reviews, and when asked how she acquired the part of Player Queen in such estimable company, Kay quipped, "By lying a lot—to the right people."[15] *The New York Times* favorably commented, "the point about this new production is that, for the most part, the acting has body and polish." *Time* magazine stated, "Though not distinguished by a star, the company was far more capable than is usual with production of the play…It turns out to be as Shakespeare meant it, a credible, relatively shrewd commentary on human weaknesses…without the bewildering mass of scene and costume."

To stay in the modern spirit before going on stage each evening, "Player Queen" Kay afforded herself tango lessons with a guy named Willy. But, after *Hamlet*'s moderate success, running 88 performances, Kay was back on budget. She didn't have any delusions of grandeur about the tango or her theatrical career. She wasn't the type. Kay explained her rational approach to being an actress saying, "[Mother] effectively stripped the profession of any false glamour it might have had for me, while I was still in my teens…"[16] Kay simply stated that she wasn't the "stage-struck" type. "When I first went on the stage, I didn't know—whether it was to be merely a temporary way of earning my living or whether it was to be something more. I just went at it calmly and to the best of my ability, not with any of the feverish, pushing anxiety of the usual stage-struck girl. Probably that's why I was lucky. Perhaps if I'd been all tied up in knots about it, I'd not have had half as easy a time."[17]

During rehearsals for *Hamlet*, Kay connected with a Cathedral School classmate, Virginia Farjeon, and took an apartment. Kay also began fashion modeling. This short-lived career ran her into a snag on one occasion.

> I had been spending the week-end visiting friends at Southampton and arrived in town early Monday morning just in time to check in on my new job. Everything went very smoothly all day and I was just congratulating myself on my quick adaptability when six dresses were reported missing from the racks. Of course, no one accused me BUT…I was a new girl…I had arrived that morning with a valise…the evidence was *all* against me. If I had stolen the entire store I couldn't have felt, or looked, more guilty. I was so embarrassed I never went back. I'm sure to this day they suspect me of 'taking ways.'[18]

Kay's poise, affinity for clothes and unique looks, attracted the attention of two well-known artists. One of them that Kay posed for, Leo Mielziner, would end up being her future father-in-law in 1931. (Mielziner's commissioned portrait of President Woodrow Wilson resides today at New York City's Democratic Club.) Another portrait of Kay that attracted much acclaim was done by Sir Gerald Kelly in 1925. Andrew Potter, research assistant at the Royal Academy Library, wrote to me in 2003. "In 1924 Kelly went to the USA with his wife to undertake several commissions of American society. He stayed there for nine months but did not enjoy himself and found his living expenses to be very high. The portrait he painted of Francis in 1925 was considered to be his most successful of this period."[19] Sir Kelly had been exhibiting at the Royal

Academy since 1909. Kay's exquisite portrait was a sensation at the Academy in their 1926 exhibition. Kelly was later commissioned to paint the State Portraits of King George VI and Queen Elizabeth. In 1959 Kay wrote Kelly, reminiscing about posing for him.

> 'Shades of 1925'—How kind you were to me when I came to your studio on Central Park South—but also—you frightened me most to death when you said 'One day you are pink—One day you are yellow—Why does your skin tone change?' Do you remember? So many years have passed and now you are Sir Gerald and I am Kay Francis.[20] [Letter dated 9/16/1959]

The third artist to capture Kay on canvas was Charles Baskerville in October 1925. He was an illustrator for *The New Yorker* and wrote their cabaret news column using the name "Top Hat." Baskerville, a Cornell graduate, had studied art at Academie Julien in Paris. (He would do commissioned portraits for Prime Minister Nehru and the Duchess of Windsor.) Baskerville illustrated Kay with poise and a graceful, catlike presence. She is seen as a modern-day Eve with her arms carefully positioned upon white fur, pearl bracelets on each wrist. A hand holds an apple from which two bites have been taken—a *fate accompli*. She stares, looking somewhat detached, off into the distance. Kay later bequeathed her portrait by Baskerville to close friend Jetti Ames.

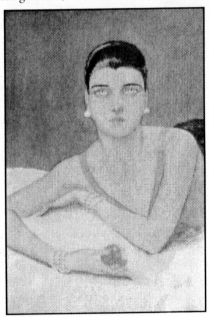

A few years later, Kay's provocative looks and demeanor would compel the hand of James Montgomery Flagg to sketch her in caricature. Flagg's famous WWI poster of Uncle Sam, "I WANT YOU—For U.S. Army," became an American icon. Flagg reveled in the company of beautiful women from the theatrical world, but found Kay to be the most striking among the cinema's glamour queens. *Vanity Fair* noted, "His favorite actress is Kay Francis, who appears in practically every Warner Brother film...which keeps Mr. Flagg in a state of chronic contentment."

(Fall of 1925) Katharine Francis by Charles Baskerville. Kay tempts the viewer after she has taken a bite out of an apple. (Courtesy of Jetti and Lou Ames)

Kay's modeling stints not only attracted attention in the galleries, but, according to close friends Lois Long and Charles Baskerville, Kay herself was a *living* work of art. On a subsequent trip to Paris that the three made together, Kay was always a stunner. Lois, a former actress and graduate of Vassar, wrote for *The New Yorker*. She was noted for her coverage of the fashion world and inventing fashion criticism—a task none too easy as *The New Yorker* did not publish photographs. She used words alone to describe clothes in detail. Long's expertise in fashion rubbed off on Kay. Long later recalled to reporter Harry Evans the days she and Kay rented a two-room Greenwich Village flat and ate meals out of tin cans. "Lois, who is a very handsome person herself," noted Evans, "does not resemble Kay except in coloring, but the similarity of their voices is perfectly amazing. Over a telephone you cannot tell them apart, unless you know their mannerisms of speech."[21] Decades later, Lois talked to George Eells about Kay's sparse wardrobe purchased in Paris. "Kay was five feet nine [sic] inches tall, had tiny feet—I think she wore size three or four. I know I was able to get her sample shoes—whatever the size was then. She loved shoes. And her head was twenty and a half. She was terrific-looking. Before we left Paris, she managed to get a beige Patou outfit and hat, a black Patou outfit and a hat and a black lace evening dress—and that's what she wore for two years. And always looked stunning."[22] Charles Baskerville also marveled at Kay's ingenuity:

> [Kay] was an extraordinary person. That summer she had no wardrobe, and neither of us had much money. But she took a paisley—gray, black and white Persian shawl and had it made into an evening wrap. Whenever we were going to any swell place, she would put the paisley wrap over her gown, and she was a knockout. She carried herself beautifully; her hair was cut as short as mine, and she wore no jewelry, only lipstick. No eye-shadow or anything; she didn't need it. People were stampeded by this creature…They thought she was a maharani on the loose or something like that.[23]

Kay and Lois let a flat at 140 East 39th Street in New York. Lois had fond memories of that time saying, "We had a tiny apartment with no kitchen and a bedroom so small you had to crawl over the end of one bed to get to the one near the wall. But we had three telephones, and they were always ringing."[24] Katherine Swan, who would later work on the scenario staff of Paramount Pictures, became a third roommate. Kay said that neither Lois nor Katherine had much confidence in her acting ability. George Eells gave an insider's look at Kay's whirlwind life at the time. "A clique developed—three women and eight or nine men. Although no dates were made, around 5 p.m. the group would gather at some apartment…After a few drinks they would go their separate ways and meet again around midnight at a popular watering spot, Tony's, to drink sidecars." Lois elaborated to Eells:

> Then we'd split up, and finally some of us would meet again at the Owl Club. It was Negro entertainment, a low-down place where the girls scooped up dollar bills in unmentionable ways. One night Kay and I were there with a couple of gently reared fellows when the place was held up. Fortunately, one of these gently reared fellows wasn't so gently reared that he didn't get the table top between us and the gunmen before the bullets started flying, or I might not be telling you this now.
>   We all drank heavily. It was wild generation…Kay—always had a tumbler of gin for breakfast. We got it for twelve dollars a case from Frankie Costello, who was our bootlegger. She wasn't too knowledgeable about alcohol. I remember her saying once, 'I'm so sick of champagne, and brandy. Isn't there any light alcohol I could drink?' Some clown asked if she'd ever heard of Pernod. So, she started carrying a flask of it because clubs didn't seem to stock it. When I was first living with her…Kay'd get home at six in the morning, and there was no way you would win. If I took the rear bed,

I disturbed her when I crawled over her to go to work. If I took the front one, she woke me when she arrived home at dawn. We were really quite innocent. I wasn't sleeping with any of the gang. I was too busy dancing all night. Kay did some…Anyway, a couple of them confided she was a big disappointment in the hay.[25]

Kay's own notations in her diary confirm Lois' memories—the parties, getting "terribly drunk," and debating whether or not to spend the night with her current beau. Lois' claim that Kay was "a big disappointment in the hay," is debatable. Kay's diaries confirm that her beaus *always* came back for more "disappointment." Kay typified New York's Jazz Age youngsters who questioned everything they had been brought up to believe. Drinking alcohol in public during Prohibition was an especially brave act for a woman. Wearing make-up (which previously had only been the territory of actresses and prostitutes) was also a mark of independence. There was a lack of caution as they explored what felt like new territory and the blur of illegal booze seemed to keep them from having any sort of epiphany about their experiences. They seemed hellbent on being out for the fun of it. If Kay judged herself, it was only as an afterthought. Her diaries are peppered with comments like, "What an idiot I am!" "God, I ought to be shot … !"[26] But, Kay "the lover" always won out saying, "My God he does know how to kiss!"[27] She felt akin to the excitement and promise that surrounded her. She sensed her life was her own. Oddly enough, it was self-reliant women like Kay that paved the way for the modern woman to emerge as an integral part of the Western civilization.

After *Hamlet* closed, Kay was tempted to try her luck with the movies. D.W. Griffith, whose controversial *The Birth of a Nation* became the first film extravaganza, was on location in Long Island, New York, filming Marie Corelli's 1895 moralistic novel *The Sorrows of Satan*. The book's success made Corelli the best-selling author in the English language since Charles Dickens. A relic in the making, *The Sorrows of Satan* featured Adolphe Menjou as Prince Lucio de Rimanez (Satan) who tempts a young author played by Ricardo Cortez into a world of sin. When released in 1926, it flopped at the box office. Griffith was fired from Paramount. Wearing a blonde wig, Kay had tested for the Russian Princess vamp role, Olga Godovsky. Kay lost the part (to Lya De Putti), and was horrified at her screen test. She vowed never to appear in the movies.[28] In 1936, Griffith, by then a relic from a bygone era, would be welcomed by Kay when he paid a visit to the set of her starring vehicle, *The White Angel*.

Before her next shot at Broadway, one of Kay's more profound psychic experiences took place at the movies. It regarded an old classmate named Alice. Kay was watching a film that showed a cross-country race on horseback. "As the horse took the first jump," Kay recalled, "I felt faint and ill and asked my escort to take me home. Arriving home, I can't even *describe* my feeling. I was in a daze and went immediately to my room. But before retiring, I wrote something on a piece of paper and tucked it away in a book. Three days later the news reached us of Alice's death from a fall from her horse…I found the book and read what I had felt impelled to put down on paper. It was a prophecy of Alice's death, describing in full details exactly how it happened. *And coinciding to the minute with the date and hour.*"[29]

In the New Year, 1926, between acting and modeling assignments, Kay took time out to promote the American debut of Spanish singing sensation Raquel Meller. With Kay's social connections, she proved a capable young champion. In her youth Meller (pronounced "May-aire") had wandered through villages collecting melodies woven into Spanish life. The King of Spain heard her and proclaimed her the cardinal vocal artist of her country. Sarah Bernhardt, who once heard Meller sing in a private audience, told her she would some day be "as great as I think I am."[30] The quality of Meller's voice was a source of heated debate, but she put the song-style known as the *cuple*, a mix of Cuban and Spanish influences, on the map.[31]

The *Time* magazine review of Meller's debut, "Her Hands Are Like Faces," noted that the audience fell into an "expensive hush" (at $27.50 a seat), as she took to the stage. While she sang "Flor del Mal" (Flower of Sin), Meller, her hair disheveled and wearing the rags of a hopeless street girl, moved onto a little platform and lit a cigarette. She smoked, singing her song, then walked over to the stage wall where she leaned, dejected. "The song ended and she disappeared. The charm of an irresistible personality fulfilled her promise [and] had burned home its deep impression."[32] When she sang her most famous piece, "Violetera," Meller went into the aisles of the Empire Theatre with little bunches of violets that she bestowed impetuously upon the starched and bejeweled Manhattanites, who rose and cheered.

Today, the *cuple*, along with Meller, is a buried and forgotten nostalgia. However, Kay was so impressed by Meller that during her early Hollywood years she would often mention their association. She was proud of her success as a promoter. After all, Meller's Broadway show broke all box-office records at the Empire Theatre in April 1926. *And,* she also made the coveted cover of *Time.*

As fate would have it, *Hamlet* director James Light finally took note of Kay's *own* star potential. He made arrangements for Kay to audition for the Stuart Walker Company. Beforehand, Kay had followed the advice of her friend Dwight Deere Wiman, a fledgling theatrical producer, to see a speech therapist to modify her lisp. Kay's trouble with saying "r's" (known as lallation) became much improved and bolstered her confidence. Stuart Walker, whose career started with David Belasco, had managed his Portmanteau Theatre Companies since 1917. Walker liked Kay's reading and signed her in February 1926. His troupe of players included Peggy Wood, Elizabeth Patterson and McKay Morris. Kay trouped through Cincinnati, Dayton, and Indianapolis with the stock company, polishing her acting skills. Throughout the rest of the year Kay was offered a variety of bit parts, walk-ons and second leads.

Kay's first assignment for the company was *The Chief Thing* starring McKay Morris. She was also in the cast of *Candida, Polly Preferred, White Collars* and *Puppy Love.* Even in brief roles, as in the popular Parisian love story *Seventh Heaven,* the critics took note of Kay. "Katharine Francis is saucy and 'Frenchy' as Arlette," said *The Indianapolis Star.*[33] Kay took note of the leading man, George Gaul. "Slept with George like a damn fool," she wrote. "God, I ought to be shot…"[34] After the Dayton opening of *Puppy Love,* Kay stood out as the slangy stenographer. Instead of being shot, she gave her first interview as an actress, to the *Dayton Daily News.* After pointing out that Kay was being featured in important roles, the article, titled "The Storm Gave Her Courage," mentioned Kay's vision regarding a stage career when she was aboard the *S. S. Lapland.*[35] The following week,

Kay received more accolades playing Lottie in George Abbott's *The Fall Guy.* "Katharine Francis is sensitive to the demands and necessities of her part, which she plays very well," wrote James Muir.[36] Kay reported years later, "My real training in acting came with Stuart Walker. Sometimes, while I was playing in Cincinnati, I'd get up early to take a train to Dayton, rehearse the next week's bill and get back to Cincinnati in time to appear that night. My parts were heavies, but I always wanted sentiment. Once, when I was begging for a weepy part, Stuart Walker actually shook me. 'I'll shake some sense into you,' he said. 'If you learn to play heavies well, leads will come easy to you.' I later found that this was true."[37] Kay's association with the Walker Company provided her with a repertoire of stories to tell. Reporter Dick Mook was partnered with Kay at a Hollywood party in 1930 and immediately noticed what he referred to as her gift for entertaining and making people feel at home. "Kay is one of the few women I have ever met who doesn't at all mind telling a joke on herself," Mook commented. "My first meeting with her occurred at the Fredric Marchs'...she kept us all in stitches throughout the evening with tales of her days in stock companies and the madcap things she used to do."[38] One of her escapades landed her in police court and a $15-fine for disorderly conduct. Roommate Katherine Swan, who found Kay to be very genuine and anything but high-hat, had her own story to tell of Kay's antics. "We were a bit haywire in those days...Dances and parties not being exciting enough, we invented new amusements. Indoor Polo held our interest until Kay broke her collarbone...The night Kay was hurt, there was a four-hundred-pound football star in the game. In the excitement...someone yanked at his knees to bring him down—and all of his four hundred pounds fell on Kay!"[39]

During the summer of 1926, Kay fell in love. McKay Morris, a notable Broadway performer from 1915-1946, had studied with David Belasco and played opposite Ethel Barrymore in a 1922 production of *Romeo and Juliet.* He also had a part in the aforementioned *Shanghai Gesture.* Lois Long described what happened between Kay and McKay after their return to New York from the road.

> The whole episode was something. [Kay] broke her collarbone...she was in a plaster cast to here...she went to live with McKay at the Hotel Carlton on Eighth Street. She was madly in love with him. Neither one had a job, and she had no money. He was a great actor and very handsome but impotent, which didn't really seem to make a great deal of difference to her. I don't think sex meant that much to her, I really don't. Anyway, she behaved so well and was so broke that Bill Lebrow and I got eight of the gang to put in one hundred dollars, and then Bill bought a cashier's check for one thousand dollars and sent it to her anonymously. She had no idea where it came from, and it took her ages to find out.[40]

A couple of years later, when Lois was in need of financial help, she wired Kay. She didn't receive an answer, but $1,000 was suddenly deposited in her bank account. Kay herself was generous to a fault when friends were in need. Kay's fling with Morris was a short-lived disappointment. That fall, after her collarbone healed, Kay's diary reflected a definite party mode. She shared quarts of gin and got cockeyed while quietly patronizing the usual places: Club Avalon, Texas Guinan's, Cerutti's, Tony's and The Owl Club. Kay's prerogative for "painting the town red" may have been simply to be noticed. In 1931, *Vanity Fair* captioned under her photograph, "Although she had played with Stuart Walker, and in a few minor roles on stage, Kay Francis was chiefly famous, in New York…as the lady who was going about doing a good deal of what is known as 'creating a stir' when she entered crowded restaurants and nightclubs."[41] Kay's nightclubbing actually proved profitable. She became a ghost writer for *The New Yorker*. Roommate Lois, using her pen name "Lipstick," included Kay's observations in her columns for the magazine. Reporter Dick Mook elaborated, "Lois was making much more money than Kay and had a much more extensive wardrobe. As part of her job, she was required to cover the New York nightclubs. It was physically impossible for her to visit all of them, so, if she had five to cover one night, she assigned two to Kay and she took the other three. Kay made shorthand notes which Lois incorporated into her reviews. For her trouble Kay had the privilege of wearing Lois' clothes!"[42]

There was yet another reason behind Kay's binges, aimless nightclubbing, and "creating a stir." What very few people knew during this time (1925-26) is that Kay had secretly married again. In fact, she had been married for over a year! It was something that she refused to divulge until the mid-1930s—partly because of her own uncertainty about the relationship, embarrassment, but mostly, according to Kay, for political reasons. His name was William "Bill" Gaston. Lois Long rather succinctly summed up the relationship. "I was introduced to Kay at a Beaux Arts ball after her first divorce. She was nineteen [sic], just back from Paris, and she met Bill Gaston, a very good-looking bastard. She had a wild affair with him, thought she was pregnant and married him. They were keeping it a secret from his family until the baby came. *And*—two days after the marriage she got the curse. Oh, boy! *Then* he wanted a divorce. Eventually he married Rosamond Pinchot—and *that* ended with her suicide."[43]

When Kay finally confessed to the marriage in 1933, she still wouldn't mention Gaston's name. Kay divulged her well-kept secret to Gladys Hall for the August 1933 edition of *Motion Picture Magazine*. Kay was vague about the exact dates and was hesitant to divulge the story at all, saying, "I have a story—one that has never been told before, one that I thought I should *never* tell. I don't know whether I ought to, or not…it might not be quite fair to him…*There was a second marriage*…I haven't *tried* to keep it secret. It just *was*. For political reasons, marriage was unwise and all but impossible for him. For political reasons, I cannot, even today, divulge his name."

Kay met Gaston (the man with no name) just before she sailed to Paris in 1925 for her first divorce. After a very brief introduction, she had one of her strong psychic premonitions that she would marry him. Kay said, "The instant this man entered the room, the very instant I laid my eyes on him, I said to myself, '*I am going to marry this man!*' … It was a stark and simple and unequivocal FACT. That is all…I didn't know who he was, what he did, or where he came from. It wouldn't have made any difference." Coincidentally, Gaston was in Paris during Kay's final week there. The two saw a great deal of each other. Gaston changed his sailing to go back with her on the same boat. Kay's first mention of the marriage, in her diary, was on October 19—"Married to BG, my God!"[44] The newlyweds kicked Kay's roommate out of the apartment for a honeymoon. Their relationship remained sporadic. Her diary entry for the New Year 1926 aptly summed up her situation. "1925 has been a very big year in my life—and on the whole I have behaved like a damn fool!"[45]

Kay added further details of the unusual husband-wife relationship:

He arrived bright and early one morning and, with scarcely a word spoken between us…we found an obliging parson. I had been divorced, you see, and that closed many doors to us. We didn't have a ring. There were no friends or family. Our colored chauffeur was one of the witnesses and the other was someone drafted from the minister's household. I had to be in the theatre immediately after the ceremony. I was in rehearsal [*Hamlet*]. He had to catch the noon train back to Boston. He came down for the marriage that day. The next day he came down for the honeymoon.

Only two people in the world were ever told about that marriage during the whole two years of it. One was the chauffeur, and the other was the girl who shared my apartment with me. She had to know, of course, because when he came down for week-ends or for a day or two during the week, she obligingly vacated and left us to ourselves. I really don't know just what did happen to us, what broke us apart. Separations, I suppose. Divided interests. The impossibility of having a home together, of sharing each other's lives. Shortly after our marriage, I went out with the Stuart Walker Stock Company.

There was another divorce—very quiet—and then it was as though…the stone of our deep secret had been dropped in the depths of some sea. No one had ever known. No one asked. It was over, and hidden and finished—*until now, until today.*[46]

William B. Gaston, "Bill," was a barrister, well known socially, and from a prominent Boston family. His grandfather, William Gaston, had been governor of Massachusetts (1875-76). Bill Gaston himself entered the world of politics—starting as Assistant District Attorney of Suffolk Co. He was tall, good-looking, with a ruddy complexion, and weighed in at about 190 lbs. He had been a Harvard athlete and had developed an interest in the art of boxing. During their brief association in Paris, Kay was attracted to his knowledge of fine art and classical music. He was also a great collector of rare books and first editions. Gaston loved the theatre and the people in it. Kay claimed that Gaston had connections and provided her with a letter of introduction to director James Light, which led to her first important part on Broadway. Twenty-year-old Kay's deep impression of the twenty-nine-year-old Gaston may have been simply another attempt to recapture the lost romance of her first marriage. In her words, she let the episode with Gaston sink "in the depths of some sea," until it emerged in the news during her 1934 divorce proceedings from her *fourth* husband. Kay and Gaston divorced in Paris in 1927.

Gaston and Dwight Francis were birds-of-a-feather in many respects. Gaston, a real womanizer, was involved in a dramatic relationship with his next wife, the tragic, socially prominent actress, Rosamond Pinchot. Gaston introduced Rosamond to Kay in 1928. Kay made a point of paying a visit to the Gastons when their first child was born in early 1929. The couple had another child, but was separated by 1934. The failure of their marriage devastated Pinchot, who committed suicide in 1938.

During his marriage to Pinchot, Bill Gaston leased his summer place off the coast of Maine to Clare Boothe Luce (author, playwright and future Ambassador to Mexico under Eisenhower). Luce's summer on the 15-acre property was attended by a succession of visitors, all male, and mostly all intimate in nature, including Gaston. The island was appropriately named: Crotch Island. Luce's biographer, Sylvia Jukes Morris, gave some details on the landlord-tenant relationship. "Never was a place more aptly named, for the summer of 1932 turned out to be one of sensual and sexual indulgence...Bill Gaston was suave, devastatingly handsome, and sexually dangerous. His marriage to Rosamond Pinchot was breaking up, and he had the reputation of a confirmed woman-izer. Between him and Clare the air was always heavy, and she tried to avoid his blan-dishments. She knew that they were the same kind of animal."[47] Oddly enough, Luce, who always favored male companionship and society, is most famous for her play *The Women*, in which there are *no* male characters. Gaston would remain a loyal friend and supporter of Kay's through the 1950s. He often would bring friends to Kay's stage performances after she relocated back east in the late 1940s.

With her second divorce behind her, Kay surged ahead with her career. Al H. Woods came to the rescue once again by offering her the part of Marjorie Grey in the play *Crime*, which opened in February 1927. The play distinguished itself as one of the longest runs of the season, with 186 performances at the Eltinge Theatre. Kay's co-stars were Sylvia Sidney, Chester Morris, Kay Johnson, Jack LaRue and Douglass Montgomery—all future stars of the Hollywood cinema. The underworld melodrama told the story of a dewy-eyed salesgirl (Sidney) and a naive young elevator operator's (Montgomery) involvement with a criminal mastermind. *The New York Times* thought the show to be "spectacular and fast-moving...well acted and excellently put together." To the end of Kay's life, Sylvia Sidney maintained that Kay had stolen the play from her.[48] Robert Benchley, writing for *Life*, was most impressed by *Crime's* robbery, calling the scene, "a masterpiece of direction. While police are decoyed to...a brawl next door, men rifle Goldberg's jewelry store in full sight of a pop-eyed audi-ence." *Time* magazine cautioned, "It is the sort of play that sends small boys and big boys out of the theatre hoping some day to work up to the nobility of banditry." *Crime* was made into the Lowell Sherman-directed 1930 film, *The Pay-Off.*

When *Crime* closed, Kay picked up another modeling job and found time for another major love affair. On August 1, after a dinner date, Kay agreed to marry Allan A. Ryan, Jr., the grandson of millionaire Thomas Fortune Ryan. Ryan was a student at Yale when he and Kay became engaged. On August 5, Kay and Allan were canoeing all day and sailing at night. She met Allan's mother for cocktails on August 8. Feeling quite confident about her future fiancé, Kay put an amusing slant on their August 11 date. "Slept with him to sort of consecrate our engagement! He can be taught a few things!"[49] Then it was off to Montreal, Canada to meet with Allan's father for a "long talk." He insisted she give up a part in a new play. She followed the instructions, but felt "rotten" about it. On August 22 she and Allan "consecrated" their relationship once more, but Kay was wary. "Gee, we are taking awful chances," she told her diary.[50] Kay had agreed to wait eighteen months before the marriage would take place!

Even though Kay "flashed a solitaire large enough to illuminate Madison Square Garden," her marriage to Allan A. Ryan never took place.[51] Elsa Maxwell herself was puzzled as to what happened to the Ryan-Francis engagement, saying, "What kept Kay from becoming the first Mrs. Allan Ryan, Jr., I'll never know."[52] Most likely, the Ryans didn't find Kay a suitable match for their son. If so, they failed to realize that she was cut from the same cloth as Thomas Fortune Ryan, who, from his early humble beginnings, would personify the classic American success story. Homeless at age fourteen, he went from errand boy and messenger to become one of the wealthiest men in the United States (with financial backing from his father-in-law). He died leaving $200 million from controlling the Washington Life Insurance Co., and the largest diamond fields in the Congo. Kay, on the other hand, whose memory of one-nighters on the road in cheap hotels, eating popcorn for dinner and knowing the struggle of poverty, would, through her intelligence and talents, become a self-made millionaire *on her own*, with the help of no man. She would also develop a successful career on stage, film and radio. Kay's mother observed, "Kay found all her own jobs, made her own way and deserves all the credit. I will say that only a tremendously hard worker could have done so much in so short a time."[53] Kay's passing up the Ryan name and her handsome, young fiancé was no loss to her. The youthful Ryan sported the same roaming eye that would characterize Kay's first two husbands. But the two remained close. Ryan often came to Kay for counsel. Elsa Maxwell noted this, saying, "I do know…they are still friends and that Kay often goes out of her way to help and advise her former fiancé." In fact, Kay and Allan's continued friendship sometimes bordered on the scandalous. Maxwell alluded to one 1937 incident that attracted a lot of brouhaha in the press. "Some people thought it rather strange that he [Ryan] should have taken Kay to the Cotton Club in New York on the very eve of his marriage to Eleanor Barry but I wasn't even mildly surprised. Knowing both as I do, I understood that Allan simply had to talk it over with Kay."[54]

During their long engagement, Kay and Allan saw one another frequently, but the bloom began to fade. Kay had another abortion in May 1928. The lack of birth control was a real dilemma for someone as liberated as Kay. She loved the intimacy that she and Allan shared and wasn't willing to give it up for convention's sake. Still, they seemed to enjoy one another's company and things weren't officially *fini* until December 1928.

Kay's next role, as the lady villain in *Amateur Anne* (October 1927), closed after tryouts in Wilmington and Hartford. The play, about nightclub life, was right up Kay's alley. For a complete turnabout, she was then offered the part of Sharon, the ethereal prophetess, in *Elmer Gantry*. The part was based on the popular evangelist Aimee Semple McPherson. When that didn't happen Kay was cast in a sci-fi, futuristic experiment written by Rachel Crothers. She sought advice for this role from none other than Charles Lindbergh! Lindbergh, who had just returned from his spectacular solo flight to Paris, was hiding out from publicity hounds with Bill Maloney, who was a member of Kay and Lois' gang. George Eells described Kay's encounter with "Lucky Lindy":

> Lindberg…agreed to meet a group of Maloney's friends. Among them was Kay, who mystified everyone by asking such question as: 'Tell me, were you scared?' or 'What makes a man become an aviator?' or 'Are fliers unique in any way?' Lindbergh, who obviously suspected her motives, politely evaded the banal questions. Friends remained puzzled at her gaucherie until Rachel Crothers' *Venus* opened at the Masque Theater on December 26. *Venus'* premise was that a pill had been developed that made men experience feminine desires and women masculine drives. After taking one, the character Kay played was seized by an urge to become an aviator.[55]

Venus also tackled such bold topics as equality of the sexes. The futuristic play cast Kay as Diana *Gibbs*, an aviatrix whose character comes closest to representing sexual equality. Kay, as Diana, was to exhibit natural intelligence and spiritual perception balanced into a male-female personality. Reviewer J. Brooks Atkinson found the result to be "an uncommonly imaginative theme…Miss Crothers posits her questions of sex equality [but]…they remain questions rather than answers. And before the play is concluded they begin to seem distractingly tedious. Last evening the unfinished performance of the actors made for scanty enjoyment."[56] The cast included Tyrone Power, Sr., whose wife had died tragically before the opening. Power went on with the show, which required him to dance a fandango and weep into his handkerchief. Dwight's parents drove over from Pittsfield to see their ex-daughter-in-law's debut in *Venus*. Also in the audience were her almost future in-laws, Mr. and Mrs. Ryan. The play closed a few days later when the elevator broke under the stage. According to Kay, her biggest thrill was her *mother's* thrill of seeing her daughter's name on Broadway in electric lights for the first time. "Mother went down to that theatre and walked around the block a dozen times, just so she could look at it. She even took a camera with her and made a picture of it…"[57]

Kay's last role on Broadway, until 1946, was Ring Lardner's *Elmer the Great*. The play, produced by George M. Cohan, opened September 24, 1928, at the Lyceum Theatre and ran for 40 performances. Columnist Frances Kellum described how Kay instantaneously nabbed her role in *Elmer*…"When Kay attended the first rehearsal for *Elmer the Great*—she saw a tall, gaunt man pacing up and down. 'Excellent!' he said, observing her. 'If you act as well as you look, the role is yours!' That was her introduction to the most wonderful Man friend she was ever to know. Walter Huston."[58]

Walter Huston and Katharine Francis in Elmer the Great *(1928).* Variety *noted Kay made her "level-headed show girl stand up." (author's collection)*

Kay said of Huston in 1935, "I owe my entire career to him. We were cast together in *Elmer the Great* and he did more for me than any coach ever could have done."[59] In *Elmer*, Huston played a not-too-bright baseball pitcher who is tempted to throw the "big game." Huston's girlfriend was played by his real-life mistress, Nan Sunderland. The comedy came on strong, but the play struck out in the last inning when Huston foiled the bad guys. *Drama Magazine* summed it up saying, "Elmer…consistently drawn during two acts as a prize bonehead, is suddenly not a bonehead at all. It is incredible. Yet in spite of this…*Elmer the Great* is full of brief scenes that ring true…" Kay played the part of Evelyn Corey—one of Huston's flames. A British critic noticed Kay and commented, "She was arresting from her first entrance.

She had stage presence, personality, and a smooth assurance..."[60] Backstage, the comedy turned into fiery dramatics when Huston's wife, Bayonne, accused Nan Sunderland of "living with my husband!" Replied Nan, infuriating the hysterical Bayonne, "I certainly *am*."[61]

Walter Huston and Kay learned important skills from their producer, George M. Cohan, who emphasized timing and pausing for effect. He asked Ring Lardner to write a new scene for the actors, which they learned. Cohen then cut the scene, asking the actors to *think* the scene without dialogue. The ploy encouraged the actors to pause and convey real life by holding onto silence.[62] Huston claimed it was one of the most valuable acting lessons he ever learned. "Without exception, [Cohan] is the greatest stage manager I ever worked with," said Huston. "Actors who have the good fortune to work under him will carry traces of his influence the rest of their lives."[63] When the play closed, Kay recalled that it took her by surprise. "We opened in Chicago and did fine," Kay remembered. "Then we flopped on Broadway. I'd been a fool and didn't have a cent. All I had left was $3.25. Then and there I vowed to climb out of that mess *myself*. If you cry for help you'll never amount to beans. I'd been an idiot. There were many friends to whom I could have turned, but I refused to consider borrowing."[64]

Though Kay wasn't getting the shining notices that Huston did, it really didn't matter. The fates were looking out for her and the only person that really mattered, when it came to noticing Katharine Francis, was co-star Walter Huston. Through Huston's keen eye for star power and his affection for Kay, she was catapulted overnight into what *Photoplay* magazine called, "one of the most astonishing first performances in the history of motion pictures."

❈ WILLIAM "BILL" GASTON ❈
Born: 1896, Mass.
Died: August 30, 1970, New Canaan, Conn.
Married to Kay Francis: 1925-1927

Bill Gaston was born into a politically prominent family. His grandfather, William Gaston, was the mayor of Boston (1871) and governor of Massachusetts (1875-76). Bill Gaston's father, William Alexander Gaston, was the Democratic candidate for Governor (1906) and in 1922 he was a candidate for U.S. Senator from Massachusetts.

A "chip off the old block," Bill Gaston, after completing Harvard in 1923, became a member of the Boston Bar Association. Bill's career in law was often put on hold, because of his interest in theatre. Kay had mentioned that Bill knew James Light who staged her Broadway debut in *Hamlet*. It was Gaston's letter of introduction to Light, which got Kay motivated. During their marriage Gaston penned a play, *Damn the Tears*, which ran for 22 performances on Broadway in January 1927. Nine years older than Kay, Gaston, for whatever reason, asked Kay to keep the marriage a secret from his family.

After Gaston's divorce from Kay Francis in 1927, he met his next wife, Rosamond Pinchot, another actress, who also happened to be the niece of Giford Pinchot, a former Governor of Pennsylvania. A more "suitable match," there was no need to keep *this* marriage a secret from anyone. The couple was married on January 26, 1928. *The New_York Times* claimed Gaston was writing a new play at the time and had already written several plays. The paper also mentioned that he had a previous marriage which ended in divorce in 1927 "on the grounds of desertion and incompatibility." Kay's name was not mentioned. Gaston and Pinchot had two sons, but the failure of their marriage drove Pinchot to commit suicide.

After his marriage to Pinchot, Gaston quit his Boston law practice to enter the firm of Lehman Brothers, Wall Street Investment brokers.Much later, his political heritage carried him into the running in November 1948 for Congress on the Democratic ticket. He lost. Bill Gaston married once again, to the former Lucile Hutchings. The couple also had two children. When Bill Gaston died on August 30, 1970, he was residing in New Canaan, Connecticut. His age was listed as 74.

✳ ALLAN A. RYAN ✳
Born: July 4, 1903, New York City
Died: October 13, 1981, Palm Beach, Florida
Engaged to Kay Francis: August 1927—December 1928

Allan Aloyshius Ryan was the son of Allan A. and Sarah Teck Ryan. He was also the grandson of multimillionaire Thomas Fortune Ryan who lived up to his middle name by co-founding the American Tobacco Co. The Ryan home was in New York City; however, Allan, Jr. went to Canterbury School in New Milford, Connecticut. He graduated from Yale in 1924. During 1927-28, Ryan was engaged to Kay Francis. He and Kay never made it through the 18-month-long engagement agreement, but remained friends. Ryan often went to Kay for counsel and her diary indicates their visits through the 1940s.

Allan A. Ryan, Jr.'s first marriage was to Janet Newbold in 1929. They had two children. He married a second time, to Eleanor Barry, in January 1937. The eve before the couple's nuptials, Ryan took Kay Francis nightclubbing in Harlem. It caused a scandal, but apparently Ryan simply needed his morale boosted and trusted Kay's advice. Kay wasn't exactly the best person to ask for advice on marriage. Within four years Ryan was headed for the altar again, marrying a Priscilla St. George in 1941. They had a daughter. Ryan's fourth marriage, to Grace M. Amory, in 1950 was his last. Ryan managed to match Kay in the matrimony sweepstakes.

Ryan worked for the New York Stock Exchange after his first marriage. He then acted as director for the Royal Typewriter Co., Inc. (1932-54) and as chairman of the board for Royal McBee Corp. (1954-65). Ryan was a member of the New York State Senate from the 28th District (1938-42). He played tennis and golf. Ryan retired to Palm Beach, Florida and died on October 13, 1981.

Chapter 3

Kay Vamps Hollywood: "You'll Just Love My Pekingese"

"Are you the editor?" the striking, well-heeled young woman asked.

"Sorry, no," said the newsman at his desk.

"Then get him…get him down here!" she demanded, then added very impatiently, "Get all the editors down here! I'm suing this dirty paper for $50,000 libel. And I'll get it too!" Opening her fur-collared coat, she places hand on hip and declares, "You can't print lies about *me*! Naming *me* a correspondent in that Cummings divorce suit!" She then ups her ante. "I'm suing for $100,000!"

Fascinated by this enticing creature, the newsman inquires if she is not the Myra May that Mrs. Cummings had specifically named. "Mrs. Cummings is a liar!" she hotly replies. She then visibly softens and adds defensively, "Mr. Cummings was merely a dear, dear friend of mine." Her guard is suddenly up again, and just so there was no misunderstanding, she repeats herself, "…unless you retract the story I'm suing for *$150*,000."

The by-now bedazzled reporter eagerly agrees with her and invites Myra May to sit down. She does, while conveniently arranging her coat, defiantly, and very much off-the-shoulder. "I'll take charge of this case *myself*," he promises her. "You have an occupation?"

"Oh," she hesitates. "Uh, I'm here from California doing…secretarial work, just temporarily of course." She looks at him directly. "I'm not an ordinary secretary."

"No," he smiles. " I can see that."

After offering her phone number, Myra seems much relieved. She even begins to melt. "I didn't know newspaper men were as *nice* as you."

After a pregnant pause he assures her. "No…they're not."

"Then you understand why I came, don't you?" she pleads, pulling him closer into her net. "A girl…all alone in New York simply *must* protect her reputation."

He brightens. "Oh, then you live all alone?"

"Nooo!" she says playfully. "That is—with my *dog*." She smiles broadly. "You'll just love my Pekingese!" she smolders.

The newsman is practically ga-ga. "Yes," he finally utters. "I'm *sure* I will."

Gentlemen of the Press *(1929) Kay convincing Walter Huston that she's "not an ordinary secretary." (Paramount)*

The story continues. The newsman loves her "Pekingese" several times, before he realizes Myra May is bent on seducing his own son-in-law!

The scene was Katharine Francis' knockout grand entrance into the world of motion pictures as Myra May. The film: *Gentlemen of the Press*. How did Kay get the part? She told Ed Sullivan a few years later:

> It was while I was playing in *Elmer the Great* with Walter Huston on Broadway. He had signed with Paramount and he asked me to come over and take a test. A silent test. The studio and Walter raved over it, but when I saw myself on the screen I thought I looked horrible. My face was shiny, and I looked…like the devil. For ten days I hid on Long Island. Finally, my mother got me on the phone and said, "Kay, Paramount is offering you a contract for $300 a week with a five-week guarantee." And I *rushed* back to town. For $1500 I would have jumped off the Woolworth Building. Then I caught cold and could hardly talk. Millard Webb was all for throwing me out of the cast, but the chiropractor got me in shape by cracking my neck. My voice was so deep that I sounded like Ethel Barrymore. They liked it so much that they wanted me to keep my cold. No fooling![1]

Ward Morehouse, theatre critic for the *New York Sun*, wrote the Broadway hit *Gentlemen of the Press*. He asked Paramount director Millard Webb and dialogue director John Meehan to go on the prowl with him and find a new face for the film version. Morehouse later reminisced, "So, we all immediately went to Tony's [a popular bar] and there, in the haze of that famous backroom…we found Kay Francis. She was resting comfortably behind a Tom Collins. She was tall, dark and interesting-looking but had made far more appearances in Tony's than she had on the Broadway stage. She looked the part of Myra, all right. But the day of just looking it was gone forever. Could she act, and how was her voice? She was hustled over to Astoria. In the first test her voice came through strong and clear and vibrant. Her career began that very day."[2] Margaret Reid, for *Picture Play*, reported that, "Meehan and Huston made life miserable until [Kay] satisfied them by going over to the Paramount studio for the test. Kay was equally determined that she shouldn't." Kay explained, "The very thought of movies scared me off. D.W. Griffith had made a test of me three years before and it was a notable fiasco. I was convinced that the screen was not for me, and tried to forget it."[3]

Kay often gave credit for her consistently riveting and strong performance in the film to Walter Huston and dialogue director John Meehan. Meehan was pretty thick with Huston and both were pulling for Kay. Kay complimented her friend and mentor, Huston, saying, "I'm not sure just how I would have come through all this if I had not been able to draw encouragement and inspiration from Walter Huston. Maybe, we sustained each other, for this was the first film venture for us both. I would not have signed…if Walter hadn't advised me to. He has been the most remarkable and kindest friend a person could have."[4] Meehan, the film's dialogue director, gave Kay *more* than assurance. Paramount had paired the two to work on Kay's confidence before the camera and microphone. Kay and Meehan met over cocktails just before her December "Lucky 13th" (Kay's favorite number) screen test. The two spent long hours "rehearsing," which started rumors. While filming, Kay told her diary, "John M. is going to be difficult I am afraid."[5] Meehan wasn't half as difficult for Kay as her being able to deny the two were ever married. "But he was never her husband as some of the columnists have inferred," wrote one reporter in 1936.[6] In 1939, Kay was still denying the marriage, saying, "My supposed third marriage was to John Meehan, a writer. When this news broke, he sent me a kidding wire: 'When did all this happen? I must have been asleep or on a trip around the world.' He was dialogue director on my first picture and while we're good friends we were never married."[7]

Hollywood still reverberated from the 1920's scandals involving Fatty Arbuckle, Barbara La Marr and the murders of directors Thomas Ince and William Desmond Taylor. Film studios were on guard and Paramount counseled Kay to remain silent on the subject of her personal life. Some insisted she was living with Meehan. Kay did concede that it was Meehan who gave her confidence before the camera and turned her into a film actress. Her relationship to Meehan continued to puzzle when his name showed up, along with Dwight Francis and William Gaston, in the legal citation posted after her death. Most of her obituaries listed Meehan as her third husband. The assumption is that he and Kay *were* briefly married. She was simply hiding the fact of having chalked up another hasty marriage.

Kay's diaries mention Meehan and the arduous rehearsals at Long Island's Astoria studio, but they surprisingly place more emphasis on her relationship with her director, Millard Webb! On January 22, Kay wrote, "Dinner Millard—had fit of hysterics. Got quite tight and then I spend the night there…"[8] When she left for Hollywood, Kay was feeling "blue as hell" upon leaving Millard who kept busy telegramming her all across the

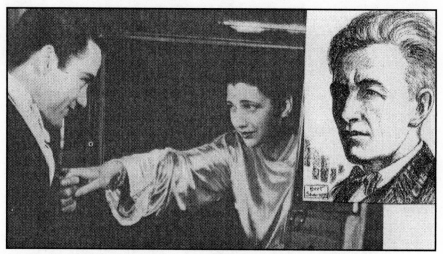

Kay's "lost" film, Illusion *(1929) with Buddy Rogers. At right—Kay's mystery husband, director John Meehan (New York Times sketch by Bert Sharkey)*

U.S. What's even more mystifying is her entry on May 13, 1929: "Took off Millard's ring afterwards so that's that—well, it was very nice in New York—Now I must find another man!"[9] Were she and Millard engaged? Was the hasty marriage to Meehan annulled? Was Meehan the key to Kay's mystery Las Vegas divorce in 1945? If so, did Kay's fourth marriage in 1931 make her a bigamist? It's no wonder that Kay could never articulate the complexity of her love-life.

So, what became of Myra May in *Gentlemen of the Press*? Her life seemed almost domestic compared to the real-life Kay. Myra is hired as newsman Walter Huston's secretary. He acquires a posh job as publicist for the National Mausoleum Association, which is in the process of being re-christened *Heaven*—"the ideal resting place"—*Heaven*—where cocktails are served after heavy dictation. When Huston catches Kay smooching his son-in-law (Norman Foster), he forgives her, but becomes intent on keeping the two apart. Myra's onto Huston's scheme and soaks him for all he's worth. We finally see Myra interrupting him at work with a phone alert. "Say! What's the idea?" she shouts at him. "Did you forget to send up that *gin*?" She fires him an ultimatum. "Say, listen, baby. You get that gin up here and you get it up here quick, or I'll come down with the gang and stage the party *there*!"

Myra has reeled Huston in on her hook, but not for long. He calls his bootlegger, telling him, "I don't care how bad it is…anything but poison." This is followed by news that his daughter has died in childbirth. Myra's no longer a threat, but he's left with the sobering realization that looming headlines and deadlines had been the *real* culprits governing his life. Kay's direct, sharp demeanor is as compelling as it is frightening. She's definitely showing Myra's true colors. And, you don't soon forget her at the film's fadeout.

Paramount executives were so pleased with Kay's performance in the dailies, that they actually squeezed her into a second feature before *Gentlemen of the Press* (filmed in both silent and sound versions) was completed. She began rehearsing with the Marx Brothers for a film of their Broadway hit *The Cocoanuts*, playing a similar kind of vamp. Paramount decided Kay's vivid aristocratic looks gave her potential to become a popular star. She was signed at $500 a week. Kay's being cast with the Marx Brothers would bring her to the attention of a more diverse group of moviegoers.

With a budget of $500,000, *The Cocoanuts*, with music by Irving Berlin, had French *avant-garde* director Robert Florey and Joseph Santley at the helm. Despite the limitations of a studio with no soundproofing, the film managed to capture some of the Marx Brothers' best routines. The wired-for-sound four-

Kay and Groucho Marx in Cocoanuts *(1929) (Paramount)*

some had hit Broadway with the play in December 1925, and it ran for 377 performances. George S. Kaufman hardly recognized his play when he saw the film. The Marxs' ad-libbing forfeited the script with hilarious results. Groucho, as a mis-manager of a Florida hotel on the financial skids, is trying to auction off some land. He mentions to his partner-in-swindle, Chico, "Now here is a little peninsula and here is a viaduct leading over to the mainland." Chico, as usual, has to put a twist on the translation. Viaduct becomes the perplexing question, "Why a duck?," a classic Marx Brothers' routine.

While Groucho insults and abuses the few hotel guests there are, he proceeds to read aloud an outlandish telegram, "Aunt Fannie had an eight pound boy. Can you come to the wedding?" He then brazenly propositions a wealthy guest (Margaret Dumont), saying they should find a bungalow where they could "Bull and cow." Kay is thrown into the ring, for a farce within a farce, playing a jewel thief. When juxtaposed against the Marx Brothers, Kay's sophisticated demeanor provides much of the same comic potential as Margaret Dumont. Kay tries to seduce Chico for an evening rendezvous, saying he reminds her of the Prince of Wales. She wants him in her room at a certain hour in order to incriminate him in the heist of Dumont's necklace, but her ploy backfires.

> "Don't you *dare* come to room 320 at 11 o'clock!" Kay coos encouragingly.
> "All right," Chico pipes up, "I come at a half past ten!"

Kay's part as the sleek jewel thief, Penelope, did not go unnoticed amid the knockabout Marx Brothers' farce. Leonard Hall, writing for *Photoplay*, wrote in raptures about Kay's roles in *Gentlemen of the Press* and *The Cocoanuts*. "This modern, up-to-date man-killer of the screen must be a far smoother and more seductive article…Others will come, do their dirty deeds, and pass, but as the pioneer of the clan, Miss Francis will occupy a sizable place in the yet unwritten history of the talkies. She takes her stance with a steady gaze…there is an air about her that says, 'Well, you fool, take it or leave it—but if you leave it you're an idiot!'"[10] As Kay is ushered in for the film's costume banquet, she dons a magnificent Raquel Meller-like costume complete with tall comb and *mantilla*.

A New York reviewer raved about the film, saying, "Audiences are rolling in the aisles over Paramount's *The Cocoanuts*, the Marx Brothers' madcap movie debut…Kay Francis and

Kay and Harpo Marx "cutting up" in The
Cocoanuts (1929). *Years later Kay laughed, "I
think back to the falls that I took with the Marx
Brothers and have a nice quiet giggle." (Paramount)*

Margaret Dumont bring up the rear and attempt to maintain their battered dignity amid
the non-stop craziness."[11] Kay delighted in
her memories of working with the Marx
Brothers. When once asked her most amusing recollection, she offered, "Playing the
'heavy' with the Marx Brothers in the film
version of *Cocoanuts*. Chico pulled lingerie
out of my hat. Harpo chased me all over the
screen. Groucho wrestled with me. When
they talk of me as the dignified Kay Francis,
I think back to the falls that I took with the
Marx Brothers and have a nice quiet giggle."[12]

In the late spring of 1929, after Kay
finished retakes for *The Cocoanuts*, she was
told by Paramount to pack her trunks and go
to Hollywood. As neither of her films had
been released, Kay had her doubts about success in tinsel-town. She also had doubts about
the people there. She felt she couldn't brave
it alone. Kay confessed to writer Ben Maddox,
"I may well admit that I was scared stiff of the 'iniquities' of Hollywood as well as being
financially low when I came here. My friends had warned me I'd probably be inveigled into
taking *dope*, so I actually brought a girlfriend from New Orleans along to stay with me as
protection for awhile! When I got acquainted, I found Hollywood wasn't a bit dangerous."[13]
    While passing through Chicago, en route to Hollywood, Kay got more reinforce-
ment by engaging a new maid, named Ida. Kay later referred to Ida, who was black, as "a
lady's lady, if ever there was one. To Ida, it is always 'our career,' and she shares its every
phase, and she is an ardent picture fan, too, never missing a preview of my films."[14] Apparently, Kay's friend from New Orleans, Katty (Katherine Stewart), was also an ardent fan of
Kay's. "Slept with Katty only because she wanted me to—Damn!"[15] Kay wrote aboard the
train. An affair with Katty was the furthest thing from Kay's mind. However, it is important to know that Kay truly cared about Katty. The two had known each other since their
Cathedral School days on Long Island when Katty wrote the school play and cast Kay
opposite her as the male lead. The flame of love still burned in Katty and she accompanied
Kay everywhere while Kay established herself in Hollywood. Katty returned to New Orleans on June 2. The night before her departure, the two had stayed up until 5:30 a.m.
"talking." Kay wrote sentimentally, "I really adore her—and I guess she really loves me."[16]
Kay's soft spot for Katty would be rekindled the next spring, when Kay vacationed as the
Stewart family's house-guest in New Orleans.

    Kay and her entourage arrived in Hollywood April 15 with her three trunks and ten
suitcases of clothes. She had three days to settle in and learn how to drive a car, before she
began work on her first film on the Paramount lot. Paramount had been home to many of
the great silent stars such as Valentino and Gloria Swanson. The studio was the brainchild of

Hungarian-born showman Adolph Zukor. In 1912, he stretched the average 30-minute feature to well over an hour, when he financed the French film *Queen Elizabeth* with Sarah Bernhardt. He watched "audiences gather to see the famous actress as if she were Niagara Falls brought to their town."[17] The response was tremendous. Theaters were upgraded to accommodate a more sophisticated clientele. By the 1920s Zukor was the man in charge of Paramount Pictures. Under his determined guidance, Paramount set up the monopoly pattern of filming, distributing and the ownership of theaters. The studio's claim to fame was its sophisticated, witty, glamorous and stylish product. With directors like Lubitsch and von Sternberg, spectaculars created by Cecil B. DeMille, and an eclectic mix of popular and sophisticated stars like The Marx Brothers, Gary Cooper, Chevalier and Claudette Colbert...Kay Francis was in good company.

For her first film on the west coast, Kay was co-starred with Paramount's top female attraction, Clara Bow, in a 1929 release titled *Dangerous Curves*. Kay was pleased with her role in *Dangerous Curves*, as it allowed her to act out her childhood fantasy of being a trapeze artist. Kindhearted, hoydenish Clara helped the dignified-looking newcomer by suggesting that the studio change Katharine, as the actress had been billed, to Kay, which would fit marquees better. Just before their first scene together, Clara counseled: "Now look, Kay, I'm the star, so naturally they train the camera on me. But if you cheat a little, you'll get in it just right too. You've got to keep that face in the camera, darling."[18] It must have worked. Many felt that Kay's alluring Zara stole the picture. Bow, who had been a top star in the silent films, had difficulty facing the mikes. Bow's biographer, David Stenn, wrote about her trauma on the set of *Dangerous Curves*. "The mike overhead loomed like an enemy, and in take after take Clara would involuntarily stare at it in terror...her confidence was undermined to the point where, during the shooting of one especially talky scene, Clara could endure no more. Frustrated and ashamed of her mistakes, she swore violently at the mike, then burst into tears and sank to the ground, sobbing and whimpering. Though word of the incident never reached the press, details spread throughout the studio and fueled rumors that Clara could not cope with sound technology."[19] For all her advice to Kay, Bow seems uneasy in her part. Her performance is filled with nervous pauses and girlish gestures. Still, Bow had her fans, and at this point her films made tremendous profits for Paramount. Her fear of the mike would eventually prove her undoing.

Dangerous Curves, originally titled *Pink Tights*, was the first of five outings for Kay and director Lothar Mendes. Billed third, she sauntered around in aerial gear while two-timing Richard Arlen, who takes to the bottle. We see Kay kissing Arlen and within ten seconds of his departure she is smooching another aerialist, David Newell. Bareback equestrienne Clara Bow worships Arlen. When he passes out drunk in his dressing room, she makes herself up like a clown and doubles for him on the high-wire! By the end of the film, Kay's character gets tired of all the fuss and lets Clara Bow have Arlen. Kay's own impression after the preview of *Dangerous Curves* was summed up in her diary with one word, "Ouch!"[20] But, the film was good exposure for Kay, who would repeat a similar role in her next Mendes-directed film, *Illusion*.

Writer Dick Mook dropped in on the set of *Dangerous Curves* and found Kay offering Arlen her therapeutic touch. "I walked on to the set one afternoon to see Arlen. He was lying on a bench complaining of a backache and the dignified Miss Francis, in black tights...was astraddle him, vigorously massaging the aching portion of his anatomy!"[21] Mook later reported that Kay became fast friends with Arlen and his actress-wife Jobyna

Ralston. A great deal of Kay's spare time that first year was spent with the Arlens. The couple was down-to-earth and spoke Kay's language. Kay's diary mentions taking along Katty to the Arlens' for enjoyable days canoeing and swimming in the lake. Kay was also mixing with other Broadway transplants to Hollywood such as Ruth Chatterton, Basil Rathbone, and a now amorous Walter Huston. Kay preferred keeping Walter, whom she adored, at a friendly distance. When Kay invited him over for dinner, he proceeded to get "too drunk to get home." Kay wrote that Huston "slept between Katty and me. Good old Walter."[22] Soon afterwards, Kay went over to Huston's for drinks and he was persistent. "Kissed him like a damn fool," she moaned. "That is the last person I want to have an affair with—not because he isn't sweet, but—not that way! Thank God."[23]

While renting a modest little bungalow, Kay started a little family by acquiring two canaries which she named Sears and Roebuck. She also bought a little Scottie pup—the first dog she ever owned. William Powell named it "Snifter." Kay bought her first car, a Ford, and christened it "Rabbit." Trying to impress no one, she was determined to save money. Kay was comfortable at Paramount and told *Picture Play* magazine,

> I like living alone. I have to be alone at times and the only chance I get is when I'm at home. I don't see how people live who are never alone. I couldn't do it. Besides it's convenient. I like a small house. Even if I had a lot of money, I wouldn't want a big one. Why complicate existence? Aren't there enough things you have to do without taking on a lot of extraneous ones? I make a swell bachelor girl, really, I'm not domestic. I want to live simply. Work happens right now to be the important thing to me. It's filled my life. I'm mad about it. I love it. I love acting. Every thing about the studio is marvelously lovable to me. I'm beginning to understand what acting can be. I love to come home at night and work out a part, visualize it, think up business, get inside the character. I love shooting, when we work hours to get results. It has satisfied me completely. And it seems to me something that cannot fail me.[24]

However, one thing Kay did find puzzling was that everyone in Hollywood thought of nothing but films. It was a state of self-centeredness that struck Kay as bordering on insanity. She was determined not to become like that. Her solution was to flee to New York whenever she could. Kay's first real escapes from Hollywood were San Francisco and Hawaii. Five days after completing *Dangerous Curves*, Kay, Katty, and Snifter drove Rabbit up to San Francisco to view the Golden Gate Bridge, Nob Hill and the Twin Peaks. She mentions some location shooting, and co-star Richard Arlen and his friend Gary Cooper joining in the sightseeing. On her way back to Hollywood they took a sojourn to Yosemite. After saving Snifter from arrest for chasing peacocks at Fresno City Park, Kay, a little bewildered by the traffic laws, was followed through three towns by a speed cop. He clocked her driving at 62 miles per hour near school grounds, crosswalks, through intersections, "riding in the middle of the road…and, [she] had passed ten cars in three miles."[25] Despite Kay's plea that she had only been in California three weeks, Rabbit was hauled into court. Kay paid the $25-fine, and they took off, only to be stopped a few miles later by another officer. Kay had sped through a stop sign. When her vacation rolled around in September, Kay forsook driving and sailed to Honolulu.

The two-week holiday included a visit to Hilo on the Big Island and surfing lessons from the legendary and handsome Hawaiian big wave rider, Bill Hollinger.

Illusion seems to be the only film of Kay's to have bitten the dust and not be circulating among collectors. The film, with Buddy Rogers and Nancy Carroll, had a circus-vaudeville theme. When the pair tries to break into showbiz, Rogers is distracted by society girl June Collyer. Fourth billed, Kay plays a bit part as the beautifully gowned charmer, Zelda Paxton, whom the *New York Times*' reviewer, Mordaunt Hall, overlooked completely. It was just as well. Hall found the film "a dull offering…sadly lacking in imaginative direction." He found the dialogue distressing, as well as the nature of the Rogers-Carroll vaudeville act in which four men took aim at a girl with army rifles loaded (they suppose) with ammunition. Hall does raise a valid question. "One wonders in what theater they could get four men to fire at a girl…?" Needless to say, a *real* bullet is loaded into the script just before an improbable "happy ending." *Photoplay* was puzzled by Kay's presence in *Illusion*, and commented, "if you can discover what Kay Francis is supposed to be we'll mail you a prize."

Otto Dyer's camera captured Kay in 1929. "I'm terrified," Kay reflected on Hollywood. "After being here awhile…People think of nothing but themselves. I've already deteriorated to the point of going around with my make-up on…If I stay out here very long, I haven't the slightest doubt that I'll be wearing feathers in my hair."[26] (Paramount)

It had been announced in May 1929 that Kay would play a society vamp who influences a young musician in *The Genius*. Paramount had also planned to put Kay opposite handsome newcomer Phillips Holmes in a picture titled *Youth Has Its Fling*. Instead, in her next film, Kay played a film star vamp named Zinnia La Crosse. Again, Lothar Mendes directed. The film's adaptation of Edith Wharton's celebrated novel *The Children* was given a racier title: *The Marriage Playground*. The story is set in Italy and tells of a group of six American siblings from different marriages, whose pleasure-seeking parents leave them in the charge of the eldest (Mary Brian). The parents return to find that Brian has fallen in love with an older man (Fredric March). The much-married mother who is raising the brood of kids is played by Lilyan Tashman, who would become a good friend of Kay's. When Kay finally arrives on screen, she refers to herself as Lady Wrench. On her arm she sports a Marquis and shows him off to her precocious daughter, Little Zinnie (the impish Mitzi Green).

"Did you bring me a present?" little Mitzi asks her mother.
Kay smiles. "First, you must meet your new papa!"
"*Another* one!" Mitzi sneers. She looks at the Marquis and blurts out,

"I bet you got money! 'Cause Zinnia wouldn't get married if you didn't!"

Handing Little Zinnie her present, Kay muses, "Isn't she a *scream?*" Seconds later Kay's batting eyelashes have discovered Fredric March.

The Marriage Playground's most climactic moment is when Lilyan Tashman and Kay Francis discover they are wearing the same designer outfit.

"How *dare* you copy my suit!" Tashman accuses Francis. "Anastage designed it *especially* for me."

"You mean he designed it for *me*!" Kay fumes. "I suppose you bribed him for one just like it!"

The ensuing catfight is dissolved when something as inconsequential as cocktails are announced. The Francis-Tashman fashion feud couldn't steal the picture from the children in *The Marriage Playground* and everyone appeared to be having a good time. This may have been due to Mendes' technique of putting actors at ease. He told his cast "When they yell 'Camera!' it means *relax.*"[27] The technique didn't exactly work for Kay, who noted during filming, "Horrible afternoon. Seven hours on one damn dumb scene! Went to pieces."[28] Robert Landry in *Variety* thought *The Marriage Playground* "A peach of a picture...the kind that leaves a sense of full-hearted human pleasure behind it." Kay always regarded the film as a rotten apple, her *worst* film. The story was remade in 1990 using the original title, *The Children*. Its all-star cast included, Ben Kingsley, Kim Novak, Geraldine Chaplin, Karen Black, and Britt Ekland playing Kay's Lady Wrench.

Reporter Dick Mook mentioned that Kay's slick coif she'd sported since 1924, was still pretty extreme for 1929 Hollywood. "Practically every employee on the Paramount lot heard of her as soon as she set foot on the place," wrote Mook. "Groups of executives, directors and writers who had stopped to talk to each other lost all track of conversation when she approached. No one has ever been able to pass this girl with the gray-green eyes without looking twice. The studio was not slow to capitalize on Kay's ability to wear clothes."[29]

Ironically, Tashman and Francis *would* become rivals for "best dressed" woman in Hollywood. Designer Travis Banton had already put Kay in the "best dressed" league as early as November 1929, and reported, "Kay Francis, who has been given the title of 'America's best dressed woman,' appeared at the Coconut Grove wearing a frock of coarse net in the new shade, dahlia. The skirt at the back and front swept the floor with four inches of material. When dancing, Miss Francis solved the long-hem problem by the good old-fashioned method of holding her skirt in her left hand. Miss Francis calls it the 'waltz-gesture.'"[30] The fashion rivals of 1929-30 also included the slender, sophisticated Constance Bennett. The three of them, Kay, Lilyan and Constance, were often seen sitting, not far from one another, at Hollywood Stadium's "Friday Night Fights." Wearing extremely chic outfits and eyes that sparkled with challenge—the fighting spirit prevailed, although Kay really couldn't have cared less. Kay groaned from the beginning about being "best dressed" anything and fired, "I can think of nothing more tremendously unimportant than being the best dressed woman in pictures—or anywhere else, for that matter. I have absolutely no ambition, in that direction. Neither do I want to be a dowd. I'd make a terrible frump. I like clothes...And I propose to dress as I have always dressed—carefully, correctly and as smartly as I know how. But I shall never make it a ballyhoo."[31]

At the end of 1929, after being fifth-billed in *The Marriage Playground*, the fashionable Kay found herself vamping again in the dark-edged, comedy-drama, *Behind the Make-Up*. It turned out to be another very small role. Elsie Janis seemed to sum up Kay's career at Paramount at this point, saying Kay "went along adding a dash of studio-made menace to this and that film. They admitted that she was a 'comer' but they had too many 'goers' on their hands to concentrate on this slim, chic Francis."[32] True, the studio was occupied with trying to satisfy the thespian appetites of William Powell, Ruth Chatterton, Maurice Chevalier, Jeanette MacDonald, and many others. *The New York Times* would comment that Kay, "rose to fame in roles that Lilyan Tashman didn't have time to fill." In *Behind the Make-Up*, Kay's dash of menace was brief, but deadly. Fourth-billed, she was the money-hungry vixen who drove an oily Italian (William Powell) to suicide. *Behind the Make-Up* was based on the 1926 *Redbook* story "The Feeder" by Mildred Cram and dual-directed by Dorothy Arzner and Robert Milton. The real star of *Behind the Make-Up* was Hal Skelly who plays a comedian and artist of hokum. Skelly, who wears his heart on his sleeve, befriends Gardoni (William Powell), who is down on his luck. Before Skelly knows what's happening, Powell has stolen his bizarre comedy act of parading around in high-heels and a white-fox fur wrap. By the end of the reel, Powell has also stolen Skelly's girl (Fay Wray).

Kay, as Kitty Parker, a racy man-eater, entices Gardoni with her dark mannish hairdo, low necklines and multiple strands of pearls. She becomes the great inspiration who "elevates" his soul. The elevating soon takes a tailspin dive. Kay ropes Gardoni in with her long strands of pearls, wiping both him and Skelly out of their savings. She has

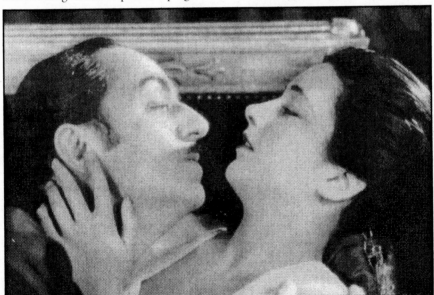

Behind the Make-Up *(1930) Kay's first teaming with William Powell. As an actress, Powell found Kay* "as responsive as a violin." *(Paramount)*

found a new source of revenue in Boris (Paul Lukas). When Powell comes to her at the casino desperately asking for help, she's dismissive:

> "I'm leaving for London…and *Boris* is going with me!"
> Gardoni pleads, "I *need* you!" Kay watches the overwrought Gardoni emote while she patiently enjoys her cigarette. As usual, his "performance" has taken on Shakespearean proportions.
> "But, *I* don't need you," she says, matter-of-factly, adding, "I might remind you that you're *quite* exasperating."

The distraught Powell rewards Kay with a new ring for her heavily bejeweled hands, before he jumps into the river. Inadvertently, Kay has solved Skelly's problems by driving Gardoni to suicide. The film has a *noir*-ish feel to it. It's fascinating to watch Powell as the heavy in such a seamy story. He cheats, he lies, and he's an adept backstabber. Kay is a knockout—confident and engaging in the six minutes of film time allotted to her. One reviewer took note of her subtle and convincing maneuvers: "Kay Francis slithers seductively through the siren scene."[33] *The New York Times* agreed that "Kay Francis does nicely as the adventuress." *Hollywood Daily Citizen* reported, "*Behind the Make-Up*…has pathos, characterization, and a good plot…Skelly gives a most pathetic and appealing characterization…Powell is superb in his role of the egotistic Gardoni. Kay Francis plays her usual vamping role."

William Powell took an immediate liking to Kay and confided to Adela Rogers St. Johns, "I hate talking to blank faces. You say something. Nothing happens in the face opposite you. So you say it again, with more detail. Finally you find yourself running on and on and growing more and more annoyed. *Kay is as responsive as a violin. I … love to talk out scenes and business with her. She's a wonder, really.*" St. Johns verified Powell's observation and

Paramount on Parade *(1930) Kay plays Carmen for a comedy sketch in her only Technicolor appearance. (Paramount)*

found Kay to have a "recklessly expressive face…When you are talking, she listens with her eyes and her mobile red mouth, and her very pretty nose, as well as with her ears…If you say anything, she shows you just what impression it has made. Her vivid interest stimulates you to talk and to talk better than you can. William Powell, who has worked with her in three fine pictures, told me to watch for that."[34]

Kay's self-assured approach to playing screen vamps impressed audiences. She was interestingly independent and more human than her vamp sisters from the silent films. *Behind the Make-Up* was her sixth such role and she must have wondered if Paramount had anything else in mind for her. They surely recognized her growing popularity when they added her to their all-star line-up in *Paramount on Parade*—an all-star extravaganza of music, skits and dance numbers. Kay was featured as the alluring Spanish beauty Carmen in a musical-comedy Technicolor sequence titled, "Isadore the Toreador," with the Marion Morgan dancers.

In another sketch, titled "Impulses," she was a mouthy party-girl—an entertaining farce with George Bancroft. The sketch is easily one of the best bits in the film's hodgepodge. It has George Bancroft visiting a party where he and hostess Cecil Cunningham use all the social graces while interacting with the guests. Kay plays herself and is seen commenting on the exquisite pearls worn by her companion. They are interrupted when William Austin (who had played Kay's Marquis in *The Marriage Playground*) poses a riddle to Bancroft. After this bit of nonsense, Kay approaches Bancroft, and gushes, "I think you're simply marvelous!" The party suddenly ends when an insufferable musician insists on serenading everyone at the piano.

After a fade out, Bancroft poses a question to the movie audience. "What would happen if everyone followed their impulses at such an affair?" The scene is then re-enacted with everyone in a different frame of mind. All pleasantries have vanished. Bancroft re-enters, gruffly greets the hostess and makes a few insulting remarks about her dead husband (much to her delight). Kay asks her companion if the pearls she's wearing are strung on telephone wire and proceeds to yank them off her neck—pearls scattering everywhere. When Austin mentions to Bancroft that he has a riddle, Bancroft grabs him by the neck and chokes him, while everyone laughs. When the hostess asks Bancroft if he'd like to meet Kay, referring to her as a drugstore beauty, Bancroft balks, saying, "Not while I'm conscious!" As soon as Kay spots him, he has no choice. "Hey Bancroft!" she yells across the room. "Come here!" "What do you want?" he asks, irritated. "*You* heard me!" she repeats. "*Come here!* I got something for you." Bancroft walks over, gazes down at the flowers Kay is holding, smiles and bends over to sniff them. Kay wallops him over the head with a vase which shatters to pieces. While the dizzy Bancroft is rubbing his head, Kay gives him a shove. "Go on *Bozo!*" she sneers. The aforementioned musician only gets to play one chord before the battered Bancroft grabs him by the seat of his pants, carries him across the room and throws him out the window! The partygoers wildly applaud his bravado. As rough as it sounds, it's really very funny.

Nineteen Twenty-nine had come to an end. Kay's career and life had taken unexpected and promising directions. If she had any apprehensions about having to repeat *another* vamp part for Paramount, she had nothing to fear. Her next role, in *Street of Chance*, was the antitheses of a vamp and definitely put her on the map as a versatile actress. According to the press releases, Kay also began a new romance with her co-star, William Powell. Nothing could have been further from the truth.

✳ JOHN MEEHAN ✳ – Kay's *Mystery Husband*
Born: May 8, 1890, Lindsay, Ontario, Canada
Died: November 12, 1954, Woodland Hills, California
Married to Kay Francis: (1929?) (Divorce—1945?)

John Meehan made his acting debut on Broadway at age 12 in a play titled *Soldiers of Fortune* (1902). By 1917, he had written a Broadway play, *The Very Minute*. A 1928 *New York Times* article said Meehan was "the image of George M. Cohan."

> He has trouped since he was 16 and knows every phase of the theatre as actor, director and playwright. As an extremely young man he was stage director for David Belasco's production of *The Girl of the Golden West* and he is among the few individuals who have worked both for Florenz Ziegfeld and George White. Meehan having directed a *Follies* and a 1922 *Scandals*. When Meehan was acting in *Abraham Lincoln,* he turned out a play called *Friend Tom* in which the late Arnold Daly became sufficiently interested to show the script to Mr. Cohan. The upshot was that two days later Meehan became Cohan's general stage director, in which capacity he has served for seven years.

Meehan's biggest success was teaming up with Robert Riskin for the play *Bless You, Sister* (1927). The play followed in the wake of the popular hit *Elmer Gantry* and the Aimee Semple McPherson religious tent revivals. *Bless You, Sister* was filmed in 1931 as *The Miracle Woman* with Barbara Stanwyck. While working as dialogue director in Kay's 1929 film debut in New York, Meehan and Kay were "secretly" married. Kay always denied the marriage, but legally, had to list him along with her father and other husbands in her will.

Once in Hollywood Meehan contributed his writing skills to such classics as Norma Shearer's *The Divorcee* (1930) and *Boys Town* (1938). He was nominated for the Oscar's best writing category for both films. His last assignment was on Jeanette MacDonald's *Three Daring Daughters* (1948).

Meehan had married an actress named Helen Scott in 1920. According to a 1926 press release, Meehan had abandoned his wife "after they had been married only two months." Meehan was arrested in 1923 in a separation suit. His wife claimed she was unable to get employment, "because managers fear that Meehan will use his influence against them if she is employed." Helen finally filed for a Paris divorce in December 1926, while Meehan was living at Chicago's Hotel Ambassador.

Meehan died in Woodland Hills, California on November 12, 1954.

Chapter 4
Street of Chance

She looked at the stucco castles and Spanish haciendas with twenty rooms, swimming pools, landscaped grounds, tennis-courts, and garage space for a fleet of cars, in which the majority of the successful film people—and those who *wished* to create an impression that they were successful—lived, and vowed that she would *never* inhabit such a place…this is the finest comment that could be made on the way Kay Francis has kept her head and her balance in that dizzy film world of unreality and pretentiousness.[1] (*Picture Show*)

Hollywood had Kay Francis pegged. In spite of the town's enthusiasm for Kay's talent and signifying her as one of the best dressed women in America, everyone noticed that Kay was hesitant to buy a house and settle into the film community. Her reasons were twofold. Firstly, renting seemed more practical. Kay was determined to save her salary. Memories were still fresh of being constantly broke in New York and she vowed never to be in the same predicament again. Putting on any kind of "Hollywood swank," as she liked to call it, was pretty unrealistic considering the Crash of '29 and the Depression looming ahead. The times called for simple, practical living. Secondly, Kay felt her roots were back in New York. Columnists mentioned her numerous trips to The Big Apple, where a close-knit circle of friends awaited her with open arms and good-times. Hollywood had a personality that didn't meld with Kay's. Her affinity for New York compelled her to return again and again. When Kay was unable to get away, many of her friends from back east crossed the country to assuage her homesickness.

Kay's rented, modest, six-room bungalow on De Longpre Avenue was serving her well. She didn't care if it wasn't in the fashionable part of town. Her home reflected her lack of pretension, yet showcased her appreciation of fine things. As modest as Kay's bachelor-girl pad was, it demonstrated her distinct talent for color and design. Friend and writer Dick Mook observed that her home was "furnished in exquisite taste. Nothing in the place screams at you, 'Look at me! I cost thousands,' but most of the pieces would make a collector's mouth water."[2] A tour of Kay's boudoir, with its canopied bed and French night tables lit with Art Deco glass lamps, was easy on the eye and verified her expertise. Her bed, a fine fixture of Louis XIV art, was upholstered in green moire

Kay at home in her bungalow on De Longpre Avenue. Her Louis XIV-style boudoir, in shades of apple-green, maize and deep orchid, was her favorite room. (1931)

and painted with maize-yellow roses. Above the bed were dusty orchid drapes, which matched the carpet. The windows were treated with cream lace and over-drapes of apple-green taffeta.[3]

Even more important to Kay than fine trappings were her feelings about what a home should consist of. She commented,

A home should be a haven. A place for real living, a congenial environment that is at once, restful and stimulating to new ideas. Here I find complete rest after filming scenes all day at the studio that revolve around the splendors of multi-millionaire mansions…In screen portrayals, I wear gorgeous costumes and I adore them. Yet, after dressing up all day for the cameras the feminine desire for pretty clothes is fully satisfied and I like to slip into slacks and sandals when I leave the studio…My idea of a pleasant evening is to spend it with six or eight congenial friends, where we can sit in the patio or before a fire, and carry on a really interesting conversation.[4]

Kay economized with a minimum of hired help. In her first seven years in Hollywood she drove only Fords. She eventually traded in her 1930 model for the 1934 (christened "Rabbit II"). Kay often drove herself or Ida would be at the wheel. Occasionally, free-spirited Kay would turn up for work riding the pillion seat of her gardener's motor bike. Ida, who according to one reporter had *quite* a personality, was Kay's personal maid and secretary for eight years. Their devotion to each other became legend. Later, when Kay was at Warners, Sara Hamilton reported on the duo for *Photoplay*. Hamilton requested of the reader, "Let me lay bare for you, if you please, a section of the lady's heart for your inspection." Hamilton tells of the time Ida was taken ill and a frantic Kay stayed at her bedside for hours at a time administering cold towels. Riding in the ambulance, a faithful Kay kneeled next to Ida, offering her soothing voice and comfort. Hamilton reported that during the operation, "outside the door, waiting, handkerchief torn to shreds, eyes wide with suffering, stood Kay Francis."[5] The next day, the studio gateman dropped back at the sight of Kay's white-strained face at five a.m. The cold, rainy, morning held no peace for her as she paced the office floor of her friend and make-up artist, Perc Westmore. When Perc arrived at seven, Kay was desperate, "Look Perc, I—I just want to talk about

Ida. You think she's going to be all right? Talk to me about her, Perc! Should I call in any other doctor?"[6] Ida survived while basking in Kay's love and attention.

Kay's compassion for those she was close to became the *root* of who she was. Love, according to her, meant love of many things. "It means love of friends and it means love of charity," Kay would explain. "I don't mean the charity of giving things to certain organizations or persons; I mean the charity of giving *yourself* to those who need you. I mean meeting with other people in tolerance and kindliness; trying to give something of yourself; trying to give something of which no disaster can ever deprive them."[7]

By the end of 1930, Kay and Ida extended their "charity" by surrounding themselves with a loving menagerie of pets. Joining her dog "Snifter" were two Persian cats, "Mitzi" and "Tibs"; a canary named "Napoleon"; a Boston Bull christened "Caesar"; and seven fish—known as the Seven Vestal Virgins. There was also a noisy bull frog Kay christened "Basso Profundo." When asked about her hobbies, Kay always said she had none. "Hobbies seem to be terribly important," she explained. "And I haven't any. I have a dog and a cat and a canary and a lot of goldfish, but they aren't hobbies. But I suppose, sooner or later, I'll be caught in a weak moment and they'll run a picture of Miss Francis, that irrepressible child of nature, romping among her goldfish."[8] Over the next few years, Kay did actually develop a genuine hobby: collecting ornate boxes. All kinds of shapes and textures. She loved it when someone would prowl around funny little shops and find one for her and place her favorite brand of cigarettes in it.

Kay's lack of interest in publicity was discovered early on by the fan magazines. They did not consider her good copy. Still, she was a popular cover-girl favorite. In November 1930, Kay was selected for the cover of the premier issue of *Modern Screen* which would continue publication for more than sixty years. Kay graced many covers, but would not volunteer meaty stories about her private life. Instead, she enjoyed talking about ideas. Kay liked expressing her philosophies about how to live life to its fullest. She refused to provide the type of fodder the average fan thrives upon. One ex-publicity man noted, "[Kay] wasn't like some of the great beauties who never smiled because they might develop lines. She wasn't vain. She was warm and funny about herself if she trusted you. ... She just didn't want to bother with publicity."[9]

One of Kay's less intellectual, safe, and favorite topics for interviews was her fascination with numbers. Seemingly an inconsequential subject, Kay gave it a great deal of significance in *many* a fan magazine interview. "13" was her lucky number. She was born on the 13th on the 13th hour of the day on the 13th month of her parent's marriage. She announced her engagement to Dwight on the 13th and divorced him on the 13th. Kay would go on and on, fudging here and there and by 1935 had convinced her directors that her important scenes must be shot at the 13th hour of the day (one o'clock p.m.). Kay told reporter Jack Grant: "You think I am silly to believe in luck in numbers…This has nothing to do with the science of numerology. It is merely what concerns and influences me…The most important point is that the most significant events of my life have occurred on thirteenths…Ten is a very bad number for me. Or five. Or anything divisible by five or ten. Eight is also unlucky, while seven is pretty good. This extends to street addresses and telephone numbers."[10] Paradoxically, Kay would admit that her fascination with numbers was "very, very silly and doesn't mean a thing." "But why take a chance?" she mused.[11]

Whatever numbers surrounded Kay's next film assignment were in her favor. *Street of Chance*, which she would consider one of her best films, took Kay out of the vamp category. It was her first opportunity to play a sympathetic and complex character. David Selznick was bent on teaming William Powell and Kay Francis together and helped create a screenplay that was tailored to their physical qualities and talents. He felt that they both could become very important stars. Selznick thought Kay's husky voice and sophistication would make her Powell's perfect leading lady. Both stars were clients of his brother Myron Selznick. After the Selznicks completed a fine scenario for *Street of Chance* (it would be nominated for an Oscar in 1930 for best writing), they hired director John Cromwell. Cromwell did not want Kay in the lead. The Selznick brothers rallied for Kay, in what David referred to as, "a bitter struggle against John Cromwell," and won out.[12] Cromwell, later conceded that the film, "did very well and created quite a stir, and stirs were not too frequent in those days. Many [films] were just routine..."[13] Kay was grateful to Selznick and later commented, "David Selznick did more to buoy my self confidence than anybody else...[he] was the only one who always believed that I was capable of playing leads."[14]

Street of Chance was loosely based on New York's mastermind gambler, and kingpin of the Jewish underworld, Arnold "The Big Bankroll" Rothstein. The 1919 Black Sox baseball scandal tainted his reputation and he moved into even seamier venues where he finally met his end, shot in the abdomen while playing cards. The parallels between Rothstein and Powell's character are peppered throughout the film. Powell's slightly shady character had charm, was sophisticated, and thoroughly likable. As Rothstein, he provided the prototype for Hollywood's popular villain-heroes such as Gable, Cagney and Bogart. Powell's character wasn't the only one to be inspired by Rothstein. Damon Runyan modeled the character Nathan Detroit in *Guys and Dolls* after him.

On screen, Powell's Rothstein-like character, "Natural" Davis, was a successful, but compulsive gambler. His devotion to his wife Alma (Kay) and brother (Regis Toomey) are foremost in his mind when he decides to quit gambling for good after a particularly "big killing" at the table. Kay convinces him they would be much happier if they left New York and settled elsewhere. However, Powell's intentions to quit go awry when his brother unexpectedly shows up to enter a big game. Powell feels compelled to teach the boy a lesson. In the process of throwing a game to disillusion his brother, Powell becomes a marked man.

Kay was finally given more allotted screen time for *Street of Chance*. While *Gentlemen of the Press* showcased her nicely, the following five films featured her only briefly. As Powell's wife, Alma Marsden, Kay's character was the antithesis of Myra May. Like Myra, Alma was intelligent, she could take care of herself, yet she had a soft, vulnerable edge—a natural tenderness. Early in the film she is *resolved* to let go of her marriage. She's tired of the nagging worry for Powell's safety and the uncertainty of their future. When Powell phone-calls telling her he's turning a new leaf, she almost believes him. Kay puts it bluntly. "I know you better than you know yourself," she tells him. "In a few weeks you'll go back and expect me to lead the same old impossible life. No, I've had enough of being a gambler's wife...I'm not so naive any longer." Powell assures her they will leave New York. Kay shows Alma's emotional struggle as she conjures up one last hope. She is quite touching. "Don't disappoint me this time, Jack," she pleads. "I won't...I *can't* give in like this again." Later, when a newsboy knocks on the door asking for Powell, Kay suspects the worst. Powell excuses himself yet again. The camera leaves Kay in tears as she sits on the edge of the bed.

Kay's sympathetic portrayal in Street of Chance *(1930), with William Powell, helped diversify her career. (Paramount)*

The role was familiar territory for Kay. With three broken marriages, she had gone through the torment of separation and reconciliation, and could well grasp the situation and disappointment found in the Marsden relationship. Alma's struggle had once been *Kay's*, it showed in her voice and body language. Her fine acting did not go unnoticed.

In reviews, *Street of Chance* was an unqualified success. *The L.A. Evening Herald* raved, "The big-time gambler has his day in Paramount's *Street of Chance*, a fine picture, that without doubt will be a candidate for the 'ten best' of 1930…it has photographic realism, taut suspense, unobtrusive sentiment and superb acting." Charles Lang's excellent camerawork in *Street of Chance* was fluid and inventive, capturing the quiet menace of the underworld without the usual bluster. *Street of Chance* has a polish rarely seen in films before 1932. *Photoplay* praised, "Bill Powell's finesse and Kay Francis's sincere emoting would be highlights in any picture." Louella Parsons noted, "If Rothstein had half the charm that William Powell gives 'Natural,' it's easy to understand why so many of his underworld friends have sworn revenge on his murderer." Parsons' review gave high praise to Kay, saying, "But no woman on the screen could be more stunning than Kay Francis as 'Natural's' wife. She wears her clothes like a thoroughbred and she adds interest to a story in which men are featured." Kay's sympathetic portrayal diversified her career. The emotional simpatico between Kay and Powell fueled their performances. His touch and her response were compellingly genuine. As we watch their lives torn apart by the world of gambling, we *believe* that they are losing what matters most to them: each other.

Powell's biographer, Charles Francisco, commented, "Bill Powell and Kay Francis were both pleased that the studio had agreed to co-star them in David Selznick's next special project *(For the Defense)*. During the filming of *Street of Chance*, they had developed a relationship that continued off-screen. They became an 'item' in the gossip columns, although both issued the standard denials of any serious romance. Even the most casual observer could see that Powell was giving more time and attention to Kay Francis than he had to any of the attractive young women who had decorated his arm earlier."[15] Powell's association with Kay was just that—a woman who decorated his arm on occasion. Paramount's publicity department had a field day when the two were seen together, but her diary only mentions a few instances where they got together for dinner, drinks and long talks. If anything, the two had a mutual admiration society. A couple of years later, Kay commented on what she found attractive about William Powell: "He's generous to work with, has an unfailing sense of humor, is witty, has a fine code of honor, and is so essentially a gentleman under all conditions. We always laugh and joke when we are together; our humor seems pitched in the same key." She also commented that she had profited, as an actress, by working with Powell. "We are very serious when making a picture, for we feel it requires all our concentration. Bill has taught me to keep from getting a one-track mind regarding my role. In studying his characters he likes to twist the story around, figuring out different angles in the psychology of the persons involved, and you would be amazed how this broadens one's understanding of the drama as a whole and of your own role in particular."[16] Kay also emphasized, "Despite his flippancy on the screen, [Powell] takes his work immensely seriously. He tries to make not only his own performance, but the picture as a whole as good as it possibly can be. It is a pleasure to work with him."[17]

When asked, Powell's observations about Kay were insightful. "Kay is deliciously feminine, with a thoroughly unconscious lure that captivates everyone," Powell told reporter Maude Cheatham. "She's a very real person, vital, alive. She's well-read and is a stimulating conversationalist. Kay also is blessed with a gorgeous humor, and with an uncanny understanding of a man's mental processes she always gets his viewpoint. She's sincere, a square-shooter, a real comrade. Playing opposite Kay has been one of my happiest experiences since coming to the screen."[18]

Powell also appealed to Kay's penchant for chivalry, which was fast-fading in the post-WWI world. In a frank interview with Jack Grant, Kay explained:

> Perhaps I am being sentimental, but it is my opinion that another generation will see a decided change in the social relationship of men and women…a direct reaction to the conditions imposed in 1914 by the World War…chivalry never depended upon man alone…No man cares to indulge in a foot race with a girl for the privilege of opening a door that she seems determined to open for herself. He will not rise at her approach nor offer her the seat he has been occupying if he senses in her attitude a contempt for such "old-fashioned nonsense." Poor devil! He doesn't want to be held in derision by being conspicuous in his act of gallantry. Small things, these, you may think—trifling courtesies that are unimportant in the breathless rush of the world we live in today. Yet our lives are made up of the little things that give us happiness or sorrow. It is only when we lose appreciation of the little things that we begin to die.[19]

If ever there was a gentleman to bestow Kay small courtesies offered so flatteringly, it was William Powell. The fact that he found Kay a "stimulating conversationalist," was in his favor. This enhanced their on-screen and on-the-set connection. Powell knew *how* to listen. This was very important to Kay, who declared:

> I resent more than almost anything else the attitude of those men who do not treat women as if they were individuals. They do not consider us *people!* To such men their wives are servants, their women friends are mere diversions. If you advance an opinion or an idea, they smile indulgently and pat you on the head—as if it were awfully cute for "a little woman like you" to try to think! They will make love to you, but they won't exchange views with you…They will pay you elaborate compliments—but they haven't the slightest respect for your opinion on any subject. In fact, they grow pretty restive if you try to express an opinion! It's their vanity, of course. If they admit you to anything like an equal basis, they cannot feel as superior as they want to feel. All they want of a woman is that she shall be a good audience. It is the old-fashioned masculine attitude—and it irks the modern woman immeasurably.[20]

Kay made it known that she didn't like the "big out-door type" of man who is "bombastic" and "*so* likely to want to perform stunts to show off his muscles!" Effete men? Kay volunteered, "Well, there is nothing especially irritating to a woman about effeteness, I think. It all depends upon the sort of mind he has and what he talks about and what his interests are."[21]

The only fault that Kay could find in Powell was his inability to be on time. "He even kids himself by keeping his watch set exactly thirty-one minutes fast," she merrily explained to *Screenland*, "but even that doesn't help much. He's quite hopeless in this."[22] One did not keep Kay waiting. It's no wonder there was no real significant emotional involvement between the two. Kay's mother had once mentioned with pride, "Kay's punctuality is famous. She will help a mechanic change a tire if it means arriving at the studio on time."[23] Kay's reputation was to arrive on the set as scheduled "on the moment, not before, not after."[24] While the unpunctual Powell and Kay kept mum on their own non-affair, Paramount fueled plans to re-team them. Warner Brothers also had their eye on Kay and wanted her to reprise the "modern" vamp that she had so expertly perfected.

In the Warner Brothers' feature *The Notorious Affair*, Kay played her last notable vamp: Countess Balakireff. It's really too bad, because her vamp characterizations were intriguing, impressive creatures. Adapted from the play *Fame* by Audrey and Waverly Carter, *The Notorious Affair* is about a violinist, Paul Gherardi (Basil Rathbone). His new bride, Patricia (Billie Dove), comes from a socially prominent family who snubs the yet unheralded Gherardi. Countess Olga Balakireff (Kay), London's most daring horsewoman, comes to the rescue, introduces him to the right people and he is an overnight sensation on stage *and* in her boudoir. His obsession with his music is soon transferred to Olga. This works out perfectly for her since her recent flings with the stableboy and the butler have turned sour. Before long, poor Gherardi can't take the pressure that accompanies fame. He gets dizzy while playing for Olga and has to be taken home in an ambulance. On the verge of a nervous breakdown, he becomes psychologically paralyzed and is unable to play the violin at all. It's preposterous stuff. Rathbone plays way over the top, pouting, whining and complaining that his milk ("meelk") has become cold. While recuperating, Gherardi attempts to play the violin. Kay

Notorious Affair *(1930) Scheming Countess Kay is shown stealing Basil Rathbone from Billie Dove.* The New York Times *thought Kay also stole the picture. (Warners)*

interrupts him, complaining, "Is *that* necessary?" He whimpers that he is worried that his public will forget him. Kay coldly consoles him by saying, "How will they *ever* forget you when you make such *terrible* noises?" She turns her back to him and looks out the window where she notices a handsome police officer—her next victim.

The critics concurred that Kay Francis was the best thing in *The Notorious Affair*. "One of the most subtle husband-stealing 'vamps' of the screen is Kay Francis," cheered *The Los Angeles Examiner*. "It is quite obvious that once she makes up her mind to 'get' a man, there is no way out. She plays her role with the cool assurance becoming her type. There is no undue eagerness displayed on her part, which is especially pleasing to the opposite sex." After a few unkind words about Billie Dove's performance, *The New York Times* declared that "Kay Francis, as the scheming countess, puts Miss Dove somewhat in the shade." Dove herself recognized Kay's talent, saying, "Kay Francis is the best bet in pictures! She not only knows how to wear clothes, she knows how to act."[25]

Variety thought Kay the standout in *A Notorious Affair* and made comment on her promising career. "Kay Francis, whose upward rise has been very rapid since last summer…sufficiently supports, merely by her presence, the story's suggestion of a seductive countess of definite nymphomaniacal tendencies…" At the time, Kay made a projection about the type of acting challenges she desired beyond the vamp category. "What I'd like to do, is women of the sort Katharine Cornell plays. They are living, breathing people, women whose very vitality makes them dramatically interesting. When you get such characters to analyze and project, then you really know why you insisted on turning actress."[26]

Asked if she had requested any such roles from her bosses at Paramount, she emphasized, "I'm no fixture yet. Give them *time* to find out whether or not I am a potential flop. Doing a few plays doesn't necessarily qualify me for pictures. I'm still learning the trade."[27] A modest assessment, considering the way she was being singled out with glowing praise.

Paramount placed their lovebirds, Kay and Powell, in a follow-up picture in hopes of repeating the success of *Street of Chance*. Their screen chemistry continued to intrigue David Selznick and he reversed their images in *For the Defense*. Bill Powell would play the innocent and Kay would have the ambiguous morals. Selznick supervised the story, which was based on a true incident. John Cromwell was again in the director's seat and Charles Lang repeated the fluid camerawork. *For the Defense* was written by the skilled pen of Jules Furthman, who would later write such classics as *Nightmare Alley* and the Bogart-Bacall hits *To Have and Have Not* and *The Big Sleep*. Running 65 minutes, the film was shot in two-and-a-half weeks.

The parts for Kay and Powell provided excellent opportunities. Powell plays a controversial, slick attorney for racketeers. In a sizably larger part from her previous role as Alma Marsden, Kay plays an actress who is Powell's sweetheart *and* lover. In definite shades of pre-Code Hollywood, Kay is a nice woman in an intimate relationship without the benefit of marriage. Such a storyline would not pass the censors a few years later. Still, the story has her hoping for something more permanent with Powell. When she asks *him* to marry *her*, her heartfelt request is ignored. Powell quietly dispels any of her hopes by saying, "After all these *months?* Don't you think that would be rather silly?" Unhappy with his response, Kay decides to rendezvous with her pal Defoe (Scott Kolk), who she has kept in the wings just in case her affair with Powell fizzled. When Kay drives the inebriated Defoe home, he can't keep his hands off her. The car swerves and a roadside bystander is killed. In desperation, Kay summons Powell and begs him to defend the wealthy Defoe, who is taking the rap for her. When Powell hesitates, she pleads with him, "You know how juries hate rich people!" Powell finally agrees, but is suspicious of her feelings for Kolk. "Baby," he warns her, "Don't ever pull anything on me. If you did, I'd never see you again. I'd never even want to *hear* about you." Powell bribes a juror and gets Defoe off the hook. But, he pays a price—his career. The film was chock full of emotional complexities for Kay.

One of the more interesting side-notes on *For the Defense* was the character Powell plays. He is loosely based on the lawyer William Joseph Fallon, also known as "The Great Mouthpiece." Fallon represented Fanny Brice's boyfriend, Nicky Arnstein. He also represented the very character that Powell's "Natural" Davis in *Street of Chance* was based on: Arnold Rothstein! In 1924, the Hearst newspapers put Fallon out of business when he was suspected of jury tampering. Fallon fought the mighty news baron, saying that he was framed by Hearst because he "uncovered birth certificates of twins that Hearst had fathered with a movie actress."[28] Although Fallon was found not guilty, clients shied away from him thereafter for fear Hearst would be following Fallon's every move.

Across the board critics were in favor of *For the Defense*. "Kay Francis is interesting and varied in her portrayal of the actress who indirectly and unwittingly brings [Powell] to his downfall," wrote the film critic for the *Hollywood Daily Citizen*. The *Los Angeles Illustrated Daily News* noted, "Miss Francis, remembered from her effective work in *Street of Chance*…gives good account of herself." *The New York Times* stated, "*For the Defense*…is essentially a New York picture…there is a story present and a good deal of acting that is *better* and more appropriately attuned to *life* than most. Mr. Powell carries his role well, as does Kay Francis as the lady of the case."

How did the film end? Critic W. E. Oliver put it aptly, stating, "Much of the public favor of *For the Defense* will rest on director Cromwell's smart handling of the story…[and] of being let in on the inside of things. The last scene, as [Powell] enters the penitentiary and finds [Francis] there in the rain to tell him she loves him and will wait for him, is a masterly bit of realistic pathos."[29] Suspenseful, sophisticated and fast-moving, *For the Defense* did well at the box-office and reinforced the team of William Powell and Kay Francis.

During filming on the Paramount lot Kay was confronted with some real-life pathos. She had just alighted from her car before the studio door when Snifter decided to take an exploring sniff of a bush across the street. (Kay often brought one of her dogs with her on the set.) She heard a screech of brakes and an agonized howl before rushing over to little Snifter lying in the street. Kay fell to her knees and bundled him up in her arms, tears rolling down her cheeks and upon the stricken Scotty. Someone drove them to the dog-and-cat hospital, but Kay couldn't stay. The actors and director were waiting for her. Kay worked without complaint, but after shooting was completed she rushed to the hospital with her make-up still on. She was greeted by a fully recovered and cocky little Snifter.[30] Snifter was Kay's constant companion. On her trip to San Francisco she had to stay at the Francisco Hotel "because of Snifter." Her love and admiration of dogs is well documented; she equated them with people, referring to the male of the species as gentlemen. In truth, Snifter was more of a bum. He continually ran away from home and cost Kay a lot of money in rewards and advertising for his return. Kay even had an appeal broadcast over the radio for him. It wasn't too many more months before Snifter did a thorough job of it and never returned.[31]

William Powell left behind "publicity sweetheart" Kay in July 1930, to explore the historic and scenic wonders of Great Britain. At the same time, Kay had the opportunity to co-star with Powell's close friend, Ronald Colman. Colman, also a bachelor (divorced), was dynamite as far as women fans were concerned. His co-star from the silent version of *Stella Dallas*, Irene Rich, crooned, "I had some lines to say, but when I turned to him, he was so beautiful that I forgot every word I was supposed to say, didn't remember a darn thing—just sat there and looked at him!"[32] While working with Colman, Kay had a similar reaction to him and jotted in her diary, "God, Ronnie excites me."[33] Kay's opportunity to co-star with the "exciting" Colman was a real coup. A Colman picture was always a "Class A" production. Kay later commented "I didn't really get into my stride until I played opposite Ronald Colman in *Raffles*."[34] The prestigious Samuel Goldwyn production of *Raffles*, is now considered the forefather of *The Pink Panther*. It was the third film to be based on the E.W. Hornung novel. (John Barrymore had done a 1917 version). As *Raffles*, Colman played an elite English cricketer who does some fancy filching on the side. As Lady Gwen, Kay was on to Colman's game. She was also smitten with him and fascinated by his ability to burgle her wealthy friends with such finesse. *Raffles* was a natural hit. Goldwyn had originally signed the brilliant Harry D'Arrast to direct. After three days filming, Goldwyn tactlessly complained to D'Arrast about a scene he thought was being played too fast. D'Arrast's temper flared and he yelled, "You and I don't speak the same language, Mr. Goldwyn!" Goldwyn answered him, without missing a beat: "I'm sorry, Mr. D'Arrast, but it is my money that's buying the language!" D'Arrast was fired on the spot and replaced by George Fitzmaurice.[35] Filming continued without a hitch.

Upon release, *Cinema* magazine reviewed *Raffles* saying, "Colman keeps the interest up more than would seem possible, and Kay Francis manages to give the impression that the most entertaining part of the story will come after she and Raffles are safely on the Continent." *Raffles* was the last picture Goldwyn produced in both silent and talking versions and it grossed more than $1 million. The film also garnered an Academy Award nomination for best sound (1930). The topnotch photography was by Greg Toland, who later filmed *Citizen Kane*. *Raffles* would be filmed again, less successfully, in 1940 with David Niven and Olivia de Havilland playing the Colman-Francis roles.

For her work in *Raffles*, Kay continued to receive excellent notices. *Variety* commented, "Kay Francis is a happy choice—an actress with that suggestion of reserve vitality that makes her stand out strongly." *Film Daily* commented that Colman "is given beautiful support by Kay Francis, whose sophistication and charm make her an ideal team-mate for the star." Norbert Luck for *Picture Play*, thought Kay a standout. "There is nothing lacking from the perfection of *Raffles* ... it is Miss Francis who reveals the surprising performance. Always interesting, arresting, here she is sympathetic, charming, delicate. The admirable dialogue provided by Sidney Howard…enables her to show how the modern girl reacts to finding herself in love with a thief. There are none of the tremors of sentimentality of a bygone day, but a brave facing of facts that is far more romantic."[36]

Kay was modest regarding such praises. "No one could give a really bad performance in a Colman picture," Kay told an interviewer. "He is so delightful to work with that the whole company is keyed up to him. Although I did attempt to demolish him one day, poor dear. I had on a very elegant gown, with train, and was to make an entrance. I swept in, feeling quite effective—and tripped over a rug and fell headlong, bringing Ronnie and a couple of chairs down with me. Francis, the human butterfly!"[37] The director and crew gasped. Kay howled with glee, "Everyone falls for Ronald Colman!"[38]

Raffles *(1930) Kay felt she got into her "stride" playing opposite Ronald Colman. A 1930 diary entry gave good reason. "God Ronnie excites me!" she swooned. (United Artists)*

   With the completion of *Raffles*, Ronald Colman joined Bill Powell in Paris. The two bachelors would sail home together. According to Colman's daughter, they arrived back in the U.S. "in time for Ronnie to emphatically deny rumors of an engagement to his leading lady, Kay Francis."[39] It must have seemed odd to Powell that *Colman* had to deny any romantic involvement with Kay. Powell biographer, Charles Francisco, wrote, "Back in Hollywood, William Powell discovered that his romance with Kay Francis had come to an abrupt end. Unlike the character she had played in *For the Defense*, Miss Francis had decided not to wait for him and had taken up with another man. Whatever his private emotions may have been, Powell kept them to himself because plans were in the making for more Powell-Francis screen teamings."[40] If Powell had, by some chance, bought into the publicity about Kay and him, it was high time to face the truth. Since July 1929, it was obvious to those close to her, that Kay was spending most of her time with one particular actor, albeit a lesser known one.

   After completing *Raffles* Kay escaped to New Orleans to visit Katty Stewart and her parents. Katty's father was a prominent cotton broker and Kay's arrival received a great deal of brouhaha in the local press. A large delegation assembled at the city's Union Station. Kay was quite an eyeful as she debarked from the train wearing a green-tailored frock, a fur neck piece, tan chapeau and shoes and brandishing a tennis racket in her hand. (Kay was an avid tennis player). "She won the entire audience, as in the movies," said one reporter, "with that broad and spontaneous smile."[41] Katty was late arriving for the festivity, and as one newshound noticed, "dashed through the crowd and grabbed Miss Francis in her arms."[42] Another reporter commented, "The meeting of Miss Francis and Miss Stewart, old friends, would have won over the entire city for her had they been able to see it."[43] Kay remarked to the crowds that she intended to play a "considerable" amount of tennis during her two- to three-week stay and added, "The visit to New Orleans really is a God send, because I am run down…People are all wet about the wildness of Hollywood…If the Hollywood folk are hopheads, I don't know about it and they are much too busy to throw wild parties. How can they dissipate when they work 14 and 18 hours a day? The movie people have their dinner parties, but they are really more circumspect than some in New York. The Hollywood wives go to parties with their own husbands."[44] After some rest, tennis, and a boat trip through the bayou, Kay would return to Hollywood and what she called "working my head off again."[45]

   If *Picture Play* had thought *Raffles* to be perfection, Kay's next film was the antithesis. With the title *Let's Go Native* and a capable director like Leo McCarey (who later did the classic Irene Dunne-Cary Grant comedy *The Awful Truth*), you would think a great laugh-fest was in store. Seen today, *Native* is an amateurish embarrassment. Gag after tiresome gag catapults the film nowhere until a volcanic explosion forces it to glub, glub into the sea. The film opens with Jeanette MacDonald, a costume shop proprietor, waking up to find all her belongings being repossessed. For some reason she is inspired to sing the jolly ditty "My Mad Moment" while her piano is hauled away. Her "mad moment" turns into an extended holiday when she high-tails, via oceanliner, to Buenos Aires to collect from her debtors. Her beau, James Hall, and his pal, Jack Oakie, follow her aboard ship. Kay, happens to be onboard—she also happens to be Hall's fiancee. Kay has the film's best line when she greets Hall on deck with Jeanette. "I didn't recognize you with your clothes on!" Kay smiles naughtily. Suddenly, the viewer's interest is piqued. But, after the cast is stranded on an island inundated with gyrating native girls with Brooklyn accents—what follows gives new meaning to the word "dumb."

In spite of the film's ineptitudes, the *Hollywood Daily Citizen* noticed that "Kay Francis was attractive in becoming costumes and is heard in an alluring song." The song was a duet with master ham Jack Oakie. MacDonald's biographer, Edward Baron Turk, wrote, "Perhaps the best reason for viewing this anarchic comedy today is to see and hear Miss Francis join in on the flirtatious second chorus of 'I've Gotta Yen for You.'"[46] Kay's mezzo-soprano is pleasant and shows an uniquely appealing musical ability. (Kay and Oakie's second duet, "Don't I Do," was deleted from the final print.)

During production of *Native*, director Ernst Lubitsch asked Jeanette how the filming was going, because Paramount was pressing him to take over from McCarey. She was hardly optimistic and unfortunately the Lubitsch touch never found its way to the set.[47] Kay, however, felt that director McCarey helped develop her characterization beyond the script. After release, a reviewer for the *American* commented, "It is really something of a shock to find the heroine of *The Love Parade* [MacDonald]…in such shoddy surroundings." *Let's Go Native* was the beginning of MacDonald's disenchantment with Paramount. After a stint with Fox she found her greatest success at MGM. *Let's Go Native* was exactly the kind of film that made musicals box-office poison in the early 1930s. *The New York Times* signaled the film's death knell, saying, "a ludicrous hodge-podge…Miss MacDonald gives as pleasing a performance as is possible…Kay Francis and others add to the wild gayety." Jeanette MacDonald carried off her pop tunes with her inimitable style and élan. It's a pity the script didn't provide her and Kay a few good barbs to banter back and forth. They got along well and apparently had forgotten all about Jeanette's earlier tantrum during the filming of *Monte Carlo*. Reporter Dorothy Herzog said MacDonald's face was "contorted with rage" as she "split the silence" using a few choice expletives before cussing some more and flouncing off the set. The reason? Jeanette had been informed that her hairdresser was occupied at another studio caring for Kay Francis. "Dear me," the astounded Herzog surmised, "the tribulations of the celluloid art!"[48]

Why Paramount would dump Kay into such an atrocity as *Let's Go Native*, after carefully building her up in such quality vehicles as *Street of Chance* and *For the Defense*, must have puzzled her. Most likely it infuriated her. There she was, vamping *again*, in something titled *Let's Go Native*, *seventh*-billed, and at one point being swung around like a sack of potatoes by Jack Oakie and William Austin. In protest, she eventually would align herself with other stars on the lot and become part of the "Infamous Warner Brother's Raid on Paramount."

Chapter 5

Paramount's Passion Flower

Virtuous Sin. The title provided an oxymoron to challenge Kay's acting skills. The film also brought her face to face with her next husband, Kenneth MacKenna. The tall, talented, mustachioed MacKenna had an intellect and charm that appealed to Kay. She had known Kenneth casually back East. He was born Leo Meilziner, Jr., and came from an artistic and theatrical background. His great-aunt, actress Charlotte Cushman, was much acclaimed for conveying "all the power and energy of manhood" in what was referred to as "breech" (pants) roles. She played Hamlet and Romeo to adoring audiences filled with female admirers. Cushman also founded a Sapphic artist community in Rome where she spent many of her later years.[1] Kenneth's father, Leo Meilziner, was a well-known portrait artist for whom Kay had posed in the 1920s. Kenneth's younger brother, Jo Meilziner, was a prominent theatrical designer. Kenneth had been on the New York stage since 1919 and first went to Hollywood in 1929. Soon after arriving in Hollywood, and before filming *Virtuous Sin* in 1930, he and Kay began what writer Frances Kellum referred to as "one of those swift, tumultuous romances that ended up with MacKenna practically kidnapping her!" [2]

After the buffoonery that surrounded Kay in *Let's Go Native, Virtuous Sin* seemed like a masterpiece. Based on Lajos Zilahy's play *The General*, the story had already been filmed in Sweden. George Cukor, whose career would include such classics as *The Philadelphia Story* (1940), tackled the script. It was his second attempt at directing. *Virtuous Sin* was co-directed by Louis Gasnier whose most famous film is the unintentionally hilarious cult classic *Reefer Madness* (a treatise on the dangers of marijuana). Jean-Pierre Cousodan commented in his book *American Directors*, "*Virtuous Sin* breaks through the barrier of the ridiculous into a kind of loony, surreal romanticism, which is more than most of the filmed plays of the early sound period can claim."[3]

Virtuous Sin opens in St. Petersburg, Russia, January 1914. A reunion for two students of science, Marya and Victor (Kay and MacKenna), prompts a proposal of marriage. "I have great affection for you, Victor," Kay confesses. "But, it isn't love. I don't think I know what love is—I may never know." Her somber confession triggers MacKenna's determination for what he calls a "scientific union." He's willing to take the risk and they marry. Their "real-life" attraction translates well on screen.

When Victor is ordered into the infantry, he becomes part of what he calls "a

64

machine for taking lives." "No point in saving them," he says with disdain, putting aside his work with serums and cures for humanity. Once inducted, it isn't long before he verbally lambastes the iron-willed General Platoff (Walter Huston). Victor is arrested, court-martialed and sentenced to be shot. When Kay visits him in solitary confinement, she wants to help him. "What can you do to this machine that I'm caught in?" he wails. "Throw in a monkey wrench," she answers. Kay's "monkey wrench" is formulated upon seeing officers enter a boisterous establishment next to the inn she's staying at. When she inquires of the innkeeper if it's a restaurant, he hesitates. "Well," he replies, "they have *food* there. The prima donnas can't sing," he explains, "and the chorus girls can't dance." The next morning, Kay makes her way to see the madam, who confides, "The general hasn't fallen for any of my talent." Kay seizes the opportunity and pays cash to become a "prima donna who can't sing."

One of the real virtues of *Virtuous Sin* is the costumes and hairstyles. Travis Banton, who was a great influence on Kay's fashion-sense, designed an exquisitely authentic vintage wardrobe. Margaret J. Bailey noted in her tome to fashion, *Those Glorious Glamour Years,* "Kay Francis stole the show in *Virtuous Sin* in her stunning dinner dress of lamé, sable, beads, jewels, and lace. Despite the extreme lavishness of the ensemble, Francis's face and screen character are not overpowered and in fact are enhanced. Few women have this magnetic power."[4] Bailey is referring to the costume Kay wore for her bordello scenes and it *is* a knockout. The jeweled headdress turns Kay's face into a striking cameo. She throws Huston for a loop. When Houston shows up at the bordello one evening, he immediately starts making demands. He barks at the hefty soprano who is bellowing an aria. "Stop that infernal noise!" Kay, who is busy flirting with other officers, steals Huston's thunder. Throwing her chair against the wall, she storms over to him and calls his bluff. "I suppose you call *that* a dignified exhibition," she chastises

Kay leads Walter Huston toward Virtuous Sin *(1930). (Paramount)*

him. "Everybody enjoying themselves. Everybody having a good time…and then *you* walk in! The ghost of 'Old Man War' himself !! And then *boom*! We're in a graveyard!" Dead silence fills the hall. It doesn't stop her. "You'll find he has nothing under his sleeve, ladies and gentlemen," Kay sneers, yanking at his uniform. "Only a wet blanket hidden under his coat!" Kay is charged with attitude. She bowls everyone over.

Huston is stunned. After he motions to the soprano to continue warbling, he takes Kay's arm and pulls her toward a table, tossing her into a chair. She laughs, as if mocking him. He gets up to leave. She pulls him back. He lights a cigarette. She lights one. She mimics his every move. It's an amusing little ploy. Soon after they leave to walk in the moonlight, the madam announces to the guests, "I'll take bets on who's running the army now!"

Kay's character continues to fascinate and perplex Huston. Her mercurial behavior gives away that she's attracted to him, defeating her own purpose. It isn't long before the hard-nosed Huston also senses a profound change in himself. He releases a soldier whose mother has lost all her other sons in war. Kay again visits MacKenna, who suspects her of doing favors to get him out of prison. He insists she be fair to him. He would rather die. She promises. Her promises do not die hard. She is soon being seduced by gypsy music and the taste of long-stemmed cherries in Huston's boudoir. Kay is feeling exactly what she does not feel for her husband, love and desire. She falls into Huston's arms until dawn. As predicted, she now controls the army. When Kay asks him the favor of saving MacKenna's life, Huston is outraged. "You've cheated us both!" he declares, and asks her to get out. After the inevitable confrontation between the two men, the script provides a lasting reunion for Kay and Huston. A perfect pre-Code ending, where sin, albeit virtuous sin, is rewarded with a happy ending.

Kay and Huston offer *Virtuous Sin* rich performances. Cukor enjoyed working with Kay and encouraged her to develop a real character. She succeeded. MacKenna, although high-strung in his acting technique, also makes his character believable. Jerry Hoffman for *The Los Angeles Examiner* wrote, "Relentless, and yet fascinating in its dramatic power…*Virtuous Sin* [brings] a new twist to an old story…absorbed by the splendid performances of Walter Huston and Kay Francis…the climax brought an angle, possibly not new to fiction, but surely rare on the screen…The greatest credit belongs to Walter Huston and Kay Francis, and by all means, Kenneth MacKenna…the entire cast makes a very unusual collection of quality performances."

Emanuel Levy, a Cukor biographer, commented, "[*Virtuous Sin*] stands on the eloquent portrayal of Francis, who excelled in the climactic scene, when she meets the general with whom she has fallen in love."[5] *Variety* pointed out that *Virtuous Sin*, "should do much to help Kay Francis on her way…the picture…is all Miss Francis'. As the well bred but humbly parented girl who goes into a censor proof brothel to meet the general, this legit brunette probably turns in her top film contribution to date…Feature is not overly strong on theme, so it's no twist of fancy to say that Miss Francis holds it to-gether." It was unanimous: *Virtuous Sin* provided Kay her most complex role as an actress to date. She met head-on the range and demands required of her, and was very much on par with Huston in the confidence and relish she put into her performance.

Kay and Kenneth consummated their affair just after she moved into her new house at 8401 De Longpre—July 13, 1929. Kay noted in her diary that he was lover #24—a fact that seemed to amaze even Kay.[6] Number twenty-four also seemed to be a perfect match for her. Over the next year Kay's shorthand entries are all about Kenneth. August 1—"Kenneth came back and we had a very nice time. He's sweet in bed."[7] During her rumored affair with William Powell, the diaries attest that Kay's heart, body and soul belonged to Kenneth. "Bill Powell for dinner. Late. Talked till 2. Over to spend night with Kenneth...he's a RAM!!!"[8] There was also a spirit of fun about Kenneth. They enjoyed taking baths together and making love before the fireplace. Kay knew she was into something good. Her closing entry for 1929 read: "Well, 1929 is over. I have a good job, but I must try to save money this next year. My love life is very happy. Kenneth is terribly sweet and I should be a very content woman!"[9]

Kay and Kenneth were sensitive to each others' moods and looked out for one another. "So often I am drunk," Kay wrote in January 1930, "and Kenneth is a dear about it and takes care of me."[10] "God, I really do love him," Kay confessed to her diary in July.[11]

During the summer months, while filming *Virtuous Sin*, Kay and co-star Kenneth were seen regularly sharing her box seats at the Hollywood Bowl. That fall, after the film's release, the couple were regulars at the opera. In November, Kay and Kenneth bought a boat together and so began her lifelong interest in sailing. It was another passion that cemented their relationship. But, Kay was uncertain about marrying again and vacillated about accepting Kenneth's marriage proposals. She explained later, "Even when I realized how deeply I was in love with Kenneth, I was afraid. I asked myself questions about it. I discussed problems with [Kenneth]. He finally had to abduct me from a hospital bed...telling me not to be a little fool, that we loved each other, and what else was there to do about it?"[12]

After her minor operation, Kenneth rode with Kay in an ambulance to the courthouse! They visited just long enough to apply for a marriage license. On Catalina Island (Avalon), a few days later, Ken swept her into matrimony. A cook from the hotel was their witness. *The New York Times* (January 17, 1931) headlined on the entertainment page, "Film Stars Flee on Yacht." "Kay Francis and Kenneth MacKenna...were believed to be on their wedding trip tonight aboard his yacht Pamet Head bound for Ensenada, Mexico...In departing shortly after noon aboard the yacht, they made good their promise to keep their affairs to themselves. Their plans became public on Monday when they appeared at the Marriage License Bureau and filed intentions to wed under their legal names, Katherine Gibbs and Leo Meilziner Jr.... Under California law they had to wait three days before they could be married..."

As they sailed south, Kay was preparing an elaborate honeymoon meal when the stove ran out of gas. Tears welled up and she cried, "I can't think God would let this happen to me on my wedding night." Miraculously, within minutes a friend's yacht pulled up alongside *Pamet Head*. "I knew it," Kay called out, "here comes God!"[13] They dined on the friend's boat. Kay expressed her hopes for the marriage in her diary. "Married. Oh my god, please let it be very happy, and let me make Ken happy."[14]

Legend has it that on their first evening home together, Kay and Kenneth had a surprise visit from the Earl of Warwick. The newlyweds were in their bedroom sipping champagne when it was announced that his Lordship was waiting without. Kay, amazed, *en negligee*, went downstairs and graciously began to converse with her surprise visitor, whom she had never met, wondering "what was up?" After some idle chatter about the decor and her paintings, the eager, but somewhat anxious Earl asked, "You're delightful Madam Francis, but would you mind bringing in the girls?"[15] As a prank, someone had

(1932) Kay and actor/director Kenneth MacKenna. The couple, who married in 1931, shared an interest for yachting, New York City, Cape Cod, and passionate lovemaking. "Kenneth's a RAM," Kay joyously reported to her diary.

given the royal visitor Kay's residence in lieu of the address of Madam Lee Frances, owner of a famous bordello. Kay was one step ahead of him, however, and had been stringing him along before revealing her true identity. The Earl later took a fling into films himself, as actor Michael Brooke.

For all appearances, Kay seemed happier in this fourth marriage than she had in her previous three. She considered their real anniversary to be July 13—on that day she noted, "Ken and I have been together for two years today! Gee, that's swell!! Grand!!"[16]

She had told Gladys Hall, "I can never be thankful enough that I was abducted. I have never been so happy in my life. I believe that on the background of experience I have built something *enduring*."[17] Kay and Kenneth enjoyed their passion for yachting and spent many happy hours together on *Pamet Head*, a thirty-six-foot sailing schooner. Many Sundays would find them headed toward Catalina. The boat was not a luxury. During 1932, the boat cost them a few cents under one thousand dollars for the entire twelve months. There was no crew, no cook and no maids. When Kay wasn't basking in a bathing suit, she was doing crew-work in overalls, or playing chef, while Kenneth sailed or spent the day diving beneath to clean off barnacles. It was great fun and an opportunity to get away from it all. Kenneth shared Kay's sense of economizing and probably wasn't at all surprised when she insisted that he agree to sign a legal document that would counteract the community property laws of California.[18] This was, after all, her *fourth* marriage and she had learned to exercise caution no matter how deeply in love she was. Kenneth's closest pal, Humphrey Bogart, had arrived from back east in early 1930 and often joined the couple for sailing and dinner. Kay's mother also relocated to the west coast in October 1930. Kay looked out for her, but kept her at arms length from socializing with her crowd. This didn't seem to bother Mrs. Gibbs, who kept herself busy with her own circle of acquaintances.

Kay leased a new and roomier home for her and Kenneth. It was the former residence of silent cowboy star, William S. Hart. She got along well with Hart, who signed his letters, "your tyrant landlord." The house was on the same street and a few blocks away from her bungalow on De Longpre Avenue. The history of the neighborhood alone appealed to Kay. The street was named after a native painter whose studio in the area was a popular gathering place for the intelligentsia. When questioned by reporters why she hadn't selected one of the newer more impressive areas such as Beverly Hills or Bel Air, Kay answered, "What was good enough for the old silent stars is good enough for me."[20] She was only a few houses away from the former homes of Wallace Reid and William Farnum. Reporter Ruth Rankin explained Kay's penchant for familiar surroundings:

[Kay] likes to deal with the same market, the same service station, the same cleaner—she likes familiar surroundings and persons. She is, she says, like a cat. Wants to be comfortable…a sane and logical system, and possessing a certain element one finds all too seldom in Hollywood, *stability*…Kay's home is small and lovely…A partition was taken out to make the living room a little larger. But the furniture—fine pieces of Sherton and Hepplewhite—is her same old furniture, selected…carefully and thoughtfully…The carpet is a soft green, a cozy fire burns in the fireplace…a well-bred room which looks as if people really talk in it, and say things worth hearing…Kay prefers books to be intimate possessions and does not have them on display. Most of her books are lined around the bedroom…some even in the bathroom…she likes to read in the tub.[21]

Kay said, "No house can have more than comfort, convenience, and an inviting atmosphere. Beyond that is vanity. My friends take me as I am, and I have no desire to impress strangers." Kay and Kenneth's inviting atmosphere, became larger within a year. They moved to 1010 Benedict Canyon after Kay's close friend Jessica Barthelmess redecorated. (Later, when Kenneth's work relocated him to New York, Kay moved back to her smaller, more compatible home on De Longpre.) Reporters still ribbed Kay regarding her reasons for driving a Ford instead of the standard Hollywood star limo. "If I wanted a show window for myself," she explained, "I would hire one and get it over. I certainly wouldn't have it on wheels. A car is simply transportation, to me."[22] Kay and Kenneth avoided comparison between their acting careers when Kenneth's passion turned to directing films. He found more satisfaction behind the camera and jumped at an opportunity given him by Fox studios. He had six directorial credits to his name over the next few years, directing such talents as Joan Bennett and Elissa Landi. Unfortunately, none of his efforts received much attention.

Among the titles that Paramount announced for Kay's next assignment included Rouben Mamoulian's inventive and visual *City Streets*, although the part was ultimately given to Wynne Gibson.[23] Another misfire was a part that went to Frances Dee in *Rich Man's Folly* (a modern dress version of the Charles Dickens novel *Dombey and Son*). According to Helen Hayes, Kay was offered the lead in MGM's *The Sin of Madelon Claudet*. Kay rejected the role stating, "I would have to be out of my mind to play that silly French prostitute. Why that dumb little bunny actually walked the streets so that she could buy clothes for her son. Phooey! How can you generate sympathy for such a shallow woman?"[24] Instead, dumb bunny Kay hopped over to MGM for a less stellar role in *Passion Flower*, based on Kathleen Norris' popular novel. Helen Hayes took over *Madelon Claudet* and walked away with an Oscar.

Passion Flower takes place in San Francisco and California's Napa Valley. Directed by William C. deMille (Cecil's brother), the film is a smart, intelligent soap-opera about a young woman, Cassy (Kay Johnson), who falls in love with the family chauffeur, Dan (Charles Bickford). As the film opens, Cassy urgently announces to her cousin, Dulce (Kay), that she has fallen in love. When Kay learns he's the family chauffeur, she's nonplused. "No family? No money?" Kay exclaims, "It's worse than murder!" Kay is wed to a much, much older and wealthy Napa Valley land baron

(Lewis Stone). She refers to her husband as square, upright and grand. "That makes him three kinds of pianos," she jests. It is evident from her expression, that the marriage lacks passion.

After Johnson-Bickford marry, Kay assists the struggling young couple to relocate near her in the Napa Valley. Kay finds all kinds of projects that keep her and Bickford busy *together*. When husband Stone suspects her motives, Kay is defensive. "It hasn't been heaven, living like this!" she rationalizes. Shamed, Stone lowers his head. As the energy between Dulce and Dan gets "hot and heavy," both marriages begin to unravel. The couples separate. Kay and Bickford head for Europe. Their romance doesn't last long.

Kay makes a statement by underplaying her role as Dulce. She's not the typical, manipulating "other woman" so prevalent in Hollywood product. She manages to generate compassion for her situation. Instead of being defensive, she consoles Bickford when he decides to leave her. "It's easier for me," she tells him. "I can run away from the harm I've done. You've got to stay…and face it."

The *Hollywood Daily Citizen* noted, "Miss Francis…who uses her beauty, wit and charm to win Dan away from Cassie, enacts the role with realistic fervor." *The New York Times* agreed, "Kay Francis does exceptionally well as the fashionably-clad Dulce," but felt "the good work of the players and the competent direction of William de Mille are somewhat vitiated by strained psychology…and uneven dialogue." But, *Passion Flower* wasn't all pathos and psychology. It had just the right ingredient of comic relief from Bickford's son (Dickie Moore) and housekeeper (ZaSu Pitts). Pitts amusingly prefaces everything she says with the worse case scenario. Dickie Moore is a delight trying to remember his evening prayers, reciting, "Now I lay me down to sleep, I pray the Lord my soul to keep. If he hollers let him go, eeny meeny miney-mo!" The frequency of ZaSu's and Moore's one-liners adds just the right mix into *Passion Flower's* dramatics.

Passion Flower (1930) was directed by Cecil B. DeMille's brother, William C. deMille. Kay, top-billed, is seen here with Kay Johnson and Dickie Moore. (MGM)

Charles Bickford snorted his attitude about *Passion Flower*, saying, "It's just another one of those pictures—poor boy marries poor girl and they have kids and a terrible time. Along comes a rich vamp and he leaves the wife…so the wife sits down and writes him a letter telling him the daffodils are blooming in the front yard and Junior can write 'cat.' So he goes back to the wife. Boloney, with a capital B!" Bickford was not a happy camper in Hollywood, a place he thought was full of "ridiculous people." His animosity toward "tinsel-town" was stronger than Kay's. "Collectively," Bickford stated, "they're absurd. They take themselves too seriously. Oh, I understand how they get that way…surrounded by a swarm of sycophants; yessed to death…besieged by autograph hunters; get thousands of sappy fan letters—no wonder they get to think they're big shots. And if I ever get that way, I hope somebody shoots me!"[25]

Exhibitors were discovering that Kay's name on the marquee meant top business. But, Paramount *just didn't get it*. She returned, from being top-billed in *Passion Flower* at MGM, to her own studio for another supporting role. This time, she was again paired with George Bancroft. Although not a personable actor, the film focused mostly on him.

Bancroft played a ruthless editor of a scandal-oriented newspaper, hence the title, *Scandal Sheet*. He is oblivious to his lovely, loving wife (Kay) and her afternoon trysts with her pickled-puss lover (Clive Brook). After one such sexual interlude, Kay asks Brook for twenty-four hours to decide whether or not to run off to Europe with him. He promises to call her at 4:00 p.m. the next day. "Will you be close to the phone when I call?" he asks her. "If I decide to go, Noel," she says tenderly, "…I'll be *inside* of it."

A key scene shows Kay's revulsion for Bancroft's work ethic and penchant for lurid headlines. "Your story's responsible for wrecking an entire family," she scolds. "Haven't you any feelings at all? I hate it!" Bancroft is unapologetic. When Brook, a bank president confronted with a faulty stock situation, becomes a victim of Bancroft's *Scandal Sheet*, Kay is filled with vengeance. She defiantly confesses to Bancroft her feelings for Brook. "I love him!" she exclaims. "Now splurge *that* all over your paper!" Although she establishes her unfaithfulness, one wishes the script had allowed Kay to read Bancroft the riot act, ripping into his own lack of scruples and the behavior that had destroyed her love for him. The film concludes with Bancroft living happily ever after as editor and chief of the *Sing-Sing Herald*. And what got him there? He went ballistic, killed Brook, and ended up a headline in his own paper. The contrived finish in Sing-Sing leaves us wondering what happened to director John Cromwell's common sense and puzzled as to what became of Kay's character.

Kay registered well in the few scenes allotted her in *Scandal Sheet* and the critics noticed. The *Los Angeles Record* gave Kay kudos, saying, "Miss Francis has what can be most nearly described as 'sensible seductiveness' in this part. There is none of the incredible, overheated emoting commonly associated with the word in the days when vamps were just too bad to be true. She has an emphasized femininity that is charmingly human, and as natural and unaffected as the wind. Besides that, she has been given lines to say that are extremely clever in their extreme simplicity." *Variety* didn't care for the film, but complimented Kay. "One saving grace is…the presence of Kay Francis…because of her suave playing of an impossible role…" Once again, Kay, in a supporting role, was selected as the standout. Now she was *definitely* looking for something more than what Paramount was offering her.

Publicity shot (ca. 1930) Kay's natural persona translated well on screen. (Paramount)

After the release of *Scandal Sheet*, Kay made the headlines. She and Powell became a mutinous screen-team and a part of the infamous "Warner's Raid on Paramount Studios." Paramount had been too preoccupied with their vehicles for Maurice Chevalier, Jeanette MacDonald, Clara Bow and George Bancroft to pay much attention to Kay and Powell. Writer Elsie Janis, who was privy to the inside scoop, later commented, "I sat in an executorial office and heard Paramount's side of a conversation with Warner Brothers, who wanted to borrow Kay Francis for a picture [*Notorious Affair*]. I watched the Francis stock soar as they discussed terms and, above all, what sort of part she was to play. It was finally arranged to give Paramount's rising star all that Paramount had *not* given her. Kay was again cast as the menace…but the tendency to take care of something borrowed is a natural one, so they not only paid attention to her personality, they took a borrower's inventory of her possibilities. Almost before anyone could tell whether the ink of the gentlemen's signatures would prove to be in the red or black, Warner Brothers staged their famous raid on Paramount…William Powell and Kay Francis moved their make-up kits, box-office values and protests about unsatisfactory roles over to Warner Brothers."[26] In spite of the gentleman's agreement for studios not to raid competing studios' contract stars, there was nothing Will Hays or the powers that be could do. Facing bankruptcy, Paramount was dealing with insurmountable financial woes. Their hesitation at a strategic moment in renewing Kay's contract proved a mistake. When Paramount tried to reclaim her, the court sympathetically ordered Warners to loan Kay back to Paramount at a future date. (In hindsight, this punishment was a godsend for Kay. The loan-back turned out to be what many consider her best film, *Trouble in Paradise*.)

Paramount was unhappy about Kay's defection and was determined to squeeze as many performances out of her as possible before her contract expired. The first of these, *Ladies' Man*, co-starred William Powell. Kay recalled,

> I remember when we started *Ladies Man* we were neither one so enthusiastic over the story, and we've often laughed at B. P. Schulberg's clever strategy in arousing our interest. He patted us on the back and told Bill that no other actor was as capable of endowing the difficult character with the

necessary qualities. Then he explained that there were three reasons why he put me into the picture. First, the movie audiences wanted to see us together again. Of course, this was his trump card and it pleased us immensely. Then he said my part was a sappy one and he was sure I would make it less sappy. The third reason was that Bill died in the end and left me and that was what the fans expected from us![27]

Powell pulled no punches in announcing why he *shouldn't* play the part of a gigolo. "I'm offering a direct challenge to the movie public, playing this part. I'm throwing down the gauntlet. I'm not a ladies man. I haven't the physical characteristics, for one thing. I'm not handsome. Someone like Valentino should have played this part, not Bill Powell."[28]

What fans *didn't* expect were the somber mood and the unusually dark portrait of New York's high society that permeated *Ladies' Man*. It may have spelled film art, but it didn't spell box office. They stayed away in droves. Which is too bad, as *Ladies' Man* is an incisive psychological study of individuals caught in a web of disillusion about love, money and pride in a so-called super-civilized world. It was a world that middle-America knew nothing and cared nothing about. The script was penned by the creative genius of Herman J. Mankiewicz, who largely created the character of *Citizen Kane* for the later Orson Welles film.

Ladies' Man has a sorrowful William Powell living off the generosity of lonely, wealthy women. His own intelligence tells him his life is a sham that fosters nothing but emptiness and disappointment for all concerned. A glimmer of hope comes along when he is confronted with Norma Page (Kay, appearing twenty minutes into the film). Kay knows the inside dope on gigolo Powell and feigns disinterest. Wearing a stylish ensemble of black velvet and white ermine, she looks quite irresistible. After toying with Powell's proposal for a "night on the town," she eventually gives in. They are both swept into a romantic whirl wherein Powell confesses about his empty life *and* his love for Kay. "I've fallen into the clouds," he says hopefully. "Heaven help me if I start to drop." He speaks prophetically. At the film's finish Powell is tossed off a hotel balcony to the relief of the film's detractors. Elizabeth Yeaman for the *Hollywood Citizen News* was among them. "It's incredible that William Powell should jeopardize his screen popularity by appearing in a role which is unsympathetic," blasted Yeaman. "[Powell's] portrayal of the gigolo is contemptible from start to finish. Carole Lombard…drags the story into the mire a little more with her disgustingly drunken scenes. Kay Francis is also an object of disgust…because she…falls in love with him like all the other women." Yeaman was an odd duck. She often took potshots at Kay's performances over the next few years and never had a good word for her.

The *Los Angeles Examiner* was less reactionary to *Ladies' Man*. "Powell plays the role with consummate delicacy…a less skilled actor would have been offensive…Beautiful settings, an unusually adroit cast, and no end of lovely gowns give the picture a high production value. Carole Lombard does some of the most important dramatic work of her career…Olive Tell is very fine as the society matron who turns to the gigolo for flattery. Kay Francis completes the feminine triumvirate as the woman Powell really loves. Her role, the least showy of all, is the most human in the story."

Ladies' Man was the first film Kay and Powell made after their publicized breakup. The simpatico was still very much in tact during their confessions of on-screen love. Any disappointments Powell may have had regarding Kay were assuaged by his new romance with Carole Lombard. The Francis-Powell-Lombard combination turned the set of *Ladies' Man* into a feast-fest for gossip columnists. Powell and Lombard were actually secretly engaged. They married six weeks after the film's official release. Lombard's biographer, Larry Swindell, noted, "Winning his heart was easy enough for Carole; winning his friends was rather more difficult. They tolerated her with an unmistakable note of condescension, regarding her as a typical social-climbing starlet."[29] The gregarious and spirited Lombard told Powell his friends (particularly Ronald Colman and Ruth Chatterton) were awfully stuffy, and did he have to see so *much* of them? Lombard acquired Powell's liking for good Scotch; otherwise, they could hardly have been less alike in tastes. They divorced after two years.

Critics were finally taking note that Paramount was not using Kay to full advantage. She still ended up in what appeared to be glorified bit parts, such as her next role in *Vice Squad*. *The Los Angeles Evening Herald* noted, "Paul Lukas, manages to put a sincere note to everything he does…He is aided by Kay Francis in her most splendid fashion, but seen much too briefly on the screen." "Much too briefly" translates to twelve minutes in an 81-minute film. We first see Kay, for about three minutes, as she is being jilted at her own engagement party. Her character is petulant, self-absorbed and only concerned about what people will think. Her almost-fiancé is a foreign ambassador, played by the morosely serious Paul Lukas. When the orchestra strikes up the tune "Out of Nowhere," Lukas suddenly appears to break his engagement with Kay. Stunned and perplexed, she grabs her furs and asks her brother (William B. Davidson) to take her home.

Vice Squad then focuses on Lukas, who loses his ambassadorship and unwillingly becomes a stool pigeon for a police racket that hauls "vagrant" women into night court. Coincidentally, the women are sentenced by Kay's brother, a judge, who is opposed to the tactics of the vice racket. Neither Kay nor her brother know of Lukas' whereabouts or his new line of employment. When next we see Kay (much later in the film), she appears less pretentious. Matured. After Lukas unexpectedly shows up at her apartment, she listens carefully to his excuses, fully aware of his discomfort and hesitation. When her brother turns the conversation to his dislike for stool pigeons, Kay changes the subject. "Oh well," she exclaims, "who cares about stool pigeons, when we can go out on the roof and be cool?" They leave the room. When Lukas bemoans to Kay, "I don't belong with decent people!," she confronts him. "You mean," she replies, "about your being a stool pigeon?" When he balks, she is insistent. She still loves him and beseeches him to put up a fight. He does. He makes public his work for the racket, which isn't what Kay had in mind. Lukas loses her once more in the process of gaining his self-respect. In spite of her allotted time, Kay made an impression in *Vice Squad*.

While Fay Wray was being groomed to take her place on the Paramount lot, Kay, as usual, had to be loaned out in order to acquire a more sizeable role. This time she headed for RKO for her first of four pairings with Ricardo Cortez. Cortez usually spelled trouble on screen and he managed to be murdered in each film he made with Kay. They worked well as a team in spite of the ludicrous plots. *Transgression* set the tone for their work together and had Cortez repeating the role he had filmed in 1924 for Paramount.

Transgression was adapted from the 1921 play, *The Next Corner,* by Kate Jordan. It tells the rather fantastic tale of a naive British wife, Elsie Maury (Kay), who finds passion while under the spell of an unscrupulous womanizer. Her husband, the imminently stiff

Paul Cavanagh, goes off to India on a year-long business trip. Kay escapes her overbearing, live-in, sister-in-law and sails for Paris. Kay transforms herself from a dowdy-looking, insecure matron, into a sleek, captivating creature. Latin lovers are seducing her with slow tangos. By the time she is reunited with Cavanagh in England, Kay has had a scintillating affair with Don Arturo (Cortez) and is being blackmailed because of his murder!

The *Los Angeles Evening Herald* commented on the emotional challenges the film provided Kay, saying, "The pangs of illicit passion call upon Kay Francis, as the wife, for distraught emotions all through the picture. The pain of it all was never more vividly set forth. If you have known her chiefly for gay, seductive parts, the novelty of this over-emotionalized role might intrigue. Ricardo Cortez likewise spends his moments in the strained agony with which Latins, we are told, pursue their love conquests. *Transgression* has a lot of the breathless quality that palpitated in an old silent film…"[30] Aptly put!

Transgression is one of the most dated, stilted films of Kay's career. Director Herbert Brenon never quite mastered talkies. He was unable to duplicate the expertise he showed in films like *Beau Geste* (1926), or the Oscar-nominated *Sorrell and Son* (1927). The lifeless script and stiff direction produced a plethora of pregnant pauses. Seen today, it's pure camp. When Kay has a rendezvous with Cortez at his Spanish estate, he pursues her like Valentino. After a passionate kiss, Kay assumes one of her trademark poses (hands clasped at the side of her cheek) and croons, "Oh Arturo, love me like this always!" Cortez grabs her, "Always and forever! Cara Mia. Above all in life! Above all the world I will adore you!" As an afterthought, Kay hastily writes her husband a confession. She explains to Cortez that she doesn't want to feel guilty during the heat of passion. It might spoil their pleasure. When the ink has dried, Cortez's devoted manservant, Serfin, carries it away. Kay is feeling refreshed and relieved, sighing, "Oh, Arturo, with that letter gone I have no one, but you…I'm so happy. So *very happy!*" In what is possibly the briefest "very happy" interlude in film history, we are confronted with the father of a 16-year-old girl Cortez has impregnated. A gun goes off. Cortez collapses. Kay does a grand job going hysterical. Once back in England, husband Cavanagh is almost as hysterical upon seeing Kay wearing makeup. He is adamant with disapproval. "That stuff on your face!" he exclaims. "I don't like it!" "Well, my dear," Kay counters, "you'll just have to get used to it!" Under these gloomy circumstances, one feels sure that Kay would look back on her time with Cortez as the highlight of her life.

The *New York Times* stated the obvious, saying *Transgression* was "not endowed with any great degree of subtlety…," but thought Kay stood out among the cast, noting, "Miss Francis gives a clear portrayal. Ricardo Cortez…is too much given to smiling through his part." Cortez could have been grinning for actually getting *paid* for the role.

Paramount kept Kay on loan-out while lining up new scripts for her. She returned to the MGM lot to be second-billed to the formidable talents of Lionel Barrymore. The picture was titled *Guilty Hands* and Kay held her own with the stage and screen veteran. Woody Van Dyke directed this unusual whodunit, and Broadway playwright Bayard Veiller wrote the screenplay. In *Guilty Hands*, Barrymore plays a lawyer who has specialized in murder trials. "We haven't morals anymore," he scoffs to his cronies, "we just have laws!" He believes there are instances where murder is justified and gives himself the opportunity to prove it. Invited to an unscrupulous client's estate to change his will, Barrymore is shocked to discover the infamous womanizer's plans to marry his daughter (Madge Evans). He tells the client, played by Alan Mowbray, that he intends to kill him. "You ought to have been killed years ago!" says the defiant Barrymore. "I can kill *you* and nobody will know anything about it!" The sly Mowbray threatens, "I'll come back after I'm dead, and I'll get you!" Barrymore remains confident and replies, "All right, old man, meet you in hell!"

At that evening's dinner party, Mowbray announces his surprise engagement to the guests. Among them is one of his lovers, Marjorie (Kay). She looks at him with disbelief. Later, in the drawing room, Kay sits at a harp plucking what must feel like her own solemn heartstrings and trying to piece things together. When she is finally alone with Mowbray, she confronts him, "I guess that's the end of us!" "Probably not," Mowbray confesses, "I've *always* come back to you." The camera dissolves as they embrace.

During a convenient thunder and lightening storm, Barrymore shoots his future son-in-law. The body is discovered and Barrymore proclaims it must be suicide. He explains that Mowbray was guilt-ridden by his sordid past and his abuse of women. Kay, looking chic in black satin and a long strand of pearls, challenges Barrymore's suicide theory when they are alone. He challenges *her* with the fact that she is the sole benefactor of Mowbray's will. She watches in horror as Barrymore enacts a mock trail that would send her to the executioner. Kay's dilemma is resolved during the police investigation just as she is about to expose the real assassin. The dead Mowbray's hand, which still holds the gun Barrymore placed in it, clenches suddenly as rigor mortis sets in. A shot rings out and Barrymore falls to his death to keep his promised rendezvous in hell with Mowbray. The police inspector looks at Kay. "Well?" he inquires. "You were going to say something. What was it?" Kay looks stunned. "Well, well!" he persists, "What *was* it?" Kay glances somberly at Barrymore's daughter holding her father's body. A look of sorrow for the girl plays across Kay's face, followed by a puzzled expression. "I don't

In Guilty Hands *(1931) Kay spars with Lionel Barrymore.* The Los Angeles Examiner *raved, "Kay Francis is splendid…It is not an easy role, but Miss Francis is always believable in the emotional fireworks." (MGM)*

know, Chief!" she says finally, trying to grapple with the situation, amazed at the finality of what has just occurred. She looks sadly at her lover's corpse, then raises her head and shakes it, trying to reach some sort of resolve. It's easy to read her thoughts. She realizes that Mowbray's life has been avenged. "I just can't remember...now," she says with finality. The camera comes in for a close-up of a woman who has accepted what is, and who can go on with her life.

Kay's performance in these last 30 seconds is remarkable. From the time the inspector questions her until the fade out, Kay does a fine job of registering a complexity of emotion that influences the audiences' own feelings and conclusions about what has occurred on screen. *The LA Examiner* praised her performance. "Kay Francis is splendid as the friend of the murdered man. It is not an easy role, but Miss Francis is always believable in the emotional fireworks." *The New York Times* was also impressed with *Guilty Hands* saying, "Bayard Veiller has shuffled the ingredients of the murder mystery into a fresh and arresting story...not a word is wasted. There is an excellent scene between the murderer and the woman who has 'discovered' him, in which he proves to her that there is sufficient evidence to convict *her* of the crime...Kay Francis in this latter role plays well...W.S. Van Dyke also deserves a word for his direction..."

Kay was impressed with Van Dyke as a director and as an individual. She wrote about him, "W. S. Van Dyke...a hard-boiled hombre...A leader of men, a soldier of fortune, he is truly adventurous in this modern, tame world. His kindness is unexpected and so all the more potent. Virile, dominating, he has tramped the by-paths of the world and, somehow, this seeps through."[31] Kay was well aware of Van Dyke's work for on-location filming in Tahiti (*White Shadows in the South Seas*) and Africa *(Trader Horn)*. Kay had an opportunity to work with him again at MGM in 1941.

After initially mismanaging Kay and subsequently realizing how much other studios valued her talents, Paramount finally found four films worthy of her. These films provided an impressive exit for Kay's departure from the studio. In the aftermath of Warners' raid on Paramount, little did *anyone* know that the FBI was keeping records on Paramount's "Passion Flower," Kay Francis. Evidentially, J. Edgar Hoover had an interest in her off-screen performances and private life.

✳ KENNETH MACKENNA ✳
Born: August 19, 1899, Canterbury, New Hampshire
Died: January 15, 1962, Santa Monica, California

Kenneth was born into an artistic family and educated in London and Paris. His father, Leo Meilziner, was a well-known portrait painter. Kenneth recruited his younger brother, Jo Meilziner, into theatre work, which led Jo to becoming one of the masters of modern stage design. Kenneth's great-aunt was the famous actress Charlotte Cushman, known for her versatility playing male and female roles. Declaring her emancipation from men, Cushman later on created a woman-centered community in Rome.

Kenneth made his Broadway debut in 1919's *At 9:45*. He changed his name when theatrical producer William A. Brady said it wouldn't look well in lights. His other acting credits on stage included *Immodest Violet, Mad Honeymoon,* and *What Every Woman Knows* with Helen Hayes. Kenneth made a few silent films at Paramount's Astoria studios in 1925-26. He and close friend Humphrey Bogart vied for the same girl, Mary Phillips, on stage and off, during 1924's *Nerves*. Bogart won. (When Bogart and Phillips divorced in 1938, Kenneth and Phillips exchanged vows.)

Kenneth's sojourn to Hollywood in 1929 led to a few leads, as in John Ford's *Men Without Women* (1930), a submarine epic, which *Variety* claimed to be "a stunning, realistic picture." After making *Virtuous Sin* (1930) and marrying Kay (1931), Kenneth ventured into film directing for Fox Studios (1931-34)—not quite making the grade. After divorcing Kay (1934), he returned to Broadway in productions of *By Your Leave*, *Othello* (Iago) and *MacBeth* (Macduff).

His obituary in *The New York Times*, January 17, 1962, gave further details about his life:

After service in World War II [MacKenna] was an MGM producer for a short time and then became editorial director of the studio . . . selecting written material for pictures, as well as the top man in editing the screen plays. In 1959, Mr. MacKenna quit his movie position and returned here to star in a Broadway play, *The Highest Tree* [co-starring a young Robert Redford]...after that he portrayed a judge in the 1961 motion picture *Judgment at Nuremberg*. In 1956 Mr. MacKenna gave a collection of George Bernard Shaw works to the UCLA library. [Wife] Mary Phillips, survives. His only other survivors are his mother and brother. MacKenna was 62, and living in Los Angeles, when he died of cancer.

Chapter 6
Girl About Town

Writer Louis Bromfield was part of Kay's social circle during the '30s and '40s. He had written a piece titled "Moon Madness" for her in 1930, but Paramount never got the project rolling.[1] The following year, an adaptation of Bromfield's *24 Hours* provided Kay with one of her most intriguing roles. The opportunity to play Fanny Tower, the bored, adulterous wife of the wealthy and inebriated Jim Tower (Clive Brook), provided Kay the grave wistfulness and glamour that befitted her. Bromfield's philosophies are cleverly integrated into the script, particularly in the beginning when, over cocktails, the young couples are discussing what it means to be a newcomer in New York. Kay's husband, Brook, a hopeless dipsomaniac already in his cups, surprises everyone by saying, "A newcomer is a person whose ancestors were not thieves." He then volunteers an explanation, politically correct and way ahead of its time. He points to a portrait of a Dutch ancestor of their host, and makes comment: "He landed on the island of Manhattan from Holland, murdered an Indian family and took a grant of land for $18 in glass beads. Today, the land is loaded with skyscrapers, honeycombed with subways and the ancestors are perpetuated in our charming host!"

Film historian William K. Everson noted that *24 Hours* has the look and feel of a 1932 film. "It was in 1932 that Hollywood really learned to weld picture and sound...which exuded a polish and above all an elegance. With its good musical score [Anton Rubinstein's "Romance"] and its ultra glossy art direction and cinematography, *24 Hours* is way ahead of most Paramount 1931 releases, and well up to the visual standards of their 1932 films."[2] Ernest Haller's camera seemed to adore Kay in this film. (Haller's cinematography for *Gone With the Wind* would win an Oscar.) At the aforementioned cocktail party, we first see Kay musing over a goblet of Napoleon brandy. After she dons an amazingly designed, wraparound fur coat we follow her out of the hotel where she maneuvers through snowflakes into her limousine. Next, we watch her gloved fingers wistfully write her lover's name, her name, then her husband's, on the limo's frosted window pane. At home, in her elegant penthouse, we see her stoking the fire as she watches old letters from her lover burn. Rubinstein's music swells to compensate for her disappointments. Sitting on the edge of her husband's bed, she tearfully cries out to a man who isn't there. "Oh Jim, help me...help me now!" Kay is mesmerizing. There is little or no dialogue during these sequences, just her profound presence.

The excellent 24 Hours *(1931), based on the Louis Bromfield novel, captured Kay's allure, sincerity and poise. Seen here with Clive Brook. (Paramount)*

After we witness Kay and Brook's faltering marriage, we are introduced to Brook's main squeeze and mistress, cabaret singer Rosie Dugan (Miriam Hopkins). Hopkins is impressed with Brook. "Even when you're drunk, you're a gentleman!" she marvels. Gentleman Brook is *so* drunk he passes out on Rosie's bed. The next morning he wakes to discover her body, strangled. He is arrested. Kay stands by him, though unsure of his innocence. When fingerprints finally implicate Rosie's estranged husband (Regis Toomey), Brook is freed. He rejects Kay's willingness to save their marriage and try again. He calls her a "thoroughbred," which apparently was a big compliment for wealthy women. He books passage on an ocean liner for Europe, but soon realizes that Kay is "so deep, deep" in his heart. We then see him welcoming her aboard with the ominous toast, "Let's drink to my last drink!" The film has a very downbeat, hopeless feel of despair that envelopes every scene, yet still manages to fascinate. William K. Everson noted: "With its taken-for-granted adultery all around, non-stop illicit drinking, drug addiction and a murder that goes unpunished…typical of the crime and sex related amorality that was treated so casually in pre-Code movies…It's the lack of exploitation of these elements, the tasteful handling of them and the implication that they are in fact a part of contemporary life…that is in a way more shocking than scenes of explicit sex or violence in contemporary movies."[3]

Upon release, *The New York Times* observed, "Those who hope to see more ideas from the book may be disappointed, but they will not be disappointed in the portrayals of Clive Brook…Miriam Hopkins…and Kay Francis. It is beautifully photographed…Mr. [Marion] Gering invites one's attention to the passage of the hours with no little artistry." Harriet Parsons wrote for *The Los Angeles Times*, "Kay Francis as the society woman is alluring and poised as ever, and brings great sincerity and feeling to her role…Clive Brook seemed to me a trifle stiff…" *Variety* commented on the film's "deft touches of detail" and that Kay's "vividness of style and personality somehow manage to make her a positive individuality." Hopkins was really in her element in *24 Hours*. She's believable as the energetic cabaret singer and she puts over her songs with, if not the greatest voice, gusto. At a Los Angeles preview of the picture, *The Los Angeles Record* reported, "Miriam Hopkins, as the cabaret entertainer, walks away with the entire picture in our opinion."

Designer Travis Banton once again put Kay on the map as fashion guru in *24 Hours* and her next film, *Girls About Town*. After commenting on the mercilessly designed Rus-

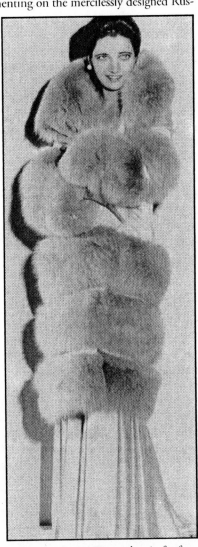

sian chipmunk trim on Kay's coat, hat and muff worn in the final scene of *24 Hours*, fashion archivist Margaret J. Bailey noted in her book: "Francis became one of Hollywood's most envied clotheshorses after she stumbled onto Travis Banton's services. No star spent less time, money, energy, or thought on her wardrobe—initially, that is. Banton remembered that she wore a black lace dress for an entire season and a black felt hat for two years just because she hated to shop. Banton provided Francis with a new hat and coaxed her into the lead of Hollywood's best-dressed list."[4]

As mentioned, Kay was indifferent to the best-dressed lists, but was grateful for Banton's attention to her wardrobe on and off screen. By January 1932, Kay was doing fashion layouts for the likes of *Hollywood Magazine*. "Kay Sports a New Wardrobe," shows her in six lovely creations by Banton for *Girls About Town*. These included a chartreuse crepe evening dress; molded-to-the-figure flesh-tinted pajamas; and a sumptuously trimmed, platinum fox evening wrap of white satin. Photo spreads like this were enticements for women to see the film, which they did, in droves.

Director George Cukor's *Girls About Town* was the first real chance to show off Kay's forte for light comedy. It brought out the brighter, more carefree aspects of Kay's personality. *Girls About Town* is high on the list of favorites among her fans and film buffs. Cukor's biographer, Emanuel Levy, commented that writer Zoe Akins, "bathed the film's heroines in a charming innocence. The women had lovely wardrobes, money, and a succession of rich men, but at the end of the evening they just smiled and said good night— as if this were the extent of their activities.

24 Hours (1931) *Wrapped up in fox fur, but not in herself.* "Hollywood is an incredibly smug place," *said Kay.* "And the worst of it is they're so satisfied...If I start talking about me, me, me, I hope someone will give me a smack." *(Paramount)*

'What if the audience wonders where do these girls get all those fancy clothes?' Cukor sarcastically teased Akins. Despite the material's underlying dishonesty, Cukor finessed highly polished acting from his cast...Lilyan Tashman...had never before been given the opportunity to tap into her comic persona. Kay Francis's natural elegance...complemented Tashman's inherent vigor."[5]

Playfully amoral on screen, our heroines in *Girls About Town* were good friends off-screen. Kay and Kenneth often entertained Lilyan Tashman and husband Edmund Lowe. Photographer Steichen, for *Vanity Fair*, captured both couples cavorting near the beach at Malibu in early 1932. In November the photographer would feature Kay solo for the magazine. The papers often mentioned the MacKennas and Lowes' "togetherness" at social activities. Tashman and Lowe, who were both gay, had an unconventional marriage and were among the elite "lavender couples." When drag queens reigned at the nightspots in 1931-32, Kay and pals like William Haines, Lowe and Tashman, etc., were reported as visiting the very profitable "pansy clubs."[6] Lowe and Tashman had frequent dinner parties with the more sophisticated set that also included: Ruth Chatterton, Arthur Hornblow, William Haines, George Cukor and various writers, directors and personalities from Broadway. These are the names that are frequently repeated on Kay's engagement calendar. Filming started for *Girls About Town* in August. The cast was chummy. The buoyant feeling on film was a reflection of the off-screen antics. On location at Catalina, Kay noted, "Lil terribly drunk all day!"[7] Kay, Cukor, Joel McCrea and Andy Lawler would go out for dinner at the High Hat before returning to the studio to watch the day's rushes. Upon the film's completion, Kay celebrated by buying herself a little dachshund and named him "Weenie." Snifter, by this time, had disappeared for good.

Girls About Town opens with frothy fun as the girls gossip in the powder room about the aging Romeos that their "agent" (Alan Dinehart) has lined up for them for that evening. "I've got calluses on my knees from my boyfriend's subtle approach!" Kay chuckles. She then confesses the routine gets "duller and duller"...an opinion that Tashman doesn't share, she thrives on it. After their evening out, the girls arrive separately at their apartment. "I only live in *some* of it!" Tashman responds when her date inquires, "Is this where you live?" Their black maid (Louise Beavers) poses in the window as "mother" so she and Kay aren't obligated to invite their wealthy beaus inside. When Kay arrives home, Tashman is admiring her $500 check for services almost rendered. Kay confides to Tashman, "I'm sick of being pawed by a bunch of middle-aged Babbits." But, late the next afternoon, as they are just waking up, she is coaxed by Tashman to attend a yacht party that Dinehart has lined up for them. Lucky for Kay, the fates intervene this time.

Once on board, Tashman takes a shine to Mr. Thomas, a.k.a. Benji (Eugene Pallette), a prankster and, unbeknownst to her, a tightwad. When she finds out that he's a Gemini, she tells him, "I must keep away from you!" She then explains that the combination of a water baby and a fire baby would never work. "You'd have too much *influence* over me," she says coyly. He's hooked. Kay's heartstrings are being plucked by a young, handsome bachelor named Jim (Joel McCrea), who is suspicious of the whole set up. Determined to get under his skin she suggests they pretend they are in love. After a prolonged, passionate, pretend pucker, Kay falls for him. The next day, Kay suddenly collapses while swimming and Joel comes to her rescue. Before long they embrace for real. When the girls arrive home, love-struck Kay quietly tears up her $1,000 paycheck.

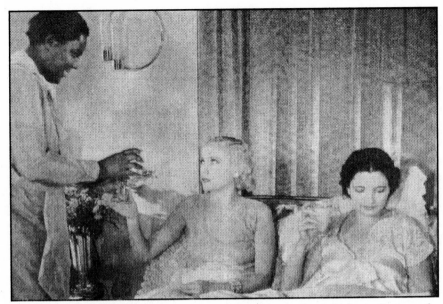

Director George Cukor's Girls About Town *(1931). Kay is seen here with Louise Beavers and lesbian-about-town Lilyan Tashman. (Paramount)*

Kay is honest with McCrea about her estranged husband (Anderson Lawler) and he encourages her to ask for a divorce. She does and Lawler seems agreeable. In the meantime, Tashman befriends Mrs. "Benji" Thomas, a matronly middle-west housewife, and convinces her they are "the same type." They are soon scheming to get Benji to spend some of his millions. When Benji overhears his wife tell the proprietor of an expensive jewelry store what a "small town cheapskate" he is, he goes ballistic. He spends $52,000 on jewelry and gold watches for Tashman.

The Kay-Joel romance hits a snag when husband Lawler shows up and tells Joel that he and Kay are in cahoots to get $10,000 out of him. He threatens to name Joel as correspondent in a divorce suit. McCrea believes him, writes the check and storms out of Kay's life. After the girls throw a yard sale, parting with their fine jewels, frocks and furs, they raise the $10,000 to pay Joel back. Tashman reluctantly concedes to give Mrs. Thomas the $52,000 worth of bangles. Mr. Thomas is flabbergasted, warning his wife, "You'll just turn out to be one of those *girls about town!*"

"Jim and I are going to live in Lansing, Marie!" Kay announces happily after she and Joel patch things up. Tashman replies, "Can't you two stay *mad* at each other!" She picks up the phone and calls her agent. "My telephone number is still the same," she informs him. "But, from now on I work...*alone!*" The number Tashman gave was actually for the Brooklyn Paramount Theatre.

Louella Parsons, quoting the good book, indicated that Kay and Lilyan weren't exactly "lilies of the field." "You would be amazed how hard these two gold-diggers *toil* in *Girls About Town*," she wrote. "Fat men, lean men, bankers, oil magnates, one and all come under the spell of Kay Francis and Lilyan Tashman. It's all very amusing and entertaining, too. The fun is riotous, the dialogue smart and the characterizations excellently contrived."[8]

Girls About Town (1931) Kay and Joel McCrea. (Paramount)

The romantic development between Kay and Joel provides a nice contrast to all the hi-jinks going on. Both humor *and* love prevails in the end and both girls are winners. "There's an unwitting and unintended punch scene in this picture to draw whimsy laughter," said *Variety*. "It's where Kay Francis shows off her figure in undies while explaining she's through with the gold-digger racket and intends going straight." William Mann, commented on *Girls About Town* (and, in many respects, Kay herself) in his book *Behind the Screen*: "When Francis strips down to reveal skimpy lingerie, it's a declaration that sex and sexuality are defined here not by moralists and tradition, but by people who break rules and make up their own."[9] Films like *Girls About Town* appealed to a more sophisticated, urbane American audience. Kay's role was written by Zoe Akins with the outlandish Tallulah Bankhead in mind. Bankhead, an unapologetic lesbian, was a star on Broadway. Mann noted that in New York "she flouted all rules of public behavior and convention, reveling in her status as iconoclastic rebel. Hollywood never knew quite what to do with her, either on screen or off."[10] If the truth were told, middle America, and the scions of society, would look down with scorn on such charmers as Wanda and Marie in *Girls About Town*. The vice squad, or worse, the FBI, would be hot on their trail. One's private life in the United States was open to the scrutiny of the government as well as fodder for gossip and scandal. What was chic, accepted, or at least tolerated in European cultures, was forbidden and often illegal in the States. So much for diversity.

When Marlene Dietrich arrived on the scene, her playful attitude regarding sex created quite a stir. She was flirting with both men and women. Biographer Diana McLellan noted that Dietrich "experimented with the film world's established lesbian crowd, centered around [Dorothy] Arzner and her choreographer lover, Marion Morgan…Dorothy's widely known crush on her was in vain."[11] Dorothy Arzner was a talented and inventive director. She had co-directed Kay in *Behind the Make-Up*. Kay had also worked with Arzner's lover, Marion Morgan, on the Carmen number in *Paramount on Parade*. McLellan writes that in the summer of 1931, "Marlene instigated a couple of affairs—one with actress Kay Francis (then playing Tallulah's role in *Girls About Town*), another with a leading Hollywood wife. For public consumption and emotional novelty, she had an affair with Maurice Chevalier."[12]

Impossible as it seems today, these incidents and their details are located in the FBI's Marlene Dietrich files: officially, FBI file no. 65-42237, part 25, page 10. Such reports, as the one on Dietrich and Kay Francis, were instigated under the auspice of the department's chief, J. Edgar Hoover. Cukor biographer Patrick McGilligan wrote that "Decades later, it became known that…Hoover hoarded information about people's sex lives, which interested Hoover almost as much as their politics."[13] Many believe that Hoover himself was gay. He and his lifelong bachelor friend and favored co-worker, Clyde Tolson, were constant companions from the time Tolson joined the bureau in 1928 until Hoover's death in 1972. Hoover left the bulk of his estate to Tolson. But, regardless of his sexuality, his obsession with the sex lives of Hollywood stars and collecting voluminous files on their private lives, can only be seen as the brainchild of a prurient purveyor, a very repressed man. Hoover would go so far as to even blackmail his own agents if he discovered they were homosexual, forcing them to be informants, or "listening posts" in the Federal Government.[14]

Kay certainly found Dietrich intriguing. Any relationship she may have had was the result of a free spirit and a curious nature. In 1937, Kay told an interviewer that she would like the company of Dietrich on a desert island, but then reneged on the idea: "I'd like to take Marlene Dietrich as a thing of perfect beauty. But I don't know…I'd be afraid that Marlene would be the cause of revolution among the men. She'd stir up violence just by being. They'd all be fighting among themselves for a date by the lagoon with Marlene. Think we'd do better to leave Marlene on the *mainland*."[15] J. Edgar Hoover would rather Dietrich had never left her *fatherland*, Germany. According to *The Guardian* newspaper, J. Edgar Hoover "largely mistrusted" Dietrich: "For years Hoover ordered that the Hollywood star's every move be trailed and her mail opened…FBI officials who followed the German star noted with puzzlement that, despite her marriage to Rudolf Sieber, Dietrich was 'promiscuous, albeit in a rather cool and glamorous manner' … Particular interest was shown in the 'affairs which shifted away from the norm…' said to include Kay Francis, to whom the notes stated Dietrich once presented 'a sapphire ring in a nightclub on the Sunset Strip.'"[16]

My suspicions were aroused upon reading *The Guardian* report regarding Kay's preferences. Her affinity was for *emeralds*, not sapphires. Upon acquiring the files from the FBI on Dietrich (they had no files on Kay), I learned that Dietrich had actually given the large sapphire to a producer's wife who was "a known lesbian." No name given. The quote on file regarding Kay and Dietrich stated, "During her Paramount days, she [Dietrich] verged from the norm for an affair with Kay Francis (known lesbian), and since that time has been involved in similar experiences, although less known." The report was submitted in July 1942.[17] The other mention of Kay occurs in FBI file no. 65-42237-29, listed under "Gossip Concerning Dietrich." Here it was repeated that Dietrich had "veered from the norm and had had affairs with well-known women in Hollywood, one of these being Kay Francis."[18] Kay's diaries give *no* indication of an affair with Dietrich or any other woman. Experiences, yes, but no emotionally involved affairs. Kay wasn't shy about writing the intimate details of her love life into her diary. These were usually entered in shorthand—with no holds barred. Kay had been adventuresome on three occasions with women and had told Kenneth about it. On January 21, 1930, she noted, "Told Ken about the three women I had slept with—probably was a God damn fool, but it seemed to excite him a little."[19] For Kay, her experiences with women were out of curiosity. On one occasion the outspoken Tallulah Bankhead called her a lesbian at one of Kay's dinner parties. Kay confessed that she and one of the guests "were very next to getting queer! Damn fool."[20] She never took offense to the fact that some women found her attractive. She dealt with these situations with care and understanding, but rarely acquiesced to their wishes. When she did, she would be angry at herself.

Kay expressed her puzzlement concerning the keen interest in the personal lives of stars exhibited on the west coast. She was used to mixing with the more openly sophisticated, "anything goes" crowd in New York. She commented to reporter Margaret Reid, "In the theater, no one particularly cares where, when, how or why you were born, what your favorite salad is, or your opinion of the Indian salt strike. And they don't give a whoop about your sex life. You have one or you haven't—it's all the same to them. They have sex lives of their own and would be terribly bored by a recital of any one else's." Reid observed that when Kay arrived in Hollywood she was disconcerted by the "clinical curiosity" regarding film stars. Kay found it rather odd that in the middle of preparing for a big scene, an "eager-penned son or daughter of the press" would suddenly appear and demand her theories on career versus marriage. Kay explained to Reid, "In the first place, I don't theorize about marriage. It works or it doesn't, depending only on the participants. In the second place, I never have theories of *any* kind when I'm about to go into a big moment for the camera and posterity." Kay shook her head and laughed, "One idea at a time is all I can manage!" Reid concluded that, "Kay...the possessor of steady nerves and a sense of keen amusement," found the whole situation to border on the ridiculous.[21] Kay reiterated the same feelings to Ben Maddox, and added, "I don't mix the professional and personal. I'm willing to do what I should in the line of duty. So long as I do that, my very private life is all mine!"[22] Writer Dick Mook observed that there was nothing phony about Kay, "she's genuine."[23] But, Mook had to admit:

> "[Kay] is one of the moodiest people imaginable. Either her spirits are in the clouds or she is down in the depths...Once...she came into a friend's office at the studio, slumped down in an easy chair and started opening some mail. Suddenly she burst into tears, rose and left the room. We never found out what she was upset over. You don't ask Kay things like that. There is no one in Hollywood more reticent than she about her personal affairs...Once I referred to the fact that so little of her personal life finds its way into print. Her explanation was simple. 'Most actors are afraid to open their mouths in front of writers or reporters for fear what they say will get into print. I have found it isn't the writers and reporters who circulate the stories about us—it's our friends ... If I keep my troubles to myself, I know they're not going to be broadcast.'"[24]

Kay did share her emotional ups and downs with her diary. It provided a cathartic effect during her career, from 1922-1953. The diary was her choice of venue to share private matters—and it served her well. As she pointed out to Mook, reporters weren't being singled out *not* to share details about her private life. Kay chose not to divulge personal matters even to close friends. Kay would later refer to Fred Astaire as her male counterpart in this regard. "He never reveals much about himself," Kay said, "but when he does care to talk he has something worth saying...I have been so pleased with the way he has behaved in Hollywood...he relied on merit to bring him his deserved attention. Nor did he discourse wildly on his private life to gain publicity."[25] Uncertainty surrounding Kay's "private life" lent an air of intrigue and mystery to an essentially un-mysterious person.

Proof that Paramount was unable to pinpoint Kay's screen persona was evident by the studio's choice for her next film, *The False Madonna*. In her largest role to date for the studio, they disguised 26-year-old Kay as a matronly mother of a 17-year-old son! At least the film reunited Kay with her old mentor from the stage, Stuart Walker, who directed. Walker came west in 1930 after finishing a season at the Cincinnati Repertory Theatre. *False Madonna* was based on May Edington's magazine story, "The Heart Is Young." Louella Parsons reported that Edington "might have unconsciously...written ['The Heart Is Young'] for Kay Francis."[26] That's quite possible, since it appears she was unconscious when she wrote the preposterous plot. Kay plays Tina, who impersonates the mother of a wealthy seventeen-year-old boy to get control of his multimillion dollar estate. This ruse is the brainstorm of Kay's lover, and partner-in-crime, William Stage Boyd. Naturally, she has her misgivings. "It's almost fantastic!" she tells him. "The *idea* of impersonating some long lost mother! I'd never get away with it!" She almost does. Fortunately, the boy is had been blinded two years previously.

The reunion of this highly improbable mother-son pair is really quite touching. The boy descends a winding staircase on his own, gazing blindly into some imagined happiness. Kay is shocked to realize his condition. "Oh, you poor boy!" she exclaims. "You've come a long way," he tells her, "haven't you?" Kay, realizing the gravity of the situation and what her life has actually come to, gives a telling expression. "Yes...," she says quietly, "...a long way!" Once she establishes a presence in the boy's life, the lad grows extremely fond of her. Kay begins to feel remorseful as she follows through with the charade, especially when she discovers he hasn't long to live. She looks at the greeting he wrote her in Braille: "I hope you will stay." Heartsick, she sits in her bedroom and stares. The boy's guardian (Conway Tearle) is convinced Kay is not the legitimate mother, but he is hesitant to do anything due to the boy's fragile health.

There are tender scenes of Kay and the boy walking through the gardens, silhouetted by the pond, and singing "In the Gloaming" together. Kay's low-throbbing soprano is accented with her tears as the boy accompanies her on the piano. The plaintive lyrics, "When the lights are dim and low..." seem to parallel the boy's own life. Kay reconsiders her plans to take advantage of him. She has become a *False Madonna*—and she wants out.

Boyd is outraged when he learns Kay has had a change of heart. He arrives, armed with a gun, intending to at least blackmail her, but Kay feels no threat. She is attuned to something deeper. The boy had a relapse and died. Kay brilliantly plays her reaction to Boyd's misguided passions. "I've nothing more to live for...now!" she tells him. "That boy believed in me. I forgot that such things existed. For the first time in my life I learned the joy of giving...not taking! Go ahead...shoot!" Before Boyd pulls the trigger, the boy's guardian unexpectedly enters the room and Boyd runs off. Out of the blue, the rather bland, unemotional Tearle decides to take this opportunity to declare his love for Kay! "Wouldn't you like home and peace?" he asks. Kay seems unprepared for such a sudden turn, as is the audience. She reluctantly embraces him as the music swells for a contrived happy ending.

The False Madonna was selected for the grand opening of Oakland, California's new three million dollar Paramount Theatre. On December 1931, a Hollywood contingent consisting of Kay, George Bancroft, Elissa Landi, John Boles and Francis Dee attended the gala premier. Cast members, Conway Tearle, Marjorie Gateson and William Stage Boyd, were also on hand. The speeches and other entertainments were broadcast to the throngs of 10,000 that crowded the roped-off streets in front of the floodlit theater. The advertising headlines blared: "Her Face—A Carnal Lie! She tries to make a mockery of humanity's most sacred emotion!" Had Kay succeeded?

The reviews for the film were surprisingly respectful considering the unlikely nature of the plot. Perhaps there had been a deluge of "False Madonnas" invading the lives of blind, wealthy orphans during the Depression. The LA Evening Herald Express thought, "The False Madonna…convinces mostly because of its understatement and its gentility of mood…at times you're in a state of mixed feelings watching the youthful Miss Francis develop maternal love for the youth…If the film were not acted with such quiet sincerity, you'd feel the boy was about to regain his sight and fall in love with the pseudo mother at any moment. Stuart Walker directed. His hand shows welcome repression and a sureness many a Hollywood veteran still has to learn." Eleanor Barnes for the Los Angeles Illustrated Daily News gave credit to Kay, saying the "picture…is given some substantiality by the brittle and tailored beauty of Kay Francis…Miss Francis, always smartly costumed, and convincing in parts of this type, is up to her standard."

With The False Madonna completed, Kay assumed her job at Paramount was over. She now had more time to enjoy yachting with Ken. They also had ample opportunity to see the latest 1931 releases at the cinema. "When work permits, Kenneth and I go to see three or four films a week," Kay told a reporter. She then elaborated on being star struck herself:

> It probably sounds silly, but I still am a hopeless movie fan. Before there was even a possibility of my becoming a screen actress, I adored certain movie stars, with abject worship. I built up all the glamorous illusions for which fans are noted, and the fact that I am now a screen actress myself hasn't changed those illusions one bit. Take for instance Pola Negri. She held me enthralled when I was growing up. I thought she must be the most marvelous person in the world…when I met Pola Negri not long ago, I was so awed that I could scarcely speak. I am quite sure that if I should meet Greta Garbo I would be speechless with admiration and unable to utter a syllable. I adore her as much as any movie fan and I don't suppose I shall ever be able to look upon her as just another human being.
>
> No one cries in a movie theater more than I. When Jimmy Dunn enacted the scene in the doctor's office in Bad Girl, I cried so copiously that I very nearly ruined my dress. And all the time I was crying I tried to argue with myself that Frank Borzage spent a whole week making that particular scene. Most ridiculous of all, I can make myself cry. When I go to a preview of one of my pictures, if there is a sad scene I can cry over my own plight up there on the screen just as if I were weeping over the sorrows of another person. Yet by some strange paradox, I can at the same time criticize my

performance and see where I could have improved my acting so that it would make me cry a little harder.[27]

Bad Girl had won a Best Director Oscar for Frank Borzage. In 1935, Kay would have an opportunity to work twice with the skilled, "love triumphs against all odds" director. Over the next few years, movie fan Kay would also mention her crush on James Cagney (her favorite), the grace and allure of Anna May Wong, and the "amazing forthrightness" of Joan Blondell.[28]

Hoping to profit from Kay as much as possible before the year closed, Paramount announced two more films for Kay, teaming her with Fredric March. The first was *The Master Key*, in which she would play the richest girl in the world. The project was shelved for lighter fare, the cleverly entertaining, *Strangers in Love*. In November 1931, Kay gave reporter Elizabeth Yeaman a rosy assessment regarding her departure from Paramount. "In a way I am a little frightened at the thought of going to a new studio," Kay said. "I know Paramount and like the entire organization. And I was so pleased and happy when they asked me to make one more picture than my contract called for. *And* they offered to pay me the salary that I will receive at Warners. It is mighty nice to know that I will leave Paramount with good feeling on both sides and that there will be no resentment over my departure." God only knows what Kay thought of interviewer Yeaman, who would eventually throw many a nasty barb at Kay's film performances. Their first encounter, however, proved complementary with Yeaman saying that Kay was "suave, sleek, sophistication…extraordinary chic," while curiously adding that Kay had "the candid emotion of a child and a boundless enthusiasm."[29]

Strangers in Love attempted to capitalize on Fredric March's Oscar-winning, dual-role, performance in *Dr. Jekyll and Mr. Hyde*. The film offered him another opportunity to delineate two distinct personalities. In *Strangers* March played twin brothers, one good, one bad. Kay is the bad-one's secretary. Although the focus was on March, Kay managed to steal the audience's attention throughout. Kay, as Diane, has been working for a wealthy, cold-hearted miser, Arthur Drake (March), who scorns the "Benevolent Society" and the misfortunes of needy friends. As he dictates a very dry dissertation on Egyptology (his expertise aside from swindling), he suddenly grumbles upon hearing street musicians playing outside the window of his mansion. "They leave," Kay advises, with a note of disdain for her employer, "if you toss them a dime, you know." Responding to her sage counsel, he manages to part with the sum. We soon learn that Kay suspects Drake of defrauding her father out of his fortune. She works for him in order to discover the truth.

Enter Buddy Drake (March) and his pal Stan (Stu Erwin). Buddy's return home after twelve years finds him on the dole. He ventures to ask brother Arthur, who has a heart ailment, for $50 to tide him over. Arthur smugly assures Buddy that he's been left out of their father's will and angrily offers a check for $1,000. Buddy smells a rat and confronts Arthur, who goes into a rage followed by a complete and fatal collapse. Buddy takes Arthur's place and soon finds out that Arthur's life was not a "bowl of cherries." Buddy is threatened by the people with whom Arthur was in cahoots. But, before he can decide whether to stay put or flee, Arthur's lovely secretary (Kay) arrives. The butler warns her that Mr. Drake "hasn't seemed like himself." "Well," Kay deduces, "*that's* an improvement!" Kay's reaction to the transformed, bad boy imposter is essential to the film's humor. Her display of confusion, disbelief, frustration and amazement are fault-less and give March some real onscreen competition. The plot thickens when Kay learns the truth about Buddy and falls for him. She gets more than she bargained for when the pair finds themselves in a boat chase, with the police in hot pursuit. The boat catches fire and the two are forced to dive overboard. Once apprehended, Buddy's true identity is restored. We see a dripping, disheveled Kay embracing Buddy for the fade-out kiss.

The film never fails to entertain. The script, based on William J. Locke's *The Shorn Lamb*, supplied what the *New York Times* called, "a heap of good comedy...Kay Francis is charming and alert."[30] Critic Harry Mines aptly summed up Kay's role, saying she added "vividness to an ordinary heroine role. This combination of Francis and March is successful. Both being tall, brunette and somber, they are nice to look at..." *Movie Mirror* complimented Kay's comic sense, saying, "Kay Francis is no slouch, either, when it comes to dragging out the hahas." "Miss Francis gets everything possible out of her sec role," cheered *Variety*. "She works with a nice restraint throughout, pacing her part with just the proper shading."

Paramount included Kay in their special featurette for the 1931-32 season titled, *The House that Shadows Built* (1931), in which stills of Kay from *Girls About Town* and *24 Hours* were prominently displayed. Her marathon of filming at Paramount com-pleted, Kay headed for the studio that would endeavor to make her one of the most popular and biggest moneymaking stars in Hollywood, and also do its damnedest to bring about her downfall: Warner Brothers.

Chapter 7

One Way Passage To Stardom

"As part of the star-loot from the famous Paramount raid, Kay is getting plenty of attention from Darryl Zanuck and his associates," reported the *Los Angeles Evening Herald Express*. "She'll go over big, if they can swing it." "Plenty of attention," however, did not include script approval. "Going over big" meant hard work. Kay had three films in the can at Warners before her last Paramount feature, *Strangers in Love,* was released. Reporter Jewel Smith summed up Kay's busy life, saying, "You can cease calling her 'Clothes-horse' right now, and more appropriately rename her 'Race-horse.' Kay has never worked so hard, so untiringly, so ambitiously. In two months, she has completed three pictures at Warner Brothers under her new contract—a record to quake the strength of a male, let alone that one of one hundred and twenty-eight pounds of feminine flesh…Kay has kept up her athletic attainments through the equally strenuous game of tennis. She is Hollywood's most excellent player."[1] Kay was as earnest about her film work as she was her tennis game. She detailed a typical day at Warners for *Collier's* magazine.

> I get up in the morning at a quarter to six if I'm going to wear an evening dress. An evening dress means a body make-up. It takes time…By nine I am at the studio, made up, and on the set for work. We stop usually at six-thirty in the afternoon. Then comes a talk, probably with the director and the leading man…so that we'll be ready with everything thoroughly understood for the next day. After that, we see the rushes of the day's take. At about eight, it's time to go home. I jump into a bath, and am glad to have dinner on a tray in bed. If I don't get to sleep before eleven, I have only seven hours. This round-the-clock schedule goes on for four or six weeks at a stretch. Just let anyone try to persuade me to go out any evening except Saturday! It can't be done when I'm working…[But] I'm like everyone else in every other business—I wouldn't advise anyone to go into it and nothing could drag me out of it…I'm happy right where I am…[2]

Many of Kay's co-workers at Warners referred to their studio as "The Factory" and some called it the "Burbank Branch of San Quentin." Bogart biographer A. M. Sperber wrote, "The studio was Jack Warner's empire and he was its tyrant…a man whose word was as good as his need."[3] At 46, the trim, thin-mustachioed, vice-president at Warners, had, along with his five older brothers, worked his way from nickelodeon owner in Pennsylvania to the founding of Warner Brothers in 1923.[4] Warner prided himself on the studio's low salaries. A supporting player, like Joan Blondell, Glenda Farrell, or Lyle Talbot, might find themselves working in three pictures at the same time. The hectic, creative atmosphere made an environment that some, such as Kay, found exciting. Although she was overworked, Kay was philosophical about accepting the strict routine. She told Maude Cheatham, "I have to adopt this regime in order to give my best to the screen and remember, it is my profession. I'm tremendously serious about it."[5]

In January 1932, it was reported that Warners had bought *A Dangerous Brunette* for Kay. Her previously announced role as a wealthy divorcee in *The Rich Are Always With Us*, was given to Ruth Chatterton. Producer Darryl Zanuck (using the alias Melville Crossman) had written *A Dangerous Brunette* with Kay in mind. Zanuck would also write *Baby Face* (1933), the classic pre-Code shocker, for Barbara Stanwyck. *A Dangerous Brunette* translated to the screen as *Man Wanted* and it still has a contemporary feel to it. A breezy, truthful comment on marriage and relationships, Kay finds herself with a philandering husband, a male secretary who adores her, and her emotions grappling with the human thing to do. In spite of the film's mature attitude, and Kay being "tremendously serious" about her work, David Manners and Andy Devine acted like juveniles on the set. "Andy Devine and I behaved very badly," Manners commented years later. "We were whooping it up one day and Kay Francis walked off the set. She sent back word that she'd return to work when those two 'apes' quieted down."[6]

Man Wanted was a complete turnaround from the featured status that Kay usually received at Paramount. Every quality of Kay's that was persuasive was shown to advantage and her screen-time far exceeded any of her Paramount films. In *Man Wanted,* Kay was the *star*. She worked well with director William Dieterle and gauged her performance with naturalness and appealing gestures that were uniquely hers. Her technique drew audiences and fans into what felt like her charmed circle. As dangerous brunette Lois Ames, Kay is the officious, very responsible editor of the exclusive "400 Magazine." She's enthusiastic about her job. She's fond of her husband (Kenneth Thomson), whom she supports, while he plays polo and philanders. He mostly philanders. She's aware of his infidelity, but wants to be a good sport and not nag. Her fulfillment at work compensates for what her marriage is lacking. Almost. Enter David Manners, whom Kay hires as a secretary.

For some comic relief, we learn Manners is being pursued by Una Merkle and eager to get away from her henpecking clutches. When Merkel calls him at work, Manners, using Kay's desk phone, attempts to politely bring the conversation to a close. "Yes," he tells Merkel. "Yes. Yes. Yes. Yes." Kay interrupts, "Are there many *more*?" To which the embarrassed Manners gives an abrupt, "Goodbye." Delightful and amusing moments like this abound in the film as the romance between the two develops. When Kay invites Manners to join her and husband Thomson at a Bar Harbor resort, business culminates with Manners kissing his boss as she's about to fall asleep on a chaise lounge. Not ready to acknowledge her feelings, Kay thoughtfully dismisses the kiss, saying, "it can be forgotten, because it has no meaning." We are then privy to the fact that Thomson's mistress, Claire Dodd, also made it to Bar Harbor. Dodd informs Thomson that she wasn't there just to dance and supplies him with the key to her room.

The direction, script and creative camerawork (Greg Toland) are fluid and compliment the story. The scene where Kay and her husband Thomson decide to part is intelligent, simple and honest. We see Kay sliding a conciliatory note under his bedroom door. Before he reads it, he invites her in only to announce that he would like to go to England, alone. "Divorce," Kay says finally. "We can't change ourselves," he pleads. Disappointed, Kay sadly retreats toward her room. When Thomson picks up the note, she's embarrassed and asks him not to read it. He reads it anyway, feels remorseful and bows his head. Laying her head on his shoulder, Kay comforts him by saying, "Freddie, I feel like crying too..." The scene is thoughtfully handled, and objective, although sympathies lean in Kay's direction. Realizing what a team she and Manners make, Kay invites him for a catered dinner for two at the office and the inevitable fade-out kiss. *Man Wanted* is a delightful mix of humor and romantic wistfulness.

The New York Times raved that "Kay Francis radiates so much charm throughout *Man Wanted*...that the familiar theme somehow does not matter...the screenplay is the very thing for Miss Francis...the comic relief is injected in well-measured doses...the directing work of William Dieterle seems to be another feather in his cap." Other reviews echoed the film's delights. The *LA Illustrated Daily News* wrote, "It's a topsy-turvy version of all those stories about the private secretary and her boss. This is good light material which has the benefit of luxurious settings, pleasing dialogue, rather clever situations and some good performances. Miss Francis photographed well and wearing stunning costume creations, as usual, contributes a smooth, svelte delineation as the wife who found happiness in the world of business rather than in the smart set."

Kay's next venture was an intelligent piece titled *Street of Women*. The connotation was simple. Mistresses, not wives, are the real impetus behind all the great achievements of men, in this instance skyscrapers. If that seems daring, it was, but usual fodder for

The very pre-Code Street of Women *(1932) purported that mistresses, not wives, were the inspirations behind a man's achievements. After his afternoon trysts with mistress Kay, Alan Dinehart erects the "world's tallest building." (Warners)*

pre-Code Hollywood. After June 1934, it would be impossible to film a story where the sympathies lie with the "other woman" and the wife is shown to be a pretentious social-climbing bitch, especially when it was established that the "illicit" relationship was definitely sexual. Based on a novel by Polan Banks and directed by Archie Mayo, the film held interest, but lacked the fluid momentum of *Man Wanted*. Ernest Haller's photography had some nicely done shots of the daring men who were building with steel up in the clouds. Anton Grot's characteristic arched and curved-lined interiors and windows enhance Kay's surroundings, as if she resided in some sort of Art Deco heaven.

Kay's influence behind the realization of the Baldwin Building ("the world's tallest") is understood early on. Her three-year liaison with Mr. Baldwin (Alan Dinehart) was established in the bedroom and made its way to the board of directors of Baldwin Inc. Her *real* job, however, is as the proprietor and designer for "Madame Natalie," an exclusive salon that has afforded her a hefty income and the ability to support her brother Clark's education at the Paris School of Architecture. When Clark is due back home, Kay tells Baldwin that he can't visit anymore. Her brother might not understand the finer aspects of their relationship. Baldwin is finally motivated to ask his wife for a divorce, but first confides in his daughter, Doris (Gloria Stuart), who is horrified. It turns out that she and Clark are secretly engaged. Mrs. Baldwin (Marjorie Gateson, in a brilliant exhibition of pretension) overhears her husband's confession to their daughter and is more concerned about "social ruin" than the loss of a husband.

Gateson makes a point to visit her rival at "Madame Natalie." It's evident she feels Kay is beneath her. She asks to see "something *men* like." She peppers snide remarks, as models parade by her in Kay's creations. "Red seems such an *obvious* color!" she smugly observes. "Quite in the *modern* spirit!" she says sarcastically. "I've seen everything I was interested in seeing," she tells Kay dismissively. Hurt and torn inside, Kay returns home only to find Baldwin's daughter, who begs Kay to give up her father. Before long, brother Clark spins out of control and crushes Kay's spirit by asking whether he should thank *her* for his education or the man who paid for her services.

Thankfully, Roland Young is on hand as Kay's confidant to add some levity to the soapy dramatics. While Kay is down in the dumps, he whips up a plan. He draws a "pessimistic rabbit" to cheer her up. It works. "Look at that dumb thing!" she laughs, finally agreeing to go out for dinner. The plot quickly reverts back to dramatics and is finally resolved with a car crash, which inadvertently unites the two-sets of lovebirds. Roland Young convinces Mrs. Baldwin to head for Reno. Clark and Doris head for the altar. Mr. Baldwin and Kay forego ceremony and sail to Europe.

Harry Mines wrote a review saying that *Street of Women* was, "an exceedingly well-done drama, both from a directorial and acting standpoint....The studio is giving [Miss Francis] good vehicles and evidently spending money on her production judging by the exquisite setting and the line up of talent in the supporting cast. Archie Mayo has made an engrossing picture...Miss Francis wears stunning clothes and has been photographed advantageously. Her performance is warm, sincere and charming."[7] *Film Daily* also emphasized that *Street of Women* was a "superior production...Kay Francis delivers with distinction...The production is punctuated with many clever situations, and some unusually intelligent and witty dialogue...It seems a pity to put such a cheap title on such a worthy film." *Film Daily* had a point. One promotion read, "Where every address is the 'right' number...Where every woman was once a lady...Where passion masquerades as love." A prominently nippled, slouchy woman, wearing a negligee, is sketched below Kay's beaming photograph. Kay's own reaction upon seeing the film was simply, "Preview—*Street of Women.* Ugh!"[8] Audiences reacted differently. Many were fascinated by Kay's screen persona. It prompted author Faith Baldwin to pose the proposition, "If You Want to Be Like Kay Francis," for *Modern Screen* magazine. Baldwin promised, "any girl could be like Kay Francis—if not physically, then spiritually or mentally," and wrote in raptures about Kay:

> Who wouldn't want to look like her? The day I saw her we sat before a bright coal fire in the living room of her brother's [sic] charming New York house...I asked her if she'd mind if I sat and looked at her for a couple of weeks. For that's the way she affects you. And she laughed, and said she wouldn't mind...She said it in her low, pretty voice, which can't quite manage the R's and so slides over them, much to her horror.
>
> To be like her, you must be vital. You must be interested in strange people and strange places, you must be ready to embrace change and adventure when they come your way. You must be a hard worker. Only a hard worker could have accomplished as much in a time as comparatively short. You must have a sense of humor, which laughs with others, and at yourself. She is entirely of this world, poised, sure of herself, friendly...a good listener, an excellent conversationalist, as styled and chic and charming as one of the frocks Banton so brilliantly designs for her. If you want to be like Kay Francis...you will be faintly amused and more than faintly disgusted at the people who swagger in their talk, and who, having themselves won a certain position, look *down* instead of at other people...If you want to be like Kay Francis you will be yourself. That is the paradox I suppose, as perhaps you know your real self does not resemble Miss Francis in the least. But if you are yourself you are like her in one very basic quality. For she is herself, quite perfectly, and does not try to be like anyone else.[9]

Baldwin was observant as to Kay's demeanor and personality. But, inventing a brother for Kay must have been an inside joke. (It's possible that Kay was staying with her brother-in-law, Jo Mielziner). Kay had been considered for the Baldwin story *Week-End Marriage* in 1932. The role went to Loretta Young. It would be six years before Kay filmed a Baldwin story, the unremarkable *Comet Over Broadway.*

In July 1932, Kay's third release for Warners hit the theaters. It was the fifth outing for the Kay Francis-William Powell team. *Jewel Robbery,* based on a 1925 play by Ladislaus Fodor, was a fun, racy, satirical romp with a sophisticated edge. The ads promised, "He stole her jewels—but that wasn't all!" *The Los Angeles Evening Herald Express* tattled that "Kay is naughty again. I mean naughty! She plays Terri, the vivacious Viennese in *Jewel Robbery.* It is quite the naughtiest role she has done in pictures!"

Jewel Robbery was probably the "naughtiest" film anyone associated with it had ever made. Kay (a replacement for Barbara Stanwyck) played the pampered wife of wealthy Henry Kolker. She has a lover on the side (Hardie Albright), whom she's ready to dispose of, and spends her time and husband's bank account on jewels and furs. Kay plays her role with the enthusiasm of a frivolous coquette whose most cherished desire is a new thrill. When she meets her husband at the jewelers to buy the 28-carat Excelsior

Jewel Robbery (1932) Kay watches William Powell deftly steal an entire jewelry store from proprietor Jacques Vanaire. Afterwards, Powell kindly offers both of them a marijuana cigarette for "any inconvenience," but Kay declines. (Warners)

Diamond, they are confronted with an attractive, sophisticated jewel thief (William Powell). She is captivated by him. He flirts with the same finesse he uses to rob the store. Considerate to a fault, he supplies marijuana cigarettes to everyone to calm their nerves. Kay declines, saying, "I prefer to keep my wits about me, thank you!" (The studio was bombarded with letters asking the contents of the curious cigarette). When Powell escorts her to be locked in the safe, she asks him to join her. "What would I do in there alone?" she queries. As an alternative, Powell offers to drop her off in the suburbs, untouched. "Untouched in the suburbs! Oh, no!" Kay refuses. When she slaps him for taking the Excelsior Diamond off her hand, Powell smiles, saying, "How intimate!"

Back at her mansion, Powell appears out of nowhere after watching Kay change into her negligee. "You were everything I anticipated!" he compliments her. In gratitude, a surprised Kay offers him cognac. Powell tries to seduce her, saying he lives "only for the present." Peeking into her bedroom he suggests, "if you wish, at dawn we shall have a secret behind us." Managing to conjure up a smidgen of self control, she refuses. Through an amusing ploy, Powell and Kay end up at *his* hideaway, where his man-in-waiting escorts them to the bedroom. Powell shows some protocol. "No, no, no," he admonishes the valet, "supper first!" Kay agrees. "There are so many pleasant, intervening steps," she says happily. "Show me your jewels!"

Their rendezvous is cut short when the police arrive. Powell escapes to Nice after inviting Kay to join him there at the Hotel Negresco. When Kay's husband shows up, she feigns that she's been kidnaped. Her nerves are "shattered, simply shattered." She must get away "for a *long* rest." She walks toward the camera with a smirk on her face saying, "I think I'll go to Nice! Yes, Nice. On the first possible train." Placing her index finger to her lips, she admonishes the audience, by looking straight into the camera as if we're privy to her little secret. A very funny, original ending.

Kay's sleek lines and fashion-sense were complimented throughout *Jewel Robbery* by designer Orry-Kelly. Like Kay, Orry-Kelly was an east-coast transplant, who had been Cary Grant's roommate in the 1920s. Kelly and Kay got along famously. Margaret J. Bailey in *Those Glorious Glamour Years* commented: "Kay Francis was a favorite of the costume designers because she rarely questioned anything they made for her. She never told Orry-Kelly to change a line or redo the skirt folds. Kelly once commented on professional stars like Francis to *Motion Picture Magazine*: 'They know that I know my business, which is to make them look superlatively well on the screen. They understand to the point where they know, too, that if they look badly on the screen, if their clothes fail to bring them distinction, that they are not as much at fault as I am.'" Bailey emphasized that Kelly's reputation was secured when Kay's donned such creations as the velvet negligee she wore for *Jewel Robbery*. "Kay Francis was queen of the matinee audience," said Bailey. "Women would stand in line, come rain or shine, to see what their favorite star wore because it was terrifically important to them ... Francis kept them coming back for more. It was Hollywood glamour, and moviegoers loved it."[10]

Filmgoers still favored the team of Kay Francis and William Powell. Kay commented,

> I shall never forget when we started *Jewel Robbery*. I was worn out having made four pictures in a row, finishing the last one at seven o'clock one night and starting *Jewel Robbery* early the next morning. We were on location and it was frightfully hot and I became cross, really, very irritable. Finally I blew up in my lines and went all to pieces. Bill sauntered over and sat down beside me saying, quietly, 'Kay, if I didn't love you and understand how utterly exhausted you were, I'd, well, I'd—I'd *spank you!*' That made me laugh. We both howled at the imaginary picture his words suggested and this broke the tension I had been on. Everything was serene after that.[11]

Jewel Robbery is now a cult favorite amongst pre-Code aficionados, but when released it got mixed reviews. Some critics couldn't decide whether to take it seriously or not! From the "oom-pa-pa" polka music of the opening credits to Kay's tongue-in-cheek look into the camera at the finish, it's hard to understand how *anyone* could misconstrue the film's intent. Elizabeth Yeaman didn't get it. She complained, "*Jewel Robbery* is one of those pictures which you decide not to take seriously and suddenly find that you are expected to take it seriously...it is not a little puzzling." The confused Yeaman then gives her first full-blast lambaste against Kay's acting. "Kay Francis...is required to speak lines of flip sophistication. But they sound pretty unnatural coming from her. For some reason Miss Francis seems to have forgotten how to act. She is self-conscious, and a little silly. At no time can you believe in her or her type. Helen Vinson...has only a small role, but she reveals charm, beauty and acting ability. Perhaps if she did not handle her sophisticated dialogue so well the deficiencies would not be so apparent."[12] (Ouch!) It was a typical Yeaman ploy to compare Kay with a female co-star in order to point out what she saw as Kay's deficiencies. Over the next few years Yeaman never let up on Kay. Harrison Carroll was charmed by *Jewel Robbery* and reported, "That old cinema favorite, the gentleman thief, is viewed through the eyes of humor in *Jewel Robbery*...an unmoral tale, but one so completely tongue in cheek and so continental in flavor that who shall condemn it?…Both Kay Francis and William Powell enter thoroughly into the spirit of the occasion and William Dieterle adds the proper touch to the direction."[13]

After completing her first three Warner features, Kay had plans for sailing. She told reporter Jewel Smith about her idea to take Kenneth with her and get away from it all. "Ever since my entrance into films in 1929," Kay sighed, "I have hoped against hope that the studio program would afford me sufficient leisure to make a hurried trip to Havana…no doubt it is the Spanish blood of my grandmother stirring in me, which suggests Havana…I have had what amounts to a hunger for it ever since I went there for the first time…I'm going to complete as many pictures as they'll let me in the least possible time—and then, for that long vacation—Havana—my honeymoon."[14]

Before *any* travel plans materialized, Kay was given a fourth assignment at Warners. It would prove to be the personal favorite of her career. Kay garnered nothing but accolades for her sixth and final pairing with William Powell: *One Way Passage.* The film's sentimental script had been rewritten several times before director Tay Garnett got the right mix of wistfulness and light comedy. When Zanuck quibbled about Kay's speech impediment in such a serious tearjerker, Garnett persisted. He felt he could write around her difficulties. Zanuck snapped, "It's *your* problem," and it was a go. The film boosted Kay's popularity to where she would roost for several years. She brought a genuine vulnerability to a role that would have eluded many of the era's high-strung actresses. Her performance as Joan was the key that allowed the film its patina of pathos and brought out the handkerchiefs. Without Kay, Tay Garnett's career would be minus a major achievement. *One Way Passage,* along with *The Postman Always Rings Twice* (1946), has been called the best of Garnett's career.

With strains of the W. Franke Harling melody "Where Was I?" floating in the background, *One Way Passage* is a melancholy dream of two souls on a final and unexpected romantic voyage. Terminally ill Joan (Kay) bumps into Dan (Powell) just as he is about to sip his exquisite "Paradise Cocktail" at the International Bar in Hong Kong. "I'm so sorry," she apologizes. His disappointment dissolves when he looks into her soulful eyes. "*I'm* so *glad*," he tells her. The attraction is mutual. He notices there are a few drops left. "Always so precious," she philosophizes, "the last few drops," a comment which parallels their very lives. They part hesitantly, saying "Auf Wiedersehen," and, breaking their glasses, leave behind two stems crossed upon the bar for good luck. Powell is nabbed by the law once he steps outside the bar. Thickheaded San Francisco detective Steve Burke (Warren Hymer) has finally got his man and Powell is doomed for execution at San Quentin. Once they are at sea, Burke mercifully allows Powell to roam free aboard the ship bound for Honolulu. Kay and Powell are reunited at the ship's bar, but neither divulges their personal dilemmas. They grasp at one last chance for romance.

Powell finds reinforcements on board in the form of two old cronies—"Barrel House Betty" (Aline MacMahon), who is posturing as Countess Barilhaus, and Skippy (Frank McHugh) who's usually three-sheets-to-the-wind and up to some minor con game. They both agree to help Powell escape once they get to Honolulu. When Betty looks out a portal window and notices Powell romancing Kay at sunset, she poignantly observes, "Death ain't *tough* enough. He's got to fall in love!" "He's just a ghost," she

Director Tay Garnett's superb One Way Passage *(1932). Kay and William Powell enjoy the brief spell of a doomed romance. Kay was awarded* Photoplay's *"Best Performance of the Month," and the film would remain her favorite. (Warners)*

adds sadly. In the evening's twilight, Powell and Kay comment on time, and whether it matters, or if it even has any meaning. "The world and *time* seem somewhere else," Kay says dreamily. Love has enveloped them in a lovely euphoria, regardless of what awaits them. It's a poetic moment.

Once in Hawaii, everything starts to unravel. The two lovers have a romantic interlude near the Pali (Oahu's best scenic view) where Powell promises her, "Whatever happens we belong to each other, always." However, when Powell explains to Kay that he won't be going back on board, Kay has a relapse. Even though Powell knows it will cost him his life (he's wanted for murder), he returns Kay to the ship. Kay's physician lets Powell in on Kay's secret—she hasn't long to live.

Arriving in San Francisco, Kay learns indirectly that Powell is to be executed. Realizing the other's fate, their poignant parting glances upon debarking create a touching farewell. They promise to meet in Agua Caliente for New Year's, knowing it's impossible. The final scene takes place at an Agua Caliente bar on New Year's Eve. Two bartenders are talking shop when they hear the shattering of glass. They turn around to see the stems of two cocktail glasses crossed together, but no patrons. It's as if Kay and Powell's soulful desires had reached across time and space to keep their promise. "We made the ending twice," Kay later said. "Once the imaginative way, with glasses tinkling before an empty bar, the other with hazy figures standing there...[they] used the better ending, with its *Outward Bound* quality."[15]

Although the authorship for *One Way Passage* is credited to Robert Lord (who won an Oscar for best original story), Tay Garnett often took credit for most of the screenplay's comic touches. Filming wasn't easy while Kay, Powell, cast and crew were far out at sea aboard the *S.S. Calawall*. Aline MacMahon later commented, "Warners engaged a broken-down iron boat for location shooting and sent the cast offshore, allowing us some fantastic sum like thirty-seven cents a day for food. It was an uncomfortable assignment, and we were all pretty miserable. It was boiling hot. The food was terrible. The kids got drunk, and Tay Garnett took this occasion to be difficult…Finally, the studio lost patience and brought us back to the lot to finish it. Through it all Miss Francis behaved with great dignity and did her work without complaint."[16]

Kay's diary confirmed MacMahon's report. On June 1, 1932, Kay wrote, "Bill Powell and I got cockeyed in dressing room waiting to work."[17] MacMahon paid tribute to Kay and her achievement of star status, saying, "After you say talent, then you have to ask, 'What does the audience want?' The audiences wanted what Miss Francis had. After all, Kay Francis was in a special class. She was very elegant, and she had taste and special clothes, and she fulfilled a need audiences felt."[18]

MacMahon's countess, teamed with Frank McHugh's Skippy, are two of the film's delights. McHugh brightened many a dark corner in Warner Brothers films, with endearing bits of "little business." Using what he referred to as his nonsensical one-two-three laugh (ha-ha-ha) made no sense at all, but everyone loved it. Ultimately, it's the tragic romance of Kay and William Powell in *One Way Passage* that haunts the memory. Kay's determination to "go out in a blaze of glory" registers as if she were the sunset. Her femininity has grace and intelligence. Powell responds accordingly. His gentlemanly strength is never lessened by the inevitable doom that awaits him. Or, as the film suggests, is it really doom? The audience suspends their disbelief, willingly, and enters a transparent world where the lovers have been reunited with their Paradise Cocktails.

Orry-Kelly was assigned to design Kay's wardrobe for *One Way Passage*. After interviewing Kelly, years later, George Eells wrote that Kelly thought Kay,

> …was one of the most generous, down-to-earth stars he ever had worked with. Their eventual relationship, he felt, was summed up in an incident which happened later, at a time when Kay's career was faltering and he was drinking heavily. A great deal of confusion occurred during one fitting, climaxing when she tried on a hat he had designed which was at least two sizes too large and sank to her eyebrows. It was the last straw "What's the matter with you? Are you drunk?" she demanded. And the hung-over Kelly snapped, "NO! Your head's shrunk two sizes since your last couple of flops!" which caused Kay to burst out laughing and embrace him.
>
> "In the beginning, she was very reserved but well mannered and knew exactly what she wanted," Kelly said. "I designed simple unadorned evening gowns in velvet, chiffon and crepes for *One Way Passage*…At first, only those with sensitive taste were impressed. Luckily, Kay was the essence of good taste."[19]

The physically fit Kay commented on how her wardrobe for the film enhanced her performance of the terminally ill Joan.

> In *One Way Passage* I wore a white organdie…It was quite the wrong dress for the occasion. But it happened to be the only dress that would do for the scenes I had to play…William Powell had to pick me up and carry

me…Now I'm a pretty hale and hearty creature, and I couldn't look as if I were dying in a sports dress! I had to wear organdie to create an illusion. And so the dress, though terribly wrong for the boat, was right for the scenes I had to play.[20]

Harrison Carroll wrote praises for *One Way Passage,* saying it was "persuasively acted…by that satisfying team, Kay Francis and William Powell. For a story with such a tragic undercurrent, *One Way Passage* develops an unusually rich vein of humor…Tay Garnett's direction is excellent."[21] "By far the best movie that Kay Francis and William Powell have turned out as a team," raved *Photoplay,* which also awarded Kay by listing her in their touted "Best Performances of the Month" category. Mordaunt Hall for the *New York Times* said, "In its uncouth, brusque and implausible fashion *One Way Passage*…offers quite a satisfactory entertainment. Besides the capable performances of Mr. Powell and Miss Francis there is some good comedy contributed by Frank McHugh as Skippy, Aline MacMahon is excellent as the 'Countess'…Tay Garnett's direction…keeps the story on the move with its levity and dashes of far-fetched romance."

Audiences' copious tears would again turn into box-office gold five years later when *Passage* was re-released. In 1939, Jack Warner wanted Bette Davis to film a remake titled *'Til We Meet Again.* Davis had done plenty of successful dying in *Dark Victory* (which was originally purchased with Kay in mind), and refused. The shipboard romance eventually paired Merle Oberon and George Brent, with Frank McHugh repeating his role. *'Til We Meet Again* (1940) failed to reap the raves of its predecessor.

Over the years *One Way Passage* would be *the* favorite of Kay's to show her beaus. Her diary entries showed a similar notation after each screening: "Showed Del *One Way Passage.* He loved it." "Erik very moved by *One Way Passage.*" "Ran *One Way Passage* for Don."[22] Kay complimented *Passage*'s photographer Bob Kurle, who had experimented with light and shadow to flattering effect. "When I saw that," Kay admitted, "I felt the one pang of pure pleasure I've ever experienced when I looked at myself on the screen."[23]

After completing *One Way Passage,* Kay did not head for her fantasized Havana trip or her much planned for honeymoon abroad. A few hours before their scheduled departure for Europe, Kay received word that she was wanted by Ernst Lubitsch for a big role in his next film. Her salary: $26,000. Upon accepting the part, some assumed the money was more important to her than the honeymoon. Kay told reporters, "Twenty-six thousand dollars was *not* worth more to me than my honeymoon…the money had absolutely nothing to do with it. I proved that because, shortly before Lubitsch asked for me, I had had an offer of another picture on the Paramount lot. The same sum of money was involved. I turned it down. I wouldn't even consider it. But when it came to working for Lubitsch, when I weighed my honeymoon against the honor this meant, against the things I would learn under his direction—well, Lubitsch won. He tipped the scales."[24]

Before the Lubitsch film began, Kay and Kenneth took a quick trip to New York. Kay made a point to visit her Francis ex-in-laws in Pittsfield. She met ex-fiancé Allan Ryan for dinner to see Gerswhin's *Of Thee I Sing.* She also went to a party at ex-husband Bill Gaston's. Leonard Hall, a reporter who had been impressed with Kay since seeing *Gentlemen of the Press,* visited her and Kenneth in New York. In 1929, Hall had been "*kerflummuxed*" by Kay Francis' beauty, keenness and charm." Now, at New York's Hotel

Elysee, Hall described the festivity of Kay, Kenneth and Co., after he was greeted by a smiling Kay—"hand outstretched."

> The doorbell is ringing like a xylophone—callers, cracked ice, packages and pals. MacKenna leaps from phone to door with all the agility of an adagio dancer, while Kay holds court. Mr. Clifton Webb, the noted dancing comedian, tail-coat type, is sitting on a sofa talking fourteen to the dozen…The room is a bedlam of bells, conversation, and cries of "My DEAR!" Kay, it appears, has acquired a tough case of "rheumatic sore throat"…"It started in my pharynx," she says, "and then it got into the larynx." "My dear," says Webb, "I know. I've had it. You're lucky if it doesn't get into your trachea! … It's all caused by acidity. You mustn't eat red meat."
>
> And so it goes. "I liked that piece you wrote about me three years ago," says Kay to me. "Do you want to go into the other room and talk a few minutes?" "No," says I, "let's just sit here. I'm getting a good story this way." She looks at me quizzically, wondering what is going on inside my thick skull. Finally I rise to go. "Goodbye, Kay—thanks for the visit and take care of the throat." "Goodbye," she answers. The rest of the crowd chatters on. A word of ta-ta to MacKenna, and the door closes on the steady thunder of small talk, dotted with ringing bells. Kay Francis, 1932 model. Still lovely, much more sure of herself, still with wide-frank eyes—and with the shining veneer of hardness with which Hollywood coats its hectic, successful children. Heigho—Kay's a star now. She lives in the midst of madness, which is one of the wages of fame and fortune.[25]

Amidst such clamor, flippantly observed by Hall, Kay and Kenneth were determined to make their marriage work. Kenneth turned down an opportunity to play with Katharine Cornell on Broadway. "After all," he told reporter Harry Mines, "I'm happy—or rather *we* are happy—in Hollywood." MacKenna added, "To work on the stage again would mean my having to live in New York while Kay remained on the coast. It would upset our domestic happiness and all we've worked for. I don't think I've made a mistake…In a few years when Kay is fed up with pictures we can return east to the theater, and possibly do a show together. But all our interests are out here now and there's too much to be done."[26]

Kenneth had even taken up tennis under the tutelage of a pro. Kay's own passion for the sport was legend. As was her claim to good sportsmanship. Her friend, New York reporter Harry Evans, played doubles with Kay over a period of a few weeks in 1936, while she was shooting *The White Angel*. She was so enthused about the game that she rushed from the studio without removing her make up—from the neck up, she looked like the character she was playing, Florence Nightingale. On one occasion, as Evans and Kay played against British actress Evelyn Laye and Count Alfredo di Carpegna (who had been a member of the Italian Davis Cup team), Evans noted,

> Kay was playing so well that she was making up the difference between my game and that of Alfredo—and quite a difference it was, I can assure you. We knew—and our opponents knew—that we had no right to beat them. But here

we were about to do it. The score was one set all, and we were leading eight games to seven in the third set. Kay was serving, and the score was 40-30…we needed one more point to win the match. Her first service was in, and Alfredo returned it deep to her backhand. She made a fine get, but her return was weak, and, rushing in behind his shot, Alfredo smashed to the side-line. Kay was in position to see the ball when it struck, and she immediately called it good. Both Alfredo and I looked at her sharply, but she just walked over and prepared to serve to Evelyn. As we passed, I said, "Gosh, Kay! That certainly looked out to me." "Maybe," Kay replied. "But it was too close to take." And that sums up this girl's attitude toward life. She is always willing to give the other fellow a break. As a consequence, we finally lost the match.[27]

Kay and Kenneth's passion for boating continued to flourish and they spent many happy hours together hoisting the sails. The couple enjoyed their colonial-style home set on four acres in Benedict Canyon, a quiet residential section between Beverly Hills and Hollywood. Kay still drove her Ford "Rabbit" and Kenneth sported a luxury Cadillac car that Kay gave him for his birthday. But, behind this scenario was *another* dream. Kay had already purchased a two-hundred-year-old farmhouse near Cape Cod where she and Kenneth could escape from the spotlight. "That farmhouse is to be our home," Kay declared. "It still has its old-fashioned oil lamps. There are quiet, charming neighbors near at hand…we fit in quite well with those people as we do with our Hollywood friends." Kay was vocal, as well as prophetic, about her and Kenneth's indifference to Hollywood, saying, "Our bodies are in Hollywood, but our roots are in the East. We shall remain in Hollywood just so long as we are wanted, so long as we have jobs. We will not stay one minute after our bell has rung. That is definite."[28]

In the summer of 1932, reporter Ruth Allison for *Movie Mirror*, thought Kay appeared "to have found herself." Kay responded without hesitation as to "Why?":

> Companionship, first of all. There can be a great romantic love between two people, but it cannot last unless there are other bases of enjoyment. I learned that the first time I married. I'd rather not say anything about that first episode…it is of the past and this is today. I was seventeen then. I am twenty-seven now. I have learned a great deal and I am a different person. I was in love then. I am in love now. I believe sincerely that one can love several different people for different things. I believe if one marriage doesn't work out, that it should be tossed overboard, discarded. Maybe the next one will. In that first marriage, we could find no common tastes. I loved the theatre…he couldn't stand it. It was cruel to inflict it upon him; it was cruel that I should not be permitted to enjoy it. And so it went.

Allison described Kay and Kenneth's *real* passion, their boat, saying, "They tear away from Hollywood like two mad children over week ends. It is no uncommon sight to see Kay rushing from the studio to the market of a Saturday afternoon, tucking a couple of lamb chops, some lettuce, and a loaf of bread under her arm, and rushing for San Pedro to meet Kenneth and go out on the boat. They love that boat." As far as marriage and Hollywood not mixing, Kay answered, "Divorces are brought on by people, not by a town. If a marriage is going to crash, it will crash anyway, no matter what the city or the country. Sometimes outside conditions hasten the split, but they never cause it. Marriage is an individual, not a community proposition. I think if two people can realize that, can realize that their happiness depends upon *them*, how they adjust themselves to each other, they won't have any trouble. We don't."[29]

When she was questioned regarding "children-to-be," Kay was upfront. "What have we to give a child as we live today? When I come home from the studio at night, I am full of it. I am dead tired, I can think of nothing but getting into the tub and removing my make-up. I know that I could not, at the same time, be full of the nursery and imbued with a desire to get the *baby* into the tub...We'd like to have a baby. Because I feel that it would be a pleasant thing to have—not at all because I feel that I *must* have the experience in order to have 'lived,' as so many women do. I'm not a bit sentimental about it. But, in the first place, I do not believe that a baby would enjoy *being had*— right now." Although the "right" now for Kay to have a child never came, she accepted her choices unequivocally, saying, "I know that the kind of person we should be, according to Hoyle, is not always the kind of person we can be. I know that there is not that poetized thing, 'one love in a life-time.' I have proved that—by loving twice [sic]. ... I find whatever kind of person this makes me, that the joy I get from working outweighs the things I lose. But I do know that I lose them."[30]

Kay and Kenneth's relationship in the fall of 1932 was also profiled by Kay Roberts in a *Photoplay* article, titled "They Hope to Stay Married." They attributed their formula for marital success to the credo, "Business is business, and marriage is marriage." When asked about Kay's current film project, Kenneth responded, "we never discuss each other's work. She never says what she's doing or tells what happened during the day. Neither do I. I'd be the last person to know about Kay, professionally." He informed Roberts that he and Kay had made two pre-nuptial agreements. 1) Neither was to ask the other to attend a Hollywood opening no matter what the picture or who the star. 2) Neither was to make a social engagement without first consulting the other. Ken explained the first agreement, "Openings are ballyhoo; definite exploitation stunts for picture people to be seen. We believe in other forms of advertisement." Kay also elaborated saying, "When we go out together we do so to have fun. I don't like to be grabbed or yanked around by crowds or packed into a lobby like the proverbial sardine so that I can't even light a cigarette during intermission without burning my dress. Pictures are work, and Kenneth and I are not in business together!" Kenneth continued, "Kay will come in and say, 'I had a terrible day. How are the dogs?' And we are off into a canine discussion. So, her bad day is forgotten. Or, I will come home and say, 'Damn. When can we get over to Europe?' and we are into a travelogue. It's just a form of selfishness for a husband or wife to bring home professional troubles...Kay is so irritatingly honest! If I sat down to dinner and told about a scene I'd had to make thirty times and blamed some temperamental actress, she'd probably say: 'And what did you do or not do to make her temperamental?' She knows about directors, of course, being an actress!" Kay nodded and added, "Kenneth would do the same. He knows about actresses, being a director!" Kay did acknowledge that she loved hearing the stories about the clever little canine actor in *Careless Lady*, but wasn't aware that Kenneth was directing Joan Bennett in the same film! Kay also recalled the French girl in one of Kenneth's films, who had proudly shared a series of her latest portraits. They were all impressive. She was fired afterwards, for no apparent reason, other than the photos were all...*nude. Quel dommage!*

Interviewer Roberts questioned Kay's status as fashion queen. She heard that Kay had few clothes, because her passion for sailing had narrowed down her wardrobe to yachting costumes. Kenneth laughed. "Kay can't help but be best-dressed. You know what I mean? She puts on a pair of blue trousers and sweater on the boat and washes dishes and she still looks swagger!"[31] Ending on an optimistic note, Kay and Kenneth's "hope to stay married" story showed no premonition of what would follow toward the end of 1933 – "trouble" in their little paradise.

Chapter 8
Trouble In Paradise
"Shut Up, and Kiss Me!"

"Champagne reflected in moonlight" aptly describes Paramount's *Trouble in Paradise*. Director Ernst Lubitsch's satirical treatment of jewel thievery translates to many as a cinematic love letter to Kay Francis and is considered her best film. She was Mariette Colet, a delightfully feminine captain of industry, smart and knowing. She seems bemused when she finds herself in the midst of a tantalizing erotic triangle. And how does this happen? She loses her enormously expensive handbag at the opera and discovers, with an air of delight, that its "honest finder," Gaston Monescu (Herbert Marshall) is not only *tres charmant*, but compellingly attractive as he murmurs his way into her employ and boudoir. Lubitsch disregarded Aladar Laszlo's play, from which the film was

Director Ernst Lubitsch's exquisite Trouble in Paradise *(1932). Miriam Hopkins observes Herbert Marshall and Kay lock eyes. "Miriam Hopkins may receive first billing," columnist Jimmy Starr wrote, "but Kay Francis...steals the honors." (Paramount)*

loosely adapted, and concentrated on the intriguing situations and characters. The play, *A Becsuletes Magtalalo* (*The Honest Finder*), opened in Budapest in December 1931. The central character, Monescu, was based on the famous Hungarian swindler Georges Manolescue, whose *Memoirs*, published in 1907, had inspired several films.

The famous Lubitsch touch is felt everywhere, from the opening shot of an operatic trash collector maneuvering through Venice in his gondola, to Monescu's fond farewell to Mariette. By the *finis* one sees Monescu as a professional, whose skills and manipulations are simply poetic justice. The elaborate lifestyle of Mariette Colet and her well-heeled crowd is begging to be robbed, preferably by an equally elegant, clever master. What sets Mariette apart, is that she seems to realize this necessity, hence her gracious attitude upon Monescu's departure. At his leave, she nods dreamily to his query: "Do you know what you're missing?" The audience understands exactly, the content of her reverie, before Monescu lovingly, playfully, reaches for the pearl necklace tucked away in his pocket. "No," he tells her, holding up his farewell heist. "*That's* what you're missing...your gift to *her*." Without skipping a beat, Mariette graciously complies with his confession, and the intended gift for the *other* woman in his life. She replies, bittersweetly, "With compliments of Colet and Company."

The third party of Lubitsch's triangle is the zesty, if high-strung, Miriam Hopkins. She is Monescu's comrade in crookedness, Lily. It's difficult to believe that Monescu prefers her to the shimmering Kay Francis. The answer to this incongruity is best put in the words of Lubitsch author Scott Eyman. "Love and larceny not only coexist, they positively bask in each other's company."[1] Monescu and Lily are addicted to the thrill of thievery and the competitive edge that compels them.

After rejecting the casting choices Paramount gave Lubitsch for the picture, he had no trouble coming up with his own. He had already written parts for specific actors: Edward Everett Horton and Charlie Ruggles. Lubitsch had considered working with Kay earlier that year in *One Hour With You*. When he realized the male lead, Maurice Chevalier, had his hungry eye on Kay, Lubitsch avoided the inevitable complications. He cast Jeanette MacDonald instead. Lubitsch was well aware of Herbert Marshall's reputation with women. "While very much married, Marshall managed affairs with both Kay Francis and Miriam Hopkins," says Eyman, "as well as a serious relationship with Gloria Swanson, all within the pace of a few years." If Marshall and Kay *did* have an affair, it was not mentioned in her diary. As for Hopkins, Lubitsch was also attracted to her. He liked her. "He may have been the only person in show business who did," Eyman clarified. "Hopkins managed to simultaneously entice him and keep him at arm's length. Photographer John Engstead referred to her as 'that old...bitch. You should have seen how cute she was with Ernst Lubitsch. And Lubitsch never saw through her.'" As a reward for taunting him, Lubitsch kept casting Hopkins in his films, which propelled her into the realm of top-ranking stars. Hopkins was a handful. According to Eyman: "There were the usual...complications, courtesy of the frantic Miriam Hopkins. In one scene, Hopkins ruthlessly upstaged Kay Francis by slowly turning the chair in which she was sitting until her profile had magically become her entire face."[2] After Kay complained to Lubitsch, the problem was resolved simply by nailing the chair to the floor. Onscreen, Francis seems amused by the perpetually agitated Hopkins. The contrast between the two provides a silkier edge to Marshall's scenes with Francis. Francis and Hopkins weren't necessarily feuding throughout the making of the film. They were frequently on one another's dinner guest list during the 1930s and a few years later it was Kay who accompanied Miriam and Miriam's adopted son to Reno when Hopkins divorced director Anatole Litvak.

Trouble in Paradise establishes sexual innuendo in the opening credits with its title superimposed above an elegant double bed. We are introduced to the gentleman-thief Monescu (Marshall) in his posh hotel room ordering a "most marvelous supper" that he and his guest Lily (Hopkins) "may not eat." We then relocate to the environs of Colet and Company, a French *perfumerie*. Their motto is: "Remember, it doesn't matter what you say, it doesn't matter how you look, it's how you smell." The head, the beautiful and frivolous head of the company, is Mariette Colet (Francis). As to the board's decision on salary cuts, she simply announces "Leave things where they are!" Business bores her, and besides, she has a luncheon engagement. The two plots are joined together at the opera where Monescu steals Mariette's bejeweled purse. The opera score itself spoofs love relationships. Performed in English—we hear an ACT I aria in which the soprano warbles, "I love you. I love you. I love you." Pages of the conductor's score fly by to ACT III and we hear the inevitable "I hate you!"

Responding to an advertisement for the return of the lost evening bag and a reward of 20,000 francs, Monescu, guised as Monsieur La Valle, shows up at Mariette's home. With flirtatious charm he critiques her love letters, offers advice on the correct shades of lipstick and powder for her complexion, and chastises her for not having more than 100,000 francs in her safe. "If I were your father, which fortunately I am not," he advises, "and you made any attempt to handle your own business affairs, I would give you a good spanking. In a business way, of course." Kay responds with, "What would you do if you were my secretary?" "The same thing," he assures her. She leans back, smiling and *very* interested. "You're hired!" she declares. As Mariette and Gaston's affair ripens, Lubitsch teases the viewers' imagination using a series of visuals: an Art Deco clock defines the length of the romantic interlude; a telephone is left unanswered; and nearby, a champagne bottle's cork has been "popped." Parting glances contain revelations of unspoken dialogue. One interlude finds Mariette postponing her departure for a dinner engagement. Gaston reluctantly encourages her to leave. "I don't want people to talk," he tells her.

> "Talk, about me? About us?" she queries.
> "Precisely," he says.
> "Afraid I'm ruining your reputation, Monsieur LaValle?"
> "No, yours, Madame."
> "I wouldn't hesitate one instant to ruin *your* reputation," she says, seductively snapping her fingers, "like that!"
> "You wouldn't?" he asks, their lips only inches apart.
> "No, I wouldn't."
> He snaps his fingers and echoes, "Like that?"
> She snaps her fingers again. "Like that," she assures him. She puts an end to the dialogue commanding, "*Shut up and kiss me!*"

Kay's character employs some of the "Lubitsch touch" when two of her suitors (Charlie Ruggles and Edward Everett Horton) propose marriage. With self-assurance, she rejects both of them. "You see, Francois, marriage is a beautiful mistake which two people make together. But with you, Francois, I think it would be a mistake." To Ruggles, she logically offers, "Don't be so downhearted, Major. You're not the *only* one I don't love."

Throughout the film Lubitsch establishes the tentative nature of romantic relationships. At the film's *finis*, Mariette discovers Gaston's secret: he's an imposter. She is saddened, but philosophical. What could have been, simply wasn't meant to be. Their parting is a gracious one. He escapes into the unknown with his "sweet little pickpocket," Lily.

From the get-go, reviews for the film were glowing. Columnist Jimmy Starr pointed out, "Miriam Hopkins may receive first billing on the credit card, but Kay Francis, borrowed from Warner Brothers...steals the honors."[3] Previewed for the *Los Angeles Record*, Llewellyn Miller wrote, "*Trouble in Paradise* is as fragile as an orchid and just about as rare. It is pictures like this which make people like me decide that life spent in theaters is worth while after all." *Variety*, missed the gondola all together. "Swell title, poor picture," said the reviewer. "Will have box office trouble." On the east coast, *The New York Times*, concurred with the L.A. critics about "the alert-minded Ernst Lubitsch's...shimmering, engaging piece of work...the only person in Hollywood who could have turned out such an effective entertainment from such a feathery story." Happily, *Trouble in Paradise* provided Kay the opportunity to prove herself as a captivating comedienne. Her sleek energy and wry wit leave the viewer intoxicated, satisfied.

Cheerfully amoral, when *Trouble in Paradise* was up for reissue in 1935, it was rejected by the Production Code. The Code forbade a story focused on sexual swapping and unpunished crime. Lubitsch had a world view that embraced, wholeheartedly, the sexual being. When it was reported that his brother, Richard, had died of a heart attack while visiting a brothel, Lubitsch wasn't fazed in the least. "Kings and princes die in whorehouses," he told his niece. "Why should we be ashamed?" The rest of his family remained embarrassed and appalled.[4] The scourge of the Production Code kept *Trouble in Paradise* out of circulation for decades. It was only shown at private film festivals, which kept its reputation alive as one of the best film comedies. Lubitsch was in attendance at a 1947 screening presented by the Great Films Society at Rexford School in Beverly Hills. Buoyed by an appreciative audience viewing *Trouble in Paradise*, Lubitsch knew it would always be a consensus classic. He died a few months later. Film critic Leslie Halliwell wrote with rapturous delight about the film. "It has been in my mind and my heart since the Sunday morning in 1949 when Cambridge's Film Society, a thousand strong, rose to it as one man and gave it a deafening ovation; later I booked it at the Rex as a double bill with *French without Tears*...we had to turn hundreds away, after which it became as firm a favourite as *Genevieve*, *The Lavender Hill Mob*, or anything starring the Marx Brothers."[5] Lubitsch and his cast captured an elegance and effortless grace that escapes modern filmmakers. The film's intelligence and polish remain unmatched.

When Kay returned to Warners, she was supposed to have had a lead in the grandfather of the modern musical, Busby Berkeley's *42nd Street*. The filming of *Trouble in Paradise* had gone over schedule. Kay was understandably upset and let the front office know about it. She had been replaced with Bebe Daniels (who, incidentally, Kay had replaced as Hollywood's foremost bridge champion). Kay was compensated by the studio with a loan out to Samuel Goldwyn for one of the best marital dramas of the 1930s, *Cynara*.

Adapted for the screen from the 1930 British play, which alludes to Ernest Dowson's line "I have been faithful to thee, Cynara, in my fashion," the film is told in flashback. It was one of the earliest uses of this technique in the sound era. Considered daring for its time, the courageous production was under King Vidor's direction. Vidor was responsible for such classics as *The Big Parade, The Champ,* and *Stella Dallas*. In *Cynara* he creates a film with great feeling and emotional texture. At the film's outset we are confronted with a married couple, Ronald Colman and Kay Francis, in the process of separating after seven years together. His infidelity has caused a public scandal and ruined his career as barrister. Kay inquires in earnest to Colman, "What happened to you? Inside you?" This prompts the flashback that details Colman's relationship with a poor shopgirl (Phyllis Barry). The affair took place while his wife, Clemency (Kay), was chaperoning her sister in Venice. Colman cautioned the girl of his marriage and that any relationship with him could hold no happiness for her. Sadly, the girl becomes *obsessed* with him. There's something foreboding about her as she pleads to Colman. "Nothing matters if you're fond of a person. I'd never be a nuisance." Well, it *does* matter...and she *is* a nuisance...a dangerous one. There are shades of *Fatal Attraction* when the girl threatens to kill herself. For 1930s' audiences, sympathies are thrown in favor of Colman, after all, he wasn't the girl's *first*. The film's moralistic views almost make it a timepiece. It's the acting and the sense of compassion experienced between Colman and Francis that stand the test of time.

When Kay and Colman are reunited after her return from Venice, she senses something is amiss. Her inquiries as to his activities in her absence provoke his guilty conscience. "Why do you want to talk of all this?" he says with agitation. Taken aback, she quietly says to herself, "Sometimes I wonder if one ought to be so sure." Together, Kay and Colman create a sustained emotional integrity and *connection*. The final shot of their reunion aboard the ship is done without dialogue, but has pages of feeling to create a powerful moment for the film's finish.

The New York Times praised the film, saying, "King Vidor...gives to his scenes effective and restrained guidance...Kay Francis and Phyllis Barry do their share to make this tragic tale quite convincing...Mr. Colman gives an ingratiating portrayal..." *Film Daily* thought *Cynara* to be a "strikingly done drama...looks like a candidate for listing among the "ten best." Louella Parsons cheered, "A great team, Ronald Colman and Kay Francis. She is particularly charming and effective as the wife. No one on the screen can play the lady with more finesse and more realism than Miss Francis. King Vidor does a superb piece of direction...one of the finest of the 1932 product."[6]

In the biography *A Very Private Person,* Colman's daughter, Juliet Benita Colman, commented on the similar acting styles of her father and Kay. "Kay Francis had the same wide, generous brown eyes as Ronnie, and was equally adept in projecting her thoughts in such a manner that each member of the audience felt he alone really knew what the character on screen was going through."[7] Initially, Colman was hesitant to play an adulterer. Producer Arthur Hornblow impressed him otherwise. When asked to comment on her role of Clemency and if modern women would similarly overreact, Kay responded:

> Not sophisticated wives. But they are a minority. There are thousands
> of women all over the country who could never bring themselves to live
> with their husbands again after finding out an infidelity. As in Pittsfield,
> Massachusetts, where I once lived. Women in that town...would have felt
> the blow to their pride too severely to make up after a public scandal such
> as followed the husband's affair in *Cynara*. I think that's true of so many
> divorces. It's pride that goads women on to an unforgiving attitude. They

simply can't believe it, and they can't walk out of the house and know the neighbors are whispering.[8]

Kay's reference to Pittsfield is telling. She still harbored disappointment from the collapse of her marriage to the philandering Dwight Francis. Her friend Lois Long commented on the difficulty Kay faced in her marriages. "Kay had this exotic exterior, and people who were attracted to that were always disappointed because she was a regular guy...one of our gang said later that Kay should have married, had lots of children, run the Women's Club and everything else in some small city. But the kind of men who would marry a gal who would do that were frightened by her exterior. She always said, 'I'm not an actress, I'm a personality.' But she would have fared better if she could have been just a wife."[9]

Cynara, Trouble in Paradise and *One Way Passage* were all featured when the "best lists" for 1932 were published; a banner year for Kay, as far as quality films were concerned. She would give credit to the directors of these successes, saying, "The story is not the most important factor. It is the director who has the greatest influence on both the film as a whole and an actress's individual performance in particular. I owe a lot to the men who have directed me and have brought out acting abilities which with less understanding direction, I might never have shown."[10]

Kay's modest appraisal of her abilities was typical of her. Social enigma Elsa Maxwell called Kay a "veritable Hollywood phenomenon because never, not for a split second, does she kid herself into believing that she is the world's greatest star. And this...is rare indeed, in that part of California where egos grow faster than oranges and taller than palms."[11] However, Kay did admit to *Woman's Fair*, "I'd be horribly disappointed if no one ever wanted my autograph. I like fan mail and the more I get the happier I am. Not simply because it feeds my vanity, but because I get a great deal of pleasure from the thought that people are interested in me."[12] "But on the other side," Kay admitted to Faith Service, "well, there is the time Ken and I went to Coney Island...I wanted, awfully, to ride on the roller coasters, and to have a bicepy male with an East Side accent guess my weight...and I wanted to ride the unicorn on the merry-go-round and...I wanted to buy lemonade and popcorn and have *fun*. I couldn't do *anything*. We were recognized. We were followed from place to place. *We* had to go. I felt quite bitter and childishly disappointed about it all. That night, Fame seemed to weigh almost nothing on the scales."[13] Kay's experiences in crowds had staying power. In the late 1940s Kay attended Broadway's *Annie Get Your Gun* with her close friends Jetti and Lou Ames. Lou noted how leery Kay was of being recognized and mixing out in public.

Although fans were deprived of consuming stories about Kay's personal life, they were privy to her intelligent responses on a variety of subjects. She liked talking about *ideas*. Among her favorite authors (she was always reading) were Hemingway and the psychological-sexual jottings of Arthur Schnitzler (Kubrick's *Eyes Wide Shut* was adapted from Schnitzler's *Traumnovelle*).[14] She may have made the best-dressed lists, but Kay was always included among the most intelligent women in Hollywood. In 1933, *The New York Times* listed Kay among the ten 'brainiest' women of the screen. The selection was made by Maxwell Arnow, a casting director, who saw himself as an authority on the subject. He met with the women only on a business basis. Arnow commented, "They know what they want, they know how to get what they want, and they know what to do with what they wanted when they get it."[15] Kay's comrades in brains also included Aline MacMahon, Ann Harding, Helen Hayes, Miriam Hopkins and Katharine Hepburn. Dick Mook, who interviewed all the big names in Hollywood, said matter-of-factly, "Kay is one of the most intelligent women I have ever met—anywhere."[16] "You cannot talk to her five minutes without being conscious of it," Mook emphasized. "Although she talks glibly, she doesn't talk just to be talking. Except when she's kidding, everything she says *means* something. Once when I commented on her intelligence she looked vaguely alarmed. 'I don't know that I *am* particularly intelligent,' she said slowly, 'but if I am, please don't ever stress it.' 'Why not?' I asked, amazed. 'Because there is nothing that frightens people so much as a reputation for intelligence. It makes them afraid to talk to you—to open up and be themselves.'"[17] Mook felt Kay was "Far too intelligent not to give a great deal of thought to her career and everything concerned with it."[18] Kay gave a tongue-in-cheek reason for *not* divulging personal information to interviewers. "Business training teaches one *not* to volunteer information," she declared. "Thanks to my training in the business world I keep a secretary-like silence about…my employer, who happens to be myself."[19]

While on the set, Kay didn't care to entertain publicity hounds with opinions about *anything*. It was her approach to concentrate and sustain her role's character between takes. Kay compared her concentration to a switchboard operator plugging cords in and out in a rapid maze. "Plugging your own emotions in and out at the same rate all day," Kay claimed, "is infinitely more wearing."[20] Reporter Dick Mook noted, "There are few actresses who concentrate between shots on their next scene as Kay does. So, when the publicity departments persist in bringing writers up to her on the set she closes up like a clam. She can't help it and she doesn't bother to explain. 'Explanations always sound so fishy,' she says."[21]

While still at Paramount Kay had a scheduled interview and when the newswoman walked onto the set Kay let out a scream at the very sight of her. The poor reporter became so distraught that she was sent home in hysterics.[22] A few years later, Kay wasn't faring any better with newshounds on the set. While concentrating on her most challenging role as Florence Nightingale, reporter William Fleming French incredulously came up to her and asked the clam-ish Kay how she managed to keep her morning freshness. Kay sat there in 90-degree heat wearing a cumbersome nurse's uniform and wool shawl. "Get plenty of sleep," she snapped, trying to control herself. "Without it you are sure to have that tired look, and that, if I may say so, is…very uninteresting…" When he dared ask her about dieting, Kay, who never had a weight problem, said that diets led to food binges. "What this does to beauty," she added dismissively, "is something too sad to discuss."[23] As the confused French tried to avoid the glaring sun he failed to get the *real* message and leave her alone. Kay brusquely commented, "Squinting eyes may be attractive, but I've never met anyone who thought so."[24] The bewildered French managed to concoct an article out of Kay's remarks, referring to them as "beauty hints." Kay's views on the subject of writers dropping in on actors in the middle of their work, was given a very logical explanation to reporter Harry Evans. "What if I tried that on one of them?" Kay queried. "What if I went charging into the newspaper office of a columnist when he was trying to make a deadline, proof-reading his copy, or trying to think up an idea? Do you know what would happen? I do. I'd be thrown out on my ear—that's what."[25]

Back at Warners for the New Year 1933, Kay was teamed for the first of six times with George Brent. "In their day," wrote James Robert Parish, in his 1974 book *Hollywood's Great Love Teams*, "Francis-Brent were Warner Bros. melodrama equivalent of MGM's droll Myrna Loy and William Powell, and were regarded by the bulk of steady filmgoers as the height of refined, upper class romantics; personified, sartorial elegance."[26] Michael Curtiz, who would go on to direct the classic *Casablanca*, was at the helm for the Francis-Brent feature *The Keyhole*. *The Keyhole* was originally slated for a seventh teaming of William Powell and Kay. While no *One Way Passage*, the provocative adult drama solidi-fied the look, feel, tempo, atmosphere and essence of what became the trademark of a Kay Francis Warners feature. Sporting a newly designed hairdo by Perc Westmore, Kay was ready for the graceful entrances, lingering exits, the showcasing of Orry-Kelly gowns, the employ of unique Francis gesture—all of which provided the viewer a pulsating world of romance nicely underscored with compelling music.

In *The Keyhole*, Kay's oily ex-husband (Monroe Owsley) sends her a suicide note to get her attention. Arriving hurriedly to his cheap hotel room, she finds him cheerily drinking milk in lieu of poison. Yanking a costly necklace from her elegant fur-lined neck, he threatens to blackmail her. Repulsed by his behavior, she makes him a propo-sition. "The next time you try to kill yourself," she snarls, "let me know. I'd love to help you." Wanting to keep the incident from her rich, elderly husband, Kay flees to Havana after hatching a scheme to rid herself of Owsley.

While on deck, bound for Havana, Kay meets George Brent who is tailing her at her husband's request. Even though Brent is the least dynamic of actors, the camera picks up a wonderful energy between he and Kay. With the classic tango "La Cumparsita" playing in the background, the camera pans across the ship's deck to discover Francis and Brent basking in the moonlight. The dance floor is just behind them, the song ends, there is applause. Brent comments that there is a mere half-inch between them and the unfathomable ocean depths. "Sounds dangerous," responds Kay with a sensuous, knowing smile. It's a lovely vignette— the very kind that audiences came to expect from a Kay Francis picture. And the *clothes*...Warners was well aware of Kay's unique ability of inviting the audience to notice what she was wearing and somehow enhance the proceedings in doing so. It meant box-office. It sold. In *The Keyhole*, Kay's costume changes consisted of twenty-three eye-catching creations, out-topping Ruth Chatterton's competitive twenty-two outfits in 1932's *The Crash*. That would average three minutes per ensemble for *The Keyhole's* sixty-nine minutes.

The Francis-Brent chemistry in *The Keyhole* held the story together nicely. Their scenes were juxtaposed with the frothy antics of Glenda Farrell's blonde shill and Allen Jenkins as Brent's numbskull assistant. The story is resolved when Owsley conveniently plummets to his demise from Kay's second-story hotel room and her elderly husband storms off in a huff and out of her life. The camera then retreats through the keyhole leaving us with a Francis-Brent clinch sealed with a kiss. *The Keyhole* was revamped in 1948 for Doris Day's Curtiz-directed film debut, the Technicolor musical *Romance on the High Seas*.

Critics may not have been overly enthusiastic, but the *New York Times* thought *The Keyhole* had "many amusing moments; Miss Francis acts her role with the desired lightness; a good-natured piece of work." Jerry Hoffman in the *Los Angeles Examiner* wrote, "Aside from the usual display of wardrobe given Kay Francis, there is Kay herself, as warm and appealing a personality the screen has to offer. There is a lack of artificiality about Miss Francis that makes her refreshing."

Mary Stevens, M.D. (1933) Kay arrives to deliver a baby. She also happily has one of her own...out of wedlock. (Warners)

While audiences were lapping up *The Keyhole*, Kay helped William Powell lap up beer to celebrate the demise of Prohibition in April 1933. Congress signed the "Beer Bill" on April 4, "declaring that 3.2% beer was not intoxicating."[27] (In 2005 most marketed beers were 2.5-2.8%). Powell threw a "My First Legal Drunk" party at the Little Club of the Ambassador Hotel. Kay, Powell, Carole Lombard, director Wesley Ruggles, among others, smiled for photographers and drank their darnedest to see if Congress had made the right decision. "Drunk as Naldi," Kay wrote into her diary after one such 1933 festivity.[28] Kay was referring to silent screen siren Nita Naldi who had turned to drink and referred to herself as "Dracula in Drag." Kay herself was no slouch when it came to the drinking sweepstakes and occasionally got upset with herself. After one of Ruth Chatterton's dinner parties, Kay wrote, "Me <u>very</u> tight. <u>Damn it</u>," then added in shorthand, "I got really disgracefully drunk. And I am very ashamed." [29]

In the eye-opening *Complicated Women: Sex and Power in Pre-Code Hollywood*, author Mick LaSalle comments on 1933 being the "last frontier presenting women on screen as successful professionals. Kay Francis, in the final stage of the era, emerged as an actress at home in such parts."[30] Kay's next film, *Mary Stevens, M.D.,* was such a role. The film was to be the second Francis-Brent team effort, but instead, Kay found herself playing opposite Lyle Talbot. They played fellow medical students who open an office together after graduation. Much to Kay's chagrin, Lyle doesn't see her in "that way." Instead, he is lured by a society blonde and the perks accompanying a social position. When his marriage goes sour he and Kay are reunited, romantically. There are complications with Talbot's divorce and Kay becomes pregnant. LaSalle adds, "If poverty made pregnancy difficult for her unmarried sisters, making a comfortable living turns pregnancy into an unalloyed joy for Mary Stevens. In one of the more unexpected moments in pre-Code cinema, Francis tells her assistant, 'Take a good grip on that desk, plant your feet firmly and prepare for the shock of your life. I'm going to have a baby…What's so funny about it? I didn't invent the idea. Women have been having babies for a long while.' When her assistant (Glenda Farrell) asks her if she is happy about it, she answers, 'Walking on air.'"[31]

Francis leaves for France to have her baby, giving time for Talbot to work things out. LaSalle noted that "as for sex, Francis was no prude on screen, and she was hardly a victim…She was also a real live actress…competent and emotionally honest—and she brought a natural authority to her roles as a professional woman…The movie ends with an affirmation of Mary Stevens as both a woman and a professional."[32] After the Code the film was not allowed a reissue as Francis was simply seen to be nothing other than an immoral woman. Virginia Kellogg, who wrote the story, would have to wait until 1949 after the easing of the Production Code for her Academy Award-nominated screenplay successes. Her equally complex and adult themes registered with solid impact in such classics as *White Heat* and 1950's *Caged*.

After the absorbing *Mary Stevens, M.D.* was released, Kay's diary indicated she was "up all night" using her doctoring skills on her dog Weenie. The importance of Weenie's recovery took precedence over the news of the film's mixed reception. *The New York Times* found *Mary Stevens, M.D.* to contain, "disagreeable circumstance…one of the shabbiest of the Hollywood contemplations of the medical profession. Kay Francis…is a woman physician who has a startling amount of trouble preserving a professional detachment toward the primitive emotions." The critic's bias and sexist opinion was not shared by the Los Angeles press who felt the production had excellent performances. *Variety* stated the film was, "exceptionally good adult entertainment…Kay Francis is always dignified, yet very personable, as Dr. Stevens…she avails herself of an unusual opportunity…which should add considerably to her popularity." Indeed, Kay's fan mail took a sudden leap and her sympathetic nature took some of her fan's jottings very seriously. Kay seemed down when Virginia T. Lane met her for an interview. She looked up at Lane from a letter she was holding, written by a young woman who had just seen *Mary Stevens, M.D.*; was afraid of losing her husband; and, was pleading Kay for advice. "I wish there was some way I could help," Kay said solemnly. "If there was *something* I could do about it…"[33] Lane acknowledged the difficulty getting Kay out of her doldrums.

Before Kay started filming *Mary Stevens, M.D.*, the studio amplified a part for her in Somerset Maugham's novel *The Narrow Corner*, co-starring Douglas Fairbanks, Jr. Those plans were set aside. A loan-out to MGM was set up for Kay to join Ann Harding in *When Ladies Meet*. Her part went to Myrna Loy. In its place, MGM gave Kay their most opulent treatment in the turbulent love triangle *Storm at Daybreak*. It would be her last loan-out from Warners. *Storm at Daybreak*, originally titled *Rhapsody*, was taken from the Hungarian play "Dark-Stemmed Cherries." Kay was replacing, of all people, Greta Garbo. Although she had not met Garbo, Kay did find her fascinating and remarked, "There's a different quality about Garbo…although she is giving everything when she expresses her emotions for a film scene, she simultaneously is a woman apart from everyone and every thing…I don't give a hang whether she's brilliant or dumb, or whether it's a magnificent act she's putting on about wanting to be alone. I believe that Garbo has utilized all kinds of artificialities to enhance her film glamour…so skillfully that she gives the impression of being a stern realist. She exudes beauty and strength."[34]

Storm at Daybreak contains one of Francis' most touching, complex and poignant performances. Unfortunately, Richard Boleslawski's uneven direction almost obliterates her fine intentions. The story is told of a Serbian mayor (Walter Huston), his wife Irina (Kay) and a dashing Hungarian cavalry commander (Nils Asther). The lavish film surrounds events of World War I with authentic-looking sequences of the assassination of Archduke Franz Ferdinand in 1914. Out of this turmoil an affecting romance emerges between Kay and Asther. Poetic interludes between the two are inviting: at the piano, she serenades Asther by candlelight; silhouetted behind a veiled window they share a stolen kiss; a light-hearted moment finds the pair under a tree as Kay feeds a playful colt—these scenes are nicely set up for the camera and performed emotionally on cue. Kay was given another opportunity to sing on screen with her husky contralto voice. This time she prerecorded a William Axt/Gus Kahn song, "Two Lips Like Cherries," with good acoustics which amplified her voice to a pleasing effect. The *LA Examiner* noted: "Kay adds a fine singing voice to her other accomplishments."

There is a touching climatic moment when a conflicted and guilt-ridden Kay urges Asther to leave and find, "some lovely, hateful girl. I hate her now," Kay sighs, "just thinking about her." The emotions run strong. The tears, real. Nils Asther is solidly in place as Kay's romantic interest. He finds himself torn between loyalty to his best friend (Huston), his attraction to his best friend's wife (Francis) and his role as commander of the invading army. Asther is as charismatic as he was riveting in *The Bitter Tea of General Yen*. Unfortunately, the script works against the full impact of Kay and Asther's work.

Bertram Millhauser's screenplay keeps drawing energy *away* from the romance and war background. Tossed in is some ridiculous nonsense in which Asther's regiment shows up at mayor Huston's mansion in the middle of the night to announce, "We came to look up a word in your dictionary!" What follows is like something out of a Marx Brothers comedy. A madcap gypsy band cavorts through the festivity, while Louise Closser Hale and Eugene Pallette mug their way through a senior-citizen flirtation! All of this takes away from the impact of the Francis-Asther-Huston triangle. In spite of the distractions, *Film Daily* took notice. "The development of their irresistible passion is beautifully and delicately handled in some finely restrained scenes that both Kay Francis and Asther handle well." According to Kay's diary their love scenes were less restrained when the camera wasn't rolling. On June 23 she entered, "Retakes MGM. That was the day I had lunch in Nils' dressing room at studio. Many kisses."[35]

On July 13, before Kay returned to Warners, she and Ken celebrated the fourth anniversary of consummating their relationship. The couple also benefitted from her prophetic powers and strong "premonitions." She told reporter Jack Grant about driving Kenneth out of Pismo Beach. "I had a foreboding of danger," she told Grant, "and slowed down to a few miles an hour while I attempted to see what the danger might be. There wasn't a thing to be seen. So I shook off the feeling and started to speed up again. Just then an orange truck came down a blind hill and ran into us…had we been going at any speed, we would all have been killed…if I had obeyed my hunch implicitly and not tried to regain speed, there would have been no accident at all. You can rest assured that I have never disobeyed since."[36]

Kay also developed a penchant for square dancing and encouraged Kenneth to help her throw a big barn dance. The hoe-down turned out to be the talk of all Holly-

wood. For an "oink oink here" and a "cluck, cluck there," Kay included real pigs, chickens, rabbits and geese and led her guests in a "do-se-do." Of the foray of stars that came
dressed accordingly, most notable was Gloria Swanson disguised as a very annoying
Huckleberry Finn. Swanson used her water-pistol on all the guests—it was loaded with
milk! Along about dawn, with hayseeds in their hair, a few celebs were taking punches at
each other. Kay would later top her Barnyard Brawl by concocting the *most* famous
Vendome party—she turned the entire restaurant, inside and out, into a luxury liner.

In June 1933, it was announced that cowgirl Kay would next be singing "Home on
the Range" to Edward G. Robinson in the David Karsner story *Red Meat*. Robinson was
set on having her co-star. It turned out to be a case of Robinson getting what he wanted,
but not wanting what he got. A month later Elizabeth Yeaman reported, "Kay Francis
fought strenuously against playing the feminine lead opposite Edward G. Robinson in *Red
Meat*, but she finally agreed…"[37] In her diary Kay wrote of her rebellion, "Big fight with
Hal Wallis re: *Red Meat*."[38] This was unusual for her. She usually agreed to whatever roles
the studio handed her. Kay's hesitation was actually more of a strong premonition of hers,
according to producer Hal Wallis. Wallis reflected in 1980 that Robinson "and his
costar…were oddly matched. Kay was so tall that we had to put Eddie on a box in some
scenes to bring him level with her and, understandably, he was humiliated. Irritable and
self-conscious, he argued with Kay frequently. But he was a gentleman, and years later,
when he wrote his memoirs, gave credit to her fine acting."[39]

I Loved a Woman anticipates *Citizen Kane*, as Robinson's character (John Hayden)
changes from an idealistic, artistic young man into a ruthless, unscrupulous businessman.
He is thrust into a career in the meat packing industry and we witness how he is transformed
into a conscienceless man who sells embalmed beef to the U.S. army. His wife (Genevieve
Tobin) is only interested in high society and he soon is distracted by a lovely opera singer,
Laura McDonald (Kay, vocals dubbed by Rose Dirman). Kay asks him for a loan to sponsor
her career and her studies in Europe. "I've come to talk to you as one giant to another!" she
announces. "Here's my proposition. I'm as sure of success as I am of death!" He shows
interest. A great deal of interest. She understands, perfectly. She invites him to her flat for an
"aria." Upon hearing her voice he tells her, "You *compel* me to think it's beautiful." Later, after
one of their trysts, he confesses that he loves her. "There's no reason why you shouldn't," Kay
says matter-of-factly. When he proposes marriage, she discourages him. "If you really knew
me, you wouldn't want to marry me," she cautions. She encourages him instead to dream on
a large scale with what life and his heritage has given him: the meat packing business. "Our
love will lead us to greater things," she says determinedly. He listens. He now has two obsessions: his mistress and financial gain. He gives up on the losing proposition of selling quality
beef and goes for the jugular of condemned and embalmed beef. He makes millions. When
chastised about his "new" ethics, his peers call him a madman. He simply states the obvious.
"It's madmen who run the world today!"

The pre-Code flavor is heavily accented in a scene where Robinson happens upon
Kay entertaining another man. Robinson is upset, angry and confronts her. Author Mick
LaSalle noticed that "Robinson is disillusioned, but the point of the scene is not that she's
a whore but a grown-up. 'You've lost nothing,' she tells him, 'because you never *were* the
only one.'"[40] Kay is confident and self-assured. She has exactly the kind of outlook that
would be obliterated from filmmaking after the Production Code took effect. "I'm trying
in my way to be honest with you," she assures Robinson. "I never cared how many loves

you had besides me." Today, Kay comes across as the sanest member of the cast. Her character is honest and straightforward.

Eleanor Barnes, of the *LA Illustrated Daily News,* wrote, "In the gallery of Edward G. Robinson—the portrait of John Hayden will stand out as a strange and much-discussed one." Barnes made of point of saying, "Kay Francis...voices no regret when the man who backs her career discovers her ability to philander." *Film Weekly* referred to Kay's ability in turning her characterization, "to brilliant account." In 1973, Robinson published his memoirs, *All My Yesterdays,* and paid Kay a belated tribute after viewing *I Loved a Woman.* "Let me give a small bow to Kay Francis...She had that indefinable presence that somehow enabled her to be convincing as well as beautiful."[41] According to James Robert Parish, "*I Loved a Woman* gave a glimpse of the career problems Kay was to face at Warners. Third-billed Genevieve Tobin, as Robinson's wife, received equal screen time to Kay. Three of Kay's best scenes were deleted from the release print and despite her lofty status the studio gave her only featured billing."[42]

Warners next tried to please Kay by offering a project tailor-made for her, *Newspaper Woman.* It was axed. Then, Kay and Paul Muni were considered for the leads in *Ever in My Heart,* which became a Barbara Stanwyck feature. Jesse Lasky wanted to borrow Kay for *The Worst Woman in Paris* at Fox. Finally, Kay was given a Ruth Chatterton reject for her last release in 1933: *The House on 56th Street.* Lawrence J. Quirk's 1974 volume, *The Great Romantic Films,* paid tribute to the film.

> *The House on 56th Street* is not only the perfect Kay Francis vehicle— it is a touching nostalgic romance that haunts the memory. The film also contains Kay Francis's finest performance, in the type of role that made her a household name in the 1930's. Miss Francis keeps expertly abreast of the story line's downward trend, running the gamut from bright hopefulness...to the embittering realities of an aging woman buffeted by fate. The film does full credit to the distinctive talents of Kay Francis, one of the more underrated stars of her era. A handsome, poised woman with... considerable technical resource as an actress, portraying the many ways of love with an eloquent sincerity of cool authority.[43]

A film with many twists and turns, *The House on 56th Street* afforded Kay the opportunity to be implicated in the manslaughter of her former paramour, then sent to prison for a twenty-year stretch. Upon release, she adjusts to the Jazz Age world of the 20s and gets a fresh start as a card-shark. As if this isn't enough! She finds employment in a gambling hall that had been the very home she had once cherished as a young bride. Poker-face Kay is very convincing, she never breaks and her portrayal has authenticity.

Jerry Hoffman of the *Los Angeles Examiner* commented, "Ruth Chatterton is said to have refused *The House on 56th Street* as a vehicle. Kay Francis finds in it an opportunity to do some of the best dramatic work of her career." Some viewers commented that there was too much story and not enough time. The early scenes establishing Kay's marriage to Gene Raymond were abrupt. However, the final moments of Francis' reunion with her long-lost daughter (Margaret Lindsay) have an electric edge. Francis' skills as a card-shark place Lindsay's marriage in jeopardy. But Lindsay, a compulsive gambler, learns an important lesson from a woman (Kay) she doesn't realize is her own mother.

Photoplay thought *The House on 56th Street* had an epic quality. "Kay Francis' superb performance of a rich role, lift this tale into poignant, compelling drama...it's grandly done by all and Kay is superb throughout." Critic Frederic F. Van de Water had definite convictions about Kay's ability to bring out the best in her co-stars. "Good acting by all concerned makes this a good picture...thanks to the glamorous art of Kay Francis...in [her] smooth performance as Peggy. Miss Francis is one of the blessed who never overact. She has converted the rest of the cast, who behave like human beings throughout." The phenomenal financial and critical success of *The House on 56th Street* was repeated overseas. "Kay Francis read *The House on 56th Street* with an open mind, and accepted it," observed Britain's *Film Weekly*.

The House on 56th Street *(1933) was a box-office giant for Kay. She runs the gamut from young wife, to prison inmate, to embittered card-shark. Kay was paired with Gene Raymond in the 69-minute "epic."* (Warners)

"She did not feel slighted because she was second choice for the vehicle. The finished film did more for her than any other picture she has made at Warners. She became emphatically a power to be reckoned with at the box-office."[44] Kay joked about the epoch saga, saying, "If it does better than my other films, it's because I parade thirty-six costumes instead of sixteen."[45]

By the close of 1933, Kay's arduous regimen at the studios was nothing to joke about. Her schedule had taxed her, physically and emotionally. Kay's diary entries denote the toll it took on her. By the time she left for New York in December 1933, she was eager to leave the Hollywood routine behind.

Before leaving for New York, Kay and Kenneth threw a party at Arrowhead Hot Springs. It was one of Kay's favorite getaways. She would often escape her weekly schedule to spend weekends at a friend's cabin at Arrowhead Lake. Ninety minutes east of Los Angeles, at an elevation of 1800 feet, the climate at Arrowhead was invigorating. Steam caves were carved into the heart of the mountain and were reached within elevators from the main hotel building. Mud baths and gurgling hot and cold springs were a favorite natural resource of pleasure for the film colony. Kay and Kenneth's party consisted of Kay, Kenneth, Bill Powell, Carole Lombard and Richard and Jessica Barthelmess. Aside from enjoying the springs, the revelers sported mountain togs and ate dinners barbeque-style outdoors. But the revelry was not necessarily reflected in the depths of Lake Arrowhead. Kay and Kenneth's marriage was in trouble.

A few weeks later, before departing for New York, Kay and Kenneth attended the Eddie Cantor film *Roman Scandals*. The couple seemed happy and contented. So, it came as a complete surprise on December 20 when the newspapers reported that the two were "amicably separating." Kay's diary marked September 30, 1933 with the first mention of real trouble. She wrote, "Kenneth and I had big fight. We are going to get divorce!"[46] In spite of Kenneth's intention of staying on the west coast, his work frequently took him to New York. While Kay's career soared, he had been fired from Fox, which seemed to sour his attitude about Hollywood and his marriage. Kay had moved back to the W.S. Hart home on De Longpre. Their relationship was held together at this point by Kenneth's occasional visits from back east. They had little opportunity to nurture their relationship and preserve what Kay referred to as a "fragile sense of reciprocation" that keeps a marriage alive. That June she had told Virginia Maxwell for *Photoplay*, "Granted two people are well mated, the loveliness of that marriage relationship need never become tarnished if each one remembers that the beauty of love is an illusion. Each must work to preserve that intangible thing, and it is the little courtesies, the little exchanges which grow into every marriage, which are stronger than tangible bonds. Only when this fragile sense of reciprocation has fled...do we realize what had been given us—to preserve or destroy."[47]

While promoting the release of *The House on 56th Street* in New York, Kay's diary told of the underlying tension in the relationship, referring to Kenneth as *Mister MacKenna*. Her use of his surname, as she now often referred to him, indicated there was no love lost between them. On one occasion Ken had hit her and when the going got too rough she spent the night at the studio. Kay would sometimes go for the jugular herself, knowing that Kenneth had qualms about changing his name from Mielziner to MacKenna. She referred to him as a turncoat Jew. The next day she would regret her remarks and refer to herself as a "pretty stupid, unattractive person."[48]

When Kay made one last attempt to mend things with Kenneth in New York, he wasn't reciprocating. She found solace while attending *The Dark Tower*, a new play by Alexander Woollcott and George S. Kaufman. It told of an actress who is in top form, except when her sinister husband induces a trance-like state in her! By coincidence, the murder-mystery's scenic designer was Kenneth's brother, Jo Mielziner. Kay also attended Miriam Hopkins' *Jezebel* and the critical disaster *The Lake*, starring Katharine Hepburn. Hepburn's co-star, Colin Clive, soon got a hurried call from Hollywood for a lead role in a film planned for Kay and William Powell, titled *The Key*. (The Michael Curtiz picture, about the Irish rebellion in the 1920s, was filmed later without Kay.) Kay's sad-merry romp continued, as noted in her diary for December 31, "Bee's lunch for gang...Tennis later...then to Jo Forrestal's for dinner and on to Winthrop Aldrich's party at the club. Swell fun!"[49] George Eells gave his slant on Kay's crowd: "Bee was Beatrice Ames Stewart, a Santa Barbara society girl who had married writer-wit Donald Ogden Stewart. The guest lists of Bee Stewart, Jo Forrestal and Winthrop Aldrich...were composed of a sprinkling of Old Society, Café Society, playboys, artists, playgirls, writers, songwriters and assorted bohemians. These were the lucky ones, who at the height of the Great Depression were still clinging to the merry-go-round that had rudely dislodged so many riders in 1929."[50] Underneath the "swell fun," Kay was still hurting. This was her second trip to New York in an attempt to save her marriage. There were days when Kay wasn't feeling up to the social whirl and she retreated to her farmhouse near Cape Cod.

After a final attempt at reconciliation, Kay returned to Hollywood. A stewardess commented that Kay cried all the way across the continent. Dick Mook reported that a well-known prizefighter bragged about accompanying Kay en route and was puzzled by her behavior. The prizefighter had been trounced at Madison Square Garden two nights before and came west on the same train as Kay. Mook added that the fighter,

> had a couple of the most beautiful black eyes I have ever seen. When he arrived in Los Angeles Mushy Callahan introduced me to him and he began telling me about Kay—and raving over her. "Sumpin' was wrong with her, too," he said, "because she was wearing dark glasses like me—only her eyes was red and swole from crying…we gets to Chicago and dere's de press. Me and Miss Francis had never been introduced, but dey sticks us up on one of dem trucks dey use to haul baggage around on and gets ready to take pictures of us. Den dey says, 'Off wit de glasses!' an' Miss Francis says to me, 'You keep those glasses on. If people see a picture of you with eyes like those you're cooked,' and den she turns around to de photographers and says, 'all right, boys, I'll take mine off, but he's keeping his on.'" "I wish," he finished, "some of de guys I've fought was good a sport as she is."

Mook emphasized that the photographers resented Kay, "because even though she had kept a fighter from losing his prestige, it meant they had lost what they considered a scoop."[51] They were unable to appreciate that even amidst her lowest of lows, Kay could take her mind off herself and come to someone else's rescue. Kay, surprisingly, shared a few intimacies to media magnate Harry Evans regarding her separation from Kenneth. It was a subject that Evans would never have broached, but Kay offered him an explanation, "Knowing Ken and me as well as you do, I suppose you were a bit surprised when I first told you about our decision. We tried very hard to make our marriage a success. We gave it every possible chance. I know it is quite possible for a husband and wife to work and still not let their careers interfere with their domestic relations. Ken and I have friends who have made a go of it. But the situation is never easy, and in our case—well—we never found the formula."[52]

Back at home, Kay mended her emotional wounds. In the New Year of 1934 Kay and Kenneth's marriage resolved itself. On February 21, a subdued Katharine Mielziner testified in court that Leo Mielziner nagged and harassed her. "He didn't like my selection of a home, my manner of dressing, or even my acting. He assumed an air of superiority and for months made slighting remarks about me." The gallant MacKenna maintained his silence. The divorce was granted in three minutes. Kay commented to a friend regarding the notoriety of her divorce, saying, "They want to know everything *now*—in six weeks they will have forgotten we were married."[53] Kay decided never to marry again.

Chapter 9

Pre-Code Kay:
Trollop, Mistress, Obstetrician, Revolutionary

1934—A year of transition for the Hollywood Community. The transition took place not only in the films that were produced, but in the lives of the performers and artists that created them. Kay's first three pictures released in 1934 had the raciness and atmospheric touches that made the early Warner talkies such a delight to watch. All of this came to an end July 1, 1934. Onscreen, women were no longer allowed sexual relationships or pregnancies outside of marriage. Their careers, if they were allowed one, were secondary to their husbands. Author Mick LaSalle summed up the situation for the female star roles of the era. "The price for non-conjugal relations was either death, permanent loneliness, or a profuse, protracted, and degrading apology. If a husband strayed and wanted to return, a wife not only had to take him back, she had to smile as she did it."[1]

Joseph Breen, who ran the Production Code Administration (PCA) as of June 1934, was a lay Catholic with strong ties to that organization. Breen, a crusader, was the impetus behind the church's critical attitude toward Hollywood. Breen targeted Warner Brothers. Through his influence, a church boycott of Hollywood product took place on May 23, 1934, in Philadelphia. The City of Brotherly Love's Cardinal Dougherty announced that all Catholics in his diocese were "forbidden to patronize any movie house, by 'positive command, binding all in conscience under pain of sin.' The result was an immediate fifteen to twenty percent drop in movie attendance."[2] The Catholic Legion of Decency was organized and had the power to forbid Catholics to see pictures considered immoral. The aftershock of the boycott terrified the studios. The threat of losing twenty million Catholic customers coerced Hollywood to acquiesce to the Legion's demands. Breen's unbridled homophobia and anti-Semitism also acted as a catalyst upon studio executives. Fox executive Sidney Kent shared the opinion, "I think the quicker we get away from degenerates and fairies in our stories, the better off we are going to be. I *do not want any of them in Fox pictures*."[3] By July 1934, the concern about gays in the film industry had led to their invisibility on screen, as well as off. In his well-researched book, *Behind the Screen*, William Mann wrote that the homophobic purge, "wasn't just directed at the *portrayal* of homosexuality, but against homosexuals themselves...Such active discrimination was a large part of the Production Code clampdown of the early 1930's."[4]

One friend of Kay's who felt the chill as the PCA approached was the very popular William Haines. Haines was the top male box-office attraction in the country in

1930. The story goes that when MGM's head honcho, Louis B. Mayer, asked Haines to give up his relationship with his lover of several years, Jimmy Shields, Haines said he would…if Mayer would give up his wife! Whatever was said, Haines career as an actor was *finished*. Kay's diary attests that her friendship with Haines and Shields was consistent up until she left Hollywood in 1947. Kay was well aware how the Code effected the lives of her immediate social circle. Author Mann commented on Kay's relationship with the more sophisticated, gay-friendly crowd. "Kay Francis…turned up in the gossip columns often linked to gay men, who were in truth merely pals and escorts…Costume designer Miles West recalled an 'all-gay' pool party at Francis' house in the 1930's…Supporting player, Anderson Lawler, was one of her most frequent companions."[5] Lawler had met Kay when his friend, director George Cukor, gave him the part of Kay's husband in *Girls About Town*. After the clampdown Lawler sacrificed his acting career, but studio executives made use of Lawler's talent as a social gadabout and escort. Mann says Lawler's scrapbook collection is like, "a walk through gay Hollywood: he arrives with Zoe Akins and Kay Francis at a party thrown by Lilyan Tashman and Edmund Lowe, and at another with Francis, Billy Haines, and Eddie Goulding…At a Countess di Frasso gala, Andy arrives with Kay Francis, Marlene Dietrich and Cary Grant. These were the names that were linked together over and over in the fan magazines and gossip columns. These were the 'smart set.'"[6] Kay's diary noted a particular festive dinner-party she threw for Cole Porter, several male friends and their pals. Afterwards, she merrily noted in her diary, "Never saw so many really *nice* fairies!"[7]

Kay's first feature of 1934, *Mandalay*, was released before the PCA took effect. It was not allowed re-release after its initial run. Most of Kay's Paramount films were *never* allowed re-release. Kay didn't specifically comment on the Code, but one interview reflected her animosity toward the industry's treatment of its talent. Four months of the PCA's impact had opened her eyes. Kay saw the toll it took on many of her friends and co-workers. In November 1934, she expressed her concerns to her friend Dick Mook. The interview is appropriately titled: "Kay Francis on The Real Tragedy of Hollywood." Mook noted that Kay's eyes were brooding as she spoke:

> When I think of Hollywood, it's the tragedy of the place I think of. Look at the young people around you—young— whose lives are finished. Why people who three or four years ago were not only important, but who were also part of the screen. They're not even working today. They can't get work. It's appalling. I hope when my time comes and I'm through, I'll have vision enough and sense enough to clear out.
>
> It's this *place*. Here is one of the largest, most active industries in the midst of a semi-tropical climate. In other places with a climate like this, people take things easy…Not here! Everything is intensified…there is none of the leisurely, take-it-easy manner of going after things…That's why we're all keyed up to breaking point all the time. The moment a person does the least thing out of the ordinary, everyone else is at his throat.

Kay tapped the table in front of her with her forefinger to emphasize her words. "All of us should *get away* from Hollywood at every possible opportunity," she declared.

"It's the only way we have of staying sane. I rush to New York whenever I can."[8] Kay's sojourns to New York were so frequent that Louella Parsons referred to them in her columns as regular commuting trips. Other contemporaries of Kay's followed her advice during the rough climate of 1933-34. After reports of a live-in male friend cashing bad checks from Nils Asther reached the papers, Louis B. Mayer fired Asther, who left for England. Kay's friend, producer David Lewis, was vocal about the studios' intolerance of his and director James Whale's relationship, saying they had no choice but to retreat from Hollywood's social scene. Cary Grant withdrew himself from the gay-friendly crowd around 1935. Lilyan Tashman, the most colorful woman from Kay's circle, made her final exit from Hollywood a few months before the Code took effect. Author William Mann thought it ironic and fitting that Tashman died when she did, saying she was a creature of pre-Code Hollywood, "Her films, her outlook, her lifestyle: it's hard to imagine her existing in the era that was to come…The town, the community, the industry, had once looked to her—as outrageous a lesbian who ever lived and worked among them—as its social arbiter. Now those same forces would increasingly turn in on themselves, forever altering the gay experience in the land of myth and make-believe."[9]

Kay's comments to Dick Mook underscore the oppression and stifling aftershock that surrounded her from the PCA's effect. *"Look at the young people around you…whose lives are finished…the moment a person does the least thing out of the ordinary everyone else is at his throat."* Kay was opposed to the restrictions imposed by the PCA regarding the portrayal of working women on screen and stated, "I am a working woman myself. I'm proud of it…and I prize pretty highly the compensation attached to earning your own money and being able

Respite from Hollywood—Two views of Kay Francis in Yosemite (May 1932). "All of us should get away from Hollywood at every possible opportunity," Kay declared. "It's the only way we have to staying sane."

to do what you want with it."[10] Fortunately, for working woman Kay, Warners was preparing vehicles that would bring her greatest box-office successes over the next three years.

Hal Wallis started the ball rolling for *Madame DuBarry* to star Kay. *Picture Show* magazine headlined that Warners had cast Kay as the Empress Josephine opposite Edward G. Robinson's Napoleon Bonaparte. Later in the year, the studio's enthusiasm for newcomer Errol Flynn garnered him a leading role opposite Kay in *A Present from Margate* (later filmed as *The Widow From Monte Carlo* with Dolores Del Rio and Warren William). Kay was also slated to star in Willa Cather's *A Lost Lady*, a role turned over to Barbara Stanwyck. Other studios were creating projects with Kay in mind. An RKO biopic was in the works of the Bronte sisters to star Kay, Ann Harding and Jean Muir. F. Scott Fitzgerald, contemplating a screen treatment of his just-published *Tender is the Night*, jotted down Kay Francis for the vamp part of Baby Warren—a calculating, arrogant woman of many affairs, reminiscent of Kay's work at Paramount. Carole Lombard's lead role in *Twentieth Century* was originally considered for Kay. But, Warners simply *would not* loan Kay out.

What did materialize for Kay was another Ruth Chatterton reject—an incredulous, but entertaining melodrama. (Chatterton was tired of playing "bad" ladies.) Titled *Mandalay*, the steamy locale and storyline are a film connoisseur's delight. In the opening shot, Kay, as Tanya, is aboard a small yacht in the Rangoon harbor waiting for her lover, Tony (Ricardo Cortez). Once Cortez is aboard, we see her stepping out of her bath and him staring at her lovely naked body. Her sensuality is complemented by a sweet vulnerability. Producer Hal Wallis cautioned screenwriter Robert Presnell and director Michael Curtiz about the scene. "When you show Kay Francis...stepping out of the tub and going into Cortez's arms...stick to the script...For God's sake, Mike, you have been making pictures long enough to know that it is impossible to show a man and woman who are not married in a scene of this kind."[11] Presnell solved the problem by having Kay step out of the tub, into a towel, and kiss Cortez through the window while the towel falls to the floor. With scenes like this, it's no wonder the Secretary of the Navy, Claude Swanson, and a gang of Admirals, visited the set. Patricia Keats wrote that Kay, "led the distinguished visitors over to the [set's] bar and cordially invited them to have one on the house...after one sip they all set the glasses down as if each and every one contained ginger ale...and, shiver me timbers, they did. The Sec and the Admirals were good scouts, though, and posed for pictures, all of them tried to get as close to Kay as possible...the photographers had a field day."[12]

Mandalay allowed Kay to get away with murder while suffering in some fascinating Orry-Kelly designs. Her lean figure and small chest streamlined an intriguing wardrobe. After she is abandoned and sold in exchange for munitions by lover Cortez, she finds herself as the main attraction and "hostess" at a local brothel-nightclub. Kay's soft, sweet Tanya has become the hard-as-nails main attraction at Nick's Place. Wallis made note that the nightclub "should be shot carefully, that is making it more of a nightclub house than...a hook shop...people will put their own interpretation on it and know what kind of establishment it is and what Francis is doing there."[13] When Cortez and Kay arrive at Nick's, she asks, "What *are* these girls?" Cortez replies, "Just like café girls anywhere." Kay looks surprised, "You mean...?" "I mean *exactly* that, my dear!" he clarifies.

Unhappy, Kay manages an escape from her environs by blackmailing one of her one-night-stands who just happens to be the police commissioner (Reginald Owen). He wants her deported. She quickly turns the tables by exposing her garter decorated with the Com-

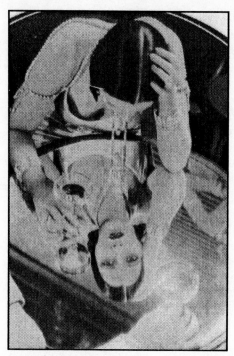

Mandalay *(1934) As a trollop along the Irrawadi River, Kay murders her ex-lover before venturing into "Black Fever" country in hopes of redemption. (Warners)*

missioner Owens's medals. She reminds him of their encounter at a masked ball. "You called me your itty-bitty baby," Kay coos. The commissioner writes a hefty check for 10,000 rupees to retrieve his reputation. "Not a bad price for *not* being deported," she sneers. Kay, money in hand, escapes aboard a steamship to Mandalay.

The exotic locale was filmed along the sandy beaches, freshly planted with palms, up the San Joaquin and Sacramento Rivers. The sternwheeler *Capital City*, famous along California's Delta in 1933, played an integral part in the film. While on the set, Kay told Patricia Keats, "all the dirty work is done on a river boat up near Stockton, which, unfortunately, is over a night's ride from Hollywood. We took some early scenes in the picture over on Catalina Island—which also is a bit far for commuting. I wonder what the location chooser for this picture has against me."[14]

Onboard the *Capital City* for *Mandalay*, Kay cuts her hand while unpacking. A porter calls for Dr. Gregory Burton (Lyle Talbot, in a role intended for George Brent) who treats the wound with a poison antiseptic. Talbot has been drinking himself to ruination. While Kay and Talbot hatch plans to redefine themselves, Cortez unexpectedly shows up on board. When confronted with Cortez's scurrilous plans for her, Kay is shocked and repelled. She slips him some of the aforementioned poison. We soon see Cortez's convulsing body conveniently falling out the window and into the Sacramento (Irrawadi) River. Much to his credit, Cortez plays the perfect slimeball and garners no sympathy. The film ends with Kay and Talbot heading for the jungle depths to fight an epidemic in black fever country. If redemption counts as a happy ending this one scores an easy 10.

The New York Times mused that "they have set the sultry picturesque-ness of the East down on the screen so neatly that a New Yorker is tempted to throw his overcoat and earmuffs away, and cut a bee-line through the opium smoke to Nick's." The review thought Francis "highly decorative." The *LA Evening Herald Express* saw more to Kay's performance. "*Mandalay* is her most melodramatic to date. She creates a real illusion as the seductive Spot White, charmer of all races, with a few overtones of that flamboyant humor lately regarded as Mae West territory. Crammed with melodrama…Miss Francis disposes with tragic-eyed competence. Make no mistake, you'll like Kay Francis in her clothes, her rich, exotic lure, her drama, no matter how you quarrel with the over-wrought story." *Variety* thought *Mandalay* a "meaty first-run property…thoroughly entertaining film fare in the hands of Miss Francis…" The film made a whopping $325,000 profit.

The role of Tanya was quite an amazing characterization to pull off. Atop the stairs at Nick's place, dressed in an eye-popping lamé gown, Kay does a grand job of letting it be known, *this* woman has lost touch with her soul. She uses men the way they had used her. But, once aboard the steamer to Mandalay, we see that Francis hasn't totally given up on herself. She sings (dubbed this time), "There are so many dreams to be mended, when tomorrow comes..."

When reporter Patricia Keats arrived on the set of *Mandalay*, she heard Kay's *own* voice singing Kipling's popular song of the same title. What followed was an amusing story in itself:

Kay was captivating in the Ruth Chatterton reject, Mandalay (1934). On the first take of this scene Kay tripped down the stairs in her size 4 shoes. (Warners)

'Pipe down you dope!' a voice roared right under my nose as I tip-toed onto a stage at the Warner Brothers film factory ... there was a discordant crashing piano chord and the contralto voice that had been gaily caroling Kipling's famous song choked...A smartly coiffed raven black head appeared out of the dimness, and a very meek voice said, 'So sorry.' The assistant director's eyes nearly popped out of his head, and an expression of horror swept over his face. I thought surely he must be seeing Frankenstein—but no, it was only Kay Francis. 'Oh, Miss Francis, I-I-I didn't know it was you,' he muttered.

'I'm—awfully—'

'Forget it,' said Kay with a grin. 'I'm used to being shushed when I break out in song. Why I've been shushed out of the best places in Hollywood.' Contrite at having bawled out the star, the assistant director backed away. I never saw Kay so exotically charming as she was that day. She wore a glove-fitting silver gown that didn't spare the details...'I'm supposed to be Spot White from a hot spot in Rangoon,' Kay explained. 'I'm the principal reason why men leave home—and stay away. And this is supposed to be the most notorious night club in Rangoon.' She went on, pointing out the colorful Oriental motifs of a huge café set...I gazed in dismay at a flight of steps that rose steeply to a balcony...The steps were set at uneven intervals, which is an old Oriental custom I learned. And they looked pretty tough going if a person had to navigate them in a hurry.

A call for 'Lights' and 'Quiet' and Kay was back on the set again to do her 'tripping' scene down the jerry-built stairway and I'm here to tell you it was a real 'trip.' Hollywood's best dressed actress started down the steps, looking languidly toward the dance floor. One heel got caught in the train of her gown, and down she came, bumpity bump BUMP. And pride goeth before the fall. '*-*-*!' said Miss Francis.

Director, cameraman, assistants, extras, dancers, everyone, even I, rushed forward to help her. 'Hurt?' Director Curtiz asked solicitously. 'What do *you* think?' Kay groaned rubbing a tender spot…She really was considerably bruised, but as she remarked to me, 'The bruises *aren't* where they show.'[15]

The boys at the Production Code office were neither fascinated nor charmed by Kay's portrayal. They were horrified. They axed its re-release in 1936. *Mandalay* remained a movie memory for the next 50 years until Ted Turner's networks brought it out of the vaults. The same fate awaited Kay's next film for Warners, *Wonder Bar.*

Wonder Bar, was directed by Lloyd Bacon with musical numbers by Busby Berkeley. The film's narrative takes place in the course of one night in a Montmartre cabaret known as the *Wonder Bar.* 1995's documentary *Celluloid Closet* includes one of the film's most celebrated scenes. A slender, dark-haired young man descends upon a crowded ballroom floor, taps a blond gentleman on the shoulder and asks, "May I cut in?" The blond man looks pleased, smiles, and abandons the lovely young lady with whom he is dancing. The two men dance off together. The disgruntled girl leaves the floor. Bandleader Al Jolson has been enjoying the little episode and announces to the crowd, "Boys will be boys! Wooo Wooo!" When Joseph Breen heard about the scene, he angrily sent a letter to Jack Warner demanding a screening of the film. Warner didn't reply. *Wonder Bar* fueled Breen's fire. Four months later the film would never have been released. Breen's only consolation this time was that the state censor boards in Ohio and Pennsylvania cut the scene. If *anything* in the film was offensive, it was the closing musical number of Al Jolson doing his blackface shtick in "Goin' to Heaven on a Mule." It was a lengthy racist vignette of blacks eating watermelon, munching on the meat from "pork chop trees," amidst a perpetual song and dance fest. *This* didn't seem to offend Mr. Breen. His other big concern was the "irregular sex relationship" between Ricardo Cortez and his dance partner, Dolores Del Rio. The main ingredient to their dancing art is Cortez's use of a whip on Del Rio. Its strong intimations of sadomasochism is pretty shocking, even by today's standards. Del Rio gets the satisfaction of mortally wounding Cortez with a knife during their act—her crime going unpunished at the film's end.

So where was Kay Francis amid all this? She plays a spoiled, wealthy wife who's having an affair with Cortez. Many thought Kay was displeased with her part, because she has little to do, scowls a great deal, and her anger seems to be eating away at her. Although accepting of the roles afforded her by Warners, Kay did not want to repeat being featured in brief appearances like she had at Paramount. Kay herself explained the situation to writer Dick Mook in November 1934.

The one I objected to most was *Wonderbar*, not because I felt it wouldn't be a good picture but solely because I felt it wouldn't give me enough to do. And, speaking of that film, I've read a number of items such as 'Kay Francis didn't want to do the part and her aversion to it was apparent in her work.' I didn't scowl my way through the picture because I didn't like the part. I felt the woman would be spoiled, petulant, sullen, and I played her that way. I was trying to characterize. I hope I'm too intelligent to let any dissatisfaction I may feel over a part reflect itself in my work.[16]

Kay's attitude was generous given her less than seven minutes screen time in an 84-minute film. Kay complained again about *Wonder Bar* when she went over to England the next year. "I had a very small and thankless part in it. People knew that I didn't want to take the role…All I had to do was to look sullen throughout the picture. Everybody expected me to look that way, anyhow, so I didn't even get credit for acting!"[17]

Kay needn't have defended herself. She plays the character on cue. Spoiled, tired of her husband, suspicious of Cortez, seeking satisfaction in riches and relationships that will go nowhere—she's a fascinating creature. Given her allotted time, Kay establishes a far more complex and interesting character than Del Rio's woebegone passion dancer. Still, the camera seems to linger on Del Rio's striking looks. It's easy to appreciate Kay's dissatisfaction with her role. Del Rio's role was expanded at Kay's expense.

William F. French wrote about the making of *Wonder Bar* for *Photoplay*. Titled, "Only Al Wanted to Play," French talks about the famous photo of the five major stars raising their glasses at the *Wonder Bar*, toasting the film. Ricardo Cortez, in gaucho gear, sits next to the smiling Dolores Del Rio. Al Jolson, grinning from ear to ear, is in the middle. A scowling Kay Francis is to his left and sweet-cheeked Dick Powell rubs elbows with Kay:

Director Busby Berkeley's Wonder Bar *(1934) was all about Al Jolson. Kay thought her part "small and thankless." Seen here with Ricardo Cortez, Dolores Del Rio, Al Jolson and Dick Powell. (Warners)*

All five raise their glasses to a toast. Happy, happy set! "Click," goes the still camera. The players at the bar change their pose—and that is not all. Kay shrugs, glances about her and settles back with queenly indifference. Ricardo's toothful smile straightens into a thin, hard line and friendly Dick Powell grins sheepishly at his director. Meanwhile Al Jolson edges a little forward in the center of the group and Dolores keeps discreetly silent. The almost inevitable friendly repartee that follows a shot is strangely missing. "Just one big, happy family," I suggest to Director Bacon. "Yeah," he returned, dryly. "But we are going to get a good picture out of this."

French reports on Jolson's intimating a walkout if he didn't get his own way; Kay's queenly hauteur; and, Dick Powell's demands to be released from the picture. "Every player came in handcuffs, so to speak," claimed French. That is, except Del Rio, whom Jolson had handpicked for the juiciest part. French's mention of Kay was very telling:

Kay, meanwhile, had been told a little fairy story about the really charming part which was being re-written for her, and which Mr. Jolson was going to have built up big. Al, you know, happened to own the story—the picture being made from his New York show of the same name, which had a moderate run. "I didn't like the part the first time it was suggested to me," explains Kay, "and after I got the script I liked it less. In the first place, there was really no part there for me at all. Just a bit—nothing more. It was a part any one of twenty girls on the set could play just as well as I. Naturally, I told them I didn't want to do it. They insisted…No actress likes to play an insignificant part—especially if it…could be cut out entirely without hurting the story…Not only was I cast to a role in a picture I did not want any part of, but I was put in a picture in which the male lead is not recognized as a screen star and the girl with the only feminine part that can be called a part, is borrowed from another studio…Dolores is a good friend of mine,…but she is not under contract here and I do not think I should be asked to support her at the cost of playing a weak bit. Poor parts hurt an actress more than the average person can realize…No star on the screen can play four bad parts in succession without meeting disaster. And, personally, I think I had my share for the time being. I could understand being cast to such a role if the studio did not value my services and had not renewed my option, but, under the circumstances, it seems inexplicable to me.

French reported that "almost unanimously" Kay's co-stars agreed with her. Dick Powell also felt slighted, saying, "Gee whiz…I thought I was due for a good break…When they talked to me about *Wonderbar*…I knew Al Jolson would never let another singer do anything in it … he took the good song that was assigned to me and gave me in exchange the eight bars he didn't like…I've been teamed with Ruby Keeler for three pictures—and I thought *maybe* Al would want to see me built up a little. But I guess I guessed wrong, because he's going over all the scripts suggested for us—as Ruby's manager and I'll probably be whittled down in *them*." French concludes with the consolation that at least the cast wasn't required to raise hands in salute saying "Viva Yoelson."[18] Kay later admitted,

"My anger at the studio…being *made* to play in *Wonderbar* never reached very actionable heat. I began to wonder what I would do if the studio informed me that my option would *not* be taken up and that I could go."[19] After seeing Kay in the film and on the set of *Wonder Bar*, columnist and fan Jimmie Fidler felt the film benefitted from all her venting and wagged, "Kay is very beautiful, particularly when she is a bit annoyed."[20]

In spite of *Wonder Bar*'s sea of tension and battling egos, the dazzling musical numbers, the gowns, the variety of characters, the subplots all added up to a quintessential Warner Bros. '30s musical. Some of the film's progressive themes thankfully led the viewer to non-moralizing resolutions, which wouldn't be the case for films released a few months later. *Motion Picture Herald* thought *Wonder Bar* a "worthy successor to *42nd Street*, *Footlight Parade*, and *Gold Diggers*…In many ways, it tops any one of its predecessors."

While the PCA was clamping down on Hollywood, Kay, in her own private life, continued to rebel against the moralistic climes of the times. Just before her divorce from Kenneth was final, she had a *very* brief fling with Count Alfredo Carpanga, a tennis pro who provided Kay stiff competition on the court, but not in the boudoir. By all accounts the affair only lasted one night. "Slept with Alfredo. Very dull," she wrote disappointedly.[21] To the rescue from her dull evening came Maurice Chevalier, whose marriage to Yvonne Vallee was on the skids. Chevalier happily preoccupied himself with Kay to escape his marital woes. From January 1934 through March 1935, Maurice was foremost in her thoughts. "God, hope I am not caught again," Kay wrote after their first night together.[22] Kay spent many nights at Maurice's. A typical day might find her playing tennis with opera diva Grace Moore, after which Maurice would join them for dinner and poker. The press kept hinting that the pair would be married, but Kay liked her newfound independence and denied the possibility of such an entanglement. When asked about Chevalier Kay was prone to pun, "Maurice Chevalier? I adore him. Is that plain enough? He's the most charming person I know—almost…"[23] Writer Harry T. Brundidge inquired about the huge portrait of Kay encased in a silver frame adorning Chevalier's dressing table at MGM (during the filming of *The Merry Widow*), then asked, "Is it true that Miss Francis is your big moment?" "No," Chevalier answered. "Miss Francis is a very good friend of mine. But so is Ruth Chatterton and Grace Moore. We are all pals."[24] By May 1934, Chevalier was feeling comfortable sharing some of his fantasies about his "pals" with Kay. She noted in her diary, "Maurice for dinner. Swell evening. Very exciting, discussing about lesbians and a threesome. Not practical, I'm afraid."[25] Before Kay left for Europe that June, she had some hesitancy about leaving Maurice behind. "Maurice here for dinner. Good-bye. Wonder when will be the next time I see him. Terribly sad!"[26] As usual, she wasn't "terribly sad" for terribly long. A few royal highnesses were waiting with bated breath for her in Italy. In the meantime, Kay's last pre-Code film was released in the United States.

Dr. Monica, directed by William Keighley, had been a moderate success for Nazimova on Broadway in 1933. The film was hailed by one New York film critic as "superior to the parent work. It moves apace and the acting is excellent…the women in the case are Trojans and the man is—well, one might almost say, vile."[27] Kay plays Dr. Monica Braden, an obstetrician, who, unable to have a child of her own, is confronted with the fact that her husband, John Braden (played by Warren William), has impregnated one of her best friends (Jean Muir). The ads read, "Only a super-woman could have lived this story…Only

Dr. Monica (1934) Obstetrician Kay maneuvers cocktails and cigarettes before delivering the child of her husband's mistress. With Verree Teasdale. (Warners)

a super-star could bring it to the screen! You'll marvel as you watch the supreme artistry of Kay Francis sweep triumphantly through a role only the greatest dared to play! …the story critics warned could not be screened!" After release, the PCA demanded *Dr. Monica* be pulled from theaters due to the references to adultery and pregnancy out of wedlock.

Dr. Monica was a sensitive exploration of friendship between three women and how they dealt with conflicting feelings about men, motherhood and professional obligations. The only drawback was the drastic solution for Jean Muir's character: suicide. Author Mick La Salle thought Kay brought a "natural authority" to her roles as a professional woman. He points to the scene where Muir "hints she wants Monica to perform an abortion. Monica gets angry and says, 'Don't you *ever* talk that way again—don't you ever *think* that way again.' The outburst is completely in character and calls to mind Francis's own experience [with Dwight Francis]."[28] Oddly enough, *Dr. Monica* was banned in Pittsfield, where Kay and Dwight had lived. Kay's ex-mother-in-law, Mrs. Henry A. Francis, protested against Mayor Bagg's decision. She was still very good friends with Kay and told reporters, "I am as much opposed as any one to vulgar and gangster pictures, but *Dr. Monica* does not come within either of these categories. It is a clean picture, well acted."[29] Mayor Bagg admitted he had not seen the film. It would be many years before any mention of abortion would be included in a screenplay again.

When Monica learns that the child she is to deliver belongs to her own husband, she loses all sympathy for Muir's character. Their mutual friend, Anna (the sharp-edged Verree Teasdale), confronts Monica.

> "She's your patient right now. Her life and reputation are in your hands."
> Monica rebels. "Do you think I'd touch her?!"
> "You're going upstairs," commands Anna.
> "I'd kill her! I have the right!" Monica declares.

Anna swiftly slaps Monica's face. "The woman upstairs is nothing to you but a patient. You're a doctor under oath to deliver her child. Go upstairs, Monica!"

Monica finally relents, lets go of her stubborn pride, and begrudgingly utters, "Thanks."

It's a powerful scene. Kay carries the film emotionally and reaches into her own experience and complexities. One may not like the anger she directs at Muir instead of her blundering fool of a husband with his mindless grin, but Francis makes her choice of scapegoat believable. Film historian Janine Basinger commented that in *Dr Monica*, "the women do everything and the man is little more than a sperm bank."[30] Jacalyn Dufflin, professor in History of Medicine at Queens University, Ontario, commented in 1999 that *Dr Monica* was, "a riveting account of 1930's professional women...the issues of working women, extramarital sex, single parenting, suicide, and marital dishonesty are treated with astonishing frankness..."[31]

Reporter Harry Evans asked Kay how she liked herself in *Dr Monica*. She was honest. "I don't particularly like myself in anything any more," Kay responded. "Seems to me I'm always doing the same things with my hands and eyes and face. It makes you wonder just how much there is and is not to this acting business." She mentioned her tendency of placing her left hand on her forehead. "Just think how many times I do that in a picture!" Kay said despairingly. "But directors like it. They say it's characteristic of me." Regardless, *Screenland* saw her performance as a minor triumph, saying, "There are moments of heartbreaking realism between Miss Francis...and Miss Muir (who) finally strikes her stride as a dramatic actress...extra competition is provided by Veree Teasdale...But La Francis, as you know, always holds her own, and this film is no exception..."

Ruth Chatterton had turned down *The House on 56th Street, Mandalay,* and *Dr. Monica*. Kay's part in *Wonder Bar* had originally been assigned to Genevieve Tobin. For her next release, *British Agent*, with Leslie Howard, Barbara Stanwyck had been pursued to play Lenin's secretary. When confronted about the roles she had been assigned, particularly her last five, which had been rejected by other stars, Kay was responsive:

> I was skeptical of some of these pictures and some of them I didn't want to do simply because I didn't feel I was suited to the part. But I've been in Hollywood six years now, and do you know the conclusion I've reached? ... That the studios usually know better what's good for us than we do ourselves! We're so concerned with whether our roles are good that we lose our perspective on the picture as a whole. The studio sees it as a complete unit—or should. The only fly in the ointment is that Warners is primarily a man's studio. MGM is first of all a woman's studio...Our executives and writers understand men thoroughly, but they have no grasp whatever of woman's psychology. Don't misunderstand me. I love this studio. After all, they made a star of me. That feeling of gratitude is one reason I haven't complained more over some of the roles given me.[32]

Kay's mentor, Walter Huston, put it more bluntly, "Never set your heart on anything in Hollywood. Just take the money, and do what is expected of you." As would be expected,

Hal Wallis, production head at Warners, complimented Kay to *Film Weekly*. "The vital factor in this girl's success," he said, "is her sound common sense…and the fact that she realizes that stars themselves are never the most competent judges of their screen stories from a box-office point of view…Kay is possibly the only star in the entire history of the Warner studios who has realized this fact, and who has been ready to meet us more than half way."[33] Easily said. Wallis failed to mention that Kay did not have script approval.

Surprisingly, Kay hoped that Warners would meet her half way and grant her permission to do a play in the fall of 1934. "I do want to return to Broadway," Kay told Jimmie Fidler. "To begin with, I feel the need of *audience contact*. There is something electric and inspiring about stage work. The *feel* of an audience lifts one. That inspirational touch is lacking in motion pictures, where acting is a cold, cut-and-dried proposition."[34] Both *Dr. Monica* and *Wonder Bar* had been adapted from plays, and, as Kay had once so adroitly pointed out, there was very little *original* product coming out of Hollywood.[35] Kay would have to wait another twelve years before again facing Broadway audiences.

Kay sailed on the *Rex* for Naples in June. Before her trip, Kay had commented to Dick Mook that she had a strange affinity with Italy and predicted, "I'm going to Italy…and you'll see a vastly different person when I return than you're saying good-by to today."[36] After arriving in Europe, Kay's feelings for Maurice quickly dissolved into the lovely scenery of Pompeii, Rome, Acque Albule, Venice and the handsome faces of three princes and a duke! She also attended the third Venice Film Festival. Kay and Marion Davies were the very first Hollywood stars invited to attend the affair. But, Kay found herself unable to fully concentrate on the festivities as she had already been swept away with a particular married Crown Prince, whom she referred to as Paolo in her diaries and found "damn attractive." The intense affair lasted several weeks. Kay ran through her usual emotional gamut amid much lovemaking and what she referred to as a "miserable farewell." She left His Royal Highness behind and took the train to Paris where the doctor told her she was four weeks' pregnant. Kay, "the vastly different person," seemed to be stuck in a very familiar dilemma.

Kay then rendezvoused in Paris with Maurice, but after her experience with a Crown Prince, Maurice came across as "dull." On September 16, *The New York Times* insisted the Francis-Chevalier affair was in full sway and that the lovebirds were motoring about the French capital. In October, Kay returned to New York on the Italian liner, *Rex*. She laughed away reports that suggested an engagement to Chevalier, replying she had no intention of marrying again, "unless it is when I am old and doddering."[37] Back in Hollywood, Kay went directly into the hospital for an abortion. With exasperated humor, she entered into her diary, "Bed all day—operation! Last of the Mohicans. I hope!"[38] Kay's "operations" took an emotional toll as well as physical, but she thought herself fit and gallantly continued her pursuit of love and romance fueled by a healthy sexual appetite.

Just before Kay's return home, Warners released her final film for 1934, *British Agent*. Her part was a switch from anything she had played before. With the Bolshevik revolution as a background, the story focused on the relationship of a British agent, Stephen Locke (Leslie Howard), and his affair with a Russian woman, Elena Moura (Kay). Kay's character was loosely based on the Ukrainian-born baroness, Moura Budberg. Budberg was a favorite of the Empress Alexandria and knew Rasputin before befriending Russian revolutionist Kerensky. A personal friend of Stalin, she became the mistress of Russian folk hero and playwright, Maxim Gorky. By 1918 she was having an affair with British agent Bruce Lockhart (both were married) and in 1920 she started her affair with author H.G. Wells (*The Time Machine*) and functioned as his secretary. She also had an abortion by Wells.[39] Budberg was a suspected double agent for Britain and Russia. She popped up in the 1950s and '60s as technical advisor on films for Anatole Litvak's *The Journey* (1959) and Sidney Lumet's *The Seagull* (1968). Budberg's life was a tall order for any one film—the stuff of *British Agent* was a mere escapade in this woman's life. Besides, the Breen Office would have chopped her story up into impermissible bits.

As Elena Moura, Kay's character abandons her aristocratic roots for the Bolshevik revolution and the welfare of the common man. As Lenin's secretary she's become a mover and shaker for the cause. When Stephen Locke (Howard), an unofficial diplomatic agent from England, arrives on the scene, Kay finds herself torn between love of country and love of another human being.

British Agent was based on the autobiography by R.H. Bruce Lockhart (*Memoirs of a British Agent*). Lockhart was sent to Russia in 1917 to prevent the new Soviet (Bolshevik) government from signing a separate peace pact with Germany. We first see Kay aiming a pistol at a Cossack who is beating a woman and child during a street riot. She shoots to kill. She misses. Howard watches this action from inside the British Embassy and manages to rescue her from the situation. Before long she is sharing with Howard her belief in the Red Army's takeover: "The people have found their voice," she proclaims, "tomorrow the Red government will be in power." Howard mocks her saying, "And the day after that the blue, then the white I suppose?" She looks at him directly in the eyes, and coldly replies, "Perhaps you don't know a great deal about it."

As fate would have it, Kay and Howard come to realize all they really want is to be truly happy together. He admits he sees her as a sort of Joan of Arc, but would rather have her as a woman. Their respective loyalties continue to present a major conflict in their relationship. They keep locking political horns. Of the two, Francis seems more torn by the situation. She opposes Howard's scheme to lend British monies to the White

British Agent *(1934) Besides an off-screen tryst, Kay and co-star Leslie Howard achieved what* The New York Times *deemed, "striking dramatic values." (Warners)*

counterrevolutionary army and feels that he is meddling in other people's business. Howard never really shows any empathy or appreciation for what she feels and accuses her of "running the red flag." Later, Kay informs the revolutionary government that Howard is *not* an authorized representative of England. When Howard finds this out, he feels she has betrayed their love. He tries to convince her that England is "fighting for the world." "*England's* world, not ours," she clarifies. Francis' arguments are more persuasive than Howard's. She has abandoned her wealthy inheritance and privileges. Howard, on the other hand, is merely a political opportunist and intruder. Francis sums up Howard's character when she consoles him about their situation. "You're clever, Stephen," she tells him, "but not clever enough. Weak, but not weak enough. Strong, but not strong enough." Her observation is on target. By the film's end, Elena has grown multi-fold, thanks to Francis' portrayal, while Howard, as Locke, seems stuck in his world view. At a 1960 screening of *British Agent*, film historian William K. Everson noted, "It's rather difficult to have too much sympathy for the British agent—or his American cohorts—who are clearly...diverting another nation's affairs for reasons of their own country's politics. The underhanded tricks that Leslie Howard and Co. get up are the kind of things that we are now told only those sneaky Communists perpetrate."[40]

The film's climax has Francis retreat to Howard's hideaway knowing it is about to be bombed by the Boleshevik. The film would have had far more dramatic impact had the lovers been sacrificed in the bombarded building. Instead, we get a contrived twist for the end and the lovers are off to England and "happiness." Of course, Lockhart and Budberg's actual *survival* preclude the more climatic ending. Unfortunately, any dramatic impact is lost amid some nonsense about chewing gum, and smiling farewells at a train station. *Variety* made note of this, saying, "Picture cries for a tragic ending, and had it been allowed to end two minutes earlier, with an explosion killing both leads, it would be a much finer picture." Otherwise, the reviewer thought *Agent*, "both artistically and cinematically good entertainment...excellent acting...Leslie Howard and Kay Francis handle the two chief roles tellingly."

Overall, the press was enthusiastic about *British Agent*. W.E. Oliver wrote, "*British Agent* accomplishes a rugged dramatic power...authentic in feeling, and for such a large canvas, the picture strikes a very intimate response...This is due of course to the love story of Miss Francis and Leslie Howard being made important and to the two stars' ability of playing sincerely in well-cast roles. Miss Francis' straight, breezy charm is well suited to the role of Elena."[41] Shortly after filming, Kay explained her success in such roles as Elena in *British Agent*: "I try to strike a balance, to make these women thoroughly rounded individuals. Professionally, they must be competent, but it mustn't make them hard or cold or destroy their appeal in their scenes of private life."[42]

It is ironic that Leslie Howard lost his life, as an "unofficial" British Agent, while on a lecture tour in Spain and Portugal during World War II. Howard's son, Ronald, commented years later, "Germans in Madrid—without doubt on instructions from Berlin...may well have wanted to establish a motive for liquidating Leslie. He was Britain's most powerful and effective propagandist, he had ridiculed the German hierarchy in *Pimpernel Smith*, he had broadcast against them and he was, certainly, on Goebbels' black list..."[43] Howard's death in 1943, made headlines worldwide. The shooting down of his plane was given prominence in Goebbels' newspaper *Der Angriff*. Under blazing headlines the paper celebrated the victory, saying, "Pimpernel Howard has made his last trip!"

Kay made headlines while shooting *British Agent*—for breaking into her own home! The previous evening she and Maurice had quarreled. The next morning, she took Weenie out for a walk and when she returned she found all the doors were locked. How she remedied the situation was unusual. *Hollywood Citizen News* reported, "Kay Francis reported at Warners for work today in *British Agent* with Leslie Howard, despite the fact that she bears 25 stitches in her right arm…the laceration occurred when she took her dog out for an airing and the door slammed shut behind her, locking her out. She…felt too much consideration for her sleeping servants to waken them, so she plunged her arm through a window pane and unfastened the catch to let herself back in…An artery was cut and she might have bled to death if her maid…had not improvised a tourniquet…" Kay and Maurice made up the next day. Also, to the rescue, came her co-star Leslie Howard. He offered more than just sympathy. Though married, Howard kept an eye out for the ladies. On June 8 he brought Kay home from the studio. "And, like a damn fool," wrote Kay after she and Leslie had a nightcap, "I slept with him. Hell!"[44] Kay "thanked God" when *British Agent* wrapped up filming three days later.

In November 1934, when asked once again about Chevalier, Kay replied, "I have no intention of remarrying while I have a career. My marriage with Kenneth MacKenna taught me that."[45] In December, Kay was reported visiting Maurice on the set of *Folies Bergere*. Her diaries indicated that the affair was petering out. In early January 1935, Kay had dinner with Maurice and then he asked her to spend the night. She noted, "He could not do anything for ages…he cried like a baby and I felt terribly sorry for him."[46] Chevalier's fellow countryman, director Robert Florey, recalled, "When all was going well in his love affair [with Kay], he could be very gay; he would dance around and hum [Victor] Schertzinger tunes or some of his early songs. But then, when he was unhappy, I would find him despondent and talking about returning to Paris immediately."[47] By the end of January, Kay and Maurice's love-life appeared to be back on track. Kay wrote, "Maurice here at 7. Very sweet to me about everything. God damn it."[48] Soon after a miscarriage in February (for which Kay was very grateful), the lovers were *again* at odds when Maurice blamed Kay for "a pimple on his god damn prick."[49] In early March they both realized the end was at hand. They were very sweet with one another, because Maurice had decided to leave Hollywood for *good*.

In 1960 Maurice reminisced in his autobiography, *With Love*, about his departure from Hollywood after filming *Folies Bergere*. Insulted by losing top billing to Grace Moore in an MGM project, he cancelled his contract and left for France. After mentioning his more serious entanglement with Marlene Dietrich, Chevalier lumped Kay into a group of beauties he had his eye on. "Happily there was no dearth of other alluring women to encounter," he wrote. "Merle Oberon, Claudette Colbert, Miriam Hopkins, Kay Francis— stars whose intellect matched their beauty." Chevalier did confess that his last evening in Hollywood was spent with Kay. "You'll never come back, Maurice," Kay told Chevalier unhappily over dinner. She was silent for a moment and then, as if being held by one of her premonitions, added, "I *know* it." Thalberg had predicted that one day Chevalier would return "bigger than ever." Chevalier pondered, "Irving Thalberg had thought one way, this beautiful woman another. I wondered which of them would ultimately be right." In a sense both of them were. Chevalier did come back, not as a screen star but with his very successful one-man show in the 1940s and '50s.

Later in 1935, when Kay returned to England, Louella Parsons could only think of another romantic escapade for Kay and Chevalier. That April, Parsons wrote, "Kay Francis who has more admirers than we have room to print names of, off for Europe in another two weeks; Kay isn't saying whether it's Maurice Chevalier or the Italian Count who is the attraction; probably both."[50] In truth, it was *neither*. Something had happened between Kay and Maurice to cause a *permanent* rift. When she went to London in 1935, the newshounds assumed she was going to France to marry Chevalier. During her extended stay at a London nursing home to have an infected wisdom tooth and salivary gland removed, reporters sought out Chevalier to ask if the wedding would be postponed. Chevalier called his and Kay's relationship a "Franco-American friendship alliance" and nothing more. He added they weren't even thinking of marrying, at least to each other. For some reason Kay took offense at his statement and ended their friendship. Kay's romantic liaison during the 1950s, Dennis Allen, would say, "I could never understand it. I know she had various pieces of jewelry from him, and I noticed when he died there was a picture of Kay in his den, but she never saw him again, never, ever. She wouldn't even let me take her to his one-man show twenty years later."[51] (Kay *did* see Maurice's one-man show in 1947.)

Never *completely* burned out on love, Kay put forth her liberated feelings regarding relationships and wrote an article for *Motion Picture Magazine,* titled, "My Design for Happiness." After briefly describing her ideal dinner party for eight *at* eight, she confessed that, "Three nice beaux are a part of my design. Beaux who will take me places when I want to go, who send me flowers and candies and theatre tickets; beaux who make the world the kind of place a woman believes it should be; beaux who lay more stress on fun and companionships and little attentions than they do on love-making!" Although her "design" downplayed the physical attraction in relationships, her diaries confirm that the art of lovemaking was very important to her. She told reporter Ben Maddox, "no woman who is smart is ever *too* definite in her private life relationships with men!" Kay's views were frank stuff for a Hollywood under restriction from the Production Code. A voice ahead of her time, Kay was asked by *Screen Book* for her opinion about nudism in films. Early in 1934, producer Bryan Foy released his film *Elysia,* which documented the benefits of life in a nudist colony. Kay saw it as a new trend. "I think nudism will have its effect on motion picture making," asserted Kay. "Pictures reflect modern life and conditions. The nudists…are pioneers, and without pioneering there is no progress. Nudism will liberalize thought and action, and some of these days we may wonder why we were shocked. Pictures are much more liberal now than they were a few years ago simply because the industry had pioneers who dared defy conventions and silly restrictions." Kay wasn't going to compromise her style for the Breen Office, the Legion of Decency, or religion. "I would not say that religion is a part of my design," she emphasized. "*Philosophy,* I think, would be the better word—the philosophy of finding happiness in myself and of giving as much of myself as possible to others."[52]

Marriage and Hollywood did not appear to be important in Kay's design. Her life had turned a new leaf. "I am not domestic," she wrote. "I don't want a home of my own—not now. I don't know yet where I want to live…I know that I should prefer living in New York if it were not for my work."[53] And, with the New Year of 1935, Kay was perfectly content enjoying the company of a new compatible lover. A new beau under contract at Warners, became her *only* beau: film scenarist Delmer Daves.

Chapter 10

Queen of Warners –
"Lousy Wife—Happy Lover"

By 1935, Kay had taken over as Queen of the Warners' lot. The dethroned Ruth Chatterton had been a big disappointment to the studio. Kay was now their highest salaried female star at $4,000 per week. But, Bette Davis was nipping at Kay's regal heels. Davis had garnered much acclaim for her strong performance in *Of Human Bondage*. What Kay needed was a big hit, both critically and commercially. Instead, Warners placed her in a series of run-of-the-mill, light melodramas with George Brent.

Before the release of her first film of 1935, *Living on Velvet*, Kay celebrated her newfound royalty at Warners by throwing one of the most talked about parties ever given in Hollywood. She hired the Vendome Café, at 6666 Sunset Boulevard, and had the front of the building converted into the semblance of a luxury liner. On the hull was the inscription, *S. S. Francis*. A gangplank greeted the guests as they pulled up in limousines. They were met by their hostess, Kay, dressed as an admiral. She gave the official maritime salute to each reveler only after they had descended a slide that brought them to the floor where the party was going on full-sway. *The Los Angeles Times* reported on February 18:

> Nearly every feminine star-guest wore white shorts and blue sweaters, with their male escorts attired in varied sea-going costumes, running largely to natty blue and white officers' uniforms. There was Fredric March as a blue-jacket...Joan Blondell made her appearance in a little girl's dress, with socks, starched shirt and hair ribbons. Joan Bennett, her husband, Gene Markey, Virginia Bruce, Walter Wanger, Samuel Goldwyn...and numerous others wore the striped sweater and beret of the French sailor. To carry the nautical theme even farther, guests danced on a floor that occasionally tilted slightly, simulating the motion of a ship at sea.

Kay was seen with her arm around her "screen crush," Jimmy Cagney, and looking *far* more smitten with Cagney than her current beau, Maurice Chevalier. There were no reports of seasickness among the revelers, but there was one mighty case of pneumonia: Kay Francis. One newspaper headlined, "Parrish Spanks Film Star for Flu Menace."

February 17, 1935. Kay's nautical party. She is sandwiched between her "screen crush," James Cagney, and her current lover, Maurice Chevalier. At far left is Richard Barthelmess, at far right, Joan Blondell.

Kay Francis, film star, got a good scolding from Dr. George Parrish, head of the city health department, for appearing at her party in a Hollywood café last Saturday night when she was suffering from influenza…Dr. Parrish wrote Miss Francis a letter telling her that she 'used anything but good judgment…Probably you gave the influenza to many of your guests. The city spends the taxpayers' money to educate people to remain at home when they have influenza…and the fact that you are a screen star gives you no right to do a thing like that.'[1]

The article claimed Kay could not be reached for comment, as she was resting up in the hospital "after a lot of hard work on a picture." Kay claimed that her nautical party had a ship's doctor aboard keeping an eye on her temperature. And besides, Kay told the newspaper, "It was such a *little* bit of flu."[2] Rumor had it that Kay had spent beaucoup bucks on her nautical romp. She scoffed at the very idea saying, "If anybody believes that party cost me $10,000, they don't know their Kay Francis."[3] Two days later, Kay was up and horsing around at the Santa Ana races for the $100,000 handicap. Her appearance, along with that of Clark Gable, Marion Davies, Al Jolson, and Dolores Del Rio ended up in a ten-minute Vitaphone short titled *Kings of the Turf.*

Fans and columnists were hopeful for Kay's new project, *Living on Velvet*, with the reputable Frank Borzage directing. Author James Robert Parish thought George Brent (who had just divorced the dethroned Ruth Chatterton) and Kay "did some of their best tandem work in *Living on Velvet.*"[4] Director Borzage had the ability to give his films a poetic quality and was always concerned with the presence of spirit behind reality. Author John Belton wrote that Borzage's screen lovers "go beyond their initial mutual sexual desire to a more spiritual, quasi-religious awareness of and dependence on one another."[5] This is best illustrated in the subtle, moving impact of his 1933 film *A Man's Castle*. One of the best films made in the thirties, *Castle* carefully establishes a bond between Spencer Tracy and Loretta Young that is tied in with the pulse of life itself. "Birds have nests, don't they?" the pregnant Young tearfully asks Tracy when he is about to abandon her for the wanderlust and fear that seem to propel him nowhere. Young's query is a wake-up call for Tracy. He has a sudden awareness that allows him to appreciate the beauty of their interdependence.

The spiritual quality in *Living on Velvet* is evident in the rebirth of George Brent's character, Terry Parker. After a plane he was piloting crashed, killing his parents and sister, Terry appears to be a lost soul. He is preoccupied with a fascination for flying, and taking risks. His meeting up with Amy Prentiss (Kay) doesn't alter his aimless manner, as he sees himself living on borrowed time...living on velvet, as he puts it. The kind of bond that Tracy and Young had in *A Man's Castle* doesn't seem available to him.

Brent and Francis' characters first meet at a party she is giving. Screenwriters Jerry Wald and Julius Epstein sneaked in some sly, pre-Code humor, as Brent passes by two attractive women, gazing into each other's eyes. One says to the other, "I've been reading the most *interesting* book." "Oh?" the other woman's interest is peaked. "Um-hm," replies the first woman. "It's called *The Well of Loneliness*." The book, by Radclyffe Hall, is a 1920s' classic of lesbian fiction—a popular and sympathetic story of a young woman's coming to terms with her sexuality. The Breen Office would have bristled had they caught on. As the party proceeds, the fluid camera movement and close-ups reveal, with no dialogue, that Francis and Brent experience some sort of love at first sight. One senses that both lives are about to change direction. The two speak only briefly, stumbling over words that don't seem to matter. Brent says, "I'd like to say something...something..." Kay smiles, "I *know*. It isn't necessary." They concur that the ideal time to leave any party is at the beginning. Kay grabs her mink, abandons her guests and soon finds herself being teased atop a double-decker bus. Wald and Epstein provide a delicious opportunity for Kay to poke fun at herself and her r-less nature. Brent comments that he likes the sound of her voice and asks her to say something nice and long.

> She begins: "Thirty days hath September, Apwil..."
> He interrupts: "Apwil! Apwil?" (Kay nods.) "Hmm, I see! Repeat after me, please. Say: 'Around the ragged rocks the ragged rascal ran.'"
> She obliges: "Awound the wagged wocks the wagged wascal wan. There! You see? Now you know everything!" (She smiles. He's delighted).

Kay could have suppressed such an interlude, but went along with it, and turns her impediment into an asset. The audiences loved her for it.

After a whirlwind marriage, Kay realizes that Brent's demons have a stronger hold on him than her love does. She is confronted with a series of seemingly whimsical challenges. *Pate de foie gras* was easy enough for Kay to pronounce, but there was little she could do with the *case* of it that silly goose Brent brings home. She finally squawks when Brent squanders a financial windfall on a new plane instead of new furniture. Their love-nest collapses. "There's a void in your life," a frustrated Kay tells Brent. "I thought that when I married you I could fill that void. I've failed. I haven't cured you of your trouble. Why, I haven't even made you happy."

Director Frank Borzage's Living on Velvet *(1935). Kay ingratiatingly makes light of her lisp in this scene with George Brent. (Warners)*

The film tries to resolve its issues for the two lovers, as Brent once again escapes death in an automobile accident. He realizes that it's *Kay* that he wants more than anything else. "Everything seems different," Brent declares, as if awakening out of a haze. In the fade out Kay repeats a phrase of Brent's, at the very spot they had once rendezvoused. Looking up at a statue of General Sherman she says, "Love, General, something I learned from an old Indian chief whom I befriended as he lay dying in the Black Hills of South Dakota." The camera pulls back and ascends. Borzage's biographer, Frederick Lamster, surmised that Kay and Brent's characters became "a single spiritual unit. Their repetition of each other's words reinforces this…and echoes their transcendence into a sphere of greater spirituality, understanding, and love."[6] The Borzage formula was at work.

Was the pat, love cures all, ending completely satisfying? Some critics felt the ending fell flat. *The New York Times* reported, "With all the advantage of a rather neat plot situation, some brittle dialogue and the presence of the amiable George Brent and the attractive Kay Francis, the new photoplay…dwindles off to an unconvincing and rather meaningless ending…and it's too bad, after all the bright qualities that had gone into the film, that a more scintillant climax could not have been contrived. Mr. Brent's performance is excellent, and Miss Francis displays…a somewhat surprising talent for comedy…It is not the fault of the cast that the picture does not merit unqualified praise."

Flat ending or not, the film did well at the box-office, even in jerkwater places like Preston, Idaho where the owner of the Grand Theatre raved, "What a honey! I would like to have one like this on every program for a while. Perhaps I could lift the old place out of the mire."[7] Promotion over the airwaves also helped the film's success. Film fans had had their interest piqued by Francis and Brent's reenactment of their outstanding scenes from *Living on Velvet* on radio's *Hollywood Hotel.*

Film critic Kent Jones wrote an article on Borzage's work for *Film Comment* in 1997. He said Borzage, "had something rare in Hollywood: a philosophical formulation of life that, at a certain point in his career, took precedence over the delivery of a satisfying piece of entertainment..." Jones continues that Borzage's outlook was possibly "nourished by Masonic teaching and...exposure to the Mormons when he was growing up in Salt Lake City, but he believed it and sometimes bent plots inside out to accommodate it. Simply put, to find love is to find one's true self, and hence to create an invincible paradise on earth...Few meetings in the cinema are as charged as Brent and Francis locking eyes in *Living on Velvet*...but it's so forceful that it goes beyond the merely sexual. [Borzage] never treats sexuality in the 'frank' sense of, say, Delmer Daves, a zealous missionary on behalf of the honest proclamation of sexual appetite..."[8]

After Maurice left Hollywood for France, Kay and her diary were feeling "very sad" and "very unhappy." But, as usual, her mourning only lasted a day or so. As a "zealous missionary" and new beau in Kay's life, Delmer Daves, brought much more than a sexual appetite. He was a mentor, a playmate, a fellow traveler, and took a sincere interest in her career. If it wasn't for Kay's lisp, they may have never gotten together. Daves, who had studied law at Stanford, was a tall, nice-looking, sandy red-haired, easy-going guy. He was sent to help out on Kay's second Borzage-directed release of 1935, *Stranded*. Daves later recalled:

> Hal Wallis was production head at Warner Brothers during the thirties, and it was he who was Mr. Fate with Kay and me. He asked me...to go to her house and rewrite all the lines of the script that had the embarrassing r's which Kay would turn into w's in most instances...I hadn't even met her at that time, went to her house, introduced myself and the object of my visit...and it became one of Cole's [Porter]...'one of those things,' for we hit it off so well I never left, and we were devoted to each other solely for the next three years, traveled together between films, to New York, Europe...During those years Hedda and/or Louella (both close friends of ours and very tactful in their reporting of our wanders, etc.) would make us Best Bets in their annual matrimonial Derby columns. When our affair started I had been a bachelor with no permanent attachments for my thirty years, and Kay, on the contrary, had been married four times...and she laughed as she designated herself: lousy wife-happy lover.[9]

After Delmer Daves made his surprise visit, Kay was smitten. "He is a darling," she wrote on March 16, and a week later, "Christ, he is a good lover...my God, all hell broke loose. He came in his trousers."[10] Luckily, Daves turned out to be a match "made in heaven" for Kay. Her diary attests to their marathon of lovemaking and laughs—and Kay, happily falling asleep on Daves' shoulder. In April Kay queried, "Am I really falling in love with Del?"[11] Daves, whose contract allowed him to write at home, had never been noticed on the set of his previous film, *Flirtation Walk*. While he penned *Stranded*, he was on the set with Kay all day long.

Due to the production schedule for *Stranded* Kay was unable to accept her engraved invitation to attend the first get-together of the Nudist Club of New York. *The*

Kay and Delmer Daves (c. 1937). Scenarist Daves claimed that upon meeting him Kay declared herself "Lousy Wife-Happy Lover."

Los Angeles Examiner cunningly commented, "Being one of the screen's most famous clothes horses, this is vaguely incongruous, furthermore, she has no intention of going, first she's too busy and secondly because she hasn't that much curiosity." Kay sent the nudist club her regrets, and after shooting wrapped up on *Stranded* she ventured to Europe. Kay's scheduled departure on the *Aquitania* for France was headlined as an epochal event by *The New York Times.* Kay's friend Andy Lawler designated himself as her manager and told reporters that Kay would receive the press and give them refreshments in her stateroom. The reporter then described Kay's arrival: "Miss Francis came up to the waiting group. Her hand was out-stretched...'Hello, there! I'm glad to see you...Well, what shall I do for you?'...The hat she wore was made so that it looked like the top of a black cat's head. There was an emerald on the little finger of the right hand, set in sufficient platinum to cover the entire third joint."[12] (Unbeknownst to everyone, this "little gem," was one of Kay's favorites. A late Christmas gift from one of her New York pals, Kay loved the fact that it was entirely made of candy!) The reporter then described the surmounting chaos.

> 'Let's take a picture of you sitting on the rail,' one of the photographers said...After a few minutes of posing, the party adjourned to the Francis cabin...Meanwhile the 'hall' was filling up with autograph seekers...Miss Francis was very polite...She explained her circular idea of life. 'Everything goes in circles,' Miss Francis said. 'You have a round of bad pictures and then a round of good pictures. The principle applies in everything else, too,

don't you think?' ... One of the reporters started asking personal questions...which flustered Miss Francis, who has for years been a firm believer in the privacy of the public figure.[13]

A philosophical discussion about the cycles of success was of far more interest to Kay than talking about her *love* life, a subject that would have probably given half the nation apoplexy. It is interesting to note that Andy Lawler was posturing as Kay's manager on this trip. He was paid $10,000 to accompany her. And, according to Lawler, his services went well beyond the norm. Upon his return from Europe, Lawler, who was gay, circulated a story that Kay made sexual demands on him while in London, which he dutifully fulfilled.[14] So much for his valor and discretion. As previously mentioned, Kay spent much of her time on this trip convalescing from an operation for the removal of a salivary gland. The operation was given royal treatment by Sir Thomas Dunhill, surgeon to the royal family.[15] Just before her hospital visit, Kay's Italian Prince Paolo, who, according to one report, had been calling her frantically and long distance from Rome, got a different kind of "treatment" when he had greeted her. She was pining for Delmer and wrote, "Paolo at station. Dead tired. Bed. Slept with P. in afternoon and hated it. Told him everything at night then telephoned Del. I love him."[16]

While in London, Kay told Britain's *Film Weekly*, "I get a long vacation once a year...a holiday of two or three months in which I can get right away from Hollywood and even America and come to Europe. This annual trip is very important to me, for it gives me not only a change of scenery and climate, but also a change of outlook. In Hollywood there is a danger of not seeing the wood for the trees. You live too close to films to know what your work really looks like to others. Coming to Europe gives me a chance to check up with your views on my work and compare them with mine."[17] In Italy, after her hospital stay, Kay enthusiastically enjoyed a "change of outlook" and relished the moment. She put aside her love life and romantic obsessions just long enough to really relax into what life could offer. She treasured one particular incident and mentioned it to reporter Jerry Lane:

Bon Voyage, 1935. Kay off to Europe, where, she noted: "I feel my complete unimportance and yet, somehow, renew my faith in myself and in my potentialities." On this trip, Kay "renewed her faith" in a "bowl of grapes," rather than resume her "steamy" affair with a married Italian Count.

There were four of us that wanted to rent a boat. We were in a tiny Italian fishing village, and our Italian friend began arguing with the boatman over the price. They heckled over *two lire* for an hour. And loved it! It became almost a battle royal. When they had settled, the boatman's wife, who had known all along her husband would have to come to terms, brought us a bowl of magnificent grapes. She did it with a gesture that was half apology, half pride. I couldn't help giggling inside because the whole thing was so funny. And it stands out now as one of the highlights of the entire trip! When you live as if there wasn't any future you can get pleasure out of anything. Even out of a bowl of grapes![18]

While Kay found Hollywood "vitiating," she compared her trips to Europe with beautiful music—"as something into which I can sink myself," Kay rhapsodized. "My cares and problems and hurts are, somehow...healed [giving] me a new vision and a new perspective...I feel my complete unimportance and yet, somehow, renew my faith in myself and in my potentialities."[19] Kay was adamant about not spending time in big cities. On this adventure, aside from her stay in London, she visited exactly two cities—for a day and a half. "You can't get the *feel* of a country by exploring the bigger towns," said Kay. After putting on a fresh pair of slacks and goggles, she would spend most of her time bicycling through the countryside, while warbling tunes with her throaty voice. (Kay had built up her stamina at home for this adventure, by riding an electric stationary bicycle she had purchased in New York.)[20]

Revitalized, Kay returned to the U.S. and met with Delmer Daves. The couple escaped for a romantic getaway to Banff in the Canadian Rockies. Kay registered as "Mrs. Gibbs" and Daves as "Mr. Davis." The year-round wilderness playground was popular among Hollywood Stars and International Royalty. The park encased the spectacular kind of jewel that could take Kay's breath away: Lake Louise (originally named Lake Emerald). Kay's affinity for emerald green was reflected below Victoria Glacier in the lake's unusual opaque waters. Kay found diamonds "cold, hypocritical and egotistical." "If I have a favorite," she told a reporter, "it is the emerald, because it is warm, honest and friendly."[21] Kay and Daves' romantic, relaxing escape included the comfort and old-world charm of the lakeside hotel, Chateau Lake Louise. Kay was in good spirits and ecstatic about Daves. "I love my room. I love my bed. I love, love, love, Del," she wrote.[22] The majestic surroundings acted as a catalyst and she soared. "Snow snow snow. Fun day—quiet and Oh thank you dear God for (Kay and Delmer)—everything! Walk four miles in snow before lunch."[23] After two weeks of mountain air, canoeing, exploring the Plain of Six Glaciers, and much lovemaking, Kay reported back to Warners refreshed. Poor Delmer simply returned with a bad back!

When Kay and Delmer returned to Glendale, the press was waiting for them. Kay was dismissive to their queries for photos and details of her new relationship. Was there a romance? "My heavenly goodness, no!" Kay answered as she disappeared into her taxi. Daves stayed behind simply to report, "I have nothing to say."[24] Del's back soon recovered and Kay was elated to have her lover "back." But, lack of birth control once again came to haunt Kay in August. "God damn it, I am caught! ... Mrs. Wilson performed the abortion! No fun."[25] Mrs. Wilson did not succeed and the operation was repeated on August 21. "At last got the bambino! Home and bed. Anytal [sedative]. Doped. Del with me."[26] By the end of the month Kay's life was back to normal. Del was with her every night and she was happy. Over the next three years Kay and Daves' travels coincided with their work schedules: nine months on and three months off on vacation. Their compatibility was well documented in the fan magazines.

Stranded was released upon Kay's return from Europe. As usual, Kay was adorned in handsome frocks in every scene. The real shocker was that her character was allowed to maintain her integrity, her profession, her individuality and her beliefs at the film's fade-out. Such scenarios for women were practically nonexistent as a result of the Production Code. Daves' input into *Stranded* was evident throughout. He had the ability to develop a film around an important social theme with a direct, uncomplicated narrative.

Stranded was adapted from the story *The Lady with a Badge* by Ferdinand Reyher and Frank Wead (who would write *Test Pilot* for Gable and Loy). Kay and George Brent find themselves solidly on ground in San Francisco, building bridges out of steel and human relationships. The story was more down-to-earth and their connection more feasible than it had been in the airy *Living on Velvet*. Francis worked with people for the Traveler's Aid Society, while Brent worked with steel, as foreman on the new construction of the Golden Gate Bridge. (Exciting footage was incorporated into the film of the bridge, before the span across the bay was completed.) As usual, there is the instant attraction of Kay and Brent upon meeting and the inevitable conflict in their world view. Brent disapproves of Francis' social work. He insists that she quit and take care of his needs as a homemaker. "Only weak people need help," he argues. Kay has a more compassionate viewpoint and simply states, "I see life in terms of human beings." Kay seems well rid of Brent and his stubborn attitude. The Golden Gate Bridge itself becomes a metaphor for Brent's eventual change of heart. Amazingly, he learns to appreciate her work and her individuality. She concludes that their respective careers complement each other. "You build with steel," she tells him, "and I *try* to build with people." This is a complete reversal of *Living on Velvet*, where she was given the hard-to-swallow line at the film's conclusion, "I'll be what you want me to be...I'll do what you want me to do."

Usually, as prescribed by the PCA, the woman inevitably gave up her career for the man. Audiences would have to accept this message for decades. So, miracle of miracles, in *Stranded*, Francis is able to continue her work. Throughout the film we see the details of her profession: guiding travelers at a station terminal; making sure a young woman, unwed and pregnant, gets proper hospital care; listening to an elderly woman bunked in the poorhouse talk of her glorious past; and, accompanying some immigrant brides to their prospective husbands. Kay even storms a union meeting to defend Brent of charges made against him. Through the combined effort of Daves' script and Borzage's direction, love once again redeems those who find it, with a feminist twist.

Kay was impressed by the performance of a young actress in *Stranded* named June Travis. Travis played the desperate, expectant, unwed mother, with heartbreaking realism. As was typical of Kay, she marched into Jack Warner's and producer Hal Wallis' offices to promote the career of a young hopeful. "I tell you that girl has something," Kay told them. "Give her a chance. Give her better roles."[27] As a result, Travis ended up with a steady career in films.

The Los Angeles Evening Herald Express took note of the unusual female-male plot line in *Stranded*. "Clash they do from their first meeting, and the audience thoroughly enjoys the arguments, the swift give-and-take of repartee and the un-stereotyped love scenes between the two." *Variety* noted Kay's "smooth and sensitive performance." Kay wasn't always the darling of the critics. As usual, Kay could count on Elizabeth Yeaman of the *Hollywood Citizen News* to take a few potshots at her expense. For *Stranded*, Yeaman stated, "Miss Francis does not vary her usual performance…with a change of raiment she effects…transition…Clothes, as usual, do most of Miss Francis' acting for her." That wasn't all Kay had to contend with. *The New York Times* reviewer for the film thought, "The Francis-Brent team…a happy combination," but quoted Kay as saying, "Nevah wose youah awwogance!" On viewing the film the line is distinctly spoken as, "Never lose your arrogance!" It's odd that professionals would stoop to get a laugh at Kay's expense, but it became typical of the kind of flak she had to put up with.

Kay had enough champions not to pay much attention to her detractors. Chiefly among them was Warners' make-up artist, Perc Westmore. He told one reporter that Kay was the "best friend he ever had." Perc acknowledged her loyalty and explained that Kay's "appeal to men flings forth like a magnet from the screen…subconsciously men always respond to the real article…that can't be downed in the shimmer of bleached hair, cupid lips, arched brows…Something in the deep heart of every man applauds the *real* in every woman."[28] Kay often mentioned her admiration for Perc. She told *Modern Screen* in 1935:

> He excites me because he is a man who started from the bottom and built up a splendid organization and yet has time to be absolutely crazy about children. Great tenderness in a self-made success is a very bewildering quality to me. Very thorough, extraordinarily conscientious, Perc has gathered about him in his business, people who are nice as well as artistic and capable. That's a reflection on his own intrinsic worth, in my estimation. But I can't get away from his love for children. He has three, two of whom are adopted, and his love for them is marvelous. It denotes much that is beyond mere words.[29]

In the spring of 1935 Perc ran out of funds to complete his House of Westmore which would promote a line of cosmetics. His brother Frank revealed years later, that Perc,

> …one morning at Warner Brothers…was making up Kay Francis for a movie in which she was starring called *Stranded*. He told me later that it probably was the irony of the name of the film which prompted him to tell Kay that his 'monument,' as he liked to call it, now would never be completed. Right then and there, with one eyelash on and the other still in Perc's hand, Kay reached into her purse, brought out her checkbook, tore out a blank check, signed her name at the bottom of it, and told Perc to fill in whatever amount he needed. He filled in $25,000, rushed to his decorators with the money, and the job was completed on schedule.[30]

It was no surprise when Kay's generosity gave her the honors on April 13, 1935 (notice, it was the "13th") to officially open the golden doors of the two-story Tudor-style House of Westmore on Sunset Boulevard. The press reported, "Kay Francis, a reigning queen of the silver screen, turned a golden key which opened this magnificent salon of beauty. Joan Blondell threw the golden switch which flooded the interior of the salon with light…everyone stood dazzled and dumbfounded by the spectacle that met their eyes. Claudette

Colbert...pressed a gold button to light the exterior."[31] Marlene Dietrich, Carole Lombard, Clara Bow, Myrna Loy and other celebrities joined Kay to spend the day being coiffed, painted, and groomed by their favorite Westmore brother. It was a dream made possible by Kay's generosity. Although she held a tight purse string on her own budget, she had a reputation for reaching into her pocketbook when friends were in need.

Kay often spent weekends, the summers of 1935-36, at Perc's beach house. Frank Westmore, who was twelve at the time, remembered watching Edmund Lowe and John Boles, "playing heated games of bridge with two of Perc's closest pals, Ann Sheridan and Kay Francis."[32] This happy seashore scene bubbled over into her next film assignment, *The Goose and the Gander* (which was actually filmed before *Stranded*).

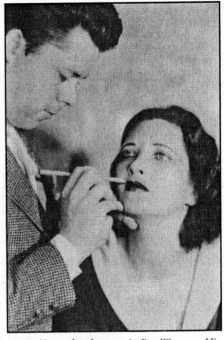

1935. Kay and make-up artist Perc Westmore. His "House of Westmore" would never have opened its doors without Kay's generosity. (Warners)

The Goose and the Gander was a short, tight bit of froth that had many a chuckle and good ensemble playing by Kay, George Brent, Genevieve Tobin, Ralph Forbes and Claire Dodd. The film opens at a seaside resort where Kay finds herself eavesdropping on the romantic getaway plans of a frivolous, married woman (Tobin) and George Brent. When husband Ralph Forbes confronts wife Tobin regarding her escapades, she informs him, "I've been flirting with *every* man I meet!" And reassures him with a flippant, "Shall we just trust each other with a beautiful blind faith?"

Kay and George meet officially after spilling cocktails on each another. Brent offers a peace-offering for his clumsiness. "A war might be more exciting," Kay suggests. At this point we learn that Forbes is actually Kay's ex-husband. Kay's mind starts scheming immediately and just when we are wondering what she's up to, two jewel thieves are heisting Kay's emeralds in her hotel room. As planned, Brent and Tobin inadvertently end up at Kay's cabin home pretending to be man and wife. A madcap plot ensues with merry mayhem when the robbers show up. At the *finis* Kay and Brent end up in jail for stealing *her* emeralds. This jaunty romp is funny, amusing stuff. Alfred E. Green did a fine job of directing the sparkling 65-minute feature. It was a switch for Green who was noted for his work with contemporary dramas such as Barbara Stanwyck's *Baby Face* (1933). He had worked with Kay on *I Loved a Woman*. His turnabout success in *The Goose and the Gander* was appreciated by the public and the press alike.

Jimmy Starr wrote for the *LA Evening Herald Express*, "The screen hasn't enjoyed such a delightful farce and marital mix-up since *Private Lives*...What a lot of fun director Al Green has made of it, too. He deserves special praise for his surprise maneuvers and the

Kay and George Brent flirt after spilling cocktails on each other in The Goose and the Gander *(1935). (Warners)*

manner in which he kept the half-dozen main characters revolving in a circle of amusing incidents…Kay Francis is quite lovely as the heroine and fixer-upper…Genevieve Tobin does splendidly as the flirty wife." *The New York Times* liked the mad scramble of *Goose* saying, "The narrative is so deviously complex that if you stop to light a cigarette or talk to your neighbor it requires five minutes to reorient yourself in its labyrinthine ways. Its chief impediment…comes from its insistence on cramming the dialogue with r's, which have an embarrassing habit of becoming w's when Miss Francis goes to work on them." It almost seemed to be the vogue to comment on Kay's speech, warranted or not.

Kay rated the number two position in *Variety's* popularity rating of Warner stars for 1935. The studio rewarded her with a new dressing room. Lloyd Pantages covered the news-worthy event in March, noting, "we discover that in Kay Francis' new dressing room…which is actually a suite of rooms, the walls of the main room are hung with…autographed photographs of her most intimate motion picture friends, but in her sitting room, the walls are as bare as a monastery, the only bit of adornment being a photograph of her maid, which is framed and placed well on a table near the door. The effect is somewhat startling, for after you gazed upon the placidity of this faithful person, she suddenly arrives in person to bring you a dish of tea."[33] The prominence of Ida's photograph was understandable. After all, according to her—it was, "our career," *not* just Kay's.

As usual, Kay's name continued to pop up in the best-dressed columns. When told she was in the same clotheshorse class as Norma Shearer or Dietrich, Kay suggested "old workhorse" was a more apt description. After Lilyan Tashman passed away, Louella Parson's thought it *vital* to devote a lengthy column to her likely successor as best-dressed woman. With the help of leading fashion designers, Parsons narrowed the contest down to: Dietrich, Lombard, Shearer and Francis. The columnist proclaimed, "Now let's hear from the

The New York Times *thought* The Goose and the Gander *(1935) "deviously complex." Kay and George Brent would team together in six films. (Warners)*

world…Marlene Dietrich, Carole or Kay Francis…?" So, Kay came up with her own list and humbly omitted herself. She told reporter Harrison Carroll that she was impressed with: Constance Bennett, Claudette Colbert, Marlene Dietrich, Carole Lombard and Myrna Loy. "But please list them alphabetically," said Kay. "I don't want to get in any more jams with my friends." When Kay's mother was queried about Kay's fashion sense, she readily replied, "Kay has always been clothes-conscious since a baby. When she was four I found her changing from a pair of plain, play panties into party panties trimmed with ribbon and lace. 'I ain't going to wear panties without trimming,' she declared." Kay was so mortified by this tidbit of information that Mrs. Gibbs was never allowed another interview. Lloyd Pantages supplied the ultimate fashion topper for Kay in his news column stating: "Kay Francis wears her skirts thirteen inches (Kay's favorite number) from the floor on her street costumes, because she has definitely decided that such a length makes street walking a pleasure!" Kay merely tolerated all the attention and occasionally relished risking her lofty status. She told reporter Harry Evans about the Eastern society matron who had reservations about including Kay on the guest list. "The woman who was giving the party had asked one of my friends to drop me a hint about what a *nice* party it was going to be," Kay sneered. "She was having some people who were veddy, veddy prominent socially. She told my friend, 'I am sure Miss Francis is not the strictly Hollywood type.' I promptly got together everything fancy I own…added a gay touch here and there. I walked out looking much like one of those white French poodles when they are washed, trimmed, powdered, and fluffed for a dog show." Kay reveled her hostess's displeasure.

In August 1935, Kay began working on *I Found Stella Parish*. The film was high-gloss soap and a very popular vehicle for her. Robert Osborne, host of television's Turner Classic Movies, noted that the film was the "perfect example of what was known as the

'Kay Francis Formula,' peppered with bizarre situations and worlds they [audiences] were never privy to." Osborne also cautioned, "You have to be careful, because they can become very addictive." (Hmm…) The "Kay Francis Formula" made a great deal of money for Warners over the next few years.

In *I Found Stella Parish*, Kay worked with the reputable Mervyn LeRoy whose versatility had scored him hits with *Little Caesar* (1930) and *I Am a Fugitive from a Chain Gang* (1932). The John Monk Saunders' story allowed Kay to play a famous, American-born, London stage actress with a secret past she keeps hidden from her daughter (Sybil Jason). As the story unravels, we find all kinds of rats in the cellar, including an ex-husband who had killed Kay's leading man back in 1930. Due to circumstantial evidence Kay is forced to have her baby in prison. Years later, the husband shows up out of nowhere to blackmail her, so she does the sensational and disappears. The press and radio bulletins have a field day. She is then tailed by Ian Hunter who plays, as he puts it, "a newshound first, a gent second." Amid the film's dearth of reality checks, their mutual attraction and love complicate the situation into further tragic results. Somehow it all works, except for Kay's shouting match with Caligula (!) in her London triumph, *This Brief Hour*. Fortunately, it was only a brief few seconds. After Caligula promises her that the beasts were growing hungry for her "soft flesh," Kay proudly confesses her love for the ruler's captive slave. "In death you give me life!" she exclaims defiantly.

Variety thought the film to be a "powerful story of an actress and mother love. Kay Francis…is shown to be an actress of much ability." The reviewer also found Kay to be a "cameo of loveliness." Throughout the picture Sid Hickox's camera seemed to adore her. Andre Sennwald for *The New York Times* thought *I Found Stella Parish* was relentless in,

I Found Stella Parish *(1935) Before Caligula's lions eat Kay's "soft flesh," co-stars Paul Lukas and Ian Hunter give her a pep talk. (Warners)*

"wringing the last tear from the reluctant duct," in a story that was, "too, too tragic." Sennwald had to acknowledge that the ploy had worked, "from the sobs of the departing audiences."

Sybil Jason, a disarming little emotional actress, does a splendid job. After being separated from Kay, she inquires as to when her mother is coming back. "Is she lost?" she pleads to Hunter. The scene is a real heart-tugger. When I contacted Ms. Jason, she was heartfelt in her praise for Kay:

> How much I admired and dearly loved Kay! She was one of the most warm and sensitive people I ever had the pleasure of knowing and working with. Ironically, I played her daughter in two different Warner Brothers movies and she was the spitting image of my own mother. Kay got such a kick out of that fact. Kay always referred to me as "my daughter, Sybil." I just wish Kay Francis had received her full due on her contribution to film and stage. She was an amazing woman both on and off the screen. I shall never forget her. I will be ever grateful to her for the kindness and love that she showed me when I was a child.[38]

Stella Parish gave audiences the added thrill of seeing glamorous Kay hitting the skids. She ends up in seedy burlesque houses acting out her sordid past and commenting, "Americans pay most anything to look at a freak!" Tears well up again, when Paul Lukas shows up backstage and offers her a London comeback. On film, Kay gives a convincing portrayal of a woman who has been humiliated, humbled, broken, hardened and finally, acquiescent to a helping hand.

Kay had a rapport with the director Mervyn LeRoy. He respected Kay and went along with her theory about shooting important scenes on the 13th hour of the day— Kay's "Lucky 13." Jack Grant reported from the set before one of Kay's important scenes:

> "Kay has an affinity for certain numbers," Merv explained. "It's really her only superstition, if you can even call it a superstition. She particularly likes the hour of one o'clock and while she never complains about working at times she doesn't like, you sometimes can sense a slight tenseness that detracts from her best work. She has had to weep now in every scene for three days and this is the most important 'take' of the lot. That is why I postponed it until today-Friday the thirteenth—and this hour. The scene requires a terrific emotional intensity, actually the highlight of the whole performance. With all the numbers in her favor, she will go into it without a worry. Just watch."
>
> We watched—fascinated. The scene was a six-minute close-up and in it, Kay Francis did one of the most beautiful pieces of acting that we have ever seen. The thing rang completely true. She wept real tears and when the scene had ended, the set thundered in applause, a spontaneous ovation that is never accorded a star by the hard-boiled workers of Hollywood unless they have been deeply and sincerely moved.[39]

I Found Stella Parish did record business in New York. Kay and Ian Hunter did excerpts from the film on the popular radio series, *Hollywood Hotel*. Louella Parsons reported that Jack Warner was smiling dollar signs from Kay's success and that he had rewarded her big time. "Not all the movie contracts are signed with struggle and strife," reported Parsons. "Kay Francis, whose contract had not expired with Warner Brothers, was handed a new one. Jack Warner told her that she had accepted any story given her without a word and had always been gracious and lacking in unpleasant temperament, that he wanted to show his appreciation by handing her voluntarily a three-year contract."[40]

As pleased as Jack Warner was with Kay's attitude, she had ambitions for roles that were more challenging. She sought opportunities to widen her range. Sam Goldwyn wanted Kay to play Edith Cortright in the film *Dodsworth*. It was an excellent opportunity to re-team with Walter Huston. "No can do *Dodsworth*. Much fuss!" Kay entered into her diary when Warner refused to loan her to Goldwyn.[41] The part went to Mary Astor. Kay also persuaded Delmer Daves to write a scenario for Mildred Cram's novella *Forever*. The story appealed to Kay's ethereal side. Fitting into the rare film genre of *Death Takes a Holiday* (1934) and *Peter Ibbetson* (1935), the story tells of two lovers, Julie and Colin, whose souls meet in a half-world awaiting life on earth. Years later, in physical life, they both are mysteriously drawn by an unexplainable longing to Mont Blanc in France. Upon meeting, they, "revel in the ecstasy of this seemingly new found love." Fate steps in. After their lives are claimed in a skiing and car accident, the lovers are reunited in cosmic space. No union is eternal, the story claims, "*This*, is forever."[42] Daves was reluctant to do an adaptation of the story. Not because he didn't like it. He simply wasn't in favor of mixing their professional and private lives. He was relieved of the responsibility when it was made known that Norma Shearer owned the rights to the popular novel.

Daves later said, "Kay's greatest ambition was to do *Tristan and Isolde*, but I discouraged this, feeling her metier was modern life. I was certain the public wanted the more glamorous Kay Francis, the Kay with the wondrous husky voice, with or without her r's."[43] To imagine Kay in the legend of *Tristan and Isolde* (best known as Wagner's 1865 opera) is provocative. Aboard ship from Ireland, Isolde is taken against her will by Tristan to meet her future husband, Cornwall's King Mark. Isolde and her captor unknowingly drink a potion that awakens their mutual undying love for one another. Kay pursued the idea of *Tristan* with Delmer, but got nowhere. Delmer was never again required to work on one of Kay's films at Warners.

Kay's quasi-spiritual bent in reading was further reflected when she plugged her favorite read of 1934-35, *All Men Are Enemies,* by British author Richard Aldington (of *Les Liasons Dangereuses* fame). She sent columnist-screenwriter Elsie Janis a copy of the romance novel. The story concerned the protagonist's attempt to escape life in a post-World War society and recapture the idyllic pastoral life of prewar England with his first love Kathy. Janis commented that, when filmed, Kay would be perfect for the part of Kathy. *All Men Are Enemies* included a commentary on earth-life by the gods of Mr. Olympus, which, again, captivated Kay's sense of the ethereal.

Author Faith Baldwin observed that Kay "knows which parts she can feel, and feeling, play. She has an excellent grasp of the mechanics of screen writing, the perfect construction which should go into the making of the perfect picture, and she is quick to see flaws in technique or characterization."[44] If Kay envisioned herself as Julie in *Forever,* or Isolde, it was because she felt she could make them *real*. Kay commented that, "Acting brings a peculiar satisfaction because it permits one to creep into the very heart of different characters. I've portrayed many women...a few saints and several very lurid ladies, and each one reacts differently to love and romance because custom and environment effect the expression of their emotions. This is fascinating to an actress—a woman's imagination is limitless, and, too, it tests her histrionic ability. I always enjoy foreign characterizations because invariably the backgrounds are an integral part of the drama and this adds a 'feel' to the emotions."[45] Kay felt that her range went well beyond the modern metier.

Kay's distinctive thespian skills were acknowledged by theatrical legends Max Reinhardt and Peggy Wood in two *New York Times* articles in 1935. Producer Reinhardt listed Kay among the twelve greatest artists in talkies, along with Cagney, Laughton, Hepburn, Garbo, Robert Donat and others.[46] Peggy Wood, a fine stage actress and dialectician, listed a select *seven* best screen-acting voices, saying, "Kay Francis speaks extremely well—when she wants to. That throaty, emotional voice is decidedly effective and she is *always* interesting."[47] Wood listed Kay in the same league as Helen Hayes. Compliments from Reinhardt and Wood were indeed feathers in Kay's cap.

As for the contemporary roles she had played, Kay emphasized that *mental attitude* is what kept her characterizations human and feminine. She felt a similar attitude could be reflected in the real lives of women who went to the movies. She commented, "It's all a matter of their own understanding and response. And I know enough of work outside the fiction of the films to assure you that it is just as possible in *real life*. Business and this thing that people call glamour or charm—are *not* incompatible except as the woman herself makes them so."[48] Kay mentioned in interviews that a tailored masculine image for businesswomen was not necessary and certainly needn't extend beyond the eight-hour work day. She wanted to present an image for young women on screen that showed responsibility and intelligence enveloped with feminine attributes. While in New York, in early 1935, Kay elaborated further on the subject for *Collier's* magazine, "The trouble with so many women in business is that they persist in being business women after hours as well as in the office...When a man finishes his day in the office...he closes the door on it and relaxes. He has the wisdom to shake himself loose, change his viewpoint and become a social being. But do most women do this? No, they take their business home with them...It doesn't make them a bit more efficient and no one wants them to do it."[49] Kay's diaries attest to the fact that she rarely brought her work home with her. In her own words, she could "shake herself loose" and "become a social being." Kay saw herself as on par intellectually with men, but holding on to her feminine qualities. She admitted, "I am sometimes called 'a man's woman,' and I think I am. Men have definitely helped me in my life far more than women have. Whatever I have done, whatever I have been or hope to be, I owe, for the most part, to men. For the most part, too, I prefer the company of men. I prefer to talk to them, argue with them, work with them, plan with them."[50]

In the fall of 1935, businesswoman Kay was part of a highly embryonic group of stars combining to make films along the lines of United Artists (which was made up of Chaplin, Pickford and Fairbanks). The new group was headed by Richard Barthelmess, along with Kay, Ronald Colman and Clive Brook. Although the plans never materialized, Kay, being "a man's woman," was a logical choice for such a venture.[51]

How did Kay's personal attitudes regarding men translate on screen? Hilary Lynn, for *Photoplay*, attempted an answer, and wrote, "Kay Francis accepts men and their passions as a necessary part of the scheme of things. So she *allows* them to make love to her. Their companionship, their admiration are important to her…But she has an automatic, collected control over herself and her emotions…She seems to have learned that no good can come of allowing a passion to consume one…She responds to the amorous advances of her lovers—but she never abandons herself."[52] Lynn's observation is exactly what kept the real-life Francis-Daves liaison thriving for as along as it did. Kay didn't have to abandon herself. Theirs was not an all-consuming passion. The relationship avoided much of the dramatic fireworks of some of her previous entanglements and allowed for a healthier intimacy. Kay's New Year's entry for 1936 acknowledged her gratitude for Delmer Daves. "Beginning the New Year with my lover. May he be in the same bed with me next year at this time."[53]

When opting to name her fantasies for onscreen passion and new leading men, Kay made some interesting choices. She told *Film Weekly*, "Charles Laughton and Clark Gable are actors whom I have not yet worked with, and would like to. But my real screen ambition is to play opposite James Cagney. He is the leading man of my dreams. Unfortunately, I am afraid Warner Brothers will never be able to find a story with suitable parts for us both. And, anyhow, perhaps I'm a little too tall for Cagney to give me a really effective and affectionate sock in the jaw?"[54] Apparently, Kay's crush and admiration for Cagney was on the level. She included him in an article she wrote, titled, "The Eight Most Fascinating People in Hollywood."

Jimmy Cagney simply enchants me on the screen. He is my favorite actor and so I'll admit I may be prejudiced! It's an instinctive liking that I have for him. I often try to analyze his appeal. He isn't handsome. But every single muscle of his seems to be taut. Jimmy is like a leopard, ready to spring. I sit through all his pictures twice because I get such a kick out of watching him…We are only casual acquaintances and I run into him just at the studio and at actors' meetings and parties. He is astonishingly quiet and modest, a strange contrast to that fiery self the camera tempts forth. I guess it's a good thing he isn't as devastating 'off' as 'on,' for Cagney in celluloid is irresistible to me![55]

It's very unlikely that Kay's Cagney crush was based on any of his gangster roles. Kay's aversion to guns was no secret. Reporter Sara Hamilton made a point of saying that Kay "never attends a gangster picture. The shooting leaves her prostrate."[56]

As they approached the first anniversary of their meeting, Kay and Daves were still determined to keep their relationship under wraps. Harrison Carroll reported in late 1935, "The campaign of Kay Francis and Delmer Daves to avoid photographers is as good as a spy melodrama…When *Shipmates Forever* was sneak-previewed…the pair hid themselves in the balcony. Not taking any chances, they didn't leave with the preview crowd, but sat through the regular picture on the program. Then Daves came down first and…finally gave Kay the high sign and the two faded away like the G-men were after them."[57] (Daves had scripted the popular Dick Powell-Ruby Keeler feature, which was directed by Frank Borzage.)

Daves also gave the "high sign" for what the studio claimed to be Kay's most challenging role. She had been selected to play Florence Nightingale. The proposed film was to be a companion piece for the studio's successful screen-bio *The Story of Louis Pasteur*. James Robert Parish wrote, "The selection of Kay for the prestigious production delighted Delmer Daves. It was he who reputedly 'sold' her on the idea of tackling the offbeat assignment."[58] Kay's spirits were soaring on Christmas Eve as she went a-caroling through Brentwood and Beverly Hills with Jeanette MacDonald, Jimmy Stewart and Allan Jones.[59] What transpired next was totally unexpected. All the hopes that Kay, Delmer and director William Dieterle had for the Nightingale film were shattered at all turns. A saga in itself, the production of *The White Angel* demonstrates how the power of the Production Code, coupled with further restrictions from outside sources, and the demanding expectations of Jack Warner, could cripple a story, a film and a star's career.

❊ DELMER DAVES ❊

Born: July 24, 1904, San Francisco, California
Died: August, 17, 1977, La Jolla, California
Kay's companion: December 1934—October 1937

Delmer Lawrence Daves had an intimate connection with the wild west. His grandfather, fresh off the boat from Ireland, assisted Mormon wagon trains to Salt Lake City where he went into the freight business and rode the Pony Express. Daves' grandmother was born in California in 1854. His family left San Francisco after the quake in 1906 and headed for Los Angeles. At age 10, he had bit parts in silent films and served as prop boy in James Cruze's 1923 classic *The Covered Wagon*, on location in Utah. While working as a draftsman for the City of Palo Alto, he studied law at Stanford University. After graduation in 1927, Daves wanted to connect with Native Americans so he ventured to Arizona and lived among the Hopi and Navajo tribes. Upon his return, he joined the Pasadena Playhouse and reconnected with director James Cruze, making appearances in silent films, such as a boxing champion in James Cruze's *The Duke Steps Out* (1929) with William Haines. The husky 6"2' Daves was also technical director on the film. More promising was his serious pursuit as a screenwriter for Warner Brothers in such film gems as *Dames* (1934), *The Petrified Forest* (1936), and RKO's *Love Affair* (1939).

Daves first met Kay Francis in 1934 while working on the script for *Stranded*. The two hit it off and became an item. After their amicable separation, Daves married actress Mary Lou Lander in 1938. When WW II broke, he devoted himself to directing patriotic films that focused on emotional challenges rather than heroics, such as *Destination Tokyo* (1943) and *Pride of the Marines* (1945). His films put "a very human face on the battles." Daves continued producing and directing his own scripts, many noteworthy and box-office successes such as *Dark Passage* (1947) with Bogart and Bacall. He returned to his roots and early experiences with Native Americans with a Western film cycle. 20th Century-Fox's *Broken Arrow* (1950), was one of the best pictures dealing with the displacement of Apaches by white settlers.

In 1957 Daves reworked his 1939 script from *Love Affair* into the memorable classic soaper *An Affair to Remember*. Daves most successful film, *A Summer Place* (1959), challenged Hollywood and contributed to the liberalization of the Production Code. In the 1960s Daves directed a series of popular soaps such as *Parrish* (1961) and his final film, *The Battle of the Villa Fiorita* (1965). Daves was well liked, open and easy-going. His cabin in the San Bernadino mountains bore a motto over the hearth, saying, "Know Thyself." He passed away in La Jolla, California in 1977. Daves was survived by his wife, Mary Lou, a son, two daughters and three grandchildren.

Chapter 11

Well-Bahaved Women Rarely Make History – *The White Angel*

On the Crimean warfront of 1854, we see Kay Francis as Florence Nightingale storming the Scutari supply store, after hours, taking what she needs from a disgruntled supply clerk. She is soon confronted with her "superior," Dr. Hunt, a misogynist, who feels Nightingale is far beneath him. He chastises her saying "she should behave like a soldier." Very much in charge, Francis fires back, "I'm not *here* to behave!" In many respects Nightingale was not *anywhere* to behave and this is exactly what allowed her to make a difference—to make history.

As Queen of the Warner lot and top female box-office attraction, Kay had a great deal of clout for acquiring the role of Florence Nightingale. After Warners' astounding success with *The Story of Louis Pasteur* with Paul Muni, they looked for a follow-up biography from the field of medicine. In December 1935, entertainment news across the country announced: "Kay Francis For Florence Nightingale—Will Do Greatest Role of Her Career for Warners." *The San Francisco Chronicle* commented, "Kay Francis is beautiful enough and glamorous enough to transcend the monotony of a nurse's uniform. And, by the way, that is something few Hollywood actresses can do...I might add there is a fine humanity in Kay Francis which transcends dress and circumstance. One other woman on the screen completely dominates the situation by merit of her light and spirit, and that woman is Garbo."[1]

Kay's intelligence and reputation for having concern for others had preceded her. Like Nightingale she was uniquely unconventional. Both women preferred the intellectual society of men and thrived on being independent. However, the announcement of Kay's plum role in what was then titled *Angel of Mercy*, did not please Warners' contract player, Josephine Hutchinson. While *Pasteur* was shooting, the studio told her she would play Nightingale. Hutchinson later commented, "When Kay Francis was announced for Florence Nightingale, after it had been promised to me, I was with Bette Davis at the studio, and she told me, 'Go up and do something about it!' I do think my quality would have been better for it, but the fighting didn't interest me—I just wasn't that ambitious."[2] Hutchinson's sharper features made her a better look-alike for Nightingale. Nightingale biographer Lytton Strachey depicts her as a powerful, albeit demonic eagle. Unlike Nightingale, Kay's face was softer. Her presence was more like that of a swan.

Kay as Florence Nightingale in The White Angel *(1936). London's* Film Weekly *stated, "Kay Francis has at last found a role to test her powers and measure her stature as an actress…she appears once more as a whole person." Warners)*

After *The White Angel* was released, Kay received many praises for a memorable performance: *Variety Daily*—"Kay Francis steps into high niche as an important actress in her superb portrait of Florence Nightingale…her fine, sensitive and altogether impressive performance opens up new screen cycle for a personality already high in popular esteem"; *Motion Picture Daily*—"Kay Francis captures the indomitable courage of the character and gives a performance which stirs the emotions; London, *Picturegoer Weekly*—"Kay Francis enlists full sympathy as Florence Nightingale…she plays the role with easy and convincing naturalness…the excellent modulation of her voice and the dramatic yet effortless intensity with which she plays the part…fulfills the object of paying tribute to a woman who brought honour and recognition to the nursing profession"; *Literary Digest*—"Three persons could easily have flooded such a story with syrup and tearful hokum. Scenarist [Mordaunt] Shairp yielded to the peril only momentarily and in scenes where honest sentiment was no plague to the story. Director William Dieterle, followed through by disciplining the cast into sharp…performances. Miss Kay Francis, in the title role…made a forthright, stirring performance. The film is a triumph for all three."[3] Some critics felt that Nightingale's drive and ambition were missing from the benevolent, yet determined presence that Francis brings to the screen. There was *no question* that strong forces prevented her from portraying Nightingale any differently.

The offer to play Florence Nightingale was presented to Kay by Warner Brothers as an opportunity, albeit a double-edged one. Not only was she to effectively bring to life a historical legend, her efforts had to be reflected in impressive returns at the box-office. Kay grabbed at the chance to play in a prestigious production and redefine her acting career. Scenarist Mordaunt Shairp tried to eliminate lines that gave Kay trouble. Kay later said, "The only real trouble was when we got to the nurse's oath that was full of r's. I learned it so every 'r' came out clearly. When the picture was released, I waited for the notices. Always before some critic said something like 'the r-less Miss Francis is back in a new film.' This time the sillies wrote, 'Kay Francis complete with r's in new film.' After that I gave up trying to overcome the lisp."[4]

With the harrowing r's gone, one interviewer found Kay bubbling over before filming began. She was elated about her role as Nightingale. Kay explained her enthusiasm:

You have never been called one of the best dressed women or a glamorous personality, whatever *that* is…Well, I *have* and for nine years I have been trying to live it down. This role is my first chance…Florence Nightingale is a role without an alibi. All the clothes and glamour in the world could not make it convincing. It's an acting part and an opportunity that doesn't come often to an actress. The ordinary picture uses conflict as a climax, but this story is conflict from the very start. Before she takes up her career, Florence Nightingale has to fight the opposition of her own family. Then she has to ignore the wishes of the man who loves her. When she is thrust into the harrowing realities of the Crimean War, she pits her wits against scores of official enemies. Underneath all the turbulence of her life, she must show the *calm, determined* sympathy and merciful desire to serve humanity. Any actress would be enthusiastic over the chance.[5]

Was the average cinemagoer eager to see something titled *The White Angel* about the pioneering efforts of the world's most famous nurse? Was there enough "meat" to her story to create another Oscar-winning, box-office epoch ala *The Story of Louis Pasteur*? If there was, could the scriptwriters and director honestly present it under the constant scrutiny of the Production Code? And what about the imperious, nit-picking on the set by British "experts" who were hired to guarantee authenticity during filming? Considering the restrictions of 1936 Hollywood, exactly how much truth of the real-life Florence Nightingale story could be translated to film?

Born in Florence, Italy, the city she was named after, in 1820, Florence Nightingale felt herself an outsider most of her life. As a child, Florence devoted herself to her father and learning. She trained in Languages, History and Philosophy. Her thirst for and success in educational endeavors was highly unconventional for Victorian England. Such "goings on" for a female was frowned upon and her mother and sister found her to be a general embarrassment. The first few scenes in *The White Angel* are precise in showing Florence's conflicts with her environment. These scenes also establish effectively the health crisis which she would eventually help resolve.

The film opens on New Year's Eve, 1850. The bond between father and daughter is acknowledged in Mr. Nightingale's toast to Florence. With a touch of wistfulness Francis looks dreamily into her wine cup and repeats his wish for her, "*All I desire.*" The film segues to the revelry in the heart of London where, amid the throngs, a typical drunken, elderly nurse passes out in the street. There is a brief glimpse of the squalid conditions in the hospitals and the indifference of hospital administrators to the problem. Back at the elegant Nightingale home we see Francis at the piano, looking and feeling as did the real Florence Nightingale, out of place in her surroundings. Francis arises from the piano and wearily confesses to her suitor of nine years (Donald Woods, based on the real-life Richard Monekton Milnes), "I never feel so useless, so devoid of any purpose as when I get up from the piano." She complains of wasting her emotions on music and "casting away gifts of God." Francis shows the agitation in her relationship with Mrs. Nightingale, who is tired of listening to her daughter's opinions. *Years* of irritation and frustration seethe beneath Francis' lines directed at her mother. "Half our life is spent doing nothing! That's supposed to be the whole duty of a woman!"

Nightingale claimed she heard the voice of God call her to service in 1837, when she was 17.[6] Her upbringing in the Unitarian faith guided her to trust her own spiritual intuitions, whereas the Church of England (which held most of Britain's population in queue) admonished its followers to adhere to the rules handed down by authority. One cannot underestimate the Unitarian background in Florence's outlook.

Florence's "call from God" lay in limbo as she spent the next 13 years dreaming up imaginary scenarios to fulfill her desire to help humanity. She felt imprisoned and had written, "I see numbers of my kind who have gone mad for want of something to do."[7] "Passion, intellect, moral activity," she wrote, "these three have *never* been satisfied in woman. In this cold and oppressive conventional atmosphere, they *cannot* be satisfied."[8] The film is considerate of the temper and style of Nightingale's voluminous writings and letters. In 1850 Florence noted, "Today I am thirty—the age Christ began his Mission. Now no more childish things, no more vain things, no more love, no more marriage. Now, Lord, let me only think of thy will."[9] Nightingale recognized the divisive nature of organized religion and did not believe in the *divinity* of Christ. In fact, her grandfather had fought in the halls of Parliament and succeeded in decriminalizing non-belief in his divinity. The Unitarian belief was to see oneself as *Christ-like*—the emphasis was on deeds not creeds. It is for this reason that Francis personifies Nightingale's readiness for her calling to coalesce into action. The real strength of Francis' portrayal is the confident determination and a sense of "inner knowing" that follow her throughout the film.

After Francis frantically reads reports sent to her father on the pitiful conditions of London's hospitals, she defiantly announces to her family she intends to become a nurse. Her mother considers it a degradation. Her father again shows his bond with her by encouraging her. As far as marriage is concerned, Francis is adamant, "I shall never be anybody's wife! I must give my life to humanity." As to her suitor, Francis looks beyond the camera and confesses, "There's a passion in me that couldn't be satisfied in a life with him, because it doesn't belong to one person." Although subsequent films on Nightingale emphasize her romance with a Milnes-like character, she actually was indifferent to his adoration, although she admired his mind and talents. She broke off with him after a courtship of nine years. Nightingale may not have been the *type* to be swept away by romance. Still, earlier in 1846, age 26, she did write: "I have never loved but one person with passion in my life and that was *her*! That brilliant face is almost as the face of an angel."[10] Nightingale is referring to her cousin Marianne. Her infatuation with Marianne was perpetual torture. Marianne ended their friendship when Florence refused her brother Henry's proposal of marriage. "To Florence, the loss of Marianne was a catastrophe. Nothing was real but her suffering over Marianne."[11] Romantic friendships between women in the 19th century were accepted. They were looked upon as non-sexual, because women in general were looked upon as non-sexual. In *The White Angel* the time spent on any such kind of romantic notion is nonexistent. On film, Florence Nightingale is preoccupied and focused on one thing, her destiny.

After following Nightingale's footsteps through the rigors of nurse-training school, we witness a further obstacle in the attitude of a London hospital administrator who rejects her application for nursing work. Francis shows her disgust when her father inquires as to how her interview went. "He told me to go home and find *a husband!*" she groans.

At this juncture *The White Angel* introduces the conflict in the Crimea and the lack of medical care on the warfront. The Crimean War has been called the most unnecessary war in modern Europe, worst managed, poorly supplied and wasteful of life, yet it provided Nightingale the opportunity to change the course of history. In October 1854, Nightingale, age thirty-four, and thirty-eight nurses set off for Constantinople.

Sybil Jason, Kay's screen daughter from *I Found Stella Parish,* told me of an incident during the filming of *The White Angel.* Cast and crew were on location at the old Vitagraph lot where there was a large lake. It was here that the ship scenes, and the arrival at Scutari, was filmed. The nurses are shown debarking during a torrential downpour. After a morning of takes and retakes, they knocked off for lunch at noon. One of the wardrobe mistresses brought Kay a huge towel and portable heater so she wouldn't catch a chill. Kay immediately asked if the extras who were in the scene with her were going to be offered the same things. When she was answered, "No," Kay handed back the towel and stepped away from the heater. Jason emphasized, "That was just the kind of lady she was."[12] Kay refused to separate herself from the others and receive special treatment. Kay's friend, New York reporter Harry Evans, witnessed this same incident and he claimed it turned into a real confrontation between Kay, the director, the assistant director, "and everybody else and his assistant." They all crowded around a

The White Angel *(1936) During an arduous shoot, Kay stood up for 40 women extras soaked to the bone. She told the director, "You'll see that they get dry clothes and something hot to drink—or you won't get another lick of work out of me today!" (Warners)*

drenched Kay urging her to return to her dressing room. "And while I'm doing this," Kay replied, "what's going to happen to those people?" Evans elaborated,

> She pointed over to the side of the set. Standing in a group, huddled and wet to the bone, were about forty women who had worked with Kay during the morning scenes. They were all extras. And many of them were well past middle age. "The first thing to do is to get those women dried out," Kay stated. "You can't leave them standing around in those dripping clothes until you are ready to use them again this afternoon. And stop making such a fuss over me. I've got a warm place to change and have lunch."
>
> One of the men raised a loud objection. They were just extras. No accommodations had been provided for them. Nor were there any dry clothes for them. "Well, you'll *find* accommodations for them," Kay shot back, "and you'll see that they get dry clothes and something hot to drink—or you won't get another lick of work out of me today! Which means you won't be able to take another foot of film. Do you understand?" They understood and hopped to it.
>
> ...a few days later, Kay's mother answered a ring at the front door.

Standing outside was a woman holding a tremendous bouquet of flowers. As Kay's mother opened the door wonderingly, the woman stepped forward and said, "I was sent by the women who worked on your daughter's picture. The extras, you know. We want Kay to understand how much we appreciate her thoughtfulness. So we decided to give her these. And knowing Kay, we felt sure she would like it better if we gave them to her mother."[13]

The White Angel details the overwhelming conditions at the hospital at Scutari. Amid an abundance of rats and vermin, corpses were lying next to the dysentery-covered sick. Warners had hired veterans, some limbless, to lie in the berths as Kay walked through the corridors. Kay was overwhelmed by their presence and kept breaking down. She had to reapply her make-up several times before the take was finished.

Within three weeks of her arrival at Scutari, Nightingale had 2,300 patients to attend to. Francis looks at home in her simple nursing garment, a plain gray dress with a white cowl. Her neck was garnered by an actual broach that had belonged to Florence Nightingale. Francis combines Nightingale's determination with an air of confidence as she meets more opposition in the face of Dr. Hunt (played effectively by Donald Crisp). He is Francis' nemesis, with an attitude to match. He is repelled by the idea of female nurses. "You'll make the men soft...coddled," he argues. When Francis asks "is there no possibility of an understanding between us?," he simply says, "None." The conflict between the two is met head-on when Nightingale refuses to use old bandages on a patient's affected wounds. Dr. Hunt threatens her. "I shall make a very *strong* protest," he shouts. Francis quickly cuts him off saying, "Dr. Hunt! One of the most important things in

The White Angel *(1936) Kay as Nightingale "revolutionizing" Scutari, along with Ferdinand Munier and Ian Hunter. Working with her for the third time, director William Dieterle thought Kay, "potentially one of the greatest actresses in pictures." (Warners)*

nursing is *not to chatter!*" Rebuffed, he is silent and focuses on the task at hand, using clean bandages. These confrontations have the audience cheering for Nightingale.

An unexpected conflict comes up for Nightingale when she is shown returning from her rounds to find her nurses fraternizing with their new husbands. "Husbands!?!" she exclaims. "No nurse has a life of her own. This is a whole time job. I shall give orders that you will be sent back to England!" The incongruity of mixing marriage and nursing was true to Nightingale's character. Nightingale's creation of the Nurse's Vow parallels the commitment and ritual associated with becoming a nun.

During the Crimean War those who fell by disease were seven times above those who fell in battle. "Proceeding against all opposition in a tactful but dictatorial manner, Nightingale...and her nurses cleaned the patient areas, instituted procedures for sanitary waste disposal, did laundry and improved the diet of the soldiers...By the end of the war, the 'art of nursing' helped the mortality rate fall from 420 per thousand to 22 per thousand."[14] Through articles in *The London Times*, England built Nightingale into a national heroine. In America, Longfellow's poem, "Lady With a Lamp" solidified her work into legend. There is an effectively lit scene by the cinematographer, Tony Gaudio, of Francis walking through corridors at Scutari Hospital as Longfellow's poem is being read. The impact of her work is shown reaching the hearts of the English people as various households are shown reading the text of "The Lady With a Lamp."

The film underscores England's admiration to the point of worship of Florence Nightingale when it is reported that she is suffering from cholera (more probably typhus) at the Crimean front.[15] The whole nation is seen praying for her. Francis seems unperturbed as if her will had more precedence than her body. She revives with a vengeance when she learns that Dr. Hunt is busy undermining all that she has established. "If anything kills me," she tells a sympathizer, "it will be my anger against this deadly system!" She returns to Scutari in a steely rage. She dismisses the charge nurse and chastises the staff. "Take orders from me and only me," she commands. She assures them they will "work under the most severe discipline." The film is careful not to make Nightingale seem too brutal. After she vents on her staff, she receives a letter from a deceased soldier's mother, who has been waiting to hear from him. Francis reads and is compelled to carry the spirit of its content to the boy's graveside where she places flowers. "From your Mother," she says thoughtfully. There is also the young drummer boy, Tommy (Billy Mauch), a character based on historical fact, whom Nightingale nurses back to health. Following his recovery, the boy became her devoted companion, following her everywhere.[16] (In 2003, Mauch told me he found Kay to be, "kind and considerate, and easy to work with, especially with a younger person as [I] was.")[17]

Nightingale's work in the Crimean finished, she returns to England (1857) to recover from the emotional and physical strain. A reception with Queen Victoria was intended to be the highpoint of the film. Producer Hal Wallis and director William Dieterle were stunned when the Lord Chamberlain announced that Queen Victoria could not be portrayed on screen. The whole film was being built up to the meeting of these two women—the two most powerful in the British Empire. Instead we see the camera focusing close up on a diamond-studded broach, given to her by the Queen, wherein the audience sees the inscribed dedication to Florence Nightingale and her

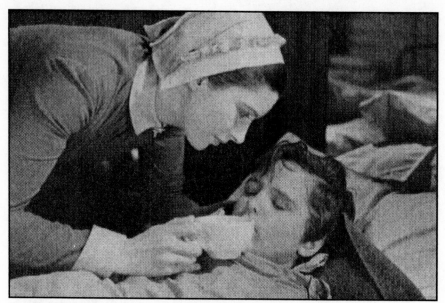

The White Angel *(1936) Kay is seen here with her devoted little drummer boy (Billy Mauch). (Warners)*

work: "Blessed are the Merciful." *Finis.* The compromises in this final scene seriously affected the impact of the film's emotional climax. As *Variety* noted, "In *The White Angel* the triumph is vague and dramatically unsatisfying." Nightingale's story certainly didn't end here. The fact was she had a complete mental breakdown. After meeting with statistician William Farr, Nightingale discovered that during the first months of her stay at Scutari the death rate actually *increased* at her hospital. Her insistence on bringing in more patients under her care exposed them to the hospital's defects.[18] For a time, Nightingale had been running a death camp. After learning the facts, she started a crusade to make them known at the expense of her glorified reputation. This put her at odds with the government and Queen Victoria. Nightingale's anguish provided the impetus for all her great reform works such as the International Red Cross, which Kay herself volunteered countless hours of service from 1939-1945. Kay's own proclivity for being of service to others (which was demonstrated over and again during World War II), was much in line with Nightingale's belief in "deeds not creeds."

William Dieterle felt the full complexity and controversy surrounding Nightingale was not satisfied on film. In 1928, he had been perfectly at ease filming the German release *Geschlecht in Fesseln (Sex in Chains)*, about the hothouse of passions between men in prison. In 1936, with the PCA hovering over him, his ability to honestly direct the story of a nurse, felt stifled. Dieterle commented on what *The White Angel* was up against and later recalled, "That was a beautiful story, but it was, shall I say, written by the wrong people—they wanted to be so correct with the English. We had so much trouble with the English censor; in the end it almost killed the story…The film itself could have been a lot better, but one of the things that we had to face at Warners, a mark, a shadow upon us, was that we hardly ever made a retake after a preview…at Warners the attitude was 'Just let it go, it will sell.' We really never took care."[19]

In his autobiography producer Hal Wallis reflected on the setbacks they ran into while filming and stated, "We were faced with problems at the outset. Told by the Lord Chamberlain that we could not portray royalty on the screen, we protested that Florence Nightingale's presentation to Queen Victoria was a high point of the production. The same day, the Breen office told us we could not have any brutality on the screen. And this was the story of one of the most horrifying wars in history."[20] Indeed, there were brutal scenes filmed that were deleted during editing. Kay told reporter Harrison Carroll about a harrowing scene that ended up on the cutting room floor. She sat between takes, knitting and concentrating, as usual, and related the details: "They were going to show an amputation, and…selected a man who had really lost both legs at the ankle. As the actor playing the army surgeon hovered over him with a sharp knife, [the man] became nervous. 'While the operation is being performed,' [Dieterle] said, 'two men will hold your shoulders. I want you to struggle.' The crippled man looked up at Dieterle and his eyes were full of remembering. 'When I was on the table,' he said, 'they didn't have to cut my legs off. One of the doctors had them in his hands. And I didn't struggle. There wasn't a move left in me.'"[21] The completed scene was considered too brutal by the British advisors.

The film's limitations were compounded extensively by the Production Code. Florence Nightingale accomplished many things that, according to the Code, women are not supposed to do. Warners had to obtain the Breen's office "Certificate of Purity" before they could release the film. They were attempting to tell the story of a woman who had little use for organized religion, did not believe in the divinity of Christ, saw *herself* as Christ-like, fought discrimination in hospitals, fought for the health care of prostitutes, and had no interest in marrying a man. Her career took precedence over absolutely everything. According to the Code, a woman like Nightingale should be punished, put behind bars, or shot at the finish. The solution that Warners came up with is best expressed by Jeanine Basinger, professor of film studies at Wesleyan University where the Kay Francis archives are stored. Basinger wrote *A Woman's View: How Hollywood Spoke to Women, 1930-1960* (Kay's portrait graces the book's cover), in which she said:

> There is one interesting subdivision of good sportsmanship that lets a woman out of her dependence on men—nobility. Such a woman goes out among mankind and does good instead of marrying…She loves and serves all men instead of just one, so it is all right for a woman to reject men and love if…she has a higher purpose in mind…something that will serve all humanity. Women of noble purpose are to be admired by everyone—not necessarily emulated, but admired. A typical example is the story of Florence Nightingale made as *The White Angel*, starring Kay Francis as the heroine of the Crimea.[22]

The noble edge to Kay's performance mirrored the image *expected* of a heroine. Through a subtle kind of subterfuge Kay's performance still manages to get the message of Nightingale across. In the words of Basinger, Nightingale's message is perpetrated that "Women not being allowed to express themselves is wrong, wrong, wrong. Throughout its running time, it will clarify the issue of the woman's place in society by suggesting that those who try to restrict a woman, prevent her from doing meaningful work, are hopelessly misguided and, what's more, slowing the progress of civilization."[23]

Throughout *The White Angel*, Kay's unwavering strength and determination are seen questioning what she is being asked to do as a woman. As Kay herself had stated, she focused on, "the calm, determined sympathy and merciful desire to serve humanity...underneath all the turbulence" in Nightingale's life.[24] Her performance, as it stands, was unusual film fare for cinemagoers. Audiences were more used to *men* being the movers and shakers. Still, the repercussions for not garnering an unqualified critical and commercial success were tough on Kay. *The White Angel*, compounded by weak promotion, proved to be a box-office failure and seriously sabotaged Kay's opportunity to score as a dramatic actress. Once *The White Angel* was "in the can," Warners' publicity department had the difficult job of selling it. There were many educational tie-ins, but by the time the film was released at the end of June—school was out. The film's pressbook had preposterous publicity suggestions such as a Florence Nightingale look-alike contest. On a more practical publicity note, Kay and director Dieterle both addressed 15,000 nurses at the American Nurses Association Biennial Convention held at the Hollywood Bowl. But, the initial review of *The White Angel* from *The New York Times* didn't help matters. Critic Frank Nugent thought the film worthwhile, but with qualification:

> A respectful—in fact worshipful—history of Florence Nightingale. The picture is dignified, reasonably accurate, deeply moving and dismayingly pompous...Miss Nightingale, when she speaks, she is speaking for posterity. She was, no doubt a woman of infinite compassion...but she was, too, a lively, forceful, direct, sarcastic and present-minded personality, who, in all probability, did not regard herself (as Miss Francis would have us believe) as a Joan of Arc, mystically responding to the promptings of heavenly voices and moving with an air of lofty serenity and other-worldly detachment on a pre-ordained mission...Miss Francis's performance is sincere and eloquent, however we may regret its reverential tone. The sincerity of the Warners' attempt deserves our respect, even if the picture does not fully achieve its destiny.[25]

Nugent obviously knew nothing of Nightingale's obsession with having "a calling." Her spirituality had bite and it often left her on her own. Mrs. Gaskell, an acquaintance of Nightingale's, wrote, "She has no friend—she wants none. She stands perfectly alone, halfway between God and His creatures."[26] (Francis' portrayal to a fault.) The script and the censors weren't trying to *humanize* Florence Nightingale and were in fact honoring her. Anything that lacked dignity for the role would be questioned and inevitably discarded. The end result softened Nightingale's image on film.

The reception of *The White Angel* in England was characterized by a review in London's *Film Weekly*. The magazine's editor, Herbert Thompson, stated, "Kay Francis has at last found a role to test her powers and measure her stature as an actress...It is the first part Kay Francis has had for some years which gives scope to her dramatic talents and personality. The result is that she gives her most satisfying performance since *One Way Passage*...she appears once more as a whole person. The heroine of *The White Angel* is a real woman, of intelligence, depth and vigorous character."[27] Kay appreciated the favorable response to the film in England. A year after the film's release, Kay admitted to English reporter W. R. Mooring, "In some respects I liked 'Nightingale,' but I know the subject, historically, must have been so near to the hearts of the British people as to tempt their resentment against the screenplay and against me. The story obviously had to be tempered to the American taste and adapted with a better eye on drama than on history." Mooring added a rather insightful comment about the production *and* the script. He was on the Warner set himself during filming.

> I shall never forget seeing her on the set one day…she had some specially sentimental lines to deliver. In the middle of one take her memory failed her. Or was she overcome by the heart-tugging dialogue the screen writer had given her? It doesn't matter. While the cameras and sound recorders were still running she stamped her foot and shouted a few colourful words which certainly were not in the script and were almost certainly never in the vocabulary of any sweet Nightingale, least of all Florence. It is only the artist who feels in a false position who "blows up" the way Kay did that day. Something in the situation, or in her lines, did not ring quite true to her…she reached something in the script which didn't seem to work out easily, she had tripped across a flow and something should have been done to repair it.[28]

Perhaps Kay's initial reaction to Mordaunt Shairp's scenario had been a foreboding. Upon receiving it on January 2, 1936, she simply wrote, "Read my new script. Dear God!"[29]

Reporter Richard Lawson protested when Kay and William Dieterle weren't acknowledged Oscar nominations for their work in *The White Angel*. When he approached Kay the following year, asking about the Academy, she threw up her arms in mock terror. "'Don't ask me about Academy awards,' she pleaded, but added seriously, 'honestly I think an Academy award is a great honor. It is unfortunate when such brilliant artists as Ruth Chatterton (*Dodsworth*) and William Dieterle are lost in the shuffle, but there are so many fine things being done in pictures today that it is impossible to please everybody.'"[30] Kay added that Dieterle, "is one of the very few really great creative directors in pictures today." According to Richard Lawson, the feeling was mutual. Dieterle firmly believed that Kay was "potentially one of the greatest actresses in pictures."[31]

Since 1936, one British film, 1951's The *Lady With a Lamp* with Anna Neagle, and two TV attempts at Nightingale's life were made. The Neagle version, without the restrictions of the Code and so-called advisors, allowed greater scope to Nightingale's story. Neagle was even allowed to say the word "prostitute" on film. (For this reason, *The Lady With a Lamp* had limited distribution in the U.S. where use of the word was still forbidden.) In 1964, Julie Harris was nominated for an Emmy in the televised presentation *The Holy Terror* directed by George Schaefer. It takes awhile for Harris to touch base with Nightingale's strength and determination, but once she does, she is riveting. In 1985, Jaclyn Smith got to carry the lamp in *Florence Nightingale*. In contrast to *The Holy Terror*, romance was emphasized. Smith managed to indulge in a few of Nightingale's accomplishments amid *nine* romantic interludes with Timothy Dalton, filled with stolen kisses. The viewer was left with the unsettling notion that *something* was contrived. *The New York Times* commented that Smith, "single-mindedly earnest…looked good while reading her lines…then there is the matter of romance. Television movies, it would seem, must have love interest; no matter what the truth may have been concerning their real-life heroes and heroines. The producers have carefully expanded her very close and

The White Angel *(1936) "Kay Francis' work in the title role is easily the best she has done and will deserve much consideration in the Academy voting for best actress." (*Film Daily*)*

very platonic friendship with Richard Milnes into a palpitating question of will she or won't she marry him." A similar mistake was almost repeated in 2001 when it was announced that Kate Winslet (of *Titanic* fame), would play Nightingale in the "romantic drama," *Florence*. Joaquin Phoenix was being considered to play her "lover."

In many respects Nightingale's story, in all its complexity, is still waiting to be told. However, in spite of the script, Kay Francis' portrayal in *The White Angel* resonates to the very core what sustained Florence Nightingale: *tenacity*. Nightingale's struggle, her accomplishments that changed the world as we know it, are all intact in the 1936 film. A more recent acknowledgment of Kay's performance came at the 1999 Oscar ceremony when astronaut John Glenn presented a tribute to the actors who portrayed "Historical Figures in Cinema." Through these performances, Glenn emphasized, "we found our heroes…and were made a little more idealistic." Sandwiched between the likes of Greer Garson, as Madame Curie, and Paul Muni, as Louis Pasteur, was Kay, as Florence Nightingale arriving at Scutari. A voiceover of Kay saying, "I have shown beyond doubt that nursing is woman's highest vocation," was followed by a close-up of her witnessing the appalling conditions of the barracked hospital for the first time…a determined woman whose odds were against her from every direction. In many ways it was a close-up of another woman with the odds against her, Kay Francis. The failure of the film to create a box-office sensation and garner unanimous critical acclaim and awards, put Kay face-to-face with the beginning of the end of her reign at Warners.

Chapter 12

Highest Paid Actress In Hollywood – "Money, Nobody Appreciates the Stuff Any More Than I Do"

Kay's diary became a lexicon of woe during and after production of *The White Angel*. The days were long, "terrible," exhausting, and the studio lighting damaging to her eyes. Her entries focused on work and her relapses, but when filming completed on April 22 she managed to throw a party for the crew. It was clear that Kay felt responsibility for making *The White Angel* a critical and commercial success. She had stated, "It is not the artistic triumph that counts in the success of a film player; it is the public reception of their performances that is the decisive factor. Without popular acclaim, no artistic triumph is anything but an empty and unprofitable one."[1] Kay's initial enthusiasm for the project wavered once she realized, along with director William Dieterle, that pressures from outside were altering the overall effect of the film and her performance. Her first reaction to the troubled script was less than enthusiastic. After the film's release, Kay rarely mentioned *The White Angel*. Realizing that the film's lack of success *wasn't* because of Kay's performance, Warners cooled plans for another bio-pic with Claudette Colbert as Joan of Arc.

Still riddled with doubts about the reception the film would receive, Kay was asked by Louella Parsons to do *The White Angel* on radio. Kay was apprehensive about playing the role live, especially after the film's mixed reviews came in from New York. Her frustration was compounded by impacted wisdom teeth and codeine that did "no good." To top it off, Kay endured yet another abortion in June. She moaned, "Jesus, it's awful. Why do I always get caught and have so little fun?"[2]

Delmer Daves felt Kay's anguish. He acquired his own physical complications and had an abscess lanced. "We are a pair!" railed Kay. "Del home and nursed him all day...Christ!"[3] In late June, Kay noted that her dog Weenie joined in on the act. "Poor wiener had foxtail and we had to operate."[4] Before long, Kay and Delmer found themselves quarreling over such insignificant things as pinochle. Kay would regret their contretemps, calling herself a harridan. The real capper was when Delmer, upon turning on the front porch light, caught Kay kissing another man named David. (Most likely David Niven, who was a frequent escort of Kay's.) "Big fight upstairs and Del goes home!" Kay frantically entered into her diary. "God damn fool that I am!"[5] The angry Delmer then vanished, and after two weeks Kay was miserable. Finally, she went over to Del's house. "We had long talk and made up!" Kay wrote. "Thank God!"[6]

Kay was determined that her ills and love life in no way detracted from her work as an actress. However, there was an occasional slip. When visiting her on the set of *Give Me Your Heart*, Jimmie Fidler was witness to one of Kay's tirades, and wrote, "Changing as April weather is Kay Francis. Like the sun darting in and out of clouds. This morning I came across her in a fret. She was denouncing Director Archie Mayo, and at the end of a snorting tirade she flounced from the set. I was amazed that work did not cease immediately, and asked why. 'Oh, she'll be back sorry as a spanked child,' I was told. Sure enough, ten minutes later Kay returned, a bashful smile on her face. 'I'm sorry Archie,' she said to Mayo, and kissed him on the cheek. I left before the next change of weather."[7]

If Kay was aware that she had hurt someone's feelings "there would be no stone left unturned," commented one observer, "no trips too many to take, no deeds too humble to perform to make amends. She has an almost unbecoming attitude of humility where her friends are concerned."[8] Writer Frances Kellum caught Kay in one of her better moods on the set of *Give Me Your Heart*. Kellum describes what it took to "get it right" for the camera.

He had been kissing her for two hours. Each time more rapturously, until the fifteenth kiss stirred the cockles of your heart...Then the director [Archie Mayo] called, "Cut. We'll print that one!" Kay Francis slid out of George Brent's arms and they smiled at each other. How do stars feel after such a love scene that has lasted through fifteen "takes?" I wondered. And then I heard Kay say in that rich, throbby voice of hers, "D'you suppose we could send the prop boy out for some ice cream? I'd like vanilla."

Everybody laughed. And "props" trotted off. With a single gesture Kay had swung the tempo back to normal. She hasn't an ounce of the coquette in her. Just as George Brent told me later, "Kay is one of the few women I know who speaks a man's language. He gets from her the same firm, steady friendship he gets from other men—and yet she's so deeply feminine along with it."[9]

Brent's observation of Kay was exactly how she saw herself. During filming, Kay came up with what she called the "Romantic Age Codes and New Ideas" for the British publication *Picturegoer Weekly*. Her vision was a "magnificent blending" of the old and new guaranteed to "stir the gallantry of men." At the forefront of Kay's philosophy she listed: "*Train yourself to love*...Not only the man who might conceivably love you in return but also the aunt or cousin or friend who needs you. *Put imagination back into the world*...Let yourself thrill to the sweet, spicy smell of a wood fire burning on a cold evening, mimosa in the moonlight. (Don't laugh at sentiment. We need it.) *Know that the newest thing in Feminism is becoming very feminine.* It emphasizes charm and intelligence—and it takes votes and jobs pretty much for granted."[10]

The woman Kay played in *Give Me Your Heart*, Belinda, was too problem-ridden to enjoy the fruits of Kay's codes and new ideas. Kay's own life, however, was providing a wellspring of pathos she could access for the character's inner turbulence. In *Give Me Your Heart* Kay comes across with heartbreaking vulnerability. The story begins in England where Kay's romance with a titled and very married man, Robert (Patric Knowles), produces a child. Her lover's father, Lord Farrington (Henry Stephenson), persuades her to turn over the boy to his son's invalid, childless wife (Frieda Inescort). He claims, "You don't stand on moral ground," and begins to preach about "codes that hold civilization together." She counters that his attitude is merely a pack of superior intolerant words. "Your point of view is easy to see," she accuses him. "What about mine?" When Lord Farrington confronts her with the wealth, status, and privileges that would be available to the boy, she feels defeated. She convinces herself that those advantages would certainly outweigh anything she could provide. Kay sails for New York, a new life, and a new nickname, "Bill."

On the train out of London, Kay meets James Baker (George Brent), a New Yorker. The film then carries us two years later where we witness their troubled marriage. In an actual reversal of the situation in *Living on Velvet*, this time it's Brent's character who can't reach into the troubled world in Kay's mind. He

Give Me Your Heart (1936). Kay combined her dramatic powers and beauty to the tune of big box-office and a new contract at $5,250 a week. (Warners)

claims she keeps "walking out" on him emotionally. Resolve is in the air when Kay has an unexpected reunion with her former lover, Farrington, and his no-longer invalid wife. Kay is confronted with the couple head-on at the hotel. Instead of being cordial, she is sullen, moody and rude to everyone around her. When Lady Farrington puts two and two together, after watching Kay's reaction to a photograph of the child, she makes a point of having a private "talk" with her. The film's most powerful sequence is between the two women. When Inescort compassionately tells Kay that she hopes they can like one another, Kay indignantly responds, "Like you? ... I *hate* you! You've probably hated me as much as I did you." The scene continues with gripping intensity until Kay softens, realizing her boy is in loving hands. When told that he is upstairs asleep in the hotel and is asked if she would like to see him, Kay opens to the opportunity. The two women agree to keep in contact, through letters and visits. Afterwards, Brent is baffled by the sudden turnaround in Kay's demeanor. She tells him, relief shining in her eyes, that her old bogey has turned "into something lovely."

It's clear upon viewing the film that Kay had become lax in pronouncing r's. Her unwarranted w's were peppered throughout the film. "You sound like the cwown pwosecutor!" she wails, when confronted with the elder Lord Farrington. It was evidence of what Kay claimed, that after *The White Angel* she had given up trying to please the critics with perfect enunciation.

Frank S. Nugent for *The New York Times* complimented the film, calling it "an affecting, mature and sophisticated drama of mother love and applied psychiatry." He noted the especially riveting scene where Kay comes face to face with Lady Farrington. "The picture comes electrically to life when Belinda and her husband meet the new Lord Farrington and his wife, now recovered and intuitively aware that she is facing her boy's real mother. Out of the meeting, out of the touching womanly talk of the child and his pony cart and fear of loud noises, Belinda wins release and surcease from anguish. It is a crackling scene they have contrived." Nugent thought the film handled the heavier scenes with restraint and found a genial form of humor to balance its tragedy. Nugent compliments Kay not only for being "amazingly gowned," but also for the "pathos and reticence" she brought to her role. The film was the premiere feature for the opening of the elegant new theater on Broadway, The New Criterion.

Film Daily thought *Give Me Your Heart's* delicate subject had "been handled with good taste and intelligence. It gives Kay Francis a strong emotional role and she does unusually good work…" *Photoplay* commented that the film, "proves a perfect vehicle for the dramatic power of Kay Francis…her dramatic ability and beauty combine to offer a perfect result." *Time* magazine smugly reported, "*Give Me Your Heart* exhibits Kay Francis enjoying the rewards of illicit romance. Having borne a bastard to a married sprig of British Aristocracy, she travels De Lux to New York and marries a millionaire." *Time* be damned. Somehow, the Breen Office had on blinders. In spite of her character's proclivities Kay didn't end up in jail or jump off a bridge by the film's ending. *Give Me Your Heart* had been a successful play, *Sweet Aloes,* in London (Diana Wynyard played the role on stage). Playwright Joyce Carey (using the more "acceptable" masculine alias, Jay Mallory) supports, with convincing skill, her theory that ghosts exists when kept in dark corners.

Louella Parsons gave kudos to *Give Me Your Heart* and invited Kay and George Brent to enact scenes from the film on radio's *Hollywood Hotel.* "Kay Francis, who has that rare gift of playing a suffering heroine, keeping herself attractive and interesting at the same time," Parsons raved in the *Los Angeles Examiner,* "has never given a better performance…with all the tears she has to shed, it is indeed a feat. Archie Mayo, who excels in these human heart-interest stories, does a really beautiful job. If Warner Brothers can continue to turn out box-office attractions of this type [they]…need never worry about the good old box office returns."

Jack Warner was happy with the "good old box office returns." He looked at the profits from *I Found Stella Parish* and *Give Me Your Heart* and decided Kay's niche would be limited to glamour roles that emphasize fashion and tears. Granted, such roles were her forte. However, her diary entries showed her disappointment in what the studio offered ("Script from studio—BAD! Too sweet—old hat"). But, she wasn't being singled out. Bette Davis had a dozen so-so roles between *Of Human Bondage (1934)* and hitting her ultimate dramatic stride in *Jezebel(1938).*

Kay's first "old hat" for 1937 had the working title *Mistress of Fashion.* The film proved an *almost* happy marriage of fashion and a high-level swindling scandal that had rocked the French government a few years before. The event was known as the Bayonne Pawnshop Scandals/Stavisky Affair. Multimillion-franc swindler Stavisky was protected by police officials and legislators whom he apparently paid off. Claude Rains is brilliant as a Stavisky-like character named Stefan Orloff. He hires Kay, a fashion model, as a cover for his fraudulent interests. She establishes her own legitimate dress salon while he, unbeknownst to her, weaves his web of deceit. After his empire unravels, the film's

After the completion of Stolen Holiday *(1937) with Claude Rains, Kay was officially recognized as the "Best-Dressed Woman in America" by the prestigious Fashion Academy in New York. (Warners)*

climax has Orloff unconvincingly killed off, only because the PCA would not allow for a suicide as the real Stavisky had committed. The film was remade as *Stavisky* in 1974 by director Alain Resnais. Jean-Paul Belmondo starred—suicide in tact. Unfortunately, the 1937 version diverts midway for a romance between Kay and Ian Hunter. Aside from similarities to the real Madame Stavisky (a former model) Kay's character was loosely based on Gabrielle Chanel, who revolutionized the fashion industry. Chanel's torrid love affairs, which included a British nobleman, were the talk of café society. The film was re-titled *Stolen Holiday* to give some credence to Kay and Englishman Hunter's unimpressive interlude (filmed on location at Lake Arrowhead). The main draw, however, was Kay modeling Orry-Kelly designs, and a scheming, devilish Claude Rains.

The *New York Times* had only praises for Rains and Kay's parade of fashions. "If the picture is at all distinguished, it is because Claude Rains does a superb job with the character whom the film's producers would have you believe is not patterned after the late…Stavisky; and because…as a successful *modiste*, Kay Francis parades the most striking wardrobe that Hollywood's couturiers can conceive in the Paris manner." Warners released a plethora of publicity stills for *Stolen Holiday*, which Kay *hated* posing for. "The still camera lens, for some reason or other," wagged one reporter, "brings out the worst in Kay and she can usually be counted upon to go into a temperamental rage and tell off everybody in sight." As usual, Kay would harbor much guilt after such diatribes. "The night after these stormy gallery sessions," the same reporter added, "Kay usually spends calling up everybody she bawled out and telling them quite meekly that she is very, very sorry."[12]

Kay's aversion to visitors on the set was temporarily put on hold when she paid homage to a visiting Dowager during the filming of *Stolen Holiday*. An attuned Kay noted "a little ghost of a secretary" trailing the Dowager. The secretary's eyes "were alight like candles." Kay un-cornered herself from the Dowager and gently asked the little ghost, "Is there anything you wanted particularly to see on the set?" "Oh, Miss Francis, if I—I could just take a peep at your make-up table." Kay laughed, "That's simple." When they returned, the girl was no longer a ghost—she looked radiant. Kay had spent time making her up. "And somehow you had the feeling that she had reached a remarkable 'Turning Point' in her entire life…"[13]

In the fall of 1935, Kay was recognized as one of the 20 best dressed women in the world. The poll was taken by the leading Paris dress designers. In November 1936, Kay's affinity for wearing *haute couture* was honored officially. The prestigious Fashion Academy of New York recognized her for being the "Best-Dressed Woman in America" and awarded her a ribboned-medallion. Kay was the first actress to be so acknowledged. The previous year's winner was Mrs. Harrison Williams (Mona—Countess of Bismarck), an eastern society beauty who, in 1933, had already received accolades as the couture world's best dressed. For news coverage of the event, Kay chose an Orry-Kelly ensemble from *Stolen Holiday*. It was a large-tasseled pillbox hat complemented by a lengthy poodle-cloth coat. Her kid-leather-gloved hand held her medallion from the Academy. Poodle-cloth was considered the "cat's meow" for the 1936-37 season.

Reporter Elizabeth Davis said, "What the red flag is to the bull, the word 'Best Dressed' became to La Francis. But it stuck like adhesive tape."[14] Kay never relished all the pretense, but said she *was* surprised and pleased at the Academy's decision. She felt that it was her attention to small details of grooming that made them notice. In a down-to-earth interview with Reine Davies, Kay revealed that too much attention is given to fashion in real life. "I'm of the opinion," cautioned Kay, "too much attention to clothes sometimes indicates lack of self-assurance and real ability. Young girls with screen aspirations frequently have the idea that they can attract attention by going to extremes in their dress. I'm not prone to giving advice, but if I did get around to it I would advise the young actress to waste no thought on clothes beyond the point of achieving good taste. For so arduous is the struggle that she can't spare any more thought than that and still have enough left to make the grade."[15] However, Kay did cop to paying a lot of attention to shoes. "I have a shoe fetish," Kay confessed. "I am mad about them. I may be said to collect them. When I started to pack for Europe—just started—I had forty-eight pairs of shoes stowed away before I was half-through. By the time I finished, I had shoes enough to *walk* around the world."[16] Kay's truest colors emerged when she told Faith Service about her fantasy to live on a remote island. "I would *not* take clothes," Kay emphasized, "[or] pins, patterns, or anything to remind me of the years of endless fittings I have undergone. Fittings—fits—fits—fittings—phfft to 'em! I'd sling a piece of old banana palm about me and stab it with a thorn. If the Hollywood influence should overcome me, I'd stick a hibiscus flower in my hair, make a lei of passion flowers and hang a couple of clam shells over my ears for earrings."[17] Kay also revealed her most bizarre fashion-*fantasy* accessory: snakes. "I like them; I admire them," Kay said bluntly. "I feel no revulsion whatsoever toward them. I have had them twine about me and have enjoyed it. I don't know what this makes me, but there it is!"[18]

Kay not only emerged from 1936 as "best dressed," but as the highest paid employee at Warner Brothers. Her annual salary registered at $227,500. She managed to soar past the nation's top business salary, Harvey S. Firestone, chairman of the tire and rubber company he founded. He was listed in the papers with a paltry $85,000 for the year. When *Stolen Holiday* was released in 1937, Kay was listed sixth, in *Variety's* listing of favorite female stars. The top ten were Myrna Loy, Loretta Young, Claudette Colbert, Ginger Rogers, Alice Faye, Kay Francis, Barbara Stanwyck, Joan Crawford, Jeanette MacDonald and Janet Gaynor. Kay's accumulation of personal wealth was more know-how, than simple penny-pinching. She always acknowledged that acting was also a business. She was in it to make money and to perform as a professional. William Powell and James Cagney echoed Kay's attitude. Powell told Ben Washer of the *New York Telegram*, "I'm in this racket for the shekels that are in it…any job worth doing is worth doing intelligently."[19] Cagney was just as blunt saying, "With me a career was the simple matter of putting groceries on the table."[20] Jimmy Starr discussed Kay's affection for "shekels" in his widely circulated column for June 9, 1936: "Kay Francis is in the movies for money and no other reason. She makes no bones about it; ask her and she will shrug her shoulders and answer, 'Why not? Why do *you* work?' Thus it is that Kay rarely upsets studio routine with temperamental outbursts. If higher-ups feel inclined to call her on the carpet, that is quite all right with Miss Francis as long as the pay check arrives promptly. Most of her money goes into sane investments, and annuities…Quietly enough, she has amassed one of the most sizable film fortunes."

Reporter Ruth Rankin concurred, "Kay is an economical lady, with planned economy, and will some day be, undoubtedly, one of Hollywood's wealthiest women…she seems to subscribe to the theory that one's first duty to the world is to take care of one's self."[21] Kay was logical and to the point regarding her lack of extravagance saying, "I live with unusual modesty in Hollywood because I am saving my money to secure my financial independence."[22] Rankin also observed, "So far as discussing business, money, or politics—take heart…Kay loves to talk about all three, and enjoys the man who can converse intelligently on these subjects. But the man who tries to run her business annoys her excessively. He is unthanked, who interferes with a woman's career or job, unless she asks for advice…At all other times, man, allow her the benefit of the doubt that she *knows* what she is doing."[23]

It wasn't that Kay would do anything for a buck, either. One trip to New York had her bombarded with commercial offers and radio appearances—most of which she turned down. The hefty sum to perform on a radio program she considered poorly written could not sway her. She told reporter Harry Evans, "Now don't misunderstand me about this money business. Nobody appreciates the stuff any more than I do, but it seems that most of the people in New York think a person will do *anything* for a dollar." Kay no sooner finished saying this, when the phone rang. "Who did you say is calling?" Kay asked the operator. "No. I do not want to speak to him," Kay snapped, "and tell him my answer is 'No' and will be any time he calls." Evans watched Kay slam the receiver down groaning, "that one was a *hip reducing* company!"[24]

Elsa Maxwell commented that Kay would be on the eastbound train from Hollywood the day the money stopped coming in. Her statement turned prophetic eight years later. Maxwell respected Kay's frank attitude about cold cash and didn't take offense when Kay refused to raise stakes at one of Maxwell's poker parties. "I work hard for my money, and I'd hate losing it, just as I'd hate taking yours," she told Elsa.[25] This was a brave thing to say to such a social powerhouse as Maxwell. But Maxwell appreciated Kay's bluntness—which once saved Maxwell from social ruin. When Kay arrived at Maxwell's first Hollywood party, she looked around the room and saw the Goldwyns, the Selznicks, the Mayers, the Gary Coopers, etc. Kay took Elsa aside and confided, "Elsa, your party is a dismal failure." "Don't I know it," Maxwell sighed, "but whose fault is it?" "Yours, of course," answered Kay. "You forgot to invite the photographers." Kay told Maxwell to phone Hyman Fink to hightail it over there and photograph the famous faces for the newspapers. Elsa said afterwards, "By one in the morning everybody was beaming and laughing. At 2 a.m. I discovered that I had given the greatest party of my career!"[26]

As far as poker was concerned, it was a good thing Maxwell conceded to Kay's wishes. Kay was a cutthroat player who won large sums. Kay's game, during which she sported bone-rimmed glasses, was excellent and serious. Constance Bennett had 24-hour poker marathons where she and Kay out-bluffed studio heads like Selznick, Zanuck, Goldwyn, and Jack Warner. Bennett once caught Kay complaining about the money she spent supporting her mother, and groaned, "Oh, come off it, Hetty. We all know you support your mother on your poker winnings."[27] Hetty Green was known as the Witch of Wall Street at the turn of the century. As one of the country's wealthiest women, she lived a Spartan existence.

Kay's 1936 successes were rewarded with a three-month European holiday. She shared her good fortune with her mother by presenting Mrs. Gibbs with a round-the-world ticket for her birthday. Kay also finally broke down and bought her first luxury car, a 1937 La Salle (she liked the color). But, still far more exciting to Kay than her La Salle, according to reporter Frances Kellum, was the little dachshund Kay rescued from the Humane Society back in 1931. "Weenie" showed gratitude by her keen interest in Kay's acting. Kay, draped in ermine and jewels, kept busy between takes "plying needle and yarn" to make "Weenie" sweaters. "Come here, you—'Weenie, '" Kay kept calling. "How can I drop the right number of stitches if you don't let me measure your neck? It's the longest part of you!" Kellum noted that underneath the glass top of Kay's dressing table was an assortment of candid shots Kay had taken of her "Weenie"—who, according to Kay, was the "most comforting pal she ever had."[28] "Weenie," in fact, was her top priority. Kay stated, "Luxuries mean nothing to me. *Things* mean very little to me…Because, when things become important to you, you are a slave. The only 'thing,' if I may call him that, that really matters to me is my Dachshund dog."[29]

Kay and Wiener (circa 1936) Kay had rescued "Weenie" from the Humane Society in 1931.

Kay had no problem showing her gratitude for her good fortune. She created a tradition for expressing it by acknowledging cast and crew members. Frances Kellum mentioned the little red book that Kay carried around during the making of every picture. "In it," Kellum noted, "are scribbled the most amazing quotations. Like this: 'F.G.—Deep dish apple pie. Grip 1—Thick rare steak. B. L. N.—Filet of Sole marguery.' They are the favorite foods of every member of the company from the prop boys to the director—

which Kay discovers in an oh-so-casual manner. And at the end of the production Kay gives an enormous dinner…at which everybody sits down to the dishes they like best!"[30]

Rumors still abounded regarding Kay and Delmer Daves. Daves had spent considerable time on the set while Kay filmed her next release, *Another Dawn*. The fall of 1936 had scores of columnists predicting their nuptials. Elizabeth Wilson reported, "Before her recent departure for Europe, and she has been to Europe more than any other actress in Hollywood, Miss Francis made a statement for the Press. 'I am not going to get married while I am in pictures.' Ten days later she was on a plane for New York, where Delmer Daves, who, not by accident, caught the same boat she took for France. When last heard of, they were celebrating Christmas together at St. Moritz, along with the Douglas Fairbanks' and Merle Oberon. Your guess is as good as mine."[31] In Paris, Kay and Delmer saw Raquel Meller perform at the Café de Paris. After London, they spent New Year's in the Austrian Tyrol sleigh-riding, skating and playing Tripoli with the Fairbanks' and Merle. Kay also bought yodeling Tyrolean dolls for her friends back home. Sadly, she had to leave behind a surprise male suitor, of the four-pawed St. Bernard variety, who, according to Merle, took quite a fancy to Kay. On January 13, when Kay returned on the *Aquitania*, she found her completed film, *Another Dawn*, in need of retakes.

Harrison Carroll reported: "All movies are shot piecemeal, but the final scene of *Another Dawn* probably holds the record. Kay Francis and Errol Flynn did the first half of it before her departure for Europe. This week, they did the tag. In the meantime, Miss Francis had taken a three months' vacation and had traveled 20,000 miles. This Warner film has the distinction with being photographed with two endings. In one, Errol Flynn dies and Ian Hunter is left to console Miss Francis. In the other, the two men exchange fates. Warners are waiting for preview reactions to decide which ending to use."[32] *Another Dawn* had been purchased for Bette Davis, who was fighting Jack Warner when filming began. In September 1936, Kay took over the role of Julia Ashton. The film was based on a Somerset Maugham storyline (*The Ambassador's Wife*). Warners had often used the fictitious title "Another Dawn" on marquees in feature films. All that changed when producer Hal Wallis couldn't come up with a new name for the Maugham story and used *Another Dawn*. The film is an

Kay "concentrating" on the set of Another Dawn *(1937). (Warners)*

exquisite example of love caught in the midst of a triangle. A remote location in the British Empire provided an exotic background for romantic, as well as military, conflicts. British film expert Stephen Luscombe thought *Another Dawn*, "revealing and illustrative of inter-war imperial outposts. Authentic attitudes, props and ideas filter through the Hollywood gloss and cutting room floor. Treatment of the natives, stiff upper lip attitudes and gung-ho daring-do were very much part of the imperial tapestry of the era."[33]

Filmed on location in Yuma, Arizona, the Imperial Valley and Lasky Mesa Agoura in California, *Another Dawn* reunited a dozen members of cast and crew from *The White Angel*. Errol Flynn was seen making his own personal 16mm version of the film and it was reported he would dub with sound-effects and narration. This was Flynn's fifth starring release at Warners, and he was emerging as one of the great cinematic heroes. Flynn and Francis make a beautiful visual duo, and their scenes together have an eloquent chemistry. Although director William Dieterle disliked the Maugham story, his direction, Tony Gaudio's camerawork, and the score by Erich Wolfgang Korngold provided a fluid, absorbing, and compelling romance-drama.

We meet Kay (as Julia Ashton) aboard an England-bound liner, being annoyed by a persistent boor who inquires as to whether she finds the trip, "not very amusing." "At the present moment," Kay answers, "I find it *revolting*." Ian Hunter, on leave from a remote imperial outpost, is sitting nearby. He gallantly provides an excuse for him and Kay to leave together. That evening, on deck, Kay's sequined gown glitters in the twilight as she graciously listens to Hunter's dreams for his desert home. There is a reserve and undertone of wistfulness about her. Philosophical in her outlook, observant, and a step removed from life, Kay seems devoid of any particular pursuit. Hunter is intrigued. It's Kay's portrayal and distinct personality that set the tone for the film.

By coincidence, Kay and Hunter meet again as guests at an English manor. It is here we learn the reason for Kay's subdued, serene sensibility—her lover of three years, Duncan Hitchens, had died while piloting across the Irish Sea. She feels her love for Duncan will last a lifetime and in her words, "compensate for never being able to love again." Hunter quotes an Arabic phrase that mirrors Julia's situation, and is beginning to mirror his own feeling for her: "The hopes for tomorrow, die today." Days later, Hunter proposes marriage over tea. "One day you'd grow to hate me," Kay tells him, reminding him that she still loves Duncan. Hunter persists. "I can't be jealous of the man who never came back." After she agrees to marry, he promises her that with time, "the past will seem not quite real." This mystical edge is carried throughout *Another Dawn*.

Irishman and daring-do pilot Errol Flynn is stopped dead in his tracks upon seeing Kay at the desert station. He takes the opportunity to introduce himself and inquire if she would give him the chance to do his daily good turn. Amused, but firm, she gives him the order, "Left about turn!" Rebuffed, he obeys. The two are formally introduced by new husband Hunter, Flynn's superior officer and best friend. Once settled in, Kay sports a safari hat and jodhpurs. She asks Flynn to prepare a horse for her to ride part way with Hunter who leaves on detail. When the horse startles, Flynn laughs aloud. He turns to find Kay staring in shock. "I used to know someone else who laughed *just like that*," she says solemnly. With Hunter gone, Flynn and Kay are left to their own devices. They soon find themselves enjoying cigarettes and listening to Bedouin music. As the melody weaves around them, Kay comments that it's like "a melodic will-o'-the-wisp, that dares your emotions to follow it…compelling…beckoning." She makes a parallel

Another Dawn (1937) Kay commented on co-star Flynn, "To look at he's grand. That boy hasn't one camera angle that isn't perfect. It's quite appalling!" (Warners)

between the music and the spirit of Duncan who lived solely to "fly into his tomorrows." "I wish I were like him," Flynn confides. "I'm afraid you are," Kay confesses.

Cinematographer Tony Gaudio's slatted lighting picks up and carries the film with an exotic, poetic visual edge. His camera work is stunningly beautiful, and it softens the romantic scenes with a dreamlike quality. When Flynn escorts Francis to a dinner-ball there is an exquisite interlude between them in a garden court surrounded by palms and the rippling sounds of a fountain. Francis is elegantly draped in a short cape of ostrich feathers. Francis and Flynn fall into an embrace and kiss as Korngold's music underscores their true feelings. Francis struggles with her attraction while Flynn picks a large gardenia-like flower and hands it to her.

After a climatic battle with a desert sheik, from which Flynn is slow to recover, the two lovers realize the futility of their situation. Flynn repeats to Kay, Hunter's Arabic phrase, "The hopes for tomorrow, die today." They both realize the quotation applies to their newfound love. The original ending, with Flynn meeting his doom, was scrapped. Preview audiences preferred the version of Hunter sacrificing his life for the two lovers. Running 73 minutes, the film's mood has definite staying power long after the final credits roll. For years the film was mainly acknowledged for its fine score by Erich Wolfgang Korngold. Sadly, when the film was cut before release much of the music was trimmed along with it. The original masters of Korngold's music disappeared, but were fortunately reconstructed by John W. Morgan for the acclaimed October 1995 recording of the Moscow Symphony Orchestra, conducted by William T. Stromberg.

The *Los Angeles Evening Herald Express* praised *Another Dawn*, saying, "Flynn and Miss Francis...have keyed their performance nicely to the mood...Dieterle has made a picture of strong emotional appeal...It would be unfair to reveal the ending, but it finishes off the picture tersely and dramatically...it has the lure of adventure in strange places and of a love theme that scratches deeper than the surface." James P. Cunningham of *Commonweal* was observant of the film's intentions. "*Another Dawn* brings another triangle, but a most restrained and dignified triangle, sophisticatedly treated. Kay Francis, Errol Flynn and Ian Hunter work seriously and intelligently. Smart dialogue is the main medium for interpretation, with frequent discussions explaining the viewpoints of the principals on ethical and unethical love."

The New York Times review was bent on making sarcastic jibes at the film. "Not since the fabled phoenix," remarked the reviewer, "has the Arabian desert blossomed into anything quite so stunning as Kay Francis and her exhaustive wardrobe in *Another Dawn*. Miss Francis walks with love and some mysterious form of Yogi in her eyes, in long flowing gowns...that go sweeping—more effectively than a vacuum cleaner. [She is] assisted in her metaphysical meanderings from the path of strict marital rectitude by that swashbuckler and devil-of-a-fellow, Errol Flynn...[who] revolves around her too-yielding form. Miss Francis, in a kind of mystical trance which seems to relieve her of moral responsibility, walks into the arms of Captain Flynn—pretending he is a reincarnation or something...The picture is not entirely without merit, of course...the California sand dunes have rarely if ever been photographed more beautifully."

As far as being swept away by her co-star Flynn, Kay saw too much of his boyish mischief to be fooled by his charm. When interviewer Faith Service asked Kay if she would take Errol to a desert island with her, Kay just laughed. "No. I don't believe that I would. Errol is an adventurer at heart, you know. He would be apt to decide that he'd like to go fishing or hunting on the other side of the island and would forget to come back. He'd see another island just over the horizon. Of course, to look at," sighed Kay, "he's grand. That boy hasn't one camera angle that isn't perfect. It's quite appalling!"[34]

On the other hand, Kay told Service she would definitely take beau Delmer Daves. "It would be necessary; it would certainly be terribly desirable to have a strong, practical, sort of desert-island-minded man along. And for that man I'd choose Delmer Daves. He has the strength, the practicality, the ability to do well all the things which would have to be done. He could chop down trees, build tree houses, build fires, draw water, know what to do about everything. You could almost do without the manual if you had Delmer along."[35] Kay wasn't kidding. Daves once listed himself as having 28 hobbies.

Ad for Confession *(1937) (Warners)*

Next up for Kay was her third teaming with Fredric March in the European melodrama *Mazurka*. Based on a true incident from 1930, it provided Kay with one of her meatiest assignments. By the time filming was started, March, who had a commitment with David Selznick, was replaced by Basil Rathbone, and the story was retitled *One Hour of Romance*. William Dieterle, who was originally slated to direct *Mazurka* was replaced by German director Joe May. Anita Louise was usurped by Jane Bryan to play Kay's daughter. Upon release the film was called *Confession* and told in flashback. The poignant story tells of a young girl (Jane Bryan) mesmerized by the concert pianist, Michael Michailow (Rathbone), who is encouraged by him to rendezvous at a nightclub. It is there a jaded, blonde cabaret singer Vera Kowalska (Kay) notices him kissing the girl. Upon their leaving, Vera takes a gun from one of the cabaret acts and kills Michailow. The question the story tries to answer is—why?

After the murder (a scene which took two hours to shoot—May insisted that Rathbone roll down the stairs ten times in order to get the perfect shot), the film uses flashbacks during the courtroom proceedings to unravel Vera Kowalska's story. We learn that, years earlier, Vera was the victim of Michailow's betrayal and that the girl is actually her daughter. In recent years *Confession* has been newly appreciated. William K. Everson reviewed it as a rediscovery for *Films in Review*:

> The plot…pre-dates *Citizen Kane* in its narrative structure…it is almost impossible to understand fully all of the plot ramification at one sitting…Kay Francis, perhaps piqued by the knowledge that Bette Davis had turned the property down, professed not to like it at all, and reported that May was impossible and tyrannical to work with. *Confession*'s finest moment is also its most old-fashioned. After the trial, mother and daughter meet accidentally in the cheerless prison corridor. Both stand silently staring at one another, the daughter unaware of the other's relationship to her…the mother unable to reveal her own emotions without giving away her secret. Then a ghost image leaves the mother's body to bestow the wish-fulfillment embrace that she cannot bestow in actuality. It is one of the most poignant and moving moments I can recall in any movie. Kay Francis is surprisingly good. For once it's a role for an actress rather than a personality, and she does well with it…Joe May believed in what he was doing and didn't feel superior to its tear-jerker category. *Confession* is one of the very best and most handsomely mounted genre films…a needed reminder [of] the German influence on Hollywood.[36]

May's precision direction was not easy on the cast. He was so fond of the 1936 film original (*Mazurka* with Pola Negri) that he used a stopwatch to insure that each scene ran exactly as long as the original's! Jane Bryan would later recall, "We were all marching through the film like sleepwalkers. There was absolutely no spontaneity."[37] Kay, who rarely commented on work specifics in her diary, noted on March 2, "Joe May driving us all crazy!"[38] And, by March 9, entered, "For first time in nine years refused to work!"[39] Regardless of the regimented atmosphere and fireworks between Kay and May on the set, *Variety* thought Kay's haunting portrait one of her best performances, commenting, "*Confession* is a finely produced vehicle for Kay Francis, and a picture that is

Flashback scene from Confession *(1937). Kay disliked Joe May's regimented technique. "Joe May driving us all crazy!" she told her diary. (Warners)*

likely to put her forward in favor as a dramatic actress...Responsibility for the commercial career of the picture is tossed right into Miss Francis' lap. Despite some very fine supporting acting, the picture is all hers. It is her most important production in several years, and is ideal material for any dramatic star."

Confession also had the novelty of showing Kay in a curly blonde wig in the opening cabaret scenes. The idea must have appealed to her. Kay thought having her hair done a chore and would sometimes don a wig. When a friend mentioned that medieval prostitutes sported pubic wigs or 'merkins' for use in their profession, Kay bawdily christened her wigs "Miss Merkin."

Projects announced for Kay during 1937 included *A Prayer for My Sons* (with Billy and Bobby Mauch), *The Sisters* with Miriam Hopkins, and a Bette Davis reject by Faith Baldwin, *Comet Over Broadway*. In June, Kay attended Jean Harlow's funeral and during the months that followed made a point of inviting the distraught William Powell (Harlow's lover) to her house for dinner. By the end of the year, Kay and Delmer were experiencing a low-ebb in their relationship. The fertile couple were confronted with yet another abortion that May. "My God, am I caught again?" Kay moaned. "Dear God, please-no!"[40] Soon afterwards, Kay requested Del return to his own home at night, and was resolved to keep it that way. An August entry read, "Fight with Del...No Call from Del. So what!"[41] Her mood carried over into her usually enjoyable social outings. "Dinner for Grace Moore at Lily Pons. Awful! Strange females."[42] Daves commented later that his relationship with Kay was mostly tranquil, and said, "None of them (columnists, casual friends, reporters) knew that Kay and I had a no-marriage pact between us when our love affair started...Thus, our happy pact and our rather enchanted life for the next three years. We broke off in much the same manner...Kay was accustomed to planning another adventure whenever she finished a film—and I was able to accompany

On the set of Confession. *Kay wearing a "Miss Merkin" (wig) next to Jane Bryan.*

her since I was a free-lance writer or a short-term contract writer during that period. But now my career was becoming increasingly important, my contractual obligations forbade the up-up-and-away life. So we had to face this change…I went to Europe alone—and suggested she find a new love while I was gone, so Louella and Hedda would write items such as 'Delmer had better cut that wander in Europe short, else he'll lose his Kay to a handsome wooer.'"[43]

And a handsome wooer he was. In the fall of 1937, at an evening soiree at Countess di Frasso's, Kay was introduced to Baron Raven Erik Angus von Barnekow, an attractive, distinguished-looking, charismatic, forty-year-old German businessman. It was a mutual attraction. Although as late as October 1937 Kay and Delmer attended a party thrown by Grace Moore for Beatrice Lillie and newlyweds Miriam Hopkins and Anatole Litvak, she was seen more frequently with her new baron. After Kay was escorted by Delmer to Pat O'Brien's wrap party for *Women Are Like That*, also in October, Delmer, for all intents and purposes, drops out of the picture. He left for Europe November 27.

Kay moved from *Confession's* onscreen romance-drama to a political farce based on the popular Broadway play (that starred Jane Cowl) *First Lady*. Kay had seen Cowl's New York performance. Kay's nemesis, Elizabeth Yeaman, was appalled when Kay was selected for the plum role. "Apropos of Warners, I was distressed to read that they were negotiating with MGM to buy the screen rights to *First Lady*, as a Kay Francis vehicle…the role is by no stretch of the imagination suited for Miss Francis…Miss Francis is not a comedienne…I never remember seeing her in a humorous mood."[44] On the contrary,

Kay on the set of Confession *(1937) doing needlepoint.*

Kay's own sharp wit had buoyed many a Hollywood party. Kay told reporter W. R. Mooring of the British Press that she looked forward to filming *First Lady* and added, "I am ready to admit this is going to be such a pleasant change for me. I don't believe I have to weep once from beginning to end."[45] Mooring had observed Kay on and off the set and saw a totally different Kay Francis than what flickered across the screen. He felt that Kay had one outstanding characteristic, an "irresistible tomboyishness that had seldom if ever been permitted to seep into her screen work." Mooring liked Kay's buoyancy and "she-devilishness." "She has the fun inside of her," he said. "All she needs is the right story to bring it out."[46] *First Lady* was *not* the right story. Unfortunately, Yeaman's foreboding harbored some truth regarding Kay's performance.

To offset the inevitable jibes at Kay's wardrobe, Orry-Kelly kept her designs for *First Lady* simple. The only fur in the picture would fly. It was a verbal cat-fight as two Washington, D.C. wives vie to be "First Lady." Contrary to popular opinion, author Roger Dooley thought *First Lady* to be "the wittiest political satire of the decade…Lucy Chase Wayne (Kay Francis), vaguely suggestive of Alice Roosevelt Longworth, is the wife of Secretary of State (Preston Foster), whom she hopes to make the next President. She suspects, however, that her dearest enemy, Irene Hibbard (Verree Teasdale in a deliciously catty performance), the bored heiress wife of an elderly Supreme Court justice…is about to divorce and marry a young congressman whom she will maneuver into the presidency. How Lucy and her cohorts try to prevent this…makes a hilarious film."[47]

Kay's character had her roots in Teddy Roosevelt's politically-minded daughter, Alice Roosevelt Longworth. Longworth's rivalries and smoldering animosities with fellow eminent Washington, D.C. hostesses, would often break into flame and much talked about feuds. Longworth, who lived to be 96, was often referred to by wags as "Washington's *other* monument." Writer Jason Vest gave his analysis of the D.C. of Alice's era. He told how sexual shenanigans of upper-class women were only threatened with, "genteel titters, not journalistic scrutiny." Vest mentions the time *Washington Herald* publisher Cissie Patterson, "trysted with a male dinner guest in Alice's upstairs library." Alice wrote Cissie a snide note the next morning: "Dear Cissie: Upon sweeping up the library this morning, the maid found several hair-pins which I thought you might need and which I am returning. Alice." With an upper-hand, Cissie replied: "Dear Alice: If you had looked on the chandelier you might also have sent back my shoes. Love, Cissie."[48]

Unfortunately for Kay, her Lucy never seemed to get the upper-hand, or give the final zinger, to her Cissie-like rival, Irene Hibbard (Teasdale). Teasdale's sharp barbs ripped and curled around Kay, who had somehow been misguided into a more flighty, happy-go-lucky characterization. Kay often threw away lines that needed more punch and sarcasm. In fairness, the lines themselves lacked much of the irreverent wit that Alice Roosevelt Longworth was known for. A staunch conservative, Longworth often referred to her distant cousin FDR as being, "one-third sap and two-thirds Eleanor."[49]

Kay explained away her misfire in playing the part of Lucy Chase Wayne. "I know that I've got one special quality to see on the screen, as most actresses have," Kay said. "Fans expect sincerity from me, a certain warmth, and if they don't get it, they howl. They didn't like me in *First Lady* worth a cent. They told me so by the hundreds." A San Francisco fan wrote at the time, "I have always said that Kay Francis is the most miscast star in pictures. And after seeing *First Lady* I repeat it again. *White Angel* and *One Way Passage*—incidentally the only two good pictures she's ever had—proved it. But, she's no comedienne as they tried to make out of her in *First Lady*. Why the whole supporting cast walked away with the picture. Kay Francis, capable, brilliant, charming...dying on

Kay and Preston Foster in First Lady *(1937). The role was not her cup of tea. (Warners)*

the vine because of miscasting."[50] In retrospect, director Stanley Logan needed to nudge Kay toward the art of insult. Some attitude would have made her a better match for Teasdale. Logan's first venture into solo film directing held little promise.

The New York Times confirmed that Kay had blunted the film's fine cutting edge. As expected, to her defense came Louella Parsons. "Kay laughingly said that Verree stole the show, but while Verree gives a performance you won't forget, you couldn't steal a picture from Kay." Variety agreed, saying Kay was "splendid and witty." Kay was indeed splendid in the outtakes from First Lady. In one, Kay, graciously pouring tea, flubs her line, slams down the teapot and blurts disgustedly, "Oh, Dammit!" Not exactly the protocol of a D.C. hostess. Another scene has her surrounded by dignitaries who are babbling niceties. After a long, long, long pause of no one saying anything, Kay realizes she has the next line and lets out a hilarious, agitated, "Aaaaaaa!" They all "break up" afterwards. Lucy Chase Wayne just wasn't Kay's cup of tea. Today, the film as a whole seems dated and riddled with caricature.

Before First Lady was released, Kay became embroiled in a dispute with Warner Brothers. She had negotiated a new three-year contract with the understanding that she would play the lead in Tovarich opposite Charles Boyer. Anatole Litvak, fresh from his critical success with Mayerling, was to direct. Kay was enticed by the role of Grand Duchess of Imperial Russia turned Parisian servant, and incensed when the part was suddenly handed over to Claudette Colbert. After an exchange of legal letters with Warners that resolved nothing, Kay took them to court. In retrospect, Kay needn't have worried. Tovarich exhibits a pleasant fizz rather than the much needed sparkle, of say, an Ernst Lubitsch production. Lawrence J. Quirk observed that, "Colbert was third or fourth choice for the role...Kay Francis was ruled out...because her box office had dwindled."[51] (Quirk overlooked the fact that Kay was still the studio's top female draw.) Tovarich co-star Basil Rathbone was interviewed by Quirk in 1954 and had some telling comments about the production. "I don't think Charles [Boyer] was really at ease in the role...and as for Colbert...there was tension between her and Litvak. Litvak was not the right director for her or for the picture itself. Litvak was arrogant and peremptory after his recent success. Claudette...didn't get the personal consideration on the picture that she felt she was entitled to. The critics were kind to the film." Colbert told Quirk regarding Tovarich, "I've done better, and I have certainly done worse, a lot worse."[52]

Stories popped up about a feud between Kay and Claudette. Kay refuted them. "The stories about Claudette and myself being enemies are silly. We are the best of friends. As you know, she's one of the nicest persons out here."[53] If Kay had been expecting Tovarich to be another Trouble in Paradise, she was mistaken. What could have been much ado about nothing, was practically a death knoll for Kay's screen career. What transpired next, left a bitter memory that would follow Kay the rest of her life.

Chapter 13

Glamorous Martyr –
Kay Francis vs. Warners

Warner Brothers had established a tradition of punishing their top talent. Jack Warner bristled mightily when James Cagney and Bette Davis chose to go on suspension rather than acquiesce to the studio's demands. Warner's behavior wasn't always rooted in logic. To punish a box-office star like Cagney was like cutting off his nose to spite his face. Kay's suit against the studio was the last straw. Jack and Harry Warner decided to make Kay an example of what other contract players could expect if they didn't tow-the-line. Warners' machinations against Kay and her career were ruthless. What it did to her *inside* she would carry with her the rest of her life. Her close friend in later years, Jetti Ames, said Kay would not talk about her battle with Warners, and only referred to it as "her great struggle."[2]

All of Hollywood was aware that the lead role in *Tovarich* had been acquired especially for Kay Francis. When the part was assigned to Claudette Colbert, Kay found Warners' dishonesty demeaning. On September 3, 1937, Kay summoned her bosses to court and asked to dissolve her contract due to the studio's reneging on its promise to cast her in *Tovarich*. She claimed it was, "a foolproof part...which would automatically enhance the reputation of anyone playing it."[3] She also charged that Warners had assigned her

Calm Kay amid chaos. As she battled Jack Warner, Kay bitterly spewed, "I hate all the attention a star is supposed to give her precious self...I not only do not enjoy seeing myself on the screen, but I don't even see myself anymore when I look in the mirror...I know there's a face there. And it's probably mine. I know that I must go through the motions of pulling it together, and I do..."[1] (Warners)

189

inferior parts and listed her in an inter-studio register as not being available for loan-out. The British press had already pointed out that Kay was Warners' "greatest single problem in story selection" and could profit by allowing her "to take on films for other studios, on the much favoured policy of loaning out."[4] Not being released from Warners to do a prestigious film like *Dodsworth* had been a major disappointment for Kay.

As mentioned, James Cagney had run up against a brick wall the year before, when Jack Warner refused to loan *him* out. Studios were offering Cagney as much as $100,000 per picture. Attorneys warned him that winning his case meant never working in motion pictures again. When Cagney finally did sue, he was blacklisted and inactive for a year. Other studios were afraid of being blackballed from the Warner chain of theaters. Cagney's motives got mixed reviews in the press. "Bad Boy Cagney"—screamed the conservative *Motion Picture Herald*. There was no guarantee that fans and the press, in the aftermath of the Depression, would be sympathetic to Hollywood's highest paid actress, Kay Francis. *Film Weekly*, a British publication, came to Kay's defense. "For the last three years she has been served with many of the most driveling stories a star could be offered. Until now she has been loyally uncomplaining…without judging the issue in question, a lot of people will sympathize with Kay Francis for breaking out at last; and will hope the result is better stories for her at Warners or elsewhere."[5]

After heavy news coverage of Kay's trial, came a shock that riveted the Hollywood community. Once in court, for some inexplicable reason, Kay decided *not* to break her contract. Whatever transpired behind closed doors between Kay and Warners angered her to the point where she dropped her suit. Officially, it was announced that her suit to cancel her contract had been amicably settled. Amicably? The announcement was merely a cover-up. Kay's diary entries during the trial (September 3—15) are curiously filled with blank pages. Some say Kay stayed with the studio out of pure spite.

Bette Davis, whose suit with Warners had followed Cagney's, recalled in her memoirs, "Our contracts were outrageous and the security I dreamed of…had become the safety of a prison. I was being handed crumbs by the studio, financially as well as artistically."[6] Before her death, Davis gave her slant on why Kay dropped the suit and completed her contract in films unworthy of her talent. "Out of the blue, it was announced she would complete her contract by starring in B-pictures!" Davis related. "It was simply unprecedented, and no reason was ever given. A huge embarrassment for such a star— she had many, many fans." Davis then confided, "It all boiled down to another woman— in *her boudoir*. Jack Warner was despicable to Miss Francis. I felt awfully sorry for her, and it certainly scared every actress in town. [Kay] said what she had to: that she was looking forward to retiring. Or, at least taking time off after having worked so hard. No one dared question her explanation, but it was known."[7]   Davis' comments and the speculation of blackmail being used against Kay are especially disturbing when one considers the effect the Production Code had already inflicted on the film community. Years later, George Eells, also came across the rumors surrounding Kay's sexuality, but discovered nothing concrete. "Perhaps her lusty humor, lack of vanity, low voice, boyish hairdo and tailored suits—plus the inevitable rumors that surround celebrities," wrote Eells, "gave rise to the widely held but false assumption that she was bisexual…But both her private diaries (agonizing over Dwight, Allan, McKay, Billy, John, Ken, Del, Don and later Hap, Joel and Dennis—to mention only a few of her romantic attachments) as well as assurances of her friends lay this rumor to rest."[8] An acquaintance of Kay's also rebuffed the idea, saying, "Oh there may have been some occasion when she was very, very drunk. But that wasn't where her head was...There was never the slightest doubt that she was man-oriented, and don't let anyone persuade you otherwise."[9]

If Kay's sexual dalliance with a woman was used as a threat by Jack Warner, it was indeed a despicable thing to do. She had provided the studio with a great deal of box office revenues and had cooperated for years in vehicles that had been rejected by the studio's *real* prima-donnas. If the rumors carry some semblance of truth, it simply means that Kay was open-minded enough to include women in her romantic experience. After all, she *did* mention her few experiences with lesbianism to Kenneth MacKenna and Maurice Chevalier. Kay had also been very close to Katty Stewart, but the passion that Kay usually reserved for men was missing from that relationship—a fond, schoolgirl crush. One may wonder what all the fuss was about when the bisexuality of such stars as Garbo, Dietrich and Tallulah Bankhead were common knowledge within the industry. Of course Bankhead was no longer filming since the Code took effect, Dietrich toned down her behavior, at least in public, and Garbo...was Garbo.

It's ironic that Jack Warner would use sex as a weapon. Warner himself indulged in and demanded numerous sexual dalliances with the studio's actresses.[10] No one was threatening to expose *him*. His own marriage had "withered into a charade of formality and custom," while he was living under the same roof with his mistress (starlet Ann Page, who was also married).[11] When he finally married Ann in 1936, none of his brothers showed up for the ceremony. "Thank God our mother didn't live to see this," exclaimed Harry.[12] Jack Warner targeting Kay was the double-standard in full throttle. It didn't matter to him that he was destroying the career of one of the studio's biggest moneymakers. Having his highest paid star rebel was just too much for Warner to contend with.

Kay's salary for 1937 topped producer Hal Wallis' and made her Hollywood's highest paid female star. According to the public and theater managers, she deserved it. Fawcett Publications polled thousands of readers over several weeks in 1937 in a Screen Popularity Poll. Kay and Errol Flynn were the *only* two Warners' stars that made it in the top 20. In January 1938, Kay also made the top 15 honor stars in a popularity poll among British theater managers. *Hollywood Citizen News* mentioned, "the stars who rate in the upper brackets of the international poll are the real moneymakers for Hollywood producers, who count upon 40 percent of their revenue coming from foreign countries, in which the British Empire is the dominant contributor."[13] In spite of Kay's success in the movie polls, Warner Brothers seemed bent on disposing of her services. After Kay's court case, and an attempted final financial offer of a 50% settlement on her remaining 18-month contract, which she rejected, Jack Warner focused on getting her to break her pact with the studio and *force* her to quit.[14] The studio announced that Kay would finish out her contract in *B* programmers. James Robert Parish later commented, that "Not since MGM and John Gilbert had a studio so garishly given a former star the kiss of death."[15] The announcement made Kay even more determined to wring every cent out of her remaining ($5,250 weekly) salary, "even if they put me in a bathing suit," fumed Kay, "and have me walk up and down Hollywood Boulevard!"[16] Instead of doing that, Warners insisted she compromise herself and her talent for something just as demeaning. Screenwriter Stuart Jerome, who worked at Warners during Kay's ego-withering departure, referred to her ordeal as "one of the more sordid chapters in our history…"

Her next assignment, she was notified, would be to assist a number of young hopefuls who were to be screen-tested for stock contracts. It was unthinkable to use high-salaried actors, let alone stars, for the embarrassing task of playing second fiddle to raw newcomers, but her refusal would have resulted in an immediate suspension. Swallowing her pride and pocketing her pay check, for the next six days she reported to the test stage to…feed lines to the youngsters…the camera shooting over her shoulder. Uncomplainingly, she spent her days sitting on the sidelines, knitting and drinking gin from a silver flask, and we wondered if, like Dickens' Madam Defarge, she was inscribing into her afghan the names on her hate list. An old-timer, Hobart Bosworth, a star in the silents…commiserating about the way she was being treated, concluded that she was still better off than the stars of his day. "Back then," he recalled, "if you offended any of the moguls, they could order you to clean out toilets. Our contracts only stipulated that we were hired 'for services rendered.' Kay's lucky that the Screen Actors Guild made them change that clause to 'for acting services,' otherwise they could force a showdown by ordering her to report to, say, the commissary as a waitress." To which another old-timer who had worked with her commented, "Knowing Francis, she would not only report, but she would also keep the tips, right down to the last goddam dime!"[17]

So, what was the reaction of Kay's co-workers after her court ordeal? "Within the studio, sympathy was mostly for Francis," wrote Stuart Jerome. "It was necessarily muted sympathy except for two vocal champions."[18] Openly vociferous, Bette Davis (sometimes referred to as the 4th Warner Brother) and Jimmy Cagney (who spent breaks in his dressing room reading law books) let it be known that they considered the studio's behavior despicable. Deliberately going over Jack Warner's head, they sought an audience with Harry M. Warner, who as president had the power to override any decisions he disapproved of. Harry was supposedly sympathetic, but said that since all production matters were under Jack's jurisdiction, he was unable to interfere. However, a series of freshly typed copies of memos, all strictly confidential, disclosed that *Harry* had been the instigator of the campaign against Kay Francis. Jack Warner, inexcusably, had carried out the orders. Screenwriter Wilson Mizner, who supplied many a bright remark for *One Way Passage*, best summed up working for Jack and Harry when he said, "Working for Warner Brothers is like trying to fuck a porcupine. It's one prick against a hundred."[19] Stuart Jerome also emphasized that Kay's *real* nemesis was Harry M. Warner…something few were aware of.

Whereas J.L.'s [Jack's] studio reputation was that of a bastard, H.M. [Harry's] was seen as the benevolent good guy. But, we wondered, was that really so? Many of the firing and suspensions were ordered by H.M., even though it was Jack who carried them out…through the hiring of private detectives, Harry had acquired some particularly gamy evidence of sexual misdeeds on the part of some of our top talent. He instructed his brother to use this evidence whenever necessary to keep them in line. It was no wonder that our studio was known in the industry as "The Burbank Branch of San Quentin"...[20]

Regardless of whatever, if any, evidence was being held against her, Kay was determined to get every penny coming to her at the cost of putting up with Jack and Harry Warner's enforced indignities for the next two years. Kay wasn't a voracious fighter like Cagney or Davis. It wasn't her nature to go for the jugular. Instead, she left behind her legacy as the glamorous martyr of Warner Brothers studios. Oddly enough, it was *her* attitude that set a precedent for many others. Columnist Bob Thomas wrote, "If Jack Warner's abuse of Kay Francis was designed to make other stars compliant to his will, he failed. They recognized that the studio's treatment of Francis would befall themselves as their careers ran down. They resolved to get what they could while they could."[21]

During Kay's screen test marathon, the studio moved her belongings from her plush dressing room, under the pretext it was going to be redecorated. It was—for newcomer John Garfield, who also rewarded himself by stealing silk shirts from the wardrobe department. Kay knew better than to complain and adjusted to the stark new reality of one room in the Featured Players Dressing Room building. From her new cubbyhole on the lot, she reported to work for the previously announced film assignment, aptly titled, *Return from Limbo*. The casting for the film was an uncomfortable and strange mix. Pat O'Brien's bravado and abrasive edge didn't gel with Kay's graceful, sophistication. Still, O'Brien considered playing opposite Kay to be a real coup. Years later, O'Brien recalled, "One of the most glamorous leading ladies I played opposite was Kay Francis. Not only was she a big dark beautiful creature, but she was endowed with a wonderful sense of humor. I saw Kay a few years ago when I was playing in Falmouth, Massachusetts. She and Eloise [Mrs. O'Brien] and I dined together and I reminded her how completely uninhibited she was." "Whenever you played love scenes," O'Brien told Kay, "you always took off your shoes." Kay, looked the stocky actor in the eye and quipped, "I was *taller* than most of the men I played with."[22]

Kay also cut O'Brien down to size in the contrived plot of *Return from Limbo*. The story tells what disasters can befall a happy marriage when the wife shows too much interest in her husband's career. Penned by Albert H.Z. Carr for the *Saturday Evening Post*, the story vacillates between an odd mix of feminist misogynist theory. Any intended sympathy for the husband (O'Brien) turns into disdain. Kay was well rid of him when he pounds his fists and leaves in a huff upon realizing *her* business savvy for *his* failing advertising agency is far keener than his own. The best scene in the film has Kay speaking at a Professional Women's Business Forum. She refers to her husband as having an "ego built about him like a mausoleum" and when she tried to help him she was, "met with a volcanic explosion." Bolstered by good dialogue, she caps her speech by saying it took her only a full moment "to understand the awful thunderings were only those of her husband's collapsing vanity." That evening, Kay relates with delight her success at the forum to her father. "I bet half the married women in that room went directly home and beat up their husbands!" she laughs. What *then* follows is completely out of character for the woman she is playing. The bullheaded O'Brien joins up with a rival firm to help destroy the agency Kay has been diligently carrying on for him. Amazingly, she concedes to his innate something-or-other—the film is unclear on what it *is* exactly and falls into his arms, cooing, "This is lovely!" Her concession is both surprising and appalling—a puzzlement that left the audiences reeling with a bad aftertaste. Just as distasteful was the new title they gave the film: *Women Are Like That.*

Stanley Logan, who had also misguided Kay through *First Lady*, cringed at the film's reviews. His career as director came to a sudden and permanent halt. *Photoplay* was indignant. "Poor Kay Francis certainly got a dirty deal in this. Unbelievably gauche and tiresome…Maybe we'd better pretend we didn't know about it." *Variety* put it bluntly. "Shoddy direction holds down a good cast of players in *Women Are Like That*, which marks another disappointment for Kay Francis…Pat O'Brien enacts a character that is unconvincing in both attitude and action, Miss Francis garnering most of the sympathetic interest. Her speech at a business forum is a bit touching." *Film Daily* thought the film sank into an "unsatisfactory conclusion."

As with *First Lady*, the best thing about *Limbo* was the outtakes. One showed Kay arguing with O'Brien as he's packing his bags to leave her. Kay marches over to him declaring, "I married you for better or worse. If this is the worst, I—I—Oh, *goddam it!*" In another outtake, O'Brien accidentally squirts a somber, glamorous Kay right in the puss with a heavy dose of seltzer. Surprised, she wakes up from the daze of a dull script, looking delighted by the mishap. The outtakes alone would have been worth the price of admission. Kay's only consolation during filming had been pal Andy Lawler. He was on the set in an uncredited bit part. It was a good thing Andy was close by. There were reports of suspicious accidents contrived to unnerve Kay. A few years later reporter Robbin Coons mentioned that during this period Kay "began to feel uneasy about falling arc lamps, collapsing sets, or other hazards…" and that Kay insured herself with Lloyd's of London.[24]

Women Are Like That *(1938) Nearing her contract's end, a struggling Kay declared, "I have loathed being a star. There's too much heartbreak to it…too much publicity, which means too little privacy, too much of everything I detest, and far too little of everything I value."*[23] *(Warners)*

Before her first "B" film, the studio paradoxically announced Kay for some "A" productions. First, she would be reunited with Errol Flynn in *All Rights Reserved* penned by Wallace Sullivan who was responsible for MGM's classy hit *Libeled Lady.* The papers then announced that Bess Meredyth had been hired to create a lady gambler role similar to *The House of 56th Street* for Kay. In February 1938, Warners announced that Jane Bryan would join Kay and Miriam Hopkins, as leads, in *The Sisters.* Kay instead reported to Bryan Foy's cheapie unit in February. This meant that Kay left behind the supervision of Hal Wallis' prestige

"A" productions, which usually took 40-plus days to film with a budget of a third to one million dollars. The Foy unit films were rushed through production and shot in 15 to 20 days with a cost of $50,000 to $125,000. These films were often retread storylines and the directors were almost always minor-league.

Kay's first B film release, *My Bill*, was hands down her best among the five films she made under the Foy unit. Adapted from the successful 1928 Broadway play *Courage*, the first film version had starred Belle Bennett. Kay's version had a well-written screenplay by Vincent Sherman and was under the capable direction of Australian-born, and future Oscar-nominated (*Wake Island*) director, John Farrow (father of Mia). *My Bill* became such an audience favorite that it warranted a *Hollywood Hotel* radio presentation in May 1938 and a repeat broadcast in 1941 on Cecil B. DeMille's *Lux Radio Theatre* (both featuring Kay).

In the film, Kay has three ungrateful stepchildren and her own, very disarming, and *suspected* illegitimate son, Bill (Dickie Moore). The original play had eight children, one *definitely* illegitimate. The Breen Office expurgated that little detail. Still, even with four children in tow, widow Kay is beleaguered by financial woes that expose her ineptitude. Her lack of "know-how" fosters the resentment of her spoiled stepchildren and pompous sister-in-law (Elisabeth Risdon) who force Kay and Moore out of their home. (One wonders if Risdon and Kay discussed the one role they had in common: Florence Nightingale. Risdon had been the only other actress to previously play the nurse icon on film, in 1915.)

The scenes between Kay and Dickie Moore define the word "heartwarming" and give the film its innate appeal. The inevitable reconciliation of the family at the film's end kept it in line with family fare. Audiences walked away in the feel-good spirit intended. Kay's optimism and resilient spirit, coupled with a dash of disarming featherbrained sincerity, worked well for the film. *Photoplay* commented, "That director John Farrow and his cast, working together, have made sympathetic entertainment from this is a small cinema miracle. Bonita Granville, Anita Louise, Bobby Jordan...all form good background for the nice performance of Miss Francis." In 1984, Dickie Moore commented, "Kay Francis played a mother of four in *My Bill*. I was Bill, and twelve, when we did the low-budget Warner Brothers film, which won unexpected critical acclaim. Kay Francis was pleasant, but she worried that her role was not sufficiently important."[25] Jimmie Fidler's column acknowledged

My Bill (1938). Kay's first "B" film was an unexpected surprise "hit." (l-r) Bonita Granville, Bobby Jordan, and Dickie Moore. (Warners)

Kay's courage and success in tackling the part:

> If Warner Brothers forced Kay Francis to play a middle-aged mother of four adolescents in *My Bill,* in an effort to discipline her, their plan has boomeranged laughably. The picture, previewed a few nights ago, is a triumph rather than a humiliation, for Kay. As a production, it is strictly class B…But Kay Francis shines the more brilliantly by contrast with so mediocre a setting. She makes it all class A entertainment…In it, for the first time in years, she is denied star-billing…It took spunk for a woman whose whole success has been built on "glamour" to accept such a role, and it took a lot of ability to turn it into a personal triumph.[26]

Chagrined by Kay's unexpected success in *My Bill,* Jack Warner assigned her a supporting role in a spy-story starring, of all people, Boris Karloff! Bryan Foy assisted Kay in her attempt to escape from Karloff's *Devil Island. Film Weekly* reported the incident in their July 1938, issue, "Kay Francis will go out of Warners in a blaze of authordom. The prospect of being teamed with Boris Karloff stirred her to creative effort. She scribbled a three-page synopsis and handed it to producer Bryan Foy, who had it substituted for the Karloff spy-story as Kay's last picture. Called *Lady Pilot,* title tells all. She gets lost on a desert island going round the world."[27]

Kay's next film, *Lovely Lady,* was actually filmed before *My Bill,* but shelved. The film was re-titled *Secrets of an Actress,* and finally released in October 1938. The ads for *Secrets* claimed that Kay had, "a mood for every man and a man for every mood." It was more of a tag-line for Mae West and had nothing to do with Kay's character in the film. The feature would be the last under Kay's contract to be advertised in *The New York Times.* Warners didn't bother much with publicity for her final three films. Frank S. Nugent's *Times* review summed the story up: "*Secrets of an Actress*…is one of those apparently effortless concoctions of the Warners in which several well-dressed people drift pleasantly through…cocktail bars, penthouses and offices until it is time for Miss Kay Francis to rush down to the pier and tell George Brent everything is going to be all right—Carla will give him his divorce. Ian Hunter is left in a gallant lurch. Mr. Hunter has been in the lurch for years now. It didn't seem to surprise him at all. Nothing in *Secrets of an Actress* is surprising except possibly the realization that its plot still is making the rounds and getting away with it."

Nugent did have compliments for the dialogue and underplaying of key scenes. He added, "Miss Francis herself is content simply to rumple an emotion, instead of tearing it to tatters…" Nugent was more impressed with Claude Rains' ex-wife Isabel Jeans for "majoring in a minor role." As Kay's inebriated roommate, Jeans plays *way* over-the-top—a perpetual madwoman looking for a drink. *The Motion Picture Guide* also rallies behind Jeans, saying, "She stands out like a diamond in a mud hole."[28] Theater owner A.E. Hancock, of Columbia City, Indiana, didn't want anything to do with the film, the story, let alone Kay's secrets. He claimed: "There is absolutely no excuse for releasing such a picture…If Vitagraph wants to kill off Kay Francis, they are doing a swell job of it. More walkouts than we have had for some time, and I'd have walked out too if I could have left the theatre unattended. Boresome, extremely so."[29] With comments like that, and the lethal concoction of "B" films Warners had thrust upon her, Kay's popularity took a dramatic nosedive.

In May 1938, the Independent Theatre Owner's Association included Kay on their list of box-office poison. According to the Association's president, Harry Brandt, Kay, Garbo, Dietrich, Astaire, Mae West, Hepburn and Joan Crawford weren't drawing in the customers. Brandt's slur, which the press devoured, received a lot of publicity and plummeted the status of these stars at their studios, and elsewhere. The news fueled the dismissive attitude Kay seemed to have regarding her own career.

Secrets of an Actress was Kay's last film with frequent co-star George Brent. After filming was completed Brent began his role, without Kay, in *Dark Victory*. The lead part of a terminally ill young woman had originally been offered to Kay before her ruckus with the studio. Producer Walter MacEwen had written Hal Wallis regarding *Dark Victory*, saying, "I think you would have a good Kay Francis picture, moreover…Kay herself is very much in favor of it."[30] Jack Warner made sure that Bette Davis was cast instead. Davis' move into "Kay Francis turf" proved to be a gigantic success in more ways than one. During the filming of *Dark Victory* Davis was able to consummate a longed sought-after affair with George Brent. But, the Davis-Brent romance abruptly ended after Brent listed the ten most glamorous women in Hollywood. He included Kay, Greta Garbo, Norma Shearer, Loretta Young, Marlene Dietrich, among others, and Davis blew her top when left off Brent's list. Harmless stuff, but it was all over for Bette and George after that. Kay and Brent would be reunited next on 1940's *Lux Radio Theatre's* presentation of *The Rains Came*.

Kay's next "B" venture was directed by musical genius Busby Berkeley. Warners' big cover-up for Berkeley in 1935 further illustrates the studio's lack of scruples in order to get what they wanted. When the drunken Berkeley smashed into an oncoming car killing three passengers, Jack Warner told an underling to "Fix it." The man who investigated the accident was soon assigned to the studio's security force with an impressive salary. While at odds with the studio, Kay was indeed getting a different *kind* of "fix." She was handed another Bette Davis reject. *Comet Over Broadway* was based on a *Cosmopolitan* magazine story, "Curtain Call" by Faith Baldwin. Davis told author Whitney Stine, "This was the first nothing script I was given since my court battle in England. It was heart breaking to me. After winning an Academy Award…I was asked again to appear in junk…nor could I afford, career wise to make films such as *Comet Over Broadway*."[31] For refusing to work on it Davis was put on suspension, which meant loss of salary. She held out for four months (something Kay would *never* do) and was rewarded with the part (intended for and promised to Kay) in *The Sisters*. It was another of the great roles in Davis' career, wherein she exhibited grace, sensitivity and distinction, attributes that were usually attributed to Kay. James Robert Parish thought *The Sisters* "would have been a nice showcase for Kay. Miss Francis did at one point break down and virtually beg Warners to cast her as Empress Carlotta, the lady who lost her wits, in the studio's *Juarez* (1939) with Paul Muni in the title spot. Kay should have known better than to ask—the assignment would go Bette Davis."[32] Kay told the editor of Britain's *Film Weekly* in 1936 that the story of Carlotta and Maximilian of Mexico was the *only* pet suggestion she had ever requested of her employers. When the studio finally acquired the novel in October 1937, Warners was only thinking of Bette Davis.

Of course, Kay had made her choice. She had decided to collect her salary regardless of what roles were given her. In *Comet Over Broadway* Kay got to do her usual shtick of suffering nobly, while being flatteringly photographed by James Wong Howe. A real camp-fest with an ample plot, *Comet* only ran 69 minutes. During filming, the stress Kay was under was beginning to take its toll. She developed a kidney infection and experienced side effects from prescription drugs which ruined her complexion. When Warners suspended her she drank enough gin for another flare-up. "So discouraged about my face," wrote Kay on August 8, 1938, "I fell off wagon—very quietly."[33] Upon completing *Comet* a frustrated Kay commented, "Finished picture. Buzz mad at me. Oh, well!!"[34]

Sybil Jason, who had played Kay's daughter in *I Found Stella Parish*, had also been having a difficult time during 1937. When Kay found out about it, she campaigned to have Sybil assigned for the role of her daughter in *Comet Over Broadway*. The South African native Jason found the role to be a godsend and provided her with long-needed encouragement. In the 1980s Jason recalled Kay's gesture. "I hadn't been assigned to a film for three months, and that wasn't a good sign. Kay Francis helped me. She said she wouldn't do *Comet Over Broadway* unless I played her daughter. She was kind."[35] Apparently the two had a connection. After the film's opening, the *Los Angeles Examiner* noted there were three reasons to see the film: "Stately, usually fashionably gowned Kay Francis in the spangles of a burlesque queen, 12-year-old Sybil Jason's murderous impersonations of Kay Francis, and a story certain to tug at the heartstrings of every mother's heart."

In 1991, Leonard Calanquin wrote about his own experience seeing *Comet Over Broadway* in 1938. His article in a 1991 issue of *Classic Images* was titled, "Falling in Love With Kay Francis."

> I was a sixteen-year-old high school student when I first fell in love with Kay Francis. I entered the theatre at 3 P.M. and stayed until the lights went on at 11 P.M.; seeing the film three times. I remember going home to two irate parents. My memories of the situation were very vivid for the next couple of weeks, particularly when I tried to sit down. What was there about Kay Francis that made me look upon her as the most beautiful woman in the world and the greatest actress on the American screen? I know puppy love had a lot to do with it. But there was also her beautiful deep voice, stunning figure, and fabulous wardrobe…her performances always left us with the desire to see her again.

Kay may have seemed the "most beautiful woman in the world" to Calanquin, but her beauty couldn't counter the fact that she was starring in one of her most bizarre, surreal film roles. Absurdities abound throughout the convoluted plot of *Comet* and one simply can't resist the story's ridiculous twists and turns. Small-town actress Kay becomes hopeful when a famous (and lecherous) actor manages to catch the tail-end of her starring role in a local production. Hammy Ian Keith, with his usual wild-eyed lunacy, plays the Barrymore-like Lothario who compromises Kay. Her suspicious husband, John Litel, catches the duo in a clinch at Keith's bungalow. He manages to slug Keith with such impact that Keith is thrown *over* the front porch, *sailing* into a nearby lake where he experiences a brain-concussion and drowns! After a scandalous trial, the "dumb, patient and trusting-like-a-dog" Litel (as the lawyer describes him) lands in prison for life. Kay is left alone to care for herself and their little girl. She does what anyone else in such a situation would do. She joins a carnival.

After four months on the road, her agent suggests Kay hop a train and join a burlesque troop. She does—but soon tires of parading around in spangles and beads while ogling eyes lust after her talent. She befriends an older burlesque queen, Tim (Minna Gombell). Gombell, who by some miracle—tips?—has quite a nest-egg built up for her retirement. If you believe that, then you can also believe she wants to raise Kay's daughter while Kay achieves unimaginable success as a London stage star! Years later, Kay and daughter (Sybil Jason) are reunited so Kay can face the music of her past. Of course, she must sacrifice her career and her newfound true love (Ian Hunter, in his seventh and last screen paring with Kay). Upon finding out the whole truth behind Kay's dilemma, Hunter sums up the picture with one line: "This whole thing doesn't make sense!" With or without sense, Kay must now devote herself to her daughter and her jailbird husband, who hopefully won't live long with his convenient heart ailment. So, Kay courageously returns to her hometown, takes her daughter by the hand and marches over hill and dale toward the prison gate for a family reunion. The ending is a real jaw-dropper. Film expert Robert Osborne, had this to say of *Comet Over Broadway*:

> This movie really pushes logic to the limit. There's not one scene in *Comet Over Broadway* that has any relation, whatsoever, to reality. It so defines what a lot of movies were about in the 1930s. Fantasy. Pure Fantasy. And boy, does this film deliver.
>
> There's just one unbelievable thing that happens after another and it's all played very seriously. A friend of mine saw this movie for the first time and said after it was over, "That is the stupidest film I think I have ever seen...and I just loved it!" But, I think *my* favorite moment in the movie is the last one. Kay and that kid walking up the hill to the prison with a suitcase. I mean, couldn't have *somebody* given her a *ride* in a *car* from the train station? Is that too much to ask? That is great stuff. Just amazing. And people got paid for that script.

Although *Comet Over Broadway* premiered as a second-feature in New York, it did get reviewed. After witnessing a showing at the Palace Theatre the reviewer for the *New York Times* found it to be "as unendurable as Kay Francis in ready-to-wear clothes. Not even the hint that the husband has developed heart trouble in prison can comfort us; we're that romantic. Some of these cardiac cases hang on forever, you know...the authors...were obviously all broken up when they thought of the heroic, sacrificial years ahead."

Years later, Busby Berkeley commented on working with Kay, and said, "Kay had a reputation for being a bit difficult...but I saw no evidence of it on this picture. I do know she was unwilling to participate in the publicity game. That didn't interest her at all. And it seemed to me she lacked that driving ambition an actress needs in order to get the best parts in the best films. I found her to be cooperative and humorous, perhaps because she knew this was one of her last films for Warner's...I think she was rather glad the grind was coming to an end."[36] Indeed, any ambition Kay did have, at this juncture, had been knocked out of her. After their aforementioned squabble, Kay and Berkeley managed to patch things up. On August 17 Kay jotted down, "Talked to Buzz Berkeley after nice letter from him."[37]

Amazingly, Busby Berkeley sailed from the ridiculous *Comet* into the director's seat for the sublime crime melodrama, *They Made Me a Criminal* (1939). That film, along with Kay's dressing room, made John Garfield's star shine a little brighter. Garfield's occupancy in Kay's dressing room was brief. After her success in *Jezebel*, Bette Davis asked her attorney to acquire Kay's two-story, cottage-style dressing room as a symbol of her ascension. The cottage had five rooms, two baths, and a real fireplace. By the time Davis completed *Dark Victory*, her mother, Ruthie, had completed the decor of Kay's former roost with French and English antiques and a grand four-poster bed as centerpiece.

In spite of her own predicament Kay was, as always, very generous in her support and encouragement of co-workers. Dick Mook commented that Kay's "charities are legion but they never find their way into print."[38] In the summer of 1937, she had learned that her wardrobe attendant (Ida Greenfield, who had assisted Kay on *Confession, Another Dawn,* and *Stolen Holiday*) had been saving for a car for two years. Kay bought the car and gave it to the girl herself. Author Doug McClelland also mentioned Kay's generosity and encouragement to other, lesser-knowns, during her Warner years. "Jane Wyman was asked by an interviewer [Rex Reed] if anyone had given her a hand up the ladder of success, and Jane replied that Kay Francis had. She said that Kay was always helpful to all aspiring actresses. Susan Hayward was by all reports one of the young actresses Kay Francis had encouraged when Susan had a bit role in Kay's 1938 vehicle *Comet Over Broadway*."[39] Wyman's interview with Rex Reed was from October 1968—two months after Kay passed away. Wyman reflected on her Warner days, saying, "We all got along and helped each other. We were trained by pros. Kay Francis helped me the most when I got started. And we weren't afraid to get out there and get our feet wet. These kids now can't learn. There's nobody around to help them."[40] Kay was unusual in this respect. Other big names on the lot suffered from what Glenda Farrell called a "star complex." "Bette [Davis] was always an outsider," Farrell would say later.[41]

One Hollywood writer mentioned that the studio's "hired help" kept their distance whenever Kay appeared moody or was concentrating on her work. But, he emphasized, "Miss Francis is also one of the most thoughtful and most generous of the movie stars to the same 'hired help.' Her generosity is not accompanied by a fanfare of trumpets and banner lines in the newspapers. Her generosity, my dears, belongs to that sacred private life, and it took a deal of prying about before I could discover it. Kay Francis may be Hetty Green to the jewelry salesmen and the real estate brokers, but she's the Good Samaritan to many a bit of broken humanity."[42] And, Kay did more than her fair share for broken humanity. She simply stated, "I am one of those who may be said to have a 'Mission in Life.' And I believe in helping people to take their minds off themselves and their own problems, even for a little alleviating space of time."[43]

Perc Westmore shared a couple of instances from Kay's "mission" to reporter Sara Hamilton. One day, according to Westmore, Kay was worried to distraction, growing even more so as the day progressed. Westmore said that Kay finally asked him, "'About that poor woman and the baby—how much do you think we will need?'" "*We'll*, need, you notice," Westmore emphasized, "only it's Kay Francis' name that goes on the check. I could tell about trips to San Bernardino, miles away, where one of the girls from the publicity office lay ill— a girl Kay knows but slightly. Time out of Kay's busy life to drive there to be a comforting presence. What makes a woman like that, I wonder, so real in a place so unreal? ... I know the worry and heart-ache that's brought it on. I know its climax too. It always ends with an open check book and a whispered conference of—'How much will we need?'"[44]

In 1938 Kay backed and financed the adoption of a baby for a childless couple who worked at the studio. She would not reveal their name, but the woman had a bit part in *Women Are Like That*. It wasn't always a checkbook that Kay reached for—like the time she marched into the executive offices demanding that an electrician be hired back on the set of *Another Dawn*. Film production was halted until he returned. He had a family to feed. Kay was grateful to be independent to do for others and it was an odd predilection of hers not to give Christmas presents. She stated that the "very spirit" of Christmas was "being murdered by the hard, commercial spirit of exchange which has crept into the world."[45] Instead, Kay gave presents throughout the year as she discovered items that suited a particular friend.

Kay's concern for young hopefuls in the film industry was so profound that she took pen to paper and wrote a succinct, from-the-heart account of what they should expect if they venture to Hollywood unprepared. Published in the January 1937, *Pictorial Review*, and titled "Don't Try Your LUCK out here!" Kay minced no words about the heartache she had witnessed first hand on the studio lot:

> While we were gathering "extra" people for background in *The White Angel*, two little girls, one twelve and the other eight, travel-stained and hungry, appeared at the offices of the Central Casting Corporation in Hollywood…They explained that they had been sent to work as "extras" in the movies. Their mother in Ohio had scrimped and saved to give them dancing lessons. Then she put them on a bus, unaccompanied, and sent them two thousand miles across the country. Two or three days later, I am told, they were on their way back home, their fare paid by one of the charitable aid associations…When things like this happen—and they are happening right along—I see red. Mothers and daughters have written me countless letters asking about "extra" work. I have been beseeched for advice. Can a girl live on her wages as an "extra"? Can she hope for featured work, eventual stardom, after an apprenticeship as an "extra"? My answers have been blunt and to the point. I have told them—and I hope to heaven they have believed me—that "extra" work means grief, disappointment, hunger…the beginning of the steep downhill road. And the chances against its meaning stardom, or anything like it, *are a million to one!* I haven't wanted to be cruel. I like "extra" girls. I have met hundreds of them. I respect them for their ambitions and their dreams. But I pity them as well. I started at the bottom rung of the ladder, too. Most of them know that. But not as an "extra." I was a stenographer…as remote from screen-acting as the north pole from the equator…But believe me when I say that "extra" work is even more distant, *and less of an apprenticeship to acting than any form of office work!* This may sound like a wild statement now. You'll understand it more fully as I go on.

Kay encouraged youngsters to take, "the longer road to the studios which is shorter in the end…" via the stage. She then told her own story—her gradual success in the theatre which made her more visible to those who counted. Kay recommended amateur theatricals, along with capable coaching. She concluded saying: "You are just as likely to be 'discovered' while getting this training and experience…enroute to your goal: motion picture acting. Which is something that is not inherent in the life of an 'extra' girl."[46]

What was behind all of Kay's concern for others? One studio employee felt that Kay had, "the pain of the world riding high in her heart. She's born a woman...in whom...the pitiful humanity finds an answering echo and the pleas of the unfortunate find a sympathetic lodging."[47] Kay herself put it more simply. Her love of charity and helping others wasn't confined to giving money or things. She emphasized, "trying to give something of yourself; trying to give something of which no disaster can ever deprive them."[48] In another interview Kay declared, "When I say my only ambition is for a life worth living. I mean by that a life in which I'll make the most of myself and a life which will be of some service to others."[49] Kay added to her humanitarian credo:

> I have a motto that reads, "Never hurt anybody if you can help it." I add to that motto, "And you *can* help it!" It may sound very smug, but I do sincerely believe that one way to be happy is never to hurt anyone else; and the reason it is a way to be happy is because it is retroactive. If you do not hurt others, you are very unlikely to be hurt, yourself.[50]

Unfortunately, Kay's compliance with Jack and Harry Warner since 1932 had not retroactively protected her from a meanspirited attack on her person and career. But, a few years later Dick Mook verified that her motto had flourished with her Warner co-workers:

> The crew on her pictures have always been Kay's staunchest friends. What spare time she has between shots she spends laughing and kidding with them. And I happen to know that in all the years she was a star at Warner's, she never finished a picture that she   didn't have a party for them and give presents to everyone who had worked on the film with her. And to show how Kay stands with her fellow workers, I don't believe she ever finished a picture there that they didn't take up a collection among themselves to buy something for her. But she would never permit any publicity to be sent out about those parties.[51]

The degradation of seeing her films' premier on the lower-half of a double bill and her dressing room usurped by Warners' new "Queen Bette" was somewhat alleviated for Kay by her new romance with Baron Barnekow. Their romance had intensified before Delmer was completely out of the picture. Kay and Erik consummated their affair the day before Delmer left for Europe. In the New Year of 1938, her diary notes were ecstatic: "Erik here for dinner—Long talk re: his projects. Big night of love...Erik is very good."[52] Kay now had a hopeful future and could leave Hollywood far behind and to its own devices. Kay promised Louella Parsons that she would be "the first to know," as Parsons was devotedly following the couple's romance. Upon Delmer's return from Europe, Kay and Erik met privately with him. Daves gave the baron his approval. Kay authorized Parsons to announce the betrothal *and* her retirement from films at 10:30 p.m., March 1, 1938. Soon afterward, columnist Sidney Skolsky translated the announcement into "Hollywoodese": "Humphrey Bogart will marry Mayo Methot in September when his divorce from Mary Phillips, who will marry Kenneth MacKenna, who was formerly married to Kay Francis, who will marry the Baron Barnekow..."[53]

Surprisingly, on that same day, Kay stated in her diary reservations about the marriage. "Announcement of Erik and my marriage. Well, I can't go very wrong, but no marriage and baby until I know where Erik is going!"[54] At times she was puzzled by his behavior. For his birthday she gave him a money clip, birthday cake and ice cream. "He seemed very nonchalant," wrote Kay. "I was hurt, but should understand when he says he was embarrassed."[55]

Louella Parsons raved about the "new Kay" in her May 22 column after a tanned Kay, with new short haircut, had driven in her station wagon to meet the columnist.

> What's happened to Kay?…She is like another girl—so happy and care-free. My guess is that it's *love* and also the knowledge that she has mapped out her life as she wants to live it…She has learned that there are other things in the world besides success and international fame. It takes a strong person to turn away from the adulation and the excitement of a movie career…she and her Baron will go to Europe on a honeymoon as soon as that Warner contract is completed…the Baron, tall, blonde and charming, seems to be a companion who will be a worthwhile substitute for an exciting movie career.[56]

In July 1938, Kay reiterated to Ted Magee of *Screenland* that she "was giving up her career for the man she loves." Magee describes Barnekow as "unassuming and charming…he is giving up his German title to be plain Erik Barnekow, American aviation official." Barnekow had arrived in Los Angeles on a deal for the TWA airlines. Magee gave a brief synopsis of their romance.

> The fall social season was in full whirl when "Erik," as Kay calls him, walked into her life. He was a guest at a party being given by Countess di Frasso, one of Kay's closest friends…when these two looked at each other…a vague and inexplicable something passed between them…It must have been a wonderful thing for Kay…I have watched her   many times on the set at Warner Brothers, knitting endlessly between shots…Those busy hands, ceaselessly plying the needles, seemed to give away something she would never admit—that there was a vast, empty void which only could be filled by some new and overwhelming interest…and then she met the Baron…that fateful night was the beginning of it all…I have never before seen Kay Francis so radiant. There is new strength in her words, in her actions.[57]

Magee did manage to get Kay to talk about what she and Erik had in common. She mentioned enjoyment of the same sports. They both played and loved tennis. They both shared an equal dislike for nightclub life. Kay's intention at this point was to give up her career and make the marriage stick. Magee pointed out that Kay had managed to put enough savings aside to be independent for the rest of her life, calling her a shrewd business woman. She had just built a beautiful home in Coldwater Canyon, in a location she fondly referred to on her stationery as "Gopher Gulch" (which Kay derived from a U.S. Geodetic Survey Map). The previous Christmas Eve she noted in her diary that she and Erik had "baptized the library floor" making love. After she hired the new household staff, Kay made plans to refurbish and provide Erik with a new office for his business venture. She was swept away by Erik to the point of confessing to Magee the usual sentiments surrounding women giving up careers. "I am determined that once we are married, I shall devote myself to being a good wife, to considering only his wishes and plans. Don't you think that is any woman's duty? If I should ever again make a picture, it would be because there was no possibility of its interfering with my private life…I never would make one anyhow if Erik objected…He will always come first, regardless of any role I am offered."[58] Previously, Kay would have choked on such sentiments. Her romantic nature was definitely in full bloom. Be that as it may, Kay had no interest in becoming Baroness Barnekow. Erik had taken out U.S. Citizenship papers and planned to drop the baron title. The couple wasn't certain they would stay in Hollywood after their wedding. "I don't know where we will live or what we will do," Kay said, "but whatever the answer may be it is all right with me." Magee concluded:

> It is a mystical and wonderful thing to see how two personalities can meet like this, and alter each so deeply. And no matter how badly you may feel over the prospects of Kay's retirement, it would make you happy to see her suddenly young and gay again, with that old hint of loneliness banished completely from her makeup. All her fans the world over will be wishing her luck as she rounds the turning point into a new and precious phase of her life.[59]

✳ BARON RAVEN ERIK VON BARNEKOW ✳

Born: March 10, 1897, Pomerania
Died: October 25, 1942, Altmarrin, Pomerania
Kay's lover and fiancé: October 1937-October 1939

During the 1930s Hollywood, Barnekow acknowledged he was heir to his father's castle and country estates in Pomerania. His mother was the oldest daughter of Count Sholto Douglas, famous philanthropist and owner of the Westeredeln Potash Mines. After his childhood and schooling, seventeen-year-old Erik joined his father's regiment in the Royal Horse Guards. At nineteen, Erik was attracted to the glamour and risk-taking associated with aviation during the Great War. By February 1917, he had joined the Luftstreitkrafte and flew in the first Richtofhofen Pursuit Squadron. Barnekow served under Kurt-Bertram von Doring, along with his lifelong friend Ernst Udet, who was the highest-scoring German pilot to survive the conflicts of World War I. After several victories Erik was wounded in action on August 23, 1918, but returned to score many more victories by the end of the war.

Barnekow's interest in aviation brought him to New York in 1922. He was employed by several of the cities stock houses as a broker. While in New York he met a 18-year-old German girl, Ingeborg Wendroth. Ingebord had lived with her grandmother in New York for a number of years and had gone to school there. The couple married in August of 1924. The newlyweds returned to Baden-Baden, Germany, where Ingebord gave birth to a son in 1926. They named the boy Erik.

In 2003, Erik reflected on the relationship with his father. "In 1926, when I was around six months old, my father left her (and me) in Baden-Baden, where we lived at my grandmother's estate, Mariahalden. My mother and father never met again. My grandmother's estate was a well-known social center in those days. She loved to have interesting guests and give 'small' lunches for 80 people. My father evidently did not like that at all...neither would I. My parents divorced when I was one-year-old. I most unfortunately never met my father, though he always seemed very close to me and a most inspiring example of a man who was a loyal friend, extremely brave and willing to sacrifice almost anything. After World War II, I saw a great deal of a most wonderful lady, Brita, my father's sister, finding out more about him. His other sister, Jutta, shot herself in Pomerania when the Russian army overran our estate. So much suffering on all sides. About my father's activities in the U.S. I know nearly nothing. Except that he was super-interested in wonderful and fascinating ladies, and known never to raise even a finger in order to conquer. Sort of a master of the art of letting happen what should happen. 'Wu Wei' is the Chinese word. Kay Francis was a remarkable and wonderful actress with whom my father had an intense love relationship during the time he lived in Hollywood. My father never remarried and had no other children."

Chapter 14

Bogie and the Baron

While Kay was contemplating her future with Erik and making major life decisions, her next screen assignment, *Dr. Socrates*, underwent a major sex-change. The story, from *Collier's* magazine, had been filmed in 1935 starring Paul Muni. As good-guy Dr. Lee Cardwell, nicknamed Dr. Socrates, Muni foiled some notorious gangsters by injecting morphine into their veins. Muni had said the plot was nuttier than a walnut ranch. The story was retreaded at the Foy unit in 1938, re-titled *Lady Doctor,* and placed Kay in Muni's shoes. Typecast, Humphrey Bogart filled in as the notorious gangster. Kay joined Orry-Kelly to create a variety of tailored suits befitting her call. Filming was touch and go.

Vincent Sherman was brought in to create a screenplay on *Lady Doctor* that could be shot in the twenty days allotted. Sherman got along fine with Kay and thought her a nice lady. Bogart biographers Sperber and Lax pointed out that Kay and Bogart assisted Sherman with the script, "tooling away at the unfinished scenario and trying to make sense of a story about a killer with a Napoleonic complex (Bogart, of course) and a physician (Francis) who subdues him with toxic eye drops. Director Lewis Seiler, a house director with a predilection for glacial pacing, never bothered to consult the script the night before and arrived on the set each morning not quite knowing what to do. The picture was being shot as it was being written, a routine disquieting to studio hands, who cherished predictability."[1]

Lady Doctor was suddenly shelved. After a few months it was dusted off for re-takes, which beefed up Bogart's part, and re-titled *Unlawful*. Next, the film went through another sex-change, in star status. Bogart, whose drawing ticket with the studio was still nebulous at this point, was given star billing for the first time—more out of spite for Kay than anything else. Shortly before the picture's release in January 1939, the embarrassed Bogart was billed above a new title, *King of the Underworld*, and Kay, was demoted below the title in much smaller print as a featured player. "It was conceivably the first time that the supporting player drew nine times the salary of the ostensible star. Even the usually cynical industry was stunned, as was the press."[2] Bogart's top-billing was truly a non-achievement and a slap-in-the-face to Kay. Bogart had the added discomfort of having to live up to the impossible task that the ads for the run-of-the-mill feature promised: "Humphrey Bogart blasts his way to stardom!"

One must remember that during the filming of *King of the Underworld* Humphrey Bogart was *not* the icon we know him today. Far from it. Sperber and Lax felt that by 1939, "the coming decade held little promise for Bogart. He was going nowhere. Duke Mantee was passé."[3] Bogart's character in *King of the Underworld* was a carbon-copy of the Mantee character Bogart had first portrayed for the Broadway stage in 1935. Director Vincent Sherman commented, "The word was, if it's a louse-heel, give it to Bogart." Bogart was used by a studio that repeatedly put him in roles where he was toting a gun.

In spite of fattening Bogart's part as gangster (Gurney), the film's focus still remains on the story of physician Carole Nelson (Kay). She attempts to redeem her career after her husband's association with Gurney results in his being killed in a police raid. Kay leaves town to hunt down Bogart and gain evidence to prove her innocence. Arriving in Wayne Center (supposed hideout of Bogart and gang), Kay's reputation had preceded her. The self-righteous, crotchety local doctor gives Kay flack for being there. "This is a small town ya' know!" he wails. Kay sizes him up and replies, "With *small people* in it!" It isn't long before Bogart shows up at Dr. Kay's doorstep wounded from a shootout. When he brags about not feeling pain, Kay caters to his unbridled ego. "Some people aren't sensitive to pain," she tells him, "especially the moronic type." Bogart takes it as a compliment. "Wait'll I tell the boys!" he crows. "I'm the moronic type!" Humor is really the saving grace of the film, intentional or not, especially when Kay shoves a thermometer in Bogart's mouth, in front of his gang, and tells him, "Keep your mouth shut!" Bogart, who sees himself as the "Napoleon of Crime," is amazed and impressed at

Humphrey Bogart and Kay, whose ex-spouses had recently married each other, struggled through the filming of Lady Doctor. *The picture was re-christened* King of the Underworld *(1939). Bogart felt like a heel taking top-billing from Kay. (Warners)*

her effrontery. Kay finds her opportunity to roundup Bogart's gang when his wound's infection spreads to his eyes. She claims the highly contagious germ could blind Bogart *and* his gang. Bogart is miffed. "I gotta get mixed up with some cockeyed germ!" he bellows. Kay puts drops of the liquid "cure" (which creates temporary blindness) into the eyes of Bogart and his boys. Soon the police are surrounding the house and Bogart, as usual, ends up dying on the staircase pleading. "Do me a favor will ya?" he gasps with his last breath, "Don't tell 'em that a dame tripped me up!"

King of the Underworld was a formula gangster picture with some amusing incidental horseplay by gang members. Such shenanigans probably weren't too far off the mark. Producer Bryan Foy's connection with bookies and con men proved resourceful when filming crime pictures. To add some convolution to the storyline, Bogart kidnaps a British author, played by James Stephenson, to co-write his autobiography. Stephenson also adds romantic interest for Kay, which is finally consummated at the film's finish by the sudden appearance of their seven-year-old child!

Bosley R. Crowther, of *The New York Times,* took the studio to task in his January 7, 1939 review for the film:

> It never occurred to us that one day we might be the organizer of a Kay Francis Defense Fund. But after sitting through *King of the Underworld*…in which Humphrey Bogart is starred while Miss Francis, once the glamour queen of the studio, gets a poor second billing, we wish to announce publicly that contributions are now in order…we simply want to go gallantly on record against what seems to us an act of corporate impoliteness. *King of the Underworld* is said to be the farewell appearance of Miss Francis…considering the plot and everything, it is our settled conviction that meaner advantage was never taken of a lady.

CBS Radio news commentator Jimmie Fidler also came to Kay's defense:

> Out here in the once-chivalrous West, the studio czars have a way—a sort of mean way, I might add—of "getting even" with players who have been quarrelsome and are about to leave their employ…The bigwigs avenge their hurt by giving the departed star a thorough beating in the advertising. For example, *King of the Underworld* is currently being screened. In the local theater ads, you have to read carefully to find the name of Kay Francis, in much smaller letters, buried way down in the reading matter. You grasp the psychology, of course. The intention is to make Kay feel very, very small indeed—as small, even as the type in which her name is printed…I imagine that Miss Movie Fan's opinion of Kay must have taken a certain slump when she reads that advertising. It's all so absurd. Studios employing such tricks are like small boys, who, being displeased at something mama has done, sneak off around the corner and stick out their tongues.[4]

Among the rich and famous who saw how the studio seized every opportunity to kick her while she was down was Noel Coward. After witnessing the film and her undeserved demotion, Coward pointedly asked Bogart, "Have you and Jack Warner no shame?"

Bogart retorted, "None."[5] Funny, but not very true. Bogart had misgivings about the picture and the way Francis was being treated. While filming a trailer for the picture, Bogart, as gangster Gurney, told of fighting his way to the top in the world of crime. At the finish, he capped his speech saying, "Now I'm *King of the Underworld*, and nobody is better than I am!" Without missing a beat, Bogart pointed a threatening finger at the camera and sneered, *"And that goes for you, too, Jack Warner!"*[6]

The Hollywood Citizen echoed the sentiments of those coming to Kay's defense saying, "Miss Francis…handles a thankless role capably, and deserves better than the secondary billing the Warners have given her in this last of her pictures under the Warner contract." (Kay actually had one more release for the studio.) *The LA Evening Herald Express* gave compliments, saying, "Kay Francis handles [the] role of the wronged woman and turns in a convincing performance, better than many of her recent efforts."

Sperber and Lax, commented on the Francis-Bogart team, saying, "On the set, they were professionals making the best of a bad situation, with Bogart determined to see his co-star through the process as quickly and painlessly as possible. They got along well. They also had ex-spouses married to one another."[7] Kay and Bogart's ex-spouses (Kenneth MacKenna and Mary Phillips) were honeymooning in Canada during the filming of *King of the Underworld*. MacKenna was now a film editor for MGM in New York. Another bond between Kay and Bogie was their friendship with Pulitzer Prize-winning author Louis Bromfield. They often visited Bromfield's 715-acre home, called Malabar Farm, near Mansfield, Ohio. Kay was a familiar sight at the environmental friendly utopia, carrying pails of milk while wearing her mink coat. During the 1940s Bromfield's Malabar would play a significant role in both Bogart's and Francis' lives. Malabar was the location for the much publicized marriage of Bogart and Bacall. In 1948, Kay would retreat to Malabar after an unfortunate and scandalous accident.

While earning her final paychecks at the studio, Kay was prominently featured in the news while being courted by the Baron Barnekow. When the marriage failed to take place in the fall of 1938, as previously announced, columnists began to wonder—especially when Kay sailed for Puerto Rico without her baron. Kay told reporters in San Juan that she was seeking, "rest, not people." A special cable to *The New York Times* stated, "her attempt to avoid people was not wholly successful, as a crowd filled the Plaza Colon when it was learned the movie star was having her hair done at a beauty shop. Miss Francis said she was through with pictures and was likely to marry again soon. She would not name the time, the place, or the man."[8]

In October, Louella Parsons quelled any rumors and reassured readers that Kay's adventure to the West Indies was purely therapeutic. "Kay Francis telephoned yesterday to say *au revoir* until December," gushed Parsons. "She and her secretary, Dorothy Wagner, are taking a tramp steamer on Saturday for a trip to the West Indies…a rest which Kay sorely needs after her unprecedented run of continuous picture-making these many months. Her fiancé, Baron Erik Barnekow, also leaves Saturday for a two months' business trip which will take him around the country via airplane. He returns here in December and, as we told you, the marriage is now definitely set for the first of January."[9] Kay and Erik exchanged gifts before separating. Kay noted on October 12: "Erik for dinner. Brought me very beautiful soap box and I gave him his belt and studs. Had a

Kay attending the premier of Kentucky *(1939) with her fiancé Baron Barnekow, along with Jessica and Richard Barthelmess.*

good cry—I *do* love him—bless him. Very sad night but *close.*"[10] According to her diary Kay spent the rest of the trip (through December 5) reading Erik's letters. On the train to Galveston a letter from Erik provided her with a four-leaf clover that his mother had given him years before. But, lady luck was not on her side.

On December 1, Parsons changed her tune. "Some of Kay Francis' Hollywood pals have received cards from her from South America…Kay said when she left she would return in January to marry Baron Barnekow. But, personally, I will be surprised if that marriage ever takes place, for it does not seem to this writer that she would be content to remain away all these months if she intended to marry. Talk is that Kay may sign with RKO when she returns. There are several movie jobs in the fire for her, and I look to see her back hard at work before many months, with her romance with the Baron a closed chapter in her life."[11] A week later, Parsons did another turnaround. "The marriage of Kay Francis and Baron Barnekow is by no means off, and it will take place, according to Kay, who planed into town yesterday, either in January or February…The good-looking baron met her at the plane and, from the welcome he gave her, it was easy to see that he was glad to have her back."[12] Two days later the couple was seen window-shopping for the holiday season.

Over New Year's weekend, Kay and Barnekow were guests at Myron Selznick's mountain retreat along with Myrna Loy and her husband producer Arthur Hornblow, Errol Flynn, and the three prospective Scarletts for *Gone With the Wind*: Joan Bennett, Paulette Goddard and Vivien Leigh. Parsons failed to mention if Kay was consulted on who she thought best for the coveted part. Parsons' co-worker for the *LA Examiner*, Erskine Johnson, did more intensive snooping and reported on January 21: "Baron Barnekow can't make up his mind about fiancé Kay Francis. One day he tells friends they'll be married soon, and the next day he's doubtful."

April 1939 saw the release of Kay's final Warner feature under contract. Originally, Warners announced she would be in the all-star cast of *The Gay Nineties,* a mammoth musical for her last film. Lloyd Bacon of *42nd Street* was set to direct. The project was to have included Dick Powell, Ann Sheridan, Humphrey Bogart, Olivia de Havilland and George Brent. Instead, Kay tackled the Francis Walton story, *Women in the Wind*, which was a fulfillment of sorts for Kay's envisioned *Lady Pilot*. The studio had purchased *Lady Pilot*, a story Kay authored about a globe-girdling aviatrix, in 1938. Women in aviation were a popular topic since Katharine Hepburn's role in *Christopher Strong* (1933). Ruth

Chatterton was Hollywood's most avid aviatrix and sponsored the Ruth Chatterton Derby in which she flew cross-country. In 1939 Twentieth Century-Fox released *Tail Spin* with Alice Faye in the pilot's seat. *Tail Spin* was similar to *Women in the Wind*, and revolved around a trio of women aviators competing in a "Powder Puff Derby." Author Roger Dooley designated the films as pioneering efforts. "One can see by hindsight," he wrote, "how easily these films about supposedly heroic women led into such wartime epics of selfless WACs, WAVEs or nurses as *So Proudly We Hail* (1943)."[13]

The trio of aviatrixes in *Women in the Wind*, also included Sheila Bromley and Eve Arden. Arden recalled in her 1985 biography, *The Three Phases of Eve*: "I had a very dramatic scene in the plane, struggling with the controls, oil spurting in my face, and then the plane crashed. Finally, I was carried on a stretcher past Kay Francis and urged her to 'go on and win for me!' It was one of the few premiers I was 'requested' to attend and, to my horror, after the oil-in-the-face scene, I saw them cut to a plane in a completely vertical dive, flames shooting from every angle, ending in a crash to forecast the atom bomb. A little fanciful work by the special-effects man who had not watched the rest of the scene! As they carried me on a litter across the screen, virtually untouched and every hair in place, the audience howled!"[14] The scene *is* laughable, but the film holds interest throughout, with some good technical shots and well-seasoned playing by Francis, Arden, William Gargan, Eddie Foy, Jr., and Bromley (great as Gargan's evil, bitchy, ex-wife). A theatre owner in Indiana commented that *Women in the Wind*, "was a very good aviation action picture...the audience liked a great deal."[15]

On film, Kay, a chicken rancher (!), impresses Gargan with her aviation skills in order to borrow his plane and enter a $15,000 derby sweepstake. Kay needs to fund an operation for her injured aviator brother. She and Gargan hit it off, but it isn't long before Kay over-

Victor Jory and William Gargan joins Kay in her swan song to Warners, Women in the Wind *(1939). (Warners)*

hears him brag to his buddy that she was no different from other dames he's gone for. "My motto is to 'Feed 'em, fly 'em and forget 'em, '" he puffs. When Kay gets him where *she* wants him, down on her farm surrounded by her chickens, she lets him know she's onto his little scheme. "I feed 'em, fry 'em and forget 'em," she tells Gargan while looking him directly in the eye. He finally relents and says she can have his plane to enter the Women's Derby. When Gargan's ex-wife (Sheila Bromley) hears about this, she claims the plane is community property: *hers*. Kay is miffed at Gargan who gets her access to Eddie Foy's plane. (Foy's character is a take off on the celebrated pilot, "Wrong-Way Corrigan.") Bromley is miffed when Kay shows up at the airfield with Foy's plane. "What are you collecting," she accuses Kay, "fliers?" "No," replies Kay nonchalantly. "I'm not collecting *from* them either." The race holds the audiences' attention, as does further machinations from Bromley. Kay wins the cat-fights *and* the derby with only one wheel attached to her landing gear! It wasn't *Wings*, but it was fun and had on-the-edge-of-your-seat moments.

Needless to say, there weren't millions lining up to witness Kay's skill as a cinematic aviator. Again, Warners put no ad for a Kay Francis feature in *The New York Times*, but the paper managed a tepid review, and commented, "Caught in the backwash of *Tailspin*, which flew over much the same terrain…*Women in the Wind* never quite gets off the ground, even though most of its action is in the sky…Everything happens according to formula, including the spiteful rival's last-minute change of heart which not only permits Miss Francis to land her crippled plane safely but William Gargan as well." Gargan referred to Kay as "that glorious, creamy beauty," in his 1969 autobiography.[16] The two had worked together previously in 1934's *British Agent*, and make a cozy team.

Kay and Leslie Howard's paths crossed professionally once again in 1939. "Never of This World" was a CBS radio presentation written by Steven Moorhouse Avery for the *Gulf Screen Guild Show*. Broadcast in March, the cast also included Irving Pichel and Virginia Weidler. Oscar-nominated director Sidney Franklin oversaw the thirty-minute play in which a small child (Weidler), having suffered scarlet fever, has retreated to a country home with her father (Howard). They are reclusive and live in a fantasy world. The pair is soon introduced to Martha Sheldon (Kay), their next-door neighbor. Weidler mistakes Kay as the Godmother of the Silver Prince, because she is "so beautiful" and her "chariot" (limousine) is driven by a Nubian slave (a black chauffeur). Kay is baffled, but enchanted when she hears all this.

As concert singer Sheldon, whose damaged voice has put her career at a standstill, Kay has her own set of challenges. "I'm not finished!" she declares. "I only want to prove how wrong those critics are! I won't accept defeat!" Although she has acquired a small fortune from performing, Sheldon confides to her manager her fears of losing her "whole scheme of living." These lines uncannily paralleled Kay's real-life situation.

Upon learning the truth about the child's fragile condition, "Godmother" Kay decides to join in the fantasy that Howard has created for his daughter during the time the little girl has left. After a few weeks, Kay is so taken with the experience and the child that she has forgotten about her own problems. "I must be under some kind of spell," she wonders, "because the things I thought so important, seem so very far away." A charming, bittersweet little tale, it foreshadowed Kay's future role as Godmother for *two* little princes in the 1950s and '60s, while she was dividing time between her home in New York and retreating to Cape Cod.

With the New Year, 1939, Kay appeared to have entered a fantasy world of her own, as far as her future with Baron Barnekow was concerned. She gave one of her most famous interviews with her good friend Dick Mook, for *Photoplay's* March 1939 issue. Titled, "I Can't Wait to be Forgotten," Mook sat mesmerized listening to Kay between takes for *Women in the Wind.* Afterwards, Mook understandably predicted that it might be the last picture Kay would ever make. "*I can't wait to be forgotten,*" Kay told him as she readied herself for the last shot of the last scene she would shoot for the studio she had been at since 1932. "As far as another contract," Kay said, "or making a *career* of pictures is concerned, I'm through." Mook offered that at least she was leaving at the height of her career. Kay's booming laugh rang out. "Don't kid me, darling," she said. "A year ago, yes. But not now. The parade is passing me by and I don't care. Perhaps I'd have been better off if I had fought for better stories, but the end didn't justify the means. I'd have been suspended and the time I was under suspension would have been added to the end of my contract. So, instead of being free now, I would probably have had another year to go. And, even then, I'd have had no guarantee the stories I picked would have been any better. Even if they had been, the only difference would have been that I would be retiring in a blaze of glory instead of more or less inconspicuously—and this is the way I want it. I'll be forgotten quicker this way."

Kay indicated that she had made her pile of money and if she had any sense, she would retire and enjoy it. "I've given ten years of my life to accumulating enough money to do the things I want to do," she explained matter-of-factly. "Ten years of never being able to travel when I wanted to, never being able to entertain when I wanted to, or go out when I wanted to—because picture schedules always had to be consulted before I could make plans. Now, I'm free!" Kay, who rarely mentioned her family, broke her tradition and revealed,

> My mother's future is provided for. I built a house for her and furnished it without her knowing anything about it. When it was all done, I planned to move her into it on her maid's day off. The maid, instead of taking the day off, went over to the new house. I had picked up Mother's dogs the day before and told her I was going to take them to the veterinarian to be washed. Instead, I took them to the new house. Then I took Mother driving and when we passed the house I said, "That's a cute place. Let's go in and look at it!" Her own maid answered the bell. Her dogs jumped up and down in welcome. I had arranged to have her best friend drop in for tea. Afterward, the friend stayed with her when I left and I went home to telephone her so the call from me was the first she received in her new place. I established a trust fund for her when I first began making important money…

Next, Mook asked her what everyone had been wondering about for over a year—her marriage to Barnekow. Kay laughed.

> If I did know, I wouldn't tell you. It won't be immediately though…When I built [my] house I had no intention of being married and now…it will have to be remodeled slightly in order to provide accommodations for Erik. But whether we'll be married here in Hollywood, in New

York, or eventually, in Europe, I still don't know…[Erik's] interests necessitate his spending six months of the year in Europe and six months here. We'll take side trips during the time we're abroad and of the six months we're in this country some of the time will be spend in New York (which I adore) and some of the time here in Hollywood. I have many friends in New York in no way connected with pictures…I think they are fond enough of me that they'll still enjoy seeing me whether I'm prominent or not.

Upon completing her last scene, Mook asked if he could continue the interview in her dressing room. Kay's eyes misted.

I have no dressing room anymore. I've been going to the make-up department every morning and using the dressing room here on the set. This is the first picture I've finished…that I haven't had a party for the cast and crew afterward …I knew I'd start crying and so would some of the others. I didn't want to become maudlin or sentimental. I didn't want to say good-by that way. I want to remember all these people as friends with whom I used to kid—with whom I had swell times. I don't want to remember them—or have them remember me—with long faces and red eyes. I want to saunter off the lot and out of their lives as casually as though the picture weren't finished and we'd be meeting again in the morning.

Kay held out her hand to Mook. "Good-by, darling," she whispered huskily. "You've been awfully sweet to me. Come and see me when I get back. You…" Kay's voice suddenly broke off. The surprised Mook wrote, "She dropped my hand, turned and ran off the stage—out, into her car. I watched the car move down the street and out through the studio gates. My own eyes misted. A star was dimmed."[17]

Soon after the interview with *Photoplay*, Barnekow made headlines by suing Kay's good friend Countess Dorothy di Frasso. He insisted that di Frasso had accused him of being a Nazi spy. Barnekow met with the DA in an attempt to begin a slander suit against the countess, but the DA, avoiding involvement, told him the jurisdiction fell into the Beverly Hills justice courts. Enraged, Barnekow gave the press a field day. "I am becoming an American citizen," he said, "and I am a manufacturer of motors, and such false remarks as this may damage my business." Di Frasso, when approached by the newshounds, shrugged her shoulders. "I do not know what his politics are, and I must say, I couldn't care less."[18] An apprehensive Kay asked her diary on March 28, "Cannot understand what Erik and I are headed for?"[19] She soon found out.

One source claimed that Kay was concerned that Barnekow would be interned as an enemy alien and she tried to persuade him to retire to Hawaii. His refusal was followed by his departure to New York. Then Kay learned that Erik was planning to return to Germany. She telephoned him and frantically asked him not to leave the country. This put a strain on their romance and kept their marriage at bay. George Eells explained:

Barnekow lived in a male-oriented atmosphere in which women— even independent ones like Kay were expected to be subservient. Kay and he quarreled because he criticized her for wearing makeup insisting that

German women "don't paint their faces." [This argument occurred soon after Erik's mother had died.] He forbade her to pry into his mysterious spur-of-the-moment trips. Kay complained about this to friends, and in the pre-World War II jittery atmosphere many suspected Barnekow of being a German agent. Jessica and Richard Barthelmess, Kay's closest friends, worried that the baron would involve her in scandal. But when Jessica attempted to discuss the problem seriously, Kay refused to hear any criticism. "How could I sit there and let her say such things?" she wrote in her diary. "I just gave way and had old-fashioned hysterics. Erik an angel."[20]

During the fall-winter of '38-'39, Kay's friendship with Jessica and Richard Barthelmess weathered emotional storms and arguments. Kay was often upset and depressed, not wanting to hear counsel from friends that perhaps she needed to. After an exchange of letters and meetings things were finally patched up between them in December. "Jessica here at 3 for talk," Kay wrote. "At last we can still be friends, but it is terribly difficult."[21] As the international situation worsened, Erik left for his homeland. Although Kay was defensive regarding Erik, her true feelings were underscored in her diary throughout their courtship.

> April 5, 1938 – "Gave Erik another thousand dollars…wonder if I will ever get it back?…if the aviation business will ever come off?"
> June 28, 1938 – "Worried stiff about money, about Erik being a bum…I'm licked."
> July 21, 1938 – "Long talk Erik…expenses. Oh my God, what am I getting into…Pray that it will come out all right…"
> September 9, 1938 – "Nothing happening with Erik. My wedding dress fitted and no chance of being married…I wish something would go right for me."
> September 16, 1938 – "Relations strained—wish I knew what was *what*."[22]

Perhaps if Kay had been privy to Erik's private notebook, she would have had a clue. "Never marry for money," he had written in a notebook bequeathed to his son, "You can borrow it cheaper!"[23] Erik's son, whom he hadn't seen since 1926, was then thirteen years old. He reminisced with me in March 2003, about his father's departure from the United States. "His close friend, Ernst Udet, called him in New York in June of 1939, urging him to return to Europe and rejoin the Air Force. Udet was in charge of finding and developing more advanced aircraft, *not* related to the Nazi regime. My father immediately gave up his apartment, stored a number of suitcases in the basement of the Beverly Wilshire Hotel and took the next ship back to Bremerhaven and was back flying in the new German Air force within weeks."[24]

In September 1939, Louella Parsons reported, "One of the most gallant women in Hollywood is Kay Francis, who has been frightfully worried over her fiancé Baron Erik Barnekow. Kay and Erik made all plans to be married as soon as he returned from Europe. He had his reservations for the last of August and was ready to sail when war broke out and he was detained in Berlin. He had taken out his first citizenship papers, but nevertheless he still was a German subject. Kay talked to him on the telephone in Berlin. Of course a conversation in any country in wartime is difficult. She had been heartsick with worry..."[25]

When England declared war on Germany on September 3, 1939, Kay resigned to the hand of destiny, and wrote "Oh, dear God. Good-bye, to my Erik."[26] Soon afterwards, she was under the weather and her doctor ordered her to stay in under a nurse's care. She made numerous attempts to call Barnekow in Germany. Kay finally got through, but Erik seemed distant and preoccupied. Still, after noting the second anniversary of their first meeting (October 25), she asked her diary, "What *is* the sense? No Cable. No word from Erik!"[27]

The life of Erik Barnekow would meet a cruel fate. His son commented to me that both his father and Ernst Udet, who had flown together in WWI, were in great "despair about where Germany was heading." Udet suffered from increasingly serious bouts of depression, and in November 1941, he shot himself. Shortly before Udet's suicide, Barnekow, while serving on General von Doring's staff, was himself conflicted regarding the Nazi regime and concerned about burning the bridges of friendship he had established in various countries over the years. In June 1941, Barnekow made a concerted effort to help his friend, British author P.G. Wodehouse, who after being imprisoned by German forces unwisely made several controversial broadcasts on German radio. But, Barnekow's main focus in flying was to protect his homeland in Pommerania from Russian attack.

For Erik Barnekow nothing could lessen the deep depression that seemed to engulf him. Distraught over the truth of the Hitler regime and Ernst's suicide, Barnekow met a similar fate in 1942. Son Erik wrote:

> My father shot himself on October 25, 1942, in Altmarrin, my grandfather's estate in Pommerania, where he was on a short holiday. The real reason for my father's suicide is unknown. We assume it had to do with the problems of Ernst Udet, but we only know fragments of those. I did get a letter from my father's last commander, General von Doring...stating his regrets and respect, but really saying nothing at all. I finally wound up believing that a number of developments contributed to the final decision to leave this life and enter into a next level. My father obviously had tremendous courage. Using a double-barreled rifle to shoot oneself goes way beyond what I could conceive of, if I was deciding to go. From all I know, for my father, it was his friendships with Udet and others that made him return to Germany in 1939 and rejoin the Luftwasse. I followed his example in early 1943...joined the Luftwasse and became a fighter pilot...was shot down 5 times (three times by Russian anti-aircraft). After the war I went illegally to Argentina in order to continue flying...My own motive for volunteering 18 months in the Luftwasse was to protect Pommerania from the Soviets, plus some minor motives...like to meet my father and the already active love of flying.[28]

In 1960 Erik's son returned to New York City, tracing his father's footsteps.

> When I stayed at the Gladstone Hotel...twenty-five years after my father lived there (for something like a year), eight or ten staff members

there broke into tears when talking about him. I never saw anything like it. If Kay Francis became convinced that a future together with my father was hopeless, the reason was probably mostly due to the fact that my father's heart was somewhat like an ancient castle, or a luxury hotel, with many rooms for many people. He certainly had strong relationships and was extremely loyal, willing to sacrifice comfort, lifestyle, money, but not able to focus all of that on one person. I do think he loved Kay Francis, and that she was one of the most important ladies in his life, but not the only one.[29]

Apparently not. On July 26, 1940, Kay noted the news of Erik's supposed recent marriage. She had received several of Erik's cables and letters during January through March, then nothing until the news he had been shot. "News from Schwabaher. Erik shot three times in body and left arm. Better, and going back to front. Christ!"[30] None-the-less, whatever chord was struck between Kay and Erik Barnekow had staying power. News of his marriage left her numb. Her diary entries for the next three months were blank pages, except for noting the anniversary of her and Erik's meeting. Then, nothing again, until November 8 when she noted her sailing for Honolulu. When I asked Erik's son about this second marriage, he emphasized, "I really pursued all traces my dad left. In London I visited (in 1950 or thereabout) Lady Irene Ravensdale, a charismatic, charming, delightfully nutty lady in London…supposedly she was engaged to my dad. When I met her, she invited me for a cup of tea and told me quite a bit about their love…perhaps this engagement was reported, and somewhere misinterpreted as a marriage. I am as sure as anyone can be in these matters that he never married a second time."[31]

In the mid-sixties one of Kay's fans, Bob French, was given the opportunity to meet her. He was told by a close friend of Kay's that, "Kay had been bitterly disillusioned and disappointed when a handsome, distinguished European man who had courted her and proposed turned out to be a former Nazi official and was arrested and deported just days before they were to have been married."[32] The *story* had been embellished (there is no FBI file on Barnekow), but Kay's heartache from Erik's deception obviously still carried weight after 25 years. As far as Erik's feelings for Kay, one *cannot* overlook the irony in his choosing the date of his and Kay's anniversary, October 25, to take his own life.

Chapter 15
Comeback "De Luxe"

Kay's romantic relationship and career were, from all appearances, in shambles by mid-1939. But, she knew how to take care of herself. The previous fall Kay had told reporter Ben Maddox, "Thank God I never considered myself a victim of depression or lost love. I've always had the hunch that I could find my way out."[1] She also commented that "a woman must never allow herself to be defeated by her own past, no matter what disappointments it may have brought her."[2] The fact was, Kay had been hedging her bets even while Erik was still in the running, seeing director Fritz Lang on the side! Also on the back-burner were deals with other studios that materialized into something promising. By February 1939, things were in full swing again for Kay when Sidney Skolsky reported, "Despite rumors that she was winding up her screen career, Kay Francis is set to carry on her cinema activities...today [she] signed with RKO for a featured role in *Memory of Love*."[3] Carole Lombard and Cary Grant would receive top-billing. In March, Jimmie Fidler commented in his column: "Today Kay Francis starts work at RKO—an important milestone in her career. Not only has she sacrificed her stellar rating to accept third billing but she is playing, for the first time since her climb to the top, an unsympathetic role...I have heard plenty of comment about her courage. Personally, I'm more impressed by her common sense...Contrast Kay's tactics with those of the average 'big star' who refuses to take anything less than star-billing and regards unsympathetic roles with indignant horror...they twiddle their glamorous thumbs until Hollywood has completely forgotten their existence."[4] When asked about playing the heavy, Kay responded, "Friends told me I was crazy. I said I *had* to be seen in some other type of part than the mush I had been playing."[5]

Memory of Love, re-titled *In Name Only*, proved to be a veritable resurrection of Kay's foundering career. *Time* magazine capsulated the film: "A mature, meaty picture...*In Name Only* has its many knowing touches deftly underscored by director John Cromwell, brought out by a smoothly functioning cast. No surprises are the easy ad-libbish styles of stars Grant and Lombard...Surprising to many cinema-addicts, however, will be the effectively venomous performance of Kay Francis. Warner Bros. buried her as the suffering woman in a string of B pictures...Francis in her first free-lance job shows that she still belongs in the A's..." Author Roger Dooley, in his much touted *From Scarface to Scarlett*, thought *In Name Only* to be "the best marital drama of 1939." He noted that

Francis was the perfect "cold-blooded schemer who, while loving someone else, married Cary Grant for his money and social position. In fact, she writes to the other man to explain, driving him to suicide, whereupon his mother sends the incriminating letter to Grant as a wedding present."[6] When Grant (as husband Alec) falls in love with the widowed Carole Lombard, his wife Maida (Kay) has the complete sympathy of her in-laws who are convinced of her perfection as a daughter-in-law. Kay has viewers on the edge of their seats wondering what heartless maneuver she will come up with next to maintain her status. She plays the "model" wife around Grant's parents, perpetually making excuses for his no-shows at her pretentious social gatherings. When Kay and Grant are alone after one such "social embarrassment" he tells her, "You make me feel like I want to beat you!" and threatens to let his parents know the truth about their marriage. "They wouldn't believe it, dear," Kay says coolly, reassuring herself. She's a satisfied cat, very much in control of the situation. When Grant confronts her with the letter which exposes the fact she married for money, not love, Francis admits, "I was mad about him! What of it?" She delivers an ultimatum, "I hope you don't think my telling you this will condone anything you might do."

"I didn't *know* there were women like that," Lombard says to Grant, empathizing with his dire situation. The calculating Francis toys with the Grant-Lombard relationship by promising a Paris divorce. She tells Grant, "I hope you'll be miserable. I hope you'll *both* be miserable!" After boarding a ship to Paris, Francis is confronted by her confidant, Suzanne (Helen Vinson, excellent as a man-hungry vixen who wants Grant for herself). "Now, honestly Maida! You're not going to let that girl take Alec away from you?" she queries. Kay looks at her with a smile edging toward a sneer. "What do *you* think?" she purrs. Upon her return from Europe, Kay threatens to sue Lombard for alienation of affection and involve Lombard's little girl (Peggy Ann Garner) in a nasty court case. Francis seems to be one step ahead of the game throughout the film. But she finally meets her comeuppance when she confronts Lombard in the hospital where Grant is in intensive care (pneumonia). It's a charged scene. She is a trapped tigress swathed in mink. "I gave up love for what I've got," Kay says coldly to the distraught Lombard. "Do you think I'm going to let you or anyone else get it away from me? If Alec gave me every cent he has, it still wouldn't be enough. But someday, his father is going to die…" Unfortunately for Kay, Grant's parents hear all this and are shocked to their senses. Scandalized. It's the end for Kay's character as far as her scheming goes, but a great resuscitation of a career and self-respect as far as Kay's scintillating performance.

Hollywood Citizen News commented, "It is remarkable for the fact that 'the other woman' has the sympathetic role, and remarkable for the picture of well-nigh perfect feminine villainy painted by Miss Francis as the wife…Of the three principal performances, that of Miss Francis is to this department the most noteworthy, for she has been sadly mishandled in recent films, and it is gratifying to report the compelling nature of her work in this new RKO film under Cromwell's direction…The Kay Francis role is really the key role in the film…" Carl Combs later added for the same paper, "What impressed preview critics most forcibly about *In Name Only* was the performance of Kay Francis, who has been delivering good performances for years, but hardly any one was aware of it because her abilities were stifled in inferior picture products and her frantic efforts to assert herself were without avail. In this case, she is the root of much evil, and

Kay's amazing comeback playing Cary Grant's venomous wife in In Name Only *(1939). She is seen here with Carole Lombard who plays Grant's mistress. (RKO)*

by this role wherein she inflicts the position of a hateful woman on her luckless victims, she will call attention to herself again as an actress of first rank."[7] In Britain, *Picturegoer Weekly* added another feather in her cap, stating, "Kay Francis, as the vicious wife, stole the picture. It was a magnificent performance..."

For director John Cromwell, Kay was the sentimental choice to play Maida Walker. He had guided Kay to important stardom at Paramount. Carole Lombard had insisted on RKO hiring Kay for the part of the vicious Maida, after jokingly suggesting that Rhea Gable (Clark Gable's former wife) audition for the role. Carole and Kay had remained friends since their Paramount days and were particularly tight when Kay was living with Delmer Daves. Daves later reminisced about their fun times with Gable and Lombard:

> We were all chums. Kay was a free spirit like Carole, and Clark loved women who could make him laugh. Carole would invite Kay and me up to dinner. We'd tell naughty stories and get a little drunk—not really drunk, just high. Then Carole would say—and this was inventive—'Is everybody hungry?' We'd never move from our chairs! The butler would come out and put a table with folding legs right beside you and serve the soup, then the next course and we'd go on talking and never move. We'd arrive, have drinks, eat, the tables were removed, and then we'd have our brandy and tell funny stories we'd heard on our travels.[8]

Kay Francis' Maida Walker was one of her most riveting performances and worthy of a best supporting actress nomination. Reaping in accolades must have seemed sweet revenge on Warner Brothers for Kay. The cold and hard-edged temperament she displayed as Maida would have been perfect foil for *film noir*. However, another distin-

Kay's new mountaintop residence in the Santa Monica foothills. She produced and edited a color motion picture of her building adventures. Her living room had an all-glass fireplace and the sofas were in silver damask.

guished screen role that would take advantage of her unique skills as an actress would not be forthcoming. Kay would add thirteen more features to her credit, and not one of them carried any great impact or significance. It was Hollywood's loss. As far as film roles were concerned, Kay seemed content with remaining active, taking interest in whatever came along and getting paid for it. Lombard, Grant and Francis repeated their roles for *In Name Only* for *Lux Radio Theatre* in December 1939.

While Kay was reestablishing her career, she enjoyed the sanctuary of her new residence in the Santa Monica foothills. Kay assisted in the design. During construction in the fall of 1937, Kay had apologized to Ed Sullivan for sporting heavy shoes during an interview. She had been trudging alongside the landscape architect all day and explained, "It's a lot of fun and a lot of headaches, but I'm really getting a terrible kick out of it!"[9] Her headaches paid off. The October 1939 issue of *House and Garden* featured the handsome home in an article titled "Kay Francis Lives Here."

> Kay Francis is a connoisseur. Long noted as Hollywood's best-dressed actress, she finds further expression for her superb good taste in her home in the Santa Monica foothills, near Beverly Hills. It is a low, rambling house, of white brick, gray roofed, commanding from its mountain-top site an incredible spread of surrounding hills and sea. Inside the house, one color—gray—is used throughout, creating a brilliantly sophisticated scheme highly complementary to Miss Francis's own distinguished tastes. In the living room the basic tone is enlivened by rose, mauve and emerald green; in the dining room it is accented with pink and in Miss Francis's bedroom with yellow. (Levine & Frederick, architects; Tom Douglas, decorator.)

The stunning photographs displayed a living room fireplace encased in glass mirrors; sofas that faced each other wearing a silver damask; striped white, raw silk and satin curtains pooled graciously at the blinded windows. Kay's bedroom had French Provincial antiques, accented with old silver lamps. Quilted valances introduced yellow linen for bright contrast. The powder room was a miniature French railway carriage in green glazed chintz. The overall effect was sophisticated—impressive, but soothing and comfortable. It was the perfect environment for Kay to retreat and redefine both her personal and professional life.

With her home and career on solid ground, Kay took time out to accompany Miriam Hopkins and Miriam's adopted son Michael to Reno. Hopkins had confessed to Louella Parsons that she decided to divorce director-husband Anatole Litvak so she could really concentrate on her next three pictures. Kay herself was hoping for a lead part in *My Son, My Son*. In November 1939, she tested to play the artist role that eventually went to Madeleine Carroll. The impressive, high-class soap, directed by Charles Vidor, had Brian Aherne as the novelist lead. It would be another year before Kay had the opportunity to work with Aherne. Instead, Kay was soon concentrating on a screen assignment at Universal. Louella Parsons announced in December, "Though Kay Francis plays Deanna Durbin's mother in *It's a Date*, the role is very glamorous. She'll be a very alluring actress who has a daughter in the background."[10] Parsons had always been Kay's major champion in the press. In return, Kay confided to Parsons and wanted no part of Parsons' competitor, Hedda Hopper. A diary entry of Kay's put it succinctly: "Hedda here. What a bitch."[11]

It's understandable why Kay had accepted the showcase part as Durbin's mother. The precocious young singer was featured in Universal's class "A" musical features that were extremely popular and seen by millions. *It's a Date* was good exposure for Kay. The film firmly established that she was *still* a contender with intelligence and glamour. After the film's release in the summer of 1940, columnist Ruth Waterbury raved about Kay's ploy and achievements in the part of Georgia Drake. "Give her a hand…Kay Francis beat Hollywood at its own game when she played to the hilt her role in *It's a Date*…a

Kay scored another success in It's a Date *(1940). Co-star Walter Pidgeon has his eye on her during some excellent comedy work. (Universal)*

year ago, she was taking a terrible beating…she did that most difficult of all things when the breaks are going against you…she remained a lady…she didn't pull hard cracks at any one or alibi…she did a supporting role in Carole Lombard's *In Name Only*, and now the mother to a very grown-up Deanna Durbin…she is beautiful, humorous and alluring…and a most exquisite object lesson in what the word 'dignity' means."[12]

The *Photoplay* review for *It's a Date* echoed Waterbury's sentiments: "Memo to Kay Francis: This is what is called a comeback de luxe…and we mean it. This is a great picture. It is full of charm, good music and superb performances. Deanna…plays the…daughter of a famous actress; both are approached by a producer to star in a play. To the mother, Miss Francis, the role means the triumph of her fading career. To Deanna it means the beginning of everything. There is also a man, Walter Pidgeon. Deanna thinks she is in love with him, but he is in love with her mother. The unraveling of this mess is done in the most entertaining fashion imaginable."[13]

Kay's role in *It's a Date* was hardly "the triumph of a fading career," but it placed her in good company. The talented scenarist Norman Krasna came up with some very funny situations that carried a sense of wit and charm throughout the feature. Kay fits in perfectly, in a part befitting a screen queen, albeit the mother of a warbling screen princess. Between takes, Kay enjoyed entertaining another young soprano, Gloria Jean. Fourteen-year-old Jean was brought to Universal to fill in when Durbin moved into adult roles. In 2004, Jean sent me an autographed photo of her and Kay, commenting, "I used to visit Kay Francis on the set when we were both under contract at Universal Studios. She was always so nice to me and took the time to try to teach me how to knit between shooting scenes. She was a beautiful knitter and it was fascinating to watch her knit so fast. I never did master the art and knew I would never be able to knit as well as she did or as fast. However, she tried! There are only very nice things I can say about her. She was just as lovely to be with as she was to look at."[14]

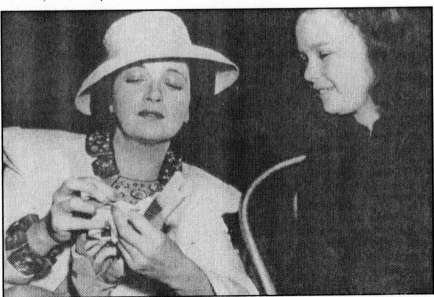

Kay on the Universal set showing Gloria Jean how to knit (1940)

Critics concurred that Kay was good to look at and *It's a Date* was another smart move for her. Kay herself stated, "When I played Deanna Durbin's mother...they were sure I'd lost my mind. But I got good notices."[15]   Hubert Cole of *Picturegoer Weekly* observed that Kay was "back in the smarter, wittier setting which she should never have left, and she is acting better than ever. The tearful, trashy roles of the past five years are, I hope, gone forever. And Kay Francis at thirty-five, is back on the road that she should never have left." Kay attended the film's premier with her good friend Louis Bromfield. Her role in *It's a Date* was re-created by Ann Sothern in the fluffier MGM Technicolor remake, *Nancy Goes to Rio* (1950), co-starring Jane Powell. Although the remake had the racy ruse of Jane Powell as an unwed mother-to-be, it sorely lacked the wit, sophistication, and class of its predecessor.

Now freelancing, Kay turned her attention to radio. She appeared on Cecil B. DeMille's prestigious *Lux Radio Theatre*. DeMille commented that many viewers had requested that she and William Powell repeat their roles in *One Way Passage*. It was sweet nostalgia and the last pairing for Kay and Powell. Host DeMille introduced Kay as a "great tennis player," and commented on the twenty-plus times she had crossed the Atlantic. Two weeks later, *Lux Radio* called again, for the much-coveted role of Lady Edwina Esketh, in *The Rains Came* (written by her friend, Louis Bromfield). Onscreen, Myrna Loy had impressed as the world-weary Lady Esketh, wife of a wealthy British aristocrat who falls for a young Indian doctor. The Lady Esketh shoe fit Kay perfectly, and reunited her with George Brent. Next up, Kay requested *Silver Theatre* director Conrad Nagel to cast her in *Four on a Match*, a clever little romp wherein she happily engages herself with two beaus. Feeling very much at home, Kay announces to her suitors, "Don't we three make a lovely couple?"

While her career was picking up on screen and radio, Kay managed to squeeze in time for frequent romantic get-togethers with Austrian-born (1890) director Fritz Lang. Lang, whose study of Nietzsche and Freud filtered into his innovative films such as *Metropolis* (1927) and the suspenseful *M* (1931), was bright and witty around women. Kay and Lang had known each other socially for quite some time. In September 1938, she had had long talks with Lang, most likely regarding Erik's troubles. Soon after Erik left for Germany in June 1939, Fritz and Kay became more involved. On June 26 Kay wrote: "Fritz here for dinner 7:30. Nice talk, what an angel he is!!"[16] The two were seen publicly for the first time at the premiere of *Jesse James* in January 1939. They were still an item a year and a half later at the preview of the Lang-directed, *The Return of Frank James* (1940). In his biography on Lang, Patrick McGillian details the couple's activity attending gala premiers for such films as *Gone With the Wind* (1939) and *Pinocchio* (1940); evenings dining and dancing; and fond farewells at the train station. As usual, Kay noted the exact date of the affair's consummation, July 13, 1940.[17] By the fall of 1940, gossip columnists were predicting matrimony for the duo.

Earlier in the 1930s, Lang had affairs with Miriam Hopkins and Marlene Dietrich. The Lang-Dietrich affair ended, according to author Steven Bach, "when Marlene reached across the pillow and picked up Lang's phone to make a date with another man."[18] Lang's courtship of Kay gave sheen to his revitalized career. Being aware of Fritz's successive affairs with other actresses, Kay let the Lang affair simply run its course. Her diary indicates no marriage proposal from him, but they occasionally got together for dinner and talks until Kay relocated back east a few years later. While the tireless, self-aggrandizer Lang completed *Western Union* (1941), Kay stumbled into some rather unpromising vehicles at her temporary roosts at Universal and RKO.

Universal was pleased with Kay's reception and added box-office appeal for *It's a Date*. She was mentioned for, but escaped being cast as "Jerry" in Randolph Scott's *Frontier Marshal* (1939) at Fox. Then, for some unknown reason, Kay accepted the hapless co-starring role opposite Scott in a rip-roaring Universal Western about the notorious Dalton brothers, *When the Daltons Rode*. The breathless climax showed the outlaw brothers in a bullet-whizzing, deadly shootout. Although the script killed him off, surviving Dalton brother Emmett wrote the book on which the film was based. Emmett's wife, Julia, was the film's technical advisor. Yakima Canutt performed one of his most famous stunts when he jumped, on horseback, from a speeding train.

So where was Kay amid all this excitement? She was probably asking herself the same question as she found herself at the stockyards counting cattle! As love interest for the trustworthy lawyer and hero of the film, Randolph Scott, Kay seemed to be playing what author James Robert Parish called, "a corseted second fiddle to brawls and bloodshed."[19] *Time* magazine had hoped the film would be a good companion piece to the very successful *Destry Rides Again* (1939), but noted, "When elegant Kay Francis is discovered perched on a corral, counting steers and fluttering her false eyelashes at buckish Randolph Scott, the parallel with the picture which revivified Marlene Dietrich with a draft of Western air is unmistakable. There the parallel ends, for *When the Daltons Rode* is no sly *Destry* but a fairly conventional Western whose big-city actors often are merely incongruous." *The New York Times* recommended the film for western enthusiasts. "We have long wanted to see one of these shootin' pictures in which the final scene is a smoking ruin with everybody dead. This one comes mighty close to being it. At the fade-out there are only a few pious and inconsequential folk, like Randolph Scott and Kay Francis, standing around...we wouldn't highly recommend the romantic byplay of Miss Francis nor the ineffectual intervention of Mr. Scott...but we will say that Brian Donlevy, Broderick Crawford, Andy Devine and others...make some fine desperados; ... for folks who like plenty of shootin', here is your gunpowder." When *Daltons* was released on DVD (2003), critic Leonard Maltin complimented Kay's portrayal, saying, "If leading lady Kay Francis was wondering how she wound up in a film like this after a decade of glamorous starring roles at Warner Bros. she doesn't show it; she's likable and believable as the hardy Western woman who comes between Scott and Crawford."[20]

There is certainly no indication in the script that Kay's role had the slightest potential of coming close to matching Dietrich's in *Destry Rides Again*. Kay just hangs around while her fiancé, Bob Dalton (Broderick Crawford), and the boys pull their hold-ups. Out of boredom she falls for Bob's best pal (Scott). Brokenhearted Broderick leaves Kay and Scott alone, while he continues to make a public nuisance of himself. In reality, Bob Dalton had actually been jilted by his first cousin Minnie Johnson. He took care of the problem by killing her boyfriend. The Dalton Brothers met their bloody doom during a dual-bank robbery in Coffeyville, Kansas. For further public humiliation their dead bodies were incarcerated in jail along with the very much alive brother Emmett.

Randolph Scott keeps the outlaws at bay while holding Kay tight in When the Daltons Rode *(1940). Kay said she did the picture, "Just for the fun of it." (Universal)*

Although *When the Daltons Rode* provided Kay with top-billing, it was a part that any ingénue could have played. Apparently, that didn't bother her. "I'd never have thought I'd be in a western," Kay told *Screenland* magazine, "yet I did *When the Daltons Rode* just for the fun of it."[21] Kay made sure her "fun" was invested wisely in the bank before going on to her next assignment. And for *that* Kay didn't even change costumes. She merely hopped back over to RKO for the lead in Louisa May Alcott's *Little Men*. The picture had been on the back-burner at RKO for seven years, ever since director George Cukor's great success with *Little Women* (1933) starring Katharine Hepburn as Jo. In *Little Men* Kay played the part of the adult Jo, which turned out to be one of her favorite roles. "*Little Men* isn't exactly up my alley," observed Kay, "but it's giving me a lot of new experiences."[22] Kay loved being surrounded by the children in the cast. George Cukor, however, was not in the director's seat and the expertise of scenarist-team Sarah Y. Mason and Victor Heerman, who had won Oscars for *Little Women*, was sorely missing. Instead, the screenplay, according to *The RKO Story* had taken "a wealth of homespun charm and unalloyed sentiment" from the original novel and negated its integrity with, "cheap jokes, anachronistic dialogue and maudlin plot manipulations."[23] Scenarists Mark Kelly and Arthur Caesar were to blame. *The New York Times'* Bosley Crowther wagged, "Miss Alcott...would shudder if she could see what these two Hollywood gagsters have done to her dear *Little Men*. Yes, she would probably weep...Instead of the sentimental and simple story which Miss Alcott's original was, this one is maudlin and smarty-smart, too obviously rigged for tears and laughs...it is played in the same synthetic vein. Jimmy Lydon is exceedingly stalwart as Dan, Kay Francis is just too sweet and good as Mrs. Jo...Elsie, at least, is true to Miss Alcott's Buttercup."

While on the set of *Little Men* surrounded by children, a donkey and a cow, Kay admitted to columnist Jack Holland, "With all this for competition, I'll have to stand on my head to get any attention."[24] She got attention all right. One of her scenes ran up against the displeasure of Joseph Breen and the Production Code office. Kay milked a cow, and Breen blew a fuse! He sent one of his lackeys to announce his udder horror to the studio. "At no time," he insisted, "should there be any shots of actual milking, and there cannot be any showing of the udders of the cow."[25] The udder woman in the film was none other than "Elsie the Cow," the famous spokes-cow for Borden Milk. The

Kay with Jimmy Lydon (far left) in Little Men *(1940). Lydon commented, "Kay was always prepared…always easygoing. Everyone loved her." (RKO)*

fawn-colored, big brown-eyed Jersey was the hit at the New York World's Fair in 1939-40. RKO offered Elsie a starring role as Buttercup in *Little Men* as a publicity stunt. (In 1941, Elsie suffered injuries while on a War Bond tour in her specially built 18-wheeler "Cowdillac" and had to be put to sleep.)

Fresh from directing the hit *Topper* with Cary Grant and Constance Bennett and its sequel *Topper Takes a Trip*, Norman Z. McLeod was obviously stumped by the confines of *Little Men*'s script and low budget. He also had difficulty directing due to the large boil on his buttocks, which required him to roost on a rubber-inflated cushion. Before long, 1940's version of *Little Men* was, along with Buttercup, laid to rest in spite of Kay's and Jimmy Lydon's substantial contributions and fine performances. They held the film together. *Photoplay* commented that "Kay Francis as Aunt Jo is very good…in a homespun story filled with laughs." Kay herself looked happy and self-assured as she managed Plumfield School. Jimmy Lydon does a standout job as the belligerent Dan, who had been trained in the fine arts of gambling, cigar smoking and singing naughty sea shanties by his wayward stepdad (George Bancroft). Kay understands Lydon, a kindred spirit of sorts, a misfit. She sees beneath his layer of self-doubt. When the other children badger him, she inquisitively asks them if they would like Dan to teach them to smoke. It appears he has no takers. But later, while the school mascot, Elsie, escapes, he demonstrates his perfect smoke-rings to the youthful, amazed onlookers. Kay punishes him for neglecting Elsie by having him whip her hand. It's a well-played scene. Lydon resists, then attempts the task while holding back tears. He finally breaks down. It is then the two reach common ground. Kay reassures Lydon that he's okay. "There's nothing the matter with you," she gently tells him. "You're just a boy." Looking at her, his self-doubt melts away. As in the novel, Kay's Jo succeeds "in finding the soft spots in boys' hearts."[26] It's a new beginning and powerful turning point in Dan's life. It's also one of the few memorable moments in the film.

Lydon, who was sixteen at the time, later commented on his pleasant memories working with Kay. "Kay was a wonderful gal," he said. "She had been a big, big star at Warners, and I already had a long career from the stage. We worked together as two professionals. She did a lot of heavies before *Little Men*. This was a tender part, which she liked."[27] Lydon made further comment to me in 2003.

> Kay was a pro and always easy to work with. She was always prepared— always ready to rehearse—always easygoing. Everyone loved her. When shooting was over, we had a set party and Kay gave me a still of her. She signed it: 'To Danny with love,' Aunt Jo; 'To Jimmy, more than my love,' Kay. I still have it 63 years later…we never worked [together] again. I was a New York kid from the Broadway theater, and I went back for a year-and-a-half—December 1950—July 1952, to do the first daytime TV soap *The First Hundred Years*. Kay was doing summer stock all over the East. I tried to get together, but our schedules never allowed us to meet. She remains a most warm memory of those years…I always felt like a kid in a candy store and Kay Francis was a part of that warm feeling.[28]

In Thoreau-loving Alcott's book, Lydon's character, Dan, was encouraged to develop his inclination as a naturalist. His transformation from a gruff, suspicious, streetwise kid to a vital contributing member at Plumfield School, whose common sense proved a positive influence on the children, was the core of the book. The film shows Dan's metamorphosis, but omits the presence of sweet, fiddle-playing Nat, who was responsible for inviting Dan to Plumfield. Alcott compares the friendship between these two boys, to the classic story of Damon and Pythias. Jo and husband Bhaer, both recognize and honor the boys' devotion to one another, and the book shows how their great love propels them to their more "heroic" selves for the benefit of all concerned. Nat, being the gentler of the two, was referred to by Mr. Bhaer as "his daughter," because Nat was "as affectionate as a girl." Jo pets him like she does her niece Daisy. Nat's "difference" in *Little Men* is celebrated. If Joseph Breen was terrified by udders, he would have had apoplexy if RKO had broached such same-sex territory as Alcott did in 1871. Director McLeod took the necessary precaution—Nat didn't get to say a *word* in the film. The real story Alcott told seems to have all but vanished in the 1940 film. Mascot Production's 1934 version of *Little Men*, on a much smaller budget, did a far better job keeping the spirit of the Alcott novel in tact. A 1998 Canadian attempt at *Little Men*, with Mariel Hemingway filling in as Jo, was, according to film critic Roger Ebert, an "innocent fable…with little depth or texture to make it interesting for viewers over the age of, say, 10."[29]

Amazingly, Darryl Zanuck wanted to keep Kay in western gear again to play one of Brigham Young's wives in Fox's big budget *Brigham Young* (1940). For the four-times wed, many-times-wooed Kay, the part would have been, at best, an incongruity. The role, thankfully, went to Mary Astor.

After Kay's affair with Fritz cooled down, she began dating Ivan Goff, whose career in Hollywood was just starting. Aside from co-writing such esteemed screenplays as *White Heat* (1949) and *Man of a Thousand Faces* (1957), Goff would co-produce such popular television hits as *Mannix* and *Charlie's Angels* in the 1960s and '70s. Kay met Goff in July 1940 and was seeing him regularly by December. A typical entry from March 1941 read, "Ivan and I early dinner. To see *Fantasia*—Wonderful! Home for short talk, bed."[30] She noted Ivan's birthday on April 17 and after a row on May 2, wrote, "Big scene with Ivan. My God, how awful!" They managed to patch things up by May 17. "Ivan here for quiet dinner, grand evening, talk. He really seemed to like me...And wanted me!!!!"[31] Kay's diary referred to September 20 as their year anniversary, but by then the affair was over and she was spending nights with a married ladies' man, and the vice-president of Vultee Aircraft, Hugh Fenwick. As usual, Kay's love life stayed *interesting*. Unfortunately, her relationships held more fireworks than the films she was selecting to star in. Kay next allowed herself to be relegated into an RKO "B" feature with the exploitive title, *Debutantes, Inc.* Why the studio didn't make a concerted effort to find a quality vehicle for her after she gave them such a strong showing in *In Name Only*, is difficult to understand. *Debutantes Inc.*, later titled *Play Girl*, gave Kay star-billing, great clothes, and the opportunity to display a tender passion for a million dollars. But, few bothered to see it.

"Why, she's said goodbye to more men than most women have said hello to!" crows *Play Girl's* lady-in-waiting Margaret Hamilton about her mistress Kay. Hamilton's also around to remind Kay that the bank account is running on empty. If Kay is ever going to get married, she "better make it sooner, than later." Kay plays Grace Herbert, an "almost over-the-hill" gold digger, who teaches the art of emptying the pockets of unsuspecting, wealthy, older men, to a young, down-on-her-luck girl she meets (Mildred Coles). As a mentor, Kay's enthusiasm for pairing up 19-year-old Coles with 50-ish Nigel Bruce, leaves a sour taste for the viewer. "Before we're through, I'll show you the whole town," brags Bruce to the playgirls as they leave for an evening at the posh spots. "Take it from me!" he crows. "Don't worry," Kay asides under her breath. "We will!"

Although it's not easy to find sympathy for Kay's ploys, a predictable humor keeps the film afloat. When Coles balks after taking Bruce "to the cleaners" for furs, jewelry and automobiles, Kay brushes it all aside, rationalizing, "We've given him the time of his life!" Then, Kay threatens Bruce for "breach of promise," knowing scandal and publicity would cost him one of his biggest clients—a company that publishes prayer books. He settles out of court for $50,000. When Coles falls for cowboy James Ellison, Kay does her darndest to keep the two apart, feeling it's a threat to her "business" interests. Margaret Hamilton, however, is in favor of Ellison and happily cheers after a deep whiff of his presence: "He smells like a stable!" Attractive and well-heeled Kay may be, but her character is frivolous and unethical. Perhaps the men get what they deserve, but as a screen role, Kay deserved better.

Play Girl's director, Frank Woodruff, capably directed many low-budget features in the early forties, and here, he cleverly uses parallelisms—the predictability of both men's and women's behaviors when it comes to the mating game. The characters also appear to be "on" to one another, which softens any emotional involvement. Nigel Bruce jokes to a fellow victim, imitating Kay's technique. "If you weally, weally want to do something nice for her—I've seen the most gorgeous mink coat!" But Kay hits a *real* sour note toward the finish. After contriving to get Ellison to marry *her*, Kay is confronted with his mother (Katharine Alexander) who implies that Kay is too old for him. After this rude awakening, Kay finds the integrity to end the affair. "I wish you were *my son!*" she says dutifully and choking on every word. (In truth, Ellison was only five years younger than Kay.) *Playgirl* simply added up to what the *New York Times* thought, "a listless comedy on a dismal subject." The British press (*Picturegoer*), who championed Kay after her fall from Warners, rated *Playgirl* as "the most *un*moral movie we have been invited to see since the Legion of Decency cut Mae West short in her prime." The reviewer thought the role undeserving for Kay and hit the nail on the head, saying, "Kay Francis, one of the screen's First Ladies and an actress who has helped to bring dignity to films, should not have to lend herself to such dubious movie material as *Playgirl.*"

After *Play Girl*, Kay's career definitely needed another shot in the arm. It was soon forthcoming. Leslie Howard's months of hard work on adapting a script from the novel *The Man Who Lost Himself*, and her friend Jack Benny, provided Kay with some promising new screen assignments. Surprisingly, Kay was no longer looking for what she referred to as "Great Moments" in her career. She felt as alien to Hollywood as she did upon first arriving in 1929. Her affinity for New York and Cape Cod held strong. She told reporter Jerry Lane she found Hollywood, "still unstable and shifting. I have the same feeling about it I had when I first came. I could never settle down here. But it has taught me a lot. *It's taught me the value of little things.* I don't live for Great Moments any more. I live for the little ones. By comparison, you learn it is the small things of everyday life that count most."[32] It was a realization that Kay would put to use hundreds of times in hospitals and on the battlefront. For the next five years she would sit face-to-face with men whose lives were shattered physically and emotionally by war. It was in acknowledging those "little moments" that Kay's giving nature flourished.

Chapter 16

The Woman Who Found Herself –
"The Small Things of Everyday Life …
Count the Most"

During England's turbulent war years of 1939-41, the British Film Colony in Hollywood had to refocus. The world was in upheaval. It wasn't only Kay who was redefining her life. She also began to see herself and her career in an entirely different light. Kay wasn't holding out for major roles. Things no longer centered on Hollywood and filmmaking. However, as a businesswoman, she negotiated sound financial deals whenever the studios beckoned. The storm clouds continued to gather over Europe and Kay's life became more involved with war-relief activity. She spent hundreds of hours lining up volunteers, collecting clothes and monetary contributions. More and more, Kay would find herself face-to-face comforting those in uniform who were convalescing in hospitals.

Immediately after war was declared in Europe, Kay was compelled to enroll for training with the Red Cross. She passed the organization's final exams on October 27, 1939. She continued with her Red Cross classes (day and evening courses) over the next three years between film assignments. Kay did radio broadcasts for the Red Cross and was repeatedly acknowledged for the countless hours she volunteered. "I felt I wanted to be doing something *useful* in this world," she told columnist Cal York. "That's why I took up Red Cross work."[1] In January 1940, long before Pearl Harbor, Kay joined other stars in committees dedicated to the British War Relief. She was part of the USO Test Shows in California during the summer of 1941. From Camp Fort Ord, Camp McQuade, Hamilton Field and six other California locations, Kay joined Marlene Dietrich, Lucille Ball, Ann Miller and the Kay Kyser Band entertaining servicemen and women as part of the Motion Picture Production Defense Committee.

Kay was familiar with the conflicting feelings of her British friends and co-stars such as Leslie Howard and Brian Aherne. Both men felt displaced and questioned their own usefulness as actors in a war-torn world. In 1969 Aherne reflected back:

> Men of my generation could never forget the horrors of the First World War or the miseries of its aftermath. In the 1920's, surrounded as we were by widows and orphans, by cripples on crutches and mutilated men in wheelchairs, and seeing as we did ex-officers of famous regiments standing in the gutter, trying to sell pencils or matches, we were all pacifists...determined

231

that never, so help us God, would we fight again, for any cause whatsoever. We were appalled as we watched the clouds of war gathering again in the 1930's and saw ourselves plunging back into the nightmare...[2]

While making personal appearances at fund raisers throughout the country for such efforts as the British War Relief, Bundles for Britain and the sale of War Bonds, Kay and Aherne managed to sandwich in a few film assignments. They soon found themselves co-stars at Universal studios. Onscreen they made a good vis-a-vis. Coincidentally, Leslie Howard had paved the way for Aherne and Francis to play together in the film *The Man Who Lost Himself*. Howard was preparing a script from the Henry De Vere Stacpoole story in the summer of 1939. He was attracted to the dual role of identical men switching identities. When war was declared between England and Germany, the financial backers for the project got cold feet. Howard decided to put energy into film projects in his native Britain that were less incongruous with world events. By late 1940, the project transferred back to Hollywood and landed at Universal with Aherne and Francis in the leads. Leslie Howard's dream project was in capable hands.

Kay faired better in *The Man Who Lost Himself* than she had in her previous Universal shoot-'em-up effort with the Dalton brothers. She was given some amusing opportunities in the entertaining screenplay and she was looking as glamorous as she had in *It's a Date*. Kay plays Adrienne Scott who's separated from her scoundrel husband, Malcolm, and being comforted by her new beau (Nils Asther). We first see her in a limo about to run down a man who she *thinks* is her husband (Aherne). Aherne has unwittingly switched identities with Kay's real husband (also played by Aherne) whom he had bumped into at the Savoy bar. He's adjusting to the fact that the switcher-roo has

The Man Who Lost Himself *(1940) was originally Leslie Howard's dream project. Kay and Brian Aherne co-starred in the cleverly entertaining film. (Universal)*

opened a can of worms. At this point he has no idea who Kay is. "Oh, it's *you!*" Kay exclaims, rolling down the backseat window. She then asks Aherne rather abruptly, "I'm on my way to the house. Will you *be* there?" He thinks she's coming onto him and cheerily agrees. "Certainly!" he says, giving her a goofy grin. "So, *please* don't keep me waiting," she emphasizes, "I haven't much time." Dismissing her terse demeanor, Aherne is absolutely delighted by the attention he is receiving from this beautiful creature and complete stranger! It's a very funny encounter.

After Kay drives off, Aherne glances at a newspaper with a story that he was murdered in the subway! (Malcolm Scott was carrying Aherne's identification.) Now Aherne is a walking dead man. Not knowing what else to do, he returns to his "new home" (where he had been dumped off the night before) to find Kay, the beautiful stranger, waiting for him. He soon discovers that she is *Mrs.* Malcolm Scott. Aherne is delighted and coos, "I think you're wonderful." Kay thinks he's making light of their being separated and storms off. At the same time, she's intrigued by the change in her "husband's" personality. When Kay pops in again, she overhears Malcolm Scott's mistress, in the library, insisting on Aherne calling her "Booby-Wooby." After Aherne complies, he notices Kay, who is miffed once again. Aherne chases her to the front door, where she warns him, "You really shouldn't leave Booby-Wooby alone in the library. She might get frightened by a book!" Before long, Aherne takes the opportunity to give Kay an impassioned kiss while they are at home getting "reacquainted." Impressed, Kay maneuvers Aherne upstairs for an evening of lovemaking. Gentleman/coward that he is, Aherne must be aware that the Production Code would never allow such a union—after all, they *really* weren't married. After he unzips Kay's dress, he zips out of the house for a night on a park bench.

Things are finally resolved when investigators grill Kay about their suspicions that Aherne's body was really that of her husband Malcolm Scott. "Comes the dawn" when Kay remembers Aherne's fantastic smooching. He must be an imposter, albeit a very lovable one. (After all, ads for the film had promised: "They looked alike...but didn't make love alike!")

The Man Who Lost Himself was a clever little romp, and it's too bad Universal didn't give it the publicity it deserved. It wasn't reviewed in *The New York Times* even though it was better than many of the comedies in theaters during the early 1940s. *Variety* thought the film, "a neatly packaged farce amply fulfilling its aim of light and fluffy entertainment. With snappy direction and a trio of interesting performances...Aherne competently handles the farcical assignment, with Miss Francis also neatly fitting into her role as the wife. Direction by Edward Ludwig is topnotch...keeping the pace zooming along merrily." Soon after *The Man Who Lost Himself* was released, Kay, along with her friend Norma Shearer and other stars, flew to Mexico City as the Hollywood delegation to the city's motion picture festival. President Avila Camacho had extended the invitation. Activities included a fiesta, sightseeing trips and a formal reception at the presidential palace.

Kay's next film, *Charley's Aunt*, with Jack Benny, was among the most successful in 1941. Benny had long been a favorite of Kay's. She praised him saying he was the main reason to have a radio on Sunday evenings. She was very pleased when Benny signed her to co-star in his first meaty (in drag) screen role. Production began in the spring of 1941. Jack Benny later reminisced about *Charley's Aunt*. "I loved making *Charley's Aunt*, because it was a classic and I wasn't going to be Jack Benny again. The only complaint I had about that picture was that with all the petticoats and girdle, I had the damnedest time going to the bathroom. And when they completed the picture, I remember seeing it for the first time in an empty projection room, and I didn't think anything in it was funny, including me. I was sick for a week. But then I went to the first sneak preview, and the audience started to laugh from the first funny thing that happened on the screen, and then they screamed throughout the whole show."[3]

Upon the release of the film in August 1941, *Newsweek* commented: "*Charley's Aunt* was first produced in London in 1892...when a movie company feels a *Charley's Aunt* mood coming on, it doesn't just go out and buy the screen rights...The heirs of Brandon Thomas, the author, are not willing to kill off the goose which has thus far earned them some $25,000,000 in golden eggs...a company can lease it only for a specified period of time—just as Twentieth Century-Fox did recently when it paid $110,000 for a five-year screen monopoly of the play after last winter's successful Broadway run proved there was more than enough life in the old girl yet...Kay Francis is the real aunt from Brazil, and the Thomas heirs have sanctioned a change in the form of a rather remotely fetched romantic ending for Miss Francis and Benny."[4]

Archie Mayo's direction in *Charley's Aunt* kept things at a brisk pace for the old chestnut. Today, it seems a bit dated, but still works. In the film Benny impersonates a matronly woman in order to chaperone two young ladies (Anne Baxter and Arleen Whelan) that his Oxford chums (Richard Haydn and James Ellison) want to propose to. Dressed as Haydn's aunt, Benny takes advantage of the situation by kissing Baxter several times and by the end of the film he and Kay (looking very svelte in Victorian finery by Travis Banton) are lip-locking on the park bench. Perhaps the Breen Office thought an old lady smooching attractive young women somehow acceptable. The story is full of mix-ups and gender-bending situations. One character sums up the coquettish Benny's allure as a woman, saying, "You can't have a past with a face like that!" The biggest surprise comes when the real aunt (Kay) shows up to see Benny impersonating *her*! Kay has her wits about her—no one else seems to. She sees through the whole charade from the outset. Intrigued, Benny is determined to get out of his costume and pursue Kay. Benny again dons his student uniform in order to be "what nature intended me to be— a Man!" *That* perhaps was his meatiest challenge.

Charley's Aunt was a huge hit (number eight) at the box-office for 1941. *The New York Times* reported the film created "a roar of laughter that must have shaken the Roxy's rococo ceiling," but found the Oxford comedy "too tightly calculated...the cue for laughter has the dismal inevitability of a grandfather clock sounding out the chimes." Chimes at the box-office rang out to the tune of $2 million. Benny noted that one critic claimed that so much of his own personality came through he should have been billed as "Jacqueline Benny." *Variety* commented that Kay, "although getting limited footage, carries off her assignment in top fashion...there's no letdown in the fast pace maintained for rollicking results. Only deft timing...can achieve that result..." The intelligence and amused charm that Kay brought to the proceedings were exactly the stabilizing influence *Charley's Aunt* needed.

During filming, Benny also pursued Kay on his popular radio show with amusing results. Benny, dressed in petticoats and curls, attempts to introduce Phil Harris to Kay. Harris, who had just become a father for the first time (with wife Alice Faye), doesn't trust himself, and balks at meeting the glamorous Kay. "You know how *weak* I am!" he cries

Kay and the always lovely Jack Benny co-starred in Charley's Aunt *(1941) to the tune of $2 million at the box-office. (20th Century-Fox)*

defensively to Benny. Benny's wife, Mary, whom he made pay admission, barges in and demands, "You charged me 25 cents and *I* want to meet Kay Francis!" Benny warns his wife, "I hear Kay is nuts about me…so don't start anything." She does. Upon meeting, she says Kay is just "too, too sweet." Kay sizes up Mary's outfit and jibes that she also, "*used* to shop at the May Company." The popular department store was well within the notorious confines of the Benny "bargain budget." Insulted, Mary demands that Jack give her the quarter back.

Benny changes the subject to *Charley's Aunt*. "Kay, here we are finally making a picture together. Kay Francis and Jack Benny! Gee, isn't it thrilling. Gosh, aren't you excited? Aren't you, Kay?" Kay is simply annoyed. "What do you want me to do?" she asks. "*Pant?*" As usual, Benny pays no attention and makes a suggestion for the next scene. "Don't you think we should embrace and kiss each other so the audience will realize we're in love?" Kay ignores him. Benny persists, saying, "A kiss would seal our relationship." "Well," says Kay with a huff, "why don't you kiss a seal?" Finally, director Archie Mayo arrives on the set and begins the scene where Kay and Benny, dressed as Charley's Aunt, meet for the first time. After numerous retakes with Benny flubbing his falsetto, Kay begins once again with her intro line. "I knew your late husband quite well," she repeats. "I wish you were *with* him!" From there utter chaos stops production and keeps the radio audience in stitches.

In the summer of 1941, between filming and her war-related relief work, Kay enjoyed sailing her small schooner on the Pacific and improving her tennis game (she was still considered one of the best players in the film colony). But, it wasn't long before she headed for MGM studios to work once again with one of her favorite directors, Woody Van Dyke, in *The Feminine Touch*. Billed above the title, along with Rosalind Russell and Don Ameche, Kay kept in toe with the pros of comedy.

The Feminine Touch (1941) had director Woody Van Dyke's swift madcap sense of fun that made his Thin Man films a success.

In *The Feminine Touch* Kay plays the lovelorn Nellie, a well-heeled New York publisher, who tries to close a book deal with new author Don Ameche. Ameche claims in his lengthy treatise that jealousy is totally unnecessary. Without jealousy, Ameche claims, there would be harmony in all relationships and between nations. Kay, however, knows what sells and wants Ameche to expand the chapter on "Marital Jealousy" into a whole book and scrap the rest. They come to terms and Ameche proclaims Kay is the perfect example of a self-sufficient, self-supporting woman, a symbol like the Statue of Liberty. Kay scoffs, "Yeh! Did you ever notice? She carries a torch!"

Tagging along is Ameche's wife (Rosalind Russell) who is concerned that Ameche's abandonment of jealousy means he really doesn't love her. After correctly deducing that Kay and business-partner Van Heflin are in love, Russell *completely* loses her grip when she walks in on Ameche and Francis all cozy on the couch drinking champagne to celebrate their book deal. Ameche is serenely non-apologetic, and Kay seems to enjoy the fuss being made "over nothing." Later, when Kay pops in on Heflin and sees him consoling Russell, she stomps out carrying her torch and threatening to halt their publishing venture. It isn't long before mayhem rules the day. Kay and Roz get into a jealousy-snarled cat-fight with the diminutive Donald Meek sandwiched between them. Meek, an innocent bystander, makes the amusing comment that jealousy "comes from reading books." He then eagerly informs publisher Kay that reading books, "rots out a man's brain cells."

Out of the four leads, Kay appears to be the most level-headed—that is, until she enters the restaurant wearing what must have been the original Mouseketeer Ears (fur-lined, of course). It was certainly the most amusing thing she ever put on her head. One completely dismisses the film for a few seconds to gape at this mouse-trosity she wears with such confidence. *The New York Times* approved of *The Feminine Touch*, complimenting the scenarists, George Oppenheimer, Edmund Hartmann and Ogden Nash, saying they had, "dropped some chortling repartee. Rosalind Russell, flip and adept...receives able assistance from Kay Francis, a lady with a torch, Van Heflin and...Don Ameche;...they all make *The Feminine Touch* seem a little more novel than it really is." *Variety* thought the film was a "major laugh-getter" and a showcase for Russell, adding that Ameche, "can also pitch comedy...Kay Francis, likewise shows up well."

Rosalind Russell made reference to Kay's insightfulness when writing her 1977 autobiography *Life is a Banquet*. In many respects, Kay and Russell were "birds of a feather." Their lives weren't focused solely on Hollywood's game. Russell commented:

> One night at Jack Warner's house...a bunch of ladies were in the powder room—which was a whole suite—and I heard Kay Francis say, "No, Roz is *in* Hollywood, but she's not *of* it." "What the hell does that mean?" I said.

Kay donned this mouse-trosity for The Feminine Touch *(1941). The surreal chapeau may have been influenced by Salvador Dali who worked on the film's dream sequences. (MGM)*

> "It means you work here," she said, "but you're not part of Hollywood, and you never will be."...I came to realize [Kay] was right. I never wanted the kind of life in which you dedicated your whole being to acting, and preparing for acting and meeting only the people who could advance your acting career. I wanted a home, a husband, children, a variety of experience. I wasn't willing to pay the price of superstardom, and my unwillingness made me very cautious.[5]

While on the MGM set of *The Feminine Touch* it was clear that Kay's priorities had refocused on something other than her film career. In between scenes, she occupied herself on behalf of the war victims in England. The MGM in-house publication *The Lion's Roar*, documented her diligence: "Kay Francis is acknowledged by her myriad Hollywood friends as irrepressible. Her famous contralto voice is likely to fling out one of her *bon mots* at any moment creating mirth among the technicians and her colleagues in the cast. She has been working industriously in the Aid to Britain effort, selling tickets to benefits, gathering clothing. In the course of shooting *Feminine Touch*, Joseph L. Mankiewicz, the producer, walked on the set where she had been disposing of tickets for some benefit affair at $1 each. Mankiewicz accepted the ticket and started to give her $1. 'Wait a minute, this costs a hundred bucks,' she exclaimed. 'That's a special price to producers.' She got the check."[6]

When Hollywood entertained heroic fliers from "The Battle of Britain" (Hitler's attempt to destroy the Royal Air Force), Kay extended the welcome mat to nineteen-year-old Richard Hough, an RAF air crew cadet. Hough was in California learning to fly. He first encountered Kay as a slightly intoxicated "lovely dark figure gliding...on a zig-zag course" across the room at a British film colony event. Everyone was tanked on cocktails. Hough slyly asked Kay the whereabouts of the YMCA. She insisted he stay with her. When they arrived at her home, his unbridled fantasies took a sudden nose-dive. Kay informed him, "We're going to put you up in the attic." Naturally, being Kay's attic, the room was well supplied with whisky, cigarettes and a silver bowl of fruit. Hough settled for a "chaste brushed kiss" against his cheek as Kay bid him a goodnight. The next morning he joined Kay for breakfast in her bedroom. She had become his "Queen Titania...lovelier than ever." Hough rhapsodized, "Her face that millions idolized looked up at me from silken pillows and her lovely white arms were spread wide in welcome."[7] But, his libido plummeted once again when Kay informed him of her busy day ahead and that she had lined him up with a "perfectly glorious girl" for Earl Carroll's nightclub that evening. Hough described his date as a "gum-chewing robot." The following day, Kay gave Hough more attention by joining him in a swim, followed by lunch at Romanoff's where she introduced him to Salvadore Dali, Joan Bennett and Merle Oberon. Before long, a party of eight, that included Herbert Marshall and Reginald Gardiner, took Hough on a shopping spree. When the British colony helped Hough celebrate his 20th birthday, "Hard liquor flowed like Niagara." Hough was relieved when Kay learned that he was *not*, as everyone had thought, a hero from "The Battle of Britain." "To her marvellous credit," wrote Hough years later, "this in no way diminished the enthusiasm of her hospitality and interest in my well-being."[8] Two years later, after he mastered firing planes like the Spitfire, Hough found himself wondering if any new spotty youths were "flaunting their white bodies beside Kay Francis's pool."[9]

In October 1941, Kay surprised everyone after Walter Huston induced Warners to accept her as his co-star-wife in the film *Always in My Heart*. Kay signed for the top-billed part. Three years had passed since Kay left the ignominious and ungracious treatment of Jack and Harry Warner. Some thought that it showed Kay's willingness to go anywhere for money, but Kay's diary bluntly stated on May 17, 1940, "Made up with Jack Warner!"[10] Kay told company executives, "I buried...[the hatchet] over here on my way out, and if you want me to work for you again, here I am."[11] The old wounds never *really* healed, but Kay enjoyed her reunion with Huston, albeit in a rather uninspired musical melodrama that takes place in a small fishing village.

Kay bolstered her courage to return to the lot by bringing along her new pet poodles, Kelly and Murphy. She posed for photographers with the white pups, while sporting a new curly coif of poodle-bangs herself. Kay even finagled getting Kelly a small part in the film (he played a birthday gift) and later on, when the plot thickened, Kelly posed as a bribe. Also, making Kay feel at home was Orry-Kelly, and cameraman Sid Hickox (focusing his lens on Kay for the fifteenth time). But, most important to Kay was the presence of Walter Huston, who still considered her to be one of filmdom's best actresses. Their scenes together in *Always in My Heart* hold the film together and confirm Huston's belief in Kay.

On film, Kay looked more Park Avenue than a resident of Fishtown, U.S.A. Just as improbable was Kay's ruse as a "pretend widow" who has long claimed that her convict-hubby (Huston) is dead in order to "protect" her two teenage children. Trouble is on the horizon, however, when Huston is suddenly "resurrected" and released from prison where he's been flourishing in rehabilitation as the prison orchestra conductor! Amid this somber fare we are treated to musical numbers performed by Kay's soprano daughter (Gloria Warren) and Borrah Minnevitch and His Harmonica Rascals. Harmonicas were big in 1942. The title musical number in the film became #1 on the Hit Parade—Ernesto Lecuona and Kim Gannon's "Always in My Heart" (Siempre en mi Corazon). The tune was nominated for an Academy Award for best song. As the film progresses, the breezy melody evolves into a gargantuan orchestral symphony to make sure the listener will never forget it.

What got in the way of *Always in My Heart's* small heartwarming story was the attempt to make it bigger. Kay and Huston's son, Marty (Frankie Thomas), flirts with an older vamp, Lolita, whose boyfriend threatens him with a knife. Things get even more turgid when daughter Warren almost drowns in a storm at sea. Huston, stabbed in the arm rescuing Marty, is then required to rescue Warren—a soggy stretch for the imagination.

Advertising for this surreal concoction was all geared to make a big star out of Gloria Warren. Kay and Huston are barely noticeable in the ads in *The New York Times*. Instead, a big blowup of Warren's face has her blurting out, "Oh Ma! *They* made me a star!" Well...they didn't. The review found her to be "a pleasing little lady [with] a reedy voice." In all fairness, newcomer Warren had a likeable timbre to her soprano voice and is always emotionally on cue in her acting. *Variety* gave a more honest appraisal of the film and young Warren, saying, "In addition to her singing abilities...Miss Warren displays both screen presence and personality...She's aided considerably by strong and able support from Kay Francis [and] Walter Huston..." It's the sensitively played scenes with Huston and Francis in *Always in My Heart* that draw the audience into the story. *Photoplay* acknowledged their team effort. "The names Kay Francis and Walter Huston lend dignity to any film and assurance of two roles well played. Their roles in this picture, that of a wife and her prison-paroled husband, despite the rather hackneyed story, carry conviction."

Kay's teenage son, Frankie Thomas, commented to me, "I really had no scenes with Kay Francis [he had at least four] and never got to know her. The pic was an attempt to create another child singing star for Warners, but Gloria Warren did not make the grade. I certainly enjoyed my stay at Warners, but can't remember anything of note about *Always in My Heart*."[12] Thomas made more of a niche in film history playing Ted in the popular *Nancy Drew* film series and as *Tom Corbett, Space Cadet* on TV.

During the filming of *Always in My Heart,* Kay made a radio appearance on Dupont's *Cavalcade of America*. She was paged for a dramatic presentation of Shirley Seifert's romantic-historical novel *Waters of the Wilderness*. Far from being typecast, Kay played Teresa de Leyba, the dark, exquisite and castanet-dancing sister of the Lieutenant Governor of Spanish St. Louis, Fernando de Leyba. Covering the years 1778-80, the story revolves around the legendary romance between Teresa and the American frontiersman and military leader George Rogers Clark. Clark had won victories against the British and their Native American allies during the American Revolution. Gale Gordon (Lucille Ball's "Mr. Mooney" on TV) played hero Clark. Odd casting, but he managed to pull it off while wooing Kay with such lines as, "Teresa, my dear. I *am* a barbarian. I *am* a savage. Living in the woods like an animal!" The story was effectively propelled by Robert Armbruster's stirring original music score.

"If only half the things they say about Clark are true," Kay says right before meeting him. "He sounds like the only interesting man in the Western Hemisphere!" This "understatement" is reinforced when Teresa hears Clark's treatise on the *Declaration of Independence*. His discourse inevitably induces a passionate love scene for the pair. After a brief courtship, Teresa comes to Clark's aid when she and her "red-cheeked, simpleton" companion, Suzette (Agnes Moorehead), discover the hiding place for an arsenal of guns Clark has been trying to locate.

The Teresa de Leyba-George Rogers Clark romance was never consummated. When Clark talks of abandoning his career and running off with her, Teresa doesn't comply. She discovers that she's more in love with the man's dreams than she is the man himself. She encourages him to continue the fight for what he believes in. At the fade-out Clark is off to a lifetime of battle while Kay (Teresa) is left rhapsodizing about "Life, Liberty and the Pursuit of Happiness." The concise presentation of these thirty-minute radio-novelettes had become a popular evening radio fare for American audiences. Robert L. Richard's script was taut and exciting. Richards would later succeed with such *film noir* classics as *Act of Violence* (1948) with Robert Ryan.

In October 1941, it was announced that Kay would join Ann Sheridan and Olivia de Havilland in the Warners picture *Miss Willis Goes to War*. Robert Buckner (soon to be Oscar-nominated for *Yankee Doodle Dandy*) had penned the script. The project never materialized. In early 1942, Kay was denying a romantic-linking with actor John Payne. He was seven years her junior. Kay's first public date with actor Payne was at the California State Guard Military Ball. Kay, along with Constance Bennett and Betty Grable, wore Bundles for Bluejacket uniforms. Kay referred to the affair in her diary as simply, "Horror Ball!"[13] It was the only mention of Payne in her diary. In August, Kay attended the wedding for a May-December romance that became legend: Norma Shearer and her skiing instructor Martin Arrouge. Arrouge was twelve years Norma's junior. Shearer, in her predictable style, was fifteen minutes late for the ceremony. The guests' anticipation of her arrival lasted longer than the less-than-ten-minute-long ceremony. Kay, along with Cole Porter, and her "old pal" Lieutenant Colonel Jack Warner, was among the select at a reception held at the home of producer Hal Wallis' sister, Minna.

Kay's diary testified she was: "working like mad" with Bundles for Britain; making appearances at San Pedro for the Merchant Marines; attending the opening of Terminal Island and the Hollywood Canteen; *and* meeting Greta Garbo for the first time. Kay also squeezed in a roller-coaster affair with Hugh Fenwick during 1941-42. She met him just after completing *Charley's Aunt* and they were quite chummy by the time Ivan Goff was out of the picture. Fenwick, in the aviation business, was still married to his wife Millicent, although the couple hadn't really lived together since 1938. His playboy reputation, fondness for booze, and charming lies were hardly compensated by his wit and exuberant personality. Decades later, Millicent became a much admired liberal Republican Congresswoman. (A former aide referred to her as "The Katharine Hepburn of politics—she could get away with saying things others couldn't.")[14]

Kay's pursuit of charming liar Hugh was worse than a scenario from one of her Warners "B" movies. "Spent night at Hugh's!!" was a familiar entry of Kay's during the summer of 1941.[15] That fall, things were quite copasetic for the pair. "Home to Hugh's and spent night and very nice, too."[16] Things turned toward the dramatic by New Year's.

"Gee…went to Hugh's and then left feeling…unwanted!!"[17] New Year's Day was rough. Down in the dumps, taking sleeping pills and crying all night, Kay wrote, "Hell of a New Year. No plans. Guess I'm a pretty stupid and unattractive person. Wonder if I will live the year out? Hope not!!"[18] Fritz Lang dropped in to cheer her up and the next day Ivan Goff dropped by for dinner. On January 5 Hugh, who resembled a solidly built bulldog, showed up for dinner and, instead of barking, was very nice for a change. The next day she was crying "all night" because of Hugh's attitude. A week later, Hugh was "mad as hell." Kay soon waxed philosophical regarding the relationship. In February, while she was on tour for Bundles for Britain, she stopped over in Nashville to meet Hugh. "Guess he and I are pretty well washed up!" Kay wrote. "He has other fish in the fire, I am sure…However, nice night together."[19] In August 1942, Hugh came back to Hollywood to discover Ivan's car in Kay's driveway at 8:00 a.m. Things finally went kaput when Kay went over to Hugh's house at night and "heard voices!" He promptly arrived at 5:00 a.m. the next morning with a bouquet of flowers. "Ridiculous!" wrote Kay, aptly describing the incident as well as the affair.[20] Thereafter, Hugh garnered no more entries into Kay's diary. Instead, she opted for a calmer, friendlier, more intellectually stimulating affair with director Otto Preminger.

For Kay's second film release in 1942, she was back at Universal to support Diana Barrymore in *Between Us Girls*. The film was designed to make John Barrymore's daughter the next screen sensation. "Tomorrow Broadway will cheer a new star!" the ads in the *New York Times* proclaimed. The next day the papers burst the balloon. The *Times* reported the sudden demise of the film, saying, "It falls, we fear, with a rather heavy thud…Miss Barrymore runs the gamut of her limitations…As a display of sheer vim and vigor, Miss Barrymore's performance is a great advertisement for breakfast food. In supporting roles, Robert Cummings…Kay Francis and John Boles are adequate." This scathing review had some minor truths in it, but was certainly undeserved. *Photoplay* said the film was, "A lambast to the funny bone. The audience shrieked. They howled and yowled from start to finish…Diana Barrymore scores a knockout in her first juicy role…Kay Francis is beautiful as the mother…Henry Koster, producer and director, can take bows in every direction for a grand job." In *Between Us Girls* Diana Barrymore *does* entertain and carries the right spirit for the part. Director Henry Koster had guided Deanna Durbin through six films successfully, but even with former Durbin co-stars such as Kay and Robert Cummings in the cast, the expected "Durbin touch" seemed to be missing. Perhaps that's why Durbin herself "rubbed" Barrymore the wrong way. Before *Between Us Girls* was cast, Deanna showed up on the set of a film Diana Barrymore was working on. Knowing they were vying for the same part in *Between Us Girls*, Barrymore caught sight of Durbin and stopped in the middle of her scene. "*Who* is that?" she demanded, pointing her finger. "It looks suspiciously like Deanna Durbin." Perturbed, Barrymore continued, "Look, Miss Durbin! This is the last scene of the picture and we're doing it over because I didn't get it right the first time. Now, would you please get out of here…"[21]

During filming, Kay had her own run-in with the antics of one of Durbin's co-stars from *It Started With Eve*, Charles Laughton. "Kay was in the middle of a scene when the lights on the set suddenly went out, and guns began to go off. Kay, who hated guns, was horrified, screamed, and grabbed Koster's arms saying, 'Somebody's shooting.' … Charles came down the stairs in a long nightgown and nightcap he had worn in

It Started with Eve, singing 'Happy Birthday, Dear Henry!' ... Koster, who had completely forgotten his own birthday, was astounded, while Kay Francis ran off the set in tears."[22] Kay, whose aversion to gangster films and guns was well known, had once said, "I don't like guns…I've never been able to appreciate the thrill of taking life, any kind of life. Men call it hunting. Why not call it murder and have done with it? I can't see the 'sport' in taking the life of wild, beautiful things."[23] Kay's attitude about guns and the loud noises of ammunition were surely challenged a few months later when she was among the first to entertain troops in North Africa's combat zones.

In spite of Kay's run-in with gunfire and Barrymore's fit with Durbin, *Between Us Girls* played for laughs. The story revolves around 20-year-old Barrymore impersonating a 12-year-old as a favor to hide the age of her glamorous mother (Kay). "Lying is a part of every woman's job," Barrymore explains to Kay. "Sometimes it's her only defense." Kay, who scoffs at the idea of hiding *anything*, suddenly begins to have doubts. When Kay's new beau (John Boles) and friend Blake (Cummings) show up, Barrymore suddenly appears in *pigtails* and a little girl's dress! Kay is amused by the ploy and goes along with it. Barrymore's "little lie" complicates matters beyond belief. The whole ruse turns out to be "much ado about nothing." Boles marries Kay anyway, proving she never needed any "defenses" to begin with.

Variety also thought the film taxed Barrymore's abilities, saying, "Miss Barrymore…hasn't the ability and the poise to sustain such a big part, nor the necessary skill to give it shading…Kay Francis and John Boles offer competent performances as amazed members of the older generation. Incidentally, Miss Francis gets off one of the film's more candid lines when she tells

On the set of Between Us Girls (1942) *Kay looked svelte and stunning in gowns by Vera West. (Universal)*

Boles, 'You'll like her once you get to know her as she really is.'" Barrymore later confessed that she wasn't prepared for the demands of such revealing a role. However, she did her darnedest for the part and commented: "I had worked hard in that picture…But the notices were mixed. They confused me. A San Francisco critic said it wouldn't surprise her if 'young Diana Barrymore was to prove the greatest of the Barrymores'…but the *Times* [New York]…crushed me. Was I good in films? I didn't know."[24]

Unfortunately, Diana Barrymore's life was filled with crushing blows and mixed reviews. Adding to her stress while filming *Between Us Girls* was the fact her father was dying in the hospital. John Barrymore had cirrhosis of the liver, from decades of drinking. Like her father, Diana had a reputation for booze. Even before *Between Us Girls* she made headlines when Alfred Hitchcock, finding her in a drunken stupor, had her thrown out of his house. By 1950, Diana showed up too drunk to host the live premier of her own CBS talk show. It never aired. With alcoholic husband number three she toured Australia in the all-girlie-show, "The Nudie-Cuties." Back in Hollywood, the couple was broke and usually drinking. Still, Diana managed to have an affair, which prompted her husband to beat her to a bloody pulp. In 1957, she had sobered up to write her autobiography. She died as tragically as she had lived, of third-degree burns from a kitchen fire. She was 38.

After her breakup with Hugh Fenwick, Kay gave herself a break from love relationships for two long weeks. She met Otto Preminger socially around this time, probably through Fritz Lang. By the end of September 1942, they were dining at Romanoff's and back home for nightcaps. On October 7 things got chummy between them. "Otto here. And excellent!"[25] They dated semi-seriously over the next year. Their relationship was enjoyable, but on occasion Kay found herself missing him and wondering how it would turn out for them. They spent New Year's Eve, 1944, together, but by the time April rolled around Kay wrote, "Otto here for dinner...What a time!!! He said he was through and then said I was through! Damn fool!"[26] Not to worry. Otto had already been replaced by a guy named Don. The relationship with Don ran through the same gamut of emotions for a much shorter duration. Kay had once expressed that "happiness is difficult to snare and to secure because happiness roots best in peace..."[27] As intelligent as she was, Kay's topsy-turvy romantic life was anything but peaceful.

Kay was back on the soundstages at Warner Brothers studios in August 1942, for the radio program *This Is Our America*. The story was an inspirational piece titled *Dark World*. Her character, Carole Mathews, had been blind since birth. *Dark World* takes place just after Carole Mathews has died. A young nurse, who had bonded with the blind woman, is quite shaken and filled with questions. "It isn't fair," she tells herself. Kay then speaks from "the other side of life," giving her own slant on being blind. She consoles the young nurse with the message that any pity is unwarranted. Carole Mathews felt her world *had* no darkness. "How could there be?" she explains. "The skies I saw never clouded, flowers never faded. I had the *world*...whenever you read to me...lonely? I had the greatest friends a woman could have...the Brownings, Shakespeare, Keats, Walt Whitman—he taught me how not to be afraid...Beethoven, Schubert, Brahms, Tchaikovsky...the days weren't long enough!" When the young nurse wishes that the woman could have seen things as they really were, Kay's voice-over poses its own question. "Would there have been happiness for me in that? Men, marching again with death at their shoulders...death for human rights...and the freedom of the human soul. Things as they *could* be. I had that!" The "dreamworld" of Carole Mathews *was* her reality—a testimony to the strength of residing "within." "What are dreams?" she queries. "What is real and unreal? We see only what we want to see. I made a world in my darkness...where all was beauty. Believe me. I was the *happiest* woman you've ever known!"

Dark World, by writer/producer Arch Oboler, fueled Kay's compassion for the blind, and manifested itself later on, after her own demise, with her generous gift to The Seeing Eye. After the program aired, host Jan Peerce greeted Kay complimenting her on a "sincere and beautiful portrayal."

"It was a beautiful play," Kay commented. "I'm glad I had time to be here."
"We're glad you *made* time to be here," emphasized Peerce. "When the

Victory Committee showed us your schedule we thought it was hopeless."

"Well, I am a little busy," Kay chuckled.

"A little busy!" said Peerce. "From what I gather you work voluntarily a great deal harder than you should. I understand you're the guiding force of N.A.A. at the U.S. Naval Hospital at Corona."

"That isn't work," Kay responded. "That's just gratifying. Almost all our wounded boys in the Pacific activities are there."

Peerce defined her work there by saying, " You're the one Uncle Sam counts on to make convalescence so pleasant that the boys won't rush away before they're well enough."

Kay laughed. "Well, something like that!"

Peerce continued. "You're going right from here to make a radio transcription for O.P.A. You're on call for sundry U.S.O. duties. All very competently sandwiched in-between running a home and a career." (The O.P.A. distributed entertainment recorded on aluminum discs, overseas.)

"To tell the truth," Kay mused, "I don't know which is sandwiched-in. Sometimes I think it's just me!"

Host Peerce introduced Kay as an actress who was, "known for her *great* goodwill." A fitting tribute. Her association and efforts on behalf of the Red Cross and other wartime efforts were extensive, and she would take it one step further. She put her own life on the line to make contact with U.S. troops and their allies. She would travel to remote parts of the world offering her support and providing entertainment. Kay's longtime friend and journalist Dick Mook noticed a *distinctive* difference in Kay since her departure from Warner Brothers. Gone were the nervousness, irritability, and bitter edge. "What's happened to you?" Mook marveled. Kay laughed, "It's not being a star that does it…as a free-lance player…I can travel where I please and when I please and no one bothers me. I'm not important anymore and I love it. It may sound like sour grapes, but I wouldn't be a star again for anything." Mook corrected her, saying, "You *are* a star. You and Lombard and Cary Grant were co-starred in *In Name Only* and you've been starred in other pictures you've made since then." Smiling, Kay acquiesced,

All right, then. I'm a star of no importance. You remember once I told you I would never sign another long-term contract? Well, I'm not only better off this way, but I'm happier…For the first time in eleven years, I'm leading my own life…I have practically given up social activities…I became interested in the Red Cross work and British Relief work and it occupies practically all my spare time. The few close friends I have I still see often and the others don't matter. I—Honestly, Dick you've no idea what a sense of freedom being nobody brings with it.[28]

With the outbreak of World War II, Kay Francis, the "nobody" from the land of make-believe, responded to a calling in a very *real* and war-torn world. She found herself a new role, which she would always consider a high point in her life. It was a part that fit a giving hand like a glove: A Jill in a Jeep.

Chapter 17
Jill In a Jeep

During World War II, the popular evening program *The Great Gildersleeve* was suddenly interrupted for what would prove a most memorable moment...to be exact, a most memorable minute. In the background, you could hear the uncanny ticking of a clock as the voice of Kay Francis asked her American radio audience, "Are we worth coming home to?" Time, suddenly became larger, more crucial, carrying the impact of her every word. "I ask your attention," she began, drawing the listener closer, "for *one* minute."

One minute isn't very long. But in this very brief minute that you're hearing my voice, men are dying for you. Dying on distant battlefields...in strange waters. Men from Nebraska, Illinois, Texas...boys from across the street....boys that you know. Right now, while I speak to you, sixty seconds in a minute, how many times are sixty men are dying for you? And, as they die, they are remembering home, remembering us, wanting to come home. Knowing they never will. Are we worth remembering? Are we worth coming home to? No. Not unless we do all we possibly can to win this war. And, our possible "all" is so little compared to what they give. We're not asked to give, but to *lend* our dollars to our government to carry our share of the Second War Loan. Lend your dollars. Right now. Right this minute. While these men are giving their lives for you. [Her voice softened as she added with tragic irony] You'll get your dollars back.

Kay's solemn, sincere delivery reflected the diligence she put into the war bond drive. The radio announcer had introduced her as a "courageous lady." "Proof of her courage," he said, "is her four-month expedition across the Atlantic this past winter to entertain our troops in England, Ireland, Scotland and North Africa." Kay had also, along with Myrna Loy, been sharing many a night shift (six p.m. to six a.m.) at the USO socializing with men and women in uniform. Loy commented on her friendship with Kay in her 1987 autobiography, *Being and Becoming*. "Kay was part of a group of friends from Arthur's [producer Arthur Hornblow, Jr., Loy's first husband] that sort of stuck with him after I came in. They were a sophisticated bunch. Kay most of all. She was a little ahead of her time, using four-letter words that shocked me terribly, but I liked her.

We shared a reality beyond titles and organizations at Long Beach, handing out coffee and doughnuts and whatever reassurance we could to draftees bound for Hawaii. We saw untrained kids inducted, all so young and bewildered, an endless stream totally unprepared for war. It broke our hearts."[1]

On yellow alert one night, Kay and Myrna were told to leave by eleven. A few days before, a Japanese submarine had shelled an oil field in Santa Barbara (February 23, 1942). "Kay and I, bordering on hysteria, were trying to drive home when we passed what is now Los Angeles International Airport...there were dozens of planes lined up ominously in the dark with their propellers just turning, waiting for something to happen." This famous false air-raid was never adequately explained. *Movietone News* documented Kay and Myrna's USO team effort in the newsreel, "Movie Colony Does Its Bit For Nation In War." The narrator commented, "Motion picture personalities like Kay Francis and Myrna Loy preside over a ceremony of coffee and sinkers in behalf of the sailors in our fleet in war." The two are shown with bright smiles serving refreshment and the spirit of support. Before long, Kay herself would be leaving the homefront.

In July 1942, the War Department was looking for volunteers to entertain in England. The first theatrical task force was stationed strictly in Great Britain. On October 25, the second task force, composed of Kay Francis, Martha Raye, Carole Landis and Mitzi Mayfair (who later referred to themselves as "The Four Jills"), were on their way—with a *difference.* Kay and the other Jills became the foundation of what became known as the "foxhole tours." They ventured into dangerous territory unexpected of them. The winter of 1942-43 became one of the most significant chapters in Kay's life. Carole Landis chronicled the Four Jills journeys. Excerpts from her diary were published in 1943 and titled, "Four Jills in a Jeep."

Kay and Myrna Loy, greeting brass at the USO, 1942. Loy liked Kay, but was "shocked terribly" whenever Kay cursed.

The journey of the Four Jills stirred the hearts of those who heard of their courage or saw their performances. Their first stop was in Bermuda, where the foursome put on two performances to packed houses at Castle Harbor. This was followed by shows at St. David's, Cooper's Island, Turtle Hill—all during a persistent downpour of rain. Landis describes Kay's role as mistress of ceremonies and her clever use of double entendre:

> Kay always...opened the show by saying, "You know, I'd rather be here than any place else in the world." She was greeted with a glorious round of boos. "No, I mean it," Kay said, wiping the rain from her face. "In a crowd like this, a girl has a chance." (Yells and screams and whistles.) "Perhaps you'd like to know a little about our trip over here. The Army flew us in a bomber from California to New York. It was a nice little bomber, a sweet little bomber, with the *cutest little ten-inch guns* I ever saw. And the pilot! Boy, he was the best-looking fellow I'd ever seen. I didn't know you could fly a bomber with *one hand*, but you can. When we got to New York...they took us to this one camp. We arrived about 11 a.m. and a Colonel came up to meet us. I looked around and didn't see anybody, so I said, 'Colonel, where are the men? We want to see them.' He said, 'Shhh— be quiet! They're still asleep.'" (This panicked the audience). "We were pretty hungry by this time, so Martha Raye stepped up to the Colonel and said, 'Sir, where do we eat?' He said, 'You mess with the men.' 'I know that,' Martha said, 'but where do we *eat?*'" The audience was roaring with laughter, and all the time the rain was streaming down Kay's face as if she were crying. "You know, we've heard a lot about buck privates," she said, wiping her tears away, "but we finally found out what the name 'buck private' means. Mitzi Mayfair went out with six of them the other night, and there was one *buck* in the whole crowd."[2]

After Kay warmed the boys up, Mitzi would come out and do some energetic dancing, Martha Raye would sing, and Carole would give her trademark sigh. According to writer Jean Maddern Pitrone, Martha Raye and Mitzi, who had never met Kay, were politely in awe of her. That all gave way as Kay warmed up to them with her wonderful laugh and bawdy sense of humor. With a 55-pound baggage limit and their itinerary blanketed in secrecy, the Jills bantered and joked crossing the Atlantic. After a stopover in the Azores, the Jills arrived in Lisbon. "Mitzi carried the war right with her," Landis wrote. "In Lisbon, she couldn't bear seeing so many Germans around. She wanted to slice them up, particularly the two men standing at the bar in the Hotel Aviz who were ordering everyone around...'Oh, the jerks!' she exclaimed loud enough for everyone in the room to hear...'Just look at 'em...they think they own the world.'"[3] The fate of Erik Barnekow must have crossed Kay's mind during Mitzi's tirades. Like many men from Pomerania, he had returned to defend his homeland from Russian attack. Unbeknownst to Kay, Erik committed suicide, not only on the date of their anniversary, but the very day Kay set out on tour with the Jills, October 25, 1942. (It is very unlikely that she *ever* knew Erik's tragic fate.)

Arriving in London, the Jills were jolted by images of the war-torn world that surrounded them. Outside of the heavily draped windows at the Savoy Hotel they witnessed a rubble-ridden city where Nazi bombs had landed. Levity somehow managed to sneak in to keep them on an even keel as when the Savoy desk clerk asked, "Pardon me, ladies. What time would you like to be knocked up?" "Beg pardon," Martha Raye chimed in. "What did you say?" "Do you wish to be knocked up in the morning?" he repeated. Before the furious Martha could take a lunge at him, Kay grabbed her and explained. "It's just an English expression. He only means, what time do you want to be awakened in the morning?" Sheepishly, Martha whimpered, "Oh."[4]

The Jills' first show in England was at a high school auditorium. More than one thousand American soldiers filled the place with cheers and whistles during the fast-paced one-hour show. Under army regulations the Jills worked six days a week and had one day off. Three days after their London arrival, Landis was taking orders from her heart. She fell in love with Captain Thomas Wallace, a young, blue-eyed charmer from Pasadena.

Before long, the Jills were putting on shows throughout Great Britain. Each night, a U.S. Army Special Forces officer would slowly maneuver their vehicle (headlights hooded) along country roads until they reached the next military camp. They would often do three to five shows at the same camp or as many as three shows at different camps on the same day. "Almost always," Landis remembered, "we tried to arrive early enough to walk around the camp and talk to the boys while they were on the job. Then, when it came time for chow, we would stand in mess line with them and take our turn with the rest." At the close of each show Kay would read a "letter" from the "folks at home" to those in uniform and then everyone joined in singing "God Save the King" and "America."

Many times the Jills were required to cut through the tension and sadness that greeted them. At one air base, half the squadron's men had been lost the day they arrived. Kay asked a Commanding Officer whether they should leave. "Please don't go," he said. "It's not that the kids don't want you here. They're all feeling rather down in the mouth because they've taken one hell of a beating today. You see that kid over there? He came in today with five dead men aboard ship. We lost quite a few planes, and we lost a man we all loved. So you see…we really *need* you here tonight, desperately." The Jills joined the men's evening meal by candlelight in a tavern with a wood-beamed ceiling. The survivors offered toasts in memory of their friends, then took candles and burned into the ceiling the names of those who had not returned from the mission. Afterwards, the boys, flying kids uncertain of their own future, broke their glasses in tribute.

When the Jills returned to London it was announced they were to perform for the King and Queen, their Royal Highnesses, and the Grenadier Guards. The day after that there would be a broadcast over the BBC, with actor Jack Buchanan. A bit unnerved at the prospect of meeting royalty, the girls had to air the pent-up feelings that had begun to pull them apart. Landis suggested they get everything off their chests. They agreed to this grievance procedure on a weekly basis and it kept them closer-knit and deepened their friendship. "Kay, bless her," Landis commented, "told me right off—and started all of us being equally truthful."[5]

"Carole," Kay said, "if you sing once more as we are going into an army mess, I'm going to kill you. Every time I turn around, you're singing, singing, singing, singing, and you're driving me batty." [Landis agreed to "put a cork" in her mouth.] "As for you Martha," Kay said, "if you don't stop talking about people, I'm going to slaughter you. You're forever chattering about somebody." "Who, me?" Martha said. "Me chatter? "And no more autographs," Kay said.

"We're not here to sign autographs." "We are, too," Mitzi said. "If the kids want an autograph, they get an autograph. That's just as much a part of our job as doing the show." Kay finally got down to the bottom of her irritation with us. She didn't like the idea of Mac and Joe (servicemen who forever kept popping up) following us around and our having dates in London. "After all," Kay said, "we're here on a military mission, and we shouldn't think of our personal desires. I've turned down numerous invitations from people I know here whom I would love to see. We're not here for a social this and that."

"Now, look, Kay," Martha said, "maybe you're overdoing this. Maybe you're being a bit too Joan-of-Arc-ish. So long as we do our job, whatever we do off the job is our own business. God knows, you can't just stew in a room. If you know somebody and you want to go out with them, you just go out with them." Kay had to laugh herself, "Well, I guess maybe I am too Joan-of-Arc-ish, as you call it," she said. "I'm sorry, kids." So we wound up with our arms around each other. Everybody loved everybody else and we were great pals again and everything was jake.[6]

The royal visit by the foursome was censored. Martha Raye was not to be allowed to sing a number titled, "Strip Polka." She was also requested not to lift her skirt so high. Kay *was* allowed to keep her Lana Turner tale about a sailor asking her if the V-neckline of her dress stood for "Victory." Kay then gives Turner's response, saying, "Yes, but the 'bundles' aren't for Britain." The Jills were taught how to "bob" before the Majesties, but as it turned out, there was one less "bob," to worry about. The King was unable to attend the Jills' performance. Aside from stress of protocol, the girls had aches, pains and miseries to contend with. Averaging five hours of sleep a night took its toll. Mitzi had dental problems. Kay found herself hobbling around with a torn ligament in her ankle, from a slip while debarking a plane. Landis herself ended up in the hospital while Kay, Martha and Mitzi did camp shows in Scotland. In late November, *The New York Times* reported Kay and Mitzi as war "casualties." Mitzi's shoulder and arm were severely damaged in a jitterbug routine (she tossed around a hulking sergeant as part of her act) and Kay's laryngitis temporarily put an end to her job as mistress of ceremonies. Both women were placed in a Midlands army hospital. Kay recovered in time to protest when Landis' romance with Captain Wallace became serious. "Carole," she said, "I just learned about your marriage and, darling, please don't get married…you haven't known him long enough." "Now look, Kay," Landis said. "Isn't that something for me to decide?" "Well, yes, of course," Kay replied. "Only don't do it right away, please. Wait a while." Perhaps, due to her own four attempts at marriage, Kay felt it her duty to offer counsel. But, more likely, Kay was aware of Landis' own shaky history with matrimony. Landis had been married twice before (the first at age 15). Kay told Landis' fiancé Wallace, "Tommy…don't take advantage of our little girl." Writer Barrie Roberts later noted, "[Carole's] closer friends and family members were well aware of her insecurity, despondency and suicidal tendencies. Affairs of the heart were her weakness. Falling in and out of love made for emotional instability and finally led to a tragic end."[7] As it turned out, the Landis-Wallace union as man and wife would be short-lived.

All during their duty in Great Britain, the Jills had made requests to tour North Africa. Finally, just as Kay, Martha, and Mitzi were about to leave for home, and just before Landis was about to "tie the knot," their request was approved. Kay finally gave

Carole and Tommy her own approval. She helped carry the veil to the ceremony—for "something blue" she tucked a ribbon inside Carole's dress. The Jills were on their way to Africa twenty-four hours after the reception. In the New Year of 1943, they boarded a B-17 toward Allied headquarters in North Africa. Flying over the Bay of Biscay to Gibraltar, two German planes attacked them. With guns a-blazing at them, the Jills escaped, but learned later their own tail-gunner had been killed. The B-17 finally landed on "The Rock" after another close call and near collision.

Their next stop was Algiers, which Landis described as, "just a dirty, mucky little town. When we got off the plane everybody's eyes popped open, and they sort of did double-takes of us and said, 'What the hell are you doing here?' Nobody was there to meet us; nobody, apparently, even knew we were due." After several hours they made contact with a Colonel who seemed baffled by their sudden appearance. "Well, I think I can get you in the hotel," he hemmed and hawed. "It's kind of difficult..." Kay was at the end of her patience. "Didn't you expect us?" she said. "I mean, is this all a big surprise? Should we go back and come in again, or what?" They eventually got rooms where they consoled themselves by eating tangerines by the dozens. In the background they could hear the constant bark of German planes on the coast. Landis wrote, "When one of the German bombers plummeted down in flames and plunged into the Mediterranean it was hard to realize this was not all part of some vast, pre-arranged spectacle." They were not comforted when told that the ruins across the street had once been a hotel.

While in Algiers the Jills were informed that all their performances were to be held at the local Red Cross Club. Their intention in coming to Africa was to get closer to the front to entertain. They were told that was impossible. Finally, General Eisenhower invited Kay and the Jills to his villa for supper. Eisenhower asked Kay if they would be

January 1943. Kay, with Carole Landis and Martha Raye, near Algiers. Kay tactfully convinced General Eisenhower to allow "The Jills" to be the first celebrities to entertain in combat zones.

willing to entertain nearer the front. Kay was emphatic. "It's the risk we took when we came here," she told him. "We *want* to get to the boys who are doing the dirty work. Please let us go." Eisenhower gave his approval, along with a fighter escort to their destination. Landis told about their flight and the reception they got at the front.

> Up we went in the big transport with the little spitfires (often referred to as "ack-acks") zooming back and forth and all around us performing every trick they knew. When we arrived at the first field they just stood around with their mouths hanging open, as if they were seeing a mirage or something. Then all at once they seemed to recognize us...and their faces broke into broad smiles and they fairly jumped with excitement...The boys couldn't find words to tell us how grateful they were that we had visited them. They wanted to give us their insignia and chevrons and practically strip themselves, just to be able to repay us in some way.
>
> At every camp we visited the officer in charge always warned us of a possible air attack. [One] night we were having a cup of coffee in a canteen hut before going on with the show. We were all dressed to the hilt for the boys, with our last remaining pairs of silk stockings, high-heeled shoes and the best dresses we could muster. Suddenly, all hell seemed to break loose. The kids...just grabbed us and flung us out of that building...across the pitch-black field, with the "acks-acks" blazing away like sixty, they dragged us headlong, in our silly high-heeled shoes, with our gas masks banging against us...We stumbled, fell and were flung into a hole, and crawled through the mud on our hands and knees...When we got out...the fact that we had gone through the air raid with them and were still there with a song and a dance and a laugh, the relief they felt within themselves that they themselves were still there to enjoy it—well, they just tore the place down with applause.[8]

There was an uncanny timing to the Jills' sudden and unexpected appearances. As the diary of Lt. Colonel Taback (a heroic pilot stationed in Algeria) attests: "Thurs. 1/21/43—A rough day today. Lost Lewis and Luddington...Boys felt quite low so most of them got drunk...I don't blame them." The following day Taback stayed on ground and didn't fly. He wrote he was, "glad of it, because Martha Raye, Kay Francis, Mitzi Mayfair and Carole Landis were here and put on a swell show. Sure surprised me, to see them here at the front."[9] The Jills stepped "out of a dream" and into the minds and hearts of men who were feeling great loss and in touch with their own mortality.

Eventually, the Jills ended up in the Sahara. Kay must have felt she was on the set of *Another Dawn* with the wind stirring up into a sirocco whirling around their faces and filling their mouths. It never subsided. The dust, coupled with the rapid drop in temperature at sundown, created what was known as sundown throat, making it difficult to swallow. Regardless, the "famous faces" vetoed the regulation "dusk masks," they were there to *entertain*. It was in the Sahara they met photographer Margaret Bourke-White, who was documenting the war. One General commented that Bourke-White didn't know what fear was. She simply lost her mind when she had a camera. The famous photographer was soon "losing her mind" taking photos of the four broken-down glamour girls as they brought the desert down with their show. For the finale, Mitzi, her shoulder recovered, carried some big bruiser off stage after wearing him out doing the jitterbug.

With their African duties complete, the Jills went their separate ways. Kay and Mitzi returned to California, Martha ventured to Casablanca to entertain more troops, and Carole Landis went back to England to see her husband. That doomed relationship soon ended in divorce. One of the conflicts that complicated Landis' life was her sexuality. She left Hollywood in 1944 to star on Broadway and fell in love with a chorus girl, Jacqueline Susann. Susann's biographer, Barbara Seaman, detailed the relationship: "Carole fell in love with Jackie and was not reticent about showing it. She sent flowers, followed by a tiny pair of perfect pearl drop earrings, even tried to present a mink coat…Jackie, no doubt flattered, reciprocated, later describing to her girl friends how sensual it had been when she and Carole had stroked and kissed each other's breasts."[10] Oddly enough, it was Susann who introduced Landis to Horace W. Schmidlapp, Jr., with whom Landis entered another short-lived marriage. When Landis ventured to England in 1947 she began an affair with Rex Harrison. That ended with the despondent Landis committing suicide. It was a tragic end for a talented and lovely lady. Years later, Susann would pattern the suicidal character Jennifer North in her bestseller *Valley of the Dolls* after Landis.

Kay and Mitzi Mayfair received a big welcome back in the United States. The first thing Kay did, unofficially, was to call Carole Landis' mother. *The New York Times* reported:

ACTRESSES BOMBED, BUT SHOW WENT ON
    Kay Francis and Mitzi Mayfair, newly returned members of a four-girl "Feminine Theatrical Task Force," yesterday described the hardships and dangers of wartime trouping…Speaking at USO headquarters with an Army

January 31, 1943. Kay and Mitzi Mayfair received a big "welcome home." Kay filed an official report and gave a coast-to-coast broadcast in Washington, D.C.

censor at her side, Miss Francis said that during the three-month journey the troupe had given 125 shows and made 150 personal appearances, sometimes close to the front lines...even attired in battle helmets, trench coats, slacks, and "Mae West" jackets, the girls caused commotion among the soldiers wherever they went. "They would have been perfectly happy if all you said was boo to them," Miss Francis declared...During their stay in Algiers they were bombed nightly. "We stood in the general's house and watched several Jerries come down in flames," said Miss Francis. Closer to the front a sudden bombing attack forced them into a dugout, after which they emerged, "powdered our noses and the show went on."[11]

Before Kay dictated an official report in Washington, D.C., she penned her own press release from New York, which was published in newspapers across the country:

Magnificent...That is the only word in my vocabulary that describes the men of our armed forces...I think I am entitled to evaluate those men...for I have just completed a tour which covered 30,000 miles by air and 7500 miles by land...There were four of us—and we played before the men of the American Army in open fields, in mess halls, in hospitals, and on the desert. We ate with American soldiers, we talked with them—and we took shelter with them in a dugout built by the Germans, while we were under fire for nearly an hour. They are magnificent—we know. When I hear people here at home discussing rationing and discussing some of the hardships, I wish they could...see our men and the spirit in which *they* meet the hardships of war...It was a great experience for us. We learned much from it. We want to go back if the opportunity comes...to keep them smiling..."[12]

Kay's wish came true. Eventually, the USO Camp Shows, Inc., the biggest booking agent in the world, got permission to send units to England. It was no easy task. Many lost their lives while on USO tours, primarily in transport plane crashes. Aside from her narrow escapes with the Four Jills, Kay had other brushes with mortality. On one occasion, Kay was en route home from a USO tour in Europe aboard a plane that was lost off the coast of Florida. No formal radio installation on the seaboard was able to pick up the pilot's signals except Chopmist Hill station off Rhode Island. Lucky for Kay, Chopmist's top-secret radio-monitoring station could intercept distant radio signals with amazing clarity and guided her plane to safety.

Kay's only celluloid release in 1943 was for 20th Century-Fox's *Show Business at War*. The documentary was part of their "March of Time" series. Running seventeen minutes, the viewer got glimpses of wartime celebrities entertaining the troops. The segment that covered the work being done overseas featured Kay, Martha Raye and Carole Landis. The narrator emphasized that, "Women stars carry on their work as near the battle line as army regulations will allow." We first see the Jills in a jeep (Raye and Francis in the backseat) with a road sign saying they were six kilometers from Algiers. The next scene shows them in mess-line fraternizing with the boys, while holding their tin mess-cans.

Upon returning to California, Kay was in demand for radio appearances and a new film assignment. Her first call was for the CBS program *Stage Door Canteen*. This was followed, by an invitation from DeMille's *Lux Radio Theatre* to appear in *The Lady is Willing*. DeMille proudly introduced Kay's return from the front, saying: "An American soldier in North Africa can't tell *who* he's going to see these days. A man rides up in a jeep and it turns out to be the President of the United States. A liberator bomber drops from the sky and out steps the Prime Minister of England. A sergeant dives into a bomb shelter and who should be sitting there calm as you please, but Kay Francis. Kay came back to Hollywood last week and tonight *Lux Radio Theatre* celebrates her return to the quiet kind of drama by co-starring her with one of our longtime favorites, George Brent. We borrowed George from the Coast Guard."

The Lady is Willing had been filmed the year before with Marlene Dietrich and Fred MacMurray. The light comedy told of a naive actress (Kay) who decides to adopt an abandoned baby girl. She enters into a marriage of convenience with obstetrician George Brent in order to adopt the baby (whom Brent informs her is actually a boy). In exchange, she helps him with his rabbits and a cure for pneumonia. A sudden riptide plummets this fluffy affair into heavy drama when the baby needs an emergency operation. Before the audience could register whether they had listened to a drama or comedy, the program was over, and Kay was praising the joys of Lux Soap. Throughout their trip the Jills had washed their own laundry—once traveling six long days without changing clothes. Kay marveled, for the radio audience, at the results she got from Lux Flakes obtained at the PX (Post Exchange) in North Africa.

More interesting than *The Lady is Willing*, and more relevant to Kay's life than Lux Flakes, was the interview George Brent and DeMille gave Kay afterwards. Brent asked how she got to North Africa. DeMille inquired if the boys were glad to see some glamour. Kay responded and added some detail.

> I flew through the air with the greatest of ease, George, and little "ack-acks" at the side. If anyone could see us in trench-coats, slacks, tin hats and boots and call it glamour...they had been out there for a *good long time*. Travel was sometimes strenuous. There was that time we were flying from one airfield to another in Africa. I was asleep...when someone took a shot at us. An officer wanted to wake me up, but Mitzi said, "Ah, let her sleep. We haven't been hit yet!" Underground, spending a few hours in a crowded air shelter is the quickest way I've ever found to get to know people! We put on shows in airplane hangers...mess halls, and...the back of trucks in the middle of the desert.

George Brent commented, "On stages like that you soon find out what entertainment can mean, don't you?" Kay brought her story home by answering, "Hearing our girls singing in an air raid shelter with bombs bursting outside, it's a little hard to worry about things we're going to do *without*, here." DeMille closed the program by complimenting Kay. "I don't believe you have much time to worry anyway. While she's at home in Hollywood...Kay is one of the moving spirits in the hospital unit of the Naval Aid Auxiliary where she's doing extremely valuable work in the Naval hospitals here and elsewhere."

Continuing in the line of duty, Kay appeared at the air base March Field for an Eddie Cantor Show broadcast. When Kay talked about the occasion she had to jump into an open dugout, Cantor interrupted her. "You mean a foxhole!" he tells her. "Well," laughed Kay, "there was a *wolf* in this one!" The show closed with Kay's request for the popular song, "Comin' in on a Wing and a Prayer."

In March 1943, Kay was offered six consecutive weeks to film a production titled *Four Jills in a Jeep* based on Landis' account of their adventures. The $30,000 contract promised her top-billing. What was released, a year later, under that title, lacked the authenticity and spirit that the four women had put into the original venture. Fox turned out a typical, wartime musical concoction, with only occasional glimpses into the heart of the four Jills' journey. Unfortunately, director William A. Seiter (who had directed *It's a Date*) and the scriptwriters, short-changed the Jills' *real* experience. The film promoted Fox studios' own roster of stars, by inserting musical numbers with Alice Faye, Betty Grable and Carmen Miranda. The cutting room floor consumed Kay at the piano as the foursome sang "The Old Army Game," and a risqué number titled, "Snafu." The innocuous "Snafu" featured Landis and Mayfair innocently asking what snafu really meant. The Breen Office feared that wartime audiences might also ask the question or worse still, know the answer. The wartime acronym SNAFU permanently infiltrated popular lingo and was used to typify a normal business day. Simply decoded it meant: "Situation Normal…All F…ked Up," which aptly described Kay's feelings about *Four Jills in a Jeep*.

Upon release, *The New York Times* zeroed in on the film. "As a piece of screen entertainment," the paper read, "it is decidedly impromptu. It gives the painful impression of having been tossed together in a couple of hours…the claptrap saga…is just a raw piece of capitalization upon a widely publicized affair." What could have been a touching documentary-style tribute to servicemen and their Jills was lost in overblown production numbers. Watching Dick Haymes sing while a bevy of beauties parade down a staircase, seemed far, far removed from the Jills' story. So did the shtick of Phil Silvers, who gave the impression the film was about *him*. The romances of Kay and a general (Lester Matthews), Mayfair and Haymes (who could easily pass as siblings), Raye (who was married) and Silvers, were contrived to say the least…and sometimes coated with unintentional humor. When Kay catches Mitzi staring dreamily off into space after an exhausting day, she asks, "What's the matter with you?" Shaken from her stupor, Mitzi replies, "I'm thinking of Dick!" Kay looks perturbed. "For heaven's sake!" she exclaims. "At a time like this?" Midway into the picture, there was another good chuckle at a Sahara

Kay, on the set of Four Jills in a Jeep *(1944) with Phil Silvers. After her death, Silvers ungallantly remarked that Kay had no interest in men. His gargantuan ego couldn't understand that she simply had no interest in him. (20th Century-Fox)*

outpost. A baffled corporal radios in, claiming he saw Kay Francis on a camel! Kay miraculously appears, slides off the monumental hump and exclaims "When I was a kid I wanted to join the circus. Hey! I take it all back!"

In 1973, Phil Silvers reminisced about the film. He referred to 1944 as a vintage year for him. His vintage memory, however, was a bit overripe. He claimed Mitzi Mayfair had written *Four Jills in a Jeep*. Perhaps Silvers did pinpoint, unintentionally, one of the reasons the film misfired. "The trouble with using the four girls was—each had her own version of what actually happened...Director William Seiter had to explain over and over that this was *entertainment*." Silvers then had the audacity to add, "Who *cared* about *reality*?" To top off his puffed-up attitude, Silvers had the effrontery to comment on Kay's sexual preferences, saying: "Kay Francis was shown falling in love with an officer. This was a tribute to her acting skill, because she had very little interest in men." Silvers had obviously failed to charm Kay. Perhaps she rebuffed him at one point. Whatever his reason, the cutting remark was the first in-print reference (aside from the FBI files) that questioned Kay's sexuality. Silvers was indeed the perfect antidote for any heterosexual urges Kay may have had during filming. Be that as it may, her pursuit for the love of men was as *strong* as ever. Kay managed to squeeze in an unproductive fling with producer Bert Friedlob—"Bert and I out...then home; he went swimming and finally came through with a lousy lay!"[13] Never one to give up entirely, Kay generously gave poor Bert one more chance. The next night she noted, "Bert F. in around 10 for nightcap," and later lamented, "Christ! What is wrong with the guy?"[14] Friedlob would later marry Eleanor Parker. Kay's most enjoyable relationship at this time continued to be with Otto Preminger. On one occasion they skipped the main course. "Dinner. Otto. Here 7:30. Never made dinner! Damn good!"[15] The relationship was one of mutual admiration. "Otto by at 5pm...Long talk! Long conversation! Long everything! But good!"[16] Kay wasn't head over heels, but she knew Otto was good for her. "Otto terribly sweet and kind and wonderful...My God, he is kind to me..."[17]

Contrary to Silvers' dimmed recollections regarding *Four Jills in a Jeep*, screenwriter Snag Werris enjoyed his daily duties on the set in what he called a "true, fun assignment." Werris remembered: "They were swell gals. Kay was a real pro and a joy to work with. Her troubles with r's were well known. So, for a gag I was asked to bring in a new page of script. I don't recall the lines, but one was something like, 'I ran into Ralph Roanoke and rapidly wrung his neck.' When Kay got to it, she read it through and yelled, 'Where is that SOB Snag? I'll kill him!' But none of the four took herself too seriously. They got along well."[18] Kay got the Jills to join in on her traditional party for the crew after filming.

Variety admitted that *Four Jills in a Jeep*, "while pleasing and diverting...is far from socko...However, the exploitation boys have plenty to work with, since the 'Four Jills' of the title afford opportunities." The "exploitation boys" succeeded. *Four Jills in a Jeep* pulled in the crowds. *Photoplay*, observed that *Four Jills in a Jeep* held interest because it was based on a true overseas adventure and noted, "As leader of the little pilgrim band, Kay Francis is given dignity and charm and comes through pleasingly...But the ending was much too abrupt...we had the feeling an important ingredient had been omitted..."

Kay also felt the film missed the mark and trivialized the real story. Drama critic Donald Kirkley reiterated Kay's disappointment about *Four Jills in a Jeep*: "She thinks," wrote Kirkley, "that the picture was unduly glamorized by the producer, and that it failed to give a true idea of the underlying seriousness of the project. She and the others were pioneers. It was the first time entertainers had been taken to the front, and the army was using them to some extent as guinea pigs."[19] Kirkley made a point of adding, "Kay…is one of those Hollywood citizens who did *more* than might be considered a fair share of duty in shaping the morale of the armed forces; and we may add that she was *not* among those who sought publicity along the way. Nor does she boast about her doings…"[20]

In the fall of 1945, Dick Terry, for Milwaukee's *Post Dispatch,* asked if Kay and the other two Jills ever got revenge on Landis' girlish and uninhibited style of telling their story, which initiated the lighthearted treatment of the film. He wrote, "Miss Francis gave me a look of silent suffering. Then she reached across the table and shook my hand. 'Some day,' she said, 'I'm going to write my own story. The true story of the things that happened on that trip.' There was something in her tone that convinced me that, if she ever does, Miss Landis isn't going to like it."[21]

Kay diligently continued her unpublicized war-related activity and entertainment duties. She was chairman of the Naval Aid Auxiliary Hospital Visiting Committee and lined up film stars to visit the convalescing men. There are dozens of diary entries logging Kay's hospital visits and goodwill. ("Leaving for Needles USO show"—"Hospital TB ward. Alone"—"Out to Fort Mc Arthur to do show for men"—"Leaving on hospital tour 10 a.m.")[22] Kay was acknowledged in September 1943, when she and Norma Shearer were awarded special medals from the Canadian government for assisting in the Canadian Fifth Victory Loan drive.

On Thanksgiving Day, 1943, Kay was in the all-star NBC special "Soldiers in Greasepaint." Bob Hope emceed. Kay introduced the Jills, who sang a parody of the tune "Sunday, Monday, or Always." A few weeks later, Kay appeared on radio's *Command Performance.* It turned out to be the Jills' most popular radio gig. Titled the "North African Follies," the Jills were again introduced by Bob Hope. He handed the foursome a sketch to act out. The surprise was—they played four guys, who were lying around, talking about the Four Jills' visit to their remote outpost in North Africa. Kay played a private named "Slim," Carole was "Spike," Mitzi played "Maxie," and Martha became "Butch." The Jills had fun sinking their collective teeth into the male ego.

SLIM (Kay):	"Say! Did you get a load of that Mitzi Mayfair dancing? Boy, whatta pair of gams!"
SPIKE (Carole):	"Yeh! That Mayfair is a dish, but personally, I'll take Martha Raye. She's a blockbuster of sex appeal. Wow! Wow!"
BUTCH (Martha):	"Sex appeal. What about that Carole Landis? Whatta 'build' on her!"
SLIM (Kay):	"Hey, Hey! Aren't you forgettin' somebody? That Kay Francis isn't exactly a dish rag!"
MAXIE (Mitzi):	"She's okay for *me!*"
SLIM (Kay):	"You said it! She may have a little bit of age on her, but Buddy…that's when *they know!*"
SPIKE (Carole):	"Hey guys! I heard a rumor this morning!"
MAXIE (Mitzi):	"A rumor? Where'd ya hear it?"
BUTCH (Martha):	"Where do ya usually hear rumors…in the army!"
SPIKE (Carole):	"Anyway, I got it straight that Frances Langford is coming here pretty soon."

BUTCH (Martha):   "Frances Langford! Boy, what a 'build' on her. Wow! Wow!"

SLIM (Kay):   "Oh, to you everybody's got a 'build' on 'em. I think that Langford's a little too skinny."

MAXIE (Mitzi):   "Oh yeh? She's not skinny where she's not supposed to be."

SLIM (Kay):   "A lot you know about dames. ZaSu Pitts is your pin-up girl!"

SPIKE (Carole):   "What are you guys arguing about? We're not gonna end up with any of those babes anyway."

BUTCH: (Martha):   "Yeh, well, I don't know about that! When I got Mitzi Mayfair's autograph, she gave me a *nice little wink*."

Capping this round of testosterone, Butch (Martha) really goes ape for *herself!*

SPIKE (Carole):   "Now, if you said Martha *Raye* gave you a wink, I'd believe you."

MAXIE (Mitzi):   "Yeh! She's really man crazy!"

BUTCH (Martha): "Ah, come on now! Break it up! Break it up! You're talkin' about the dame I love!" (lots of laughs—   Raye flubs up and ad-libs) "What a build on her! Wow! Wow!"

MAXIE (Mitzi):   "Hey Spike! Any other gals comin' with Frances Langford?"

SPIKE (Carole):   "No, just Bob Hope."

SLIM (Kay):   "*Just Bob Hope!* Now there's a guy with talent. I bet he does all right with those babes out in Hollywood." (Yawns) "Well, I don't know about you guys, but I'm gonna hit the hay. With a little luck, ya know, I might dream about 'Kay *Fwancis.*'"

SPIKE (Carole):   "Yeh, I'm tired too. Sure hope I dream about Carole Landis."

MAXIE (Mitzi):   "Gosh, I'd like to meet Mitzi Mayfair in my dreams. Hey, Butch! Who would you like to dream about?"

BUTCH (Martha):   "Bob Hope! What a *build* on him! Wow! Wow!"

1943. Kay, wrapping up her USO tour, smiles approvingly at the 10-inch cucumbers grown on the Ascension Islands.

The Jills brought down the house for their role-reversal, with a gay twist at the end. And, it was good fun to hear Kay spoof her proclivity for "w's."

Humor also snuck into a photograph taken of Kay, by the U.S. Army Signal Corps., while she on the mid-Atlantic Ascension Island. Apparently the boys were trying to impress her by showing what can be grown in volcanic lava with the aid of chemistry. There was *plenty* of chemistry in the photograph too, as they stood around watching Kay, with sheepish grins, holding handfuls of 10-inch cucumbers.

Early in 1944, Kay retreated to Mexico. She took along a notebook in which she sketched, with words, the many images that the tranquil scenery proffered. After a brief time in Acapulco, she retreated further from the *cuidad moderna* to Puerto Marques, in what her diary poetically designated "a rotten little boat." By canal, she maneuvered through the jungle toward a beachhead, while observing flying white herons. In Puerto Marques, Kay soaked up the natural surroundings and idled hours away reading mystery novels. She took a walking tour of Cuernevacca (50 miles south of Mexico City). "Saw lovely churches with gardens and shopped at Market," she wrote. "Beautiful crooked and steep streets—went for a swim—had a few drinks—bought a hat—then…a wonderful walk up a steep moonlit street into a little square with a tent show in process."[23] The same evening Kay enjoyed the music and festivity at two different dance halls. She awoke the next morning to the sounds of "thousands" of birds. (Decades later, the eternal spring of Cuernevacca would make it a popular destination for U.S. retirees.) She picked orchids in Cordoba, and then rode a third-class bus to Orizaba, where she learned how to prepare Mole´ Poblano (a delectable chili-chocolate sauce) and Ceviche (a fish marinade, with olives, tomatoes, and lime juice). Kay's Mexican journey was only a brief respite from a world inundated with conflict. Most important, it replenished her capacity to *return* to the work that mattered most to her.

Kay joined a troop of players for an "Arctic Camp Tour" in 1944, which ventured into sub-zero weather. Due to her previous overseas duty, Reginald Gardiner, Marsha Hunt, and the four other women, referred to Kay as "Sarge, Our Fearless Leader." Hunt documented the excursion in her 1993 book, *The Way We Wore*.

> [Kay] acted as MC of our shows, being breezily informal and anecdotal. With her distinctive raven hair and classic beauty, Kay was known for her fashion chic both on and off screen…no doubt her GI audiences expected more of the same. Instead, she usually went on stage in a simple dirndl skirt and blouse, but she couldn't resist trailing a long chiffon hankie…The peasant-look helped her and the boys out front feel informal and anyhow, nothing could rob Kay of her own innate glamour. Wise to the rigors of junkets, Kay traveled light…Her 5 feet 6 inch height had trouble, though, with her tiny size 4 feet…we were kept busy pulling her upright after frequent slips and spills on the ice. Miraculously, these falls left her unhurt and cheerfully resigned to them.[24]

Kay and the other players made their home in a C-47 red-winged Cargo plane where they swapped stories, napped, read, mended costumes and worked up the next port-of-call performance. Hunt was unable to recall a single sour note among the six of them for the six-week stint. The plane was piloted by Don King throughout western, central and northern Canada and Alaska. King had claim as the best bush pilot in the Arctic. Thousands of men attended performances held in mammoth unheated airplane hangars, or in the gilt-trimmed movie palaces of Edmonton and Winnipeg. Some audiences were as few as fifteen men in isolated weather observation posts. Hunt remembered, "We played to both U.S. and Canadian Air Forces, and once, in Alaska, there were Russian fliers...as well as a few German prisoners of war who'd been allowed to watch the show. Ours was the first live entertainment to reach nearly all of the bases we played, and so our coming brought the impact of an earthquake."[25]

Many times the men stood and stomped outside the entrances for hours in 40-below-zero wind and weather. In Edmonton, Kay and gang were rationed their outdoor clothing: fleece-lined sheepskin parkas with fur hoods, sheepskin parka-pants, fleece-lined heavy boots and fleece-lined leather gloves. Hunt commented, "Although lacking in chic, they were heaven-sent barriers against undreamed-of cold and fierce winds." The Royal Canadian Air Force had instructed Kay's troupe to watch one another for signs of frostbite, which could take hold in seconds. "A nose can go, just like that!" an officer warned. "Get used to the crackling in your nose," he added. "It's the moisture around the hairs...turning to icicles." They were cautioned not to pet the Eskimo huskies. The Eskimo masters kept the dogs viciously hungry in order to maximize their speed. A blood-filled hand would look like a special appetizer. Officers also warned them about the cordial Eskimos. Appetites could just as easily be lost if one got too close to them. They sewed themselves into their garments for winter, and used their own urine to wash their hair and cure their parka skins. Forewarned, but unperturbed, the troupe's visit with Eskimos included a dogsled ride *and* a venture into an aromatic, pungent igloo.

Hunt noted that, "Kay and Reggie...were the darlings of the officers, and accepted their invitation at social hours, while the rest of us mixed with 'the men.'" Because of their screen roles, Hunt emphasized, their audiences saw them "as a kind of friend-in-common with everyone else...a link with home...a reassurance to isolated,

Kay braved sub-zero weather on her Arctic Tour, 1944. Marsha Hunt and Reginald Gardiner are also seen amid enthusiastic GIs. At right—Eskimo Kay aboard the C-47 Red-Wing cargo plane.

lonely men who, more than anything else, *longed* for home." The troupe visited veteran hospitals in Canada. "There, in ward after ward," wrote Hunt, "on floor after floor, lay the still-breathing, still-pulsating human junkyard of war, the relics of World War I...Some were cheery, others vacantly staring...twisted, dismembered, emaciated survivors."[26]

In many respects Kay's diligence during the war reflected the pioneering spirit of Florence Nightingale in war-torn Crimea a hundred years earlier. A *Baltimore Sun* article praised Kay's appearances in the Arctic and her determination on behalf of naval hospitals.

> During her flights over Alaska the plane often went out of its way to pass over small snowbound camps so remote that they could be reached only by long and difficult trips by dog sled. They would circle over these camps and Miss Francis would talk with the soldiers by radio. Their extreme joy over even this remote contact with an American woman and a famous one at that was, Miss Francis said, one of the most moving things encountered on her travels.

> Between trips she made weekly visits to two naval hospitals, one at Long Beach, the other at Corona. She would take three girls with her, celebrities if they were available, and visit each one of the numerous wards, week in, week out. Hospital authorities placed great value on these visits because of their *continuity*; it gave the patients something to look forward to; and Miss Francis tried to talk with as many individuals as she could, drawing them out and relieving the tedium of hospital life with anecdotes of Hollywood; and this sort of thing, doctors agree, was far more effective than staged entertainments.

> One result of her travels has been a vast correspondence with soldiers and sailors from all over the world. She has been at pains to answer each letter and still they come. She has sent out thousands of wallet-size photographs in answer to requests and has received in return many pictures taken on various fronts, which decorate a long hallway in her Hollywood home.[27]

In April 1945, Kay made a tour entertaining in Brazil, Trinidad, Sao Paolo and Santa Cruz. The following month she seemed to shift gears, along with the rest of the world. On May 7, 1945, Germany surrendered to the Allies. On August 6, the first atomic bomb mushroomed over Hiroshima only to leave behind yet *another* human junkyard from world war. Kay Francis had done more than her share for the relief of human suffering during wartime. In spite of her arduous and much admired contributions and interest on behalf of men and women in uniform, Hollywood had somehow *lost* interest in Kay Francis, the "Woman Who Had Found Herself." The adage, "Be careful what you ask for," came back to haunt the "Woman Who Couldn't Wait to be Forgotten."

Chapter 18

Monogram Trilogy and the
Curse On *Windy Hill*

Monogram studio was bustling in the 1940s churning out low-budget Westerns, the Bowery Boys, the Charlie Chan series. The studio reached its peak in the '50s, changing its moniker to Allied Artists, with such big moneymakers like *Invasion of the Body Snatchers* (1956) and *Attack of the 50 Ft. Woman* (1958). Down-on-their-luck stars of yesteryear showed up in the studio's B programmers to keep their name, if not in the bright lights, at least in some sort of stellar twilight. From 1944-1946, Kay had a final fling as a movie star in what later became known as her "Monogram Trilogy." *The New York Times* announced on July 14, 1944: "Kay Francis has signed a deal with Jeffrey Bernerd whereby she will be starred in three pictures to be produced by him for Monogram release. She will also serve as associate producer of the stories, the first of which will be *Divorce*, a contemporary domestic drama to be filmed in September." Kay was one of the first female stars to delve into producing her own films.

Jeffrey Bernerd, a feisty cockney, had been brought to Hollywood by Monogram's president Steve Broidy. Broidy enjoyed Bernerd's "up-yours" attitude and engaged him to produce exploitation films. Broidy was thrilled to get Kay on board. "When we started in business we had less than 1,000 accounts," Broidy told a reporter. "Today our films are shown in 9,000 out of a possible 18,000 theaters...Now that our star roster can show such names as Kay Francis...we should be able to play approximately 12,000 theaters next season."[1] Kay and Bernerd used the talents of mostly the same crew on each picture. All three films credited the same screenplay writer, cinematographer, art director, and music/sound department. At least six actors were used repeatedly in the trilogy. The breakneck speed for production was 10-12 days. Bernerd was surprised by Kay's inclination to cut corners and scale down costs. She searched for low-budget vehicles, helped rewrite the script for the second feature *Allotment Wives*, and persuaded actors Paul Kelly and Otto Kruger to work for less than usual. The object was to make money. Kay planned to sit in on the first production and learn the ropes. "I'll have no office and I don't want any chi-chi about the thing," she told reporter Robbin Coons. "It's a way for me to break into the producing end of the business, which is where I want to be."[2]

Cinematographer Harry Neumann (whose crowning achievement was 1960's *The Wasp Woman*) worked on all three pictures. Neumann developed his "expertise" at Monogram, alongside directors like William Beaudine in *Black Market Babies*. Bill "One Shot" Beaudine's output was prolific and he had no delusions regarding his work. When told that his Monogram "quickie" was falling behind schedule, Beaudine feigned surprise. "You mean someone out there is actually waiting to see this?"[3] he gasped. The answer to his question, as far as Kay's trilogy was concerned, finally came in the year 2001. Yes, by then the crowds *were* waiting. Curiosity about Kay's film swan songs inspired the Roxie Theater in San Francisco to feature "The Kay Francis Monogram Trilogy" in their popular cult classics program. The second of the Francis-Bernerd productions, *Allotment Wives* (1945), had already been shown with enthusiastic response, especially from *San Francisco Chronicle* film critic Mick LaSalle:

Allotment Wives *(1945). In 2001, San Francisco* Chronicle *critic Mick LaSalle hailed the film as a "major rediscovery" and declared tht Kay's performance outshone Joan Crawford's Oscar-winning role in* Mildred Pierce. *(Monogram)*

During the long reign of censorship in American film (1934-1966) some of the freshest and most honest pictures about women were the B movies. While women in major studio films wallowed in...sentimentality—martyrs to their men...women in B pictures got to join girl gangs, run crime rings and go to prison. While A movies were big on making women apologize for any show of strength, B movie heroines could be tough as nails to the bitter end—like Kay Francis in the classic *Allotment Wives* (1945). *Allotment Wives* is the standout picture of the festival and qualifies as a major rediscovery...For years *Allotment Wives* has been written off as an embarrassing coda to the career of '30's diva Kay Francis. Guess what? It's one of her best movies...Sleek, sexy and stylish...Francis plays the head of a crime syndicate that bilks the government out of money during World War II...The story is tight; the suspense is genuine. But what makes the picture unique is that Francis— even as she's ordering contract hits and gunning down blackmailers—is the film's most sympathetic character. She's from the wrong side of the tracks and wants money so her daughter can have a better life. The plot has echoes of another 1945 feature, *Mildred Pierce*, for which Joan Crawford won an Oscar. But *Allotment Wives* is tougher, harder and stronger, and Francis' performance outshines anything Crawford ever did. In retrospect, it's amazing that Francis didn't go on to have a great second career. Notice the way she gets off her last line in the picture. It's classic.[4]

John Cocchi, in the book *Second Feature*, also praises Francis' work in *Allotment Wives*, saying the picture "was a surprisingly good crime melodrama which allowed her to be totally unsympathetic and fascinating at the same time...Although she comes to a well-deserved end, Kay Francis rewards herself with a memorable exit line."[5] In truth, Kay's character vacillates in our sympathies. Kay liked her role; in fact, the story had been her idea. The United Press reported that Kay had read about a woman who had married fifteen different sailors to collect their Navy allotment pay. Kay did further research on the matter. She got to talking to Army men on her travels and it turned out that the racket was widespread. Bernerd liked her idea and wanted Kay to be the FBI agent who cracked down on the racket. Producer Francis said, "Nothing doing!" She insisted on being the racketeer and promised, "I'll be the meanest woman that God ever made."[6] Bernerd was keen on Kay's idea of perusing the headlines for story ideas. In fact, Kay started a whole shift at Monogram. The studio's producers became headline hunters and turned topical stories into box-office gold. Although it was a moneymaker, reviews for *Allotment Wives* lacked the Midas touch. *Photoplay* wagged, "Kay Francis is stuck with the role of a bad mama who plays a lady racketeer...embroiled in unpleasant doings which aren't as bad as some we've seen, at that. Your reviewer says: 'Weediculous, weally.'" Although Kay's "r's" were intact, so were the inevitable puns. *Allotment Wives* was the only film in the trilogy that rated mention in *The New York Times* and garnered no sympathy from its reviewer. "A maximum of routine melodrama...sporadic and uninspired. As the co-producer of the picture and its distaff Fagin and mob chief, Kay Francis wears an assortment of impressive gowns and accessories and appears far too genteel for her job."

The smug attitude of *The New York Times* and *Photoplay* toward a Monogram release was an unfair assessment of a film whose pace and atmosphere hold the atten-

Allotment Wives (1945) Playing "The meanest woman God ever made," Kay blows Gertrude Michael's brains out in this scene with Bernard Nedell. (Monogram)

tion. Kay's "genteel" look is apropos to her character—a socialite and businesswoman who runs a stylish salon, fronting for her own bigamy racket to gyp servicemen out of their allotment checks. Film critic LaSalle's comparison to *Mildred Pierce* is mostly on target. *Allotment Wives'* darker, grittier edge is impressive. The film is minus a riveting Max Steiner score and a few of the big studio touches. Filmed mostly in cost-effective medium shots, one has to do without the quivering close-ups of Kay's moist eyes. It's Kay's *toughness* that holds the picture together. She says she finds the law's hot breath on her neck "more stimulating than a cold shower." When her troubled daughter, Teala Loring, goes AWOL from a private girls' school, Kay seeks vengeance. "Wait'll I work that faculty over," she snarls. Kay and her daughter get in a face-slapping confrontation and a genuinely felt, "I always loved you from the bottom of my heart" reconciliation. Kay's cat-and-mouse flirtation with Paul Kelly (on her tail from the War Department) has the audience intrigued and wondering throughout. Cast against type, Kelly was an ex-con in real life. He spent two years in San Quentin for manslaughter after bashing his best friend's head against the wall. (His wife affectionately referred to him as "Bratface.")

Kay's final scene on the staircase in *Allotment Wives* holds the tension like a tight wire. She raises a gun from behind her scarf, pointing it at "Bratface" Kelly, only to find someone else has pulled a trigger. She takes it in stride with an off-the-cuff remark, complimenting her assassin. "Nice shooting," she says, looking him directly in the eye before collapsing on the banister. A socko ending. Or, what *should* have been. We're obliged to sit through a scene where Kelly is congratulated at the Office of Dependant Benefits in Washington. He got his "man" and now the audience can go home feeling safe again—a real morale booster. This patriotic bent was used often in otherwise nicely done *noir* films. Dick Powell's *To the Ends of the Earth* (1948), which busted the Production Code wide open on the subject of narcotics, used the docu-style intro and ending. So did director Anthony Mann's *Border Incident* (1949), a well-done exposé on the abuse of migrant labor, with Ricardo Montalban. After the pompous, officious, brought-to-you-by-the-FBI-or-CIA ending, one would think that the drug cartels and migrant problems had been miraculously resolved!

The praises from LaSalle and Cocchi do not extend themselves to the first feature of Kay's trilogy, also directed by William Nigh, *Divorce*. The film was a typical exploitation flick with a hackneyed script by scenarist Sidney Sutherland (who had done so well with Kay's 1933 success *I Loved a Woman*). Of course, Sutherland was up against the Production Code. An objective, sympathetic approach to the subject matter of *Divorce* was not possible in 1945 Hollywood. During the film's production, reporter Erskine Johnson braved old territory with Kay asking, "Has anyone mentioned the embarrassing fact that you are well qualified to work on a picture titled '*Divorce*'?" Kay all but swallowed her coffee cup. "Yes, you rat," she laughed, "but I've been avoiding it." Kay explained that at first she was going to play the sympathetic part of the wronged wife, but soon realized the production was "getting nowhere fast." "So I finally offered to play the other woman," Kay said. "It made a lot more sense." Kay quickly changed the subject. "I'm having a lot of fun. I've learned that to be a producer you just have to yell louder than anyone else." Sitting nearby, producer Bernerd chimed in. "And I think Kay is wonderful, because she undresses so fast." "Pulease!" said Kay. Bernerd explained, "I've worked with a lot of actresses who spend hours in their dressing rooms and hold up production. Kay puts 'em on and takes 'em off faster than any Hollywood actress I've ever worked with." Kay explained, "When you're on a 12-day production schedule everything moves fast. We're shooting so fast that I think I'm still rehearsing when someone yells, 'That's it,' and they start tearing down the set. The way we're shooting, you better just stand by. We'll probably have the preview this afternoon."[7]

In *Divorce*, Kay pulled no stops playing a bad girl out to get happily married Bruce Cabot. At the end of the film, Bruce predictably returns, tail-between-legs, to "mama," the kids, the safety of home, and the protection of the Production Code. Preachy, to say the least, the film opens with a lecture by a judge, who claims divorce is only based on selfishness and bitterness. We are then introduced to Kay, as Diane Carter, fresh from her *fourth* divorce settlement from a rich oil millionaire, taking a sentimental journey back home. When she is reintroduced at a party to an old flame (Cabot) it seems her "endless search for something that never happened" has arrived. She's made a fortune being unfortunate in love, and now she wants to share it with Cabot in what she cozily refers to as a "mutual advisory committee." Cabot's wife, Helen Mack, gets Kay's drift after she finds out that Kay was known as "Typhoid Annie," way back when, and gave all the local boys "love fever." Kay is very much like Maida, her character from *In Name Only*. She manipulates situations right and left, giving Cabot's boys presents and reassuring Helen Mack that her interest in Cabot is strictly business. "You know what I want, and I know what you *don't* want," she cunningly reassures Mack.

Cabot walks out of his marriage, but it isn't long before he opts for respectability. The film ends with Cabot's children holding a court-martial in their home for their dad, claiming he deserted them in the face of duty and would have to leave home "unless mummy forgives you." Hokey stuff, excruciatingly painful to watch. We last see Kay leaving town, back on the train, being asked by the porter if she had changed any during her stay. "Yes, I have," she answers solemnly, "and I don't think I'm going to like it very much." Needless to say, the Breen Office gave the film its seal of purity when released in August 1945. *Variety* dismissed *Divorce*, saying, "A lackluster script grooves it for the duals. Miss Francis and Miss Mack turn in creditable performances, but Cabot appears to have lost his usual spark." Finding charismatic leading men was a problem from the outset and had delayed production. "Did you ever try to hire a leading man?" producer Kay asked reporter Frederick Othman. "They're scarcer than pearls," she groaned. "*And*, more costly."[8] The lackluster Bruce Cabot had to do. On the upside, *Film Daily* painted good prospects for *Divorce*, saying, "Here is an excellent exploitation offering, and Kay Francis scores on two counts—first as co-star and secondly as co-producer…William Nigh contributed effective, sympathetic direction." Sidney Skolsky wagged when the film was released, "Odd, but Kay Francis' picture *Divorce* is doing its best business in Reno."[9] *Divorce* was still making profits for Monogram when it was re-released in 1950.

Kay had her *own* divorce in the works during 1945. Her diaries confirm that she had conferred in July 1944 with Walter Van Pelt regarding a divorce. The *following* July, after finishing *Allotment Wives*, she headed for Las Vegas, staying at the El Rancho. On July 12 Kay had written: "Miss P. and I off to Vegas. Lord help us!"[10] She spiked the rumors of divorce proceedings by saying, "You have to be married first before you can get a divorce. I am here just to bask in the good old Nevada sunlight and enjoy a much needed rest."[11] The newspapers said she was there for an indefinite stay. Even more curious was the sudden reappearance, after 15 years, of her rumored husband, John Meehan. Out of the blue he showed up just before her departure to Vegas. Although unsubstantiated, it is likely the proceedings involved Kay's "non-marriage" to Meehan. Upon her death, court papers indicated Kay had been married and divorced four times, and mentioned Meehan, along with Dwight Francis and Bill Gaston.

During her Monogram production schedule Kay's personal love-life continued to run a very familiar course. She hadn't strayed far from the pattern she established as a young woman in New York. Still, it was a pattern that an intelligent woman such as Kay, ruefully acknowledged. Upon returning from Mexico in 1944, and her beaux weren't waiting with bated breath, she wrote, "No word from either Otto or Don! I guess that is just life!"[12] The men Kay selected weren't exactly the type for a committed relationship, and the naturally independent Kay, "in love with love," seemed to avoid concentrating on one man for too long. If she did, they had to measure up. A short-lived reunion with Hugh Fenwick, in early 1944, proved disastrous. "Finally went to bed with him and Christ, that is the end!" Kay wrote, exasperated. "The worst ever! Goodbye!!!"[13] Not to worry. Bush pilot Don King, who had safely navigated Kay and troupe on their Arctic Tour, had also maneuvered into her heart. Kay rendezvoused with Don (who was an influential force for Northwest Airlines) in Seattle and points north, during his troubled

After filming Divorce *(1945), Kay's complex love-life had her headed for Las Vegas to get her own* fourth *divorce from her* third *husband! (Monogram)*

marriage to wife Ann. Kay recognized early on that their relationship would go nowhere. "Hell, why do I fall in love with the wrong guy?" she lamented, followed by, "God, I'm tired. And so blue and lonely for Don."[14] Not surprisingly, by the spring of 1945 Don was out of the picture. "Talked to Don…told him I never wanted to see him or hear from him again…guess the whole thing is over! Well, that's that!"[15] Although her roller-coaster relationships took their toll on her emotionally, Kay remained resilient. She was *more* focused on her work and, during World War II, her commitment to war-related service organizations. Her diary entries continued to be filled with radio appearances, speech-making, traveling, and lining up entertainers to visit the wounded.

In spite of her love-life, Kay was charged by her new role as producer and seemed to enjoy all the headaches that went along with it. In a news article from 1945, titled "Producing Not Easy, Says Kay," she commented,

Actors who want to be producers just haven't the faintest idea of the trials and tribulations of a person in that spot. Say you decide to make a picture. And that's where your trouble starts. You line up a story idea. After weeks of anguish, your writers turn in an acceptable script. Then you go into the business of casting the picture. That means more headaches—and I mean real ones as well as financial. You suddenly discover all the stars you need are tied up with major producers and you can't have them at any price—even if you had the price…The director you want is busy elsewhere. You wait a few more weeks. Then you start to shoot and the weather gets nasty…then some player catches cold…[16]

When asked why she simply didn't quit, Kay answered, "Well, you know what they say about newspaper work getting in your blood. I guess it's the same with being a producer."[17] Although Kay would stick through yet another production, she soon changed her mind and got a transfusion: the stage. While shooting at Monogram, Kay was approached by former Warners rival Ruth Chatterton to star in a play she was directing, *Windy Hill*. The first reading for the new romantic comedy by silent film star Patsy Ruth Miller took place in August 1945. Kay was aware that Miller and Chatterton were working on a play. "Kay had stopped over in New York several times," related Miller, "on her way to entertain the troops in Europe, India and China, and had sort of sat on the side lines, cheering. Then, came our momentous moment of casting. Who looked the part—could play it—and would fit in with our feminine, but not exclusively feminine group? With one accord, we said it together…Kay Francis!"[18]

Windy Hill premiered Monday, August 13, 1945, in Montclair, New Jersey. Co-starring with Kay was newcomer Judy Holliday as Lola La Paz. Holliday would go on to win an Oscar for *Born Yesterday* (1950). She didn't stay long with *Windy Hill*. The reviews found the play to be a disappointment. Opening night, all seats were sold out. *The Montclair Times* reported:

> It is our unpleasant duty to report that *Windy Hill*…is a disappointing piece that makes for a dull evening, despite the presence of Kay Francis and Roger Pryor in the leading roles, and the support of Judy Holliday…The story of free love that hits a snag…centered around a returned war correspondent and a veteran newspaper woman…isn't new or very exciting. Mr. Pryor as the correspondent is excellent and Miss Francis has seldom appeared to better advantage…Miss Holliday, we thought, was the shining light of the performance…A good deal of the fault of *Windy Hill* lies in overwriting. Quite definitely the current attraction is not the hit that was anticipated by the first night audience which filled the theatre to overflowing. [19]

Variety complimented Kay, saying, "Some very good casting and good direction spark the play much more than it deserves. Miss Francis, first time in legit in about 15 years and handicapped by a laryngitis attack, nevertheless handles her playwright assignment well. She looks very smart and attractive." Kay thought they gave a "lousy performance." Patsy, unable to face the music, left town.

Jetti Preminger, who was added later to the cast, became a lifelong friend of Kay's. Jetti had a success doing *Angel Street* on Broadway and also starred in an early televised version of the play in 1946. Her memories of *Windy Hill*, which reopened at New

Haven's Shubert Theatre in September 1945, are mostly fond and amusing:

> The play was rewritten every night, literally. It was a great experience
> for me. They would get together and rewrite until two or three in the morning
> and hand it to us at ten! It got to the point that Kay and I would "get the
> gales" over it, because we'd wonder, "Now, which version are we playing
> tonight?" It was never ready to come to New York. It got so involved that I
> couldn't even tell you the plot at this point. Kay said, "I will stay out on the
> road with it. Make the money out of it. Maybe you can get it to Broadway.
> But if we went in with it at this point it would only last one performance
> and they'd say, 'what is she doing coming to New York in this turkey?'
> Everybody out on the road loved Kay and they packed the houses.[20]

Kay's former husband, Bill Gaston, brought a party by to see the show in New
Haven. From there the play went to Philadelphia. But *Windy Hill* was in trouble. The
rewrites did take their toll on Kay's patience. Patsy Ruth Miller skipped town again and left
Kay and Ruth Chatterton on their own. Even Chatterton started missing performances.
Then, as a sort of *deus ex machina*, John Van Druten, playwright of such hits as *I Remem-
ber Mama* and *I Am a Camera*, appeared. After Van Druten volunteered his sage advice, an
exasperated Kay blew up! She released her pent up frustration by breaking four bottles of
Ballantine Scotch. Needless to say, it was a sobering experience for all those present.

After three weeks of ironing out the kinks in *Windy Hill*, the cast was expecting a
reasonably smooth performance when opening at the Ford Theatre in Baltimore. Donald
Kirkley, reviewer for the *Baltimore Sun*, found, "the whole thing out of touch with reality."
Kirkley went on to say: "This is all the more disappointing, because of the excellent perfor-

Kay with Roger Pryor in Windy Hill *(1945). Co-star Jetti Ames recalled, "Every house was sold out.
They were on their feet cheering Kay. They loved her. They didn't really care how good the play was."*

mance given by the star, who is as much at home on the stage as if she had never left it, and is obviously worthy of a more substantial vehicle....the play doesn't measure up to the high demands of the theater, and must depend upon the personal charm and drawing power of Miss Francis..."[21] Kay concurred with Kirkley and jotted into her diary, "Another Horror Opening!"[22] The reviews in Pittsburgh a couple weeks later were not an improvement. Even the props showed no respect. Roger Pryor tugged at a jammed door until the substantial-looking walls shook like the San Francisco quake. Out of desperation, he entered through what had been firmly established as a closet. "The audience yelped with delight. The cast broke up, and the curtain fell on pandemonium. A moment later it inexplicably rose to reveal the elegant Kay, arms akimbo, stamping her tiny foot and screaming, 'Damn this production!'"[23] *The Pittsburgh Post-Gazette* commented:

> *Windy Hill* is the one about the two broad-minded people who are going to be gay if it kills them. No ties, no promises, no nothing...Eat, drink and be merry now, for tomorrow love may slip out the window...Miss Miller adds very little to the subject. She does have a few chuckles, but she has no play...Miss Francis is good to look at, she wears some stunning outfits and plays the newspaper-woman-turned playwright with a breezy charm. As a matter of fact, one would never guess that she had been away from the stage for so long. There's one place *Windy Hill* should positively stay away from—Broadway. Seeing as how in the hinterlands the magic of Hollywood still casts a spell over the box-office, if the Misses Miller, Chatterton and Francis just content themselves with the road, maybe they'll all make a lousy fortune.[24]

While Kay, Ruth and Patsy were making their "lousy fortune," Jetti Preminger became discouraged with playing Lola La Paz (the part Judy Holliday originated). Kay's own frustrations with the play were peppered throughout her diary. January 27: "Leaving for Washington, D.C. Chatterton rehearsing on train and rewriting. Christ!"[25] February 7: "Blew up and threw new script away!"[26] When Jetti asked for Kay's counsel, she found Kay to be "very honest and astute." Kay encouraged her to return to New York and see about doing something else. "You will always be like me," Kay advised, "you can play roles at least ten years younger than what you are. So why do this? You've had a good experience here." Eileen Heckert came in to take Jetti's place on the road. Jetti had other memories of being on the road with Kay:

> Kay was such an honest, conscientious and supportive person. We were doing one-night stands. Week-long engagements to catch our breath. Lousy little dressing rooms. It was rough. Kay took it all in stride. Every house was sold out. They were on their feet cheering for her. They loved her. They didn't really care how good the play was. And it was amusing, but it never would have made it in New York. I was in *Windy Hill* about six months. Kay was packing them in on the road. We had fun doing it. It was wild. In Baltimore we broke up in the drunk scene...she'd never done that before and neither had I, but the audience just thought it was part of the scene. We were just about to go over the breaking line. We had laughs in there

that we never had before. Kay said, "We have to pull ourselves up by our bootstraps and not do *that* again." And I said, "That's right." Kay was really cooperative with everyone. However, she was very strict about behavior. Kay liked to drink as much as anybody else, but you don't drink before you go on the stage. And if anybody showed up and had had a couple of drinks, they were, to put it frankly, on her shit-list. She was extremely professional.

One fun experience was when we were in Washington, D.C. for a week. She knew Evalyn Walsh McLean who owned the Hope Diamond. Evalyn opened her house to servicemen frequently on Saturday nights and entertained them. She asked Kay if she would bring the cast over. Kay said, "sure we'd all love to." Evalyn would always get the Hope Diamond out and walk around letting everyone handle it—then she carefully tucked it away. It was a long night. After the big party we overslept, and Kay had to charter a plane for us to get to New York.[27]

Handling the Hope Diamond was a questionable activity for the cast of *Windy Hill*. It was famous for its curse. The most famous owner who lost her head over the Hope Diamond was Marie Antoinette. Evalyn's mother-in-law had warned her to send the diamond back "before it ruins us all!"[28] If there *was* a curse, it surely followed Kay and the company of *Windy Hill*. In Buffalo, New York, they were stranded during a blizzard. Jetti Preminger tells the story:

> We played Buffalo during a terrible snowstorm. After the performance, our train started to pull out of Buffalo way out into the yard and got stuck— it couldn't back up into the station, and it couldn't go forward. They weren't going to plow in the heavy storm so we *sat* there. People were freezing. They ran out of food. They ran out of coal for heat. Kay had her fur coat on. She got up and went through her trunks. Before long, she was handing out her clothes, a fur and another fur-lined raincoat to share with other cast members. When the food ran out, Kay calmly said, "Wel-l-l-l, I think we all need a drink to warm up." So we all sat and huddled together in Kay's coats and clothes and had drinks! It could have been a *very* unpleasant nightmare, but it turned out fine—we all survived in style thanks to Kay![29]

Apparently a carload of "Kay Francises" could handle the ominous curse of the Hope Diamond. Sadly, Evalyn McLean wasn't so fortunate. A few months later, Evalyn's only daughter died of a drug overdose at the age of 25. An admitted intermittent morphine addict herself, Evalyn never got over the tragedy and died a year later. The Hope Diamond and its curse have been housed in the Smithsonian Institute since 1958.

With or without a curse, *Windy Hill* never got the script to a point that could satisfy and completely jell. Mishaps kept plaguing the production. During *Windy Hill's* opening night in Philadelphia, Kay's pistol wouldn't go off. Chatterton wisely had a second pistol waiting in the wings. They were switched, but while aiming it at her leading man (Roger Pryor), the second pistol *also* refused to go off. Kay, gun in hand, remedied the situation by wrestling with Pryor. Suddenly the weapon exploded, quite unexpectedly, and *both* of them fell to the floor. *Windy Hill* folded in Chicago in May

1946. Kay told the *New York World-Telegram* her ordeal of touring every honky-tonk in America. "What a show," she said. "I swear I had ninety-seven sides…as big as the lead in *Strange Interlude*…we kept revising…It was like doing a new play every night. But it was fun, good trouping. I really enjoyed it. I must say, though, it was a relief to get into Chicago. We played there three months, and it seemed like a vacation."[30]

Kay experienced a profound insight about "life on stage" during the run of *Windy Hill*. She was having a rough time in Milwaukee. Reporter Dick Terry caught Kay in a reflective mood, and he inquired about her return to the stage, live audiences, and the barbs of critics.

> It's interesting to be back; I like it. But I've been spoiled by G.I. audiences. They're the greatest audiences in the world. When you play to them, you just can't do anything wrong. If I had my choice now, I'd be in Tokyo. They've got to keep up the USO tours—I'd like for you to be sure and put this in your story—*because* there's nothing duller than monotony, and life for those boys overseas is going to be terribly monotonous now. The hospital work has to go on, too. You know people are letting up—they say the war's over now—but they've got to go on. Those guys have got to be taken care of.[31]

Kay missed the enthusiastic energy of the men in uniform and did what she could, while on tour, to continue with her work on behalf of the G.I.s. Aside from taking the cast of *Windy Hill* to Evalyn McLean's party to mix with servicemen, Kay and some of the cast members put on a show for the boys at Valley Forge on October 1945. Kay had also done an impressive job narrating *Warriors of Peace* for ABC on September 29. The dramatic program presented the history of the Women's Army Corps. (WACS). "Kay Francis scored as narrator on the *Warriors of Peace*," reported one columnist. "Hats were tipped to Kay for her excellent job."[32]

After the Chicago run of *Windy Hill*, Kay flew back to Hollywood to finish her last film at Monogram. "Being my own boss," Kay said, "my time is my own. I make a picture when I want to, or do a play when I want to. In the meantime, I'm usually busy catching up with myself."[33] And, the "Monogram Trilogy" kept getting better as it went along. Phil Karlson, director of Kay's third film, achieved a respectable place in the crime film genre. Among his best are *99 River Street* (1953, a brutally atmospheric *noir*), *The Phenix City Story* (1955, an advanced film for its time; bluntly pro-black), and his most controversial, commercial success, racking up $40 million at the box-office, *Walking Tall* (1973). In 1946, he was developing his technique for *film noir* with *Wife Wanted*. The film-exploiter told about a lonely-hearts club at Hollywood and Vine, used as a front for crime. The tagline read: "Here's the whole shocking story of so-called 'Friendship Clubs' that sell marriage, companionship and romance, but deliver shame and extortion!"

Kay had gathered former co-stars for the film: Paul Cavanagh, who played her husband in 1931's *Transgression,* and Veda Ann Borg, who was Kay's rival in 1937's *Confession.* Kay plays close to home as a career-slipping film star who is urged by her agent to dabble in real estate. A bit flustered by the dry spell in her career, at first Kay is hesitant. "Well," she relents prophetically, "if I don't have to give up pictures *entirely*!" (*Wife Wanted* would be Kay's last film.) She invests a hefty sum in partnership with

Cavanagh, only to discover she's been duped into a lonely-hearts "Friendship-club" racket as well. Karlson's gift for composition gives the film atmosphere and dark edges, as Kay is implicated in murder and coerced into participating in extortion. Kay catches on that she's been duped. Discouraged, she retreats to a bar. There's a cozy scene of her getting blotto and unable to confide in anyone. "Can't tell anybody," she blurts out to the bartender. "I'm like a pilot, way up high—the engine conks out and *he* forgot his parachute!" The bartender tells Kay she needs friendship. "I've got *too much* friendship," she says sourly. "I'm mixed up in a club *crawling* with friendship." She then clarifies, "Well…at least they're crawling." It's a convincingly played scene.

When Kay awakens in her apartment after her night of bingeing, she discovers a former acquaintance (Teala Loring) had come home with her! Lo and behold, the youthful Loring says she lost all her money in a friendship club. "Now I know what that old saying means," Kay muses. "Misery loves company." She cheers Teala up, while devising a plan to get them both back on track. Enter a reporter played by Robert Shayne. Shayne, a familiar face in Monogram Bs, was a testament to the dearth of available leading men at the time. In the film, he investigates the friendship club while pretending to be a sheep rancher out of Kanab, Utah, looking for a wife. (Hence, the insipid title.) It isn't long before Kay is reluctantly pulling the wool over sheepherder Shayne's eyes and unwittingly persuading him to invest in a fraudulent oil scam. While posturing as people they're not, they both manage to fall in love. In what is the most unintentionally frightening moment in *film noir*, we find Kay Francis contemplating a life on a sheep ranch…in Utah! She waxes philosophical to Shayne while they are out for a drive. "Why is life not arranged," she puzzles, "so that you can always be sure of things, others and especially ourselves?" After Shayne suggests it would eliminate the thrill of second-

Wife Wanted (1946) Kay played a fading film star in her swan song to Hollywood. Shown here with Paul Cavanagh. (Monogram)

guessing, Kay shrugs her sage shoulders. "I'll pull an old bromide," she answers. "I say live for today!" (Kay's own philosophy to the letter.) This "happy interlude" is soon forgotten when Kay is hit by a triple whammy. Loring disappears, Cavanagh is *behind* the disappearance, and Shayne gives her the heave-ho and a verbal thrashing. "On your way, sister!" he fumes, unexpectedly and *not* very convincingly.

Karlson's tight scenes climax when the menacing Cavanagh threatens Kay near a beach-house cliff. Suspense builds until Shayne expediently comes to Kay's rescue. At the fade-out, the inevitable apologies and excuses are made so the lovers can fall into each other's arms. The Francis-Shayne combination had little chemistry. But Kay, looking more mature, is dazzling in the nightclub scenes. She enters and exits bejeweled and wrapped in an amazing white fox fur. Karlson's inventiveness shows up at one nightspot where jazz pianist Edgar Hayes maneuvers through the crowd on a mobile piano!

One must admire Kay's ambition and courage to tackle producing and starring at Monogram. It was quite an undertaking, and her performances are always on target. And she *learned*. Film critic Robert Osborne summed it up when he said, "In her Monogram period, by the time she made *Allotment Wives*, Kay had obviously learned a lot about producing, because the stories were stronger, there's much more action, and the production values are also better."[34] Kay had obviously managed to loosen the co-producing grip on her purse strings. Jeffrey Bernerd enjoyed working with Kay, and in 1947 hoped to persuade her to take the feminine lead in an Allied Artists production of Maurice Sandos' mystery-horror story, *The Maze*. The offbeat fantasy, which takes place in a haunted castle, was to have been filmed in England. A 3-D version of the film finally materialized, without Kay, in 1953.

"If and when my career comes to a standstill," Kay had stated, "there are many ways to keep busy. Perhaps, I'm a fatalist. I sincerely believe what is to be will be, though I think we should keep alert for opportunity and take advantage of every chance it offers…it is foolish to sit by the roadside and expect the plums to drop into our lap." When none of the other studios were asking for Kay's services, an unexpected "plum" dropped. During her peak years at Warners Kay had predicted, "When I finish in pictures, whether it be five years or ten years, I'm going back to (the stage)—if it will have me. What I'm fearful of is that when Hollywood is through with me, I'll be unfitted for anything else." After she had been shooting for five days on the set of *Wife Wanted*, she received a call from producer Leland Hayward. He asked her to replace Ruth Hussey in the critically acclaimed success *State of the Union* on Broadway. For the first time in years, regarding a new project, Kay entered into her diary, "So excited!"

Chapter 19

State of the Union –
When "All Hell Broke Loose"

Aside from her popular run with *Windy Hill*, Kay acknowledged that it was the GIs overseas who were *directly* responsible for her return to the legitimate theater. "She frequently yearned to make another stage appearance," claimed one report, "but although the idea was enticing, the reality was terrifying...With understandable misgiving she faced the khaki-clad audiences and tried out her unfamiliar repertoire—and they loved her for it. Fortified by this experience she decided to risk a Broadway show once more."[1] The 1946 Pulitzer Prize-winning *State of the Union* proved a real boon to Kay's foundering career. The play's tour would also earmark one of the most traumatic experiences of her life.

State of the Union opened in November 1945, at one of the oldest legitimate stages on Broadway: The Hudson Theater. Intelligent and witty, the play contained the heated political argument, strategy and tactics surrounding a presidential campaign. In other words, it was a comedy. Ralph Bellamy played Grant Mathews, a wealthy industrialist who is running as the Republican nominee for President. The party machine starts worrying when Mathews speaks his own mind. Ruth Hussey left the play in September 1946, and Kay Francis took over the part of Mathews' estranged wife Mary. In many respects, Mary is the play's catalyst. She is not shy with her opinions regarding corrupt politics and disapproves of her husband's inclination to sell out to special interest groups. Mary's influence on Grant is evident when he begins to speak out more boldly. By the play's climax, she has helped transform her husband into his "real self" just before he is about to deliver a hoped for winning speech before the presidential election.

On July 2, 1946, *The New York Times* reported, "Eighteen years is too long for any player to leave Broadway in the lurch. Nevertheless, Kay Francis managed to do it quite well. But sooner or later along comes that tempting offer, which no one can afford to dismiss. On September 2, Miss Francis will align herself with *State of the Union*, a hit of the first magnitude despite the humidity..."[2] An eighteen-year absence required a period of adjustment. The demands of the theatre challenged Kay, but the warmth of an appreciative, live audience boosted her morale. Jetti Preminger Ames, who had acted with Kay in *Windy Hill*, recalled, "She was nervous. We all are. But she felt confident that she could do it. And, of course, she looked beautiful. She and Bellamy worked very well together."[3] Leland Hayward had been trying to get

275

Kay to replace Ruth Hussey since January. Before her Labor Day debut, the *New York World-Telegram* reported:

> She says she's frightened to death. She also says: "You don't get any younger," which is nonsense on both counts. A trouper like Kay will come through with, as the Scots say, "sporrans flappin." And as for not getting any younger—she gets younger and prettier. Miss Francis says she got a lucky break with *State of the Union*. A number of times she was offered the role in the play…but each time she had other commitments. Leland Hayward phoned her, "This is the fourth time we asked you to come in with us, how about it?" And this time Miss Francis was ready, and willing. It is considered one of the most coveted roles on Broadway. [4]

If Kay truly was "frightened to death" about returning to the stage, she must have found the antidote. Before her debut she appeared on WOR radio's *Exploring the Unknown*, in a program titled "How Not to Worry." As it turned out, part of Kay's cure for stage fright was taking her mind off of herself. Jetti Preminger Ames had agreed to cue Kay for her lines in *State of the Union* before the crucial opening. On a Saturday, Kay arrived in Clinton, New Jersey, where Jetti was wrapping up a stage role of her own. The plan was that Jetti would help Kay with lines during that week. It never happened. The frantic Jetti announced to Kay that a lead role in *The Male Animal* had just been dropped in her lap, because another actress had marched out of the production. "This is Saturday night, and we open Tuesday!" cried Jetti. It was after midnight when Kay cut through the small talk and said, "Stop talking about it! Get to work!" Instead of Kay preparing for her return to Broadway, she focused on helping Jetti get through the impossible. "Kay started pounding the part into my head," recalled Jetti. "This was no time for method acting…it was just a time to get lines. At 4 a.m. she said, 'Okay, it's time to stop because you're going to have a rehearsal at 9 a.m.' If it hadn't been for her I never would have made it. She came and sat out front that morning during rehearsals and took all the notes on it. We went off and worked and came back…it was just work, work, work. I had no idea who I was or what I was doing when I went on that Tuesday night, but I got all the lines out. The audience loved it. The audience never knew. I would have never been able to have done it without Kay. *Never*. She was very considerate."[5] Kay managed her lines for *State of the Union* on her own while rehearsing with the understudies. She fit right in with the seasoned cast, "sporrans flappin." "Asking for the understudies was my own idea," Kay told a reporter. "Ordinarily, you start working with only the stage manager, who reads the other parts. But you don't get much of the real feeling of the scenes that way, so I thought it would break me in a little better if I had other people to play with."[6]

State of the Union was a collaboration of two of the theatre's best craftsmen: Howard Lindsay and Russel Crouse. Previously, the duo had tremendous success with *Life With Father* and *Arsenic and Old Lace*. Originally titled "I'd Rather Be Left," *State of the Union* was a rare experience in the theatre—it was purposely in a state of perpetual evolution. A play about the political scene had to stay fresh. After all, during the play's run the nation was all a-tremble with thoughts of atomic weapons, Communists under the beds and Truman initiating a decades-long Cold War. The play kept abreast with the times by changing a few lines on a weekly basis to reflect what was happening in the news. After Winston Churchill's two weeks of speech-making in the U.S., wherein he introduced the term "Iron Curtain," he decided to see *State of the Union* on Broadway. In his autobiography, Ralph Bellamy remembered, "The theater was surrounded by Scotland Yard, the FBI, and the New York Police. I had the job to find a line that was topical and different each night. But with Churchill in the audience the line should have some reference to him, not too politically slanted, and in good taste."[7] In a scene where the Grant Mathews character began showing signs of duress, Bellamy reads the newspaper in a mock-tone voice to his wife. "Listen, Mary!" he exclaimed. "'After two strenuous weeks, Churchill *relaxes* in New York *seeing plays!*'" "I understand he loved it," wrote Bellamy. "I know the audience did."[8] The popular appeal of the play can be summed up in

Kay made a successful comeback on Broadway in the Pulitzer Prize-winning play, State of the Union *(1946) with Ralph Bellamy.*

the prologue's curtain line. After a heated emotional argument regarding the difference between the two parties, the caucus leader declares, "The only difference between the two parties is, they're in and we're out!" Bellamy makes no mention of Kay in his memoir. She shouldn't feel slighted. He completely omits the existence of his wife at the time, musician Ethel Smith. Smith was a petite blonde, famous for her organ rendition of "Tico-Tico." During the run of *State of the Union* Bellamy walked out on her. Smith charged abandonment and said Bellamy drank heavily, was moody, and became jealous when she received all the attention at their parties.

Kay's reviews for playing Mary Mathews were enthusiastic. Soon after her debut, Vernon Rice reported, "We've seen it with our own eyes—Kay Francis' performance in *State of the Union* at the Hudson—and it's good!" Rice was impressed with Kay's long speech in the third act. She speaks her mind, thereby speaking the minds of so many audience members. In the scenes where it appears Kay doesn't have much to say, the audience *felt* her reactions to the machinations of the political opportunists. She wasn't being fooled. Rice commented,

> Miss Francis not only [takes] that third act climax in her stride, but she wasn't thrown by those silent scenes. We liked her especially in the hotel scene in the second act during the time…the political manipulator, was trying to worm out of Ralph Bellamy…the subject matter of [his] speech. A bird dog scenting his prey couldn't have been more alert nor more silent. We liked, too, the marital relationship she and Bellamy established. Though the Matthews' marriage…has slipped from its firm foundation…Miss Francis and Mr. Bellamy make the audience feel that the old flame still burns…

Kay Francis can still wear clothes. She's handsome in her first act gray suit, lovely in a canary yellow crepe robe and night dress, striking in her second act green traveling suit, sensational in her black dinner dress and a DUR-EAM in her third act white crepe with sequins evening dress. If Miss Francis still maintains her fan club, now that she has returned to the theatre, we should like to submit our name for membership.[9]

In early December 1946, Kay left her successful debut in *State of the Union* and quietly returned to Los Angeles for an operation. She told Louella Parsons, "I hated to leave the show. We're such a happy group, but I was simply too sick to go on."[10] Kay had recuperated enough by Christmas to join in the festivities at director Lewis Milestone's Christmas party. In January 1947, after her return to New York, *State of the Union* earmarked its 500th performance with a photo of Kay and Bellamy in *The New York Times*. Kay had also resumed her new romance with the stage manager. Even before her rehearsals began for *State of the Union* Kay found herself taking a shine to Howard "Hap" Graham. Thirty-six-year-old Graham, who was also cast as the Bellboy in the production, was briefly mentioned in the program notes as, "Howard Graham (Bellboy)...director at the Pasadena Playhouse in California these past three years...was on the faculties of City College and Northwestern University."[11] The Francis-Graham romance intensified while he guided Kay with her blocking and stage moves. "Happy," as Kay liked to call him, began joining her for tea, dinner and drinks after the show. After several months, the relationship turned out to be a typical attachment for Kay and her diary entries began to change their tune. After seeing Broadway's *Finian's Rainbow*, Kay and Hap came home for what she called a "knockout fight." They didn't see one another during June, but Kay finally decided she wanted Hap's company on her upcoming *State of the Union* road tour.

On stage with Minor Watson and Ralph Bellamy, in State of the Union *(1946). The play ran for 765 performances.*

It was reported in January 1947 that Kay's former lover Ivan Goff, and his writing-partner Ben Roberts, were putting "finishing touches to a six-character comedy called *My Fair Lady*...with Kay Francis in mind."[12] A few days later Kay helped sponsor a memorial tribute at the Riverside Church in New York City for her friend, opera singer Grace Moore. More than 5,000 paid tribute to the diva who had lost her life in a tragic airplane crash in Copenhagen. In March 1947, Kay received another perk from her return to the stage. She was selected one of the "best dressed" women of 1947. The New York Fashion Academy's eighteenth annual poll honored Kay at a luncheon in the Waldorf-Astoria Hotel. *The New York Times* mentioned: "Thirteen gold medals were awarded in as many categories...winners...were chosen for 'their ability to wear clothes and for their selection of same in keeping with one's individual budget.' Classifications and winners are: Stage, Kay Francis...society, Doris Duke...opera, Rise Stevens...Miss Francis last was chosen in 1936 as winner in the screen category."[13] Kay was still indifferent about being a best-dressed woman. "Oh phoo! that stuff," she said, completely disinterested, to one interviewer and went back to her combination turkey and cheese sandwich.[14] She told another reporter that the war and the fact she was in uniform so long had just about destroyed her interest in clothes. "When you see fine young men lying on hospital beds with their legs missing," Kay cried, "how can you make yourself *believe* a wardrobe is important!"[15] Kay placed *more* relevance on the Damon Runyon Cancer Fund and the Sioux Falls TB Fund, making appearances at both during 1947.

When Kay, Bellamy, and company closed at the Hudson in September 1947, the total number of performances reached 765. It was announced Kay would head the company on tour beginning in Wilmington. K. Elmo Lowe took over the role for Ralph Bellamy and, according to one reviewer, was consistently impressive in the part of Grant Mathews. Lowe later became the director of the Cleveland Playhouse and Joel Grey credits him as his role model and the man who put him in the theatre. Kay, co-star Lowe, and the road company would tour more than fifty cities in the east and midwest. From New Orleans to Kalamazoo, the play was a box-office bonanza. As ticket sales soared, Kay's screen reputation preceded her. When *State of the Union* reached Harrisburg, Pennsylvania, the mayor's *wife* let everyone know who was running things by presenting Kay with the key to the city. Harrisburg's *The Patriot* gave Kay excellent notices saying, "Kay Francis...was superb as the wife...Her voice had richness and perfect control. Her acting was of the best and yet she

In 1947-48 Kay toured in State of the Union. *New York's Fashion Academy honored Kay in 1947, as the "Best Dressed Woman on the American Stage."*

was able to release her control of the scene when others were being featured."[16] While Kay played for two nights in her birthplace, the *Daily Oklahoman* commented that, "Her vitality certainly carries the comedy along at a fast clip and her years of experience on the stage and before the cameras are reflected in her stage presence and ability to get everything out of the clever Lindsay and Crouse dialogue." [17]

In December 1947, Kay's arrival in New Orleans made front page news. *The Times-Picayune* headlined, "Actress Happy to Revisit State," with a photo of Kay from *State of the Union*. Kay had been delayed after a two-passenger train collision. Physically drained from the ordeal, she kindly told reporters she "was happy to be back in Louisiana." She recalled her 1930 visit with Katty Stewart, when she took a trip by pirogue (Cajun flatboat) through the bayous near New Iberia. "That trip was one of the most beautiful I've ever been on," she raved. "I only wish I had time to take another. But then I'm so exhausted, I wonder if I can do anything *again*."[18] She did. Kay and the cast received standing ovations that evening at the Poche Theatre. Critic Albert Goldstein found the production to be a rare offering for New Orleans. "It is adult fare, quiet satire," he wrote. "Kay Francis, the star, is quite convincing…the supporting cast…give an excellent account of themselves…The machinations of politics—are so realistically portrayed that, but for the strong overtones of comedy, it might become unnerving."[19]

Although Hap Graham was accompanying Kay on tour, their relationship wasn't going anywhere. In October, Kay's diary makes mention of a warrant for Hap's arrest. After New Orleans, Kay found Hap "out of order," "terrible," and she was always on guard for another fight. In Evansville, she wrote, "Hap up for Brunch and told him I just couldn't take it anymore."[20] Although she felt the affair was ruined, on New Year's, 1948, she wrote, "All happy on the Francis Front."[21] On her forty-third birthday she received flowers from Jetti and candy from Hap. Also, on the plus side, business and

Kay and K. Elmo Lowe toured in State of the Union. *(Courtesy of Mike Rinella)*

audience appreciation were great and these carried her emotionally. In Illinois they played to an auditorium filled to capacity: 6,200 people. Five months into the tour Kay's name was *the* drawing ticket. But, when they reached Columbus on January 22, 1948, to put it in Kay's words, "All hell broke loose."[22] The headlines about Kay in the newspapers the following day leaned toward the sensational. Hap was being held on assault to kill. His victim? Kay. While she laid unconscious in the hospital for five hours, the newshounds had a field day. What had begun as a usual routine, after the show, ended up being a real tragedy for Kay, with lasting repercussions. When *The New York Times* printed the story, her situation had somewhat stabilized. The article read:

KAY FRANCIS IS ILL; MANAGER HELD, FREED

Kay Francis, star of the stage play "State of the Union," became seriously ill from an overdose of sleeping pills today, and police detained her stage manager for five hours while they investigated. Howard Graham, 37, the stage manager, was released after the 43-year-old actress regained consciousness and confirmed Mr. Graham's story of what caused her illness. He had been booked for "investigation of assault to kill." Police took Mr. Graham into custody at White Cross Hospital, to which Miss Francis was removed about 7 A.M., when they found she had second degree burns on her legs. Mr. Graham had reported that he left Miss Francis about 2:30 A.M. and was called to her hotel room about 6:30 A.M.; that she fainted and she burned her legs on a radiator when he took her to a window in an effort to revive her. He summoned a physician. Jay S. Teele, assistant chief of detectives, announced Mr. Graham's release at 3:15 P.M. and said: "The detectives talked to her and she said she had been nervous and couldn't sleep. She had been taking these pills so she took more than she thought she was taking." Miss Francis remained in serious condition. After her stomach had been emptied with a stomach pump, her condition was reported as improved. Dr. Maurice B. Rusoff, her physician, reported "her condition is serious but not critical. She is suffering from an upper respiratory infection. I believe she will live."[23]

A follow-up story confirmed that Kay was slowly recuperating from a severe cold and an overdose of sleeping pills. Visitors were barred, because she was just out of the oxygen tent. What exactly had taken place, one can't be sure. The incident had more overtones of an unfortunate accident than foul play. Kay's diary capsulated the episode saying,

January 22 – Too many pills
January 23 – *Out*—and almost out for good! White Cross Hospital at
7. Ambulance. Dr. Roussoff. Hap in jail 5 hours. Under charge!!
January 24 – Face burned and legs.
January 26 – Newspapers very obnoxious. Feeling better
January 27 – Legs not so good[24]

Kay had been suffering from a cold. After the evening's performance, the first thing she did was to order soup from the hotel's room service and have it placed atop the radiator to keep the soup hot. She and Hap went through their usual routine of having drinks in her dressing room and then headed for the hotel. After Hap left about 2:30 a.m., Kay took some sleeping pills and before dozing off she panicked. She had forgotten about the pills she had taken in her dressing room back at the theater. She frantically called Hap who immediately called Kay's doctor. The doctor prescribed cold air and hot coffee until he could get there. While Hap gave her hot coffee, he accidentally scalded her neck. When she started to faint, he became aware that the radiator was burning her legs. Jetti Preminger Ames recalled the incident and the long ordeal of Kay's recovery: "She suffered third degree burns. They did the worst thing. They gave her the wrong treatment. They put grease all over the burns, which aggravated the whole situation. She had a terrible time. After all the publicity they finally took her out of the hospital, just like in the movies, on a gurney and covered her up like a dead body. An acquaintance of Kay's [Louis Bromfield] arranged to come and get her at the back entrance and take her to his home nearby. She called us telling us where she was. She didn't want the press following her."[25]

While Kay waited for arrangements to be made for further treatment, she retreated from the stress, headlines and humiliation, to a place that was dear to her—her friend Louis Bromfield's Malabar Farm. Located in the rolling countryside of Richland County, Ohio, Bromfield had built a thirty-two-room country home where friends and family could find sanctuary. Kay had visited Malabar several times, and especially liked the activities associated with farm life. Bromfield's credo was, "Them that works, eats." On one of Kay's favorite visits, she had helped with the birth of a calf in the Bromfield barn. She enjoyed listening to Bromfield share his ideas about the unstable, rootless rush of American life. Bromfield's daughter, Ellen, kept diaries with anecdotes about the famous visitors and remembered, "It was not unusual to find Kay Francis disguised in a Greta Garbo get-up, complete with high-collared greatcoat, dark glasses and cigarette holder, stirring apple butter in a caldron at arm's length with a wooden hoe. This Endor-like performance, also on the front lawn, attracted—even way out in the country—more excited spectators than summer carnival."[26]

In contrast to her previous visits, *this time* Kay simply needed renewal. However, the tranquility of the snow-laden woodlands couldn't compensate for the fact that putting off further treatment would complicate her condition. Jetti Ames remembers that Kay contacted her from Bromfield's and asked her to meet her at the train in New York. From there, Kay was rushed to New York's Cornell Medical Center. Treatments were tedious and the pain, horrendous. But Kay was a trouper in more ways than one. She never complained, remained stoic throughout a two-month ordeal. She won the admiration, the friendship and respect of the hospital staff. Jetti recalled, "She was there two months, with both legs up in the air, having skin grafts. Awful. Just awful. She had a rough time, but she pulled through. She was a gutsy person. The business with the legs really did her in. She was in pain a lot of the time."[27]

Kay may have exonerated Hap, but the incident put a definite end to their relationship. While in the hospital, Kay wrote, "Told Hap to go home—arguments—with several drinks—I will not put up with it. Tears at midnight."[28] Hap soon disappeared from the scene completely. After two months in traction, six operations and setbacks from contaminated dressings, Kay was more than ready to be released. She could have easily left all thoughts of her stage career behind and enjoyed some relaxation with an

Kay seen nightclubbing in 1941 with her friend and mentor, author Louis Bromfield. After her accident in 1948, Bromfield rescued Kay from what she called "obnoxious" news headlines.

early retirement. She had the resources to do so. She was a millionaire. But as the skin grafts began to heal and mend, Kay's desire to return to the stage quickened. She made the decision to leave Hollywood completely behind her and set up residence in New York. Kay relocated her life and her belongings to a brownstone apartment at 31 East 61st St. The building was also home to dress designer Oleg Cassini and his actress-wife Gene Tierney.

Once she was settled in, Kay was ready for her next play. And, as a matter of course, her next beau made his usual miraculous appearance. On April 14 she interviewed Joel Ashley, fresh from Mae West's Broadway hit *Catherine Was Great,* for her new leading man. After a few months on the road, her new twenty-nine-year-old leading man, became her main man. And, for the first time since 1922, Kay became lax with her diary. There were no entries from June 14 through December 12, 1948. Just before Christmas she wrote, "Rehearsal and Joel spending night with me."[29]

In June 1948, Kay was rehearsed and ready with an old crowd pleaser for her summer stock debut. Frederick Lonsdale's *The Last of Mrs. Cheyney* had been a popular attraction on the summer circuits. In 1925, Ina Claire had sparkled on Broadway for 385 performances in the sophisticated, amusing romp about a jewel thief in high society. Norma Shearer had successfully brought it to the screen in 1929 and Joan Crawford, completely out of her element, literally stomped on all the *bon mots* in a dreadful 1937 remake. Kay was perfect for the mysterious, fascinating adventuress Mrs. Cheyney, whom men were enamored with and women found perfectly charming. As she engagingly finagles an invitation and opportunity to steal pearls at the estate of Mrs. Webley, she realizes that she actually *likes* these people and confesses to her motives. Joel Ashley, as Lord Dilling, played opposite Kay. His dark hair, moustache and handsome Southern charms were a good match for her. Together, they successfully tossed off Lonsdale's witty repartee, as when Kay tells her suitor Lord Dilling, "I don't care to be alone with you, even on a telephone!" Dilling's persistence, however, wins her over, and by the play's end, with one kiss, he establishes the last of Mrs. Cheyney and the beginning of Lady Dilling. Audiences responded favorably to the sparks of attraction between Kay and Joel. They teamed up for more plays on the summer stock circuit over the next few years.

By July 1948, *The Last of Mrs. Cheyney* was touring Massachusetts. The review in the *Fitchburg Sentinel*, felt the production "failed to give the star an opportunity to demonstrate her dramatic ability...the scene before final curtain, during which her voice was choked with emotion and her eyes were filled with tears made the spectator wish that she had attempted a straight dramatic role. Her wardrobe gave an inkling as to why she is still considered among the first 10 of the world's best-dressed women."[30] Elliot Norton, for the *Boston Post,* interviewed Kay and described her as "a trim, cool figure in slacks, her hair jet black and rather full cut." After he commented on her sunglasses, Kay took them off, explaining, "My eyes were burned by an arc light years ago, when I was first in pictures. Because of that, they water easily. I cry at the flash of a light. They found that out in Hollywood. They've never had to spray stuff in my eyes to make me cry. They just had to show me a strong light. So they took advantage of it. I cried in every picture for years...I was forever drifting through pictures, trailing furs and jewels-and crying. I was crying for the child I lost, or the man I lost. There were always tears. It got so my pictures were all the same."[31] Kay seemed amused while philosophizing about her career. Norton pointed out, "Miss Francis has made a favorable impression on her co-workers, not only actors, but also the minor people. Night before last, they had beach party...in which she behaved, they said, not like a Hollywood luminary, demanding attention, but pitching in for fun like everyone else. 'She isn't spoiled,' one of her associates said. 'She is easy to get along with. She even jokes about her age. She was born in Oklahoma, and she brags about it.' In fact, she keeps telling everyone for a joke: 'Remember, I was born in Oklahoma before it became a state.'"[32] Kay's unexpected camaraderie with her theatrical crews and co-workers would gain official recognition a few years later.

Before Kay tackled the "grind" of another tour, she appeared at Madison Square Garden along with Marlene Dietrich, Duke Ellington, and many other entertainers. The 15th annual event, titled "Night of Stars," was said to represent more than a million dollars' worth of talent. Traditionally, it was a fund raiser for disabled veterans. This 15th edition, netted more than $110,000 to aid refugees and Palestine resettlement. Also, making headlines in the fall of 1948, was a man from Kay's past. From Bridgeport, Connecticut, it was reported: "William Gaston of New Canaan, a former husband of Movie Star Kay Francis, won the unanimous Democratic nomination for Congress from the Fourth District."[33] Gaston's family, and that of his opponent, John Davis Lodge, had been political rivals since 1875. Gaston was anxious for "revenge," and predicted he would get it. He didn't. He lost the election. Gaston had visited Kay earlier in the year during her hospital stay and was one of the first visitors she had once she returned home for recovery.

By the end of the year, Kay was making a prediction of her own—a much hoped-for return to Broadway. She and Joel Ashley decided to try out a new three-act comedy. *Favorite Stranger*, directed by Leon Michel, was a first play effort by Eleanore Sellars. Set in New York, Kay played Chalice Chadwick, whose husband is overseas on a mission for the State Department. He's been gone too long. When Kay becomes depressed, a doctor (Ashley) suggests she needs male companionship. Dr. Ashley helps her pick up a naval commander and just when she finds herself with a blossoming love affair on her hands, her husband returns. When the play opened Christmas Day in Elmira, New York, most reviews found the proceedings not especially original. The publicity for *Favorite Stranger* promised that Kay's fans would have an opportunity to see her wear high fashion once again. High fashion wasn't enough.

When the play opened in Cleveland, *The Cleveland Plain Dealer* commented, "The play offers some amusing moments, but…[is] lacking in the electric quality necessary to success in the theater. Kay Francis has that quality and she may have enough of it to propel the play where the road is hospitable and wide."[34] Although the reviews were so-so, the box-office proved hospitable to *Favorite Stranger* wherever Kay toured. When they played New Orleans *The Times-Picayune* thought the play worth seeing, calling it a "good, sharp modern play," and added, "The quartet of professionally accomplished actors deftly handle it and really seemed to squeeze a bit more entertainment out of it than it actually contained…Miss Francis…does her part with lots of charm, an easy professional stage presence and a very personable smile…The play can stand some polishing and trimming, before being thrown to the New York wolves."[35]

The wolves never got the chance to howl. The final performance of *Favorite Stranger* was in April 1949, at the Nixon Theatre in Pittsburgh. Reviews for the play had continued to

In early 1949 Kay toured with Joel Ashley in the comedy Favorite Stranger. *Mixed reviews didn't deter "standing room only" crowds. (Courtesy of Mike Rinella)*

sour. Harold V. Cohen, for the *Pittsburgh Post-Gazette,* spit out the play's dismal epitaph, titled "Something From the Barrel's Bottom." "There is simply no excuse for plays like this," snorted Cohen. "Putting *Favorite Stranger* on a stage, and opening doors to the public, should come under the heading of crimes against mankind...how does such a turkey ever happen to see the light of day in the first place? ... Miss Francis has been around long enough to judge a script by more than just the number of sides there are in it for her, and Mr. Jules Leventhal, the producer, is an old and accomplished hand at feeling the pulse of the road...Miss Francis and Leventhal are not infallible. They have made mistakes before, but seldom a whopper of this size."[36] Cohen did admit that Sellar's "still-born comedy" followed some rather stiff competition: *A Streetcar Named Desire, Brigadoon, The Heiress, Harvey, Finian's Rainbow, Oklahoma* and *Born Yesterday.* To follow such blockbusters, Kay deserved a medal simply for having the intrepidity to walk across the Nixon stage.

Fortunately, fate prevented Kay from having to endure a repeat performance. She and Joel went to the Nixon Café after the show and began chatting with three men. Kay invited them over for drinks at her hotel room where they proceeded to beat up Joel! After they left, a stunned Kay and her new maid, Eunice Hawkins, tried to *doctor* poor Joel. The next morning Kay found him to be "a mess" and called in a professional. *Favorite Stranger* closed. Back in her New York apartment, Kay and a clobbered Joel had "quiet time." While she cooked for him, Kay listened to the radio and read. On April 21, she ventured out to attend Eunice's birthday party. The following day she met Jetti and Lou Ames at WPIX. (Lou was program director for the station and gave Barbara Walters her first job on TV.) The couple admired Kay very much and she could always rely on them. Jetti and Lou would remain constant in her life.

After Kay and Joel fully recovered from *Favorite Stranger*, they opened the season at the Bucks County Playhouse in New Hope, Pennsylvania. They co-starred in another "old chestnut," Rachel Crothers' *Let Us Be Gay.* A romantic comedy in a similar vein as *The Last of Mrs. Cheyney*, the play had debuted on Broadway in 1929. It opened in London the following year with Tallulah Bankhead, for whom Crothers had especially written the lead part. Again, Norma Shearer had another hit with the 1930 film version. As Kitty Brown, in *Let Us Be Gay*, Kay transforms herself into a radiant woman of the world after her husband leaves her. A few years later, she is reintroduced to her now ex-husband, Bob Brown (Ashley) at a social gathering on Long Island. Bob finds himself competing with a host of Kitty's male admirers. As for the title? When Bob gets too serious pursuing Kitty, she rebuffs him with the line, "Oh Bob! Let us be gay!"

As a play, *Let Us Be Gay* had truly run out of steam. But, audiences overlooked the dated material and concentrated on the talent and glamour of Kay Francis. Producer Harold J. Kennedy wisely dropped off the play's original prologue, showing Kitty as an unprepossessing housewife. When the play hit the Astor Theater in Hartford, Connecticut, it followed a revival of the 1928 MacArthur-Hecht play *The Front Page.* The *Hartford Courant* commented:

> Compared to the rowdy hokum of Charles MacArthur and Ben Hecht, Rachel Crothers's moralistic little comedy cannot help seeming a bit pale. But for the most part, the [players] are making a pleasant, reminiscent evening

out of it. Once again, they have secured an estimable star, in the svelte and sultry-voiced Kay Francis…Miss Francis is giving a good, polished performance as wifehood on the loose. She is lending her throaty humors to what Miss Crothers wanted to be the play's gayety, and she underscores the moral with fine, resonant emphasis. Add to that the things she can do to a snug black dress, even though she does sit down rather tenderly in it.[37]

It's interesting to note the reviewers mention of Kay's caution when sitting. One of the reasons she had selected the lighter vehicles to begin with was because they allowed her to wear the necessary long gowns that hid the heavy support stockings and long girdle-like garments that reinforced her damaged

Publicity shot for Let Us Be Gay *and* Favorite Stranger.

muscles and skin grafts. Such roles also allowed her to sit frequently, as standing up for long periods proved trying for her. Glowing praises for her performances followed her to Georgia, where *The Atlanta Constitution* cheered, "Miss Francis set the stage for the play with her performance…She had the audience on the top of their seats with her every line, her every move."[38] After the run of *Let Us Be Gay*, Kay decided to change venue and look for a more dramatic piece for her next theatrical outing.

A few years later Bette Davis turned up at one of Kay's dramatic performances (an adaptation of Maugham's *Theatre)* in Ogonquit, Maine. Afterwards, Bette and Kay went out for drinks to compare notes on their ill treatment at Warner Brothers. The harassment they experienced when the studio no longer wanted them was the focus of the conversation. Davis talked about the degradation she felt in doing her last picture at the studio, *Beyond the Forest.* (It hung like an albatross around her neck, even though it contained one of her most famous lines, "What a dump!") Francis confessed to her humiliation when Jack Warner tried to break her high-paying contract. When Davis inquired why Kay put up with it, Kay was straightforward with her. "I didn't give a damn. I wanted the money." The news took Davis by surprise. She told Kay, "I didn't. I wanted the career."[39]

One is tempted to compare notes on the two actresses' responses. Kay certainly had an interest in her career. After leaving Warners in 1938 she starred in fourteen more pictures, three of which she co-produced. Kay made many radio appearances. She toured extensively entertaining the troops during World War II. After a successful return to the theatre, she did another nine plays. She survived a debilitating accident, and continued to tour the country, always looking for new challenges and material. She added numerous television appearances to her credits. *And*, Kay liked the money. When physical limitations proved too taxing, she retired. Davis, on the other hand, always had to be doing something until the bitter end. Granted, like Kay, she had her share of flops. For every *All About Eve* there were several *Dead Ringers* and *Bunny O'Hares* (in which she was put through all kinds of indignities). In 1962, when no roles were forthcoming, Davis made what many considered a major blunder and put an ad in the Hollywood trade papers: "Mother of three...actress in motion pictures...wants steady employment in Hollywood..."[40] Davis continued accepting roles even after a debilitating stroke. She may have had more drive, but Davis wasn't always running on premium gasoline. Kay eventually made a transition that Davis simply would never consider and could *never* face. She quit.

Chapter 20

"Most Cooperative Actress" –
Along the Straw Hat Trail

During the years of Kay's popular and financially successful tours, she continued with the goodwill she had generated in her studio days. She spontaneously gave $5,000 to Ruth Chatterton, whose high-living depleted her earnings. Chatterton was performing in summer stock, with much less fanfare. When someone mentioned to Kay that a friend's summer theater was on the verge of going broke, she readily contacted him to appear in a production and, "secretly returned her salary."[1] Although incidents such as these were never acknowledged publicly, Kay's diligence, hard-work and cooperative spirit with cast and crew members, did *not* go unnoticed. Theater managers welcomed her back time and again. The theatre community would pull together and pay her homage.

On tour Kay Francis played to packed houses. During the first twenty-three weeks of their 1949-50 season, Atlanta's Penthouse Theatre asked Kay to return due to her exceptional box office draw. The Penthouse featured the new concept of "Theatre-in-the-Round," which drama critic Paul Jones described as "A new living room type dramatic presentation, which approximates the comforts of television at home...Patrons sit in a prize-fight ring fashion in elevated stands...the theatre is only seven rows deep at any point and patrons in the first row could easily shake hands with actors during the play."[2] Kay braved this new theatrical turf as did Cesar Romero, who, after his performance at the Penthouse, told

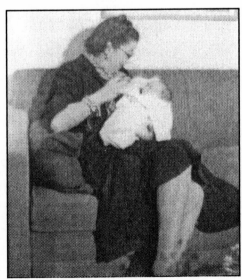

Kay, with her godson, Tabor Ames (January 1950). Tabor recalled, "When Kay entered a room...she kept your attention—and at the same time paid attention to you." (Courtesy of Tabor Ames)

reporters, "There were all those belligerent faces staring at me. They seemed to say, 'Come on, bud, entertain me; say something funny'...It's terribly frightening at first. But, then it's a thrill—there is no doubt about audience reaction here."[3]

While Kay considered a new project based on the writings of Thomas Wolfe, it was announced early in 1950 that she planned to appear for several weeks in Peggy Phillips' comedy, *Paper Moon*. Instead, Kay, Joel and Frank Albertson took the satirical comedy *Goodbye, My Fancy* out on the road for a mini-tour. Their production spent a month on New York's "subway circuit," playing in the Bronx, Brooklyn, and headlining the grand opening of the Strand Theatre in Rockville Center, Long Island. Madeleine Carroll had originally created the Congresswoman role in Fay Kanin's 1948-49 Broadway success. Ann Harding and Sylvia Sidney had already taken the play out on the summer circuit. In *Goodbye, My Fancy*, Kay finds herself in a romantic triangle upon returning to her *alma mater* (from which she had been expelled) to receive an honorary degree. On campus, she is confronted with an old flame, who is now the college president. He no longer shares her ideals. Her visit forces her to take a closer look at him. In the process the audience is encouraged to reexamine their own democratic values. Kay's tackling of the character Agatha Reed, an outspoken liberal, was a brave move, considering that the nation was in the heat of McCarthyism. When the play reached Somerset, the city's *Fall River Herald News* reported, "Miss Francis captured her audience with her dynamic personality and portrayal of congresswoman Agatha Reed. The part is ideally suited...giving her ample opportunity to display her talents as a comedienne and an emotional actress."[4] After Kay and Ashley's arrival at Norwich Summer Theatre, *The Hartford Courant* noted that they "had scant opportunity to rehearse with members of the resident company (a few hours at best), but this did not prevent the entire group from turning in a well nigh flawless opening night performance."[5] After the performance, Kay gave a heartfelt curtain speech and paid warm tribute to her supporting players. She commented they were the "hardest working and most talented summer company" with which she had performed.

Kay wrote virtually nothing in her diary-calendar in 1950. After making a few jottings during January and February she abandoned her eighteen-year habit of detailing her social and love life. At 45, was it finally smooth sailing? Kay seemed focused on keeping her dramatic turf on stage. She signed on for a dramatization of Thomas Wolfe's *The Web and the Rock*. *The New York Times* announced, "John Huntington has taken under his wing for presentation on Broadway in the fall, Lester Cohen's dramatization of Thomas Wolfe's *The Web and the Rock*...It is set for Kay Francis and Joel Ashley to undertake the principal roles. *The Web and the Rock* is Wolfe's account of his early days in New York, of the difficulties he encountered in writing and selling his novel, *Look Homeward, Angel*, and of a turbulent love affair."[6]

Cohen's challenge was to scale down the sprawling novel to the limitations of the stage. When it was ready, the play focused on *The Web and the Rock*'s second half—the story of a young writer, George Webber, and his tempestuous affair with a sophisticated older woman. George, disliking the pretension of his wealthy mistress and her friends, leaves for Europe. Disillusioned by Hitler's rise to power, George contemplates returning to the South of his childhood, but realizes *that* is futile. The story was the precursor to Wolfe's novel *You Can't Go Home Again*. When *The Web and the Rock* was first published,

Saturday Review commented: "Wolfe has illuminated a section of experience which no other novelist but Dostoyevsky and Joyce has explored more searchingly."[7] The play opened in August as the first "serious drama" for the season at the Spa Summer Theatre in Saratoga Springs, New York. Blanche Robbins reviewed the production for *The Saratogian*:

In 1950 Kay toured with the hit Goodbye, My

The turbulence of human emotions was portrayed in *The Web and the Rock*...Kay Francis, as Mrs. Jack, the theatrical designer who encourages, cajoles and prods George along the route to literary achievement, is convincing as the married career woman who finds that a great love can mean heartbreak. Miss Francis and Mr. Ashley carry the weight of the evening's performance...As the publisher who consents to print George's book, [Clyde] Waddell offers a matter-of-fact indulgence which contrasts with the tenseness demanded by the role of Esther Jack [Francis]. Lester Cohen...has succeeded in presenting the conflict, the joy, the despair, the tragedy that evolve when the lives of two persons touch. Last night's production was the world premiere of the first dramatization ever made of a Wolfe novel. After a week here and another at Marblehead, Mr. Huntington plans to present the play on Broadway...Richard Barr, who has been associated with Orson Welles, has provided understanding direction.[8]

Variety was especially generous to Ashley's performance, saying, "Joel Ashley as Webber (Wolfe) gives the top portrayal of his career...he takes full advantage of his opportunities in playing the...selfish, childish and bewildered novelist." The reviewer thought Kay underplayed her role "with the result that in several scenes of tumultuous overtones she appears to be over-acting. Further playing will undoubtedly correct this, as the role is one of great possibilities."[9] *The New York Times* touted that the play had lost none of the violent and poetic Wolfe flavor and Kay and the cast were well-received by playgoers.

Unfortunately, Kay's performance as the "remarkable" Esther Jack in Cohen's adaptation of *The Web and the Rock* failed to reach Broadway. (Coincidentally, Cohen had also written the story for Kay's first film in Hollywood, *Dangerous Curves*.) What exactly happened to the production? No one seemed to have an explanation two years later when Sam Zolotow reported, "As far as is known, only one producer, John Huntington, got to first base with a summer tryout...with Kay Francis heading the cast. Thereupon a curtain of silence enveloped the adaptation...the part enacted by Miss Francis will be undertaken by Eugenie Leontovich at the Las Palmas Theatre, Los Angeles."[10] The Russian actress, Leontovich, often compared to Duse and Bernhardt, also failed to take *The Web and the Rock* to Broadway. The Thomas Wolfe work that finally had success on stage was *Look Homeward, Angel*, which was nominated for four Tony awards in 1958.

Kay was pleased and satisfied with her stage career. Her return to the theatre had been in the back of her mind since her film heyday. As early as 1934, she acknowledged the brevity of film careers, saying, "it's a short career comparatively. In the theater you can go on acting with a double chin or lines about the eyes. Those things don't matter but with the camera, well, you know what I mean! I'm looking ahead."[11] Apparently, a number of Kay's contemporaries from Hollywood's golden era, had also been "looking ahead." J.P. Shanley of *The New York Times* best described the phenomenon:

> Like moonlight sails and suntan oils, summer theatres have become symbols of the vacation season....This year, there probably will be more stars than ever on the barn circuit. Public demand seems to be the only explanation. Lewis Harmon, who operated the Chapel Playhouse in Guilford, Conn. on a non-star basis last year, is back to a star policy...He believes now that to meet competition, he needs stars...The stars now scheduled for the summer include...Joan Bennett, Joan Blondell, Claudette Colbert, Melvyn Douglas, Olivia de Havilland, Kay Francis, John Garfield, Lillian Gish, Veronica Lake, Basil Rathbone, Sylvia Sidney..."[12]

For some reason, in June 1951, Kay left New England's "straw hat circuit" and ventured for a solo date to Pittsburgh. She once again dusted off *Let Us Be Gay* for the city's newly refurbished Arena Theatre. The *Pittsburgh Post-Gazette* reviewed the revival:

> It is a pity that some of the carpenters who worked so hard on the stage wouldn't have been employed to shore up the sagging structure of Rachel Crothers' *Let Us Be Gay*...Kay Francis and a lot of other talented actors are engaged in this comedy of week-end country-estate life of about a quarter of a century ago and they do nobly...Westchesterites of today are more engrossed in bomb shelters and legal evasion of the surplus income tax than they are in solving a triangle of manners and morals...the dialogue sounds like the Cosmopolitan magazine issue of December, 1926, but...the acting is all so acceptable that there are many pleasant moments...Miss Francis—bless her—is as attractive as ever. She looks like the proverbial million (only a half million in 1926) and makes an effective characterization as she weaves and bobs in a dusty situation...Morton da Costa's direction is brisk...[13]

Morton Da Costa, it will be noted, received acclaim for his direction of such Broadway and film classics as *Auntie Mame* (1958) and *The Music Man* (1962). His work with Kay definitely provided a much needed boost to the *Let Us Be Gay's* "sagging structure."

While Kay was touring the theater circuits from 1950-53, her agents, Mayberry and Wallace, kept an eye out for television opportunities. Mayberry recalled the ritual of Kay, her maid-assistant Eunice, and the producers, working out script and wardrobe details: "After a drink and small talk, Kay would turn to Eunice and say, 'Bring out the blue,' and Eunice brought the blue dress and a little tray which held shoes dyed to match plus a sapphire necklace, bracelet, and earrings...If the blue wouldn't do, Kay'd ask for 'the brown'—which meant a brown dress, shoes, and her rubies and topazes. That wardrobe was part of her business, and she appreciated it as that, but she wasn't ever silly or drooling over clothes. It was just a straight forward reaction."[14] Kay had assembled a classy collection of ensembles from her Warner days, like the Orry-Kelly lounging pajamas that she wore in the stage adaptation of Somerset Maugham's *Theatre*. She also consulted with Bernie Newman at Bergdorf-Goodman. Kay accomplished theatrical chic and she worked consciously to achieve it. She carried her "chic" into the relatively new medium of television on several occasions, making her TV debut November 7, 1950, in the third episode of *Prudential Family Playhouse*. The program, *Call It a Day*, had been a successful play (1935) and a feel-good comedy for Warner Brothers in 1937. Dodie Smith (who later successfully penned *One Hundred and One Dalmatians*) had written about a day in the life of a family on the first day of spring. Family members are enmeshed in affairs of the heart, with a few twists. Kay's role as the mother, finds herself pursued by a family friend who thinks she is the woman he is supposed to marry, while Kay's husband spends the day being pursued by an actress. Kay's co-player from *In Name Only*, Peggy Ann Garner, played her daughter, who laments the end of a romance with a married artist. All this, in the space of one day. Prudential's program ran one hour, the same length as some of Kay's early Warner films. Kay also appeared on Irving Mansfield's TV brainchild, *This Is Show Business* in 1950.

In January 1951, Kay appeared on the half-hour TV show, *Hollywood Screen Test*. The program was hosted by Neil Hamilton, and presented dramatic stories in which young hopefuls appeared with established stars. Kay rehearsed for three days with a young hopeful (her diaries don't indicate who). *Hollywood Screen Test* was important in jump-starting the careers of such film personalities as Jack Lemmon. In March 1951, Kay worked out a contract with her lawyer, Arnold Weissberger, to perform as Sadie Thompson in "Rain" for TV's *Somerset Maugham Theatre*. She was enthused about the role, but the project fell through on April 2 when she lamented, "Nothing happened and lost Somerset Maugham show—Damn!"[15] Kay apparently liked the new medium and guest-starred on *Betty Crocker Star Matinee* on May 22. In June 1951, Kay and her leading man, Joel Ashley, co-starred on *Lux Video Theatre*. The Lux program was a continuation of the popular radio series that Kay had appeared on in the '30s and '40s. On this "live" thirty-minute TV broadcast, she and Joel tackled roles in Lawrence DuPont's *Consider the Lilies*. They were directed by Richard Goode, who would later direct episodes of TV's popular '60s comedy, *I Dream of Jeannie*. Jerome Cowan, who was in Kay's first Monogram film, *Divorce*, was also in the cast.

Off stage, Kay and Joel (who was married) continued their three-year, steady relationship. The two had rocky moments. On March 31, 1951, Kay wrote: "Joel here, late afternoon and back again after dinner. No fights and just fun!!! What a change."[16] There were a few spats over Joel's salary, but the relationship was mostly a peaceful one. On May 17, Kay made her usual birthday phone call to her mother in Los Angeles. Joel and Eunice also talked and sang birthday wishes. It was the last mention of Kay's mother in the diaries.

Early in 1951, Kay decided to resurrect Patsy Ruth Miller's *Windy Hill*—the play with the curse. For three months the two women worked on a revival, but Kay came to the conclusion it was a bad idea. By mid-May she found a more acceptable stage vehicle—George Oppenheimer's adaptation of G. B. Stern's 1923 novel *The Back Seat*. Kay envisioned it as yet another opportunity to return to Broadway. The novel's author, London-born Gladys Bronwyn Stern, was noted for her fluid and animated style. When the book first appeared, the *New York Times* mentioned its theatrical potential, saying, "*The Back Seat* might very easily and profitably be turned into a light and rather delicious bit of comedy for the real stage. If it can be acted as coaxingly as it reads, the results will be grateful all around."[17] The story tells of the Carruthers' household where domestic order comfortably resides in role reversal. Robert, a failure in business, is supported by Leonora, his celebrated actress-wife. Hence, it is Robert who takes "the back seat" in family matters. He's a house-husband who occupies himself with carpentry. A young playwright, who is in love with the warm-hearted, sunny-tempered Leonora, writes a part for her as a young girl in a new play. From here, Robert kindly takes Leonora by the hand to face the fact that she is no longer suited for such a role. He takes the front seat, as judiciously as possible. Leonora ends up coaching her own daughter for the part. Stern's ending is not the obvious one. Robert, his flirtation with "ambition" over, reclaims his "back seat" role. Leonora, continues onward to fresh triumphs on the stage.

Kay hoped that the play Mirror, Mirror *(1951) would garner a return to Broadway. It didn't.*

The play adaptation of *The Back Seat* was titled *Mirror, Mirror* and had failed in a previous tryout. Regardless, Kay thought it had good roles for her and Ashley. Hopefully, with a few rewrites by George Oppenheimer, they could turn it around into a success. Oppenheimer wasn't a new face to Kay. He had been one of the writers for her MGM film, *The Feminine Touch*. Kay met several times with him and Richard Barr, who had directed *The Web and the Rock*. Oppenheimer somewhat bitterly recalled his association with Kay:

> Kay was great fun. Charming. I was very fond of her. The play wasn't a very good play, and the result was chaos. She wasn't the greatest person to work with because she couldn't remember lines easily…She always claimed that she never drank when she worked, but she'd quit at eight and start again at eleven. Kay was more or less the manager. After the thing opened, she wanted…me to continue touring and rewriting without expense money. I said, "Thank you very much, but no." That was more or less the end of our friendship. But I have a nice picture of her in the dressing room and remember her as a nice dame.[18]

Regardless of Oppenheimer's recollection, the play would gain momentum financially and critically. Kay returned for her fourth consecutive season to Saratoga Springs, where *The Saratogian* headlined: "Kay Francis Scores Hit in Comedy at Spa Theater: Kay Francis, favorite actress of many playgoers, is back at the Spa Summer theater, and a large audience applauded as she glided through *Mirror, Mirror*...Appearing with Miss Francis is Joel Ashley...their interpretation in *Mirror, Mirror* is possibly their best local performance...The production is a credit to all who had a part in presenting it...it offers good entertainment, and it is likely that the play will draw large audiences..."[19]

In September, *Mirror, Mirror* was still being presented as a new comedy prior to Broadway, but it did not reach its hoped for goal. Director Richard Barr would eventually have success through his association with Edward Albee, co-producing *The Zoo Story* (1960) *and Who's Afraid of Virginia Woolf?* (1962) on Broadway. He also

Third-act scene in Mirror, Mirror *from the Saratoga Springs production. Katherine Jones played Kay's daughter. (Saratogian Photo)*

helped produce the very successful production of *Sweeney Todd*. Kay's own opinion of her *Mirror, Mirror* tour was summed up in her diary after the play closed in New Hope. "Fine end to *horror* season. Joel in accident."[20]

Before Kay's "horror season" had started, she was bolstered by a long-overdue tribute from the theatre community. On April 10, 1951, the *New York Times* reported, "Kay Francis and Basil Rathbone, by a majority mail vote of members of the Stock Managers Association, have been declared winners of the newly founded awards for 'the most cooperative, serious, hard-working star who does his or her best to elevate the stock field.' The presentations will be made at a luncheon to be given by the association."[21] A bronze plaque was presented to Kay and Rathbone on May 10, at New York's Astor Hotel. The newspapers covered the event during a luncheon and announced that Kay and Rathbone were honored "for their contribution to the advancement of the summer theater."[22] Rathbone had toured in *The Winslow Boy* the previous summer stock season. For Kay, the award was an acknowledgment for twenty-five years of hard work. In January 1952, Ed Sullivan's popular TV show, *Toast of the Town*, scheduled a tribute to Kay with photo highlights of her career. Sadly, the occasion was cancelled and replaced with the announcements of the Annual New York Film Critics Awards.

In the fall of 1951, Kay got back into the swing of television. After joining in on a TV panel show, along with Ilka Chase and Bud Collyer, she made a guest star appearance on the popular *Frances Langford-Don Ameche Show*. In November, Kay made a guest appearance on the game show *Celebrity Time* with Conrad Nagel. The half-hour program for CBS was a potpourri of music, interviews and game contests. Kay ventured into a similar venue on *The Ken Murray Show* in the spring of 1952. The evening variety show, which included dramatic vignettes, also featured Lola Albright, and Victor Borge.

In early 1952, while remodeling her New York apartment, Kay made a point to rebuild her love life after Joel Ashley left. Ashley would go on to make noteworthy stage performances as Abraham Lincoln, and, aside from numerous television roles, he became

May 1951. A grateful Kay received the Stock Managers Association's award for "Most Cooperative Actress."

known to genre film buffs for his part in *Zombies of Mora Tau* (1957). By March 1952, Kay was seeing a young actor named Dennis Allen. George Eells described Dennis Allen as "a tousle-haired blond young man of catlike grace."[23] Dennis had previous experience with the Melvyn Douglas unit of Special Services during World War II and appeared on stage with Flora Robson, Jean Parker, and in the Diana Barrymore tour of *Joan of Lorraine.*

Along with Dennis, Kay ventured into one of her most successful theatrical tours— a play version of Somerset Maugham's *Theatre.* Adapted by Guy Bolton, the original 1941 Broadway production starred Cornelia Otis Skinner, and ran 69 performances. In *Theatre*, Maugham, author of such classic novels as *Of Human Bondage*, introduces the breathtaking Julia Lambert, whose poise, talent and looks have held-fast for forty-six years. She is one of the most respected actresses in England—so good, in fact, that she never stops acting. The gay subtext in such Maugham works as *Theatre* is evident to those who are familiar with the author's life. Maugham himself was prone to admire and desire younger men. Young men and middle-aged women was one of his frequently used scenarios. Maugham biographer Robert Calder emphasized that "The most common technique to mask the real sexual orientation is, of course, to reverse the pronouns and change the gender of the characters."[24] Calder noted that out of this "technique" Maugham created many of his most fully drawn characters, among them, Julia Lambert.[25] Julia always seeks variety in her numerous affairs. She happily emerges unscathed, and most important, unattached. It seems that nothing can ruffle her satin feathers, until a quiet stranger appears. She endures rejection for the first time and her ability to put on whatever face she desired for her public is finally challenged.

Maugham *Theatre* details the tensions and triumphs that arise when acting and reality merges. Dennis Allen played Tom "the quiet stranger" who disrupts the emotionally safe fantasy world of Julia Lambert (Kay). "Acting and reality" proved prophetic for Kay and her young leading man. She and Dennis' meeting marked the beginning of an intense, long-lasting, and, for Kay, final, romantic liaison. The couple toured in *Theatre* throughout New York, Rhode Island, Massachusetts, Maine, Pennsylvania, Florida and Tennessee. At Saratoga Springs, Spa Summer Theatre reviewer Blanche Robbins highlighted the play's enthusiastic reception:

> The Spa Summer Theatre is presenting the last play of a successful nine-week season, and John Huntington's choice for a satisfactory finale is *Theatre* starring Kay Francis. Miss Francis, who is playing her fifth season in Saratoga Springs, gives one of her best performances in the current offering. Very much at home in highly dramatic roles, Miss Francis also proves herself adept as a comedienne in several scenes in *Theatre.* Among the more serious moments of the play, the scene between Miss Francis, as Julia Lam-

bert, and her son, Roger Gosselyn, played by Anthony Perkins, is outstanding. Miss Francis, with her world crumbling about her, plays a heart-broken woman with commendable reserve, and Mr. Perkins, a drama major at Rollins College, is excellent as the son who finds his actress mother unreal.

Tom, played by Dennis Allen, is the young accountant on whom Julia tries her charms in a frantic effort to convince herself that her sex appeal is still appealing. Area patrons were glad to see this actor, who started out with the Mohawk Drama Festival. The play, *Theatre*, which is based on the novel of the same name, by Somerset Maugham…has much more vitality than the novel. Miss Francis, who has a reputation as a well-dressed woman, is beautifully gowned.[26]

Dennis Allen's admiration and devotion to Kay ran very deep. He felt protective of her and concerned himself over the smallest details of each production. Dennis saw Kay as a member of a school of stylish actresses that included Jane Cowl and Katharine Cornell. Dennis reflected back years later about Kay:

> Kay was a clotheshorse, and she had mannerisms. Her entrances and exits were studied, but she knew exactly what she was doing, and she always got ovations. A great deal has been made of the lisp, but it was so slight as to be charming. And I had a hunch she ought to be doing Shaw and Wilde. I began convincing her to try them—or at least Coward. If she had—who knows what direction her career might have taken? There wasn't a trace of vanity you'd expect. I guess everyone who'd seen her movies expected her to be chic in private life. You'd go into a stock theater, and the kids were appalled at the way she dressed. She always wore the same thing—a denim wraparound skirt, a blouse and little wedgies. Of course, we're talking about the private Kay—not when she was on display. She had fantastic taste when she chose to use it. But she didn't have any illusions about her position. [27]

In the winter of 1952, the play headed for the Central Florida Drama Festival. Jess Gregg, who reviewed *Theatre* on opening night, remembered: "Something terrible happened in the last act. I knew the play, I'd seen Cornelia Otis Skinner do it on Broadway, and I'd read the book, and all of a sudden Kay had stopped playing the scene and was improvising. She was a very funny, savvy woman, and she was being marvelous, but it was obviously improvisation, and I realized she was covering for someone. It went on and on, and I thought, 'They've got to bring down the curtain,' and then suddenly Tony made his entrance—but looking very different. He had no makeup on."[28] Anthony (Tony) Perkins had forgotten about the last scene in which he was to appear. He had to be found quickly and hustled on stage for the play's climax! Kay claimed it had been the worst five minutes of her life. And she kidded Tony about it mercilessly, but kindly, from then on, but admitted the boy had talent. "He's very raw in many ways," she confided to critic Gregg, "but you watch him. He's going to be big."[29]

Dennis, who often directed the production of *Theatre*, felt the third-act curtain lacked something. In it, Kay's character, Julia, has scored a triumph. She has regained her confidence. Dennis suggested that Kay exit through the front of the house, rather than the stage door, and this would add the excitement of the audience rubbing elbows with a celebrity. Kay responded, "Don't worry. I'll dress it." George Eells, noted:

> Dress it she did. Everyone who saw the production still talks of the flash of those final moments. Stage manager, Jerry O'Brien, who has worked with many of the great glamour stars, including Vivien Leigh, maintains that Kay created one of the most visually exciting pictures he has ever witnessed in the theater, "She entered an empty stage lighted with that brown jell she liked so much," he said. "There was only a rickety old chair. And she was wearing this black dornfelt cape with a little ermine collar. She moved as if she were bone-weary and sank onto a chair, saying, 'Oh, my God, I'm so tired,' or whatever the line is. Then suddenly, she threw off the cape, which was lined with ermine. She was in black chiffon and her diamond necklace, bracelet and earrings. And it was POW! Like every light in the world had suddenly been turned on."
>
> Dennis agreed. He said it made no difference that the scene was weak, because once Kay opened the cape no one heard the dialogue. "My god, there was an ovation for this woman every night," he recalled. "I don't know how her technique would hold up in the theater now. I don't think they produce vehicles for people like Kay today. But this was an era when a star was expected, as Jerry says, to be POW! And Kay was."[30]

By word of mouth and press reviews, the play's effectiveness spread. *Theatre* with Kay and Dennis was booked extensively from Bermuda to Skowhegan, Maine. She, Dennis, and her helpmate and general factotum, Eunice, would travel in Kay's station wagon from one engagement to the next. With their picnic hamper and a steady supply of martinis, life assumed the glow of one big party.

Chapter 21

Godmother of East 64th St. & Popponesset Beach

Kay's celebrated 1952-53 tour in Maugham's *Theatre* would be her career swan song. The critics were consistently impressed by her polished performance as Julia Lambert. Newport, Rhode Island's *The News* raved, "Miss Francis, every inch an actress, has here a part she can get her teeth into, and she makes the most of it from beginning to end. Playgoers are given a chance not only to see one of the outstanding figures of the entertainment world...but to watch a polished dramatic performance take shape in her skillful hands."[1] (Fifty years later, the role of Julia Lambert was magnificently essayed on film by Annette Bening and titled *Being Julia*.) In Skowhegan, Maine, the "theatrics" of Julia Lambert transported Kay into "wearing the largest summer hat ever seen" around town. She got even more inventive before stepping onto the resort area's Lakewood stage. Kay unwittingly got both feet into *one* leg of her lounging pajamas! She made her entrance and suddenly saw the other pajama leg dangling behind her. Dennis Allen recalled: "Before the audience noticed, Kay executed a graceful twirl, tossing the unused material around her shoulders...transforming it into a stole. Now *that's* class in dress. She had learned her business thoroughly and was effective."[2]

While on tour with *Theatre*, *Theatre Arts* magazine interviewed Kay about the controversy surrounding summer stock's popular "star packages." Managers were often obligated to sign for touring plays that contracted as many as five players. This cheated the local fledgling summer stock players of their opportunities. Kay gave a balanced point of view saying, "The requirements of casting make one or two supporting players necessary at times because your first interest is to give a good show. I believe in summer stock. It's a great training ground for apprentices when they can work with more experienced actors, whether they are stars or not. I call it 'the summer circus.' We all work together and have fun. But you've *got* to give a good show. And you've *got* to be reasonable, financially. You've *got* to think of the manager. If you protect the managers, the managers will protect you."[3] The truth was that many theaters were kept afloat by star packages such as Kay's.

Along with Dennis, Kay's companionship on the road included a vibrant lady-in-waiting named Eunice. Eunice, like Ida before her, was Kay's maid-secretary-helpmate during this time. Half Native-American and half black, with her hair bleached blonde—

299

Eunice, was a show unto herself. She and Kay personified the unorthodox pairing typical of theatre actresses and their maids. Their loyalty to one another weathered the
emotional storms and bickering associated with life's innate theatrics. George Eells gave
details on this very primary relationship of Kay's:

> In one sense Eunice was a paragon. She served as Kay's dresser and
> greatest fan in the theater. At home she was maid, laundress, cook, secretary
> and surrogate mother. She assumed an intensely proprietary air that pro-
> tected Kay well when she'd taken one drink too many or wished to avoid
> unwanted attentions. "Miss Kay's having a nap," or "Miss Kay's stepped
> out," Eunice would say, unless she recognized the caller as a friend. Then
> she'd whisper, "She can't come to the phone. She's got that *flu* again, but
> she'll be all right tomorrow." In another sense, Eunice was a trial. She liked
> to drink, and only a little alcohol was required to turn her into a wild
> woman. "It's the Indian in me," she explained. "It turns me savage."[4]

Some wondered why Kay put up with Eunice, but Kay was usually dismissive
about the incidents, brushing them off, saying, "Eunice is being naughty again." Eunice's
naughtiness was in full bloom when Kay and Dennis took *Theatre* to Bermuda. It had
been ten years since Kay had been to the island and entertained with the other Jills.

After the run of *Theatre*, Kay was contacted by the airline she was booked on to
do some publicity for them. She agreed. Kay, Dennis, and Eunice arrived two hours
early at the terminal to meet with photographers, which was *not* an easy task this time
for the always-punctual Kay. After a rough night of carousing with friends on the island,
Eunice was pretty tight when they arrived at the airport. Dennis elaborated years later,
on what turned out to be the makings of a Marx Brothers' farce:

> When we got to the airport, Eunice was supposed to watch the
> luggage...But she hit the bar instead and by plane time was blind-assed
> drunk. We all got on, except Eunice, who couldn't make the steps. The next
> thing we knew the pilot had bumped her. I went down to talk with him and
> got nowhere. Kay came down and explained, but no go. So we left without
> Eunice. Unfortunately, when we got to New York International, we had a
> case of liquor, and Eunice had the declaration slips in her purse. Well, Kay
> had had enough. She kept saying, "I did publicity for the airport, and they
> bumped my maid, and now you expect me to *pay* to bring this liquor in!"
> The charge was something like fifteen dollars. She screamed and yelled and
> finally slammed the money on the counter. Then she ostentatiously opened
> the boxes and passed out every last bottle before sailing out, clutching her
> handbag containing her rubies, diamonds and emeralds—which they hadn't
> even bothered to look at.[5]

Kay was protective of Eunice. Jetti Ames was quick to point out that Kay was on
guard for Eunice in a world still steeped in segregation. Jetti commented that Eunice
"was very, very light and could have passed [for white] if she had wanted to, but she said
she had never done that, and she wasn't going to do it. Kay respected that. The booking

agent always made sure that they went to a hotel where [Eunice] could stay. Kay wouldn't stay there if Eunice wasn't permitted. It shows where she stood on that subject."[6]

Although Dennis urged Kay to consider future stage projects by Shaw and Oscar Wilde, she was definitely winding down her career. She took delight in occasional developments for their current project, but was no longer interested in undertaking a new and demanding assignment. In 1953, Kay continued touring in Maugham's *Theatre* as part of the Arena Guild of America, which served theatres-in-the-round. *The New York Times* reported that Kay was one of the more prominent players on a circuit that included Ethel Barrymore, Ilka Chase and Sylvia Sidney.

After the arena tour, Kay and Dennis enjoyed quiet evenings in front of the TV, attending the ballet, and seeing the new plays. Kay also enjoyed mixing with Eva Gabor and the "Hungarian gang." She had first met Eva in 1945, and the two occasionally got together for drinks and dinner. In August, Kay appeared on the CBS radio show *Make Up Your Mind* and in September, the final episode of the popular summer TV game show *Anyone Can Win. Anyone Can Win*, hosted by cartoonist Al Capp, with a panel of four celebrities, had a quiz format. The audience in the studio would bet on which celebrity would best succeed in answering general knowledge questions. Kay enjoyed the variety-game show venue, but was even more interested in doing a TV series. Her diaries indicate meetings to pursue such a venture in the fall of 1953. While a series never materialized for her, Kay met once again with director Richard Barr to consider a role in *Late Love*, which was currently playing on Broadway. A comedy in three acts, *Late Love* would have offered Kay the role of a lady painter who is commissioned to do the portrait of a priggish novelist. Once her character arrives on the scene, she sizes up the novelist and proceeds to liberate his entire household. Kay did a reading for the part in November. It was the last entry into her diary regarding her career. She gave up on the diary altogether on December 31, 1953, with her last entry: "Dinner at home. Quiet evening, TV."[7]

During 1954, Kay put a permanent hold on her career for several reasons. She certainly didn't need the money. As Dennis had mentioned, Kay was losing interest in new projects. Life on tour had taken its toll on her. After a series of stage mishaps and falls in Richmond, Virginia, Kay, peering over her dark green glasses and blinking her eyes, told a reporter, "My eyes were blistered when I first went into the movies and since then I've been blind as a bat. Furthermore, my feet aren't any good, so I'm always falling. But, believe me, those accidents in Richmond, all in one week, were something of a record."[8] Jetti Ames "hit the nail on the head" when she told me that physically, the demands of theatre became just too much for Kay.

Theatre co-starred Kay's love-interest Dennis Allen

Kay quit theater because of her health. This business with the legs really did her in…she had trouble walking. She was in pain a lot of the time. It was a terrible thing for her to face—she never really was capable of doing anything like standing for a long time or walking. She loved the theater. It just wasn't in the books anymore. She knew that. So she tried to enjoy life otherwise. She entertained friends. We saw Dennis frequently. Dennis and she did not live together. They spent a great deal of time together and nights together, but they did not live together. They enjoyed each other's company. In all honesty Dennis probably thought she could do something to help him in theater. There's nothing wrong with that. They had a very pleasant relationship. [9]

Years earlier Kay had said that retirement coupled with independence was what she was working for. "I'll live simply," she explained. "I'll travel, I'll read…Then, and only then, will the real thrill of being an actress come home to me—when it has become the thrill of *having been* an actress!"[10]

In late 1951, Kay had purchased an apartment at 32 East 64th St. in New York City. Before she parted with the almighty dollar, she asked her longtime friend Stephie Wiman to look at it. Stephie's inspection was followed by an idiosyncrasy typical of Kay. Stephie commented, "It had been a big apartment that was divided into two. It was lovely, perfectly lovely. A big bedroom, an enormous bathroom, a hallway, tiny kitchenette, lovely library and a huge drawing room. They were only asking eleven thousand dollars for it. After we'd looked it over she asked, 'Do you think that's too much?' And I almost fainted."[11]

Dennis made comment on Kay and her pocketbook, saying, "She was very funny about money. She often laughed about Hollywood friends calling her Hetty Green because she was so slow to part with a buck. I don't mean she was stingy. She could be incredibly generous, but she did pinch pennies."[12] Once the grip on her purse-strings loosened, Kay refurbished her new home and brought in her favorite pieces from previous residences. She accessorized with her impressive collection of bibelots, boxes and *objets d'art*. George Eells noted, "About these, Kay proved meticulous as she was known to be punctual, causing Dennis teasingly to call her 'Craig's Wife.' No matter, if anything was an inch from its intended place, she could not rest until it was restored to where it belonged."[13] Old habits die hard. Sara Hamilton of *Photoplay* had observed the same thing about Kay in 1936. "I swear to you that a match box placed one-tenth of an inch from an ash tray by Kay on her dresser on a Monday late in January, is exactly one-tenth of an inch from the same old ash tray on a Tuesday in March, in the heat of an August afternoon at four o'clock and on a rainy midnight in December. Expect no deviations, no gladsome change however little." Hamilton observed that Kay was, "a soul devoted to orderliness."[14] Kay was also devoted to her favorite flower, the orchid. Jetti Ames noticed that, "Kay loved having orchids in the house. People she was close to would often send them to her. She wasn't really raising them in New York, but I'm pretty sure she raised orchids while she was in California."[15] Still in distribution (2005) from Kay's own orchid collection is a hybrid of the rare "Linda Vista," a yellow-throated, exquisitely shaped, dark purple cultivar.

Jetti shared an amusing, if harrowing, incident that occurred in Kay's apartment:

When other people would question Kay [about WWII] asking, "Weren't you afraid, flying around and entertaining the troops?" She would say, "Well, you can stay home and lock yourself up in the house and have the ceiling fall down on you! You just *go* and do what you need to do." So, in this lovely apartment in New York, the people upstairs went off for a weekend and left the water running in the bathroom. Kay got up one morning—had to go to the bathroom. While she was in the bathroom the whole ceiling fell down on her bed! Kay said, "I don't know if I made that statement too many times about how the ceiling could fall down on you. But, it was trying to show me that it *could* happen! Thank God I had to go pee!" She had a wonderful sense of humor.[16]

Jetti and Lou commented that when the elevator stopped at the 6th floor, the only resident there was Kay. She had the entire 6th floor to herself. Kay's transition to the new residence was accompanied by a new circle of acquaintances: art gallery owner Allan Brant and his wife, Priscilla, director Richard Barr, hospital administrator Eva Patton, actor Paul Lipson, and Clay Shaw, the New Orleans cultural entrepreneur whose life was ruined when he was accused of conspiring to assassinate John F. Kennedy. For the most part, her Hollywood acquaintances fell out of her social life. In 1953, when a supposed representative from Warners came backstage, saying Jack Warner wanted Kay to play the mother role to Judy Garland in the proposed *The Helen Morgan Story*, Kay wired Warner to inquire if the offer held. Warner promptly wired back: "No, Kay. We never even thought about you."[17] Kay's attorney and friend, L. Arnold Weissberger, commented, "I think the movie people forgot about her after she was no longer in the swim. It was especially true in those days that you were as important as your last picture and how much money you were earning."[18]

Kay seemed content with her new crowd, especially Weissberger's mother, Anna, whom Kay found delightful. Kay asked Weissberger to include Anna as an executor of Kay's estate. "I think the most important thing in an executor is common sense," said Kay, "and Anna has more common sense than all of you lawyers put together."[19] Weissberger handled the legal affairs of luminaries such as Orson Welles, Arthur Miller, Anita Loos, and Noel Coward. Coward commented, "The fact that Arnold always has been, is and always will be almost pathologically stage-struck naturally delights all of us who belong to the strange mad world of powder and paint."[20] Weissberger was also an avid photographer of the rich and famous. He captured Kay and his mother Anna smiling happily, arms around each other, at a party in his New York apartment. The shot was included in the tome to his work, *Famous Faces*. While Kay enjoyed the camaraderie of the older Anna, she also surrounded herself with those much younger. Dennis was seventeen years Kay's junior. Kay had said, "I've always found it stimulating to be with people who are younger than I am…when we can see eye to eye with the younger generation…without losing the things experience has taught us, we're doing all right."[21]

One of Kay's fondest pastimes after her retirement was seeing her two godsons. They were the sons of her close friends, Jetti and Lou Ames. Tabor was born in 1949 and with Jonathan being born in 1954, the boys were another venue for Kay to channel some loving energy now that her career had come to an end. She would always spend

Kay enjoying a relaxing visit with Lou and Jetti Ames and her godson Tabor, 1958.
(Courtesy of Tabor Ames)

Christmas with the Ames family. Jetti commented, "Kay always wanted to have children, and she said to me, 'You and Lou have a very happy marriage, and he's very supportive of you and your career. You shouldn't wait too long to have children. Go ahead. You can always do theatre. And she was right. Kay became a surrogate godmother to our two sons. She would always come out Christmas Day and spend that weekend with us...she was really responsible for that, because she loved children."[22] To the oldest boy, Tabor, Kay became his image of what a movie star was all about. In July 2004, he shared his "flood of memories" about Godmother Kay.

> To me, Kay represented what movie stars looked like, acted like, and talked like. The visual of red lipstick—the heavy gold jewelry, which I still remember—she was always a classic dresser. Nobody that I had ever seen looked quite like Kay. She had a very distinctive, captivating voice. I've spent my career in advertising where voice is so important, and she captivated me as a young boy. Kay was always high energy. She had a point of view on everything. When she entered a room, and she knew how to make an entrance, she kept your attention—and at the same time paid attention to you. I could see Kay in *Sunset Boulevard*. To me she was a Norma Desmond, but not as affected as Desmond. She was so *unique*. Out at Popponesset in the summer, Kay would be sitting, smoking, laughing and telling stories. She was ready to go on stage at a moment's notice. She dressed the part. I never saw her unmade-up or disheveled. She was always perfect. Kay holds a special place in my heart.[23]

Jonathan remembers that Kay always wore a red dress on her Christmas visits to their home. "We always took pictures when she was out at Christmas," Jetti recalled. "The one I remember in particular was of the three of them, the boys and Kay, sitting on the couch. A really delightful photo." To this day, Jetti and Lou pay tribute to Kay on Christmas morning. Jetti elaborated on their "Kay Ritual":

> On Christmas Day, Lou and I open our presents and then we have our Kay Francis drink. She introduced us to it the first Christmas she was coming out. 'I will bring the Christmas morning drink,' she said. 'You've got to do this!' So, we toast her every Christmas morning with Black Velvet (Stout and Champagne). It's the only way I can touch champagne. Lou mixes it, and he ices the pitcher. We continue opening presents and toasting Kay. It doesn't bother me. She swore it wouldn't, and she was right![24]

Kay had Tabor and Jonathan pegged early on and made each of them a hooked rug of a horse. The horses mirrored the boys' contrasting personalities and energy. Jonathan Ames talked about the rug with fond memories, saying, "The rug now hangs in my son's room. A white horse on a blue background. She made my brother an identical rug. Mine is jumping up in the air, because I was a hyperactive kid. I'd probably be diagnosed and on Ritalin these days. My brother's horse was…just standing there."[25]

Kay's hooked rug output was prolific. She shared her enthusiasm for the art with her new crowd at the cozy New York East Side club "Goldie's." She was a regular at the nightspot and close friends with Goldie Hawkins (accompanist for Ethel Merman's 1964 album *Merman in the Raw*) and the other half of his piano-duo, Wayne Saunders. The three of them formed the "Monday Night Hookin' Society—Kay Francis, Chief Hooker." The rugs were works of art and considered treasures by their recipients. Aside from the rugs Kay gave her godsons, Jetti and Lou Ames received a sailboat-pattern wool rug that hangs in their Nantucket cottage. Jetti commented, "The sailboat was her own design. Kay said, 'It may not *look* sea-worthy, but it is!' Or, words to that effect. It now hangs on the wall in one of the bedrooms in the cottage. We have a number of things to always look at and remember her by. She did a lot of work with her hands. She did beautiful needlepoint. When she went to the Catholic school, the nuns taught her. That's where she got started with the needle work and sewing."[26]

When I visited Jetti and Lou on Nantucket during the summer of 2004, I photographed the rug, which captures a peaceful and breezy effect. The sailboat has a single mast and is shown drifting at sea. A soft breeze engages the sails topped by a red-and-white insignia flag. Just below some fluffy clouds, three gulls serenade what appears to be a bright day. It's a hand-

Kay designed this seaworthy sailboat for Jetti and Lou Ames around 1960. The hooked rug now hangs in their guest cottage on Nantucket.

some effort, obviously influenced by Kay's memories of countless afternoons sailing along the California coastline. Kay pinpointed when her interest in needle work began. "It was during the World War that I learned to knit, and I've never given it up," she told Maude Cheatham. "It is the great social pastime; just ask any old-fashioned sewing circle. I do it automatically to keep my fingers busy while my thoughts relax."[27] Knitting, crocheting, needlework, and rug-hooking had provided Kay a lifetime avocation and creative outlet.

The "Monday-Night Hookin' Society" came to a sudden halt when Kay made a wisecrack to Goldie about a mutual friend. After a scolding from Goldie, Kay claimed he had used her name to publicize his club. Goldie, thoughtlessly, shot back, "Listen, sweetie, at this point I could get more publicity with Dixie Dunbar's name than yours."[28] Dunbar's claim to fame, on 1950s' TV, was for tap-dancing with her body encased in a huge Old Gold cigarette package—only her legs were exposed. When the flying fur settled it was Wayne Saunders who remained loyal to Kay. He would continue to faithfully communicate with her on a daily basis.

In retirement, Kay did some traveling. She spent a winter on the Caribbean's St. Thomas, while Dennis opened a nightclub. Upon returning to New York, Dennis put a hold on his own theatrical ambitions, and was employed at Bronzini's selling Brooke Cadwallaer's designer silk ties. There were trips to California. Kay's mother passed away in Los Angeles (January 1957), and Kay made another sojourn to Hollywood in 1960. (That year, Ray Stark's plans to re-film Kay's personal favorite, *One Way Passage*, never materialized.) Eventually, Kay's enthusiasm for traveling subsided due to her surmounting health problems. Her condition put a strain on her otherwise pleasant relationship with Dennis.

Kay had a series of surgeries, losing a kidney and lung. A fractured ankle bone and back injuries (requiring a brace), put demands on Kay physically and emotionally. She made a decision, ultimately a compassionate one, to end her ten-year relationship with Dennis. In the summer of 1961, while Dennis was on Fire Island working for Goldie, Kay went to Cape Cod. "The whole thing was psychologically bad," said Dennis, "and I honestly believe that she broke off with me because she realized that otherwise I'd sit there and dedicate my life to her. I loved her deeply, and I think in the beginning, she loved me. Frankly, I'm glad it was her decision, and that she did it. My life is much better. She may have sensed that. She was seventeen years older than me—that's a lot. If we'd continued, I could never have had a life other than sitting around holding the hand of a sick old lady. That fall, when I came back from Goldie's, my stuff was packed, and it was all over—*closed*. I could never get her on the phone or anything else again."[29] Dennis later married a woman whom he had met that same summer.

So, how did Kay cope with her physical challenges? She did remarkably well, considering the onset of problems which began soon after her accident in 1948. Continuing with her stage work for another six years was no easy task. When cancer was diagnosed in the early-to-mid-sixties, the strain was enormous. A mastectomy was performed, but the disease spread. Never one to complain to friends, Kay endured the consequences. As she had once stated, "I *never* discuss what might be considered my troubles."[30]

Medication provided Kay some relief, and for someone who enjoyed imbibing as much as she did, alcohol provided further alleviation. At that time, doctors would rarely diagnose alcoholism. They simply treated the side effects. Even cancer was rarely talked about and, if so, only in hushed, fearful tones. The 1960s were rather unenlightened time for what Kay was dealing with, and she did have her "episodes." Toward the end, when Kay was in the most pain and discomfort, the effects of her overindulgence were commented on by longtime acquaintances. Charles Baskerville and Beatrice Ames Stewart (who hadn't seen Kay in years) felt free to tell of incidents involving Kay's drinking. There was a scene at a restaurant (she fell down after dinner) and another tipsy episode while shopping at Bergdorf-Goodman. Baskerville said seeing Kay, "broke our hearts." Stewart, an employee at Bergdorf's, found it all "terribly sad."[31] Little did they realize that Kay was dealing with breast cancer and under much physical duress. One has to give Kay credit. She was coping with it as best she could. She even had to exercise caution with what she ate. Jetti Ames explained: "Kay had a hiatal hernia and had trouble eating. She had to have one of those beds that were elevated. They said at one point that she should really have it operated on and she looked them straight in the eye and said, 'No. I've spent enough time in the hospital. I've had enough operations and enough pain. I'll just go along with the elevated bed and watch my diet and what-have-you. I'm not having any more surgery.'"[32]

Occasionally, a die-hard fan would track down Kay, but wouldn't get very far if they broached the subject of her career. Author James Robert Parish managed to meet Kay during one of her summer visits on the Cape. Parish has since become the author of nearly a hundred books on the entertainment industry. His interest in Kay's career was actually the motivation for his first sale as a writer. It was 1963. Parish told his story:

> When I had been to Los Angeles in the mid-1960s I went to several movie still shops on Hollywood Boulevard. One had a sign out sheet asking if there were movie stars you were interested in getting stills on. I put down Kay Francis who had intrigued me since childhood when I saw her Warner Brothers films over Boston TV. I gave my address as the Cape Playhouse on Cape Cod. A few weeks later, when I was working at the Playhouse (prop master), I got a letter from Gene Ringgold in Los Angeles responding to my note at the movie still shop and telling me that Kay Francis was staying at a resort only a few miles from where I worked. I eventually tracked her down, spoke to her on the phone and made a surprise visit to meet her in person.
> She was convinced no one could care less about her past; she was still bitter at the treatment she received from Warner Brothers, and was still sensitive about her age. When we met briefly, she looked remarkably fit in her white tennis outfit, tall and regal. Her hair had turned grayish and her teeth were no longer capped, but she was the same vibrant if brusque personality...The next year, while still in law school, I worked with Gene Ringgold on a career article on Kay Francis for *Films in Review*.[33]

The career article on Kay, by Ringgold and Parish, was the first of its kind printed after her retirement. It set the tone of her being bitter and reclusive. The few who did interview Kay about her career should have had no reason to think they were being singled out as the recipients of Kay's reticence regarding her past. Even close friends shied away from talking about Kay's Hollywood years. Jetti Ames' husband Lou commented, "Kay wasn't very outgoing about *herself*. I always tried to get her to talk about Hollywood because I'm a movie buff. She didn't seem to care. She was probably bitter about leaving all that behind her. I think she showed her attitude by *not* talking about it." Jetti added, "By the same token, she didn't go around with it 'hanging out.' She *chose* not to talk about it. When you talk about her being bitter, it's *important* to mention that she didn't go around stewing about it. *Because she didn't*." On a rare occasion, Jetti said Kay would refer to her trouble at Warners as "her big struggle."[34] This refutes the stories that Kay was simply a bitter recluse, wallowing in self-pity in regards to her Hollywood past. She *enjoyed* her life and gallantly coped with the last three years when she was confronted with painfully intrusive physical illnesses.

One devoted fan who managed to meet Kay during the mid-1960s, was Bob French. Again, Kay was pleasant unless the subject of Hollywood was brought up. He wrote to me in 1997, describing how he arranged the rare opportunity of meeting her:

> Needless to say, I am a Kay Francis addict. Many years ago, as a child, I saw *Confession* and fell hopelessly and permanently in love with her...she was, to me, incredibly fascinating...I sat through *The House on 56th Street* over and over until my mother came looking for me and dragged me home...in the mid-1960s, I met a very distinguished older man and his wife, both of whom were executives at Bergdorf-Goodman, a posh department store, and somehow they divulged that they were very close friends of Kay Francis. They told me she had been bitterly disillusioned and disappointed when a

Christmas 1962. Jetti and Kay celebrate seventeen years of friendship. Jetti emphasized that Kay did not go around bitterly stewing about Hollywood. (Courtesy of Jetti and Lou Ames)

handsome, distinguished, European man, who had courted her and proposed turned out to be a former Nazi official. He was arrested and deported just days before they were to have been married…I asked my friends to let me meet her, and they kept saying—"You wouldn't want to know her. She's not the Kay Francis you remember." Nonetheless, I persisted, and one day on a summer Sunday I droved out to their home on Long Island. Miss Francis was lounging under a huge umbrella at pool-side, a cigarette in one hand and a martini in the other. She was rather into her cups, but she was charming and, in a somewhat caustic way, a little funny. I tried to talk to her about her films and her experiences, but she said simply that she didn't want to talk about that, it was all so long ago and so "rotten." These were her words. After dinner she fell asleep, having eaten only a few bites, so I didn't have the opportunity of saying goodbye. About a year later, she died.[35]

If Bob's memory is correct, this would have been 1966-67—just before Kay was confined to her New York apartment. As mentioned, the hiatal hernia kept her from eating a normal meal. His mention of Bergdorf-Goodman brings to mind that Kay had been one of the prestigious store's regular clientele since 1929. The store assisted in her new wardrobe before she ventured to Hollywood. Located in the heart of the midtown district, Bergdorf's employed eight designers in the 1940s, and provided impeccable taste to their patrons' limitless budgets. Kay splurged on occasion. In the mid-sixties, during the tipsy episode that Bea Stewart mentioned, Kay conferred with the store manager, designer Bernie Newman, before buying a mink stole—in the heat of July!

Kay's fans hadn't forgot about her, and in certain corners, neither had Hollywood. Producer Ross Hunter was known for resurrecting the careers of glamour stars, and he allegedly approached Kay in 1965 for the role of Lana Turner's stylish mother-in-law in his remake of *Madame X*. Due to health issues, Kay was unable to accept the part. The role was then offered to Myrna Loy, who was committed to touring with *Barefoot in the Park*. Finally, Kay's poker pal and competitor in the 1930s' fashion sweepstakes, Constance Bennett, took the assignment.

During the 1950s and '60s Kay was drawn each summer to Cape Cod. It was here that she would rent a cottage for the season. (Some sources say she still owned a home there.) Part of Kay's affinity to New England's coast was rooted in her own ancestry. There were memories from childhood, touring the Cape with her mother, and her first honeymoon with Dwight Francis. During her marriage to Kenneth MacKenna, they had selected Cape Cod as a place to raise a family. Starting in the late 1940s, Kay's summer stock tours kept the Cape close at hand. It was a natural for her, after retirement, to spend her summers at the Cape's Popponesset Beach relaxing and visiting friends.

Kay's cottage had easy access to a sandy beach and was located near a popular resort. Jetti recalled, "Kay used to go to Popponesset in the summertime. We'd stop and see her on our way to Nantucket. She liked to be by the sea. She was close to Hilda Coppage (who ran Popponesset Inn), but for quite a few years rented a cottage adjacent to the resort. Kay loved the sea and salt air. She had friends around from her summer stock days. Jonathan remembers the silver convertible she rented while there and her tender loving care the time he stepped on a bee walking down the wooden stairs to the beach."[36] The visit Jonathan

Ames was most fond of was the time Kay took him for a long drive:

> My biggest memory of Kay was driving around in that convertible of
> hers. She had a 1963 silver Chevy Impala with red interior. She loved red.
> That's what she drove when we visited her on Cape Cod. I was about eight
> or nine years old. Kay drove around with her cigarette hanging up in the
> breeze, you know, puffin' on her butt, driving me around. She had the
> sunglasses, the red lipstick, the scarf blowing in the breeze, hair flowing in
> the back—and the whole deal—the way Susan Sarandon did in the film
> *Thelma & Louise*. Just me and her. I was thrilled.[37]

Kay Francis happily cruising the countryside of Cape Cod in a 1963 silver convertible with a smiling godson at her side certainly shows that Kay could put her troubles
on the back burner and relish the moment. Although her health was in decline and her
Hollywood past remained a sore subject, it was *not* like Kay to dwell on either in her
daily life. Years before, she had emphasized:

> I live, essentially, for *today.* Never have I planned ahead. I try to live, daily,
> in the fullest sense, and I have implicit confidence in things being smooth in the
> long run...Surely I'm low at times. I've been broke. I've been disappointed in
> love. I've been terribly afraid. But those blue moods have never lasted more
> than a couple of hours or a couple of days. Happiness, I figured when very
> young, is a daily condition of one's own creation. It is not to be anticipated.
> Only a fool broods. We all have our misfortunes, but why take them big? Do
> that and you not only upset yourself, but you're no fun to others...I never gaze
> longingly back at the yester-years. When I'm through, I'm done. When I've
> made mistakes I profit by them, and I do *not* advertise them![38]

This philosophy, spoken as Kay approached thirty, held fast as she approached
sixty. Her friend Jetti concurred, saying, "Kay really wasn't a worrier. She lived in the
present." Jetti told of the time that Kay came to visit them, "for a nice quiet weekend in
the country," and godson Tabor had his face ripped open by a dog. "A stubborn, over-
sexed dog we had inherited," recalled Jetti. Tabor had pulled on the dog's chain in order
for his little brother Jonathan to get off the dog's back. "My husband brought Tabor in
with blood streaming down his face. This was Kay's quiet weekend. We left her alone
with Jonathan." When they returned from the hospital, Jetti said the present-minded
Kay was a godsend. She helped them through the crisis and afterwards reassured Tabor
that he hadn't done anything wrong. Jetti said that Kay helped her "work around it very
carefully and discussed psychologically how to deal with this—it wasn't his fault and so
on. She was *very* helpful and understanding. Kay had wanted children. This is one thing
that she really wanted."[39] While Kay decided to accept what she referred to as the "peculiar satisfaction" that acting brought her, the money and the independence, she felt her
lifestyle was not conducive to having a family. On this very subject, Kay had once
poignantly pointed out, "There is a fever in fame that burns up many precious things."[40]

Kay claimed that her career had made her more conscious of her existence—for this she was grateful.[41] Still, there was a strong part of Kay that longed for the *unpublic* life that had belonged to her youth. She relented that such anonymity could only exist for her on a desert island and even commented on that unlikely situation:

> I would soon become steeped in the revealing consciousness of how very unimportant I really am...how painlessly my little pretensions to being rather "special" could be stripped from me. My name in lights, reviews, my personal appearances, possessions, pride

Kay celebrating Christmas with godson Jonathan in 1961. Jonathan's favorite memory is Kay driving him around Cape Cod in her 1963 silver convertible. (Courtesy of Jetti and Lou Ames)

> would mean nothing at all...The trees, the water, the sky, the moon, the birds, the beasts would neither know nor care who I was nor where I came from. I would be, if anything, more in the nature of a nuisance...Easier by far to skin my little fame and glory off me than to remove the skin of a lowly snake. [42]

Toward the end in 1966-67, the burden of medications and physical duress kept Kay confined to her New York apartment, which finally became her imagined desert island. While being steeped in "revealing consciousness" and having the pretensions of being rather "special" stripped from her, surgery became an added drain. But, Kay was not completely alone. She did remain special to others. Lifelong friend Stephie Wiman had her own projection of Kay's last few months and commented, "No bouquets to me, but I was probably the only old friend she had had for—well, God, it would be fifty years—that went to see her. I'd go over at three or three thirty, and she'd want me to have a drink, and I'd say, 'No, I don't drink at this time of the day.' She'd insist, and as I drank vodka, I'd (actually) have a glass of water...in those last years, when she was so sick, she'd get frightened at times. She'd call, and I'd go down there at three or four in the morning."[43]

Kay's greatest support was Eunice. Jetti Ames says that Eunice, "a lovely, lovely person," stayed with Kay through the end. "She was devoted to Kay...and Kay was devoted to her, too."[44] Although they did not live in New York, Jetti and Lou Ames, and Kay's godsons, stayed close and connected to Kay. Lou mentioned the long phone conversations between Kay and Jetti when Kay was feeling lonely. Jetti's own impression during those final days found Kay drawn to privacy. "Kay remained handsome," noted Jetti. "From the time her very serious ailments caught up with her she didn't want to see anybody the last few months. There was some cancer in the liver, and things started to fall apart. We would talk on the phone. I called her before we left for Nantucket and had a long chat with her and said, 'Do you want us to come up before we leave?' She said, 'I love you, but no.' I said, 'I understand.' I left for Nantucket in June (1968) and she called in

August and she spoke in…it was really just a loud whisper, and she said, 'I just want you to know that I love you, and that I wanted to say goodbye for now.' And that was it. She was really going."[45] Kay had been in New York Hospital as a cancer patient and returned to her Manhattan home on August 24. There would be only a few days left for her.

Kay's godsons had visited her at the New York apartment that last year. From a child's eyes all that could be seen was a woman who loved them. She was the same, but somehow different—slower. In some ways even more *present*. Jonathan recalled:

> I used to visit her when my mother would bring my brother and me to New York City to her apartment—when she was probably not so well. She would be sitting in her big, big round bed with the dog. Kay had a tiny dog. I don't remember what kind. She was in her big bed, and I would lie down on it with her, and she would hug me…we would talk, just the three of us. Kay, me and my brother. She was very warm—a very warm lady. She was my mother's mentor. She taught my mother a lot about the stage. Kay took my mother by the hand and taught her the ropes of what the *real* Broadway was all about. She was a very influential person in my mother's life.
>
> Kay took a great deal of interest in my brother and myself. And, she loved kids. I have her horseback riding boots and leather jacket. She gave me the leather boots, and I was very upset when I grew out of them. I probably wore the leather jacket until I was in the eighth grade. It was a bomber jacket— a real bomber. Wore it until it didn't fit me. Near the end, Kay couldn't get up out of her bed. I remember her husky voice…a voice that had had too much whiskey and cigarettes…I remember a very warmhearted woman, hugging me…Kay Francis, was an important part of my life. [46]

What would Kay have thought of her own departure from life? Was she really the woman who wanted to be forgotten? Or, had there been things she had spent years trying to forget? Probably a combination of both. Although she never lost her bitterness about Hollywood, Kay did *care* about others and hopefully developed a sense of compassion for herself. She once said that one of the most profound and beautiful experiences in life was seeing, "the face of a dead person who has known great pain and is released…"[47] On Monday, August 26, 1968, she indeed was released from the familiarity of "great pain." Intuitively, Kay had welcomed this transition. Her will was a testament of letting go. She indicated that she wanted cremation and stated simply, "that the undertaker dispose of her ashes in any manner determined by him."[48] She wanted no memorial service or monument. She wanted to leave no trace of her existence on earth. Kay did not believe in looking back…nor into her tomorrows. "I've never been a person to look into the future," she had once remarked. "It's always been a little theory of mine that tomorrow can take care of itself…Just the present day counted. Just the moment, really." Kay elaborated:

> You have to compromise with life. I found that out. You have to get the best out of what you're given—and that "best" doesn't mean anything pretentious. It doesn't matter what you do, really—if you put your heart into it. It may be cooking or playing tennis or falling in love. But do it

simply, naturally, in good spirit. *Live for the day*...so much can happen in twenty-four hours—why should we always be seeking tomorrow? I don't know where I'm going or what the next step is. I never have known. Like the rest of the world, I want happiness and I'd enjoy giving it. But I feel I can have that happiness anywhere, no matter whether it's in China or Patagonia. All that's necessary is to adapt yourself to circumstances. [49]

Kay, displaying a Christmas gift at the Ames' (1962). "Kay really wasn't a worrier," says Jetti. "She lived in the present." (Courtesy of Jetti and Lou Ames)

Kay Francis adapted herself to the circumstances and managed an impressive career, while remaining her own unique self. During an era that was repressive to women she wisely utilized her secret: *Live for the day*. She benefitted from the awareness that results from that *kind* of living. For the patron of the cinema, the silken essence of Kay Francis continues to emanate on screen, intact, with *poignancy* and a natural vitality. As the light filters through frames of celluloid we see *spirit* rather than mere dramatics. Ironically, this essence keeps Kay Francis very much alive, remembered, and *not forgotten*.

Kay's seven-page will left bequests to twelve individuals. Among them, her lawyer, L. Arnold Wiessberger, received a drawing by her ex-father-in-law Leo Mielziner, Sr. and two drawings by ex-brother-in-law Jo Mielziner; Priscilla Brandt received Picasso's *Guitar Player*; Kay's emeralds went to Stephie Wiman. Helen Morgan of Needham, Mass. received $2,000, two pieces of sculpture, and Kay's dog, Chig.[50] The Museum of the City of New York received her collection of press notices, diaries, and film stills. Jetti and Lou Ames received Kay's custom-made desk, vanity, and accent tables. The vanity bench is covered with the exquisite floral motif of Kay's fine needlepoint. In keeping with her giving nature, Kay left the bulk of her estate to The Seeing Eye of Morristown, New Jersey. This bequest proved to be one of her greatest legacies.

Epilogue
Kay Francis—A Continuing Legacy

When I contacted the headquarters of The Seeing Eye, Rosemary Carroll, their Director of Development and Public Affairs, said, "Kay Francis did something very nice for The Seeing Eye and its important work and I am most happy to help you record and recognize her extraordinary contribution." Kay's bequest of $1 million (which translates to $5,000,000 in 2005) was placed in an endowment to provide for the long-term security of The Seeing Eye. Carroll stated that, "income from the endowment provides about 75% of the cost of our annual operations…So, indeed, the Francis bequest helps us to enhance the independence, dignity and self-confidence of blind people through the use of Seeing Eye dogs. Another way of expressing it, her bequest continues to help us to provide our specially bred and trained dogs to love and safely guide people who are blind or visually impaired." The pioneer dog guide school, with a teaching staff of highly specialized individuals, "has matched nearly 13,000 specially bred and trained Seeing Eye dogs with nearly 6,000 blind men and women from across the United States and Canada." With the help from Kay's gift (which was finally received in 1974), The Seeing Eye initiated its breeding program about seven miles from their main campus. There, they have bred German Shepherds, Labrador and Golden retrievers. After rigorous training these uniquely capable dogs make a difference in the lives of others.

When Kay's will was made public, The New York Daily News contacted the vice-president of The Seeing Eye, who found her generosity to be a splendid, if mysterious, surprise. The organization was also willed the exquisite, color portrait of Kay by Sir Gerald Kelly (which now graces one of The Seeing Eye lobbies). Few were aware of Kay's interest in the organization's work. Jetti Ames said that Kay brought up the fact many times that the national charity she believed in was The Seeing Eye. It was a subject close to Kay's heart. Kay's lawyer, L. Arnold Weissberger, also emphasized that, "Kay had thought about it and decided loss of sight was the most tragic fate that could befall anyone—hence the gift." Kay's own love of dogs was also, certainly, behind the gesture. To quote her:

> Dogs are part of my design for living. They are beautiful, too, not only
> in their shape and size, but in their faithfulness and un-asking loyalty. They
> give themselves as no human ever does. You couldn't revert to the savage

314

state so easily if you had a dog…For a dog is a gentleman, with kindliness in his heart and dignity in his demeanor—kindliness and dignity being, I think, the two qualities which make a gent a gent or not. I believe that a dog brings out the very best there is in man or woman. Dogs make me feel how shabby most of our loyalties are, how limited our patience, how easily destructible our love of one another.

Kay and Snifter (circa 1930)

Four years after her death, screenwriter Jay Presson Allen paid homage to Kay in the film Cabaret. The vivacious Liza Minnelli plays Sally Bowles, a cabaret performer in 1931 Berlin, who is rewarded with a new fur coat from her millionaire boyfriend. After putting it on, she spins around and rapturously exclaims, "I feel just like Kay Francis!" Considered the best line in the movie, it gained notoriety and is now #3282 in The Columbia World of Quotations. The line also proved a lucky omen for Minnelli—she won an Oscar for her performance. James Robert Parish commented on the line's significance not long after Cabaret's release: "To a young lady of two generations ago, there could be no higher tribute. Tall, dark, sultry Kay Francis…was soap opera's most gallant heroine…she could suffer through a celluloid weeper with more chic, style and sangfroid than any of her rouged confreres.…Kay brought the perfect touch of class …" Parish dedicated his 1971 book The Great Movie Series to Kay.

In 1974 it was announced that Joseph Zarro and Frank Pellecchia were working on a Kay Francis biography. They called Kay "the quintessential embodiment of 1930's film glamour—a wonderful combination of flesh and spirit. Her playing, marked by delicacy and reserve, projected her characters' poignancy or vitality…effortlessly, like sunlight weaving through ropes of clouds." Their poetic legacy to Kay Francis never made it to print. What finally did, was the previously mentioned George Eells 1976 epistle to six screen sirens gracing the billboards in 1933: Ginger, Loretta, and Irene Who? The Eells work was followed in 1978 by James Robert Parish's The Hollywood Beauties. Parish, who had first interviewed Kay in 1963, tackled seven Hollywood legends in his book and covered much the same territory as Eells.

Kay was one of the first film actresses to be honored with a star on the Hollywood Walk of Fame. Her star is located at 6764 Hollywood Blvd., between those of Judy Garland and Ray Bolger. The ground breaking ceremony for the "walk" was in 1960. In my research I unexpectedly came across another tribute to Kay, of the floral variety. Sauvie Island, in Oregon, lists the 1979 hybrid "Kay Francis Dahlia"—a delicate pink flower standing about four inches high, with four-inch blooms and long stems. There is also a variety of the Australian ornamental flowering plant, Grevillea Kay Francis.

Although most of Kay's co-stars and acquaintances are long gone, Jetti and Lou Ames and Kay's godsons carry heartfelt memories of Kay. Now an exhibiting artist and painter, Lou retired from his years of television work. He had been the associate producer of NBC's Today Show. Jetti still tackles two stage roles a year. In the summer of 2004 she starred on Nantucket in a production of Nunsense. A typical review for the "redoubtable" veteran states, "Jetti Ames, doesn't steal this show—she owns it…she tosses [her lines] off with shruggingly casual élan, and to devastating effect. The capacity audience loved every minute of it…" Tabor is in advertising and lives in Connecticut, while Jonathan and his wife (both physicians), and their son reside in New Jersey. This brings to mind the hours I spent deciphering Kay's handwriting at Wesleyan University. Jetti had warned me that I might have a difficult time. She and Kay always laughed about their handwriting and agreed they could have been doctors.

Over the last few years, Turner Classic Movies has made a point of paying tribute to Kay on her birthday. Host Robert Osborne, who encouraged me to "keep the flame of Kay Francis alive," has his own soft spot and admiration for Kay. It is through his efforts and the Turner library that the screen legacy of Kay Francis is kept within reach. With sixty-eight film credits to her name, it is a pity that so few of Kay's films have been released on DVD or video. As of 2005, only nine titles have been issued. The Kay Francis Film Society, in Palm Springs, which featured Kay's films and other classics, operated from 1996-2002. Marty Kearns, who established the group, told me, "I discovered Kay Francis on Turner Classic Movies. When I started seeing more of her films in such a short period of time, I really became quite fascinated. I've done private film societies over the years under DeMille's name and D.W. Griffith's. After seeing Kay Francis, I figured it was time for a switch."

Upon completing this project, I cannot help but admire Kay Francis as an intelligent, resilient, compassionate, free spirit who loved to laugh and who took her work seriously. I can also see that whatever "weapon" was used against her by Warner Brothers

Tucson, 2005. Author Scott O'Brien with Jetti and Lou Ames. Jetti had just scored in an exceptional, multilayered performance in the Israel Hororvitz's absorbing comedy-drama My Old Lady at Tucson's Invisible Theatre. (photo by Joel Bellagio)

Fall, 1936. Before the Deluge. Jack Warner (on Kay's left) celebrates his top male and female box-office stars: Kay Francis and Errol Flynn, before their completion of Another Dawn. Joining the festivities are (from left) Kay's frequent co-star William Powell, her frequent shopping companion Norma Shearer, and the film star-mistress of William Randolph Hearst, Marion Davies. The oceanliner cake is in honor of Kay's departure for a European holiday. A year later Warner was hellbent on having Kay Francis say Bon Voyage to her career. (Warners)

would not have been possible without the puritanical overlay that still burdens the American culture. Instead of blaming Jack Warner for Kay's "struggle," maybe we should take a look at ourselves. James Robert Parish noted that "the obituaries for Kay all eulogized her...for her representation of the American woman as a poised, intelligent, and admirable person. However, all marveled at the flood of bitterness that cascaded from the pages of her will, the dammed-up emotion of three decades of hurt." Ultimately, whatever Kay suffered from her mistreatment in Hollywood was simply grist for the mill—and she was smart enough to realize that. But, Kay was human—the greater truth was expressed by Kay herself to British critic W. H. Mooring, when she told him that Warner Brothers "almost broke her heart." Inevitably, Kay's Zen-like commentary from her 1933 film Keyhole not only summed up the film, but life as we know it:

"Funny thing. We worry and struggle and try to work out our little problems, and then, all of a sudden it's over." (She snaps her fingers.) "Just like that! It just doesn't seem possible."

Chapter Notes

Prologue

1. Dick Mook, "Why Kay Francis Fascinates Men," *Screen Book*, 4/36
2. Ibid.
3. Frances Kellum, "I Asked Kay Francis 1000 Questions!" *Screen Play*, 11/36
4. James Robert Parish, "Kay Francis," in *The Hollywood Beauties*, (NY: Arlington House, 1978) pg 90
5. Elizabeth Wilson, "Projections: Kay Francis," *Silver Screen*, 3/37

Chapter One

1. Ed Sullivan, "Ed Sullivan - In Hollywood," *Hollywood Citizen News*, 11/19/37
2. Donald Ogden Stewart, *By a Stroke of Luck*, (London: Paddington Press, 1975)
3. George Eells, *Ginger, Loretta and Irene, Who?* (NY: G. Putnam and Sons, 1976) pg 193
4. Maya Angelou, *I Know Why the Caged Bird Sings*, (NY: Bantam Books, 1970)
5. County of Los Angeles, Certificate of Death, District 7053 No. 1967; and, Herbert Cruikshank, "Lucky Thirteen," *Modern Screen*, 11/30
6. Helen Louise Walker, "Kay Francis Has Her Worries, Owning Nell Gwynne," *Motion Picture*, 9/30
7. Eells, pg 193.
8. Phyllis Clinton, "The Clinton Family of Connecticut and Related Families," [Online], 2002, WWW URL: freepages.genealogy.rootsweb.com
9. [Online] WWW URL: sprague-database.org
10. [Online] WWW URL: familysearch.org
11. WWW URL: sprague-database.org
12. Ibid.
13. Eells, pg 193
14. *NY Times*, 10/9/1900
15. Cruikshank, "Lucky Thirteen"
16. Sullivan, "In Hollywood"
17. "Superstition, Romance and Kay Francis," *Picture Show*, 3/20/37
18. R. S. Mook, "I Can't Wait to Be Forgotten," *Photoplay*, 3/39
19. Interview with Jetti Ames, 2/18/2003
20. Thirteenth Census of the United States, 1910

21. Film magazine article, author's collection, c. 1930

22. *Catalogue of The Tabor Grand School of Acting*, (Denver: Wahlgreen Printing Co., c1906)

23. Helen Starr, "My Daughter, Kay Francis," *Picture Play*, 3/36

24. Ibid.

25. Cruikshank, "Lucky Thirteen"

26. Dana Rush, "The Aristocrat of the Screen," *Silver Screen*, 2/32

27. [Online] Internet Broadway Database

28. Letter, Jetti Ames to author, 4/24/03

29. [Online] WWW URL: sprague-database.org

30. Ibid.

31. Ben Maddox, "Kay Francis Wants Life," *Movie Mirror*, 9/34

32. Frances Kellum, "The Men in Kay Francis' Life!" *Screen Book*, 12/36

33. Ibid.

34. Interview with Jetti Ames, 6/5/2004

35. Faith Baldwin, "If You Want To Be Like Kay Francis," *Modern Screen*, 5/33

36. Starr, "My Daughter, Kay Francis"; Eells, pg 195

37. Eells, pg 195

38. S. R. Mook, "The Authorized Life Story of Kay Francis, *Movie Mirror*, 7/37

39. Kay Francis, "The Women Men Like," *Picturegoer Weekly*, 10/23/37

40. Letter, Jetti Ames to author, 2/18/03

41. Eells, pg 194

42. Ibid.

43. Starr, "My Daughter Kay Francis"

44. Eells, pg 195

45. Starr, "My Daughter, Kay Francis"

46. Eells, pg 195

47. Mook, "The Authorized Life Story of Kay Francis"

48. Elsa Maxwell, "It's Romance Again for Kay Francis," *Photoplay*, 5/38

49. Kay Francis, diary, January 4, 1922, Kay Francis collection, Wesleyan Cinema Archives, Wesleyan University, Middletown, CT.

50. Francis Diary, April 20, 1922, WCA

51. Mook, "The Authorized Life Story of Kay Francis"

52. Eells, pg 196

53. Francis Diary, June 13, 1922, WCA

54. Francis Diary, June 28, 1922, WCA

55. Francis Diary, November 17, 1922, WCA

56. Francis, "Women Men Like"

57. Francis Diary, December 31, 1922, WCA

58. Starr, "My Daughter, Kay Francis"

59. *NY Times*, Citation, File 7558, 1968, 12/24/1968

60. [Online] WWW URL: ancestry.com. Joseph Sprague Gibbs

61. Mook, "The Authorized Life Story of Kay Francis"

62. Ibid.

63. Ruth Allison, "Two Kinds of Love," *Movie Mirror*, 5/32

64. Kay Francis, "My Design For Living" *Motion Picture*, 10/34

65. Lesley Lee Francis, conversation, 4/6/2003

66. Eells, pg 197

67. Francis Diary, October 1, 1924; October 30, 1924 WCA

68. Francis Diary, December 9, 1924, WCA

69. *NY Times*, 2/28/25

70. *NY Times*, 4/24/25

71. Eells, pg 197

72. Allison, "Two Kinds of Love"

73. Letter, Henry Francis to author, 9/23/2003

74. Kellum, "The Men in Kay Francis' Life"

James Dwight Francis: Interviews with Lesley Lee Francis, 4/6/2003; Letters, Henry Francis to author, 9/23 and 9/27/2003; *NY Times*, 11/2/32 and *NY Times* obituary 1/26/88

Chapter Two

1. Iris Foster, "Star Without Temperament," *Film Weekly*, 5/18/34

2. Rush, "Aristocrat of the Screen"

3. Margaret Reid, "Oklahoma Defied Broadway," *Picture Play*, 10/30; and Sullivan, "In Hollywood"

4. Sullivan, "In Hollywood"

5. Kay Francis, "Don't Try Your Luck Out Here!" *Pictorial Review*, 1/37

6. Francis Diary, July 8, 1925; July 16, 1925, WCA

7. Ben Maddox, "Kay Francis' Last Interview," *Screenland*, 11/38

8. Sullivan, "In Hollywood"

9. Ibid.

10. Ibid.

11. [Online] Craig Clinton, "Mrs. Leslie Carter" WWW URL: academic.reed.edu

12. Eells, pg 199

13. Sullivan, "In Hollywood"

14. Francis, "Don't Try Your Luck ..."

15. Eells, pg 199

16. Francis, "Don't Try Your Luck ..."

17. Roberts, "Acting in a Business Way"

18. Radie Harris, "Bad Girl Makes Good," *Silver Screen*, 2/31

19. Letter: Andrew Potter of the Royal Academy to author, 11/3/2003

20. Derek Hudson, *For the Love of Painting*, (1975)

21. Harry Evans, "A Dinner Date with Kay Francis," *Family* Circle, 2/9/34

22. Eells, pg 198

23. Ibid.

24. Ibid.

25. Eells, pp 198-199

26. Francis Diary, January 5, 1926; June 20,1926, WCA

27. Francis Diary, December 2, 1925, WCA

28. Harris, "Bad Girl Makes Good"

29. Jack Grant "Kay Francis' Strange Psychic Adventure," *Screenplay*, 2/36

30. "Her Hands Are Like Faces," *Time*, 4/26/26

31. Pedro De La Hoz, "Vida, pasion y olvido del cuple," WWW URL: granma.cubaweb.cu

32. "Her Hands Are Like Faces," *Time*

33. Review of *Seventh Heaven*, *The Indianapolis Star*, 6/29/26

34. Francis Diary, June 20, 1926, WCA

35. "Storm Gave Her Courage," *Dayton Daily News*, 7/18/26

36. James Muir, review of *The Fall Guy*, *Dayton Daily News*, 7/20/26

37. Eells, pg 200

38. Dick Mook, "Why Kay Francis Fascinates Men," *Screen Book*, 4/36

39. Rush, "Aristocrat of the Screen"

40. Eells, pg 200

41. "Kay Francis of the Films," *Vanity Fair*, 5/31

42. Mook, "Authorized Life Story ..."

43. Eells, pg 197

44. Francis Diary, October 19, 1925, WCA

45. Francis Diary, January 1, 1926, WCA

46. Gladys Hall, "The Marriage Secret of Kay Francis - Never Told Before," *Motion Picture*, 8/33

47. Sylvia Jukes Morris, *Rage for Fame: The Ascent of Clare Booth Luce*, (NY: Random House, 1997)

48. Eells, pg 201

49. Francis Diary, August 11, 1927, WCA

50. Francis Diary, August 22, 1927, WCA

51. Harris, "A Bad Girl Makes Good"

52. Maxwell, "It's Romance Again ..."

53. Starr, "My Daughter, Kay Francis"

54. Maxwell, "It's Romance Again ..."

55. Eells, pg 201

56. *New York Times*, 12/26/27

57. Faith Service, "It's Thrilling to be an Actress," *Modern Screen*, 7/35

58. Kellum, "The Men in Kay Francis' Life"

59. Jerry Lane, "Kay Francis' Amazing Secret," *Screenplay*, 3/35

60. Malcolm H. Oettinger, "Does Kay Mean Tashman," *Picture Play*, 7/33

61. Lawrence Grobel, *The Hustons* (NY: Charles Scribner's Sons, 1989)

62. Ibid.

63. John Weld, *September Song, An Intimate Biography of Walter Huston*, (London: Scarecrow, 1998)

64. Maddox, "Kay Francis Wants Life"

<u>William "Bill" Gaston:</u>WWW URL: state.ma.us/statehouse/massgovs/wgaston.tem; *Movie Mirror*, 7/37; *New York Times*, 1/27/28; *New York Times*, 1/25/38; Obituary, *New York Times*, 9/2/1970; Boris Nicholai, "The Untold Story of Kay's Secret Marriage," *Hollywood*, 5/34

<u>Allan A. Ryan:</u> *Who Was Who, American Biographical Dictionary; Photoplay*, 5/38

Chapter Three

1. Sullivan, "In Hollywood"; Eells, pg 202
2. Eells, pg 202
3. Reid, "Oklahoma Defies Broadway"
4. Maude Cheatham, "Not What She Seems to Be-That's Kay," *Motion Picture*, 3/37
5. Francis Diary, December 17, 1928, WCA
6. Kellum, "The Men in Kay Francis' Life"
7. Mook, "I Can't Wait to be Forgotten"
8. Francis Diary, January 22, 1929, WCA
9. Francis Diary, May 13, 1929 WCA
10. Leonard Hall, "Vamping for Sound," *Photoplay*, 10/29
11. Robyn Karney, ed., *Chronicle of the Cinema*, "8/3/29," (NY: Dorling Kindevsley)
12. Sullivan, "In Hollywood"
13. Maddox, "Kay Francis Wants Life"
14. Cheatham, "Not What She Seems to Be-That's Kay"
15. Francis Diary, April 12, 1929 WCA
16. Francis Diary, June 2, 1929, WCA
17. The New Biographical Dictionary of Film, by David Thomson, Knopf, NY, 2002
18. Adela St. Rogers Johns, "Working Girl," *New Movie*, 2/31
19. David Stenn, *Clara Bow Runnin' Wild*, (NY: Doubleday,1988) pg 170
20. Francis Diary, June 21, 1929, WCA
21. Mook, "Authorized Life Story of Kay Francis"
22. Francis Diary, May 27, 1929, WCA
23. Francis Diary, June 3, 1929, WCA
24. St. Rogers Johns, "Working Girl"
25. John Engstead, "Gotham's Gift to Hollywood," *Screenland*, 9/29
26. Elisabeth Goldbeck, "What! No Feathers?" *Motion Picture*, 8/29
27. Lawrence J. Quirk, *Films of Fredric March*, (NY: Citadel Press,1971)
28. Francis Diary, June 1, 1929, WCA
29. Mook, "Authorized Life Story of Kay Francis"
30. Travis Banton, "The Style Center," *Hollywood Citizen News*, 11/7/29
31. Ibid.
32. Elsie Janis, "Class With a Capital K," *New Movie*, 3/34
33. Film magazine, 1930, author's collection
34. St. Rogers Johns, "Working Girl"

<u>John Meehan:</u> *NY Times*, "In the Limelight," 1/8/28; Divorce, 3/6/26; [Online] Internet Movie Database

Chapter Four

1. "Superstition, Romance and Kay Francis," *Picture Show*
2. Ibid.
3. "Movie Boudoirs - Kay Francis," *New Movie*, 4/31
4. Cheatham, "Not What She Seems to Be - That's Kay"
5. Sara Hamilton, "Okay Francis," *Photoplay*, 3/36
6. Ibid.
7. Kay Francis, "My Design for Living"
8. Reid, "Oklahoma Defies Broadway"
9. Eells, pg 206
10. Grant, "Kay Francis' Strange Psychic Adventure"
11. Cheatham, "Not What She Seems to Be"
12. *Memo from David O. Selznick*, (NY: Viking Press, 1972)
13. Kingsley Canham, *The Hollywood Professionals Vol 5*, (London: Tantivy Press, 1976)
14. Sullivan, "In Hollywood"
15. Ibid.
16. Maude Cheatham, "Kay Francis and Bill Powell Talk About Each Other," *Screenland*, 8/34
17. Kay Francis, "How am I Doing?" *Film Weekly*, 5/31/35
18. Cheatham, "Kay Francis and Bill Powell ..."
19. Jack Grant, "Do Modern Women Deserve Chivalry?" *Movie Classic*, 9/36
20. Helen Louise Walker, "How Men Annoy Us," *Motion Picture*, 12/30
21. Ibid.
22. Maude Cheatham, "Kay Francis and Bill Powell ..."
23. Starr, "My Daughter, Kay Francis
24. Katharine Roberts, "Acting in a Business Way," *Colliers*, 3/16/35
25. Jerry Lane, "Plenty Has Happened to Kay Francis," *Screen Book*, 8/37
26. Reid, "Oklahoma Defied Broadway"
27. Ibid.
28. Otto G. Obermaier and Barry A. Bohrer, [Online] The New York Law Journal, "A Century of New York's Crimes, Criminals and Trial Lawyers," The New York Law Journal, 1/10/2000
29. *LA Evening Herald*, 8/15/30
30. Sara Hamilton, "The Most Baffling Brunette-Who Is She?" *Movie Classic*, 12/31
31. Mook, "Why Kay Francis Fascinates Men"
32. Juliet Benita Colman, *Ronald Colman, A Very Private Person* (NY: William Morrow and Co., 1975)
33. Francis Diary, February 13, 1930, WCA
34. Kay Francis, "I Like Being a Film Star," *Woman's Fair*, 11/35
35. Ibid.
36. Norbert Luck, "The Screen in Review" *Picture Play*, 11/30
37. Reid, "Oklahoma Defies Broadway"
38. Hamilton, "The Most Baffling Brunette"
39. Colman, *Ronald Colman*

40. Charles Francisco, *Gentleman: The William Powell Story* (NY: St. Martin's, 1985)

41. New Orleans news article, "Screen's Best Dressed Star Visits Here," 1930

42. New Orleans news article, "Film Star Here For visit Winds Heart of Crowd," 1930

43. Ibid.

44. New Orleans News article, "Knock 'Em Dead Vamp Now In N.O.: Rebels," by William Wiegand, 1930

45. Ibid.

46. Edward Baron Turk, *Hollywood Diva, A Biography of Jeanette MacDonald*, (Berkeley: UC Press, 1998)

47. Sharon Rich, *Sweethearts*, (NY: Donald I. Fine, Inc., 1994)

48. *LA Evening Herald*, 4/18/30

Chapter Five

1. Lisa Merrill, *When Romeo Was a Woman: Charlotte Cushman and Her Circle of Female Spectators*, (Ann Arbor, Mich.: University of Michigan Press, 1999)

2. Kellum, "The Men in Kay Francis' Life"

3. Jean-Pierre Cousodan, *American Directors Vol 1*, (NY: McGraw Hill, 1983)

4. Margaret J. Bailey, Those Glorious Glamour Years, (NJ: Citadel Press, 1982)

5. Emanuel Levy, *George Cukor, Master of Elegance*, (NY: William Morrow and Co.,1994)

6. Francis Diary, July 13, 1929, WCA

7. Francis Diary, August 1, 1929, WCA

8. Francis Diary, November 2, 1929, WCA

9. Francis Diary, December 31, 1929, WCA

10. Francis Diary, January 18, 1930, WCA

11. Francis Diary, July 26, 1930, WCA

12. Gladys Hall, "The Marriage Secret of Kay Francis, *Motion Picture*, 8/33

13. Hamilton, "The Most Baffling Brunette ..."

14. Francis Diary, January 18, 1931, WCA

15. Joan Fontaine, No Bed of Roses, (NY William Morrow and Co., 1978)

16. Francis Diary, July 13, 1931, WCA

17. Hall, "The Marriage Secret ..."

18. Parish, *Hollywood Beauties*, pg 75

19. Ruth Rankin, "O-Kay Francis," *Silver Screen*, 1/36

20. Eells, pg 205

21. Rankin, "O-Kay Francis"

22. Ibid.

23. *Hollywood Daily Citizen*, 1/23/31

24. *American Film Institute Catalogue, 1931-1940*, (Berkeley: Univ. of California Press, 1993)

25. Harry Lang, "Red-Head" Bickford Speaks," *Photoplay*, 12/30

26. Janis, "Class With a Capital KAY"

27. Cheatham, "Kay Francis and Bill Powell ..."

28. Francisco, *Gentleman*, pg 100

29. Larry Swindell, *Screwball*, (NY: William Morrow and Co., 1975)

30. *LA Evening Herald*, 7/31/31

31. Kay Francis, "The 8 Most Fascinating People in Hollywood," *Modern Screen*, 5/35

Kenneth MacKenna: WWW URL: .npg.si.edu; Merrill, *When Romeo Was a Woman ...*; *New York Times*, 12/20/33, 1/17/62

Chapter Six

1. WWW URL: see The Man Who Had Everything, WOSU-TV, Columbus, Ohio, 1999

2. William K. Everson, review of *24 Hours*, *Films in Review*

3. Ibid.

4. Bailey, *Those Glorious Glamour Years*

5. Levy, *George Cukor ...*

6. William Mann, *Behind The Screen*, (NY: Viking, 2001) pp 144-145

7. Francis Diary, August 19, 1931, WCA

8. *LA Examiner*, 10/30/31

9. Mann, *Behind the Screen*

10. Ibid.

11. Diana McLellan, *The Girls*, (NY: LA Weekly Books for St. Martin's Griffin, 2000)

12. Ibid.

13. Patrick McGilligan, *A Double Life, George Cukor*, (NY: St. Martin's Press, 1991)

14. Curt Gentry, *J. Edgar Hoover, The Man and the Secrets*, (NY: W.W. Norton, 1991)

15. Faith Service, "Strange Interview," *Modern Screen*, 4/37

16. WWW URL: see Guardian Unlimited @ Guardian Newspapers Limited, 2003

17. FBI File 65-42237-25, July 16, 1942

18. FBI File 65-42237-29, July 13, 1942

19. Francis Diary, January 21, 1930 WCA

20. Francis Diary, January 23, 1932, WCA

21. Reid, "Oklahoma Defies Broadway"

22. Maddox, "Kay Francis Wants Life"

23. Mook, "Authorized Life Story ..."

24. Mook, "Why Kay Francis Fascinates ..."

25. Francis, "The 8 Most Fascinating ..."

26. *LA Examiner*, 9/4/31

27. Elizabeth Yeaman, "Sad Movies Her Weakness," *Hollywood Citizen News*, 11/18/31

28. Francis, "The 8 Most Fascinating ..."

29. *Hollywood Citizen News*, 11/18/31

30. *NY Times*, 3/5/32

Chapter Seven

1. Jewel Smith, "Kay's Dream of Romance," *Screen Book*, 7/32

2. Roberts, "Acting in a Business Way"

3. A.M. Sperber and Eric Lax, *Bogart*, (NY: William Morrow & Co., 1997) pp 98-99

4.   Ibid. pg 49

5.   Cheatham, "Not What She Seems to Be-That's Kay"

6.   Parish, *Hollywood Beauties*, pg 79

7.   *LA Illustrated Daily News*, 6/17/32

8.   Francis Diary, April 25, 1932, WCA

9.   Baldwin, "If You Want To Be Like Kay Francis"

10.   Bailey, *Those Glorious Glamour Years*

11.   Cheatham, "Kay Francis and Bill Powell Talk ..."

12.   *Hollywood Citizen News*, 7/29/32

13.   *LA Evening Herald Express*, 7/29/32

14.   Smith, "Kay's Dream of Romance"

15.   Oettinger, "Does Kay Mean Tashman?"

16.   Eells, pg 211

17.   Francis Diary, June 1, 1932, WCA

18.   Eells, pg 211

19.   Ibid.

20.   Dora Albert, "Kay Francis," *Film Pictorial*, 3/18/33

21.   *LA Evening Herald Express*, 12/2/32

22.   Eells, pg 225

23.   Faith Service, "Farewell to Francis," *Modern Screen*, 7/38

24.   Faith Service, "Did $26,000 Outweigh a Honeymoon Trip for Kay Francis?" *Motion Picture*, 11/32

25.   Leonard Hall, "Just Three Years," *Photoplay*, 10/32

26.   Harry Mines, *LA Illustrated Daily News,* 8/4/32

27.   Harry Evans, "Okay Francis," *Family Circle*, 8/14/36

28.   Service, "Did $26,000 ..."

29.   Allison, "Two Kinds of Love"

30.   Service, "Did $26,000 ..."

31.   Kay Roberts, "They Hope to Stay Married," *Photoplay*, 12/32

Chapter Eight

1.   Scott Eyman, *Laughter in Paradise*, (NY: Simon and Schuster, 1993) pg 192

2.   Ibid., pg 191

3.   *LA Evening Herald Express*, 10/22/32

4.   Eyman, *Laughter in Paradise*, pg 170

5.   *Halliwell's Hundred* (NY: Scribners, 1982) pg 381

6.   *LA Examiner*, 12/30/32

7.   Colman, *A Very Private Person*, pp 117-119

8.   Eells, pg 212

9.   Eells, pp 212-13

10.   Francis, "How Am I Doing?"

11.   Maxwell, "It's Romance Again for Kay Francis"

12. Francis, "I Like Being A Film Star"
13. Service, "Did $26,000 ..."
14. Pressbook, *The White Angel*
15. *NY Times*, 12/24/33
16. Samuel R. Mook, "Kay Francis on the Real Tragedy of Hollywood," *Film Pictorial*, 11/3/34
17. Mook, "Why Kay Francis Fascinates Men"
18. Mook, "Kay Francis on the Real Tragedy ..."
19. Wilson, "Projections - Kay Francis"
20. Roberts, "Acting in a Business Way"
21. Dick Mook, "She Wanted to be Forgotten," *Silver Screen*, 4/1941
22. Hamilton, "The Most Baffling Brunette ..."
23. William F. French, "Kay Francis says: Give Yourself a Break," *Woman's World*, 8/36
24. Ibid.
25. Evans, "Okay Francis"
26. James R. Parish, *Hollywood's Great Love Teams*, (NY: Arlington House,1974)
27. Bob Ramsey, "A History of US Drug Laws," [Online] WWW URL: dpft.org/history.html
28. Francis Diary, September 9, 1933, WCA
29. Francis Diary, November 26, 1933, WCA
30. Mick La Salle, *Complicated Women*, (NY: St. Martin's Press, 2000) pg 182
31. Ibid., pp 182-183
32. Ibid., pp 183-184, 187
33. Virginia T. Lane, "Secrets of Fashion and Style," *Picturegoer Weekly*, 12/30/33
34. Maddox, "Kay Francis Picks ..."
35. Francis Diary, June 23, 1933, WCA
36. Grant, "Kay Francis' Strange Psychic Adventure"
37. *Hollywood Citizen News*, 7/3/33
38. Eells , pg 214
39. *Starmaker: The Autobiography of Hal Wallis*, (NY: MacMillan, 1980) pp 46-47
40. La Salle, *Complicated Women*, pg.142
41. Edward G. Robinson, *All My Yesterdays*, (NY: Spigelgass-Hawthorne, 1973)
42. Parish, *Hollywood Beauties*, pg 87
43. Lawrence J. Quirk, The Great Romantic Films, (NJ: Citadel Press, 1974) pp 22-25
44. Foster, "Star Without Temperament"
45. Eells, pg 215
46. Francis Diary, September 30, 1933, WCA
47. Virginia Maxwell, "Just 'Life and Love'," *Photoplay*, 6/33
48. Eells, pg 216
49. Ibid., pg 188
50. Ibid., pg 188
51. Mook, "She Wanted to be Forgotten"
52. Evans, "A Dinner Date with Kay Francis"
53. Laura Ellsworth Fitch, "The True Story of Kay Francis' Many Loves," *Picture Play*, 7/38

Chapter Nine

1. LaSalle, *Complicated Women*, pg 191
2. Ibid., pg 200
3. Mann, *Behind the Screen, pg* 127
4. Ibid., pg 128
5. Ibid., pg 83
6. Ibid., pp 107-08
7. Francis Diary, February 28, 1937, WCA
8. Mook, "Kay Francis on the Real Tragedy of Hollywood"
9. Mann, *Behind the Screen*, pg 120
10. Francis, "The Women Men Like"
11. Leonard J. Leff and Jerold L. Simmons, *Dame In the Kimono*, (NY: Grove Weidenfeld,1990) pg 38
12. Patricia Keats, "Kay Francis 'as 'eard the East a'Callin'" *Silver Screen*, 1/34
13. Mark A. Vieira, *Sin in Soft Focus*, (NY: Harry N. Abrams, Inc., 1999) pg 163
14. Keats, "Kay Franics 'as 'eard ..."
15. Ibid.
16. Mook, "Kay Francis on the Real Tragedy ..."
17. Francis, "How Am I Doing?"
18. William F. French, "Only Al Wanted to Play," *Photoplay*, 3/34
19. James M. Fidler, "Spiking the Rumors," *Silver Screen*, 8/34
20. Ibid.
21. Francis Diary, January 18, 1934, WCA
22. Francis Diary, January 30, 1934, WCA
23. Lane, "Plenty Has Happened to Her"
24. Harry T. Brundidge, "Chevalier Wants Love," *Movie Mirror*, 9/34
25. Francis Diary, May 31, 1934, WCA
26. Francis Diary, June 18, 1934, WCA
27. Mordaunt Hall, review of *Dr. Monica*, *NY Times*, 6/21/34
28. LaSalle, *Complicated Women,* pg 184
29. *NY Times*, 7/31/34
30. Basinger, *A Woman's View*, pg 414
31. Jacalyn Duffin, 4/9/99 WWW URL: endeavor.med.nyu.edu New York University, 1993-2003
32. Mook, "Kay Francis on the Real Tragedy ..."
33. Foster, "Star Without Temperament"
34. Fidler, "Spiking the Rumors"
35. Mook, "Kay Francis and the Real Tragedy"
36. Samuel R. Mook, "Unguarded Moment," *Picture Play*, 11/34
37. *NY Times,* 10/11/34
38. Francis Diary, October 27, 1934, WCA
39. Paul Minet, *Royalty Digest*, nos. 127,128,130 *Corresp. of H.G. Wells*, (Pickering and

Chatto Pub. 1998)

40. Roger Dooley, *From Scarface to Scarlett*, (NY: Harcourt, Brace, Jovanovich, 1981) pp 102-103

41. *LA Evening Herald Express*, 9/15/34

42. Parish, *Hollywood Beauties*, pg 93

43. Ronald Howard, In Search of My Father, (NY: St. Martin's Pr., 1981)

44. Francis Diary, June 8, 1934, WCA

45. Mook, "Kay Francis on the Real Tragedy ..."

46. Francis Diary, January 11, 1935, WCA

47. Parish, *Hollywood Beauties*, pg 93

48. Francis Diary, January 31, 1935, WCA

49. Francis Diary, February 19, 1935, WCA

50. *LA Examiner*, 4/5/35

51. Eells, pp 218-19

52. Francis, "My Design for Living"

53. Ibid.

Chapter Ten

1. *LA Examiner*, 2/21/35

2. Ibid.

3. *LA Evening Herald Express*, 9/7/35

4. Parish, *Hollywood Beauties*, pg 95

5. John Wakeman, ed., *World Film Directors Vol. 1 1890-1945*, (NY: HW Wilson, 1987)

6. Frederick Lamster, *Souls Made Great Through Love and Artistry*, (NJ: Scarecrow Press, 1981)

7. *Motion Picture Herald*, 4/13/35

8. Kent Jones, *Film Comment*, Sept/Oct, 1997

9. Eells, pp 218, 224

10. Francis Diary, March 16, 1935; March 25, 1935, WCA

11. Francis Diary, April 15, 1935, WCA

12. *NY Times*, 5/5/35

13. Ibid.

14. Eells, pg 191

15. *NY Times*, 5/30/35

16. Francis Diary, May 3, 1935, WCA

17. *Film Weekly*, 5/31/35

18. Lane, "Kay Francis' Amazing Secret"

19. Francis, "My Design for Living"

20. Kellum, "I Asked Kay Francis 1,000 Questions"

21. *LA Examiner*, 9/28/35

22. Francis Diary, June 29, 1935, WCA

23. Francis Diary, June 30, 1935, WCA

24. Eells, pg 219

25. Francis Diary, August 5, 1935, WCA

26. Francis Diary, August 21, 1935, WCA

27. Hamilton, "Okay Francis"

28. Ibid.

29. Maddox, "Kay Francis Picks ..."

30. Frank Westmore and Muriel Davidson, *The Westmore's of Hollywood*, (Philadelphia: J.B. Lippincott, 1976)

31. Ibid.

32. Ibid.

33. *LA Examiner*, 3/5/35

34. *LA Examiner*, 1/6/35

35. *LA Evening Herald Express*, 4/3/36

36. Starr, "My Daughter, Kay Francis"

37. *LA Examiner*, 7/4/35

38. Letter from Sybil Jason to author, 9/2/2003

39. Grant, "Kay Francis' Strange Psychic Adventure"

40. *LA Examiner*, 11/6/35

41. Francis Diary, December 12, 1935, WCA

42. Steve Margoshes, [Online] WWW URL: Famenetwork.com

43. Eells, pg 220

44. Baldwin, "If You Want to be Like ..."

45. Cheatham, "Not What She Seems to be ..."

46. *NY Times*, 2/26/35

47. *NY Times*, 2/18/35

48. Roberts, "Acting in a Business Way"

49. Ibid.

50. Francis, "My Design for Living"

51. *NY Times*, 10/13/35

52. Hilary Lynn, "How 12 Stars Make Love," *Photoplay*, 8/33

53. Francis Diary, January 1, 1936, WCA

54. Francis, "How Am I Doing?"

55. Maddox, "Kay Francis Picks ..."

56. Hamilton, "The Most Baffling Brunette"

57. *LA Evening Herald Express*, 9/20/35

58. Parish, *Hollywood Beauties*, pg 97

59. Edward Baron Turik, *Hollywood Diva*, (Berkeley: UC Press, 1998) pg 167

Delmar Daves: [Online] WWW URL: Jermey Geltzer, tcm.turner.com, John Wakeman, ed., *World Film Directors, Vol. 1* (NY: HW Wilson Co., 1987) pp 195-199; [Online] WWW URL: www-sul.standford.edu, Delmar Daves

Chapter Eleven

1. Mollie Merrick, "Kay Francis for Florence Nightingale," *San Francisco Chronicle*, 12/19/35
2. Gregory William Mank, *Women in Horror Films, 1930's*, (London: McFarland, 1999)
3. Reviews from Warner Bros. *The White Angel* Pressbook 1936, *Picturegoer Weekly*, 1/16/37 and *Literary Digest*, 7/4/36
4. Eells, pg 222
5. Pressbook, Warner Bros. *The White Angel*, 1936
6. Hugh Small, *Florence Nightingale: Avenging Angel*, (NY: St Martin's, 1998)
7. Ibid., pg 10
8. Ibid., pg 11
9. Ibid., pg 13
10. Cecil Woodham-Smith, *Florence Nightingale 1820-1910*, (NY: McGraw-Hill, 1951)
11. Ibid., pp 36-37
12. Letter from Sybil Jason to author, 9/2/2003
13. Evans, "Okay Francis"
14. Lytton Strachey, *Eminent Victorians*, (London: Chatto & Windus, 1924) pg 155
15. Gena K. Gorrell, Heart and Soul, (NY: Tundra Books, 2000) pg 81
16. Anne Hudson Jones, *Images of Nursing*, (Philadelphia: U of Pennsylvania Press, 1988)
17. Letter from Billy Mauch to author, 7/11/2003
18. Small, *Florence Nightingale: Avenging Angel*, pp 119-120
19. Parish, *Hollywood Beauties*, 97
20. *Starmaker, The Autobiography of Hal Wallis*, (NY: MacMillan, 1980) pg 57
21. Harrison Carroll, "Lights! Camera! Action!" *LA Evening Herald Express*, 3/28/36
22. Basinger, *A Woman's View*, pg 57
23. Ibid., pg 58
24. Warner Brothers, *The White Angel* Pressbook, 1936
25. *NY Times*, 6/25/36
26. Gorrell, *Heart and Soul*, pp.54-57
27. Herbert Thompson, "Kay Gets Herself De-typed," *Film Weekly*, 11/21/36
28. W.H. Mooring, "Kay Goes Gay - Comedy for Kay," *Film Weekly*, 5/23/37
29. Francis Diary, January 2, 1936, WCA
30. Richard Lawson, "The Director Hollywood Forgot to Remember," *Screenbook*, 8/37
31. Ibid.

Chapter Twelve

1. Foster, "Star Without Temperament"
2. Francis Diary, June 12, 1936, WCA
3. Francis Diary, June 25, 1936, WCA
4. Francis Diary, June 28, 1936, WCA
5. Francis Diary, October 12, 1936, WCA
6. Francis Diary, October 26, 1936, WCA
7. Jimmy Fidler, *SF Chronicle*, 9/29/36

8.   Hamilton, "Okay Francis"

9.   Kellum "I Asked Kay Francis ..."

10. Francis, "The Women Men Like"

11. Eells, pg 221

12. Wilson, "Projections - Kay Francis"

13. Kellum, "I Asked Kay Francis ..."

14. Wilson, "Projections - Kay Francis"

15. *LA Examiner* 4/16/37

16. Francis, "My Design for Living"

17. Service, "Strange Interview"

18. Francis, "My Design for Living"

19. Francisco, *Gentleman*

20. TCM Viewer's Guide, 8/2003

21. Rankin, "O-Kay Francis"

22. Maddox, "Kay Francis Wants Life"

23. Ruth Rankin, "Men—What I Like and Don't Like About Them," *Shadowplay*, 3/35

24. Evans, "A Dinner Date With Kay Francis"

25. Maxwell, "It's Romance Again ..."

26. Ibid.

27. Eells, pg 192

28. Kellum, "I Asked Kay Francis ..."

29. Service, "Did $26,000 ..."

30. Kellum, "I Asked Kay Francis ..."

31. Wilson, "Projections - Kay Francis"

32. *LA Evening Herald Express*, 2/16/37

33. Stephen Luscombe, [Online] WWW URL: britishempire.co.uk

34. Service, "Strange Interview"

35. Ibid.

36. William K. Everson, review of "Confession," *Films In Review*, 1976

37. Parish, *Hollywood Beauties*, pg 100

38. Francis Diary, March 2, 1937, WCA

39. Francis Diary, March 9, 1937, WCA

40. Francis Diary, May 26, 1937, WCA

41. Francis Diary, August 23, 1937, WCA

42. Francis Diary, August 28, 1937, WCA

43. Eells, pg 224

44. *Hollywood Citizen News* 3/9/37

45. Mooring, "Kay Goes Gay"

46. Ibid.

47. Dooley, *From Scarface to Scarlett*, pp 594-595

48. Jason Vest, [Online] WWW URL: providencephoenix.com

49. *Current Biography*, 1943, pg 458

50. Letter to magazine, author's collection

51. Lawrence J. Quirk, *Claudette Colbert*, (NY: Crown Pub., 1985) pp 98-101

52. Ibid, pp 98-101

53. Sullivan, "In Hollywood"

Chapter Thirteen

1. Faith Service, "Farewell to Francis," *Modern Screen*, 7/38

2. Conversation with Jetti Ames, 4/12/2004

3. Eells, pg 224

4. Mooring, "Kay Goes Gay ..."

5. Thompson, "Kay Gets Herself De-Typed"

6. Patrick McGilligan, *Cagney* (San Diego: A.S. Barnes & Co., 1975) pg 100

7. Boze Hadleigh, *Bette Davis* (NY: Barricade Books, 1996) pp 114-115

8. Eells, pp 190-91

9. Eells, pg 191

10. Bob Thomas, *Crown Prince of Hollywood -The Antic Life and Times of Jack L. Warner* (NY: McGraw-Hill, 1990) pg 69

11. Ibid., pp 94-95

12. Ibid., pg 102

13. *Hollywood Citizen News* 1/1/38

14. Stuart Jerome, *Those Crazy Wonderful Years When We Ran Warner Bros.* (NY: Lyle Stuart Inc., 1983) pp 37-38

15. Parish, *Hollywood Beauties*, pg 102

16. Jerome, *Those Crazy Wonderful Years...*, pp 38-40

17. Ibid.

18. Ibid. pg 40

19. Thomas, *The Clown Prince of Hollywood* ...

20. Jerome, *Those Crazy Wonderful Years ...*, pp 40, 245-246

21. Thomas, *The Clown Prince of Hollywood* ...

22. Parish, *Hollywood Beauties*, pp 102-103

23. Service, "Farewell to Francis"

24. Robbin Coons, "The Name is Kay Francis" (news article)

25. Dick Moore, *Twinkle, Twinkle, Little Star* (NY: Harper and Row, 1984) pg 168

26. Jimmy Fidler column, *San Francisco Chronicle*, 6/22/38

27. *Film Weekly*, 7/2/38

28. Jay Robert Nash and Stanley Ross, Motion Picture Guide, (Chicago: Cinebooks, Chicago, 1987)

29. *Motion Picture Herald*, 2/4/39

30. Rudy Belmer, *Inside Warner Brothers*, (NY: Viking, 1985)

31. Whitney Stine, *Mother Goddam*, (NY: Hawthorne Books, 1974)

32. Parish, *Hollywood Beauties*, pg 103

33. Francis Diary, August 8, 1938, WCA

34. Francis Diary, August 11, 1938, WCA
35. Moore, "Twinkle, Twinkle, ..." pg 175
36. *The Busby Berkeley Book* (Conn.: Graphic Society Ltd., 1973) pg 119
37. Francis Diary, August 17, 1938, WCA
38. Mook, "At Last! The Authorized ..." Part II
39. Letters to author from Doug McClelland, 4/29/95 and 5/6/95
40. Rex Reed, "OK, So It's Not 'Johnny Belinda,' But . . ," *NY Times*, 10/6/68
41. Guy Flatley, "Glenda: From Gold Digger to Grandma," *NY Times*, 2/9/69
42. Wilson, "Projections - Kay Francis"
43. Service, "It's Thrilling to Be an Actress"
44. Hamilton, "Okay Francis"
45. Service, "It's Thrilling to be an Actress"
46. Francis, "Don't Try Your LUCK Out Here!"
47. Hamilton, "Okay Francis"
48. Francis, "My Design for Living"
49. Maddox, "Kay Francis Wants Life"
50. Francis, "My Design for Living"
51. Dick Mook, "She Wanted to be Forgotten," *Silver Screen*, 4/41
52. Francis Diary, February 17, 1938, WCA
53. *Hollywood Citizen News* 3/28/38
54. Francis Diary, March 1, 1938, WCA
55. Francis Diary, March 10, 1938, WCA
56. Louella Parsons, "Kay Francis Renouncing Career for Love," *LA Examiner*, 5/22/38
57. Ted Magee, "Kay Francis Signs a Lifetime Contract," *Screen Book*, 7/38
58. Ibid.
59. Ibid.

<u>Baron Raven Erik Von Barnekow:</u> Magee, "Kay Francis Signs a Lifetime Contract"; Aerodrome Page-Internet; Letters to author from Erik Barnekow Jr. dated March 23, April 20 and April 27, 2003

Chapter Fourteen

1. A.M. Sperber and Eric Lax, *Bogart*, (NY: William Morrow and Co., 1997) pp 113-115
2. Ibid.
3. Ibid.
4. Eells, pg 227
5. *Motion Picture Guide*
6. Sperber and Lax, *Bogart*, pg 114
7. Ibid., pp 113-115
8. *NY Times*, 10/27/38
9. *LA Examiner*, 10/13/38
10. Francis Diary, October 12, 1938, WCA
11. *LA Examiner*, 12/1/38

12. Ibid., 12/8/38

13. Dooley, *Scarface to Scarlett*, pg 34

14. Eve Arden, *Three Phases of Eve*, (NY: St Martin's Press, 1985) pg 49

15. *Motion Picture Herald*, 6/24/39

16. William Gargan, *Why Me?* (NY: Doubleday & Co., 1969) pg 163

17. Mook, *"I Can't Wait ..."* pp 32, 72

18. Eells, pg 230

19. Francis Diary, March 28, 1939, WCA

20. Eells, pg 229

21. Francis Diary, December 29, 1938, WCA

22. Francis Diary, April 5, 1938; June 28, 1938; July 21, 1938; September 9, 1938; September 16, 1938; March 28, 1939, WCA

23. Letter from Erik Barnekow Jr., to author, 4/27/2003

24. Letter from Erik Barnekow Jr., to author, 3/23/2003

25. *LA Examiner*, 9/28/39

26. Francis Diary, September 2, 1939, WCA

27. Francis Diary, October 25, 1939, WCA

28. Letters from Erik Barnekow Jr., to author 3/23/2003 and 4/27/2003

29. Letter From Erik Barnekow Jr. to author 4/20/2003

30. Francis Diary, June 7, 1940, WCA

31. Letter from Erik Barnekow Jr. to author, 9/2/2004

32. Letter from Bob French to author, 7/17/1997

Chapter Fifteen

1. Maddox, "Kay Francis' Last Interview"

2. "The Love Creed of Kay Francis," *Love and Romance*, 6/38

3. *Hollywood Citizen News*, 2/22/39

4. Jimmy Fidler, "Kay Francis Passes Milestone In Career With New RKO Role", *SF Chronicle*, 3/11/39

5. Mook, "She Wanted to Be Forgotten"

6. Dooley, *Scarface ...*, pp 554-555

7. Carol Combs, *Hollywood Citizen News*, 8/26/39

8. Lyn Tornabene, *Long Live The King*, (NY: G.P. Putnam's, 1976) pp 207-208

9. Sullivan, "In Hollywood"

10. *LA Examiner*, 12/18/39

11. Basinger, *A Woman's View*, pg 154

12. Ruth Waterbury, *Photoplay*, 6/40

13. Ibid.

14. Letter from Gloria Jean to author, 7/5/2004

15. Mook, "She Wanted to be Forgotten"

16. Francis Diary, June 26, 1939, WCA

17. McGilligan, *Fritz Lang*, (NY: St Martin's Press, 1997) pp 268-269

18. Steven Bach, *Marlene Dietrich: Life and Legend*, (NY, Morrow, 1992)

19. Parish, *Hollywood Beauties*, pg 109

20. Leonard Maltin, *Leonard Picks*, 2003

21. Jack Holland, "Why Actresses Don't Fear Middle Age," *Screenland*, 11/40

22. Holland, "Why Actresses ..."

23. Richard B. Jewell and Vernon Harbin, *RKO Story*, (NY: Arlington House,1982) pg 157

24. Holland, "Why Actresses ..."

25. [Online] WWW URL: webtrading.com

26. Louisa May Alcott, *Little Men*, (England, Puffin Books, 1994) pg 31

27. Daniel Bubbeo, *The Women of Warner Brothers*, (NC: McFarland and Co., 2002) pg 97

28. Letter from Jimmy Lydon to author, 7/10/2003

29. [Online] WWW URL: Chicago Sun-Times.com

30. Francis Diary, March 11, 1941, WCA

31. Francis Diary, April 17, 1941; May 2, 1941; May 17, 1941, WCA

32. Lane, "Plenty Has Happened to Her"

Chapter Sixteen

1. *Photoplay*, 4/41

2. Brian Aherne, *A Proper Job*, (Boston: Houghton Mifflin, 1969) pg 288

3. Irving A. Fein, *Jack Benny, An Intimate Biography*, (NY: GP Putman, 1976) pp 85-86

4. *Newsweek* 8/11/41, pg 60

5. Rosalind Russell, Life is a Banquet, (NY: Random House, 1977) pg 240

6. "O-Kay for Sound," *Lion's Roar*, 10/41

7. Hough, *One Boy's War* pp 35-36

8. Richard Hough, *One Boy's War* (London, Heinemann, 1975) pp 33-37

9. Ibid., pg 138

10. Francis Diary, May 17, 1940, WCA

11. Parish, *Hollywood Beauties*, pg 110

12. Letter from Frankie Thomas to author, 7/8/2003

13. Francis Diary, April 15, 1942, WCA

14. Bruce Lambert, "Millicent Fenwick, 82, Dies; Gave Character to Congress," *NY Times*, 9/17/1992

15. Francis Diary, August 16, 1941, WCA

16. Francis Diary, October 18, 1941, WCA

17. Francis Diary, December 30, 1941, WCA

18. Francis Diary, January 1, 1942, WCA

19. Francis Diary, February 18, 1942, WCA

20. Francis Diary, August 24, 1942, WCA

21. Diana Barrymore, *Too Much, Too Soon*, (NY: Henry Holt and Co., 1957)

22. Charles Higham, *Charles Laughton: An Intimate Biography*, (London: Allen, 1976)

23. Service, "Strange Interview"

24. Barrymore, Too Much, Too Soon

25. Francis Diary, October 7, 1942, WCA

26. Francis Diary, April 12, 1944, WCA

27. Service, "It's Thrilling to be an Actress"

28. Mook, "She Wanted to Be Forgotten"

Chapter Seventeen

1. James Kotsilibas-Davis and Myrna Loy, *Myrna Loy: Being and Becoming*, (NY: Alfred A. Knopf, 1987)

2. Carole Landis, *Four Jills in a Jeep*, (NY: World Pub. Co., 1944)

3. Ibid.

4. Ibid.

5. Carole Landis, "My Wartime Honeymoon," *Photoplay*, 6/43

6. Landis, *Four Jills in a Jeep*

7. Barrie Roberts, "Carole Landis," *Films of the Golden Age*, Spring/1996

8. Landis, *Four Jills in a Jeep*

9. 82nd Fighter Group Assn. 2002-2003, [Online] WWW URL: 82ndfightergroup.com

10. Barbara Seaman, *Lovely Me, The Life of Jacqueline Susann*, (NY: William Morrow & Co., 1987)

11. *NY Times*, 2/11/43

12. "Kay Francis Gives the First Report On Actresses at the Battle Front," *SF Chronicle*, 2/15/43

13. Francis Diary, March 28, 1943, WCA

14. Francis Diary, March 29, 1943, WCA

15. Francis Diary, June 3, 1943, WCA

16. Francis Diary, October 2, 1943, WCA

17. Francis Diary, October 25, 1943, WCA

18. Eells, pg 232

19. Donald Kirkley, "The Theatre," *Baltimore Sun*, 10/7/45

20. Ibid.

21. Dick Terry, "Kay Francis as a Traveling Trouper," *Milwaukee Post-Dispatch*, 11/1/45

22. Francis Diary, May 15, 1943; July 15, 1943; July 12, 1944; July 26, 1944, WCA

23. Francis Diary, March 4, 1944, WCA

24. Marsha Hunt, *The Way We Wore*, (California: Fallbrook Pub., 1993)

25. Ibid.

26. Ibid.

27. Kirkley, "The Theatre"

Chapter Eighteen

1. News clipping, c. 1945

2. Coons, "The Name is Kay Francis," c. 1945

3. Ibid.

4. Mick La Salle, review of *Allotment Wives*, *SF Chronicle*, 5/9/1999

5. John Cocchi, *Second Feature*, (NY: Citadel Press. 1991) pp 138-139

6. Frederick C. Othman, "Wanted: 35-Year-Old Man With Sex-Appeal," (UP) 9/29/44

7. Erskine Johnson, "Kay Francis A Producer And Star With Bernerd In New Picture 'Divorce,'" (NEA), 2/1945

8. Othman, "Wanted: 35-Year-Old ..."

9. *Hollywood Citizen News*, 9/8/45

10. Francis Diary, July 12, 1945, WCA

11. "Kay Francis Spikes Rumor Re Divorce, "news article, c. 1945

12. Francis Diary, March 16,1944, WCA

13. Francis Diary, March 22, 1944, WCA

14. Francis Diary, March 28, 1944 and April, 4, 1944, WCA

15. Francis Diary, March, 9, 1945, WCA

16. "Producing Not Easy, Says Kay," news item 6/21/45

17. Ibid.

18. *Windy Hill* Program Notes, 1945

19. J.E.F. "Miller Comedy 'Disappointing,' *Montclair Times*, 8/16/45

20. Letter from Jetti Preminger Ames to author, 2003

21. Donald Kirkley, "*Windy Hill* At Ford's," *Baltimore Sun*, 10/9/45

22. Francis Diary, October 8, 1945, WCA

23. Eells, pg 234

24. Harold V. Cohen, "Kay Francis At Nixon In *Windy Hill*," *Pittsburgh Post-Gazette*, 10/16/45

25. Francis Diary, January 27, 1946, WCA

26. Francis Diary, February 7, 1946, WCA

27. Conversations, Jetti Preminger Ames with author, 2/18/03 &12/23/03

28. Hope Diamond - Becoming a Legend, [Online] WWW URL: pbs.org/treasuresof the world/hope and williamsdiamond.com

29. Conversations, Jetti Preminger Ames, 2/18/03 &12/23/03

30. "Kay Francis Returns to Broadway," *NY World Telegram*, 8/28/46

31. Terry, "Kay Francis as a Traveling Trouper"

32. "On the Dials" 9/45

33. Terry, "Kay Francis as a Traveling Trouper"

34. Turner Classic Movies showing of *Allotment Wives*, host Robert Osborne

35. Cheatham, "Not What She Seems to Be"

36. Francis Diary, June 26, 1946, WCA

Chapter Nineteen

1. "GI's Put Star Back on Stage," *Daily Oklahoman*, 11/23/47

2. Sam Zolotow, "Kay Francis to Return," *NY Times*, 7/2/46

3. Letter to author from Jetti Ames, 3/11/2003

4. Douglas Gilbert, "Kay Francis Returns to Broadway," *NY World Telegram*, 8/28/46

5. Conversation with Jetti Ames, 2/18/03

6. Helen Ormsbee, "Fame Won't Help Kay Francis To Face Her Stage Audiences," news. article c. 1946

7. Ralph Bellamy, *When the Smoke Hit the Fan*, (NY: Doubleday and Co., 1979) pg 194

8.   Ibid.

9.   Vernon Rice, "Name Submitted to Fan Club; Theatre Crime Can Be Fun," *New York Post*, 9/46

10.   Harry Crocker, "Behind the Makeup" *LA Examiner*, 12/28/46

11.   Playbill, *State of the Union*, 1946

12.   *NY Times* 1/20/47

13.   *NY Times*, 3/22/47

14.   Terry, "Kay Francis as a Traveling Trouper"

15.   "Kay Francis Knows All the Answers but Just Try Getting Her to Tell Them," news article, c. 1945

16.   R.C.W. , review of "State of the Union," *The Patriot*, 9/29/47

17.   Paul Hood, "Sparkling Wit Keeps Politics Show Moving," *Daily Oklahoman*, 11/29/47

18.   "Actress 'Happy' to Revisit State," *Times-Picayune*, 12/12/47

19.   Albert Goldstein review of "State of Union is Rare Comedy," *Times-Picayune*, 12/13/47

20.   Francis Diary, December 29, 1947, WCA

21.   Francis Diary, January 3, 1948, WCA

22.   Francis Diary, January 23, 1948, WCA

23.   "Kay Francis Ill," *NY Times*, 1/24/48

24.   Francis Diary, January 22, 1948; January 23, 1948; January 24, 1948; January 26, 1948; January 27, 1948, WCA

25.   Jetti Preminger Ames, conversation with author 2/18/2003

26.   Ellen Bromfield Geld, *The Heritage* , (NY: Harper and Bros., 1962) pg 106

27.   Jetti Preminger Ames, conversation with author 2/18/2003

28.   Francis Diary, February 26, 1948, WCA

29.   Francis Diary, December 12, 1948, WCA

30.   "Kay Francis, Excellently Aided, Stymied by Creaky '25 Play," *Fitchburg Sentinel*, 7/20/48

31.   Elliot Norton, interview with Kay Francis, *Boston Post*, 7/3/48

32.   Ibid.

33.   *NY Times* 9/15/48

34.   William F. McDermott, "Kay Francis Stars in a New Play About One woman, Three Men and Love Forever," *Cleveland Plain Dealer*, 12/28/48

35.   Ed Brooks, "Comedy Light, But Diverting," *Times-Picayune*, 3/17/49

36.   Harold V. Cohen, "*Favorite Stranger* Hits New Low For Theater Season at Nixon," *Pittsburg Post-Gazette*, 4/2/49

37.   T.H.P., "Kay Francis Tops Comedy at Astor," *Hartford Courant*, 11/1/49

38.   review for *Let Us Be Gay*, *The Atlantic Constitution*, 10/18/49

39.   Eells, pp 245-246

40.   Lawrence J. Quirk, *Fasten Your Seatbelts- The Passionate Life of Bette Davis* (NY, 1990) pg 420

Chapter Twenty

1.   Eells., pg 193

2.   Paul Jones, "Playhouse in the Sky," *NY Times*, 3/12/50

3.   Ibid.

4.   review of *Goodbye, My Fancy, Fall River Herald News*, 7/11/50

5.   H.V.A., "Kay Francis Opens Season at Norwich Theater," *Hartford Courant*, 6/28/50

6.   Louis Calta, "Wolfe Work Due in Fall," *NY Times*, 1/3/50

7.   [Online] Louisiana State University Press, WWW URL: lsu.edu

8.   B. Robbins, "Life's Conflicts Theme of *The Web and the Rock*", *Saratogian*, 8/15/50

9.   *Variety*, 8/16/50

10. Sam Zolotow, *NY Times*, 10/22/52

11. Janis, "Class With a Capital K"

12. *NY Times* 6/17/51

13. Donald Steinfirst, "Kay Francis Arena Theater Star of 'Let Us Be Gay,'" *Pittsburgh Post Gazette*, 6/19/51

14. Eells, pg 241

15. Francis Diary, April 2, 1951, WCA

16. Francis Diary, March 31, 1951, WCA

17. *NY Times*, 9/9/23

18. Eells, pg 237

19. Saratogian, "Kay Francis Scores Hit in comedy at Spa Theater" Blanche Robbins, 7/17/51

20. Francis Diary, September 8, 1951, WCA

21. *NY Times*, 4/10/51

22. *NY Times*, 5/11/51

23. Eells pg 238

24. Robert Calder, *Willie: The Life of Somerset Maugham*, (NY: St. Martin's Press.,1989)

25. Ibid.

26. *The Saratogian*, 8/26/52

27. Eells, pg 238

28. Charles Winecoff, *Split Image*, (Dutton, 1996)

29. Ibid.

30. Eells, pp 238-239

Chapter Twenty-One

1.   'Theatre,' Starring Kay Francis, Now Playing at Casino," *The News*, Newport, R.I., 7/15/52

2.   Eells, pg 241

3.   John S. Wilson, "The Small, Economy-Size Package," *Theatre Arts*, 7/52

4.   Eells, pg 240

5.   Ibid.

6.   Conversation with Jetti Ames, 2/18/03

7.   Francis Diary, December 31, 1953, WCA

8.   Mary Kimbrough, "Kay Francis Recalls Roughest Stage Week," *St. Louis Post-Dispatch*, 1/7/53

9.   Conversation with Jetti Ames, 2/18/2003 and 3/11/2003

10. Service, "It's Thrilling to be an Actress"

11. Eells, pg 241

12. Ibid., pg 193

13. Ibid., pg 242

14. Hamilton, "Okay Francis"
15. Conversation with Jetti Ames, 3/2/2004
16. Ibid., 2/18/03
17. Eells, pp 231-232
18. Ibid., pg 242
19. Ibid.
20. Arnold Weissberger, *Famous Faces*, (NY: Harry N. Abrams, Inc., 1973)
21. Holland, "Why Actresses Don't Fear ..."
22. Conversation with Jetti Ames, 2/18/2003
23. Conversation with Tabor Ames, 7/13/2004
24. Conversation with Jetti Ames, 12/23/2003
25. Conversation with Jonathan Ames, 11/25/2003
26. Conversations with Jetti Ames, 2/18/03, 3/11/2003, 12/23/2003
27. Cheatham, "Not What She Seems to Be ..."
28. Eells, pg 242
29. Ibid., pg 243
30. Maddox, "Kay Francis Wants Life"
31. Eells, pg 244
32. Conversation with Jetti Ames 2/18/2003
33. Debbie Ridpath, "Interview With James Robert Parish," *Inklings*, Issue 3.15, 7/23/97
34. Conversation with Jetti and Lou Ames, 3/2/04 and 3/11/2003
35. Letter to author from Bob French, 7/17/1997
36. Jetti Ames conversation and letter 2/18/2003, 4/9/2003
37. Jonathan Ames conversation, 11/25/2003
38. Maddox, "Kay Francis Wants Life"
39. Conversation with Jetti Ames 3/2/2004
40. Cheatham, "Not What She Seems to Be"
41. Service, "It's Thrilling to be an Actress"
42. Service, "Strange Interview"
43. Eells, pg 244
44. Conversation with Jetti Ames, 3/2/2004
45. Ibid., 2/18/2003
46. Conversation with Jonathan Ames 11/25/2003
47. Francis, "My Design for Living"
48. Eells, pg 245
49. Lane, "Kay Francis' Amazing Secret"
50. *NY Times*, 12/17/68

Epilogue

1. Letter from Rosemary Carroll, 11/15/2004
2. Ibid.
3. [Online] WWW URL: seeingeye.org

4.   Eells, pg 245
5.   Francis, "My Design for Living"
6.   Service, "Strange Interview"
7.   *Columbia Book of Quotations*, 1996
8.   James R. Parish, *Hollywood Beauties*, pg 65
9.   Joseph Zarro and Frank Pellecchia, "Kay Francis: An Appreciation," *Quirk's Reviews*, 10/74
10. [Online] WWW URL: sauvieislanddahlias.com and dahliasuppliers.com/ "Dah Big List"
11. [Online] sydneyauctions.com, 2003
12. Douglas K. Burch, Review for *The Golden Age*, [Online} WWW URL: bonniecomley.com
13. Conversation with Marty Kearns, June, 2003
14. Parish , *Hollywood Beauties*, pg 118
15. Whitney Stine, *Mother Goddam*, (NY: Hawthorne Books, 1974) pg 101

Kay Francis Film Credits

1) *Gentlemen of the Press (1929)—Paramount*—(play by Ward Morehouse)—Monte Bell (p) Millard Webb (d) George Folsey (ph); cast: Walter Huston, *Katharine (Kay) Francis*, Charles Ruggles, Betty Lawford, Norman Foster, Brian Donlevy; 75m

2) *Cocoanuts, The (1929)—Paramount*—(play by George S. Kaufman)—Walter Wanger (p) Robert Florey and Joseph Stanley (d) George Folsey (ph) Irving Berlin (m); cast: Marx Brothers, Margaret Dumont, Mary Eaton, Oscar Shaw, *Katharine (Kay) Francis*, Cyril Ring; 96m

3) *Dangerous Curves (1929)—Paramount*—(based on story by Lester Cohen)—Lothar Mendes (d) Harry Fischbeck (ph); cast: Clara Bow, Richard Arlen, *Kay Francis*, David Newell, Joyce Compton, Stuart Erwin; 73m

4) *Illusion (1929)—Paramount*—(play by Arthur Chesney Train)—B. P. Schulberg (p) Lothar Mendes (d) Harry Fischbeck (ph); cast: Charles "Buddy" Rogers, Nancy Carroll, June Collyer, *Kay Francis*, Regis Toomey, Knute Erikson, William Austin, Paul Lukas, Lillian Roth; 80m

5) *Marriage Playground, The (1929)—Paramount*—(novel: *The Children* by Edith Wharton)—Lothar Mendes (d) Victor Milner (ph); cast: Fredric March, Mary Brian, Lilyan Tashman, Huntley Gordon, *Kay Francis*, William Austin, Philippe de Lacy, Anita Louise, Mitzi Green, David Newell; 70m; remade in 1990 as *The Children*

6) *Behind the Make-Up (1929)—Paramount*—(story by Mildred Cram)—Robert Milton (d) Charles Lang (ph); cast: Hal Skelly, William Powell, Fay Wray, *Kay Francis*, Paul Lukas; 65m.

7) *Street of Chance (1930)—Paramount*—(original story by H. P. Garrett)—David O. Selznik (p) John Cromwell (d) Charles Lang (ph) Travis Banton (cos); cast: William Powell, Jean Arthur, *Kay Francis*, Regis Toomey, Stanley Fields, Brooks

Benedict; 76m; remade in 1937 as *Her Husband Lies*

8) *Paramount on Parade (1930)—Paramount*—Albert A. Kaufman, Jesse L. Lasky, Adolph Zukor (p) Dorothy Arzner, Otto Brower, Edmund Goulding, Victor Heerman, Edwin H. Knopf, Rowland V. Lee, Ernst Lubitsch, Lothar Mendes, Victor Schertzinger, Edward Sutherland, Frank Tuttle (d) Victor Milner, Harry Fischbeck (ph); cast: Iris Adrian, Richard Arlen, Jean Arthur, Mischa Auer, William Austin, George Bancroft, Clara Bow, Evelyn Brent, Mary Brian, Clive Brook, Virginia Bruce, Nancy Carroll, Ruth Chatterton, Maurice Chevalier, Gary Cooper, Cecil Cunningham, Leon Errol, Stuart Erwin, *Kay Francis*, Skeets Gallagher, Harry Green, Mitzi Green, James Hall, Phillips Holmes, Helen Kane, Dennis King, Abe Lyman and his band, Fredric March, Nino Martini, David Newell, Jack Oakie, Warner Oland, Eugene Pallette, William Powell, Charles "Buddy" Rogers, Lillian Roth, Fay Wray; 101m

9) *Notorious Affair (1930)—Warners*—(play *Fame* by Audrey and Waverly Carter)— Robert North (p) Lloyd Bacon (d) Ernest Haller (ph) Edward Stevenson (cos); cast: Billie Dove, Basil Rathbone, *Kay Francis*, Montagu Love, Kenneth Thomson; 70m

10) *For the Defense (1930)—Paramount*—(story by Charles Furthman) John Cromwell (d) Charles Lang (ph); cast: William Powell, *Kay Francis*, Scott Kolk, William B. Davidson; 62m.

11) *Raffles (1930)—United Artists*—(novel: *The Amateur Cracksman* by E. W. Hornung) Samuel Goldwyn (p) Harry D'Arrast, George Fitzmaurice (d) George Barnes, Gregg Toland (ph); cast: Ronald Colman, *Kay Francis*, Bramwell Fletcher, Frances Dade, David Torrence, Alison Skipworth, Virginia Bruce; 70m.; previously made in 1917, 1925 and remade in 1939

12) *Let's Go Native (1930)—Paramount*—(screenplay by George Marion, Jr. and Percy Heath)—Leo McCarey (p,d) Victor Milner (ph); cast: Jeanette MacDonald, Jack Oakie, James Hall, Skeets Gallagher, *Kay Francis*, William Austin, David Newell, Eugene Pallette; 75m

13) *Virtuous Sin (1930)—Paramount*—(play *The General* by Lajos Zilahy) George Cukor, Louis Gasnier (d) David Abel (ph) Travis Banton (cos); cast: Walter Huston, *Kay Francis*, Kenneth MacKenna, Jobyna Howland, Paul Cavanagh; 80m; remade in 1931 as *Generalen*

14) *Passion Flower (1930)—MGM*—(novel by Kathleen Norris) William deMille (d) Hal Rosson (ph) Adrian (cos); cast: *Kay Francis*, Kay Johnson, Charles Bickford, Winter Hall, Lewis Stone, ZaSu Pitts, Dickie Moore, Ray Milland; 78m

15) *Scandal Sheet (1931)—Paramount*—(story by Oliver H.P. Garrett) John Cromwell (d) David Abel (ph); cast: George Bancroft, Clive Brook, *Kay Francis*, Gilbert Emery, Regis Toomey; 77m

16) *Ladies' Man (1931)—Paramount*—(story by Rupert Hughes) Lothar Mendes (d)

Victor Milner (ph); cast: William Powell, *Kay Francis*, Carole Lombard, Gilbert Emery, Olive Tell; 76m

17) *Vice Squad (1931)—Paramount*—(story by Oliver H.P. Garrett) John Cromwell (d) Charles Lang (ph); cast: Paul Lukas, *Kay Francis*, Helen Johnson, William B. Davidson; 80m

18) *Transgression (1931)—RKO*—(novel by Kate Jordan) William LeBaron (d) Leo Tover (ph); cast: *Kay Francis*, Paul Cavanagh, Ricardo Cortez, Nance O'Neal, John St. Polis, Adrienne d'Ambricourt, Cissy Fitzgerald, Doris Lloyd;72m; previously filmed in 1924 as *The Next Corner*

19) *Guilty Hands (1931)—MGM*—(story by Bayard Veiller) W.S. Van Dyke II (d) Merrit B. Gerstad (ph); cast: Lionel Barrymore, *Kay Francis*, Madge Evans, William Bakewell, C. Aubrey Smith, Polly Moran, Alan Mowbray; 60m

20) *24 Hours (1931)—Paramount*—(novel by Louis Bromfield) Marion Gering (d) Ernest Haller (ph); cast: Clive Brook, *Kay Francis*, Miriam Hopkins, Regis Toomey, George Barbier, Adrienne Ames, Lucille La Verne; 66m

21) *Girls About Town (1931)—Paramount*—(story by Zoe Akins) George Cukor (d) Ernest Haller (ph) Travis Banton (cos); cast: *Kay Francis*, Joel McCrea, Lilyan Tashman, Eugene Pallette, Alan Dinehart, Lucille Webster Gleason, Anderson Lawler, George Barbier, Louise Beavers; 80m

22) *False Madonna, The (1932)—Paramount*—(story *The Heart Is Young* by May Eddington) Stuart Walker (d) Henry Sharp (ph); cast: *Kay Francis*, William "Stage" Boyd, Conway Tearle, John Breeden, Marjorie Gateson; 70m

23) *Strangers In Love (1932)—Paramount*—(novel *The Shorn Lamb* by William J. Locke) Lothar Mendes (d) Henry Sharp (ph); cast: Fredric March, *Kay Francis*, Stuart Erwin, Juliette Compton, George Barbier, Sidney Toler; 76m

24) *Man Wanted (1932)—Warners*—(story by Robert Lord) Hal Wallis (p) William Dieterle (d) Gregg Toland (ph); cast: *Kay Francis*, David Manners, Andy Devine, Una Merkel, Kenneth Thomson, Claire Dodd; 63m

25) *Street of Women (1932)—Warners*—(novel by Polan Banks) Hal Wallis (p) Archie Mayo (d) Ernest Haller (ph); cast: *Kay Francis*, Alan Dinehart, Marjorie Gateson, Roland Young, Gloria Stuart, Allen Vincent, Louise Beavers; 70m

26) *Jewel Robbery (1932)—Warners*—(play by Ladislaus Fodor) William Dieterle (d) Robert Kurrle (ph); cast: William Powell, *Kay Francis*, Hardie Albright, Andre Luguet, Henry Kolker, Alan Mowbray, Helen Vinson, Ruth Donnelly; 63m

27) *One Way Passage (1932)—Warners*—(Oscar-winning story by Robert Lord and Tay Garnett) Tay Garnett (d) Robert Kurrle (ph); cast: William Powell, *Kay Francis*, Frank McHugh, Aline MacMahon, Warren Hymer, Fredrick Burton, Douglas Gerrard, Herbert Mundin; 69m; remade in 1940 as '*Til We Meet Again*

28) *Trouble in Paradise (1932)—Paramount—*(play *The Honest Finder* by Aladar Laszlo) Ernst Lubitsch (d) Victor Milner (ph) Travis Banton (cos); cast: Miriam Hopkins, *Kay Francis*, Herbert Marshall, Charlie Ruggles, Edward Everett Horton, C. Aubrey Smith; 83m

29) *Cynara (1932)—United Artists—*(novel *An Imperfect Lover* by Robert Gore-Brown) Samuel Goldwyn (p) King Vidor (d) Ray June (ph); cast: Ronald Colman, *Kay Francis*, Phyllis Barry, Henry Stephenson, Viva Tattersall; 78m

30) *Keyhole, The (1933)—Warners—*(story *Adventuress* by Alice D. G. Miller) Hal Wallis (p) Michael Curtiz (d) Barney McGill (ph) Orry-Kelly (cos); cast: *Kay Francis*, George Brent, Glenda Farrell, Allen Jenkins, Monroe Owsley, Helen Ware, Henry Kolker, Ferdinand Gottschalk; 70m; remade in 1948 as *Romance on the High Seas*

31) *Storm at Daybreak (1933)—MGM—*(play *Black-Stemmed Cherries* by Sandor Hunyady) Richard Boleslawski (d) George Folsey (ph); cast: *Kay Francis*, Nils Asther, Walter Huston, Phillips Holmes, Eugene Pallette, C. Henry Gordon, Louise Closser Hale, Jean Parker; 68m

32) *Mary Stevens, M.D. (1933)—Warners—*(novel by Virginia Kellogg) Lloyd Bacon (d) Sid Hickox (ph); cast: *Kay Francis*, Lyle Talbot, Glenda Farrell, Thelma Todd; 72m

33) *I Loved a Woman (1933)—Warners—*(novel *Red Meat* by David Karsner) Alfred Green (d) James Van Trees (ph); cast: *Kay Francis*, Edward G. Robinson, Genevieve Tobin; 90m

34) *House on 56th Street, The (1933)—Warners—*(novel by Joseph Santley) Robert Florey (d) Ernest Haller (ph); cast: *Kay Francis*, Ricardo Cortez, Gene Raymond, John Halliday, Margaret Lindsay, Frank McHugh, William "Stage" Boyd, Hardie Albright, Phillip Reed; 69m

35) *Mandalay (1934)—Warners—*(story by Paul Hervey Fox) Michael Curtiz (d) Tony Gaudio (ph) Orry-Kelly (cos); cast: *Kay Francis*, Ricardo Cortez, Warner Oland, Lyle Talbot, Ruth Donnelly, Reginald Owen, Hobart Cavanaugh, David Torrence, Rafaela Ottiano; 65m

36) *Wonder Bar (1934)—Warners—*(play *Die Wunderbar* by Geza Herczeg, Karl Farkas, Robert Katscher) Lloyd Bacon (d) Busby Berkeley (musical numbers) Sol Polito (ph) Orry-Kelly (cos); cast: Al Jolson, *Kay Francis*, Dolores Del Rio, Ricardo Cortez, Dick Powell, Guy Kibbee, Ruth Donnelly, Hugh Herbert, Louse Fazenda, Hal LeRoy, Fifi D'Orsay, Merna Kennedy; 84m

37) *Dr. Monica (1934)—Warners—*(play by Marja Morozowicz Szczepkowska) William Keighley (d) Sol Polito (ph); cast: *Kay Francis*, Warren William, Jean Muir, Verree Teasdale, Phillip Reed, Emma Dunn; 75m

38) *British Agent (1934)—Warners—*(novel by H. Bruce Lockhart) Michael Curtiz

(d) Ernest Haller (ph); cast: Leslie Howard, *Kay Francis*, William Gargan, Phillip Reed, Irving Pichel, Cesar Romero; 75m

39) *Living on Velvet (1935)—Warners—*(story by Jerry Wald and Julius Epstein) Frank Borzage (d) Sid Hickox (ph); cast: *Kay Francis*, George Brent, Warren William, Helen Lowell; 80m

40) *Stranded (1935)—Warners—*(story *The Lady With a Badge* by Frank Wead, Ferdinand Reyher) Frank Borzage (d) Sid Hickox (ph); cast: *Kay Francis*, George Brent, Patricia Ellis, Donald Woods, Barton MacLane, Robert Barrat, June Travis, Frankie Darro; 76m

41) *Goose and the Gander, The (1935)—Warners—*(screenplay by Charles Kenyon) Alfred E. Green (d) Sid Hickox (ph); cast: *Kay Francis*, George Brent, Genevieve Tobin, John Eldredge, Claire Dodd, Helen Lowell, Ralph Forbes, William Austin; 65m

42) *I Found Stella Parish (1935)—Warners—*(story by John Monk Saunders) Mervyn LeRoy (d) Sid Hickox (ph) Orry-Kelly (cos); cast: *Kay Francis*, Ian Hunter, Paul Lukas, Sybil Jason, Jessie Ralph, Joseph Sawyer, Barton MacLane; 84m

43) *White Angel, The (1936)—Warners—*(based on biography in *Eminent Victorians* by Lytton Strachey) William Dieterle (d) Tony Gaudio (ph); cast: *Kay Francis*, Ian Hunter, Donald Woods, Nigel Bruce, Donald Crisp, Henry O'Neill, George Curzon, Billy Mauch; 75m

44) *Give Me Your Heart (1936)—Warners—*(play *Sweet Aloes* by Jay Mallory [Joyce Carey]) Archie Mayo (d) Sid Hickox (ph); cast: *Kay Francis*, George Brent, Roland Young, Patric Knowles, Henry Stephenson, Frieda Inescort; 77m

45) *Stolen Holiday (1937)—Warners—*(story by Virginia Kellogg, Warren Duff) Michael Curtiz (d) Sid Hickox (ph); cast: *Kay Francis*, Claude Rains, Ian Hunter, Alison Skipworth; 84m; remade in 1974 as *Stavisky*.

46) *Another Dawn (1937)—Warners—*(story *The Ambassador's Wife* by W. Somerset Maugham) William Dieterle (d) Tony Gaudio (ph) Erich Wolfgang Korngold (m) Orry-Kelly (cos); cast: *Kay Francis*, Errol Flynn, Ian Hunter, Frieda Inescort, Herbert Mundin, Billy Bevan; 73m

47) *Confession (1937)—Warners—*(screenplay *Mazurka* by Hans Hameau) Joe May (d) Sid Hickox (ph); cast: *Kay Francis*, Ian Hunter, Basil Rathbone, Jane Bryan, Donald Crisp, Mary Maguire, Dorothy Peterson, Laura Hope Crews, Robert Barrat, Veda Ann Borg; 85m; remake of the 1935 film *Mazurka*

48) *First Lady (1937)—Warners—*(play by George S. Kaufman and Katharine Dayton) Stanley Logan (d) Sid Hickox (ph); cast: *Kay Francis*, Preston Foster, Anita Louise, Walter Connolly, Verree Teasdale, Victor Jory, Marjorie Rambeau, Marjorie Gateson, Louise Fazenda; 83m

49) *Women Are Like That (1938)—Warners—*(story *Return from Limbo* by Albert Z. Carr) Robert Lord (p) Stanley Logan (d) Sid Hickox (ph); cast: *Kay Francis*, Pat O'Brien, Ralph Forbes; 78m

50) *My Bill (1938)*—*Warners*—(play *Courage* by Tom Barry) Bryan Foy (p) John Farrow (d) Sid Hickox (ph); cast: *Kay Francis*, Bonita Granville, Anita Louise, Bobby Jordan, John Litel, Dickie Moore, Bernice Pilot, Elisabeth Risdon, Helena Phillips Evans; 60m; previously filmed in 1930 as *Courage*

51) *Secrets of an Actress (1938)*—*Warners*—(story *Lovely Lady* by Milton Krims, Rosalind Leigh, Julius Epstein) William Keighley (d) Sid Hickox (ph); cast: *Kay Francis*, George Brent, Ian Hunter, Gloria Dickson, Isabel Jeans, Penny Singleton; 71m

52) *Comet Over Broadway (1938)*—*Warners*—(story by Faith Baldwin) Busby Berkeley (d) James Wong Howe (ph); cast: *Kay Francis*, Ian Hunter, John Litel, Donald Crisp, Minna Gombell, Sybil Jason, Melville Cooper, Ian Keith, Susan Hayward; 65m

53) *King of the Underworld (1939)*—*Warners*—(story *Dr Socrates* by W. R. Burnett) Lewis Seiler (d) Sid Hickox (ph); cast: Humphrey Bogart, *Kay Francis*, James Stephenson, John Eldredge, Jessie Busley, Charles Foy; 69m; remake of the 1935 film *Dr. Socrates.*

54) *Women in the Wind (1939)*—*Warners*—(novel by Francis Walton) John Farrow (d) Sid Hickox (ph); cast: *Kay Francis*, William Gargan, Victor Jory, Maxie Rosenbloom, Sheila Bromley, Eve Arden, Eddie Foy, Jr.; 65m

55) *In Name Only (1939)*—*RKO*—(novel *Memory of Love* by Bessie Brewer) John Cromwell (d) J. Roy Hunt (ph) Irene (c); cast: Carole Lombard, Cary Grant, *Kay Francis*, Charles Coburn, Helen Vinson, Katharine Alexander, Jonathan Hale, Nella Walker, Peggy Ann Garner; 94m

56) *It's a Date (1940)*—*Universal*—(story by Jane Hall, Fredrick Kohner, Ralph Block) Joseph Pasternak (p) William A. Seiter (d) Joseph Valentine (ph); cast: Deanna Durbin, *Kay Francis*, Walter Pidgeon, Samuel S. Hinds, S.Z. Sakall, Lewis Howard, Cecilia Loftus; 103m; remade in 1950 as *Nancy Goes to Rio*

57) *When the Daltons Rode (1940)*—*Universal*—(book by Emmett Dalton, Jack Jungmeyer, Sr.) George Marshall (d) Hal Mohr (ph); cast: Randolph Scott, *Kay Francis*, Brian Donlevy, George Bancroft, Broderick Crawford, Stuart Erwin, Andy Devine, Frank Albertson, Mary Gordon; 80m

58) *Little Men (1940)*—*RKO*—(novel by Louisa May Alcott) Norman Z. McLeod (d) Nicholas Musuraca (ph); cast: *Kay Francis*, Jack Oakie, George Bancroft, Jimmy Lydon, Ann Gillis; 84m; previously filmed in 1934 and remade in 1998

59) *Play Girl (1941)*—*RKO*—(story by Jerry Cady) Frank Woodruff (d) Nicholas Musuraca (ph); cast: *Kay Francis*, James Ellison, Mildred Coles, Nigel Bruce, Margaret Hamilton; 75m

60) *Man Who Lost Himself, The (1941)*—*Universal*—(novel by Henry De Vere Stacpoole) Edward Ludwig (d) Victor Milner (ph); cast: Brian Aherne, *Kay Francis*, Henry Stephenson, S.Z. Sakall, Eden Grey, Nils Asther, Sig Ruman, Dorothy Tree, Janet Beecher, Marc Lawrence; 72m

61) *Charley's Aunt (1941)—20th Century-Fox*—(play by Brandon Thomas) Archie Mayo
     (d) Peverell Marley (ph) Travis Banton (cos); cast: Jack Benny, *Kay Francis*, James
     Ellison, Anne Baxter, Edmund Gwenn, Reginald Owen, Laird Cregar, Arleen
     Whelan, Richard Haydn; previously filmed in 1930, and remade in 1952 as *Where's
     Charley?;* 80m

62) *Feminine Touch, The (1941)—MGM*—(story by George Oppenheimer, Ogden Nash,
     Edmund Hartmann) Joseph L. Mankiewiez (p) W. S. Van Dyke (d) Ray June (ph);
     cast: Rosalind Russell, Don Ameche, *Kay Francis*, Van Heflin, Donald Meek, Gor-
     don Jones, Henry Daniell; 96m

63) *Always in my Heart (1942)—Warners*—(play by Dorothy Bennett, Irving White)
     Joe Graham (d) Sid Hickox (ph); cast: *Kay Francis*, Walter Huston, Gloria War-
     ren, Patty Hale, Frankie Thomas, Una O'Connor, Sidney Blackmer, Armida; 93m

64) *Between Us Girls (1942)—Universal*—(play *Le Fruit Vert* by Regis Gignoux, Jacques
     Thery) Henry Koster (p,d) Joe Valentine (ph); cast: Diana Barrymore, Robert
     Cummings, *Kay Francis*, John Boles, Andy Devine; 88m; remake of the 1934 film
     Csibi, the Brat

65) *Four Jills in a Jeep (1944)—20th Century-Fox*—(book by Carole Landis) William
     A. Seiter (d) Peverell Marley (ph); cast: *Kay Francis*, Carole Landis, Martha Raye,
     Mitzi Mayfair, Jimmy Dorsey and His Band, John Harvey, Phil Silvers, Dick
     Haymes, Alice Faye, Betty Grable, Carmen Miranda, George Jessel; 89m

66) *Divorce (1945)—Monogram*—(story by Sidney Sutherland)—Jeffrey Bernerd, *Kay
     Francis* (p) William Nigh (d) Harry Neumann (ph); cast: *Kay Francis*, Bruce Cabot,
     Helen Mack; 71m

67) *Allotment Wives (1945)—Monogram*—(story suggested by *Kay Francis* and written
     by Sidney Sutherland) Jeffrey Bernerd, *Kay Francis* (p) William Nigh (d) Harry
     Neumann (ph); cast: *Kay Francis*, Paul Kelly, Otto Kruger, Gertrude Michael,
     Teala Loring; 80m

68) *Wife Wanted (1946)—Monogram*—(story by Robert Callahan)—Jeffrey Bernerd,
     Kay Francis (p) Phil Karlson (d) Harry Neumann (ph); cast: *Kay Francis*, Paul
     Cavanagh, Robert Shayne, Veda Ann Borg, Teala Loring; 73m

Kay Francis Short Subjects:

The House That Shadows Built (1931)—Paramount—preview for the 1931-32 season.
     Includes a short history of the studio from 1912-1932 and highlights an eight-
     minute Marx Brothers sketch. Clips and photos feature Mary Pickford, Adolph
     Zukor, and Maurice Chevalier. There are stills of *Kay Francis* from *24 Hours* and
     Girls About Town; 60m

Kings of the Turf (1935)—Warners—Race track featurette; Shows how race horses are
     trained. *Kay Francis*, Clark Gable, Marion Davies, Al Jolson, Dolores Del Rio,
     and Pat O'Brien are seen briefly at the races; 10m

Show Business at War (1943)—20th Century-Fox—(The March of Time, Volume IX, Issue 10) Louis De Rochemont (d) Documentary; cast: Louis Armstrong, Jack Benny, Linda Darnell, Marlene Dietrich, Irene Dunne, Deanna Durbin, *Kay Francis*, Clark Gable, John Garfield, Rita Hayworth, Hedy Lamarr, Dorothy Lamour, Carole Landis, Carole Lombard, Tyrone Power, Martha Raye, Loretta Young; Kay is shown in North Africa with the Jills. 17m.

Hidden Hollywood II (1999) Features an outtake from *Four Jills in a Jeep.* Kay is seen playing the piano and singing during the number "The Old Army Game." 90m

Hollywood Bowl: Music Under the Stars (2002) Peter Rosen co-produced this program with WDR German TV. Details eighty-year history of Hollywood Bowl; cast: John Rubinstein (narrator), Norma Shearer, *Kay Francis*, Deanna Durbin, Irene Dunne, Debbie Reynolds, Leopold Stokowski, Jascha Heifetz, Jose Iturbi; Kay is shown walking to podium with Deanna Durbin 60m

Breakdowns of 1936 (2001) A hilarious look at Warner Bros. stars' blunders from 1935-36. Kay is shown in outtakes from *Living on Velvet* and *The White Angel.* The feature is currently available on the Platinum DVD Edition of *Jane Eyre,* released by Triton Multimedia.

Breakdowns of 1938 (2003) This rare program of outtakes, from films released by Warners during 1937-38, is on *The Adventures of Robin Hood* DVD. These "bloopers" include Kay, Bette Davis, Carole Lombard, Humphrey Bogart and many others. Kay is seen in several deleted scenes from *First Lady* and *Women Are Like That.* 14m

Kay Francis on Radio:

Al Jolson—Variety
2/16/43—with Monty Woolley, Ilka Chase

Bing Crosby Show
5/9/40—with Chester Morris, William Boyd, Gloria Jean, Brian Aherne, Robert Preston

Breakfast Club—Chicago
12/16/44—with Don McNeill (Years later, the program's radio engineer, Kermit Slobb, confessed, "Kay Francis was to me, the most beautiful of the Hollywood stars I met on 'Breakfast Club.'")

Cavalcade of America—NBC
5/3/43—"Soldiers in Greasepaint"—with Martha Raye, Hans Conried
10/13/43—"Waters of the Wilderness"—with Bea Benaderet, Gale Gordon, Agnes Moorehead

Chase and Sanborn—Comedy and musical variety
1/8/39—with Nelson Eddy, Don Ameche, Edgar Bergen and Dorothy Lamour.

Kay in "Detective Play" sketch.
7/30/39—with Don Ameche, Edgar Bergen, Dorothy Lamour. Kay in "Interior Decorating"

Command Performance
12/11/43—"Special North American Show"—with Bob Hope, Martha Raye, Carole Landis

Eddie Cantor Show
3/17/43

Exploring the Unknown—
9/15/46—"How Not to Worry"

Great Gildersleeve—NBC
4/5/43—"Rabbits"—Kay made special appearance and announcement

Hollywood Hotel—CBS—Louella Parsons
1/4/35—"Living on Velvet"—with George Brent
11/1/35—"I Found Stella Parish"—with Ian Hunter, Sybil Jason
5/29/36—"The White Angel"—with Donald Woods, Ian Hunter
9/25/36—"Give Me Your Heart"—with George Brent, George Burns, Gracie Allen
11/26/37—"First Lady"—with Preston Foster, Verree Teasdale
5/13/38—"My Bill"—with Bonita Granville, John Litel

Hollywood's Open House
?/?/45- Jim Ameche and Kay appear in a skit about a lady movie producer who encounters a man with amnesia on a train.

Jack Benny Show—NBC
5/11/41—"Tribute to Jack"
5/18/41—"Charley's Aunt"—with Jack Benny, Mitchell Leisen

Larry Douglas—ABC—Variety
2/1/45

Lux Radio Theatre—Cecil B. DeMille
3/6/39—"One Way Passage"—with William Powell, Marjorie Rambeau, William Gargan
11/12/39—"In Name Only"—with Carole Lombard, Cary Grant
3/18/40—"The Rains Came"—with George Brent, Jean Parker, Jim Ameche
3/3/41—"My Bill"—with Warren William, Dix Davis
3/1/43—"The Lady is Willing"—with George Brent, Arthur Q. Bryan

Make Up Your Mind—CBS
8/25/53

Martha Deane Show
8/28/49

NBC Special
>   *11/25/43*—"Soldiers in Greasepaint"—with Bob Hope, Jack Benny and many others

Screen Guild Theatre—CBS
>   *3/26/39*—"Never of This World"—with Leslie Howard, Virginia Weidler, Mary Nash

Silver Theatre—CBS
>   *12/17/39*—"Twice Upon a Time"
>   *3/3/40*—"A Lady by Preference"—with Ned Le Fevre
>   *12/15/40*—"Four on a Match"—directed by Conrad Nagel
>   *7/4/43*—"Murder Unlimited"—directed by Conrad Nagel—host:

John Loder
>   *11/28/43*—"The Lady Grew Up"

Sky Over Britain—WOR
>   9/15/41

Stage Door Canteen—CBS—Bud Collyer, announcer
>   *2/11/43*—with Jerry Lester, Elsa Maxwell, Lanny Ross
>   *3/24/44*—with Eric Blore, Ethel Merman
>   *1/26/45*—with Bob Hope, Jerry Colonna, Vera Vague

Star and the Story—CBS—host: Walter Pidgeon
>   *4/9/44*—"Strange Victory"

This is Our America
>   *8/3/42*—"Dark World"—written by Arch Oboler—host: Jan Peerce

Troubador—KFI—*12/27/33*

Variety Show—WEAF
>   *9/19/40*—with Bob Burns, Frank McHugh

Warriors for Peace—ABC Special
>   *9/29/46*—Kay was narrator for an overview of the Women's Army Corps.

Misc.,
>   *11/17/47—KNRT—Sioux Falls*—broadcast for TB fund

Kay Francis on Television

1950:
>   *This Is Show Business—(CBS)* panel show with George S. Kaufman, Abe Burrows
>
>   *Prudential Family Playhouse—(CBS)*—"Call it a Day"—with Peggy Ann Garner (aired 11/7/50)

1951:

> *Hollywood Screen Test—(ABC)*—Dramatic stories—hosted by Neil Hamilton (aired 1/8/51)

> *Betty Crocker Star Matinee—(ABC)* (aired 5/22/51)

> *Lux Video Theatre—(CBS)*—"Consider the Lilies"—with Jerome Cowan, Joel Ashley (aired 6/5/51)

> *Toast of the Town—(CBS)*—variety show with Ed Sullivan

> *TV Panel Show*—with Ilka Chase, Bud Collyer, Peter Donald (aired 10/15/51)

> *Frances Langford-Don Ameche Show—(ABC)* (aired 10/31/51)

> *Celebrity Time—(CBS)*—game show, music, interviews—with Conrad Nagel (aired 11/11/51)

1952:

> *Toast of the Town—(CBS)*—Tribute to Kay Francis pre-empted for New York Critics Awards (scheduled to air 1/20/52)

> *Ken Murray Show—(CBS)*—hour-long variety show with: Lola Albright, Victor Borge and Mrs.Arthur Murray (aired 5/10/52)

1953:

> *Anyone Can Win—(CBS)* game show hosted by Al Capp (aired 9/1/53)

Kay Francis on Stage

1925:

> *Hamlet (Shakespeare—modern dress)*—Booth Theatre and Greenwich Village Theatre—Opening November 9, 1925—88 performances—James Light (director); cast: Basil Sydney, Helen Chandler, Ernest Lawford, Adrienne Morrison, Charles Waldron, John Burr, Elmer Cornell, Stafford Dickens, *Katharine Francis* (Player Queen)

1926:

> *The Chief Thing* (written by Nikolai Evreinov)—Guild Theatre—Opening March 22, 1926—40 performances—(produced by The Theatre Guild); cast: Romney Brent, Dwight Frye, McKay Morris, Edward G. Robinson, Estelle Winwood, *Katharine Francis* (unbilled)

On tour for the Stuart Walker Company (April 26, 1926—August, 1926) Kay played various bit parts and supporting roles in such plays as: *Candida, The Outsider, Polly Preferred, White Collars* (as Sally Vare), *They Knew What They Wanted, The Goose Hangs High, Seventh Heaven* (as Arlette), *Puppy Love* (as Ivy Green), *The Fall Guy* (as Lottie), *The Old Soak* (as Ina Heath), *Love is Like That* (as Kay Gurlitz).

1927:

>*Crime* (by: Samuel Shipman and John B. Hymer)—Eltinge 42nd Street Theatre—Opening February 22, 1927—186 performances—A.H. Woods (producer); cast: Sylvia Sidney, Douglass Montgomery, *Katharine Francis* (Marjorie Grey), Kay Johnson, Chester Morris, Jack LaRue
>
>*Amateur Anne* – (comedy in 3 acts by Bayard Veiller and Gertrude M. Fair) Opening October 6, 1927; cast: Gertrude Bryan, Allan Brooks, *Katharine Francis*, A. J. Herbert, Dorothy Cox; played in Wilmington, Delaware and Hartford Connecticut—did not reach Broadway
>
>*Venus* (written by: Rachel Crothers)—Theatre Masque—Opening December 26, 1927—8 performances—Carol Reed (producer); cast: Cecilia Loftus, Charles Hampden, Arnold Lucy, Tyrone Power, Sr., Patricia Collinge, *Katharine Francis* (Diana Gibbs), Edward Crandall

1928:

>*Elmer the Great* (written by Ring Lardner)—Lyceum Theatre—Opening September 24, 1928—40 performances—George M. Cohan (producer) Sam Forrest (director); cast: Walter Huston, Nan Sunderland, *Katharine Francis* (Evelyn Corey), Fred de Cordova, Kate Morgan

1945:

>*Windy Hill*—(written by Patsy Ruth Miller)—on tour—Opening August 16, 1945 (Montclair, New Jersey) Closed May 27, 1946 (Chicago)—Ruth Chatterton (director); cast: *Kay Francis* (Antonia Conners), Roger Pryor, Judy Holliday (later replaced by Maxine Stuart, Jetti Preminger, and Eileen Heckert), Ruth Conley

1946:

>*State of the Union*—(written by Howard Lindsay and Russel Crouse)—Opening November 14, 1945 (Kay joined the cast September 2, 1946)—765 performances (Closing September 13, 1947)—Leland Hayward (producer)—Bretaigne Windust (staging); cast: Ralph Bellamy, *Kay Francis* (Mary Matthews), Myron McCormick, Minor Watson, Margalo Gillmore, Howard Graham

1947:

>*State of the Union* (on tour)—Opening September 18, 1947, Wilmington (toured four months—Kay's final appearance, January 22, 1948 in Columbus)—K. Elmo Lowe took over the part created by Ralph Bellamy

1948:

>*The Last of Mrs. Cheyney* (on tour)—(written by Frederick Londsdale)—Opening May 24, 1948 Boston (Closing September 6, 1948, Atlantic City) Jerome Shaw (staging); cast: *Kay Francis* (Mrs. Cheyney), Joel Ashley, Sheila Bromley
>
>*Favorite Stranger* (on tour)—(written by Eleanore Sellars)—Opening December 25, 1948 Elmira, New York (Closing April 2, 1949, Pittsburg)—Jules J. Leventhal (producer)—Leon Michel (director); cast: *Kay Francis* (Chalice Chadwick), Joel Ashley, Gordon Mills, Paul Langton

1949:

>   *Let Us Be Gay* (on tour)—(written by Rachel Crothers)—Opening June 3, 1949,
>   New Hope, Pa (Closing winter of 1949-50, Baton Rouge); cast: Kay Francis (Kitty
>   Brown), Joel Ashley

1950:

>   *Goodbye, My Fancy* (on tour)—(written by Fay Kanin)—Opening May 23, 1950,
>   Brooklyn (Closing July 15, 1950, Somerset, Mass.) Ted Post (director); cast: *Kay
>   Francis* (Agatha Reed), Joel Ashley, Frank Albertson, Nancy Marchand

>   *Web and the Rock, The* (on tour)—(play by Lester Cohen—based on the novel by
>   Thomas Wolfe)—Opening August 14, 1950, Saratoga Springs, NY—John Hun-
>   tington (producer) Richard Barr (director); cast: *Kay Francis* (Esther Jack), Joel
>   Ashley

1951:

>   *Let Us Be Gay*—(written by Rachel Crothers)—Opening June 18, 1951, Pitts-
>   burgh—Morton Da Costa (director); cast: Kay Francis (Kitty Brown), Joel Ashley,
>   Ann Shoemaker

>   *Mirror, Mirror* (on tour)—(written by George Oppenheimer from the novel *The
>   Back Seat* by G.B. Stern)—Opening July 9, 1951, Westhampton, Long Island
>   (Closing September 8, 1951, New Hope, Pa.)—Julian Boris (director) Paul
>   Morrison (staging); cast: *Kay Francis* (Leonora Barton), Joel Ashley

1952:

>   *Theatre* (on tour)—(written by Guy Bolton from the novel by Somerset
>   Maugham)—Opening March 5, 1952, Winter Park, Florida—Julian Borris (Ad-
>   vance director); cast: *Kay Francis* (Julia Lambert), Dennis Allen, Anthony Perkins

1953:

>   *Theatre* (on tour)—(written by Guy Bolton from the novel by Somerset
>   Maugham)—Opening January 6, 1953, St Louis; cast: *Kay Francis* (Julia Lam-
>   bert), Dennis Allen

Photo Credits

All photos, unless otherwise noted, are from the author's collection. The author would like to express his thanks to the following individuals for the lending of photos: Henry Francis, Jetti and Lou Ames, Tabor Ames, Mike Rinella, and Gloria Jean.

Cover photo: Tom Maroudas of Australia did a fantastic job with his color-enhancement of this 1935 portrait of Kay.

Back cover: Kay's 1925 portrait by Sir Gerald Kelly was the sensation of his 1926
     exhibit at London's Royal Academy. The original now resides at The Seeing Eye
     of Morristown N.J. The magazine covers were painted by popular artists of the
     era Corinne Malvern (*Picture Play -February, 1937*) and Earl Christy (*Modern
     Screen - May, 1935*). Photo of the author at San Francisco's Hotel St. Francis by
     Joel Bellagio (2004)

Index

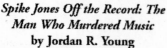
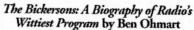

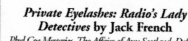